W9-CGN-622

Municipal Management Series

Management Policies in Local Government Finance

International City Management Association

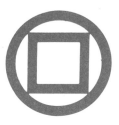

The International City Management Association is the professional and educational organization for chief appointed management executives in local government. The purposes of ICMA are to strengthen the quality of urban government through professional management and to develop and disseminate new approaches to management through training programs, information services, and publications.

Managers, carrying a wide range of titles, serve cities, towns, counties, and councils of governments in all parts of the United States and Canada. These managers serve at the direction of elected councils and governing boards. ICMA serves these managers and local governments through many programs that aim at improving the manager's professional competence and strengthening the quality of all local governments.

The International City Management Association was founded in 1914; adopted its City Management Code of Ethics in 1924; and established its Institute for Training in Municipal Administration in 1934. The Institute, in turn, provided the basis for the Municipal Management Series, generally termed the "ICMA Green Books." ICMA's interests and activities include public management education; standards of ethics for members; *The Municipal Year Book* and other data services; urban research; and newsletters, a monthly magazine, *Public Management*, and other publications. ICMA's efforts for the improvement of local government management—as represented by this book—are offered for all local governments and educational institutions.

Contributors

J. Richard Aronson

James M. Buchanan

Thomas J. DiLorenzo

Paul B. Downing

Marilyn R. Flowers

Lewis Friedman

W. Maureen Godsey

Sanford M. Groves

William W. Holder

George C. Kaufman

Julius Margolis

Alan Maynard

Wallace E. Oates

John E. Petersen

Arnold H. Raphaelson

James D. Rodgers

Leonard I. Ruchelman

Larry D. Schroeder

Eli Schwartz

Bernard F. Sliger

Robert J. Thornton

Barbara H. Tuckman

James C. Van Horne

Municipal Management Series

Management Policies in Local Government Finance

Editors

**Published for the
Institute for Training in
Municipal Administration**

**J. Richard Aronson
Lehigh University**

**By the
International
City
Management
Association**

**Eli Schwartz
Lehigh University**

Municipal Mangement Series

David S. Arnold Editor

Library of Congress Cataloging in Publication Data
Main entry under title:
Management policies in local government finance.

   (Municipal management series)
   Bibliography: p.
   Includes index.
   1. Local finance
2. Municipal finance
I. Aronson, J. Richard (Jay Richard), 1937–
II. Schwartz, Eli.   III. Series.
HJ9105.M3   1981   352.1   81–2934
ISBN 0–87326–022–8   AACR2

Printed in the United States of America.

Foreword

When the International City Management Association published the first edition of *Management Policies in Local Government Finance* in 1975, the purpose, as stated in the foreword, was to provide a "better understanding of the economic environment for decision making. . . ." That purpose continues for this book.

This book reflects the effects of three major developments in the 1970s that have recast the world of local government finance.

First are the effects of inflation, which permeate the chapters on revenues, expenditures, debt management, the property tax, cash management, pensions, and other portions of this book.

Second was the plight of New York City, which, in early 1975, was unable to raise money on the municipal bond market and was on the verge of defaulting on bonds. The effects were not confined to New York City, however; if New York City had defaulted, it would have had an adverse effect on credit instruments for federal, state, and local governments in all parts of the country.

Third was the approval by California voters of Proposition 13, the Jarvis-Gann initiative in June 1978. This property tax limitation measure has had enormous influence in other states that have adopted or are considering the adoption of various measures to limit state and local spending, cut taxes, and transfer the tax burden by service charges and user fees.

The net effect is that local governments everywhere are under tremendous pressures to cut costs and reduce services. Thus, the need for effective financial management is greater than ever.

In the decade of the 1980s, a growing number of cities are likely to operate under the constraints of severe fiscal stress. To meet conditions of financial stringency, some cities have made permanent layoffs of a significant number of employees, and many more are turning attention to direct fees and service charges to augment sales taxes, income taxes, and other nonproperty sources of revenue.

This book replaces the 1975 edition of *Management Policies in Local Government Finance*, which, in turn, replaced *Municipal Finance Administration*, which was first published in 1937 and last revised in 1962. The distinguished lineage of this book has served as a basic reference source for local government finance officers, city and county managers, budget officers, city and county planners, and teachers and students in public administration and local government finance for more than forty years.

Several points should be noted with respect to the general approach of this edition of *Management Policies in Local Government Finance*. First, economic policy as it affects management decisions is emphasized because local governments must learn to live in a national economy. Second, the discussions are set in a context of theories and issues that are applicable from the management point of view. Third, the points of view expressed by the authors are occasionally controversial and sometimes contradictory. These authors are, however, recognized authorities in their respective fields, and no attempt has been made editorially to interfere with the views expressed.

New chapters have been added to this edition on financial forecasting, the financial structure of local governments in Great Britain, evaluating local government financial condition, the interrelationships of collective bargaining and local government finance, and the management of pension funds and pension programs. All other chapters have been reviewed, revised, and brought up to date; in several instances, this involved complete rewriting.

The plan for this book is to present a balanced progression of local government finance. Thus, Part One, The Local Government Setting, provides an overview of the organizational and economic environment for financial policy. Part Two, Revenue Sources, analyzes the economic impact and administration of the major local taxes. Part Three, Intergovernmental Fiscal Relations, explores the financial setting of local governments in metropolitan and federal contexts. Part Four, Financial Management, covers specific operational and managerial aspects of local government finance.

This book, like others in the Municipal Management Series, has been prepared for ICMA's Training Institute. The institute offers in-sevice training specifically designed for local government officials whose jobs are to plan, direct, and coordinate the work of others. The institute has been sponsored since 1934 by the International City Management Association.

The Association is grateful to the editors of this book, J. Richard Aronson and Eli Schwartz, both of whom are Professors of Economics in the Department of Economics, College of Economics and Business, Lehigh University. Their work was particularly vital during project planning, manuscript review, and substantive editing.

Next, we are grateful to the chapter authors for their fine efforts and for their willingness to work with the editors in editorial reviews and revisions.

Finally, we want to thank the many city managers, finance officers, and university teachers who helped us in the preparation of this book and persons on the ICMA staff and others who worked on editing and production. These persons are individually recognized in the Acknowledgments.

Mark E. Keane
Executive Director

International City
Management Association

Contents

Part one:
The local
government
setting

The finance function in local government

How can the effectiveness of local government be assessed? In *The American Commonwealth*, a classic work of political analysis, the perceptive British observer James Bryce suggested two criteria: "What does it provide for the people, and what does it cost the people?"

With regard to his first criterion, Bryce, writing in the late nineteenth century, observed that

. . . in the United States generally, constant complaints are directed against the bad paving and cleansing of the streets, the non-enforcement of the laws forbidding gambling and illicit drinking, and the control of the police generally, and in some places also against the sanitary arrangements, and management of public buildings and parks.[1]

His findings concerning the second criterion offered no greater comfort, for Bryce was also moved to record that "both the debt and taxation of American cities have risen with unprecedented rapidity, and now stand at an alarming figure."[2]

This ominous note, sounded by Bryce close to a century ago, illustrates the deep-rooted concern in American society over the ability of municipalities to manage their problems. When the full story of American urban development is viewed from an historical perspective, this unease may not be entirely justified. Its persistence is nevertheless a fact, and it helps to explain the pervading skepticism that many people still feel about cities. It also helps to explain why state governments have been reluctant to grant urban localities greater powers of self-rule.

The continuing and widespread concern about the provision and cost of urban services is no doubt related to their direct impact on the everyday life of an increasingly urbanized citizenry. The adequacy of police and fire protection may be dramatically tested in episodes in the urban dwellers' own life-time experiences. Their life-styles may be significantly affected over the long term by the adequacy of a whole range of municipal regulations and services, from education and health to public works and leisure services, from urban transportation to environmental standards in the work place and community. The citizenry will also be constantly and perhaps painfully reminded of its role in the financing of such services through payroll deductions, the property tax, the sales tax, and a host of municipal licenses and fees. Millions of urban citizens are still echoing Bryce in asking about their municipal government: "What does it provide, and what does it cost?"

In recent decades new surges of concern over what is held to be the plight of the nation's urban communities have manifested themselves. Beginning in the 1960s, for example, numerous studies and reports were presented by presidential commissions, federal and state investigative bodies, and a variety of blue ribbon committees.[3] Almost all of them warned of crisis conditions in our cities as revealed by rising air and water pollution, growing crime rates, urban sprawl, deteriorating housing, escalating welfare provisions, traffic jams, and—a pivotal concern—racial strife. These studies and reports also clearly indicated the important role of finance at the heart of all these problems. During the 1960s local governments faced increasing difficulties in securing the resources necessary to meet their needs. It was generally true that the larger the city, the greater the money squeeze.

During the 1970s more realistic assessments may have replaced some of the idealistic urban reports and recommendations of the previous decade, but the seemingly intractable problems of urban life remain. Further, the burdens of the 1970s—economic uncertainty, energy crises, and the all-pervading tide of inflation that has gripped the industrial nations—have added to the existing problems.

Most recently, two events stand out as having major import for local government finance. In March of 1975, New York City suddenly found itself unable to raise money on the municipal bond market, and found itself on the brink of bankruptcy. Urban fiscal crisis became first page news across the nation as federal, state, and municipal agencies struggled—and sometimes fought one another—to keep New York from defaulting on its bonds. Ultimately, the United States Congress came to the rescue by authorizing federal loan guarantees. Although New York was saved, at least for the time-being, officials in many other cities were confronted by the unsettling fact that their own communities were vulnerable to some of the same conditions that had affected New York. Continued migration of middle-class persons and jobs to the suburbs, diminishing revenues, and the escalating costs of labor-intensive services are pervasive problems of most large central cities.

The second noteworthy event was the approval by California voters of Proposition 13, the Jarvis–Gann Initiative, on 6 June 1978. Named for its authors and chief proponents, Proposition 13 took effect July 1, and provides for the following: (1) Limits total property tax collections for all local governments to 1 percent of "full cash value," as assessed in 1975–76; (2) Limits increases in assessments to 2 percent each year while allowing reassessments only when the property is sold; (3) Requires a two-thirds vote of both houses of the legislature to levy any new taxes to increase revenue; (4) Prohibits local governments from imposing any new property taxes, and requires two-thirds voter approval for other new local taxes.[4]

Legislatures in several other states are considering or have approved measures to limit state spending, cut taxes, or shift the tax burden by creating new levies or increasing old ones. While the full implications of this "taxpayers' revolt" are complex and still to be assessed, local government everywhere is presently under tremendous pressure to cut costs and reduce services. The necessity for effective financial management is under the spotlight as never before.

Municipal finance traditionally has been regarded as a field that lacks the glamour that some see in other aspects of urban management. Nevertheless, municipal finance plays a key role in determining the costs and benefits of its local government's activities. Central to this role is the intricate and interlocking framework of financial flows, planning, management, decision making, municipal government structure, the problems of the metropolitan area, and those of local governmental institutions in general. The financial problems of the cities generate as much excitement, hope, and professional challenge to the urban administrator as any other field of municipal decision making.

As the effective management of available resources becomes even more crucial, those who bear management responsibilities must be prepared to perform a key role in the operation of their communities. Any attempt to come to grips with what ails America's towns and cities requires a thorough understanding of the internal dynamics of local financial management—budgeting, taxing, accounting, debt management, and related matters. It is also necessary to understand the external complexities of municipal finance in the context of intergovernmental affairs—that is, the relations between federal, state, and local governments. It is, therefore, the purpose of this chapter to provide an introductory overview of the changing financial dimensions and realities of contemporary local government. This overview will set the stage for the subsequent chapters on particular aspects of municipal finance and its administrative environment.

The urban challenge

A brief survey of urban development in the United States helps provide a perspective on the challenges that currently confront American communities.

Rapid development

With significant exceptions—notably such eastern seaboard cities as Boston, Philadelphia, Baltimore, and New York—few American cities were highly developed before the mid-nineteenth century. In contrast to European cities, American cities such as Chicago, Detroit, Pittsburgh, Cleveland, and St. Louis faced the enormously difficult task of rapidly assimilating large numbers of culturally disparate newcomers into burgeoning urban economies and building complex and viable social systems virtually from scratch. It is little wonder that so many writers, from Emerson and Henry James to the most recent critics of American urban development, have, like Bryce, emphasized the defects of the American metropolis while understating or overlooking its achievements.[5]

Lacking cultural tradition as an integrating force, and being remarkably polyglot in nature, most of our cities were put together hastily, without clear physical or social goals. Most cities functioned primarily to coordinate the country's rapidly developing productive and commercial forces. Exceptions include the cities of the West and Southwest where the urban economy was initially oriented toward the development of natural resources in mining and agriculture.

After the second world war appreciable changes took place in the pattern of urban development. As a result of technological advances in transportation, communication, and energy sources—all of which took place in a context of sustained economic growth—people and industry acquired greater geographical mobility. In ensuing decades, this mobility found dramatic expression in the growth of suburbs and an associated draining of many vital resources and influential segments of the populations from the cores of older central cities. Middle class persons in particular were able to migrate out of older city neighborhoods in search of better living conditions in the suburban hinterlands. By 1970 census figures showed that for the first time suburbanites outnumbered central city dwellers. In some areas they achieved a preponderance of as high as four to one.

Within the core areas of the older cities the demographic profile indicated an increasing proportion of nonwhite citizens. Black Americans had, of course, participated in the building of the national economy from the earliest days, though not always as citizens. Many of the older cities had long established black communities whose roots went deeper than those of late nineteenth and early twentieth century European immigrants. Black communities were swollen, particularly during and after the two world wars, by migrants from the South responding to national economic opportunities. Many of these migrants and, increasingly, their children and grandchildren have remained locked into the deteriorating economies of older city cores.

Metropolitan areas

Such patterns of migration (and lack of opportunity to migrate) gave the densely populated regions known as metropolitan areas the characteristics they exhibited in the 1970s. Each standard metropolitan statistical area (SMSA) is characterized by the U.S. Bureau of the Census as a cluster of heavily settled communities that are geographically, socially, and economically related to one another and to a central urban core.[6] Some of these functionally related regions span areas of more than one state. The New York metropolitan area, which includes parts of Connecticut and New Jersey, is an excellent example of the scant regard paid by the twentieth century urban economy to the eighteenth century political boundaries.

Census Bureau estimates indicate that people are not leaving the central cities as rapidly as before, and that some are even returning from the suburbs. Census figures presented in Table 1–1 show that suburban population gain in the 1970s (10.3 percent) was less than in the 1960s (28.2 percent). Many cities are providing incentives for migration into urban neighborhoods by making available low-cost city-owned houses to noncommercial buyers who agree to renovate them and live in them for a specified period. Under their "urban homesteading" programs, for example, Wilmington (Delaware) and Baltimore have sold such houses for as little as one dollar. The benefits of urban restoration are evident in such neighborhoods as Boston's South End, Washington's Adams-Morgan, Philadelphia's Queen Village, Seattle's Capitol Hill, and Baltimore's Fells Point.

Table 1–1   Population change in metropolitan areas

Item	1976 population estimate (millions)	Percent increase		Whites		Blacks	
		1970–76	1960–70	Number (millions)	Percent increase, 1970–76	Number (millions)	Percent increase, 1970–76
U.S. total	210.3	5.3	13.3				
Metropolitan	142.5	4.0	16.6	121.4	2.1	21.2	16.9
Inside central cities	60.7	−3.4	5.3	45.2	−7.6	15.5	11.1
Outside central cities	81.8	10.3	28.2	76.2	8.8	5.7	36.3
Nonmetropolitan	67.7	8.2	6.5	61.2	8.7	6.5	1.5

Source: U.S. Bureau of the Census, *Population Profile of the U.S.: 1976* (Washington, D.C.: U.S. Government Printing Office, 1977), Table 19.

But redevelopment has also meant displacement of the poor who are forced to relocate as rents and taxes in restored areas increase along with property values. Though still quite limited, the result of the new middle-class movement into cities could eventually generate an increased migration of inner-city minorities and poor to nearby suburbs. As the figures in Table 1–1 show, urban blacks have been moving into suburbs in growing numbers. According to Census Bureau estimates, approximately 5.7 million of the 21.2 million blacks in metropolitan areas were living outside the central cities in 1976. This represents an increase of 36.3 percent since 1970.

Interdependence

A key term, interdependence, helps to explain some of the most significant ramifications of this sprawling regional development. For in spite of the much publicized contrasts between an urban core, surrounding satellite cities, and outlying suburban districts, the differing segments of a metropolitan region are bound together in many other ways. Suburbanites, to take but one example, tend to be economically tied to the central cities, through employment, cultural amenities, and educational opportunities. At the same time many of the residents of the central cities make long journeys (often braving inadequate public transportation facilities) to places of employment in the suburban fringe. By the 1970s the expansion of suburban employment attracted workers who lived in other suburbs and outlying areas, thus adding to the complex intersuburban and interexurban commuting patterns.

Interdependence thus became a major factor in the metropolitan areas of the 1970s. It had many facets. Businesses outside the major cities depended on transportation services for the distribution of goods from the larger urban centers. City dwellers and suburbanites alike required sewage and sanitation systems, water and electricity, and health and recreational facilities. Immense—and growing—costs are involved. The provision of such interlocking and expensive public services necessitates greater regional cooperation among governments than in the past.

Megalopolis

As the nation's metropolitan areas continue to grow toward and into each other, it is possible to see another regional phenomenon, first discerned as early as the 1950s by the French geographer and urban analyst Jean Gottman. Identifying a vast urbanized complex that was beginning to crystallize along the northeastern seaboard of the United States from southern New Hampshire to northern Virginia, Gottman characterized it by the term "megalopolis." He noted:

In this area . . . we must abandon the idea of the city as a tightly settled and organized unit in which people, activities, and riches are crowded into a very small area clearly separated from its nonurban surroundings. Every city in this region spreads out far and wide around its original nucleus; it grows amidst an irregularly colloidal mixture of rural and suburban landscapes; it melts on broad fronts with other mixtures, of somewhat similar though different texture, belonging to the suburban neighborhoods of other cities.[7]

Some projections for the year 2000 extend the Atlantic seaboard megalopolis to include the lower Great Lakes region. Two other metropolitan giants, in southern California and in the Florida peninsula, are also expected to take shape by that year. Overall, these three entities, whose tentative outlines can already be observed, will cover one-twelfth of the land area of continental United States and hold no less than three-fifths of its population.

Regional movements: Snowbelt and Sunbelt

From the 1950s on, the Snowbelt cities in the Northeast and Midwest regions have been losing population to the Sunbelt cities in the Southwest and West. The 1980 Census of Population showed absolute population declines of dramatic proportions in New York, Chicago, Milwaukee, Cleveland, Detroit, Washington, and other older central cities. The 1980 Census also showed large population gains in Houston, San Diego, Dallas, San Antonio, San Jose, and other younger cities. Contributing to these massive population shifts have been the changes in the industrial base from heavy manufacturing to computers and many other forms of technology; federal government defense policies; transportation shifts to air and the interstate highway system; and a wide range of amenities in the South, Southwest, and West.

If individuals and entrepreneurs make locational decisions on the basis of these criteria, government also makes decisions that have an effect on industrial location and that influence economic patterns. For example:

. . . in preparation for World War Two and in the course of the two successive wars that were fought in the Far East, enterprises of enormous economic significance to the overall development of the West Coast were generated by government decisions.

Also, starting in the 1930s and continuing to the present time, the South has been a favored area for the flow of federal funds.[8]

Among the most fiscally distressed cities are Boston, Buffalo, Cleveland, Detroit, Newark, Philadelphia, and Pittsburgh. Along with New York, these municipalities were subject to the highest perceived risks and highest interest rate premiums during the capital market disruptions of 1975–76. Thanks to special government guarantees, New York managed to avoid defaulting on its debts, but Cleveland did go into default in December 1978—the first city to do so since the Depression.[9]

The role of small cities

In the 1940s and 1950s, migration patterns in the United States were characterized by movements of people from rural areas and small towns to metropolitan centers. These mobility patterns continued through the 1960s, although out-migration from nonmetropolitan areas was considerably smaller. In the early 1970s, Census reports showed a new phenomenon: nonmetropolitan areas were growing at a faster rate than metropolitan areas. The data in Table 1–1 indicate that from 1970 to 1976, nonmetropolitan population increased 8.2 percent compared to a 4.0 percent increase in the population of the metropolitan areas. Contributing factors to this new trend include the decentralization of manufacturing, recreational retirement developments, the opening of new resources, and the expansion of improved transportation facilities that enable persons in small towns to work in metropolitan labor markets.

As a result, small communities have been increasingly subject to rising demands for new and expanded local government services and facilities. Herrington J. Bryce finds that during the 1970s expenditures of small cities (ranging in size from 25,000 to 50,000) rose fastest in the areas of police and parks and recreation.[10] The rise in police expenditures is attributable to the fact that in the 1970s the crime rate rose faster in small cities than in all cities taken as a whole, and it has been rising faster in nonsuburban small cities than in suburban small cities. As for the rise in parks and recreation expenditures, the major attraction of small communities to visitors and prospective newcomers is the opportunity to partake in outdoor recreation. Capital expenditures have also been increasing by greater amounts in small cities than in cities as a whole. Most of this increase has been for highways, sewerage and sanitation, and public buildings. America's small communities have undergone rapid changes, changes that pose new and significant challenges for those who must manage them.

The governmental response

It is important to consider in broad terms the governmental response to the challenge presented by urban development in the United States. It is within the context of this response that the process of organizing for financial administration and financial decision making must, of necessity, take place. The capability of local government institutions to respond to and deal with the challenge of urban development in terms of governing the municipality can be approached through the principle of home rule, the fragmentation of local government, and, most pertinently, the structure of contemporary governments.

The principle of home rule

According to the Constitution of the United States, the federal government and the states share sovereign power. This basic document, however, contains no provisions defining the status of local government; municipalities possess no sovereignty—a factor that has significantly shaped national development by generating the principle of what is popularly known as home rule. Home rule may be defined as the achievement of statutory and constitutional provisions allowing municipalities to exercise all powers of local self-government. Local government units must in fact come into existence under the authority of the state by a process of incorporation. Just as a business becomes incorporated so that its organizers may carry on certain legal and financial transactions in a state on a basis other than that of individual responsibility, so a city, town, borough, or village is given legal status as a "corporate body" through an appropriate municipal charter of incorporation. Charters granted to private business corporations nevertheless differ in some important respects from those granted to municipal corporations.

Municipal and private charters First, a private charter is essentially a contract between two parties: a business corporation and a state. It can only be created, altered, or terminated with the consent of both parties. In the case of a municipal charter, however, a state has full authority over the municipality or municipalities concerned, unless the state has imposed limitations on itself through an amendment to its constitution. Many state governments are therefore empowered to alter the major features of a municipal corporation whenever they wish to do so. In such cases the state government can change the municipal corporation's powers, officers, jurisdiction, and requirements for carrying out such vital activities as borrowing money.

The second major difference between private and municipal charters is that a private business can do just about anything that is not illegal or does not violate the rights of others. A municipality, on the other hand, can carry on only those activities that are expressly authorized by state law. If no state law expressly allows the holding of a lottery, for example, then a community cannot authorize such a lottery.

Dillon's Rule Whenever there has been doubt about what a municipality can or cannot do, the courts have usually given a very strict interpretation of municipal powers. In the late nineteenth century, Judge John F. Dillon gave a succinct summary of the approach taken by the courts. His characterization, known as Dillon's Rule, is still applicable to the home rule principle. Dillon wrote:

It is a general and undisputed proposition of law that a municipal corporation possesses and can exercise the following powers and no others: First, those granted in express words; second, those necessarily or fairly implied in or incident to the powers expressly granted; third, those essential to the accomplishment of the declared objects and purposes of the corporation—not simply convenient, but indispensable. Any fair, reasonable, substantive doubt concerning the existence of power is resolved by the courts against the corporation, and the power denied.[11]

Even though most states have adopted home rule guarantees enabling municipalities to exercise all powers of local self-government, the local community thus formed is still clearly subject to the constitution and general laws of the state. The overall effect has been that, while home rule has permitted municipalities greater discretion in such routine matters of an essentially local character as recreation and zoning, the scope of municipal activity has not been significantly enlarged. For the most part, state legislatures and administrative bodies across the nation have continued to exercise the broad supervisory authority expressed in Dillon's Rule. It is instructive to note that the limited development of municipal power is in marked contrast to the broader interpretations of the Constitution made by the Supreme Court in regard to the expansion of federal authority at the expense of that of the states.

Malapportionment   Another important aspect of home rule pertains to the consistent underrepresentation of city interests in the state legislatures. Before 1962 the malapportionment, or unequal division, of legislative districts served to perpetuate the domination of state legislatures by rural lawmakers who tended to show little sympathy or understanding of the problems of cities. In 1962 the Supreme Court decision in *Baker* v. *Carr* invalidated such malapportionment.[12] The balance of political power in the following decade or so did not shift to the large, central cities, as some had anticipated, but appeared to move instead to a coalition of suburban and rural legislators. Those responsible for grappling with the problems of the largest cities have been especially vehement in their complaints about insufficient state aid and the abundance of state control.

Overseeing municipal finance   Yet another—and vitally important—gauge of the degree of state supervision of localities involved in home rule is that of the role of the state in overseeing municipal finance. Generally speaking, the states limit local financial powers, with state control manifesting itself in determining how localities may tax, how much they may tax, and how much indebtedness they may incur. Two explanations have been advanced for this tight state control. First, it has been noted that state officials share a pervasive skepticism about the ability of cities to manage successfully their resources. Second, it has been observed that the states may not want the cities to rely heavily on those tax sources that the states wish to preserve for their own revenues.

Federal and state assistance   Because the states have not fully supported local government needs, the cities have increasingly come to rely on federal government assistance. This trend was particularly evident during the 1960s and continued through the 1970s. Yet federal aid brought a host of problems in its wake. For example, during the late 1960s, the heyday of federal programming, the U.S. Advisory Commission on Intergovernmental Relations (ACIR) recorded the existence of nearly four hundred grant-in-aid and subsidy programs. Some fifty different federal agencies were involved in matters of local water supply and water pollution problems alone—more than twice the number a decade or so earlier. Thus, both the number of such programs and their administration by hundreds of uncoordinated agencies made city-federal relations extremely complex.

The new federalism of the Nixon administration represented an attempt to reduce this complexity. To phase out narrow and highly specific categorical programs and to move public decision-making responsibility away from Washington, general revenue sharing was passed into law in 1972. Additionally, in certain functional areas, individual grant programs have been combined into packages and awarded as a single block grant to state and local governments. Prime examples are the Comprehensive Employment and Training Act (CETA) legislated in 1973; the Housing and Community Development Act legislated in 1974; and Title XX of the Social Security Act legislated in 1974 (provides aid for social services).[13]

During the 1970s, federal funding to localities surged from $2.5 billion in 1971–72 to $7.4 billion in 1975–76, an increase of 197.3 percent. Increases in state aid lagged behind at 64.4 percent, but contributed almost twice as many dollars ($13.7 billion) to city budgets as did the federal government.[14]

Table 1–2 provides additional insight of the extent to which localities have come to rely on intergovernmental aid. In fiscal year 1977–78 intergovernmental revenue accounted for 39.4 percent of all municipal general revenue, compared with 32.7 percent in 1971–72. While state aid continued as the single largest source of intergovernmental assistance, its percentage share remained stable going from 24.0 percent in 1971–72 to 22.1 percent in 1977–78. In contrast, the federal share went from 7.2 percent in 1971–72 to 15.6 percent in 1977–78. The enactment of general revenue sharing (GRS) helps to explain this jump. Despite

Table 1–2 Percentage distribution of municipal government general revenue: all cities, 1977–78 and prior years[1]

Item	1971–72	1972–73	1973–74	1974–75	1975–76	1977–78
General revenue, total	100.0%	100.0%	100.0%	100.0%	100.0%	100.0%
Taxes, total	48.8	45.8	44.0	42.4	42.2	42.5
Property	31.5	29.4	27.7	26.2	25.6	24.9
Sales and gross receipts	9.1	8.8	8.9	9.1	9.2	9.9
Other	8.3	7.5	7.4	7.1	7.3	7.7
Intergovernmental revenue	32.7	36.4	37.6	39.4	40.2	39.4
From state governments	24.0	24.0	23.7	26.2	24.9	22.1
From federal government	7.2	10.8	12.4	11.7	13.4	15.6
Gen. revenue sharing	. . .	4.0	5.3	4.4	3.9	3.8
From local governments	1.6	1.6	1.6	1.5	1.8	1.7
Current charges and miscellaneous	18.4	17.8	18.3	18.2	17.7	18.1

Source: U.S. Bureau of the Census, *City Government Finances in 1977–78* (Washington, D.C.: Government Printing Office, 1980), Table 1, Summary of City Government Finances: 1977–78 and prior periods.

1 All data subject to sampling variation; interpretation of apparent interyear changes must be made with allowance for sampling variability.

the fairly fixed amount of GRS dollars dispensed annually (averaging $2.2 billion), its share of yearly revenues fluctuated from a high of 5.3 percent in 1973–74 to a low of 3.8 percent in 1977–78 with increases in other federal aid programs for cities infusing more funds than in previous years. Not to be ignored in the figures in Table 1–2 is the increased reliance on intergovernmental funds, which signifies a relative decline in revenues generated by municipalities over the six fiscal years surveyed. The dependence of municipal governments on the property tax has lessened.

Thus, the principle of home rule has given rise to a complex labyrinth of fiscal relations that shape the governmental response to urban development and urban needs. These relations are likely to become even more complicated as the results of the Proposition 13 phenomenon referred to earlier become clearer. To the extent that the California experience of restricting the taxing powers of states and localities is copied by other jurisdictions, the financial management of cities and intergovernmental fiscal relations will be more of a challenge than ever before.

Fragmentation of local government

The varying needs of communities in differing physical, social, and economic environments of a land mass of continental size must generate differences in local government forms. Different local governmental responses to those environments have been of great importance in national life; yet regional and metropolitan growth in the United States has given rise to many needs and problems that cross legal boundaries. The multiplicity of governmental units within metropolitan regions, for example, makes common solutions difficult, sometimes impossible. Many observers have noted that instead of sharing resources and seeking a common approach to regional concerns, communities have tended to guard their independence and to seek piece-meal solutions to area-wide problems. Local units, notably special districts, often have sprung up as a means of providing necessary services in the outlying sections of metropolitan areas.[15]

Students of local affairs have warned that unless this fragmentation of local governments is reversed, our large metropolitan areas, central cities, and suburbs alike will continue to experience a wide range of problems. One persistent problem is the cost of duplication that results when several different governments are performing the same type of service in a particular area. For example, communities may pay an excessive price for water if, instead of drawing water from one central source, a cluster of neighboring communities each insists on separate water supply systems.[16] Economies of scale, however, are not unlimited. Some economists and political scientists hold that public choice theories provide consumers with a way to express their preferences in a way that is efficient and cost effective.

Another problem is the unequal distribution of regional resources and services. Every metropolitan area has its wealthy and its poorer communities. Usually it is the middle and upper classes who are able to move to the suburbs. These are the people who are better able to pay taxes. In contrast the poor—those least able to pay taxes but nevertheless needing a greater measure of public assistance—remain concentrated in the large cities.

Municipal government structure

The way government is actually organized—the third vital aspect of the governmental response to the urban challenge—may be viewed as a product of the changing value systems of a society. Elaborating on this viewpoint, Herbert Kaufman has discerned three basic values that have had the greatest impact on the evolution of local government in the United States. These are: (1) representativeness, (2) technical nonpartisan competence, and (3) leadership.[17] At different periods in American history each of these three values has had a significant effect on the arrangement and organization of government.[18] It is also clear that all three have continued to have a major impact on government in the last decades of the twentieth century.

The values of government   What Kaufman characterizes as "the pursuit of representativeness" can be seen in the Revolutionary period of American history. The rising antagonism between the colonies and the English monarch, particularly as he was represented by the colonial governors, generated a deep-seated distrust of executive power generally. After 1776, therefore, executive rule—an unhappy reminder of the king's authority—was downgraded virtually everywhere. Thereafter, citizens of the fledgling democracy deferred to their legislatures, believing them more representative of their interests.[19] On the local level elected councils assumed leadership responsibilities and mayors were often reduced to little more than ceremonial figures.

The period following the inauguration of President Jackson in 1829 is noted for a strong showing of the values of representatives in national life. The essentially anti-aristocratic role of the common man was highlighted in what came to be termed Jacksonian Democracy. At that time it was widely held that "any man was as good as any other man," and the idea that a candidate for office should possess special qualifications to hold the office was frowned on. It was during this time, too, that the number of appointed officers had begun to diminish and the number of elected officers to increase as the franchise extended and elections became the primary mechanism for elevating candidates to office.

The post–Civil War era brought clarification of the ideas surrounding representativeness, which by then had serious limitations. Society was becoming increasingly complex. The Industrial Revolution was generating complicated problems of governmental management, problems that were often beyond the capabilities of part-time, amateur councilmen. The demonstrable corruption of many elected officials, and the role of the urban party "boss" in dispensing patronage, also played a major role in reassessing the values of representativeness in the late nineteenth century.

Given this background, it is not surprising that the values of technical, nonpartisan competence began to take on greater weight. New governing procedures were devised by reformers and introduced as antidotes to what were perceived as excesses of the existing system. Civil Service systems, for example, were introduced in some of the larger cities in an attempt to assure expertise; multi-member boards and commissions were created with the purpose of "taking politics out of government." The reformers assumed that where a number of commissioners held long, overlapping terms of office, special interests and party organizations alike would be denied effective influence. What was not considered by the reformers, however, was that the proliferation of elective offices from the earlier period of Jacksonian values coupled with the equally proliferating new boards and commissions would produce immense difficulties for government coordination. The opportunity for special interest groups and parties to sway decision making, far from being impeded, was, in fact, enhanced as the public became increasingly confused by the complexity of governmental arrangements.

As a result of the complexity, another shift of values took place in the field of government structure. Reformers began to urge the acceptance of a new set of doctrines to achieve integration and coordination in municipal government. With the leadership of the very mayors who had been discredited a century or so earlier, the number of independent administrative offices and agencies could be reduced. The reformers now believed that by establishing clear lines of command under a mayor, waste and inefficiency would be reduced and responsibility would be correspondingly enhanced. Under these conditions, the reformers argued, it was the mayor who could be held accountable to the electorate for the administration of the government. This new shift in beliefs and values gave mayors new powers of appointment and removal. In many jurisdictions they were given the veto for the first time. Gradually, in the twentieth century, mayoral staffs were increased, terms in office lengthened, and, in the larger cities, mayors were given authority to formulate and execute municipal budgets. In short, the values of leadership were enhanced in response to the changing values of the larger community.

The values of representativeness, of technical nonpartisan competence, and of executive leadership have played a major part in shaping governmental structures at different periods in American history. These values, however, are of more than historical significance when the formal models of municipal government that exist in the late twentieth century are considered. It is clear that they, too, were born of and continue to reflect those three basic values. The formal models are mayor-council government, commission government and other forms, and council-manager government.

Mayor-council government In noting the major characteristics of this mode of municipal government structure, it is important to distinguish between two types of mayor-council government—the weak mayor type and the strong mayor type. It is equally important to note that many cities represent variations that fall between these two forms. The weak mayor form has its roots deep in early United States history and may be characterized as reflecting community values of representativeness. As the term implies, this system features a mayor whose power in administrative matters is very weak when compared to the power of the council. The mayor, for example, has limited authority in the areas of appointment, removal, and budget making and may well be chief executive in name only. The weak mayor form persists in many mayor-council municipalities, particularly those smaller cities where the values of representativeness continue to exert a strong influence in the community.

The strong mayor system, on the other hand, reduces the relative importance of the council. The mayor's administrative powers are of greater significance. Advocates of the stronger leadership role of the mayor argue that responsibility in municipal government is possible only if administrative power is centralized in the hands of the executive. They also contend that efficiency and improved coordination result from an integrated administration under the mayor, with the council serving as a legislative body. Historically, the strong mayor form may be traced to the first model city charter drafted by the National Municipal League in 1897. This document set forth a strong, centralized executive form of government to center around a strong mayor. Ballots were shortened. Legislative powers tended to be centralized in a unicameral city council. Through the influence of National Municipal League reformers, a strong mayor form of government took firm hold in the first decades of the twentieth century.

In response to the growing complexity of the urban environment large cities such as New York, Chicago, Philadelphia, and New Orleans provided assistance to the mayor by giving him a chief administrative officer (CAO). Subject to the will of the mayor, the CAO was expected to look after the many details of interagency communication, budget preparation, personnel direction, and other similar areas. It is believed that this approach helps to free the mayor to concentrate on matters of policy.

The mayor, then, is an elected chief executive who prepares the budget, appoints and removes department heads and other principal officials, and who is responsible for both the political and administrative functioning of the city government. Proponents of the strong mayor form also point to the political as well as administrative advantages in this form of government: the mayor has a constituency to which he or she is responsible and which is likely to demand leadership from him or her. In addition, the mayor may be in a better position to use political skills and resources—notably patronage—in those very large cities where competition and conflict between interest groups are most intricate and most intense.

By the late 1970s, the mayor-council form of government was the most popular form of municipal governmental structure, existing in almost 3,600 of those cities with over 2,500 population. It was particularly popular in the very large cities; in the 24 cities of over 500,000 population, 19 had the mayor-council form. All 6 cities of over 1 million population had mayor-council governments.

Commission government and other forms   The commission form of government, on the other hand, was of only limited importance by the mid-1970s. It was the prevailing system in some 220 municipalities, and was, in fact, less popular than the town meeting form of government, which was the preferred system in some 265 cities. The two systems can be described usefully together.

The commission form of government originates with the appointment of five businessmen who were authorized by the governor of Texas to administer the city of Galveston following the catastrophic hurricane of 1900. With respect to the values underlying municipal government, the commission form stems from both those values emphasizing representativeness and those giving weight to nonpartisan technical competence. This system of government allows a small number of commissioners, between five and seven, to be elected on a nonpartisan ticket. As a group they then form the commission and are responsible for policy formation and legislation in the municipality. Each commissioner also serves as the head of an administrative department; thus, unlike the mayor-council plan, both administrative and legislative authority are placed in the hands of the same officers.

Proponents of the commission plan point to the advantage derived from the use of a short ballot, believing the ballot represents a clear, easy-to-understand form of government. Critics, however, point to the dangers of rule by amateurs and of administrative fragmentation. Since the commission form has long passed the popularity peak it enjoyed in the early decades of this century, such discussion becomes increasingly academic.

Other forms of government include the town meeting, which is largely associated with the New England region. The roots of this form reach back into the colonial period, when it played a major role in reinforcing the democratic consciousness that led to the Revolution. Although it is illustrative of the community values of representativeness, this form is of minor significance in the overall national structure of municipal government.

The council-manager form   This form of government clearly exhibits the influence of all three of the core values that have been discussed: representativeness as effected through an elected council serving as the policy-making body; nonpartisan technical competence as implemented through nonpartisan elections in most cities (and also through a professional manager who supervises administration); and executive leadership as effected by a reduction in the number of independent agencies and their integration in a chain-of-command structure headed by the manager.

In the council-manager plan the council performs the legislative function. It appoints a manager who, in turn, selects appropriate department heads and directs their activities. Where there is a mayor, his or her role may be circumscribed and ceremonial. In about one-half of the communities that elect this form of government, he or she is selected by the council from among its own membership; the remaining communities elect their mayor by popular vote.

Drawing on the experience of Staunton, Virginia—where, in 1908, a process of pragmatic experimentation led to the creation of the post of "general manager"—Richard Childs, founder of the council-manager plan, formulated a system to separate policy making from administration. Childs drew on the experience of the commission form of government, notably its integrated structure and nonpartisan short ballot features, and added the idea of a professional general manager, a concept stemming from private business structures. In essence, the council would propose and the manager dispose. In practice, as the council-manager form grew in popularity over the ensuing decades, it became clear that this distinction was not always so clear-cut. The city manager's powers—the appointment and removal of ranking administrators, preparation and execution of the budget, overall administrative coordination—imply that the professional manager cannot help exercising some degree of policy-making influence in the community. Political scientists seem to agree that the most successful managers have always been formulators of policy, although the role must be exercised with great skill and delicacy.[20] The professional manager, after all, must always be aware that he or she serves at the pleasure of the council.

Advantages of the council-manager plan include the centralization of responsibility for administration and supervision in a single individual and the emphasis on the individual's expertise. Conversely, it has been held that the plan may fail to generate effective political leadership, especially in the problem-ridden larger cities. Thus it has been argued that professional managers do not have the necessary political resources to mediate between such contending political forces as powerful unions and business interests and ethnic and racial groups.

It is clear that the council-manager form of government has achieved widespread popularity. By the late 1970s it was the preferred form of government in some 3,560 cities of over 2,500 population. Although this form existed in only 5 of the 24 cities of over 500,000 inhabitants (the remainder being governed by mayor-council systems), it was clearly the most popular form in all cities of over 50,000 population. Over 220 such communities preferred the council-manager plan in comparison to the 172 local governments that adopted the mayor-council form, and to the twenty communities that adopted the commission form of government.

Organizing for financial administration

The role played by organized financial administration within the larger managerial environment may now be considered. This chapter will discuss that role and conclude by focusing more sharply on the essential characteristics of financial decision making within the municipal context.

The historical perspective

The drive to improve financial administration in the United States has gone hand in hand with the larger processes of government reorganization already described. Thus, for example, when prevailing sentiment decreed that government should be decentralized, creating many independent offices and agencies, administration of the financial functions of municipal government underwent related structural changes. Conversely, when the strong mayor or the council-manager form became popular, unification of the hitherto fragmented functions of finance administration was, in general, also achieved.

The civic reform movement associated with the foundation of the National Municipal League in 1894 was to have significant influence in ensuing decades on municipal government. When the league drafted a model municipal corporation act in 1897, it became one of the first groups to emphasize the values of executive leadership. An important feature of the model was a budget system that was to be directed by the mayor rather than the city council. This concept was further developed by, among other groups, the New York Bureau of Municipal Research, which was established in 1906. The bureau viewed municipal budgeting as a major tool for achieving responsibility in government. Specifically, budgeting was seen as a means of realizing economies, eliminating dishonest practices, and setting fixed and objective standards of accountability. Coordination was to be achieved by making the chief executive responsible for recommending revenues and expenditures in the form of a systematic, comprehensive, financial plan. Once the budget was enacted, the chief executive would then oversee the expenditures of the agencies. With the strong support of business people who wanted demonstrable economy and efficiency in government, the budgeting proposals described eventually were adopted by many cities.

In subsequent decades some city and state governments acted to upgrade and to interrelate other important components of financial administration. Such areas as accounting, auditing, purchasing, tax administration, and treasury management were affected by this process. Gradually, the idea of a centralized department of finance to serve the chief executive as a vital instrument of municipal management emerged and took shape. As one observer of this process concluded, by the mid-1920s "most American cities had undergone a more or less thorough reform in municipal financial practices and had established some sort of a budget system."[21]

By the 1970s it appears that where the values of representativeness prevailed, certain fiscal officers—notably city treasurers and controllers—were still independently elected. Where the values of nonpartisan, technical competence were in favor, it was possible to find a variety of autonomous or semiautonomous fiscal agencies, ranging from boards of tax appeal to boards of assessors. Nevertheless, the idea of a fully integrated financial system has won increasing favor, even if the implementation of the practice has varied.

The integrated system

A convenient model of a fully integrated system has been described in the model city charter suggested by the National Municipal League. An adaptation of that model is presented in Figure 1–1. As that figure indicates, the local government manager, appointed by the council, assumes overall responsibility for financial affairs. (In mayor-council governments, the mayor would perform an equivalent role.) In this model the finance department is divided into five areas of control—accounts, budget, assessments, purchasing, and treasury. The director of the finance department is appointed by the manager and serves at his or her pleasure; division heads, in turn, are appointed by the finance director. Figure 1–1 also indicates that the model municipal charter provides for an independent outside

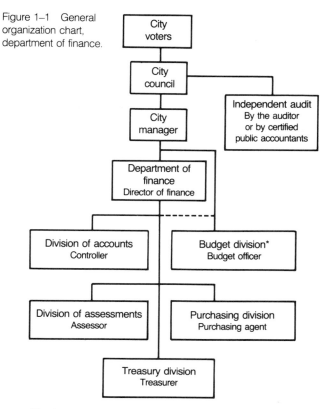

Figure 1–1 General organization chart, department of finance.

*The dotted line between the director of finance and the budget officer indicates that the latter is often primarily responsible to the chief administrator, being physically located in the finance department to prevent the duplication of records. In many cities the finance director handles the budget.

audit. Such an outside audit is in addition to the preaudit function performed by the division of accounts, which is carried out before the payment of all claims and which includes a daily checking of all revenues and receipts. The independent audit, or postaudit (taking place after payment), serves as a check on officials in the executive branch by ascertaining if any errors have been made or if any illegal expenditures have occurred. The objectivity of the independent audit would, of course, be in question if it were to be administered by persons from the branch that authorized the expenditures. In only a small number of cities this function is in fact carried out by an independently elected auditor or controller.

Within this overall framework it is possible to delineate specific components of financial management. Figure 1–2 provides an illustration of a possible breakdown by responsibility of those components. Individual responsibilities may briefly be characterized as follows:

Director of finance As a departmental head the finance director is responsible for supervising and coordinating the administration of major fiscal services. As a managerial aide to the appropriate chief executive—mayor or manager—the director advises on fiscal policy and other related concerns such as debt and investment management. In some cities this officer may also be the chief budget officer.

Accounts After the council has adopted a budget for their forthcoming fiscal year, the division of accounts is responsible for administering the budget

Figure 1–2 Detailed organization chart, department of finance, showing typical functions and activities.

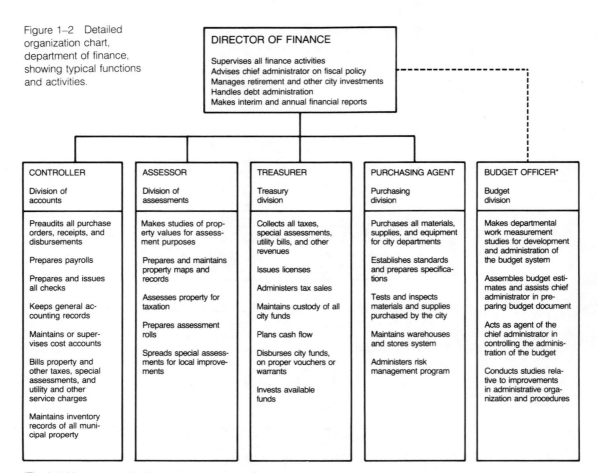

DIRECTOR OF FINANCE

Supervises all finance activities
Advises chief administrator on fiscal policy
Manages retirement and other city investments
Handles debt administration
Makes interim and annual financial reports

CONTROLLER

Division of accounts

Preaudits all purchase orders, receipts, and disbursements

Prepares payrolls

Prepares and issues all checks

Keeps general accounting records

Maintains or supervises cost accounts

Bills property and other taxes, special assessments, and utility and other service charges

Maintains inventory records of all municipal property

ASSESSOR

Division of assessments

Makes studies of property values for assessment purposes

Prepares and maintains property maps and records

Assesses property for taxation

Prepares assessment rolls

Spreads special assessments for local improvements

TREASURER

Treasury division

Collects all taxes, special assessments, utility bills, and other revenues

Issues licenses

Administers tax sales

Maintains custody of all city funds

Plans cash flow

Disburses city funds, on proper vouchers or warrants

Invests available funds

PURCHASING AGENT

Purchasing division

Purchases all materials, supplies, and equipment for city departments

Establishes standards and prepares specifications

Tests and inspects materials and supplies purchased by the city

Maintains warehouses and stores system

Administers risk management program

BUDGET OFFICER*

Budget division

Makes departmental work measurement studies for development and administration of the budget system

Assembles budget estimates and assists chief administrator in preparing budget document

Acts as agent of the chief administrator in controlling the administration of the budget

Conducts studies relative to improvements in administrative organization and procedures

*The dotted line between the director of finance and the budget officer indicates that the latter is often primarily responsible to the chief administrator, being physically located in the finance department to prevent the duplication of records. In many cities the finance director handles the budget.

through to the preaudit function. This division should provide assurance that each department has permission to spend, and that no department is spending more than is authorized. The division will also keep accounts, maintain inventory records of municipal property, and furnish financial information needed in the preparation of the next budget.

Assessments In theory, assessment does not involve decision making, because it is conceived as the mechanical application of state and local laws to the evaluation of property for tax purposes. In the uncompromising reality of contemporary urban life, assessors in fact often function as important decision makers with wide discretion in computing property values. Because these assessments can be a matter of judgment, where the state does not provide a means of handling appeals on disputed assessments, the municipality usually establishes a board of appeals or a board of equalization that can perform this function.

Treasury The treasury division collects the taxes and pays out the monies that, taken together, are the lifeblood of municipal government. Payments cannot be made, however, except after the preaudit and after appropriate certification of the controller. In many municipalities, the treasury is also empowered to issue licenses, administer sales taxes, and invest idle funds.

Purchasing Most of the supplies, material, and equipment for the municipality are procured (and then stored) through the purchasing division. This division, particularly if the municipality is a large one, will thus make the savings that are likely to accrue from large-scale centralized purchasing. The division can also administer appropriate quality control procedures, specifying standards against which purchases are then tested and inspected.

Budgeting The budget division occupies a position of paramount importance in the overall organization of the municipality. Where the role of the executive budget has become established, the head of the budget division usually becomes one of the principal aides to the chief executive. In cases where the budget officer is not in fact the director of finance, the person concerned is usually placed in the office of the chief executive so that the latter may be assured of a direct line of communication. Because of the wealth of knowledge that is acquired in the course of the preparation of the budget, the chief budget officer may well know more about the organization than any other municipal official, including the mayor or the manager. Because the budget officer should possess expertise extending beyond purely fiscal concerns, he or she may well be expected to contribute to studies and proposals involving administrative organization and management planning. The budget officer and his or her staff also assist the chief executive in administering the budget once it has been approved by the council. The budgeting amounts involved are subsequently turned over to the accounting division, which must, of course, preaudit expenditures.

The organizational forms assumed in financial administration have tended, over the course of the twentieth century, to parallel the overall development of municipal government and a more structured and efficient system geared to meet the challenge of accelerating urbanism. Contemporary financial organization may be discussed in broad terms, and the essential components of that organization may be identified and characterized with some precision. It is necessary, however, to emphasize continually that these organizational forms function in a whole range of governmental environments, from the smallest municipality to great metropolitan regions. These managerial environments represent a complex summation of the changing currents and values of history.

Financial decision making

At the heart of these interlocking managerial environments—urban, governmental, and financial—lies the decision-making process. This animates the organizational structures and accelerates or retards financial flows. The process also shapes the day-to-day existence of those thousands of responsible municipal managers who deal with financial matters in communities across the nation. It is appropriate to conclude this introductory overview of the financial realities of local government by reviewing the essentials of this decision-making process, for it is at this vital core that the modern financial management of municipalities achieves its most important expression.

As the preceding discussion has indicated, the role of the finance officer in today's world can be fully comprehended only if it is viewed in the context of community affairs and municipal decision making generally. The finance officer does not now, and probably never did, function in a social and political vacuum. The officer's roles and responsibilities are affected by underlying community values and expectations, as well as by formal rules established by government in all its forms. The modern finance officer must deal with the articulate representatives of other public agencies, with an array of interest groups, with a multitude of community institutions, and with a wide range of additional groups and individuals. Each of these groups and individuals has special needs and expectations. All may be pressing their claims in a climate of economic uncertainty.

This decision-making environment poses in its entirety a number of specific kinds of inducements and restraints that influence the finance officer's job. The modern finance officer must therefore be attuned to the realities of the external environment while continuing to monitor the equally important matters of internal organization and administrative mechanics in an era of technological innovation.

The example of the budget

An exemplary framework for analyzing both the formal and informal dimensions of the finance officer's responsibilities may be evident in the theories and concepts of the budgetary function. This method is adopted in the following brief discussion, not only because of the central importance of budget making but also because this topic has been treated in many empirical studies. A broader and more detailed analysis will be found in Chapter 5.

Municipal budgeting as an aspect of community politics Political scientists have spent much effort in trying to determine how the interplay of political forces within the community affects budgetary decisions. For example, Sayre and Kaufman in their study of New York City characterized the decision-making process as a contest involving several types of participants who strive to influence the allocation of public funds at various points in the government structure.[22] These special influences range from those of the public officials of the city to those of the mass media. The authors found that the budget director wielded substantial influence among these contending forces.[23] The example of New York is atypical, but less dramatic manifestations of community pressure may also be found in the thousands of smaller municipalities across the nation.

While community interests should affect budgeting, it is also true that budgeting has its subtle—but nevertheless significant—impact on various interests in the community. A budget cut can serve to phase out, rather than dramatically terminate, a program or an institution. "It is a quiet although often painful means of killing a program: death through starvation."[24] Again, the more manifest examples of such occurrences may indeed take place in large cities, but ripples are also felt in many smaller communities. The overall point is that, whatever the political system, the budget is a political document.

Budgeting as internal decision making Some social scientists see the budgeting process as a phenomenon that is essentially internal to the political system, one that involves compromise and conflict between ranking administrators and governmental agencies. John Crecine, for example, in a study of Cleveland, Detroit, and Pittsburgh, identified four categories of participants in this process: the chief executive (the mayor or manager); the departmental heads; the city council; and community interest groups. The influence of these participants made itself felt during the various stages of the budgetary process as given below.[25]

Stage 1: Departmental requests The department head must consider how much is needed to carry on existing functions, what is likely to be acceptable to the chief executive, and how much should be requested in additional funds for the following year. Crecine found that agency heads usually follow cues given by mayors or managers; they do not go over the executive's head to request more funds from the council.

Stage 2: Executive review and recommendations At this stage the chief executive, with assistance from the budget staff, must plan a budget in which appropriations are balanced with estimated revenues and existing services are maintained at a minimum. The executive's special burden here is that, unfortunately, requests almost always exceed resources. In deciding where to cut and by how much, the executive will usually rely on information and advice from the budget officer.

Stage 3: Council authorization   The council is now faced with the task of reviewing the executive's budget plan. Because of the complexity and the detail of the document, and because the council lacks the expert staff assistance available to the executive, it does little more, Crecine found, than adopt the budget into law. Where this is the case, it can be argued that the council is failing in the important task of assuring accountability for public performance. Jesse Burkhead and Paul Bringewatt contend that city councils should insist on performance reports, effectiveness reports, and statements of policy before voting on the budget.[26]

In observing that the municipal budget process was executive centered and executive controlled, Crecine found that participation of community interest groups in the budget-making process was minimal and that their influence was correspondingly limited. A study in Oakland by Meltsner and Wildavsky also found that the manager "is the key figure in making most of the decisions. . . . The city manager reviews all the budget and, for the most part, makes the decisions. He guides the city council in its consideration. He feels that it is his budget. And he uses it to make his influence felt throughout city government."[27]

Stage 4: Budget execution   Once the fiscal year has begun and the appropriations bill has passed, the administrative agencies are allowed to spend the dollar amounts listed. There are, however, many constraints that affect how, when, and for what public money can be spent. Assuming that agencies usually do not get all the money they request, there is a tendency for agencies to spend money faster than they should. To prevent this, many cities apportion money to the agency through the central budget office. As a related approach, performance monitoring can be established through the budget office, which periodically reviews the status of projects and activities to ascertain how plans are being implemented.

Budgeting as incrementalism   Other studies have emphasized the methods used by budgetary personnel in choosing among alternative proposals. These studies show that financial decision makers tend to rely on an incremental approach to budgeting. This method is adopted because constraints of time and cost often prevent the decision makers from identifying the full range of alternatives available and, therefore, the consequences involved.[28] In essence, this means that "the existing level of funds is accepted as the legitimate base for future decisions. Next year's budget is based upon this year's, as this year's budget was based upon last year's."[29]

Many social scientists have been critical of this incremental approach to budget making. They contend that incremental budgeting is liable to occur in terms of percentages; the content of what is being considered may therefore be ignored. As Sharkansky has observed: "The criteria employed by financial decision-makers do not reflect a primary concern with the nature of the economy, the platforms of the political parties, or articulated policy desires. . . . The criteria of financial decision-makers are nonideological and frequently nonprogrammatic."[30] Defenders of incrementalism, on the other hand, might argue that cost-benefit ratios for all alternative policies cannot be fully calculated when so many diverse political, social, and economic values are at stake.

Budgeting as rational planning   In spite of intellectual, organizational, and political constraints, the search for a rational approach to public budgeting is receiving renewed emphasis as pressures for fiscal austerity continue. Here the budget is seen as the optimal solution to the problem of allocating scarce resources. Participants list and evaluate priorities, pose alternatives for achieving their objectives, and select a mix of programs that optimizes the benefits relative to costs.

This approach is characterized by PPB (planning-programming-budgeting) systems, and more recently, by ZBB (zero-base budgeting). Derived from operations research, PPB combines a long-term planning dimension with the motivation to assess comprehensively the costs and benefits of expenditure on all program objectives. Variations on this method have been attempted by governmental bodies at all levels. ZBB means that every year each program must be justified from the bottom up. A program that has been funded in the past does not necessarily have to be funded in the future. In other words, each ongoing program and activity is expected to prove itself each year rather than being taken for granted.

Both PPB and ZBB are demanding and worthwhile concepts, but both have encountered strong obstacles, including the belief of some administrators that they are fads (and therefore ephemeral), that the terms lack precision because so many budgeting approaches have been labeled PPB or ZBB, and that there is a wide gap between idealized concepts and actual practices in government. The many variations of PPB and ZBB have, however, made great contributions toward attitudes and practices that may well be designated "program budgeting," which brings to the fore what is being *done* with the money rather than what is being *bought* with it. This approach forces all of the major "actors" in the budgetary process—the council, the chief administrative officer, department heads, program administrators, the finance and budget staffs, and major interest groups—to deal with policy issues in terms of service levels, programs, and major activities.

Unfortunately, PPB and ZBB have not been widely adopted. One student of budgeting claims that most of the obstacles are bureaucratic:

The unwillingness of agency personnel to develop meaningful work units, to learn the skills of the cost effectiveness analyst, to accept the system analyst into the decision-making circle, and the general unwillingness to change time-hallowed practices all militate against budget innovation. Additionally, lack of resources in the agencies reduces the likelihood of any kind of change.[31]

Other obstacles are rooted in relations between the administrative agencies and the legislature or city council. A change desired by the manager or an agency head may not have high priority among council members who represent different constituencies and have a different professional role orientation. Changing budget-making procedures will not necessarily change the use to which the budget is put and so may have no real effects.

The future

Looking to future directions in financial administration, we should note that the mood of the citizenry in the 1970s was conservative. The tax revolt symbolized by Proposition 13 has been gathering steam for years, with many communities vetoing increases in school and other budgets, and several states placing new limits on state-local expenditures and taxes. The pervasive feeling is that in a period when real costs of administering government have increased significantly, there has been an actual decline in the quality and quantity of public services.[32]

An important consideration is whether the tax revolt can be put to use in improving municipal finance administration. A seeming contradiction is that citizens' endorsements of lower taxes have not necessarily meant support for fewer services. The challenge ahead, then, is to achieve cost reductions through improved productivity. This means delivering more and better public services with fewer resources. Management strategies should include devising new patterns of organization and new incentives for public employees, making better use of technology, instituting more effective job analysis and personnel scheduling, overhauling antiquated civil service systems, and introducing better definitions of objectives and measures of performance.

This book deals with major areas of financial management, the economic environment of local government, and the methods for carrying out local government finance. Considerable space is devoted to policy issues, methods, and procedures; yet, it is important to point out that there is another dimension that is more subjective and value laden—that is, honest and ethical government service. In no other area of government is the temptation greater, the opportunity more present, or the responsibility more direct to apply honest and ethical government service than in finance. The stewardship of public funds carries great responsibility; the slightest infraction brings headlines. Citizens today are disenchanted with all institutions and are especially distrustful of government. Today's financial manager has a major role to play in rebuilding that trust, not only in the obvious way of obeying the law but also in setting an example for the entire organization.

Conclusion

This chapter has outlined the antecedents and the overall contemporary dimensions of, respectively, the changing urban environment of the United States; the changing governmental response to that environment; the associated changes in the organization of municipal finance; and, with specific reference to alternative modes of budget making, the crucial role of the decision-making context within which the modern finance officer operates. This overall analysis of the managerial environment will be continued in the three succeeding chapters, which present overviews of, respectively, local government expenditures, local government revenues, and forecasting local revenues and expenditures.

1 James Bryce, *The American Commonwealth* (New York: Macmillan Co., 1920), vol. 1, p. 640. (First edition, 1888.)

2 Ibid., p. 641.

3 See: National Advisory Commission on Civil Disorders, *Report of the National Advisory Commission on Civil Disorders* (New York: Bantam Books, 1968); Urban America, Inc., and the Urban Coalition, *One Year Later: An Assessment of the Nation's Response to the Crisis Described by the National Advisory Commission on Civil Disorders* (New York: Praeger Publishers, 1969); U.S., President's Committee on Urban Housing, *A Decent Home* (Washington, D.C.: Government Printing Office, 1969); U.S., National Commission on Urban Problems, *Building the American City* (Washington, D.C.: Government Printing Office, 1968).

4 On the effects of Proposition 13, see: Jerry McCaffery and John H. Bowman, "Participatory Democracy and Budgeting: The Effects of Proposition 13," *Public Administration Review* 38 (November–December 1978): 530–38.

5 Negativism toward urban government and politics, quite pervasive in the early literature on cities, and still pervasive, is illustrated in the following works: Lincoln Steffens, *The Shame of the Cities* (New York: McClure, Phillips and Co., 1904); Frank J. Goodnow, *Municipal Government* (New York: Century Co., 1909); Chester C. Maxey, *An Outline of Municipal Government* (New York: Doubleday, Page and Co., 1924). For a broader perspective,

see Morton White and Lucia White, *The Intellectual versus the City* (Cambridge, Mass.: Harvard University Press, 1964).

6 The U.S. Bureau of the Census defines a standard metropolitan statistical area (SMSA) as containing at least one city of 50,000 or more population. The nucleus of the area is the county or counties containing the core city or cities. Contiguous counties are included in the area if they are densely settled by nonagricultural workers and are socially and economically integrated with the core city. For technical criteria, see: U.S., Department of Commerce, Social and Economic Statistics Administration, Bureau of the Census, *Standard Metropolitan Statistical Areas, 1959* (Washington, D.C.: Government Printing Office, 1960), and later census reports as appropriate.

7 Jean Gottman, *Megalopolis: The Urbanized Northeastern Seaboard of the United States* (New York: Twentieth Century Fund, 1961), p. 5.

8 William Gorham and Nathan Glazer, *The Urban Predicament* (Washington, D.C.: The Urban Institute, 1976), p. 25.

9 George E. Peterson, "Fiscally Distressed Cities: What Is Happening to Them?" in *Local Distress, State Surpluses, Proposition 13: Prelude to Fiscal Crisis or New Opportunities?*, U.S., Congress, House, Committee on Banking, Finance and Urban Affairs, Subcommittee on the City, and Joint Economic Committee, 95th Cong., 2d sess., July 25–26, 1978, pp. 73–119.

10 Herrington J. Bryce, "Current Trends in Financing Smaller Cities," in *Local Distress, State Surpluses, Proposition 13,* U.S., Congress, House, pp. 95, 96.

11 John F. Dillon, *Commentaries on the Law of Municipal Corporations,* 5th ed. (Boston: Little, Brown & Co., 1911), vol. 1, section 237.

12 Baker v. Carr, 369 U.S. 186 (1962).

13 As of 1975, categorical grants still accounted for about 75 percent of all federal funds. See: U.S., Advisory Commission on Intergovernmental Relations, *Categorical Grants: Their Role and Design* (Washington, D.C.: Government Printing Office, 1977), p. 91.

14 See: Astrid E. Merget, *Untangling the Web of Municipal Finances,* Urban Data Service Reports, vol. 9, no. 10 (Washington, D.C.: International City Management Association, October 1977), pp. 2, 3.

15 A special district is an organized unit of government with substantial autonomy from other governments. It has its own taxing and usually its own bonding authority to carry out specialized services such as recreation, sewage disposal, water supply, airports, parking, and public health. It usually provides only one service, or a limited number of services, in contrast to the general service government of cities and counties. See: U.S., Bureau of the Census, *Census of Governments, 1972,* vol. 1: *Government Organization* (Washington, D.C.: Government Printing Office, 1973), p. 4.

16 See: Edward H. Hobbs, "A Problem—Fragmentation, One Answer—Annexation," *National Civic Review* 60 (September 1971): 429, 430.

17 Herbert Kaufman, *Politics and Policies in State and Local Governments* (Englewood Cliffs, N.J.: Prentice-Hall, 1963), chapter 2.

18 Ibid.

19 On the national level, the Articles of Confederation provided for no executive authority at all. Some have held that the creation of a strong presidency at the Philadelphia Convention of 1787 could be attributed to atypical qualities of the delegates.

20 See, for example: Stanley T. Gabis, "Leadership in a Large Manager City: The Case of Kansas City," *Annals of the American Academy of Political and Social Science* 347 (May 1963): 52–63; Keith Mulrooney, ed., "Symposium on the American City Manager: An Urban Administrator in a Complex and Evolving Situation," *Public Administration Review* 31 (January–February 1971): 6–46.

21 Jesse Burkhead, *Governmental Budgeting* (New York: John Wiley & Sons, 1956), p. 14.

22 See: Wallace S. Sayre and Herbert Kaufman, *Governing New York City* (New York: Russell Sage Foundation, 1960).

23 Ibid., p. 366.

24 Paul H. Conn, *Conflict and Decision-Making* (New York: Harper & Row, 1971), p. 83.

25 John P. Crecine, *Governmental Problem Solving: A Computer Simulation of Municipal Budgeting* (Chicago: Rand McNally & Co., 1969).

26 Jesse Burkhead and Paul Bringewatt, *Municipal Budgeting: A Primer for Local Officials* (Washington, D.C.: Joint Center for Political Studies, 1977), pp. 13, 14.

27 Arnold J. Meltsner and Aaron Wildavsky, "Leave City Budgeting Alone! A Survey, Case Study, and Recommendations for Reform," in *Financing the Metropolis,* ed. John P. Crecine (Beverly Hills: Sage Publications, 1979), p. 344.

28 See: Charles E. Lindblom, "The Science of Muddling Through," *Public Administration Review* 19 (spring 1959): 79–88.

29 Lewis A. Friedman and Bryan T. Downes, "Local Level Decision-Making and Budgetary Outcomes: A Theoretical Perspective on Research in Fourteen Michigan Cities" (Paper delivered at the annual meeting of the American Political Science Association, Chicago, Ill., September 7–11, 1971).

30 Ira Sharkansky, *Spending in the American States* (Chicago: Rand McNally & Co., 1970), p. 13.

31 John Wanat, *Introduction to Budgeting* (North Scituate, Mass.: Duxbury Press, 1978), p. 105.

32 John P. Ross and Jesse Burkhead, *Productivity in the Local Government Sector* (Lexington, Mass.: Lexington Books, 1974); David Greytak, Donald Phares, and Elaine Morley, *Municipal Output and Performance in New York City* (Lexington, Mass.: Lexington Books, 1976).

2 Local government expenditures

What goods and services are provided by local government expenditures? Which items in local government budgets should be expanded? Which items should be reduced? What are the appropriate criteria for budgetary allocation?

Such questions reflect the concerns of people who view municipal finance from differing, but equally valid, perspectives. The average citizen, for example, probably thinks of expenditures as buying streets, highways, schools, traffic lights, library books, and many other items and services all mixed together. He or she may not even attempt to sort out the expenditures of various units of government. Those concerned citizens who are people-oriented—that is, ministers, social workers, and the officials of voluntary agencies—may think of expenditures in terms of urgently perceived program objectives, without too much care about who furnishes the money. The United Way and the municipal budget might well be lumped together as far as they are concerned.

The finance officer or other responsible municipal officials, on the other hand, regard expenditures in precise, finite terms, as measured by actual dollars for the payment of specific services and the purchase of specific products. The astute city manager or finance officer must look at expenditures as the means of mounting programs to meet agreed upon objectives that reflect public policy. Some might think this a rather grandiose objective, but, in essence, this is largely what local government is about. Such decision making is, of course, carried out in the urban and governmental environment described in the preceding chapter.

All questions concerning expenditures nevertheless fall squarely into two sets, positive and normative. The positive questions relate to what *actually* exists; the normative questions relate to what *should* be. It is, of course, necessary to have some knowledge of the existing facts of local spending before the normative issues can be discussed. In the following discussion the existing spending patterns of local government are briefly characterized; the major issues concerning local government expenditures are introduced and analyzed; and the major individual items of local expenditure are then identified and discussed. It is hoped that this approach will contribute to an understanding of the context in which expenditure decisions are made.

Finally, it is necessary to bear in mind throughout the following discussion that there are significant differences between types of local governments and their functions. The term *local government* includes cities of all types, counties, school districts, and special districts.

Some basic points of reference can be introduced at the outset. First, an overall indication of the spending patterns of local governments can be provided. The easiest method of doing this is to look at the "cross section" provided by the outlays for a single fiscal year. For purposes of discussion, it is not necessary to take the most recent year. A fiscal year in the late 1970s is adequate to illustrate the pattern. Table 2–1 presents data on actual local government expenditures during fiscal 1977.

As the table indicates, the total outlay of all local units of government—counties, cities, townships, school districts, special districts, and other units—amounted to approximately $195 billion during 1977, or slightly over 10 percent of gross national product (GNP). In other words, approximately ten dollars out of every one hundred dollars of value produced in the national economy was spent through local government budgets. All of this outlay did not represent locally raised funds, however. Some $83 billion was expended under the direction of federal and state governments with funds made available from those higher units.

It should be noted that local expenditures have risen rapidly in recent years. Local expenditures totaled only $67 billion in 1967 compared to $195 billion in 1977. This represents an average annual growth rate of 11 percent during that ten-year span. Local government expenditures also increased as a percentage of gross national product. In 1967, they represented 8.4 percent of the GNP compared to 10.3 percent in 1977. This indicates that the local public sector was growing more rapidly than the national economy as a whole.

Several factors seem likely to exert significant influence on local government spending patterns during the decade of the 1980s. These include pressures for school finance reform, the trend toward state-imposed limits on local revenue receipts and expenditures, and the general revenue sharing program. Although some of these issues will be discussed in more detail later in this chapter, some brief introductory comments seem warranted at this time.

As Table 2–1 shows, educational outlays occupy, by far, the most important place in local budgets. As a result, changes in this category may affect the entire pattern of local government spending. During the 1970s, pressure seemed to be developing for increased centralization, at the state government level, of elementary and secondary educational financing. Local voter-taxpayers seemed increasingly reluctant to increase the burden on local revenue sources, most notably the property tax, in order to finance increased educational outlays. In addition, legal challenges were mounted in several states against the disparities in taxable wealth per student that existed among local school districts. Although the United States Supreme Court refused to hold that these disparities made reliance on local funding of education a violation of the federal constitution, in some states successful challenges were mounted on grounds of state constitution violations. Because of the dominance of education in local government spending, a continuation of current trends toward centralization of this function seem likely to result in a relative decline of local government expenditures.

A second trend that developed during the 1970s and which seems likely to continue to influence local government spending is that of increased controls on local taxing and spending decisions, imposed at the state level either legislatively or through constitutional amendment. By the late 1970s there was widespread evidence of a genuine taxpayers' revolt. Widespread voter dissatisfaction with local government taxing and spending was manifest in political support for imposition of taxing and spending limits and seemed likely to have considerable impact on the future magnitude and the overall pattern of local government expenditures.

An economic analysis of local expenditures

The following discussion focuses on three aspects of the economic analysis of local expenditures. It first of all considers some basic elements of the economic theory involved, moves on to an analysis of the role of central and local expenditures, and then discusses some aspects of the relationship between local spending and participatory democracy.

Economic theory

Local governments spend money on goods and services for the presumed benefit of the residents of local jurisdictions. Indeed, unless local residents can expect

Table 2–1 Local government expenditures, all cities, fiscal 1977

Expenditure category	Amount (in millions)
Total	$194,956
Intergovernmental	2,159
Direct	192,800
General	169,652
Education	75,733
Highways	9,239
Public welfare	11,918
Health	2,759
Hospitals	8,759
Police	8,811
Fire	4,293
Parks and recreation	3,871
Natural resources	896
Sanitation and sewage	8,873
Housing and urban renewal	3,232
Air transportation	1,139
Water transportation and terminals	508
General control	4,505
Interest on general debt	6,257
Other and unallocable	18,859
Utility	20,108
Water supply	6,637
Electric power	7,828
Transit system	4,862
Gas supply	781
Liquor stores	326
Insurance trust	2,714
Employee retirement	2,628
Unemployment compensation	86

Source: U.S. Bureau of the Census, *Governmental Finances in 1976–77.*

to secure some tangible benefits, they can hardly be expected either to pay taxes or to support the public officials who levy the taxes.

To explain local government spending in terms of economic theory, it is necessary to find out why individuals choose to purchase certain goods and services through the auspices of local government rather than in some other way. Why are services such as education, police and fire protection, and traffic controls purchased by individuals through the political jurisdictions known as local governments? Or, to put the question another way, why do individuals not purchase such goods and services as bread, shoes, houses, and haircuts through local government? What is the essential difference? To state that local governments provide a relatively more efficient means of purchasing the first set of goods and services, but not the second set, does not settle the matter; the meaning of *efficient* must be clarified.

Advantages of joint action Political and governmental institutions are devices that allow individuals to act in common, or jointly, rather than separately or independently. One explanation of government spending activity may therefore lie in just such joint action on the part of separate persons. When men and women can secure goods and services at a lower cost by acting in a group rather than acting independently, they have a valid economic reason for forming themselves into groups. For example, there may be such "gains-from-trade" in extending the size of a consumption-sharing group beyond the normal limits of a household. That is, by procuring certain goods and services through the group, each member may obtain more of those goods and services for a given expenditure than he or she could obtain by acting privately and independently.

Since there is little to prevent the formation of such voluntary cooperative groups, the mere possibility of advantages from joint consumption sharing is not in itself sufficient to explain the emergence of governmental or political institutions. The advantages of cooperatives may be, and often are, captured by such voluntary organizations as golf and country clubs, tennis clubs, swimming clubs, and gourmet clubs.

The role of "exclusion"   In certain circumstances, however, voluntary arrangements designed to capture the economic advantages of joint consumption tend to break down or not be tried at all. The circumstances are those in which exclusion is either impossible or very costly to enforce. By *exclusion* economists mean the prevention of certain individuals from consuming or enjoying goods or services without necessarily having contributed toward their purchase. (*Nonexclusion*, of course, means the lack of such prevention.) To take an obvious example, it is almost impossible to prevent any resident of an area from enjoying the benefits of a reduction in air pollution. Because an individual cannot be prevented from enjoying the benefits of this reduction, he or she will find it advantageous *not* to share the costs assumed by a voluntary group operating to reduce pollution. "Let the other guy do it" will be the individual's response because he or she will then enjoy fresher air without having to give up any of his or her own income in the process.

There also may be situations where exclusion, even if it were to be economically feasible, might negate the very objective of joint consumption. Circumstances may exist where joint action is desirable only if *all* persons in the relevant community are brought into the sharing arrangement. The enactment and enforcement of legal rules (the law) is an obvious example. It would make little or no sense to exclude some persons in a community from the operation of the legal system, even if this were somehow economically possible.

Where significant advantages of joint consumption and nonexclusion are found together, there is a logical economic explanation for the emergence of political units. Indeed, those goods and services traditionally described as public—whether provided by central or local government—normally have these properties.

The theory of public goods   The contemporary theory of public, or collective, goods[1] was developed by economists in the period after the second world war. It is based on the theoretical identification of goods and services embodying two essential characteristics: relative efficiency in joint consumption sharing and relative inefficiency in exclusion. This theory offers the analyst a way of looking at the public or governmental sector of the economy by providing a classification of observed public activity at all levels of government from a small municipality to the federal government itself.

It is necessary to qualify this statement by noting that all governments, especially local governments, provide some goods and services that are neither nonexcludable nor efficiently consumed in joint sharing arrangements. In many cases, however, these items are financed from direct user pricing rather than from taxes. Local government units may act essentially as private enterprises, for example, in the distribution of water supply, in the production and distribution of electricity, and in the provision of mass transit systems. Many local governments also provide goods and services which exhibit some joint sharing efficiencies but which seem clearly to be excludable without difficulty. Locally financed swimming pools are a good example: the costs of collecting entrance fees are relatively low, and there are no apparent benefits except to the direct users of the facilities. In this case, careful application of norms derived by economists from the theory of public goods may suggest the full financing of swimming pools by direct user charges rather than from general tax revenues.

In other instances where goods and services are provided by local governments, the joint sharing characteristic may be dominant, but some nonexcludability features may also be present. Fire protection, for example, falls into this category. When fire protection is purchased by a group rather than by separate individuals, the costs are clearly reduced. In addition, there may be advantages to nonexclusion. Because uncontrolled fires can spread, it is desirable to make fire protection available to all households in the community rather than only to those who might be willing to join a voluntarily organized fire protection club.

For still other local government functions, the jointness and nonexcludability characteristics described may carry roughly equal weights in any evaluative classification. In police protection, there are self-evident efficiencies of joint provision—a single patrol officer can protect all the houses on his or her beat. Even if individuals should voluntarily agree to finance private police protection, it proves difficult to exclude those who fail to contribute from enjoying the benefits paid for by others. Regardless of who pays the arresting security guard's wages, thieves caught by private police forces are no longer a threat to anyone.

Finally, there are local governmental functions that exhibit little or no efficiencies of joint provision throughout the entire community but which are clearly nonexcludable. Education—the single most important category of local government spending—shows such characteristics. There are no demonstrable returns-to-scale (advantages of joint buying) in education, and large school systems may even be more costly than small ones. There may, in fact, be no means of excluding all who might benefit from education. On the other hand, education offers a peculiar example in which private benefits accruing to students can conceptually be separated from the *public* benefits accruing to members of what becomes a well-educated community in general. Organizationally, government support for education, at all levels, fails to reflect this important distinction. In terms of the financing of education from general tax revenues, the implicit assumption is made that all education provides public benefits, and that private benefits are nonexistent. In light of the above analysis such an assumption is quite contrary to fact. Improvements in financial arrangements for education might well take this into account, with some increase in individual responsibility for financing purely private educational benefits.

Developing such concepts as jointness, excludability, and nonexcludability, as well as the framework provided by public goods theory, offers a useful method for analyzing the complexities of local government expenditures, as the illustrations discussed indicate.

Central and local expenditures

Although the preceding discussion concentrated primarily on local government expenditures, the theory of public or collective goods is of general applicability. Suitably modified, it can also provide a framework that helps explain the all-important division of functions between central and local government.

National defense versus fire protection   Why is there a near universal assignment of national defense to central governments, but of fire protection to local units? The common sense response to this question readily fits into the framework of public goods theory.

For different goods or services that embody the characteristics of joint sharing efficiency and nonexcludability, there are varying ranges over which the cited characteristics apply. National defense, for example, often falls at one extreme of this spectrum. In this example, the range of joint sharing includes the whole citizenry of the nation, and nonexcludability also extends to the national limits.

There is no way that individual residents of the United States can be excluded from the protection offered by a patrolling nuclear submarine. Similarly, it would not be to the resident's cost advantage to seek such services either privately or at some lower level of government.

For most governmental or public sector functions, however, the economic analysis is not nearly as straightforward as in the case of national defense. Difficulties arise in measuring the range of the properties of both joint sharing and nonexcludability.

Fire protection—characteristically a local government function—provides clear efficiency gains from its joint purchase or provision by a set of households located in an area as large as, say, a medium-sized city. Beyond this range, however, such gains vanish. Thus, Roanoke, Virginia—with a central-city population of some 100,000—should have a single municipal fire department. In the case of Los Angeles, a city of several million people, there should be many separately organized fire protection districts or jurisdictions. Similar conclusions follow when the criterion of nonexcludability is considered. There are spillover dangers of fire that warrant inclusion of all households within some locally defined area, but geographically these dangers do not extend widely. The purpose and function of fire protection suggest therefore that this service is likely to be offered most efficiently at local government levels. In fact, there is little political agitation for transferring responsibility for this function to the central government.

Most public sector activities fall somewhere between the national defense and the fire protection models described; however, the appropriate level of governmental provision becomes more difficult to determine on the basis of economic analysis alone. Although the functions traditionally performed by local units tend to be relatively limited in their ranges of joint consumption efficiency and nonexcludability, almost all exhibit some spillovers of benefits or costs to larger geographic areas or populations than those covered by local political jurisdictions. The question is one of degree, not of kind.

Police and education   Police and educational activities are both important to local government budgets.

Were a country to comprise tight, locally distinct communities with limited personal mobility, both policing and education would clearly fall within the appropriate center of local government activity. In such a nation citizens of one community would have little reason to join with those of another—through the means of a higher level, more inclusive, governmental unit—to provide internal protection of life and property. There would be no major advantages from common purchase of police services, and there would be no reasons for including citizens of other jurisdictions in the same police network. Similarly, if children educated locally were to remain permanently within the local jurisdiction as adults, the long-range public benefits, as well as the private benefits from educational activities, would largely be confined to citizens of the local community.

In contrast to a country of locally distinct communities, there is the more realistic example of a national economy made up of local communities where there are no distinct natural limits, where the movement of persons among various localities is both easy and efficient, and where migration occurs freely on both a temporary and a permanent basis. In this model, community control of the police function is not necessarily the most desirable organizational arrangement. The failure of a single local community to perform its policing function can create a haven for criminals who impose costs on citizens of other communities—as several communities run by gangsters during the Prohibition Era in the United States made all too clear. Conversely, the superior efficiency of a local police force may offer benefits to citizens residing in other jurisdictions, without effecting a method for exacting payment for those services. In short, both policing and public schooling may cause important spillovers among communities in terms of benefits and costs. One method of capturing these spillovers is to shift the responsibility for such functions to a higher level of government.

It is because of these spillovers that the 1960s and the 1970s were marked by attempts to modify the traditional responsibilities of local governments for police and educational services. A dramatic increase in crime rates stimulated various federal government programs to provide external assistance to local police authorities. Developing more effective coordination between separate localities and improving the efficiency of local police forces were among the objectives of the programs. Although the political risks of a shift to a monolithic central government police force were widely recognized, these programs concretely attested to federal government interest in the general policing function.

In education, comparable changes also took place. Until the late 1950s, the role of the central government in financing all levels of education was minimal. Federal financial participation in education grew dramatically during the 1960s and 1970s. Federal expenditures for education grew from slightly over $1 billion in fiscal 1965 to almost $7 billion in fiscal 1977. This represented an increase in the federal government's share of total government expenditures on education from 3.5 percent to 7.1 percent.

Although the bulk of financial support for education still remains at the state and local levels—though not always at the municipal level—the federal bureaucracy and the federal judiciary have increased their control over educational processes. Many local school boards and even state agencies effectively exercise their powers only within federally sanctioned limits. Nevertheless, there have been surprisingly few negative reactions to the increased federal fiscal presence in public education. Theoretical arguments against a domineering federal government bureaucracy abound; yet when solid proposals are considered, it is clear that the relative position of the central government has, in fact, grown stronger, and that of local governments grown weaker.

Other categories of public spending Pressure to transfer financial responsibility from the local government level to the federal level appears to have increased in recent decades in all of the other major categories of local public spending. Geographic spillovers are significant in the construction and maintenance of highway or street networks; the provision of public health facilities; and the maintenance of environmental control programs. Federal grant-in-aid programs recently have become more important in all these areas.

The welfare function has also been used to illustrate the desirability of an increased federal fiscal presence. Court decisions in the 1960s, for example, severely limited the powers of some local governments to establish welfare eligibility criteria in terms of residence and family status.[2] Partially as a consequence of this, local jurisdictions that offer above-average welfare benefits may face in-migration of welfare recipients and an increased burden on local tax sources.

Revenue sharing In 1972 the State and Local Fiscal Assistance Act was enacted. More commonly known as general revenue sharing (GRS), this legislation attempted to introduce a "New Federalism" by making federal funds available to state and local units of government without substantial federal controls on the manner in which the money was to be spent. Of particular interest to local units of government was the fact that two-thirds of the total revenue sharing funds were specifically earmarked for localities with the remaining one-third going to state governments. In the late 1970s, slightly under $7 billion was being distributed annually in states and localities as a result of the revenue sharing program.

Revenue sharing is a very complex program and a definitive analysis of its effects cannot yet be made. Certainly, some portion of the funds received from the federal government simply replaces local funds. It seems likely that this will continue as a result of less supportive voter attitudes toward local spending in the late 1970s. At the same time, pressures may develop to increase the size of the revenue sharing program to further ease the burden on local revenue sources.

The economic framework of analysis provided by the theory of public goods can, with appropriate modifications, help clarify vital divisions of central-local fiscal responsibility such as police, fire, and educational services. It also helps clarify the decision-making process of governmental finance at all levels. While revenue sharing introduced a new element into the picture in the early 1970s, its full significance will become apparent after a decade or so of operation.

Local spending and participatory democracy

One of the most frequently encountered arguments in support of local government autonomy is based on the claim that decisions made at this level are "closer to the people." Indeed, a central element in contemporary radical critiques of existing institutional structures is an emphasis on decentralization of political power, accompanied by an increase in citizen participation in—and subsequent control over—local governments. An analysis of political decision making at the local level is therefore essential to any discussion of the issues that affect local expenditures. In what sense, for example, is it possible to say that local budgetary decisions are more likely to reflect genuine constituency demands?

In order to discuss this question it is helpful to look briefly at an idealized local collective-decision structure, and then to critically evaluate the necessary departures from that ideal.

Unanimity   A model of collective decision making, created by Swedish economist Knut Wicksell, can provide the ideal framework.[3] Wicksell outlined a political decision process which, he held, resulted in the same efficiency in the governmental provision of public goods and services as is achieved through the market process in the provision and allocation of private goods and services.

A local community confronted with a decision about a single spending project, the construction of a municipal park, will serve to illustrate Wicksell's model. This community is small enough for all of its members to meet in one place. During such a meeting, a proposal is put forward to build a park, along with a method of sharing the cost among all the members of the community. Suppose some members object to the combined spending and taxing proposal that has been made; the proposal is withdrawn and a different scheme for distributing the costs is suggested. This sequential consideration of alternative tax or cost sharing schemes is continued until a plan is found that *all* members of the community can accept.

The requirement of unanimous agreement among individuals on the division of tax shares for the construction of the park assures that no individual is required to pay more for the "good" (the park) than his or her evaluation of the benefits received from using the park dictates. This process is analogous to individual behavior in the marketplace—no individual will ever pay a price for a private good or service that exceeds the valuation he or she places on that good or service.

If, in the example under discussion, unanimous agreement cannot be reached on a taxing arrangement to provide the park, then the park is not valued as highly as the private goods and services that the individuals of the community could purchase with their tax dollars. The park project is then abandoned because it is not worth its cost to any combination of citizens under any possible tax structure.

The Wicksellian ideal of unanimous agreement is impracticable for almost any collective decision-making group. Nonetheless, the results of unanimous consent can be approximated if alternative collective arrangements are readily available. For example, few purely private or voluntary clubs make actual decisions through a unanimity rule; yet, the final results somehow closely reflect the preferences of members simply because their participation is voluntary. If a member does not agree with the decisions that are reached by the club, and if this unhappiness is sufficiently strong, he or she can leave that club and join another. This reasoning, with appropriate modifications, may be applied to the location of governmental activities.

Perhaps the most important advantage of assigning public functions to the smallest possible governmental entity is the implied limitation placed on individual preferences. For example, the shift of a function to the national government effectively inhibits the alternatives available to those who might strongly disagree with the collective outcomes. On the other hand, the assignment of a function to a local unit of government allows individuals who are strongly upset by collectively imposed outcomes to "vote with their feet" and move to another local community. This option—which is open to all citizens—severely limits the power of any local majority coalition to impose arbitrary costs on the minority.

As with all idealistic models, the Wicksellian model offers a benchmark for subsequent analysis, and provides for the isolation of those decision-making features that are directly relevant to efficient budgetary choices. For purposes of practical discussion, however, it is necessary to identify and characterize four major areas of departure from the theoretical framework of the model. These departures are, of course, present in all governments, local, state, and national; the effect of these necessary inefficiencies at the governmental levels, however, differs.

Direct democracy   In the model, the rule of unanimity is suggested to inhibit choices that would be contrary to the genuine interests of individuals and groups. The rule of unanimity can hardly be justified, however, in any practical setting because of the costs involved, those costs being incurred primarily by a delay in any collective action. Common sense and efficiency dictate that the rule of unanimity be replaced by some less inclusive rule for reaching decisions in a local community. Majority voting is therefore accepted as the norm for democratic governments. Once majority voting is established, however, the collective decisions represent the voter whose preferences are median for the community— assuming, of course, that everyone in the community votes. In the case of a decision on the provision and quantity of a public good, for example, the median voter will divide the community in half between those who desire a greater quantity of the good than the median individual and those who desire less. As a result, no majority coalition exists to move the spending level away from that most preferred by the median voter. Obviously, majority voting rules provide no assurance that the preferences of the minority will be satisfied.

Representative democracy   Another departure from the idealized model develops when the direct democracy of the type described previously is replaced by representative democracy. In the contemporary United States, local government populations are either too large or too scattered geographically to hold direct meetings. (The town meetings of a few New England communities are virtually the only exceptions.) In most local government units, representatives of the voters are elected and fiscal decisions are made by the representatives, not the voters themselves. If the interests and preferences of representatives differ from those of the general citizenry, or even from those of the median or average voter, the collective decisions under representative democracy will be somewhat different from those that emerge in direct democracy.

Although almost all governmental units depart from direct democracy and choose some form of representation, the "distance" between the individual citizen and his or her representative in the political decision-making process varies directly with the size of the governmental unit. The town council member or the county supervisor generally "represents" a much smaller number of families than does a member of Congress or a state legislator.

Taxing and spending decisions   A third departure from the Wicksellian model involves taxing and spending decisions. If the impacts of cost and tax are simultaneously taken into account with spending proposals, citizens and their representatives generally can make rational fiscal decisions. Although the link between these two sides of the budget is generally recognized, institutional barriers nevertheless help to obscure it in the minds of the voters and to distort governmental outcomes. There is evidence, for example, that those local referenda that propose budget expansions and also incorporate supporting tax proposals secure less voter support than those that do not—even though the fact that any approved proposals must ultimately be financed is recognized by the voters.

Citizens of local governments score higher than those of state governments on recognizing the pitfalls of the idealized political process that separates taxing and spending decisions. At the federal government level, however, citizens express relatively little consciousness about the relationship between increases in budgetary totals and increased taxes. Legislation in 1974 was an attempt to remedy this problem; Congress now must set explicit limits on aggregate revenue and expenditure by functional category. Budgetary decisions on specific programs and other items are made within this framework; even so, it appears that the tie between spending and taxing is more evident to those at the local government level than those at the federal level.

Separate budgetary items   The fourth point of departure from the idealized model concerns the preparation of the budget. In the idealized model there would be many separate "budgets," one for each major spending item. A community makes its decisions on school expenditure, for example, independently of those concerning other government activities; however, the school expenditure decision would be made simultaneously with a taxing decision to raise the required revenues. A limited expression of this procedure is to be found in earmarked taxes, especially at the state and local levels of government. The fragmentation of governmental units enhances this procedure. The school district, for example, is empowered to levy taxes to be spent only for schools. The same may be true of fire departments, sanitation districts, water districts, and the like. If such mechanisms are absent, the voters and their representatives are faced with the task of making a package decision on many budgetary items, the proportionate shares of which may be tied together in ways that do not reflect the sentiments of the community.

General fund budgeting necessarily reduces the level of sophistication with which fiscal choices can be made by the electorate—despite its popularity with budgetary bureaucrats. The voter and the voter's representative are given a choice comparable to a "tie-in sale" in the private market, where proposed budgetary items cannot be "purchased" in separate accounts.

Local governments, like all other governments, do not separate fully their total expenditures into separate budgets for each item. General fund budgeting also is used at this level of government. The proliferation of local units nevertheless partially illustrates the ideal. Separate school districts, fire districts, and the like do provide separate decison-making structures, which provide for a more rational consideration of the independent items in the local fiscal mix. Even with general fund budgeting, local units often employ special devices to separate the various spending items. In the case of the general property tax, the specific assignment of mill rates (i.e., tax rates at 0.1 percent of assessed dollar value) to separate local government functions accomplishes the same purpose as the earmarking of individual items in the specific sense.

Economic theory provides the framework needed to analyze the decision-making process in a local community. The comparisons of the decision-making process at various levels of government, and the four criteria for efficient decision making, clearly illustrate that local governmental decisions more accurately reflect the genuine preferences of citizens than do decisions reached at higher levels of government. Hence, the budgets and expenditures of local governments are likely to be more "efficient" than those of other governmental units.

Summary

Many arguments may be advanced in favor of the transfer of functions to higher levels of government. Some of those arguments have been noted in discussions earlier in this chapter. Opposing arguments, such as those briefly outlined in the preceding discussion of local spending and participatory democracy, are often overlooked. The arguments for the retention of independent fiscal autonomy at the local governmental level, however, seem sufficiently strong to ensure that "local expenditures" will remain meaningful and important in the national fiscal picture for decades to come. Indeed, in spite of the extremely rapid centralization of power that has taken place (especially since the second world war) local governments remain viable entities. It appears that they will continue to be so. The following discussion of the major issues surrounding the principles of local government expenditures will help clarify the analysis of particular items in those expenditures.

The major items

The major categories of local government expenditure may now be examined in more detail. The items to be discussed are education, welfare, highways and streets, health and hospitals, police and fire protection, and other outlays. Some items are obviously more important than others. The important differences as well as the similarities among items in local government budgets will emerge as the examination proceeds.

Education

As shown in Table 2–1, outlays for education loom larger than any other item in local budgets. Out of a total local government outlay of $195 billion in the sample year 1977, nearly $76 billion (or 39 percent) went to educational expenditures. No other single item of expenditure exceeded 10 percent of the total.

Historic trends   Educational outlay, long the dominant item in local budgets (reflecting the importance given to public education in national and community life), has increased in relative importance over the three decades or so following the end of the second world war. Before that war, educational spending did not exceed one-third of total local outlays. The significance of that increase in local spending for education can be appreciated more fully when total educational outlay at all government levels is examined. Total public spending on education amounted to more than $110 billion, for example, in the sample year of fiscal 1977. The federal government's share was almost $8 billion, the state governments' share was approximately $27 billion, with the various local governments accounting for the remaining $76 billion or so.

Table 2–2 indicates the outlays made for education by all governments for selected years over the period 1940 to 1977 and serves to illustrate several interesting relationships.

Table 2–2   Federal, state, and local government education expenditures, selected years, 1940–77

Fiscal year	Total (in millions)	Level of government		
		Federal (in millions)	State (in millions)	Local (in millions)
1940	$ 2,653	$ 15	$ 375	$ 2,263
1950	7,251	74	1,358	5,819
1960	18,770	212	3,396	15,162
1965	30,021	1,050	6,181	22,790
1969	50,377	3,139	12,304	34,934
1971	64,042	4,629	15,800	43,613
1975	95,011	7,153	22,902	64,956
1977	110,642	7,836	27,073	75,733

Source: Tax Foundation, *Facts and Figures on Governmental Finance*, Table 4, and U.S. Bureau of the Census, *Governmental Finances in 1976–77*, Table 11.

The first relationship illustrated in Table 2–2 is the dramatic rise in total expenditures over the three decades covered. This increase is dramatic both in absolute dollar totals and with respect to the share of educational outlays in the gross national product. From the start of the 1950s to the beginning of the 1970s, for example, total spending on education rose at the rate of about 11.0 percent per annum. In 1977 total public spending for education amounted to about 6.0 percent of the GNP—contrasted to under 3.0 percent in 1940. Of even greater significance has been the dramatic rise in the federal share of total educational outlays. As Table 2–2 indicates, starting from a very low level in 1940 the federal outlay in this area increased more than five hundred times by the late 1970s. The major increase, of course, occurred in the 1960s in the aftermath of such events as the first Sputnik, civil rights protests, urban unrest, and more specifically, the "Great Society" legislation of the Johnson administration. From 1960 to 1969 alone, federal spending on education increased fifteenfold, from a level of 1.1 percent of total governmental outlays on education in 1960 to 3.5 percent in 1965 and 6.2 percent in 1969. Real expenditures increased dramatically, even with the erosion of the dollar because of inflation.

Table 2–2 also demonstrates that the state government's share in educational financing significantly increased in relation to local governments' share, although, relatively, not as much as the federal share. The basic overall trends in educational financing are clear. Along with a sharply increased total outlay (in both absolute and relative terms) has come an increasing shift upward in the hierarchy of governments of the financial responsibility for this vital function.

The outlook   The tradition of substantial local autonomy in the finance and control of elementary and secondary education was seriously challenged politically and legally during the 1970s. Politically, local voter-taxpayers seemed increasingly reluctant to approve school bond issues and tax increases to support increased local spending on schools. This reluctance to increase the burden on local tax sources, most notably the property tax, was accompanied by pressure for an increased participation of the state in education funding. Several states faced legal challenges to the constitutionality of traditional methods of financing education, which added to the pressure for reform in school financing.

The constitutional challenges concerned taxable wealth per student, which differed significantly across local school districts and required higher tax rates in some districts to generate identical local spending per student. Most state grants to local school districts included provisions in the funding formula that imposed a negative correlation between state funds and local district wealth.

However, these schemes did not completely offset local wealth disparities and, beginning with the famous *Serrano* case[5] in California in 1971, a spate of lawsuits in several states challenged the constitutionality of any school financing scheme that made the quality of a child's education dependent on the wealth of his or her local school district. These challenges were made on the state and national levels.

The United States Supreme Court in 1973 rejected the argument that the financial schemes violated the equal protection clause of the Fourteenth Amendment to the Constitution.[4] In California and some other states, however, similar challenges to the equal protection clauses in state constitutions have been upheld.

Regardless of the final outcome of the legal challenges to current educational finance institutions, the trend toward increased state government involvement in this area seems unlikely to be reversed. There are several ways in which state government action may influence local education expenditures. First, state grants-in-aid ease the burden on local tax sources. In addition, the structure of the aid formulas may influence local political choices regarding expenditure levels. The 1970s also saw the beginning of a trend toward state-imposed limitation on local tax revenue collections and expenditures. Between 1970 and 1977, fourteen states and the District of Columbia imposed new controls on local taxing and spending.[6] In 1978, the people of California approved Proposition 13, which rolled back local property tax levies and placed tight limits on their future growth.

Another trend that will be affecting local government education expenditures during the 1980s is that of declining school-age population. Much of the phenomenal increase in school spending that occurred during the late 1950s and 1960s was the result of the increased demands placed on educational systems by the post-World War II "baby boom." The baby boom ended during the 1960s and the current birth rate in the United States is actually slightly below that required for stable population size. Public school enrollment began to decline in the mid-1970s. With fewer children to educate, the financial burden in local school districts is expected to ease. At the same time, however, well-entrenched educational bureaucracies will undoubtedly resist sizable cuts in school spending, arguing instead for substantial increases in educational quality. Given these conflicting interests, the actual effect on school spending is hard to predict. At the very least, the rate of growth of real spending on education should slow in the future.

Public welfare

While no function in local government expenditure approaches education in quantitative importance, local outlays under public welfare—the largest expenditure category after education—nevertheless, reached an absolute sum of close to $12 billion annually by the late 1970s.

Basic features   Spending for public welfare, like that for education, has increased sharply in recent years. During the twelve-year period between 1965 and 1977, local government expenditures on this function increased at an annual rate of approximately 11 percent, from $3.3 billion in 1965 to $11.9 billion in 1977. It is important to note that, organizationally, local public welfare spending is handled largely by city (especially big city) and county governments. In this respect, this expenditure item is quite distinct from the educational outlay, which is carried out in large part through independent school districts.

It is also important to note that programs for public welfare spending cannot be treated as local government programs in the strict sense. In one major program in this category, Aid to Families with Dependent Children (AFDC), the federal government, through the use of categorical grants-in-aid, has established very specific standards that states are required to meet in order to qualify for federal funds. The state governments, in turn, transmit these funds, with matching state funds, to local governments—notably, counties and a few large cities. For the most part, the state governments have acted as "pass-through" mechanisms between the federal and local governments. The latter are, so to speak, at the end of the line and have primary responsibility for direct spending on welfare matters. They also function within a set of complex rules and regulations which govern their expenditures.

Given this framework, local governments have supplemented the grant funds with local resources whose availability has been determined by local political pressures and attitudes. As a result, major differences in political settings and acknowledged differences in fiscal capacities, have helped generate wide disparities in welfare payment levels among states.

Problems and prospects   The welfare system in the United States is generally acknowledged to be inefficient and inadequate. The various programs are administratively complex and provide weak incentives for recipients to seek gainful employment. Although there is widespread agreement that something should be done, a consensus on exactly what to do is less apparent.

The role of the federal government in the public welfare function has increased dramatically since the early 1960s. Between 1965 and 1977, for example, direct expenditures by the federal government (excluding grants-in-aid) increased from slightly over $100 million to $14.9 billion. More significantly, the federal share in total direct expenditures increased from less than 2 percent to approximately 30 percent over that twelve-year period. The share of local governments in total direct expenditures fell from 51 percent in 1965 to 24 percent in 1977. By the late 1970s, it seemed clear that whatever welfare reforms might be enacted would involve an even greater role for the federal government.

One major change that occurred during the 1970s was implementation of the federal Supplemental Security Income (SSI) program. This program established a uniform, federally guaranteed minimum income for the aged, the blind, and the disabled, and replaced a former program of categorical matching grants to the states. Although state supplements are allowed under the SSI program, the bulk of financial and administrative responsibility for welfare payments to these groups has been transferred to the federal government.

The Comprehensive Employment and Training Act (CETA) of 1973 also increased federal financial participation in the public welfare area, although, in contrast to the SSI program, localities were granted considerable administrative discretion. The two key elements of the CETA program are grants to local government units to finance training and manpower programs for the economically disadvantaged and to finance public service employment in the localities. A problem with the CETA programs and, in particular, with the public service employment programs has been to ensure that funds are actually used by localities to aid the economically disadvantaged. If CETA funds are simply used to substitute for local funding of certain local government jobs with no significant net increase in local employment and, in particular, in the employment of individuals who have difficulty finding jobs in the private sector, a primary objective of the CETA program is thwarted. The extent to which such substitution actually occurs is a subject of continuing controversy. In 1978, the Congress tightened the requirements on the use of CETA funds in an attempt to discourage such substitution.

An economic case can be made for federalization of the entire welfare program. Wide disparities in levels of provision among communities do exist. While there is no clear-cut evidence available to indicate that individuals and families make migration decisions as a result of the available levels of welfare provisions, the economic motivation for such migrations does exist. In the past local communities could control such potential in-migration by means of residence eligibility requirements, or encourage out-migration of what were perceived as marginal populations by holding welfare payments at a deliberately low level. Be that as it may, limitations set by the federal judiciary on the power of local units to set residency requirements have tended to render such discussions moot. Such judicial fiat has also placed local communities in a position where they are required to finance a large share of welfare spending without having any control over the number of claimants. Local government leaders—especially those from the larger cities—have, as a result, been active in campaigns for the federalization of the welfare function.

More generally, a trend toward greater diversification of the welfare function has emerged. A proliferation of programs tailored to the needs of particular groups, from adolescents to alcoholics and preschool children to elderly citizens, are being considered. Welfare expenditures have begun to blend into the more recently established category of human service expenditures. Finally, times of economic difficulty manifest themselves in welfare expenditures with an increase in the numbers of individuals who are unable to find gainful employment.

Highways and streets

By the late 1970s, local governments were spending a little over $9 billion annually on highway and street construction and maintenance—the third most important local spending category. The proportionate share of road spending (as highway and street expenditures are characterized) in local government budgets, however, actually declined over the twelve-year period from 1965 to 1977.

Both the federal government and the states provide massive financial support for the interstate highway system and for primary and secondary highways. Nevertheless, road and street construction and maintenance in urban areas will remain an important item in local government budgets. As inflation continues to climb, highway and street expenditures will undoubtedly increase on the local level as they increase on the state and federal levels. In contrast to education and public welfare, however, this item of expenditure appears to be a relatively stable item in local government budgets.

Health and hospitals

Local units were spending more than $11 billion annually on public health and hospitals by the late 1970s, with over $8 billion of this amount directly attributable to hospitals. Significant portions of these outlays were funded through federal and state grants-in-aid.

The 1970s were characterized by sharp increases in health care costs—increases that significantly exceeded the overall inflation rate in the economy. Many observers attributed these cost increases to undesirable features of federal medical care programs; substantial increases in the demand for medical care were generated without any accompanying programs to increase the supply. The predictable result was that medical care prices, especially hospital prices, soared. By the late 1970s health care costs were a major political issue.

As a result, direct controls on hospital costs and a program for national health insurance were under serious consideration. Either or both of these policies would have had a significant impact on the role of local government in the health area. Cost controls would increase federal administrative control of city and county hospitals, and a program of national health insurance has the potential for generating additional increases in demand for health services by decreasing the direct costs of health care to the program participants. Such a program would add to the pressure to provide cost-effective health care.

Police and fire protection

During the late 1970s local government units were spending over $13 billion annually on police and fire protection. Almost $9 billion were spent on law enforcement services.

Traditionally, police and fire protection have been the most clearly defined local government functions. To residents of large and small communities across the nation, the familiar sight of a uniformed police officer or a local fire truck probably represents one of the most tangible manifestations of local government outlays.

Trends in police protection   During the 1960s, crime became the subject of national concern. Increases in the mobility of the national population, criminal and noncriminal alike, coupled with accelerated crime rates contributed to a change in government's perception of the problem. It was no longer purely a local concern. In the late 1960s, the federal government instituted some programs of grants-in-aid for local law enforcement agencies; however, widespread fear of a national police force limited federal involvement in this area.

By the mid-1970s the crime problem appeared to have been alleviated somewhat. The upward spiral in crime rates had slowed, with a slight decline registered in 1976. The changing demography of urban areas seemed likely to contribute to more improvements in the crime rate as the number of individuals in their early teens and twenties—the age group that traditionally has accounted for a disproportionately large share of urban crime—will begin to decline in the 1980s.

The policing function in local communities is, of course, carried out within the larger internal social order. Predictions about the social order are always difficult to make, but if the trends of the late 1970s are continued, local spending on police protection should stabilize, and possibly decline in real terms, in this decade.

Trends in fire protection   Fire protection is an even more specific local function than is police protection. This function, in particular, seems to benefit the least from intergovernmental spillovers. Future trends in fire protection expenditures by local governments are especially difficult to predict given the technological advances in fire fighting and prevention that are likely to be made. The increasingly serious problem of arson, particularly in urban areas, also makes predicting trends difficult.

Other services and administration

The major items of local government expenditure have been outlined and briefly discussed category by category. A glance at Table 2–1 shows that the remaining services performed by local government bulk in the aggregate. Sanitation and sewerage, for example, required outlays of almost $9 billion annually by the late 1970s—a development undoubtedly reflecting increased interest in the environment and antipollution controls. Even with federal government grants-in-aid in this area, this item alone may require spending increases in the years ahead.

Other important services in local government budgets include such items as expenditures on parks and recreation, natural resources, housing and community development, air transport facilities, and water transport and terminals. The significance of these items is indicated by the amount of total spending in these areas, which was well over $10 billion annually by the late 1970s. The category of "other and allocable" added yet another $18 billion or so.

Finally, interest on local debt, a nonservice item in local government budgets, took on particular significance with the onset of inflation. The interest, over $6 billion annually and rising, is an increasingly important aspect of local government expenditures. No outline of the topic would be complete without reference to this difficult area of financial management.

Other local outlays

All of the local government expenditures discussed previously fall into the general fund category and are indicated as such in Table 2–1. They are financed by tax revenues at various levels of government. By the late 1970s, however, some $25 billion out of the total annual outlay of well over $194 billion fell outside the classification of general expenditures. Local governments now must make direct outlays in connection with their provision and sale of goods and services that more closely resemble those of private goods and services.

The private goods represent utility services such as power and water distribution and, in some jurisdictions, liquor store stocks. Revenues to finance these spending items and services are collected directly from the users and probably should not be included in local government budgets. In fact, many utilities and other quasi-business enterprises are handled through separate budgeting systems and separate budgeting procedures, unlike those related to local government budgeting.

Employee retirement systems

Before concluding this chapter it is important to draw attention to the area of employee retirement systems. Table 2–1 shows that in 1977 local governments paid beneficiaries of the local retirement and disability systems over $2.6 billion. This is a relatively large expenditure and one that is expected to rise over time. What has most people concerned, however, is the uncertainty attached to the future liability associated with these plans.

The level of pension benefits depends on several factors. The generosity and coverage of the plan itself, the number of workers covered by the plan, and the condition of both the national and regional economy are all important components in determining the level of the financial burden that these plans will place on the local government.

It has been the custom to define a local government worker's pension as a percent of the average salary earned in the last few years of employment. As salaries of workers (especially senior workers) rise and as the work force grows, the liability of the plan increases. Local governments attempt to provide for (or fund) the future liabilities of the benefit plans by making periodic contributions to the pension trust fund. Roughly speaking, a plan is said to be fully funded if these periodic payments are set at a level sufficient to meet the projected future liabilities. Unfortunately, most studies show that, in general, local retirement systems are seriously underfunded; moreover, inflation is likely to make the problem more severe. Although determining the precise size of the unfunded liability is an extremely difficult problem, what does seem likely is that in the near future either governmental contributions to the trust funds will have to be sharply increased or, perhaps, as an alternative the features of these plans will have to be redesigned. The pension fund problem is discussed in detail in Chapter 16 of this volume.

Summary

No attempt has been made to make a detailed examination of the major expenditure items in local government budgets; but an attempt has been made to place each item in the larger context of local government and community affairs, and to show that expenditures for local functions are not static entities but are in a constant state of flux. The differential effects of broad national trends on each item have been indicated also.

As always, in a discussion of local government affairs, the distinction between governmental responsibilities at different levels of jurisdiction must be borne in mind. A financial officer concerned with school district affairs, for example, will have a different perspective from the person responsible for a small city, and both will differ from decision makers in larger jurisdictions. All, however, are increasingly involved in the results of one another's actions and in the total financial management picture.

The outlook

This chapter, which has discussed both the general and specific aspects of local government expenditures, concludes with a few general observations on the outlook for local government expenditures.

Two factors appear likely to exert continuing and significant influences on local government spending in the 1980s. The first is the continuing problem of persistent and significant inflation that has plagued the American economy since the late 1960s. The second is the evidence of widespread voter dissatisfaction with taxing and spending outcomes at all levels of government, including local government. The number of financial difficulties in local governments has increased. As prices and wages continue to move upward, local governments will be spending larger amounts to provide their current levels of services. The possibility, if not the actuality, of inflation and recession together further darkens the future of local government finance.

Inflation, which eats at the real income of government workers, is partially responsible for the increased militancy of such workers and the mounting pressure for unionization. Faced with the shutdown of municipal services and a well-organized pressure group of public employees, political decision makers in many localities have acquiesced to strong demands for wage and salary increases. If such increases are soon eroded by inflation, the process will repeat itself, resulting in expansion of local budgets.

The growing "taxpayer's revolt" has helped offset inflation and other pressures to expand local government expenditures. Voter dissatisfaction with local taxing and spending manifested itself in political support to impose tight limits on the growth of local expenditures and tax levies. In some states explicit constraints were imposed, while in others a less restrictive requirement of "full disclosure," which requires local public officials to inform their constituents in advance of any tax increase and its effects, was imposed.

The full implications for local public finance of the tax revolt of the late 1970s remain to be seen, and undoubtedly will not be fully known until well into the 1980s. Political pressure for reduced local taxation was to some extent accompanied by support for increased financial participation to provide traditionally local services by higher level governments. This pressure may result in explicit centralization of some services. (Centralization at the state level of the education function and at the federal level of welfare were discussed in the text.) If increased centralization of finances were to take the form of increased grants-in-aid of either the bloc or categorical variety, local governments would retain final spending authority though, perhaps, within a framework of tighter higher level government restrictions. It should be noted, however, that pressure to reduce government spending was not confined to local governments. Politicians at state and federal levels of government also reacted to the call for reduced spending and taxing, and now are likely to restrict funds available for transfer to local governments.

1   Two of the seminal expositions of this theory were written by Paul A. Samuelson in the early 1950s. They are: "The Pure Theory of Public Expenditure," *Review of Economics and Statistics* 36 (November 1954): 387–89; and "Diagrammatic Exposition of a Theory of Public Expenditure," *Review of Economics and Statistics* 37 (November 1955): 350–56. See also: James M. Buchanan, *The Demand and Supply of Public Goods* (Chicago: Rand McNally & Co., 1968).

2   See, for example: Shapior v. Thompson, 394 U.S. 618 (1968).

3   See: Knut Wicksell, "A New Principle of Just Taxation," in *Classics in the Theory of Public Finance*, ed. R. A. Musgrave and A. T. Peacock (London: Macmillan & Co., 1958), pp. 72–118.

4   See: San Antonio Independent School District v. Rodriguez, 411 U.S. 1 (1973).

5   Serrano v. Priest, 5 Cal. 3d 584, 487; P. 2d 1241; 96 Cal. Rptr. 601 (1971).

6   A useful survey of the expenditure and taxing restrictions imposed on local government units by various state governments is provided by: U.S., Advisory Commission on Intergovernmental Relations, *State Limitations on Local Taxes and Expenditures* (Washington, D.C.: Government Printing Office, 1977).

3 Local government revenues

The preceding chapter offered an overview of local government expenditures. This chapter offers a similar overview of the other side of the municipal budget—the revenues, the flow of which is vital to the provision of local government goods and services.

Revenue sources can be placed in perspective only when considered in light of the theories of taxation. Thus, this chapter begins with a discussion of the theory of taxation, proceeds to an examination of the major characteristics of different revenue sources, and concludes with an analysis of overall municipal revenue. By providing an overview of the environment in which the administration of local government revenues takes place, the chapter serves as an introduction to the detailed analysis of the individual revenue sources found in Chapters 6, 7, and 8 of this text.

The theory of taxation

Taxes serve three primary functions: generating revenues to finance government goods and services; redistributing income; and, when overall demand is excessive, reducing private income and private spending. These are, respectively, the revenue, the redistributive, and the fiscal policy functions of taxation.

In other words taxes may do three things: pay for specific governmental services such as police and fire protection; take more money from some people than from other people as an equitable way of paying for government; and cut down the amount of money people can spend. The fact that the uses of taxes can be so characterized—in informal popular language as well as in the precise terminology of the disciplines of economics and public finance—illustrates that economists, municipal officials, and the general public are often thinking about the same things, even though they use different words to describe the processes involved.

The revenue, redistributive, and fiscal policy functions of taxation all raise pragmatic issues about which the contemporary manager of municipal finance should be fully aware. The revenue function, for example, raises questions about the relative values of public versus private goods, as well as the best way of distributing the cost of government goods and services among taxpayers. The redistribution-of-income function raises questions about the appropriate distribution of income after taxes. Finally, the fiscal policy function raises issues concerning the use of taxes as a policy variable contributing to the stability of the economy. Economic stability, however, remains primarily a responsibility of the federal government.

All of these practical questions can be clarified when discussed within the framework of tax principles. Many theoretical approaches are possible; some of them involve a high level of abstraction. Perhaps a better understanding of tax issues and problems is possible if the discussion focuses on the two main criteria for the evaluation of taxes, the benchmark concepts of tax equity and of tax efficiency. The essential aspects of these two criteria are described and analyzed in the following discussion.

Horizontal equity

One idea of tax justice (or tax fairness) that permeates the history of economic thought is that of equal treatment for people in equal economic circumstances. Equal tax treatment implies that taxes should not be arbitrary in nature or discriminatory in practical application. In essence, taxpayers in identical economic circumstances should be taxed the same amount. If income is taken as the tax base, then the equal tax treatment principle is obviously violated when taxpayers with the *same* taxable income pay *different* amounts of taxes. If spending rather than income is taken as the tax base, then an equal amount of spending should result in equal tax payments.

A tax distribution that adheres to the equal tax treatment principle provides for what is technically known as *horizontal equity* in the distribution of taxes. Thus, taxes are equal across income groups, or they are equal under whatever measure is being used to indicate equal economic circumstances.

Horizontal equity, however, is not without its controversial aspects. Although there is wide acceptance of the principle involved, the meaning and the measurement of "equal economic circumstances" are controversial issues. Should family size, for example, make a difference? Should wealth be considered, along with income, as an indicator of the ability to pay taxes? Should capital gains be considered as full income and be taxed accordingly? These and related questions are difficult to answer.

Vertical equity

An obvious corollary to the principle of equal tax treatment for equals is the principle of *unequal* tax treatment for *unequals*. This idea is known technically as *vertical equity*. To clarify the meaning of vertical equity, economists have developed two related principles: the ability-to-pay principle and the benefit-received principle.

The ability-to-pay principle   The ability-to-pay principle states that taxes should be distributed among taxpayers in relation to their financial capacities. Using income as a ready measure of the ability involved, this means that taxpayers with more income would pay more taxes. But how much more? Should the tax rate be regressive, proportional, or progressive?

A regressive tax simply means that the ratio of tax payments to income declines as income rises; the more earned, the *less* the proportion paid in taxes. A proportional tax means that the ratio stays the same; at any level of earnings the *same* proportion in taxes is paid. A progressive tax means that the ratio of tax payment to income rises as income rises; the more earned, the *more*, proportionately, paid in taxes. In any case, under the ability-to-pay principle, the tax liability of individuals with higher incomes should be greater than that of individuals with lower incomes. Some applications of this principle are illustrated in Table 3–1.

Table 3–1 indicates that, although it is common practice to equate the ability-to-pay principle with *progressive* taxation, *proportional* taxes likewise can be seen as consistent with the principle. In the example shown, a higher income, of course, will generate a greater *absolute* amount of tax liability even if the *proportional* liability to taxes remains the same. Even a regressive tax system can be designed (see Table 3–1) so that richer people pay a higher *absolute* amount of taxes even though their tax rate is lower than that of people with lower incomes. The case for progressive taxes, however, relies both on the ability-to-pay principle and on the belief in the social desirability of moving toward a more equal distribution of after-tax incomes.

Table 3–1 Regressive, proportional, and progressive taxes

Income ($)	Regressive		Proportional		Progressive	
	Average rate (%)	Tax liability ($)	Average rate (%)	Tax liability ($)	Average rate (%)	Tax liability ($)
5,000	10.0	500	10.0	500	10.0	500
10,000	6.0	600	10.0	1,000	15.0	1,500

The benefit-received principle The benefit-received principle of taxation represents an attempt to simulate the market pricing process in setting the distribution of tax burdens among individuals. According to economic theory, the price paid in the market reflects the benefits, or the valuation, that consumers place on an additional unit of an item and on the economic costs of producing that additional unit. Accordingly, under the benefit-received principle, taxes are regarded as "prices" and distributed in accordance with the estimated marginal incremental benefits received by taxpayers from government goods and services.

The benefit-received principle is an integrated theory that helps to clarify both the tax and the expenditure sides of public finance. In this respect, it contrasts with the ability-to-pay principle, which considers only the tax side of the tax-expenditure process. An older version of the benefit-received principle was concerned primarily with tax justice; current interest is in the principle insofar as it acts as a guide to allocating resources. Direct charges (user fees) for government goods should force individuals to reveal their true preferences or their willingness to pay for these goods. The benefit-received principle of taxation may be more useful at the local level of government (especially for municipalities) than at the national level of government. The price, or user fee, principle has practical application to many local government services such as parking, recreation, garbage collection, libraries, and utilities.

It is also important to note that application of the benefit-received principle of taxation has practical limitations. Individual benefits from such government goods and services as fire and police protection may be difficult to measure. Many services offer benefits that accrue collectively—that is, the services are social goods for which the costs are not clearly applicable to the individual. Further, the costs of collection from individual users would be high for some services (e.g., charges for the use of city streets). In some cases, the purpose of government service actually may be defeated by the benefit-received principle as, for example, in the case of public assistance.

In spite of these limitations, when it is possible to measure individual benefits with reasonable accuracy and when the purpose of the government service is not to redistribute income, many economists believe that taxes should be selected on the basis of the benefit-received principle, a procedure that is more likely to result in an equitable and efficient distribution of taxes.

Summary In short, the concept of vertical equity—unequal tax treatment among unequal persons—raises a number of questions about the practical measurement of the differing responsibilities and capacities involved. The ability-to-pay principle, in placing emphasis on the financial capacities of taxpayers, in turn raises problems associated with regressive, proportional, or progressive taxes. The benefit-received principle, another method of approaching the problems of vertical equity, attempts to construct a framework to explain the consumer's "choices" of government services. Whether used as benchmark guides, or in direct practical application, these theories help clarify the basic issues involved in taxing people to provide government services.

Tax efficiency

The concept of tax efficiency is another useful guide for clarifying the complex practical problems of the taxing process. In brief, *tax efficiency* refers to the way a given tax affects the allocation of resources, the pattern of consumption and saving, and the pattern of work and leisure. An efficient tax would change these choices only minimally. Tax efficiency also concerns the "convenience and compliance costs" to the taxpayers to determine and pay their tax liability, in addition to the costs to the taxing unit to collect taxes. In this sense, an efficient tax would be one that would not impose excess costs to the taxpayer, and that could be collected and enforced with minimum cost to the taxing unit.

General considerations   With respect to the performance of the overall economy, an efficient tax theoretically would not alter the relative allocation of resources in the private sector of the economy. The ideal tax would have neutral effects; it would transfer resources to the public sector without disturbing the relative prices of private goods.

Realistically, however, no tax is ever completely neutral in its impact on the operation of the economy. The *relative* neutrality of taxes does nevertheless vary, and the taxes may be evaluated on the basis of the variable. In the following discussion, selected revenue sources will be tentatively evaluated in terms of both tax equity and tax efficiency.

Evaluation of specific revenue sources   On the basis of the tax criteria already introduced, it appears that a proportional income tax ranks high in both equity and efficiency. A tax on income is clearly justified on the ability-to-pay principle, while proportional rates have a relatively neutral impact on the operation of the economy. On the other hand, it is possible that a progressive income tax can have some effect on the structure of the economy.

Progressive tax   Progressive rates may discourage work and encourage leisure; thus, a progressive income tax ranks high in terms of equity but fairly low in terms of efficiency. This statement, of course, implies no value judgment on the respective merits of either activity, but merely records one possible effect of progressive tax rates. Progressive rates also redistribute income away from individuals with high incomes—a process that may tend to reduce savings. Again, the structure of the economy would be affected. Most empirical studies, however, show that, up to now, the existing progressive income tax rates have not significantly impaired incentives to work and save.

Sales tax   A truly general sales tax (one levied on the market value of all final goods and services, including both consumption and investment goods) is similar in effect to a proportional income tax. The sales tax, implemented at state and local levels of government, is not truly general (even from the geographical point of view) and becomes essentially a tax on consumption. This produces a regressive pattern of tax rates on the basis of income because lower income families consume a larger proportion of their current income. Thus, the general sales tax is characterized by a low tax equity ranking and a high tax efficiency rating. Even so, in comparison to selective sales taxes, general sales taxes are more efficient because, as their name implies, they are broad-based taxes and do not affect *relative* commodity prices. Selective sales taxes, therefore, rank low on the bases of efficiency and equity.

Property tax   The property tax, primarily because of the prevailing mode of its administration and operation, is characterized by low equity and efficiency ratings. The assessment ratio (the ratio of the assessed value of property to its market value) often varies with the value, age, and type of property, thus resulting in a tax that often violates the equal tax treatment principle. Moreover, this tax may distort the pattern of land use. Improved property is taxed generally at higher rates than unimproved property, urban property at higher rates than rural property, and commercial property at higher rates than residential property. To the extent that the property tax is used to provide services to property owners, the tax may be justified under the benefit-received principle. Thus, in this case the property tax may have a high equity rating.

License tax   Licenses may be imposed as a way of regulating an activity, or as a method of raising revenue. In terms of tax efficiency and equity, the important question is whether the license is a fixed dollar amount or a variable amount. In the latter case the charge is based on the use of services or on some measure of ability to pay the fee. The charges for dog licenses and hunting and fishing licenses, for example, are generally fixed dollar amounts. Such "lump-sum" taxes usually rank high in terms of tax efficiency—unless they are very expensive, in which case the level of such activity will be affected. In terms of tax equity, however, licenses with fixed dollar amounts rank fairly low. The amount paid for vehicle tag licenses and certain business licenses, on the other hand, varies according to some measure of ability to pay. Such variation reduces the regressive effects of license taxes, so that these taxes have high efficiency and equity ratings.

User charges   Another revenue source to be evaluated is direct charges, or fees, placed on individual users of government services. These charges illustrate the benefit-received principle. However, if charges were to be completely consistent with the benefit-received principle, the charge per unit of service would have to be the same for all buyers, and the total charge would vary according to the quantity of services demanded by each buyer. When charges for services are a fixed amount (as in some systems of garbage collection), the charges may be distributed in a regressive manner, which then violates the principle of vertical equity. In any event, charges are a fairly efficient way to distribute the costs of government. They are also an equitable way, if the benefit-received principle is not seriously compromised.

Summary   Tax efficiency, the way a given tax affects the allocation of resources and compliance and collection costs, provides one useful guideline for ranking various revenue sources. Another measure of ranking is the important concept of tax equity. Tax efficiency and equity, although often characterized in theoretical terms, have a useful function in providing a framework in which the taxes employed and their purposes can be evaluated.

Shifting and incidence

A vital aspect of the theory of taxation is the process technically known as shifting and incidence. This concerns the process whereby a tax levied on one person is shifted to another. The person who actually makes the tax payment may *not* be the person who is bearing the burden (incidence) of the tax. A tax placed on a producer or a retailer may be shifted forward to consumers as higher prices for products or backward in the form of lower wages, rents, or interest paid to the suppliers of resources.

Factors influencing tax shifting   Tax shifting depends on many variables. Some of the important ones involve (1) the type of tax, (2) the price-elasticity of demand—the degree to which consumers can rearrange their purchases as the result of a price change, and (3) the size and location of the political jurisdiction imposing the tax. Taxes may be classified as direct or indirect taxes and as broad-based or narrow-based taxes. Direct taxes such as income taxes are difficult to shift, primarily because those taxes do not directly affect the cost of producing goods and services. On the other hand, such indirect taxes as excise and sales taxes do affect the variable cost of production; they can be shifted or "passed on" with greater facility.

The price-elasticity of demand (the degree of consumer response to price changes) is important when determining a tax shift. The more *inelastic* the demand—or the *less* consumers change their purchasing habits in response to a price rise—the greater the proportion of the tax that will be shifted forward to consumers. Because the quantity of the good or service purchased after the tax-induced price rise will fall only slightly, the government is able to count on the revenue from products with an inelastic demand. The demand for such products as gasoline, liquor, tobacco, soft drinks, medicine, and many food products tends to be inelastic, and makes these items obvious candidates for sales taxes if revenue stability is the primary consideration. Consumers will continue to purchase these items with little regard for price changes induced by taxes; and the taxing unit can, therefore, rely on a steady flow of revenue from the sale of items such as these.

The incidence of a tax is also determined by the elasticity of supply, as in the case of the real property tax, which has been the subject of much discussion. The general argument is that the part of the tax that falls on land values will rest with the landowner because the supply of land is fixed, or inelastic. The tax on improvements of buildings and structures, however, will be shifted forward to renters; this tax is a cost of supplying buildings for rent. If the tax on improvements cannot be covered in the gross rents, the quantity of new rental properties forthcoming would be reduced. In the case of owner-occupied buildings, both the tax on land *and* the tax on improvements remain with the owner. An important practical conclusion is that because a large part of the property tax is shifted forward in rents, the frequently heard complaint that renters are "escaping their share of local taxes" is largely without foundation.

Recent studies by Aaron and by Browning and Johnson have tended to cast doubt on the traditional theory of property tax shifting.[1] In these studies, the authors suggest an alternative view of property tax incidence in which all owners of capital would share the property tax. The argument proceeds in the following fashion. If all capital is taxed and the supply of capital is unaffected by the tax, the tax burden falls on property income rather than being shifted forward to renters as an increase in the rent. If only some capital is taxed, the economic reaction will be for assets to move to more lightly taxed areas or uses. The reaction will continue until the rate of return on capital, net of taxes, is the same in all uses. The result of the adjustment process is that the burden of tax is felt by all owners of capital and not simply by those whose property is subject to direct taxation.

The opportunity to shift a tax may depend on the geographic boundaries of the political unit imposing the tax. A city sales tax, for example, may be difficult to shift forward to local consumers if they can easily divert their purchases to nearby cities that do not have a sales tax. In such cases, local businesses must absorb the tax or locate elsewhere. Because the jurisdiction of a state embraces a larger area a state sales tax is more difficult to avoid and may be shifted forward more easily than a municipal sales tax. Nevertheless, even state sales taxes may be avoided, if there are convenient nontax or lower-tax communities just across state lines.

Formal incidence studies The assumptions used to determine tax shifting and incidence in a study of the distribution of tax burdens on income groups are shown in Table 3–2.[2] Assumptions about the directions of tax shifting are used in constructing models that show the effect of the tax system on income distri-

Table 3–2 Estimated shifting and incidence of state and local taxes

Type of tax	Shifting	Incidence
Personal income tax	No	Income receiver
Corporate income tax	Forward and backward	Consumer and stockholder
Property taxes		
Household real and personal property	No	Homeowner
Business real and personal property	Forward and backward	Consumer and owner
Farm real and personal property	Forward and backward	Consumer and owner
Highway users' taxes		
Operator's license tax	No	Operator
Motor fuel and auto tag licenses		
Household	No	Household
Business and farm	Forward and backward	Consumer and owner
Alcoholic beverage and cigarette tax	Forward	Consumer
Insurance premiums tax	Forward	Policy holder
Public utilities tax	Forward	Consumer
Inheritance and estate tax	Forward	Beneficiaries
Severance tax	Forward	Consumer

Source: Li-teh Sun, "Incidence of Montana State and Local Taxes" (Ph.D. dissertation, Oklahoma State University, 1972).

bution. These are called formal incidence models. In a recent study, Pechman and Okner state that the overall incidence of the federal tax system alone is progressive throughout the income scale, and is largely due to the influence of income taxes. However, the Pechman and Okner study corroborates the findings of most formal tax incidence models: state and local taxes are generally more or less regressive, depending on the assumptions regarding property tax incidence.[3] As Table 3–3 indicates, the regressivity of the overall tax impacts against income for major state and local taxes.

Finally, regardless of which incidence assumptions are used, Pechman and Okner conclude that the overall total "tax system is virtually proportional for the vast majority of families in the United States."[4] Even under assumptions that make taxes most progressive, the impact of the overall tax system reduces income inequality by less than 5.0 percent; and under assumptions of the least progressivity, income inequality is reduced by only about 0.5 percent.

Table 3–3 Distribution of major state-local tax burdens relative to family income size, 1976[1]

Adjusted gross income ($) family of four	Tax burden as % of family income
7,500	9.8
10,000	9.1
15,000	7.9
17,500	7.9
25,000	7.6
50,000	7.5

Source: U.S. Advisory Commission on Intergovernmental Relations, *Significant Features of Fiscal Federalism*, 1978–79 Edition, (Washngton, D.C.: Government Printing Office, 1979), p. 32.

[1] Includes the following taxes: state individual income, state general sales, local individual income, local sales, property tax on residence, cigarette excise, motor vehicle and gasoline excise.

Summary The concepts of tax shifting and tax incidence are useful in understanding the mechanisms of tax operations. Such factors as price elasticity of supply and demand, and the effect on different governmental jurisdictions, can affect the operation of individual taxes. The preceding discussions of tax efficiency and equity and the analysis of shifting and incidence rounds out the overall framework of tax theory as it applies to local government revenue sources.

Revenue characteristics

As the preceding discussion has indicated, the principles of tax theory are useful in the practical task of constructing an equitable and efficient tax structure at the local government level. Financial managers, however, must also face the task of developing a tax system capable of producing the revenue necessary to satisfy a growing demand for local public goods and services. The following discussion of the problem of raising and forecasting revenues can be structured around three items that are of major importance in this area: the concept of revenue elasticity; the problem of tax overlapping and tax coordination; and the issue of administration and compliance costs.

Revenue elasticity

During the past two decades, expenditures of state and local governments have been increasing at a faster rate than the growth in the tax base. State and local governments have had to increase tax rates and adopt new taxes to maintain a balance between growing expenditures on the one hand and slower growing revenues on the other. Over the period from 1959 to 1976 alone, for example, the U.S. Advisory Commission on Intergovernmental Relations (ACIR) reported that there were over 586 tax rate increases and 41 new taxes enacted into law by state legislatures.[5] These facts tell only part of the story; they do not take into account the actions taken by local units of government.

By the late 1970s, it had become evident that voters were not going to continue to permit state and local governments to fill the gap between revenues and expenditures by increasing taxes. This attitude was most evident in California in 1978 where the voters passed the Jarvis-Gann Initiative (Proposition 13), which amended the state constitution to limit real property taxes to 1 percent of the value of the property with the 1975–76 assessed value established as the base value. The fair market value base may reflect an inflationary rate not to exceed 2 percent for any given year. Some twenty other states have followed California's lead, most choosing more moderate measures and targeting government spending more often than taxes, yet they all reflect a strong public sentiment to slow down the growth of government, and the mounting tax bills in particular.

Historic trends The growth in state and local expenditures has occurred at a more rapid rate than the state and local tax base. General aspects of increasing state and local general expenditures are summarized in Table 3–4, which presents data for selected years from 1927 through 1975. In absolute terms, Table 3–4 indicates a rise in general expenditures from over $7 billion in 1927 to $230 billion in 1975. Most of this growth has occurred since the second world war, as indicated by the jump in the annual average growth rate during the postwar period. State and local government general expenditures increased at an average annual rate of 1.9 percent from 1927 to 1940; by contrast, such expenditures increased at an annual rate of 11.9 percent from 1970 to 1975.

The relatively slow growth in local expenditures during the 1930s and early 1940s was influenced by two major historical events: the Great Depression and World War II. Local government units neglected all but the most pressing

Table 3–4 State and local general expenditures and average annual growth rates for selected years, 1927–75

Fiscal year	Total general expenditures (in millions)	Average annual growth rate (%)
1927	7,210	
1940	9,229	1.9
1950	22,787	9.5
1960	51,876	8.6
1970	131,332	9.7
1975	230,448	11.9

Source: *The Annual Report of the Council of Economic Advisors* (Washington, D.C.: Government Printing Office, 1977), p. 273.

expenditure requirements during the Depression. In fact, in 1934 expenditures actually dipped below those in 1927; and during the war years that followed, a large part of the nation's resources was devoted to the federal war effort.

In the postwar period, it was evident that severe pressures had accumulated on state and local budgets. What came to be known as the population explosion, together with geographical changes in employment opportunities and the increased mobility of people, accentuated the strains on local budgets. The effect on expenditures resulting from these factors was presented in Chapter 2; however, some of the highlights of the pressures on expenditures will now be considered, since they impinge on the problems of generating revenues.

The population of the United States increased by just over 72 million from 1946 to 1975. Assuming that state and local governments had provided exactly the same level of service in 1975 as in 1946, the expenditures in 1975 still would have had to increase since the governments were providing services for a larger number of people. On the basis of per capita measure, state and local general expenditures increased from $78 per head in 1946 to $1077 per head in 1975. Part of this increase was the result of price inflation, which reached crisis proportions by the late 1970s. In any case, real per capita state and local general expenditures (based on constant 1967 dollar values) increased from $125 to $616 per capita over this period. In short, the demands for state and local government services have risen constantly in recent decades, whether measured in absolute, per capita, or real per capita terms.

Another well-known aspect of the postwar population growth was the bulge in the number of school-age children. The total population in the five- to nineteen-year age group increased from 35 million in 1950 to 60 million in 1970. During the most recent postwar period, the growth in this segment of the population created a serious fiscal problem for state and local governments, which not only bore the brunt of total educational expenditure but also found this item taking up some 40 percent of their total outlays. Moreover, because the absolute number of school-age children had actually declined by close to one million in the twenty-year period preceding 1950, state and local governments lacked the capital facilities as well as the personnel needed to meet the sharp postwar growth in the educational demand.

The bulge in the school-age population has become less conspicuous in the 1970s. A sharp decrease in the number of births since 1960—from 4.3 million in 1960 to 3.2 million in 1976—has led to a decline in elementary school enrollments during the seventies. Secondary schools are just beginning to feel the decline in enrollments, which is expected to continue through the middle of the 1980s. These shifts in enrollment may lead to a tapering off, at least, of the growth rate of educational outlays. However, rising costs, some of which will be due to inflation, may preclude an absolute decline in expenditures.

Another aspect of a changing population structure is that a large portion of the population moved from rural to urban areas, thus adding to the demands for services in the latter areas. Whereas in 1940 the U.S. Bureau of the Census classified 57 percent of the population as urban and 44 percent as rural, in 1970 the urban population had risen to 74 percent and the rural declined to 27 percent. As people moved from the rural areas to towns and cities, a corresponding increase in demand for services such as police and fire protection, sewage disposal, and street construction and repair was noted.

By 1970, the United States had become an urbanized nation and the portion of the urban population declined from a peak of 74 percent in 1970 to 68 percent in 1976. Since 1970 there has been a visible move away from the sixteen largest major metropolitan areas (populations above 2 million) toward the other forty-five major metropolitan areas (populations between 500,000 and 2 million). The burden of adjusting to this most recent trend falls most heavily on the largest metropolitan areas. The current need is to improve or replace what is already in place, and failure to realize these needs means flirting with financial disaster. On the other hand, the smaller metropolitan areas are still facing population growth and increasing demands for services.

Taxing and spending limits
Indicative of the public mood for limiting taxing and spending of state and local governments are the actions taken by many state governments during the first nine months of 1979.

Six states imposed spending limitations. In three states specific lids were imposed on tax and expenditure growth; in the other three states formulas were enacted to control the magnitude of allowable increases. Usually the lid was rather moderate—providing in effect that state spending should not grow faster than the overall economy of the state.

Twenty-three states either initiated or expanded tax relief measures for home owners and renters.

Twenty-five states reduced state income taxes—nineteen by reductions in the tax base and six by rate reductions.

Four states—Iowa, Minnesota, Oregon, and Wisconsin—partially indexed their state income taxes.

Fifteen states reduced the general sales tax, twelve by reductions in the tax base and three by rate reductions.

Source: John Shannon and Chris Cooper, "The Tax Revolt—It Has Hurried History Along," paper delivered to the Public Securities Association, Colorado Springs, Colorado, October 8, 1979.

The overall result of these trends has been that state and local expenditures in the postwar period expanded much more rapidly than the nation's gross national product (GNP). During the 1950s the GNP rose by an annual average rate of 5.9 percent while local government expenditures rose by 8.6 percent. During the 1960s, national output rose at 6.9 percent annually while expenditures rose by 9.7 percent, and from 1970 to 1975 the percentage increases were 9.1 and 11.9, respectively. This historical background is very important for an understanding of the current revenue environment.

The elasticity concept   The most central fact in terms of revenues is that since the second world war state and local tax systems have failed to respond to the growth that has taken place in the economy. As a result, the only way that local governments have been able to keep up with the growth in expenditures has been to adopt new taxes and to increase the rates on old taxes. Economists refer to this problem as the *income inelasticity* of the existing local government tax systems.

A tax system that is income inelastic is one in which a given percentage rise in income generates a relatively smaller increase in tax revenues from the existing tax system. The amount of money that a particular tax generates is the product of the tax *rate* and the tax *base*. Assuming no structural changes in the tax system (e.g., rate changes, new taxes, and changes in tax enforcement) tax yields will change only as the tax base changes. The responsiveness of a tax to economic growth depends on the responsiveness of the base to changes in growth. Economists refer to the degree of this responsiveness as the income elasticity of the tax. Technically, the coefficient of income elasticity is obtained by dividing the percentage change in tax yield by the percentage change in national income.

The income elasticity coefficient is *less* than 1 when the tax yield changes *less than proportionally* to changes in national or local income. It is *equal* to 1 when it changes *proportionally,* and *greater* than 1 when it changes *greater* than *proportionally*. Elasticity thus measures the way in which the tax behaves in comparison with changes in national income. For example, yields from motor fuel and tobacco excise taxes simply do not change much in relation to changes in the gross national product; a rise in national income does not produce anything like an immediate proportionate rise in the motor fuel and tobacco tax yields. The elasticity coefficient is less than 1 so that the taxes cited are income inelastic in the short run.

In the early years following World War II, some local authorities—with the Great Depression still fresh in their minds—feared a tax system that would have a large element of elasticity. Although under such a system a growing gross national product would produce a more proportionate (or elastic) growth in tax revenues, they felt that there was no guarantee that the gross national product would continue climbing. If the system were elastic and if a major recession were to occur, the result would be an even more precipitous decline in tax revenues. State and local governments would again be placed in the precarious position in which they found themselves in the 1930s.

National economic growth from the 1940s to the 1970s, however, subsided the fear of a major economic downturn. Attention shifted to the state and local tax systems, which were not generating the revenue necessary to keep pace with rising expenditures. If local officials were to produce enough revenue, state and local tax systems would have to become more responsive to changes in the level of income. The systems needed to become more income elastic.

A number of studies have been made to estimate the elasticities of various state and local taxes. A useful summary of these studies, made in the 1960s and early 1970s, is reproduced in Table 3–5.

Because there is some disagreement among the experts about the correct elasticity coefficient estimates for the various taxes cited, three estimates—one low, one medium, and one high—are provided in Table 3–5 for each category of revenue. The elasticity coefficients of most categories of taxes vary over time, and hence it would be unrealistic to expect any one estimate to be precise at any given time.[6] As with all such studies, however, the estimates do provide a guideline or benchmark. It is probably quite realistic to think of the coefficients as falling within the ranges shown in Table 3–5.

In 1975 state and local general revenues amounted to approximately $228 billion. Forty-four percent of this total came from property and sales taxes. The medium estimates in Table 3–5 indicate that the property tax has a coefficient below 1 and the coefficient of the sales tax is slightly above 1. In short, these taxes tend to be inelastic or of unitary elasticity. The most elastic sources of revenue, individual and corporate income taxes, produced only about 12 percent of total state and local general revenue.

Table 3–5 Estimated income elasticities of major state and local taxes

Revenue source	Elasticity estimates		
	Low	Medium	High
Property taxes	0.34	0.88	1.41
Income taxes			
Individual	1.30	1.85	2.40
Corporate	0.72	1.08	1.44
Sales taxes			
General	0.80	1.04	1.27
Motor fuel	0.43	0.62	0.80
Tobacco	0.00	0.27	0.54

Source: U.S. Advisory Commission on Intergovernmental Relations, *Significant Features of Fiscal Federalism*, 1976–77 Edition, Vol. II (Washington, D.C.: Government Printing Office, 1977), p. 254.

Given the demand for expenditures and given the income inelasticity of most local taxes, it is not surprising that state and local governments have had to increase tax rates, adopt new taxes, or both. This has done little, however, to solve the basic problem since local governments, when seeking new revenues, have most often turned to those taxes with low elasticity coefficients. For example, a fiscal crisis may be averted in any given year by increasing the cigarette tax. However, because the cigarette tax has a very low income elasticity, the overall elasticity of the revenue system is not improved.

Of the 627 tax rate increases and new taxes enacted into law from 1959 to 1976 alone, more than 350 involved taxes that have inelastic coefficients. Only a temporary solution has been provided if expenditures continue to rise at a rate faster than national income—and if the state's revenue system remains inelastic. Before long the local government will start once again the weary search for new sources of revenues. Similar examples could be cited for every level of local and municipal government.

The outlook What do the trends just discussed mean for the future of state and local governments? In 1965, ACIR estimated that during the preceding decade, the gross national product elasticity of state general *expenditures* averaged approximately 1.7.[7] During that same period the median revenue elasticity coefficient for the average state only increased from 0.85 to 0.92.[8] The experts argued that because there were no persuasive reasons to expect the expenditure elasticity coefficient to decrease in the near future, and because revenue elasticity coefficients are slow to increase, the fiscal crisis facing state and local governments in the mid-1960s would be with financial managers for some time to come.[9] This assumption was certainly borne out over the next decade and a half; and the crisis was actually worse during this period than the prediction.

Predictions concerning local government fiscal patterns became extremely difficult in the 1970s. Moreover, there is the added complication of the differential impact of changing revenue and expenditure patterns on the various units and structures of local government. Big cities, smaller cities, suburbs, towns, and different regions have varying problems. Even though the revenue-expenditure gap has vanished in the aggregate, a situation in which all is well with every individual state and every municipality is not to be in the near future. Less affluent communities, for example, would find it even more difficult to make ends meet if people with the ability to pay taxes move out, leaving behind a narrower tax base and an increasing need for expensive services for those remaining. On the other hand, the more affluent communities might have a fiscal surplus; however, surpluses might vanish in the face of rising demands for services. A worsening overall economic climate would, of course, aggravate the problems of those communities experiencing the greatest difficulty and would introduce new problems into affluent communities. As every city manager, finance officer, and planner is only too well aware, the demand for local government services can change quickly—and most often the demand will increase.

Elasticity coefficient   The formula for determining the elasticity coefficient is:

$$E = \frac{\dfrac{\Delta\,Tx}{Tx_1}}{\dfrac{\Delta\,GNP}{GNP_1}}$$

Where E = the elasticity coefficient; ΔTx = change in the tax yield; Tx_1 = tax yield in the base year; ΔGNP = change in the gross national product; and GNP_1 = gross national product in the base year. For example, if the tax yield increases from \$250 million to \$275 million while GNP increases from \$1,600 million to \$1,720 million, then E = .1/.075 = 1.33. In this case, the income elasticity coefficient is greater than 1, and the tax yield changes greater than proportionally to a change in GNP.

Several new trends have developed on the local finance scene. First, total tax revenue as a percent of local own-source revenue has been declining since 1970; thus, local governments are becoming more dependent on charges, fees and other types of nontax revenue. Secondly, local property taxes have fallen in relative importance as a local tax source. Finally, income and general sales tax revenues have increased in relative significance. While the property tax is still by far the most important source of local revenue, it has been steadily declining in relative importance for two decades. This is due partially to a desire among public officials to broaden the local tax base in addition to the taxpayers' unwillingness to bear higher property taxes. Local governments have had to seek alternative non-property sources to provide the marginal increments needed to keep pace with the steady rise in expenditures.

Proposition 13 has created a new climate for state and local governments. Together with a line of court decisions, which began with *Serrano* v. *Priest* in 1971, voter resistance to increased property taxes has caused a search for alternative tax sources and pressure to maintain or reduce the existing taxes. This climate has given rise to the development of a whole new set of fees and charges designed to provide local services without financing them directly by a tax source. At the same time, the willingness of many citizens to support a balanced budget at the federal level created pressure in Washington to eliminate the revenue sharing program. If the program had been eliminated, there would have been renewed cries for more adequate local financing sources. Even so, the capital outlay problems experienced in the recent past may once again haunt local governments.

The state-local fiscal sector has also become more sensitive to fluctuations in the national economy. In recent years, state and local revenue systems have continuously shifted toward income-elastic, broader-based taxes (e.g., the income tax), which tend to be more responsive to economic growth and also more sensitive to economic stagnation or decline. The increased state-local reliance on the personal income tax may produce more ups and downs in state-local budgets as swings in national economic trends occur. The national economy affects the various state economies differently, however, so that some states will enjoy surpluses while others experience deficits; this is apparently the current situation.

Summary   The preceding discussion of revenue elasticity has demonstrated that the growth in existing state and local government revenues tends to lag behind that of expenditures. Some of the historic trends underlying this situation were briefly highlighted. The concept of revenue elasticity was introduced as one method of relating changes between the variables—the gross national product, the demand for government services, and tax yields. Some of the problems arising from income inelasticity of the important taxes were examined, and some note was taken of the implications in terms of the current situation and the future outlook of a generally cloudy overall economic situation.

Tax overlapping and tax coordination

The terms *tax overlapping* and *tax coordination* refer to another vital aspect of the overall picture of local government revenue sources. In a federal fiscal system like that of the United States, two kinds of tax overlapping are bound to exist.

First, it is not uncommon for two or more *levels* of government to use the same tax base. Federal, state, and local governments, for example, may all levy a tax on personal income. This kind of duplication is known as *vertical tax overlapping*. Second, in a highly mobile society like ours, businesses and individuals carry on many economic activities and are thus liable to taxes in many different taxing jurisdictions at the *same* level of government—in different cities, for example. This is called *horizontal tax overlapping*.

Both kinds of tax overlapping can create economic inefficiencies and taxpayer inequities; yet tax overlapping appears inevitable in a society characterized by a federal structure and a notable degree of mobility. It is therefore necessary to promote effective *coordination* of the taxing efforts among the various levels of government.

Tax specialization Our federal fiscal system is characterized by extensive tax overlapping. In fact, the system is more properly characterized by tax specialization. Table 3–6 shows percentage distribution of tax collections by source and by level of government for an illustrative year.

Each level of government uses a number of different kinds of taxation. Several taxes are used by all three levels of government: federal, state, and local. Nevertheless, each level of government tends to rely mainly on one type of tax, and within this category it may have a virtual monopoly. The federal government

Table 3–6 Percentage distribution of tax collections, by source and by level of government, for fiscal year 1977

Tax sources	Level of government		
	Federal (%)	State (%)	Local (%)
Total tax collections	100.0	100.0	100.0
Property	. . .	2.2	80.6
Individual income	64.3	25.2	5.0
Corporation income	22.5	9.1	. . .
Customs duties	2.2	. . .	. . .
General sales and gross receipts	. . .	30.6	7.2
Selective sales and gross receipts	7.3	21.2	3.8
Motor vehicle and operator's license	. . .	4.5	0.5
Death and gift	3.0	1.8	. . .
All others	0.7	5.3	2.9

Source: Computed from data in U.S., Department of Commerce, Bureau of the Census, *Governmental Finances in 1976–77* (Washington, D.C.: Government Printing Office, 1978), p. 19.

thus obtains 86.8 percent of its tax collections from individual and corporate income taxes.

State governments, on the other hand, obtain the largest portion of their tax revenue—51.8 percent—from general and selective sales taxes. Finally, local governments still rely quite extensively upon the property tax—80.6 percent of local tax collections come from this source. In turn, local governments collect 96.4 percent of the total amount of property taxes paid to all levels of government.

Problems of vertical tax overlapping   One suggestion for solving the problem of vertical tax overlapping is to completely separate revenue sources. Under this plan, total tax specialization would confer exclusive use of the personal and corporate income tax to the federal government; all general sales taxes would be left to states; and the property tax would be given completely to local governments.

Such an arrangement, however, might prove undesirable for a number of reasons. First, the state and local tax systems would become more regressive. Secondly, the state and local tax systems would become even more income inelastic. A better approach might be to develop more effective methods of coordinating the taxing efforts of the various levels of government.

One method of reducing some of the inefficiencies of vertical tax overlapping is to use the procedure of joint tax administration. In recent years, both the federal government and some state governments have indeed benefited from agreements to cooperate in administering certain taxes. The first of a series of such agreements was signed between the federal government and the state of Minnesota as long ago as 1957.[10] Efficiencies and augmented revenues have resulted from procedures such as the exchange of federal and state income tax returns. Further cooperation between state and local units of government could enhance that collection efficiency.

Centralized tax administration might produce additional revenues for both state and local governments. If, for example, local communities allow the state to administer and collect a locally levied sales tax, the local governments share the costs and avoid the need to establish their own collection agencies. An increasing number of local governments has made use of the general sales tax in recent years, and many of them allow the state to collect the tax—a real benefit of central administration. ACIR reported that in 1976 more than 4,500 units of local government in twenty-two states "piggybacked" their local sales taxes onto the general state sales tax collected at the state level.

Problems of horizontal tax overlapping   The problems associated with horizontal tax overlapping may be more difficult to solve than those of vertical tax overlapping. In a mobile society, individuals frequently earn their income in one taxing jurisdiction while living in another. How should the tax claims of the two governments on a single income be resolved? One answer is to allocate the tax revenues to the various governmental units on the basis of benefits provided to the individual.[11] This recommendation, however, does not offer a precise solution to the problem. This is especially true in the case of pure public goods with social benefits that cannot be allocated to specific individuals. Social welfare expenditure, for example, cannot be allocated to individuals.

A commuter income tax is another way to solve the problem of individuals who earn their income in one taxing jurisdiction and live in another. In this case, individuals would pay for services received in the jurisdiction in which they work. On the other hand, such a tax may be an incentive for businesses to move out of the central city.

The taxation of interstate sales creates problems similar to those noted in the preceding paragraphs. Consider two states, A and B. State A levies a sales tax and State B does not. Presumably, it is possible to buy certain goods more cheaply in State B than in State A. In order to offset this competitive disadvantage, State A may levy a tax (called a use tax) on the use of the item purchased in State B. States have, in fact, attempted to collect use taxes either directly from consumers or indirectly from out-of-state vendors; but the states found many problems of enforcement.[12]

The most difficult of horizontal tax overlapping problems is how to tax the income of a multi-state business firm. In an era of growing corporate consolidations, it is not surprising that well over 125,000 firms do business in more than one state. The chances are quite good that these firms will be subject to more than one state corporation tax, which is levied by all but five states. A major problem in the administration of the state corporation income tax is the allocation of interstate income to the various states for taxing purposes. The precise components of an equitable apportionment formula remain a matter of considerable disagreement.[13]

Sales could be used as one of the determinants of the state's share of the firm's income; however, there are two major variants of this apportionment technique. One defines the sales base according to the place of origin, the other according to destination. The most popular procedure, or at least the most widespread procedure, is to allocate sales (and thus income subject to tax) on the basis of where the goods are destined or consumed. Unfortunately, this is the most troublesome standard to administer because it greatly expands the number of companies that may be subject to the variations of corporate income tax from more than one state. On the other hand, a large percentage of business firms *doing* business in many states have *places* of business in only one or a few states. Thus, if the income subject to tax was allocated by origin of sales, the number of different corporation income taxes facing the firm would be drastically reduced. The savings in terms of compliance costs would be substantial.

Another suggestion is to eliminate the sales factor from the apportionment formula, and to rely on such factors as the location of land, capital, and labor involved in producing the firm's income. This too, however, would result in definitive and administrative complications. The taxation of interstate business income is a problem far from being solved.

Summary The nature of the United States government and the mobility of its social and economic life produce difficulties in the complex administration of revenue sources. Tax overlapping, whether vertical (between levels of government) or horizontal (among the same levels of government), creates economic inefficiencies in tax collection, and each variant of tax overlapping brings its own challenges. Tax coordination represents an attempt to deal with this situation.

Administration and compliance costs

The last element of revenue sources to be considered is that of administration and compliance costs. The collection of tax revenues means that a portion of total state and local tax revenue has been diverted to pay for enforcement. If such resources were not used on enforcement, however, tax evasion might be encouraged and a decrease in total tax collections might well be the result.

Thus the question is not *whether* state and local governments should spend resources on enforcement, but rather *how much*. Economic analysis indicates that expenditures on enforcement should increase as long as the additional revenue obtained exceeds the actual cost of enforcement and as long as there are no negative reactions that might reduce volume in the long run. Pure economic analysis, however, can be misleading because it does not take into account the prospects of political opposition, tax avoidance, organized protest, and other manifestations of unacceptability. Bad enforcement leads to poor taxpayer morale, through operation of the "he got away" syndrome. On the other hand, enforcement should not become equated with harassment.

As Table 3–6 indicates, the bulk of state and local tax revenues stems from sales, income, and property taxes. It may be noted that the cost of administration, as a percentage of revenues, is surprisingly low for each of these taxes. The administrative costs of the income tax probably has a modest advantage over that of the sales tax, where costs range between 1.5 percent to 2.0 percent of receipts. With respect to compliance costs, the income tax puts costs chiefly on the individuals, while the sales tax puts them on the retailers.[14] In his seminal work on the property tax, Dick Netzer estimated that it was "entirely possible to get 'good' property tax administration in the larger jurisdictions at a cost of no more than . . . 1.5 percent of tax collections."[15]

Private resources, however, are also expended in complying with the tax laws. Business firms, for example, act as tax collecting agents for state and local governments when they withhold income taxes and collect sales taxes. In performing this function they naturally incur some costs. Business firms should, perhaps, be compensated for these costs. About one-half of the states do compensate businesses for costs incurred in collecting the sales tax, as much as 1 percent to 5 percent of the total tax collected.[16] If compliance costs are excessive and no compensation is made, tax evasion would probably increase.

An overview

The preceding discussion has outlined some of the implications of the theory of taxation for local government revenues and noted the major characteristics of different revenue sources. The remainder of this chapter presents a brief survey of the developing trends in municipal revenue through the mid-1970s, notes the role of the major items of revenue, and points out future prospects. The purpose of this discussion is to present an overall framework. Chapters 6, 7, and 8 will analyze specific items of revenue in more detail.

Municipal revenue is derived from general revenue sources (tax revenue and nontax revenue) and nongeneral revenue sources (utility, liquor store, and insurance trust revenue). During the 1950s and the 1960s the total revenue of city governments averaged an 8 percent annual growth rate. From 1970 to 1975 the average annual growth rate increased to almost 13 percent. Table 3–7 sets out the various components of this growth in absolute and percentage terms. General revenue grew at an average annual rate of 13.4 percent—about the same average annual growth rate as total revenue. Nevertheless, an investigation of the growth and trends in the two major general revenue sources, tax revenue and nontax revenue, reveals different processes at work.

Tax revenue

The historic growth patterns of city tax revenue through 1975 shows an increase of $17 billion, from $4 billion in 1952 to $21 billion in 1975. The average annual growth rate was approximately 7 percent during the 1950s and 1960s and increased to 9 percent in the early 1970s. During the 1950s the growth in tax revenue accounted for over one-half the growth in general revenue. In the 1960s, however, the growth in tax revenue represented 44 percent of the growth in city general revenue. By 1975 tax revenue growth represented only 32 percent of general revenue growth. As a consequence, the relative importance of tax revenue in the city general revenue system decreased substantially, from about 66 percent in 1952 to approximately 42 percent in 1975. Table 3–8 illustrates the percentage distribution in city general revenue for selected years and provides an overview of this process.

Table 3–7   City revenue and average annual growth rate in city revenue during 1952–60, 1960–70, and 1970–75

City revenue	Amount (In millions)				Average annual growth rate (%)		
	1952	1960	1970	1975	1952–60	1960–70	1970–75
Total revenue	8,278	14,915	32,704	59,744	7.6	8.2	12.8
Total general revenue	6,351	11,647	26,621	49,853	7.9	8.6	13.4
Tax revenue	4,183	7,109	13,647	21,135	6.9	6.7	9.1
Nontax revenue	2,168	4,538	12,974	28,719	9.7	11.1	17.2
Charges	956	2,217	5,068	9,071	11.1	8.6	12.3
Fed. and state aid	1,212	2,321	7,906	19,648	8.5	13.0	20.0
Total nongeneral revenue	1,928	3,268	6,083	9,891	6.8	6.4	10.2

Source: Tax Foundation, Inc., *Facts and Figures on Government Finance*, 19th Biennial Edition (New York: Tax Foundation, Inc., 1977), p. 251.

Table 3–8   Percentage distribution of city general revenue for selected years, 1952–75

Revenue source	1952 (%)	1960 (%)	1970 (%)	1975 (%)
Total general revenue	100.0	100.0	100.0	100.0
Tax revenue	65.9	61.0	51.3	42.4
Property	49.5	44.6	34.3	26.2
Sales and gross receipts	9.4	10.5	9.1	9.1
License and other taxes (city income taxes, etc.)	6.9	6.0	7.9	7.1
Nontax revenue	34.1	39.0	48.7	57.6
Charges (service charges and fees, etc.)	15.1	19.0	19.0	18.2
Intergovernmental transfers	19.1	19.9	29.7	39.4
State aid	16.9	16.0	23.2	26.2
Federal aid	2.2	3.9	6.5	13.2

Source: Calculated from data in Tax Foundation, Inc., *Facts and Figures on Government Finance*, 19th Biennial Edition (New York: Tax Foundation, Inc., 1977), p. 251.

The relative drop in tax revenue was, of course, made up by a corresponding growth in the revenues of various service charges and, even more significantly, by the increase in intergovernmental grants-in-aid. As Table 3–8 indicates, this last named category as a percent of total city general revenue doubled between 1960 and 1975—rising from 20 percent of city general revenue in 1960 to almost 40 percent in 1975. Federal aid as a percentage of state-local expenditures, however, reached a peak in 1978 and is now expected to stabilize. State and local governments will have to depend on their own revenue sources for an increasingly larger share of their expenditures.

The property tax   American cities have relied and, it appears, will continue to rely heavily on the property tax. Although this tax has declined significantly in total general revenue (from 50 percent in 1952 to 26 percent in 1975) the property tax still represents more than 60 percent of the local governments' own *tax* revenues. These revenues, as has been noted, make up more than 40 percent of *total* general revenue.

While Table 3–8 illustrates relative percentage *distribution* of city general revenue for selected years, Table 3–9 shows relative percentage *growth*, thus offering an additional perspective. Property tax collections increased about 65 percent between 1952 and 1960, 76 percent over the 1960s and 43 percent during the early 1970s. The growth in property tax revenue in the 1950s represented just under 39 percent of the growth in city general revenues. The growth of the property tax in the ensuing decade represented 26 percent of the growth in city general revenues and in the early 1970s property tax growth accounted for only 17 percent of city general revenue growth. The property tax is an important source of locally controlled revenues, and although its relative position may decline, it is unlikely to be replaced by other revenue sources.

There are probably several reasons for the recent taxpayer revolt against the property tax. One reason is that the property tax is highly visible compared to, for example, the sales tax, which is buried in the purchase price of a good. The taxpayer also pays the full amount of the property tax at one time compared with the sales tax, which is paid in small amounts and over a period of time. Furthermore, inflation has hit real property prices quite hard, and it is difficult for the taxpayer to understand that an increase in property value is accruing, especially when the taxpayer does not plan to sell the property. Finally, the trend toward a shorter assessment cycle (more frequent assessments) has also encouraged the taxpayer revolt. Because these problems are not likely to disappear in the near future, the taxpayer revolt may continue for some time.

Table 3–9   Relative percent growth in city revenue, 1952–60, 1960–70, and 1970–75

Revenue source	1952–60		1960–70		1970–75	
	% increase	% of 1952–60 increase	% increase	% of 1960–70 increase	% increase	% of 1970–75 increase
Total general revenue	83.4	100.0	128.6	100.0	87.3	100.0
Tax revenue	70.0	55.3	92.0	43.7	54.9	32.2
Property	65.3	38.8	75.6	26.3	42.9	16.9
Sales and gross receipts	103.5	11.7	99.0	8.1	88.1	9.2
Licenses and other taxes (city income taxes, etc.)	58.0	4.8	201.9	9.4	68.5	6.2
Nontax revenue	109.3	44.8	185.9	56.3	121.4	67.8
Charges	131.9	23.8	128.6	19.0	79.0	17.2
Intergovernmental transfers	91.5	20.9	240.6	37.3	148.5	50.5
State aid	74.1	15.0	230.5	28.8	111.5	29.6
Federal aid	225.9	5.9	282.6	8.6	280.6	20.9

Source: Calculated from data in Tax Foundation, Inc., *Facts and Figures on Government Finance*, 19th Biennial Edition (New York: Tax Foundation, Inc., 1977), p. 251.

Basically, the decline in the relative importance of the property tax reflects the failure of that tax to provide sufficient revenues to meet the expanding demand for local government services. Cities have sought new tax sources, among them the city sales and income taxes. Cities have also been forced to increase their dependency on nontax revenue sources. The fact remains, however, that the property tax is not necessarily a bad tax. It brings in a high yield; it is more stable than other state and local taxes, with the exception of the income tax; and it has a relatively easily identifiable tax base. The administration of the property tax could be improved by the adoption of a statewide assessment system and, perhaps, by the removal of the responsibility for assessment from elected officials to professional experts.

Sales and gross receipts taxes   As indicated in Table 3–8, revenue from city sales and gross receipts taxes increased slightly in relative importance from the early

1950s to 1960, but decreased in 1970 and 1975. Table 3–9 shows that revenue from city sales and gross receipts taxes grew by over 103 percent during the 1950s, by 99 percent in the following decade, and by only 88 percent through 1975.

City sales taxes include broad-based general sales taxes and also narrow-based, selective sales taxes such as those on alcoholic beverages, cigarettes, soft drinks, and gasoline. In 1976, twenty-two states allowed municipalities to levy a general sales tax. In Illinois alone, the tax was in use in over 1,200 cities. The general sales tax usually varies from 0.5 percent to 2.0 percent of the selling price of a covered good or service. By 1976, however, the rate was 3.0 percent in twenty-four cities in Alaska, fourteen cities in Colorado, and four in New York.[17] These rates are in addition to state sales taxes, which usually range from 2.0 percent to 5.0 percent.

The cigarette tax is the most common local selective sales tax. Municipalities in seven states levied such a tax in the mid-1970s. In some states, municipalities taxed the sale of alcoholic beverages and soft drinks. Some cities also taxed gasoline. The difficulty with selective sales taxes as a source of city revenue is that they may be avoided by purchasing the commodity in cities that do not have the tax. Furthermore, because the taxed items are often necessities or small vices that form a fixed part of the budget, selective sales taxes have regressive effects on the distribution of income. In contrast to general sales taxes, selective sales taxes penalize the consumer for consumption of the commodity. Sales and gross receipts taxes are about 9 percent of total city revenues. These and other aspects of local sales taxes are more fully explored in Chapter 7.

Licenses and other taxes   Revenues from municipal licenses and other taxes, including local income taxes, ranged from 6 percent to 8 percent of total general revenues during the past two and a half decades. Faced with a growing gap between their expenditures and property tax revenues, American cities turned to city sales taxes for relief during the 1950s. Because the same situation existed in the 1960s and the first half of the 1970s, many American cities sought new tax sources, namely, the income tax. The revenue from local income taxes became much more important in the 1960s and 1970s than in previous years, increasing from about 1.4 percent of local tax revenue in 1960 to almost 5 percent in 1976. Since 1939 some 4,000 local units, located mostly in Kentucky, Ohio, and Pennsylvania, have used or are using this source of revenue. In addition to these three states, cities in Alabama, California, Delaware, Maryland, Michigan, Missouri, and New York have adopted the tax as recently as 1976.

The city income tax is usually a low flat rate imposed on salaries, wages, fees, commissions, and other compensations of residents of the city levying the tax, as well as of nonresidents employed in the city. Although the range in rates runs from as low as 0.25 percent to as high as 4.3 percent, the majority of cities impose a rate of 1.0 percent on gross income. The city tax imposed on commuters is, of course, one way of taxing people who use city services but who live outside the city. It has also proved to be a productive source of revenue, representing over 50.0 percent of tax collections in more than twenty cities located in several states.

Nontax revenue

City nontax revenue is composed essentially of revenue from user charges for municipal services and fiscal transfers from state and federal governments. The nontax revenue of cities has grown significantly since the 1950s, with much of the growth in the 1960s and 1970s (Tables 3–8 and 3–9). Between 1952 and 1960 city nontax revenue grew 109 percent, an average annual growth rate of 10 percent. During the 1960s and early 1970s nontax revenue grew 186 percent and

121 percent, respectively, with average annual growth rates of 11 percent and 17 percent, respectively (see Tables 3–7 and 3–9).

The growth in city revenue from nontax sources accounted for 45 percent of the growth in all general revenues during the period from 1952 to 1960. This figure increased to 56 percent in the following decade and close to 70 percent in subsequent years. As a result, nontax revenue of cities increased in relative importance, totalling more than one-half the general revenue of cities by 1975. The growth in nontax revenues partially closed the gap between city expenditures and city tax revenues, averting for a while a severe financial crisis.

User charges   Local governments provide certain goods and services that may be financed on a quasi-commercial basis. Because these goods and services ideally provide a benefit to only the user, individual users are charged an amount that is related to the cost of providing the service. Examples of user charges are charges for municipal golf courses, park and recreational facilities, and garbage collection. Revenue from user charges and fees for city government services rose by about 130 percent from 1950 to 1970, and by about 80 percent in the next five years. During these periods, the average annual growth rates in revenue from user charges ranged from about 9 percent to 12 percent. Revenue from user charges grew faster than tax revenues grew during each of the periods.

In 1975, revenue from user charges represented about 18 percent of the general revenue of cities. Where municipal services can be related to individual consumption, charges, fees, and tolls provide an efficient way of distributing the cost among the users of the system. Although service charges do create the need for a billing system or other collection machinery, collection costs in this respect seem to have been quite reasonable. On the other hand, user charges have the potential to reduce the use of merit goods; if a user charge is placed on a good judged to be meritorious, it may reduce its consumption.

Federal and state aid   As indicated in Table 3–8, by 1975 grants obtained from federal and state governments represented 39 percent of the total general revenue of local governments. This source of revenue remained relatively constant during the 1950s. It rose sharply over the next fifteen years, growing by over 200 percent in the 1960s and by almost 150 percent in the early 1970s—faster than any other source of city revenue (see Table 3–9). Indeed, the growth in grants-in-aid accounted for more of the growth in general revenues of cities in the first half of the 1970s than did the growth in tax revenue.

Since the 1960s the implementation of revenue sharing and other programs indicates that federal and state revenues are continuing to relieve the tax pressures on local governments. Federal and state aid, of course, may be used to stimulate those local government services deemed important to society and also may be used to equalize differences in the taxing capacity of local units of government. Aid to cities should be coordinated with spillover benefits to help pay for those services that benefit people who live outside the local government unit. General education and education of the disadvantaged, crime prevention, health services, and public assistance might be considered spillover benefits.

Summary   The preceding discussion has built on earlier descriptions and analyses of tax theory and overall revenue characteristics by providing a more specific overview of municipal revenues. The role of tax revenue and nontax revenue in municipal finance has been considered, with a breakdown of major items in each category—the property tax; sales and gross receipts taxes; licenses and other taxes, including city income taxes; and the role of user charges and federal and state aid. Also, the major features of and changes in each revenue item have been outlined in relative status over the period from the early 1950s to the mid-1970s.

The outlook

The movement of people to the smaller major metropolitan areas (populations of 500,000 to 1,999,999) and minor metropolitan areas (populations of 50,000 to 499,999) in the next decade, along with rapidly rising costs of municipal services probably will continue to present the cities of our nation with severe financial problems in the years ahead. Suburban communities, too, will face the well known problems associated with inflation, national and international economic uncertainty, energy shortages and environmental demands, and continued demands by the citizenry for adequate local government goods and services.

At the same time that municipalities are trying to meet citizen demands, they will be facing a growing public sentiment to slow down the growth in government. Thus, cities are relying heavily on aid from higher levels of government, especially where the expenditures have social spillover benefits. Whether aid from the federal government will continue at current levels, however, is not clear.

Local governments remain the single most important supplier of civil goods and services. The benefits from a number of these goods and services may be restricted to individuals within the locality; hence, local governments may finance the growing demand for some of these items according to the benefit-received principle and charges and user fees. This trend has gathered momentum since the 1960s.

By the mid-1970s, only eight of the twenty-five largest cities in the nation levied a personal income tax. More central cities may look to this method of getting the commuter to contribute to city services. By "piggybacking" the city tax to the state personal income tax, local governments can collect the tax at a reasonable cost.

Federal revenue sharing will continue to play a major role in the financing of urban governments, especially in the larger cities. The search for new revenue sources and ways to use more extensively existing revenue sources will go on in the struggle to meet expenditure needs. The future of local finance will also be affected by the methods chosen to finance the public schools—the largest single item of local government expenditure. A move toward greater state financing of education may be the response to the pressures of recent court decisions affecting educational programs. Legislative, judicial, and practical experience, however, have not been extensive enough to permit any definitive judgments to be made in this area of public finance.

Change is a constant in the managerial environment of local revenues—as will be the search for revenues in the years that lie ahead.

1 Henry J. Aaron, *Who Pays The Property Tax?* (Washington, D.C.: Brookings Institution, 1975); E. K. Browning and W. R. Johnson, *The Distribution of the Tax Burden* (Washington, D.C.: American Enterprise Institute, 1979).

2 Li-teh Sun, "Incidence of Montana State and Local Taxes" (Ph.D. diss. Oklahoma State University, 1972).

3 Joseph A. Pechman and Benjamin A. Okner, *Who Bears the Tax Burden?* (Washington, D.C.: Brookings Institution, 1974), pp. 8–10, 62–63.

4 Ibid., p. 64.

5 U.S., Advisory Commission on Intergovernmental Relations, *Significant Features of Fiscal Federalism,* 1976–77 edition (Washington, D.C.: Government Printing Office, 1977), vol. 2, p. 105.

6 U.S., Advisory Commission on Intergovernmental Relations, *Federal-State Coordination of Personal Income Taxes* (Washington, D.C.: Government Printing Office, 1965), p. 41.

7 Ibid., p. 47.

8 Ibid., p. 43.

9 Ibid., p. 45.

10 George F. Break, *Intergovernmental Fiscal Relations in the United States* (Washington, D.C.: Brookings Institution, 1967), p. 33.

11 Ibid., p. 51.

12 Ibid., p. 55.

13 Ibid., p. 57.

14 James A. Maxwell and J. Richard Aronson, *Financing State and Local Governments,* 3d ed. (Washington, D.C.: Brookings Institution, 1977), p. 113.

15 Dick Netzer, *Economics of the Property Tax* (Washington, D.C.: Brookings Institution, 1966), p. 175.

16 Maxwell and Aronson, *Financing State and Local Governments,* p. 106.

17 U.S., Advisory Commission on Intergovernmental Relations, *Significant Features of Fiscal Federalism,* p. 187.

Forecasting local revenues and expenditures

Forecasting in local government is an important managerial tool and guide to what and when corrective actions ought to be taken to avoid disaster, financial and otherwise. The importance of forecasting generally has been recognized in the private sector, where it has become an integral part of the managerial decision-making process. This has not been the case in the public sector, even though the environment of the public sector is not quite like that of the private sector. Nevertheless, rational planning and analysis of what actions might be taken under a particular set of circumstances can be carried out by a public body.

Forecasting is not totally foreign to the public sector; the annual budget always includes a forecast of expected revenues as well as the level of planned expenditures. Other types of forecasts, however, could be used in the public planning and financial management process. For example, short-range (up to one year) cash flow projections, long-range (five years and over) fiscal impact analyses, and projection models designed to illustrate the potential future effects of alternative public policies in such areas as transportation and land development might be used in the process.

This chapter reviews revenue and expenditure forecasts, with primary emphasis on projections of from one to five years into the future. The varied uses of expenditures and revenue forecasts and how they might be used in discussions of overall policy issues are covered, as is forecasting as a tool for making sound administrative decisions. The chapter also describes the major methods available for medium-range (one to five years) forecasting and the administrative and political issues associated with this type of forecasting. Finally, the data requirements of several forecasting techniques are considered.

Uses of forecasts

The uses of different forecasting methods can most conveniently be classified on the basis of the length of the forecast period. This section focuses on medium-range (one to five years) forecasts. Fiscal forecasts of shorter or longer duration are briefly reviewed also.

Medium-range forecasts

The public sector, unfortunately, has often been characterized by inadequate planning for periods longer than the traditional budget year. This often results in "management by crisis" and inefficient operations. Medium-range forecasts are capable of helping to avoid such situations. For example, if budgetary problems are anticipated two years hence, planning may begin immediately to avert a potential crisis. Emergency cutbacks and tax increases may not become necessary.

The example cited illustrates one of the principal uses of medium-range forecasts—the projection of fiscal "gaps" or revenue shortfalls. Given a set of assumptions, the revenues and expenditures are independently projected. If the projections suggest a major shortfall between revenues and expenditures, policy decisions can be made immediately to balance the two sides of the budget.

If policies are implemented to eliminate the gap, then the actual revenues and/or expenditures will not be the same as the forecasts. In other words, in the usual environment where budget deficits are forbidden, the projection of a gap should bring about policies that alter revenue or expenditure such that the levels forecast originally will *not* be realized. The altered levels are not "errors" in the forecast; in fact, the changes elicited are exactly the rationale for undertaking the forecast—projections are not prophecies.

Medium-range forecasts play a role in policy analysis when the effect of a decision extends beyond the current budget period. For example, wage negotiations involving multiyear contracts obviously have fiscal implications extending beyond the current budget period. The fiscal implications of nonrenewal of a federal grant that is part of the current year must be considered by the manager as he or she plans the budget for subsequent years.

By definition, the life of capital projects is longer than that of the traditional annual budget. This means that the projects are likely to have expenditures that extend beyond the current budget year. The most obvious expenditures are debt service charges. Additionally, capital projects often require operating and maintenance expenses throughout the life of the project. Analyzing these longer-range cost implications can be an important output of the medium-range forecasts.

Short-range forecasts

The principal uses of short-range (up to one year) forecasts are associated with the construction of the annual budget and cash management. It is fiscally prudent that the flow of cash be predicted,[1] especially in a time of high interest rates and of costly and money-market investments that yield positive returns for periods as short as one day.

The annual budget, too, requires forecasting,[2] particularly the projections of revenue streams that are likely to be realized during the following fiscal year. Certain variables on the expenditure side must also be forecast; if a particular level of real inputs must be used to derive the desired level of output, the prices for these inputs must be predicted so that expenditures can be estimated.

Long-range forecasting

When planning the long-range forecast of a community, the past and present state of the local economy should first be determined. The population (its size and composition by such characteristics as age), the income structure, and the employment mix in the area are each related, directly or indirectly, to the capacity of local residents to pay taxes and to their requirements for public expenditures. An examination of recent trends in these variables may suggest whether fiscal problems are on the horizon for the city.

A commonly used technique for describing the local economic base is called *location quotient analysis*.[3] Although a full description of the technique is not within the scope of this chapter, it is based on a comparison of the industrial composition of local employment (local employment in an industry divided by total local employment) with national employment in the same industry divided by total national employment. If a locality has *relatively* greater numbers of employees in one industry than the nation has as a whole, its location quotient for that industry is greater than 1. The implication is that the locality is, in some sense, specialized in that industry. For planning purposes, policy makers may use this information to help attract new industries to the area. Specialization in one industry may suggest that industrial diversification of the area would be useful to avoid swings of boom-and-bust that often characterize particular industries. On the other hand, specialization may be used as an inducement to attract complementary industries to the area.

While the location quotient provides information on a local economic base for a point in time, more insight is gained by reviewing the changes in local employment relative to the rest of the nation over a period of time. One formal method for such study is *shift-share analysis.*[4] Shift-share analysis attempts to describe how local employment, classified by industry, has changed vis-a-vis changes in national employment. The method categorizes observed changes in local industrial employment into three components: the overall national growth in employment; the particular industrial mix within the area; and the share of total national employment growth in the locality by industry. The industrial mix suggests whether employment in the locality is predominately in slowly- or rapidly-growing industries. Changes in the locality's share of employment growth relative to that of the nation shows whether the locality is remaining competitive with other areas of the country. If the results show that local employment is predominately in relatively slow-growth industries, decision makers may want to attempt to attract new industries with brighter long-range futures to the area. Likewise, if it appears that the locality has an unfavorable competitive position relative to other areas, decision makers may wish to consider *why* this has occurred. Shift-share analysis does not, however, explain the underlying causes of change; it is only a descriptive analytical technique. While the causes of change may be outside the powers of local decision makers (e.g., a declining regional population or pressures that have made local wages non-competitive with alternative sites), some policies may be available to alter the competitive balance. Tax breaks, special services to new industries, and even aggressive salesmanship of the area by government officials may yield positive results.[5] In any event, shift-share analysis can be an important step in initiating a long-range planning process.

Neither location quotient computations nor shift-share analysis can be used for explicit long-range projections of the local economy. Recently, however, there has been considerable interest expressed in projecting the long-range implications of changes in population, income, and land use on the local fiscal situation. These methods are commonly called *fiscal impact models.*[6]

The rationale underlying these models is that as the size and composition of the population shift, as income levels and distribution change, or as land-use patterns are altered, there will be impacts on both revenues and expenditures of the locality. For example, a large parcel of vacant land might be ripe for development for low-density row houses and single-family detached units, for apartments, or for commercial development. This may raise a host of questions about the classification for the zoning district containing the parcel of land. The fiscal implications of these land development options provide invaluable information to policy makers in reviewing the present zoning classification and petitions for zoning change.

While any use of the land may require new community capital investment to provide such services as streets and sewer and water facilities, these requirements are likely to differ for commercial and residential land use. Moreover, different levels of police and fire protection services will be required for the alternative uses. The taxes, and thus, the revenue yield, will also depend on the type of land-use chosen.

Even within the general land use category, a choice may have to be made concerning the specific type of use permitted. For example, residential housing may be single-family detached houses, apartments, or condominiums. Obviously, population density and public-service costs will differ for these forms of housing; furthermore, the population and income levels of the groups demanding these different types of housing will differ. The number of school-age children who live in apartments is likely to differ from the number in single-family homes. Given the population mix, the levels of tax revenue may depend on the specified land use.

If the effect of different population groups, income groups, and land usages on government revenues and expenditures can be roughly calculated, the budgetary effects of zoning policies can be projected under alternative policy scenarios. Both revenues and expenditures under each of the zoning alternatives for future use of vacant land may be projected. Furthermore, because development of these land-use types may have differing time schedules, the flow of revenues and expenditures—including debt financing—can be forecast.

Complete consideration of the revenue and expenditure implications under a variety of scenarios is most easily accomplished with the help of a computer. Given the substantial interest in fiscal impact analysis, it is not surprising that several computer packages are currently available to derive such estimates. These packages, however, have different capabilities and data requirements; and the initial cost of these models ranges from $20,000 to $75,000.

One model, the Municipal Impact Evaluation Systems (MUNIES) model, is basically an accounting system that compiles the expected costs and revenues of a particular policy change.[7] The program uses substantial amounts of locally-prepared data concerning the timing of the proposed change, the anticipated changes in population and employment by homogeneous groups, and the estimates of revenues and expenditures associated with the different types of employment and population. The computer produces output on the budgetary implications of the proposed decision, including a breakout of capital and current expenditures and, if necessary, projects the changes in tax rates necessary to achieve a balanced budget.

A second model (actually a set of models) is the Fiscal Impact Analysis System (FIAS).[8] Whereas the previously described model is an accounting-based model, FIAS attempts to use historical data from the jurisdiction to relate changes in policies to changes in population, employment, and income. The relative changes are then used to project revenues and expenditures in the locality. Thus, the model attempts to capture the projected changes in the structure of the local economy and the subsequent fiscal effects.

As with any management or policy tool, these fiscal impact models are not capable of *making* decisions. They only provide inputs for decisions. The principal advantage of the computer-assisted approach is the speed and accuracy with which the projections can be prepared. The models do, however, require significant data-collection input; they are not likely to be general enough to incorporate all of the major variables that affect local revenues and expenditures over the long-range. The models focus primarily on the long-range impacts of general policies that affect the local budget rather than the shorter-range effects of changes in economic conditions. Thus, although the models could be tailored to concentrate on two- to five-year budget forecasts, that has not been their primary usage. For such projections, the techniques described in the following section are more likely to be appropriate.

Methods of forecasting

The focus in this section is on applicable methods for projecting revenues and expenditures from one to five years into the future. Four general forecasting methods are outlined, although the details on their use for particular revenues and expenditures[9] are not provided.

In general there is a trade-off between the cost of assembling the forecast and the amount and accuracy of information provided in the different methods. The simpler methods require less data, less time to produce, and, possibly, less expertise on the part of the forecaster. The more complex methods can incorporate the effects of a larger number of forces acting on revenues and expenditures, are more amenable to systematic analyses, and are likely to provide more useful information for analyzing particular policy choices.

Best guess or expert forecasts

Few generalizations can be made about producing "expert" forecasts because there is no single method used in forecasting.[10] Probably the key ingredient to successful expert forecasting is finding *the* expert. Often such expertise is gained only through experience; thus, the successful expert forecasters are those who know their own system extremely well and also know where they can go to obtain additional information. For example, local finance directors may be responsible for annual forecasts of all revenue streams. If these individuals know their sources, they may be more able to derive an accurate "best guess" of what the revenues will be during the following year—without a formalized method. The technique used may involve some model or specific method, but it is never made explicit.

Although the expert may produce reasonably accurate predictions, the lack of a formal technique means that it will be difficult to evaluate *why* the forecast was correct or incorrect. The forecast also may rely heavily on the subjective feelings of the forecaster, which are never made explicit. Moreover, if the forecaster were to leave, the "model" would be lost. Finally, the lack of an explicit model limits the use of the technique in estimating the effects of a variety of discretionary policy changes or of the effects of external factors. Nevertheless, one advantage of the approach is that it is likely to be inexpensive.

Trend techniques

For certain revenues and expenditures, fairly accurate predictions may be obtained simply by basing projections on the recent past. Techniques based entirely on previous levels of the variable (an expenditure or revenue source) are termed trend techniques.

Different forms of these time-dependent relationships are possible to predict: the variable will not change in the projection period; the variable will change next year by the same absolute amount that it changed during the current year (if the time series is increasing, this formulation assumes that over time there will be a slowing in the growth *rate*); and the rate of growth will be the same in the future period as it was in the immediate past. (For example, if property

Figure 4–1   Time trend chart.

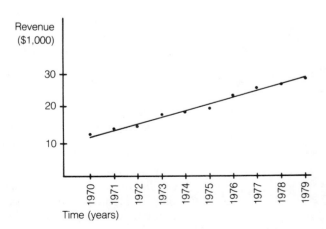

taxes grew by 7 percent during the previous period, they would be forecast to grow by 7 percent during each of the subsequent periods.)

A stronger basis for time-trend techniques is provided when a longer history of the revenue or expenditure variable is considered. A review of nearly equal annual increments in a series over the past six to ten years provides stronger evidence for the constant absolute growth assumption.

Graphical analysis is often helpful in spotting historical trends. In Figure 4–1 time has been plotted on the horizontal axis and the variable to be forecast plotted on the vertical axis. Because all points lie approximately on a straight line, the constant absolute growth assumption is reasonable. Projections of future levels of the variable would be plotted simply by extending the line.

If, on the other hand, the plotted points appear to follow a nonlinear path concave from above, a constant growth *rate* is the more reasonable assumption. This can also be easily verified by determining past annual growth rates in the variable. These rates are determined as

$$g_t = \left(\frac{V_t - V_{t-1}}{V_{t-1}} \right) 100 \qquad (1)$$

where g equals the percentage growth rate in the variable; V is the variable; and t equals the period of time. Thus, if property taxes in 1976 yielded \$5.1 million and in 1977 taxes yielded \$5.7 million, the annual growth was 11.76 percent. If annual growth for each period from 1970 through the present yields similar rates, in the range from 10.0 percent to 12.0 percent, for example, an 11.0 percent annual growth rate into the future may be assumed.

This, too, can be checked graphically, especially through the use of "semi-log" graph paper. As shown in Figure 4–2, on semi-log paper the vertical axis is constructed such that equal distances represent equal percentage changes. That is, the distance from 10 to 20 (a 100 percent increase) is equal to the distance from 20 to 40 (also a 100 percent increase). The horizontal axis is the same as it is in Figure 4–1 and is used here to denote time periods. Because all points lie near the plotted line, the constant growth rate is reasonable with projections, once again, obtained from the extension of the line to the right.

Although time-trend analysis may be useful for deriving quick, relatively short-range forecasts, it will never predict a "turning point," a severe weakness of this process. Time-trend analysis will continue to project increases or decreases throughout the projection period regardless of what may occur in the economy.

Figure 4–2 Time trend chart, semilogarithmic scale.

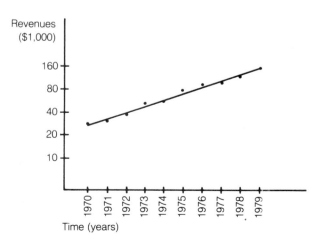

Deterministic techniques

Although time-trend forecasts basically assume that the revenue or expenditure trends are determined only by time, other deterministic techniques allow for variables other than time to "determine" the projected amount. The deterministic method does not, however, depend on any formal statistical techniques. The most common use of the deterministic technique occurs when a revenue or expenditure is determined through a pre-established formula. For example, if a city knows it will obtain $200 per pupil in state education aid, total aid can be determined as the product of the projected future school enrollment times $200.

Deterministic forecasting may also be used to review the expenditure side of the budget. The state may mandate that no more than 30 students be assigned to a single teacher. If it is anticipated that the 1,000 new residents will include 150 school-age students (and all are assumed to enroll in the public schools), then a deterministic estimate of the number of new teachers who must be hired is 5 (150/30 = 5). This technique may be applied further if analysis of personnel positions shows that, on average, there are 40 support personnel (administrators and staff) for every 100 teachers in the school system. The additional 5 teachers projected would then require an additional 2.0 (.4 × 5 = 2.0) support personnel.[11]

Each of these examples encompasses particular assumptions that should be examined before proceeding with the deterministic approach. An implicit assumption is made about the level of service being provided as well as the underlying methods by which inputs are combined to produce outputs. The requirement of one additional teacher for each thirty additional students assumes something about the level of service—that it be held at a minimal level, or if in line with what is already being provided, it be held at a constant level. Likewise, the support personnel projection is based on the assumption that input combinations (support personnel to teacher ratio) is inflexible. While this assumption may or may not be reasonable, it should be made explicit.

An issue associated with a deterministic approach to expenditure projections is the use of averages. The projection in the example was based on averages (40 support personnel *per* 100 teachers) even though the projections were in terms of additional or *marginal* amounts of inputs (5 additional teachers). The preferred method is to base marginal projections on marginal relationships. For example, rather than state that there is, *on average*, 1 fire station per 15,000 residents, it is preferable to state that if 1,000 new residents are attracted to a new subdivision located in close proximity to a group of residents for whom fire service is only minimal, an additional fire station will be allocated to serve both groups. Thus, one additional fire station would be allocated even though the average (1 fire station per 15,000 residents) would call for only .15 fire stations.

Another issue associated with the use of the deterministic approach is its applicability in cities that experience a growth or decline in population. Although cities are certain to hire more public-service employees in response to a growth in population, the assumption that the work force will be reduced proportionately in response to a decline in population is less realistic. Even so, the assumption behind the forecasts should be made explicit for careful examination by the policy makers.

Econometric forecasting

Econometric forecasting combines principles drawn from economics with statistical techniques. Conceptually somewhat more complex than the deterministic methods just reviewed, econometric forecasting is capable of yielding more useful information to both the forecaster and the policy maker. It allows the investigator to consider the simultaneous effects of several variables that ultimately determine the levels of a revenue or expenditure stream.

The most common approach in econometric forecasting is to forecast the series independently using regression techniques drawn from statistical theory. The approach is likely to involve a multi-step process similar to the one detailed below.[12]

First, a particular revenue source that is dependent on one or more "independent" or causal variables is hypothesized. Economic theory should be used to select the possible variables that influence the outcome; more eclectic or empirical approaches may be used to choose the independent variables, noting that reliance on economic theory is preferable because it is more likely to result in relationships that will hold throughout the future. For example, economic theory would suggest that the incomes, relative prices, tastes, and number of consumers are variables affecting the demand for taxable consumer goods, which, in turn, determine the sales tax revenues.

In contrast, the empirical approach simply uses the set of variables that provides the "best fit" to the historical revenue series. This approach usually involves the estimation of numerous relationships via statistical regression techniques and chooses the "best" one based on some set of criteria.

Secondly, data are collected for as many past years as is possible. The internal records of the city should be consulted for the historical data pertaining to a particular revenue series. Considerable effort must be made to ensure that the data are, in fact, measuring what they purport to measure and measuring it in a consistent manner over the entire period. For example, minor revenue sources such as service fees or charges may not have been reported in a consistent manner in the past. To the extent possible the data must be adjusted to yield a time series of data that most closely reflects the current definition of the revenue source. (This aspect of the forecasting effort is described in more detail later in this chapter.)

It is at this point that lack of data on the variables suggested from economic theory may require substitution of proxy variables. For example, many cities find that there is no reliable time series of data on city income; thus, county, state, or national income data must be used as a proxy.

The next step is to determine a statistical relationship using least squares linear regression analysis on the data collected. In linear regression analysis, the dependent variable denoted Y is specified as a linear function of the independent variables in which

$$Y = a + b_1 X_1 + b_2 X_2 + \ldots + b_k X_k \qquad (2)$$

where $X_1, X_2, \ldots, X_k$ are K different independent variables and $a, b_1, b_2, \ldots, b_k$ are parameters to be estimated using regression techniques. For example, in forecasting local sales taxes (ST) the analyst may specify that these revenues depend on real personal income (I), the consumer price index (CPI), and the population of the community (POP). The regression equation to be estimated is

$$ST = a + b_1 I + b_2 CPI + b_3 POP. \qquad (3)$$

Least squares regression analysis finds numerical estimates of a, b_1, b_2, and b_3.

Assume that local sales taxes are hypothesized to be a linear function of local income and that the values of these two variables have been plotted on the graph as shown in Figure 4–3. (Each point on the graph represents the observed values of the two variables in one year.) Least squares regression then finds the *unique* line passing through these points that *minimizes* the sum of the *squared* vertical distances between the line and all observed pairs of values. This unique line can be expressed algebraically as

$$ST = a + bI \qquad (4)$$

where a is the "intercept term" or the value of ST when I equals zero and b is the slope of the line. The slope can be interpreted as the change in *ST* associated with each unit change in *I*. For example, if the analysis yields the result

$$ST = 16.221 + .013I \tag{5}$$

the implication is that for each dollar increase (decrease) in income, sales tax revenues are estimated to increase (decrease) by $.013. (The 16.221 term has no reasonable interpretation since it suggests positive tax revenues even with an income of zero; yet it is necessary to ensure that the least squared distance criterion is satisfied.)

Figure 4–3 Least squares regression analysis.

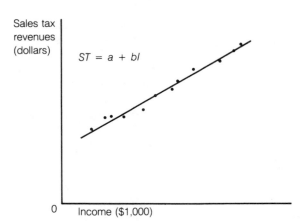

Although it is beyond the scope of this chapter to provide much detail concerning regression analysis,[13] there are several aspects of the technique that should be kept in mind. Most often revenue equations include two or more independent variables rather than the single variable used in equation (4). In such cases, the individual regression coefficients are estimates of the change in the dependent variable associated with a one unit change in the particular independent variable *with the remaining independent variables held constant*. The sign on the coefficient indicates whether the two variables tend to vary in the same or opposite direction.

Consider the following example of a multiple regression equation of the form specified in equation (3).

$$ST = 10.315 + .011I + 1.614CPI + 3.215POP \tag{6}$$

These results imply that, even if the *CPI* and *POP* remain constant, each dollar increase in real incomes is estimated to result in an increase of sales taxes by $.011. That the two variables are expected to move in the same direction follows from the plus sign (+) on the coefficient of *I*.

Although each of the examples given here has used a linear relationship of the dependent and independent variables, the same technique can be applied when the relationships between the variables are nonlinear. The most commonly used nonlinear relationship is a logarithmic transformation of one or more of the variables. Changes in the logarithm of a variable can be interpreted as a percentage change in the variable. For example, the equation

$$1n(CIG) = 5.33 + 1.007 \, 1n(CIGR) + 0.970 \, 1n(ILAG) \tag{7}$$

where 1n*(CIG)* equals natural logarithm of cigarette taxes; 1n*(CIGR)* equals natural logarithm of cigarette tax rates; and 1n*(ILAG)* equals natural logarithm of real personal income, with a lag of one year.[14]

The equation implies that, with cigarette tax rates constant, a 1.0 *percent* increase in lagged real income is associated with a 0.970 *percent* increase in cigarette tax revenues. The example also illustrates another useful transformation in revenue forecasting—the use of "lagged" variables. The equation relates revenue in the *current* year to income of the *past* year, rather than relate current revenue to *current* income. This is often appropriate when taxpayers are not expected to respond immediately to changes in such variables as income or prices. Although these transformations (and others) are extremely useful, they should nevertheless be used with care. The analyst should give some thought to whether the function chosen makes theoretical and practical sense.

Regression analysis yields other statistics that can be used to judge the final results. One of these statistics is the coefficient of determination (R^2), which can take on any fractional value from zero to one; higher R^2 values suggest a "closer" fit of the observed points to the regression equation and, therefore, suggest a more accurate forecast. Another statistic, the estimated standard error of the regression coefficient, tests whether a particular independent variable is statistically related to the dependent variable (i.e., whether the regression coefficient is equal to zero). This is especially important when the regression results are used to analyze policy questions that focus on a particular independent variable.

The cigarette tax example may be used to illustrate these two statistics. A complete reporting of the regression results show

$$1n(CIG) = 5.33 + 1.0071n(CIGR) + 0.9701n(I)$$
$$(1.26) \quad (0.172) \quad (0.163) \qquad (8)$$

$$R^2 = 0.965$$

where the number below each regression coefficient is its estimated standard error and the coefficient of determination is 0.965. The latter statistic means that over 96 percent of the variations in the natural logarithm of cigarette taxes can be attributed to variations in the two independent variables. Thus, it appears that these variables offer a good "explanation" of cigarette tax revenues.

The estimated standard errors suggest that changes in each of the independent variables are significantly related to changes in the dependent variable; nevertheless, if the estimated standard error on the *I* variable had been found to be as large as, say 0.5, rather than 0.163, there would have been insufficient evidence to conclude that changes in the natural logarithm of *I* were significantly related to changes in the natural logarithm of *ST*. Even if real income increased, there would be no response evident in cigarette tax revenues.

Finally, once the final equation is chosen, the forecaster must obtain observed values of each of the independent variables for the projection period. As is discussed in more detail later in this chapter, this step may produce errors in the projections since the resulting forecast of the dependent variable is based on variables that are, themselves, forecasted variables and, therefore, subject to forecasting error.

The statistical approach to forecasting has relative advantages and disadvantages; the approach has attributes not found in the expert, trend or deterministic methods. An econometric model bases estimates on behavioral relationships that contain a theoretical foundation and that can be evaluated by the user of the forecast—an attribute missing in expert forecasts. Furthermore, time-trend techniques only forecast in one direction, while regression techniques have no such limitations.[15] For example, if real incomes were to fall, the cigarette tax equation in (7) would project decreases in revenues.

Statistical methods also have advantages over their deterministic counterparts. Statistical inference can be used to test whether an observed relationship between variables is, in fact, statistically significant. For example, on average, there may be a linkage between income in a city and the amount of fine revenues collected; however, this relationship may have varied so greatly during the past that there are no statistical grounds on which to base predictions. Thus, the long-range relationship cannot be averaged accurately.

Furthermore, a purely deterministic approach will probably include only one causal variable (e.g., population) while several independent variables can be used simultaneously in the statistical regression approach. Thus, it is possible to estimate the effect a change in one independent variable (e.g., tax rate) will have on revenues while holding the other variables (e.g., real income) constant—an especially useful feature for policy analysis. Alternatively, each of the independent variables can be altered simultaneously to estimate the net effect of such changes on the dependent variable.

The employment of the statistical approach is, however, more costly than the simpler models discussed previously. The specification of the forecasting equations usually requires the skills of a person trained in economics and statistics, skills that are less important in the other techniques. Data collection can be costly, especially in terms of time inputs, since greater quantities of data are needed for regression analysis than for the alternatives. Although the statistical econometric approach yields results that can be evaluated systematically, it must be emphasized that the forecasts produced may contain errors. In fact, each of the four steps in this analysis contain potential for error. The equation may be improperly specified; the data used may not be appropriate for the use intended; the estimate can create particular statistical difficulties;[16] and the values of the independent variables used to generate the econometric forecasts may, themselves, be in error.

Given the available techniques for medium-range forecasting of revenues and expenditures, the analyst may find that no single technique is most appropriate for forecasting revenue and expenditure streams. In fact, some combination of techniques is most desirable. Those revenue streams that are most sensitive to fluctuations in the local economy are best forecast using statistical techniques. Trend or expert projections may be most applicable to revenues that are insensitive to local economic conditions or are so unstable that no underlying causal relationship can be specified. Expenditure projections are best forecast with some variant of the deterministic approach to ensure that both are realistic and amenable to policy analysis. Nevertheless, before undertaking a forecasting project, the various traits of the different methods should be considered carefully as should the needs of the jurisdiction, the revenues and expenditures to be forecast, and the cost associated with each method.[17]

Revenue forecasting

City revenues may be classified as tax revenues, nontax local revenues, and intergovernmental aid. Each type will be considered in turn, noting that even within these groupings no single projection technique is necessarily most appropriate for each revenue source.

Although it is possible to forecast the revenues of a local government in the aggregate, separate forecasts of each revenue source provides more opportunities to analyze the effects of a specific policy or economic change in the overall revenue structure. Furthermore, with a disaggregated model the analyst may include only those independent variables considered theoretically important to the revenue source in question and not the "hodge-podge" of data accumulated in the aggregate model. Finally, this approach provides for more extensive analysis of the sources of errors in the forecast.

Tax revenues

Most tax revenues show some sensitivity to fluctuations in the local economy. When the forecast requires the effects on revenues of projected changes in the economy to be captured, some form of econometric forecasting should be used. The first step in such a process is to specify the independent variables to be used in the regression equations.

The purchasing power of the community when measured by income (or some proxy thereof) is generally the most significant variable and, in fact, appears to be the principal variable used in those local governments that actually forecast revenues. Which of several measures of income ought to be the variable, given the availability of local income data, can be a considerable problem. Unfortunately, there are few data sources that provide income data on a timely basis for cities. The Bureau of Economic Analysis (BEA), U.S. Department of Commerce, collects income data for counties; however, the data are available only after a time lapse of at least one year. This means that if, for example, the data were needed for a regression equation, the forecast would have to ignore the most recent year. A considerable amount of relevant information is lost, especially since many cities can obtain historical revenue data series for only ten to fifteen years. The income data for the county also means that the information may not be appropriate for a city that does not coincide closely with the county's political boundaries or for a city that is a wealthy enclave in a relatively poor county. However, in the case of some revenues such as the retail sales tax, the relevant income area may be that of the entire market area, and that may coincide most closely with the county.

Another source of income data is the state; many states provide income estimates at the county level at least. Although such data may be available on a more timely basis than that from BEA, the underlying source and definition of the state data series must be reviewed carefully. For example, data based on the state income tax returns may use an income definition that differs considerably from that of the U.S. Department of Commerce. Transfer payments, including both social security income and unemployment compensation, are likely to be excluded from data based on income tax although they are included by the BEA; however, realized capital gains are generally included in income tax data, but they are excluded by the BEA. Because transfer payments are an important component of the overall purchasing power of the community, their exclusion from the income measure can yield inaccurate results if, over time, such payments constitute differing proportions of total income.

Even if local income data are available and can be used in econometric models, projections of local income have to be made in order to yield revenue forecasts. Unless there is an econometric model available that produces these income projections, a method that links the local revenues to the more accessible projections of *national* income must be used.

A local-national linkage equation that relates local income (county or SMSA) to national income has been used in revenue forecasting models. Predicted values of national income are then used to forecast local income. These projections are then formatted as revenue equations. For example, the City of New Orleans[18] regresses local personal income (*LPI*) on national personal income (*NPI*) to obtain the following linkage equation:

$$LPI = 419.02 + 2,264 \, NPI \tag{9}$$

The projections of *NPI* are inserted into the operation to derive the estimates of *LPI* values, which are then used in the revenue estimating equations.

Another approach is to use national income as an independent variable in the regression equation. The primary difficulty with this approach is that not all local economies experience recessions and expansions in exactly the same pattern as the nation as a whole. Because manufacturing industries are cyclically more vulnerable than consumer-oriented and service-based industries, communities with an economic base that consists primarily of manufacturing may lead the nation in decline. Other communities with a service-based local economy may be more resistant to a national recession. Thus, there should be some study of the linkages between the local economy and that of the nation in order to specify the most appropriate form of the national-local linkage.

Another problem with projecting the local tax base is the use of population forecasts. If national income data (which encompass effects of changes in national population) are used directly in the tax equation, an adjustment for relative changes in local population must be made. To the extent that local population grows more rapidly (or slowly) than the national population, changes in local population can stimulate or retard the growth of the revenue source. One solution to this problem is to estimate all data in per capita terms, then to multiply by the projected estimates of the local population. A second solution is to use local population directly in the estimates. Both approaches require that detailed data on the population for each year of the observation and projection periods be available.

Projecting the property tax, an extremely important revenue source for many localities, is difficult for many forecasters. The crux of the problem lies with the discretionary nature of assessment administration.[19] Where assessment practices are such that assessed values are not revised continuously to reflect current market conditions, simple time-trend techniques (or even expert judgment methods such as the judgment of the chief assessor) may be superior to the econometric models.[20]

Where assessed values do change to reflect changes in market values, the property tax base generally responds positively to the economic conditions—although not in all neighborhoods. Income, prices, population, and measures of local building activity are again the variables possible in the property tax equations. Furthermore, the forecaster has the choice of projecting the property tax base (to which an assumed tax rate can be applied to estimate revenues) or of projecting the total tax revenues directly. Projecting the base is more flexible because policy makers can estimate different tax yields associated with alternative tax rates. For example, Dallas, Texas, projects the tax base as a function of national income and then uses judgmental methods to forecast the tax rate to derive its property tax forecast.[21]

Where assessment practices are such that new properties are essentially the source of growth in the property tax base, data on new building activity should be used as the primary independent variable in the statistical relation. If these data are not available, projected increments to population may constitute a proxy variable for new building activity.[22]

Jurisdictions where there are property tax limitations may find deterministic methods most applicable for forecasting property tax revenues. Thus, if the total tax levy can be increased by only 6 percent annually, a deterministic method of projection will show a growth rate of 6 percent.

Nontax local revenues

Such diverse nontax revenue sources as charges and user fees, fines, and interest often require a variety of projection techniques to derive reasonable forecasts. Econometric forecasting techniques are most appropriate for projecting some of these revenues. Certain user fees may be closely related to economic activity, in which case assumptions similar to those used for projecting taxes can be applied in forecasting revenues. For example, sewer connection fees may depend on new building activity.

Other nontax revenues can be projected fairly accurately by using simple time-trend projections or by relying on estimates from experts. Thus, fees from such activities as the sale of maps by the planning department, can be most accurately projected by those in the planning department, particularly by the department head. Nevertheless, the department-level forecaster must be given a set of assumptions on which to base the projections; and these assumptions should be consistent with the assumptions underlying the other revenue projections.

One of the more difficult nontax revenue sources to project is interest income, primarily because of the difficulties in forecasting both the liquid-asset position of the city and the short-range interest rates. The forecaster usually will find that expert-based projections (e.g., consulting with the finance director) will be as effective as any attempt to forecast this revenue source econometrically. Even major econometric forecasters have difficulties projecting a series as volatile as short-range interest rates.

Intergovernmental revenues

Intergovernmental aid and grants have become increasingly important during the past decade. Accurate predictions of total revenues require that these grants somehow be projected. Unfortunately, the basic determining variable for projecting intergovernmental revenue is a political decision made at higher levels of government. Even so, several nonstatistical methods can be useful in estimating these funds.

One commonly-used assumption is that the dollars involved in intergovernmental grants will remain constant over the forecast period. A less conservative estimate (and perhaps a more reasonable one in a period of rising prices) is to assume that grants will rise at the rate of inflation over the period. A very conservative forecast is obtained by assuming that those aid programs scheduled to be phased out during the forecast period will not be renewed, and that other grants will remain constant in money terms. For example, if general revenue sharing (GRS) is scheduled to be retired in 1983, projections for 1984 and beyond should exclude such aid.

The forecaster may find it helpful to elicit "expert" opinions regarding particular types of intergovernmental aid programs. He or she may consult with legislators in the higher level governmental units; their assessments of an aid program—the probability of its continuance or termination—would be most useful.

A more thorough method for forecasting formula-based grants is the simulation of the distribution of revenues, which is based on probable funding levels and projected changes in the variables that enter the allocation formula. For example, if state-aid for education is based on school enrollments, projections of the number of school-age residents could be used to forecast future levels of aid. The difficulty with this approach is that the formulas for obtaining aid are usually stated in terms of relative amounts, such as the size of school enrollment vis-a-vis all schools in the state. Thus, a complete projection requires a forecast of the city's *share* of the statewide variable as well as assumptions concerning overall funding levels.

Expenditure forecasting

The most useful approach to expenditure forecasting is probably a deterministic or accounting identity approach. This method relies on varying degrees of disaggregation according to type of spending (e.g., personnel, materials, and debt service) with the disaggregated expenditures projected according to a consistent set of assumptions about service levels, productivity, and price level changes. While projections of some of the disaggregated expenditures may be amenable to econometric or trend techniques, it is not likely that a city will find the benefits of a full-scale econometric model to be worth the costs of building, operating, and maintaining it.[23]

The deterministic approach outlined here commences with a disaggregation of expenditures into subcategories. Two natural levels of disaggregation are expenditures by agency or department and by object (e.g., labor and materials). A second level of disaggregation is the division of each of these categories into units within agencies (e.g., uniformed and nonuniformed personnel expenditures within police departments) and sub-objects within objects (e.g., utilities or contractual expenditures for nonpersonnel expenditures). The forecast of these detailed expenditures can be as fine as the accounting or management system allows or as seems desirable.[24] The general categories are discussed in the following sections.

Personal-service expenditures

The total cost of labor inputs can be divided into direct labor expenditures and fringe benefits. The projections of costs are made on the basis of a functional area (e.g., budget unit, department, or program) and relatively homogeneous groups of employees (e.g., uniformed officers or white collar professionals) within that functional area. If this large amount of detail is impossible to achieve (or deemed unnecessary), the approach can be applied to broader categories.

A straightforward accounting identity is that the product of the wage rate multiplied by the number of employees will be equal to the direct cost of labor, and represented as

$$L_t = W_t N_t \qquad (10)$$

where L equals labor costs; W is the wage or salary level of employees (relatively homogenous labor) in the functional area; N is the amount of these labor inputs; and t is the year under review. Stated this way it is obvious that the projections of direct labor expenditures, L_t, require forecasts of W_t and N_t throughout the projection period.

Derivations of projected levels of employment are considered first. The amount of a particular type of labor employed depends on several factors, including the level of service desired or mandated, the productivity of the labor, and the wage of this type of labor relative to other wages and prices.

Expenditure projections are generally made using a baseline assumption of service levels. The usual assumption is that of a "constant service-level budget." This term suggests that no discretionary changes in service levels are built into the forecasts; however, in practice there seems to be little agreement about what this means under all circumstances. In communities where the population being served is increasing, the usual assumption is that employment in the functional area will increase proportionately. This assumption may be reasonable for direct-service functions such as police and fire, but it may be less applicable for projecting the service level of staff functions.

Some have asserted that one of the major "hidden" costs of categorical federal grants are the operating and maintenance expenditures necessary to keep a project in operation after it is begun. Forecasting that takes explicit account of such expenditures may then be used to determine whether the categorical grant is really a "worthy" project in an environment of fiscal constraint.

Legislated changes in service levels should be factored into the labor usage projections. Such legislation may be mandated by higher levels of government or may be due to local policies. If productivity improvements are foreseen, the possible reduction of labor inputs should also be factored into the forecast.[25]

Capital projects scheduled to come into operation may have effects on the required level of labor inputs. For example, if a new recreation center is supposed to become operational in 1983, projections made in 1981 should include the operating and maintenance inputs required to keep the center in operation from 1983 through the end of the projected period.

Estimates of the effects on employment of changes in the local population, legislated programs, new capital projects, and productivity can be done in at least two ways. One approach is to make the estimates centrally, within the office of the city manager or budget officer, for example. This approach may yield more consistent estimates, but it increases the chances of overlooking major changes, such as scheduled state-mandated expenditures. The other approach is to request the departmental units or budget centers to project manpower needs. It is important that the department administrators take the task seriously; they should not use these longer-range plans to compile an unrealistic "wish list" of projects. Thus, the centralized forecasting unit must review the projections made in the departments to ensure that the projections are realistic and consistent with the assumptions underlying the forecast.

The level of wages should be considered to project labor expenditures. The usual approach to these projections is to use the same set of assumptions concerning the level of money wages for all city employees. One assumption is that money wages will increase at the same rate as prices; thus, real wages will remain constant. Another possibility is to assume that increases in money wages will lag behind price increases by one year; however, the forecaster should analyze historical changes in wages to justify these assumptions. Whenever wage changes are based on projected price changes, price projections are best if they are consistent with the macroeconomic assumptions used on the revenue side of the forecast. A third method of projection forecasts the possibility of varying wage changes by types of employees. For example, the bargaining strength of uniformed personnel may be assumed to be greater than that of nonuniformed employees, thus larger wage increments will be obtained by the uniformed officers. The problem with such an assumption is that it must not be made public or the forecast itself may hinder the bargaining process.

A final approach to wage level projections ignores the issue entirely, and simply assumes that money wages will not change. Although this approach is likely to underestimate labor expenditures, it may be desirable in a collective bargaining environment because it limits the amount of information available to unions regarding the longer-range fiscal plans of the city.[26] On the other hand, if the public assumes that the city can remain fiscally sound under a 5 percent annual wage increase, the union usually will not be willing to settle for anything less than a 5 percent increase in wages.

Social security contribution rates can be assumed with considerable certainty; retirement contribution rates projected into the future may be obtainable from a retirement system if the city does not have a self-administered retirement program. There is, however, the additional question of what actuarial assumptions go into these projections and whether they are consistent with the remainder of the forecasting exercise.

Wages and salaries may constitute the bulk of labor expenditures, but the level of fringe benefits is becoming increasingly important. The major fringe benefits are retirement contributions, social security, and insurance expenditures. The first two are likely to be related directly to the wage bill (total direct labor expenditures) while insurance expenditures usually depend on the number of people employed. Once contribution rates for the benefits have been assumed (or projected) and the levels of employment and wage rates have been forecast, fringe benefit costs are projected easily with the deterministic method.

Other benefits to be considered by the forecaster are such fringes as vacation and sick leave. If these benefits are projected to increase and service levels and productivity to remain constant, changes in personnel must occur. Using full-time workers or labor hours as the measure of employment, rather than the number of workers on the payroll, provide a way to account for these changes in fringe benefits.

Other current expenditures

This category of expenditures includes a multitude of items ranging from stationery supplies and gasoline to contractual services. As with labor expenditures, costs of supplies, materials, and equipment can be projected for each agency by using some degree of disaggregation of the inputs. That is:

$$O_t = P_t Q_t \tag{11}$$

where O equals other current expenditures; P equals price; Q is the quantity of materials projected to be purchased; and t is the year in which the expenses are to be incurred.

The degree to which these expenditures are disaggregated depends on the desired detail of the projection, the ability of the city to disaggregate materials into relatively homogeneous groups of goods, and the price indexes of the different types of supplies. Projections of changes in quantities of materials are usually tied to projected alterations in staffing levels. (The assumption is that the quantity of materials will change proportionately to changes in manpower.) The availability of disaggregated price indexes is generally the primary constraint to a full disaggregation of other current expenditures. There is no good series of price indexes for many categories of goods used in governmental production;[27] thus, either proxy variables are used to project these prices or judgmental opinions obtained. The principal proxy variables for projecting prices include the producer price index, the consumer price index (CPI), and the components thereof. If particular materials and supplies (e.g., utility expenditures) are expected to increase at a rate faster or slower than the general level of prices for consumers and producers, the differential inflation rates should be used in the forecast. The point to be re-emphasized is that these additional assumptions should always be made explicit.

Transfer expenditures

Transfer payments to particular segments of the population (e.g., the blind and disabled) are not part of the budgetary responsibility of most cities. Where the city has responsibility for such payments, the application of trend or econometric projection techniques may be appropriate. For example, the case loads of social welfare programs probably increase when local economic activity slows. Techniques similar to methods used for projecting tax revenues would be applicable in these instances. Predicted case loads multiplied by an assumed or mandated level of payment determine these expenditures.[28]

Debt service

Debt service—interest and debt retirement—can be one of the easier expenditures to forecast. If the projection is that there will be no change in the overall level and composition of the debt over the relevant time period, future debt service expenditures are known with certainty. It is more likely, however, that there will be additions to debt as the result of a long-range capital plan; new assumptions about the structure and rates at which the new debt will be issued become necessary. The costs of servicing short-range debt and bond- or tax-anticipation notes must also be forecast. Projections from a cash management model, together with interest rate forecasts obtained from external sources, are used for these types of cost estimates.

Interfund transfers

For local governments where the entire focus of the forecasting activity is on the general fund, it is necessary to note how transfers between different funds are handled. Projected transfers to and from this fund can be based on judgmental techniques. For example, when individual departments "rent" autos or other capital equipment from other local government agencies, a special fund is created and the interfund transfers included in the overall expenditure forecasts.

If the details of the fiscal activity of all funds are forecast, interfund transfers (based on current policies concerning such transfers) can be built into the overall forecast. For example, it may be common practice for a community to transfer all excess revenues obtained from a sewer fund into the general fund. If revenue surpluses in the sewer fund are forecast in the multiyear projection of revenues and expenditures, these excess funds are projected as a source of revenue that is transferable to the general fund.

Revenue and expenditure forecasts

Given the projections of revenues and expenditures, the forecaster can construct a table or chart that compares the absolute levels of each for the entire forecast period. The purpose of the chart is to focus on projected revenue shortfalls of fiscal "gaps." Using a set of assumptions about economic conditions and revenue and expenditure policies, the forecaster may note what types of policies are available to close the projected shortfalls. For example, the rescheduling of long-range capital projects may sufficiently alter current expenditures (by changing debt-service schedules or delaying the operating and maintenance costs associated with the projects) to avoid budget deficits. The projected shortfalls may possibly be eliminated by an increase in property tax rates or by a reduction in city services also. The consequences of various policies can be very important in the policy-making process, particularly when viable alternatives need to be considered.

Once the baseline projections have been completed, a range of budgetary forecasts becomes available as changes in assumptions can be made. Alternative sets of assumptions on important variables such as the rate of inflation or the growth rate in the local economy can be studied; and five-year economic projections under "most likely" and "less vigorous" growth assumptions may be used in the budget forecasts that relate the fiscal health of the city to the economic conditions of the nation.

Data availability and usage

Internal data

Both the econometric and time-trend techniques require historical data for the projected series. A series of ten to fifteen years of observations is best for obtaining reasonable regression results. Thus, a major cost of the overall forecasting project may rest with the data gathering since data are not always accessible in a useful form. Two major problems with the historical information will be discussed here—changes in definitions and changes in the rates and bases of revenue sources that occur over a time period.

Although major revenue sources usually are reported on a consistent basis, minor revenue sources are not likely to be reported so consistently. For example, during some periods, a local government may have aggregated all of its fees into a single amount, and reported them as such in both the budget document and in the annual financial report. In other periods, the same fees may have been reported separately. Thus, the disaggregated amounts must be combined to form a single consistent time series or an attempt made to disaggregate the series during which time the fees were reported as a single number. The first approach is less complex but loses information; the second approach requires more of an effort to reconstruct the series from historical documents but may be more accurate.

Accounting for the discretionary changes in the rate or base of a tax (especially the major tax revenue sources), creates a more important problem for the forecaster than those discussed above. For example, a particular tax may have yielded $1 million in revenues for two or three years, when suddenly it yields $1.5 million. A 50 percent increase suggests that either the tax rate increased or the tax base broadened. To attribute these changes in revenues to changes in the economic or demographic variables used in the regression equation would be misleading and would lead to biased results. Thus, it is necessary to "clean" the series of purely administrative changes.

Different methods are available for this cleaning operation.[29] Essentially, the techniques attempt to factor out the effects of discretionary changes in tax rates or base definitions by estimating what revenues *would have been* without the changes. The techniques not only require substantial investigation of the legal bases and rates of revenue sources but also can involve considerable computational effort. Thus, many forecasters opt to clean only the major revenue series.[30]

The lack of correlation beween the fiscal year of the local government and the time period of the available external data (which is usually the calendar year) is another difficulty that can arise when using statistical techniques. When time periods do not correspond, it is often necessary to adjust the series to the base of one or the other. It is best to adjust the external data to fit the definition of the fiscal year since it is the internal data being forecast; however, the preparation costs of the data to produce the forecast may increase as a result of the adjustment. Except in cases with dramatically fluctuating series, these adjustments generally are not worth the effort. Nevertheless, the forecaster should consider the varying time periods when specifying the equations. For example, if the 1976 fiscal year (FY76) is from 1 July 1975 to 30 June 1976 and the data used for the independent variables are from the calendar year, whether the revenues for FY76 are made a function of the 1975 or 1976 calendar year variables may make a considerable difference in the specification. Since many economic decisions involve time lags, probably the most reasonable specification is to assume that FY76 revenues are a function of the economic data of calendar year 1975. It is, of course, crucial that those collecting the data be aware of any differences in the definitions of the time period preparing the data for analysis.

External data

External data generally do not require cleaning, but they do carry their own set of problems. (Forecasters, however, should examine the exact definitions used by the reporting agency, lest observed changes in the series be the result of altered definitions.) The problem most frequently associated with externally collected data is available sources. This holds true for both historical data and projections of series into the future.

The federal government does not provide large amounts of data on a timely basis for cities; therefore, proxies are often necessary. State agencies such as the labor department, tax or revenue department, and commerce department may also have useful information. Some local firms, chambers of commerce, banks, and universities have a wealth of information on a locality. These organizations may also have economic forecasting units that might make data available to the budget forecaster. Finally, subscribers to the major national econometric forecasting units may obtain and utilize the data compiled by the service.

Federal data sources   Many kinds of statistical data are compiled by the federal government. Among the most important for financial analyses are those covering income, population, and the labor market and prices. The sources for these data areas are summarized in the following paragraphs.

The principal agency that collects income data in the United States is the Bureau of Economic Analysis of the United States Department of Commerce. The *Survey of Current Business,* published monthly by this Bureau, contains estimates of income for the entire nation, including estimates of gross national product, national income, and personal income. Periodically, this source also publishes income estimates for states, counties, and areas within states. See, for example, "County and Metropolitan Area Personal Income," *Survey of Current Business* 59 (April, 1979) and "State Personal Income," *Survey of Current Business* 59 (August, 1979).

The Bureau of the Census, also within the United States Department of Commerce, is the primary source of

population data at the federal level. While the decenial Census presents detailed demographic information for localities, the primary source of small area data on an annual basis is from Series P–25 of the Current Population Reports, *Population Estimates and Projections.* There are approximately 70 reports issued annually, including reports for estimates of county populations and projections of state populations.

The Bureau of Labor Statistics (BLS) of the United States Department of Labor compiles labor market and price information. The *Monthly Labor Review* is published by the BLS and contains nationwide data on labor market conditions, including those on employment, unemployment, earnings, and prices. A compilation of historical data collected by the BLS is found in the *Handbook of Labor Statistics 1977,* Bulletin 1966 (Washington, D.C.: Government Printing Office, 1977) with detailed definitions of the measures provided in *BLS Handbook of Methods for Surveys and Studies* Bulletin 1910 (Washington, D.C.: Government Printing Office, 1976).

Subscription services can provide many of the independent variables required in the projections of econometric revenue forecasting. Not only does a subscription to econometric models provide forecasted variables, but it also includes access to the expertise of a staff of forecasters. Of course, such subscriptions are expensive, costing several thousand dollars a year.

If such a service is not used (and only one or two cities are currently using one), estimates of the independent variables for the forecast period must be obtained in another manner. Most often, the output of major national macroeconomic models is used, even though formal subscriptions to their services are not purchased. The national income, gross national product, and price projections from the models are publicized in business publications such as the *Wall Street Journal* and *Business Week.*[31]

Another set of projections is available from the Congressional Budget Office (CBO), which produces five-year forecasts of the national economy. The forecasts include projections of national income and prices in alternative scenarios that deal with the general rate of growth. Furthermore, because these forecasts are for five years, they are perhaps more useful than most of the forecasts from the other major econometric models.

Given the variety of macroeconomic forecasts available, the forecaster should be cognizant of what goes into these forecasts. Although econometric forecasts tend not to differ *greatly* in their final projection of the economy, different forecasters may use different assumptions to prepare their forecasts. If a "concensus" of the several forecasts for the different independent variables is used, the forecaster should be aware that the individual forecasts of the economy may not be based on consistent assumptions. For example, one forecaster may assume that a major strike by coal workers will dampen the overall growth rate of the economy during a portion of the upcoming year and, therefore, project lower growth rates than another forecaster who assumes the strike will be settled quickly. Use of national income projections from one model and price projections from the other would involve inconsistent forecasts and could lead to forecast errors.

Administrative and political issues in forecasting

In addition to the technical problems involved in forecasting, there are several administrative and political issues that should be considered when evaluating the feasibility of a forecasting project.

Administrative issues

Among the management issues that may arise in the field of forecasting are (1) the role of the chief administrative officer (CAO) or city manager; (2) the assignment of responsibility for the forecasts; and (3) the presentation of the projections.

Role of the chief administrative officer Although the chief administrative officer (mayor or city or county manager), the finance director, and the planning director are not likely to be forecasters, their roles in the process must be more than passively receiving data and memoranda. Their managerial commitment and sustained professional involvement are essential if forecasting is to have a real impact on decision making.

The chief administrator especially must ascertain and articulate his or her interests and needs vis-à-vis the decision-making process. That is to say, does the need lie in short-range forecasts, medium-range forecasts, long-range forecasts, or all three? The answers depend on what the forecasts in a given jurisdiction can and cannot do, given forecasting needs and resources of money, data availability, data access, and staff.

To work effectively, the chief administrator needs to know that forecasting is a tool, not a panacea, a means, not an end. If the chief administrator has this understanding, he or she will then be able to make forecasting do what it should do—provide systematic help in developing trustworthy policy alternatives.

An important task of the manager is to ensure that the forecast is carried through properly. The role of the manager in the process is probably most important when expenditure forecasts are based on data submitted by department heads. The compilation of projections of labor and national costs under a set of assumptions and the list of all the mandates that are likely to affect the department can be a time-consuming process. The already time-pressed department head may, therefore, be unwilling to devote much effort to the process if he or she believes the projections probably will not be used, or that the chief administrative officer has little interest in what is produced.

However, the forecasting process can force the department head to be more "forward-thinking" than he or she might be otherwise. By requiring a systematic review of what is likely to occur during the next two to five years, the department chief should develop a longer-range perspective on the operations of the department. Moreover, the review of the overall projections for the city may help the administrators develop a broader perspective of the entire organization.

Responsibility of forecasts   The office to assume responsibility for the forecasting function generally depends on the structure of the organization. In most cities, the forecasts are produced in the budget office, a logical place because the forecasts are a part of the larger budget process.

The budget office often has the most capable personnel for producing projections of expenditures, as they are the ones most intimately involved with the expenditure determination process. Furthermore, individual budget examiners are most familiar with the operations of individual departments, and therefore, are the best reviewers of the projections produced by the department heads.

Projections of revenue, on the other hand, can be derived in the budget department or in a tax-oriented department such as finance. Personnel in the finance department generally have the expertise necessary to clean data series; they are also likely to have experience in projecting different revenue series for individual budget years.

A division of effort between the budget office and the finance office may be the least costly way to produce a forecast, but it raises some potential management problems. Because the revenue and expenditure projections are to be compared, a single set of assumptions concerning the course of the local economy should be used in both sets of projections. Coordination of the assumptions is required between those involved in the projections. The chief administrative officer must see to it that such coordination occurs.

Often the question arises concerning the use of internal staff or external personnel to produce the forecast. Although outside consultants are likely to have greater technical expertise, they may lack an intimate understanding of the financial or organizational structure of the local government. Furthermore, once a model is constructed, it should be more than just a once-a-year exercise producing a single set of numbers. Having the forecast model produced in the organization facilitates its use as an on-going management tool.

Whether done internally or externally, forecasting is likely to be costly, both in the time expended by city employees and as a budget outlay to consultants. If it is done internally, the city should fully support the effort and not be content to have one individual, using his or her "spare" time, construct and operate the model.

Presentation of projections   It is possible simply to present the projected revenues and expenditures without comment, however, this is not the most effective method of presentation. The manager or CAO should be responsible for effectively presenting the forecasts.

It is extremely crucial when presenting the results of a forecast, especially if a revenue shortfall is being projected, that the rationale for the entire exercise be presented in a language that is readily understandable. That is, readers of the projection should know the particular set of assumptions under which the budgetary projections were made. These assumptions include those made about the future state of the local economy, the revenue structure, costs of services, and service levels. If a revenue shortfall is projected, the forecast document should make it clear that this does not necessarily mean the city will resort to deficit financing during the projection period. The forecasted shortfall does imply that some form of action will be taken (or at least be planned) to avoid the financing problem.

Some cities will take the forecast one step further when a revenue gap has been forecast. The forecast presentation will show, at least for the near future, exactly what actions can be taken to avoid a deficit. Tax increases, increases in intergovernmental aid, and expenditure cutbacks are possible to achieve the desired balance in the budget. [32]

Political issues

As is true of nearly all governmental decisions, there are political issues that must be resolved before forecasting can be formally undertaken. Probably the most important issue to be resolved is whether to make the forecast public. If the projection is to be used solely as an internal document, it is useful to the chief administrative officer, but it has little impact on policy making. It becomes a tool for policy making only if it is released to publicly-elected officials; however, this public knowledge can have both negative and positive effects.

A forecast of a fiscal crisis may be viewed by some citizens as an indication of poor management or poor political leadership, which (especially if seized upon by the press) could create considerable disruption in the overall operation of the local government. As noted previously, the publication of projected levels of compensation for public employees greatly erodes the collective bargaining position of a local government.

On the other hand, the publication of the forecast can be advantageous to municipalities. First, with respect to collective bargaining, a projection of fiscal problems may lower the bargaining demands of the employees' associations. That is, the union will know that the local government's lack of ability to pay is, in fact, true. Secondly, while a forecast of revenue shortfalls may initially create negative publicity, voters are likely to be impressed when policy makers react to these projections with decisions made with more foresight. Bond rating organizations also appear favorably impressed with the use of forecasting as a management technique. Thus, even if fiscal problems are projected, the fact that a forecast was produced suggests that the local government is attempting to stay on top of its financial problems and is better equipped to handle them. Finally, some cities use projections of fiscal problems to lobby for more aid from higher levels of government.

Conclusions

This chapter has shown the different uses of financial forecasting in local government. These uses include short-range cash management, budget forecasting, medium-range forecasting of from one to five years, and long-range forecasting of general trends in the city. Several different methods can be applied for medium-range forecasting. Because each method involves different data requirements, have varying costs to construct, and have differing degrees of accuracy, the forecasts should be implemented only after a complete study of the costs and potential benefits of each method has been completed. Nevertheless, the nature of forecasting is not entirely technical since its success depends on the cooperation and encouragement of both management and policy makers if it is to be as useful as possible.

1   For a complete discussion of cash management, see Chapter 14 of this volume.

2   Chapter 5 provides details on the budget process.

3   For a more complete discussion of location quotient, see: Charles M. Tiebout, *The Community Economic Base Study* (New York: Committee for Economic Development, 1962). Location quotients sometimes are used to estimate the "multiplier" effects of additional spending in a community. Tiebout also discusses this use of the technique.

4   Shift-share analysis is described more thoroughly in: Harry W. Richardson, *Regional Economics*

(Urbana, Ill.: University of Illinois Press, 1979), pp. 202–06.

5   The efficacy of many location incentive policies is, however, questionable. For a recent review, see: G. Cornia, W. Testa, and F. Stocker, *State-Local Fiscal Incentives and Economic Development*, Urban and Regional Development Series, no. 4 (Columbus, Ohio: Academy for Contemporary Problems, 1978).

6   For a thorough discussion of techniques associated with such studies, see: Robert W. Burchell and David Listokin, *The Fiscal Impact Handbook* (New

Brunswick, N.J.: Center for Urban Policy Research, 1978). A review and critique of methods are contained in: William H. Dutton, Kenneth L. Kraemer, and Martha S. Hollis, "Fiscal Impact Models and the Policy-Making Process: Theory and Practice," *The Urban Interest* 2 (Fall 1980): 66–74.

7 For a brief discussion of this model, see: Robert W. Rafuse, Jr., *State Economic Modeling,* State Planning Series, 13 (Washington, D.C.: Council of State Planning Agencies, 1977). The MUNIES model is marketed by Tischler, Marcou and Associates, Inc., Washington, D.C., and has been used by the Washington, D.C., Council of Governments; the Southeast Idaho Council of Governments; Greenwich, Connecticut; and San Diego, California, among others.

8 For a discussion of the use of FIAS in Orange County, California, see: "Fiscal Impact Analysis Forecasts Effects of Policy Changes," *State and County Administrator* 3, no. 10 (October 1978): 14–15. The model is marketed by Decision Sciences Corporation, Jenkintown, Pennsylvania.

9 Numerous books devoted to forecasting methods provide a greater degree of detail concerning use of these methods, especially with reference to business situations. See, for example: Steven C. Wheelwright and Spyros Makridakis, *Forecasting Methods for Management,* 2d ed. (New York: John Wiley & Sons, 1978); or, at a slightly higher level of difficulty: Spyros Makridakis and Steven C. Wheelwright, *Forecasting: Methods and Applications* (New York: John Wiley & Sons, 1978). For further information on econometric forecasting methods, see: Robert S. Pindyck and Daniel L. Rubinfeld, *Econometric Models and Economic Forecasts* (New York: McGraw-Hill Book Co., 1976).

10 The only formalized approach to expert forecasting is the Delphi method. It uses a large number of experts but is applicable primarily for long-range qualitative forecasting. See, for example: Olaf Helmer, *The Use of the Delphi Technique—Problems of Educational Innovations* (Santa Monica, Calif.: Rand Corp., 1966).

11 Note that this approach is not unlike that used in many fiscal impact models.

12 Since revenue forecasts are most amenable to this technique, examples are restricted to such series.

13 The underlying statistics of regression as well as interpretation of results are provided in nearly all statistics and econometrics books. See, for example: Thomas H. Wonnocatt and Ronald J. Wonnocatt, *Introductory Statistics for Business and Economics* (New York: John Wiley & Sons, 1977).

14 This equation was, in fact, used to project cigarette taxes in the City of San Diego. See: *Long Range Planning: Revenue Projection Model: FY 1979–84* (San Diego, Calif.: Financial Management Department, February 1978). The San Diego model as well as several other large city forecasting models are reviewed in: Roy Bahl and Larry Schroeder, *Forecasting Local Government Budgets,* occasional paper no. 38, Metropolitan Studies Program (Syracuse, N.Y.: Syracuse University, 1979).

15 Time trends also can be estimated using regression analysis with time as the sole independent variable.

16 Among the statistical problems encountered in econometric projections are autocorrelation, multicolinearity, and simultaneity across independently estimated equations. Discussion of these problems is beyond the scope of the present chapter, but they

are considered in nearly all econometrics books. See, for example: Jan Kmenta, *Elements of Econometrics* (New York: Macmillan Co., 1971); or James L. Murphy, *Introductory Econometrics* (Homewood, Ill.: Richard D. Irwin, 1973). For an introductory discussion of the rudiments of regression analysis, including the problems mentioned here, see: David L. Sjoquist, Larry D. Schroder, and Paula E. Stephan, *Interpreting Linear Regression Analysis: An Heuristic Approach* (Morristown, N.J.: General Learning Corp., 1974).

17 Wheelwright and Makridakis, in *Forecasting Methods for Management,* present an extensive discussion of criteria to be considered when choosing a forecasting technique and include a convenient tabular summary of several methods available for forecasting judged according to these criteria (pp. 206–7).

18 L. E. Madere, *Municipal Budget Projections, Econometric Revenue Forecasting* (City of New Orleans: Office of Economic Analysis, 1977).

19 John L. Mikesell, "Property Tax Assessment Practice and Income Elasticities," *Public Finance Quarterly* 6 (January 1978): 53–65.

20 This is basically the approach currently being used in New York City, where assessed valuation has been largely invariant to changes in market values. *City of New York Four-Year Financial Plan, Fiscal Years 1979–1982* (City of New York, 1978).

21 City of Dallas, *Long Range Financial Plan, 1978–1983,* January 1979 revision.

22 This approach is used in New Orleans. See: Madere, *Municipal Budget Projections.*

23 An econometric model of expenditures has been constructed for the city of Columbus, Ohio; however, apparently it is not actively used in the policymaking or administrative process. For details on the Columbus model, see: Wilford L. L'Esperance, John E. Graham, Jr., and Robert Kirchner, "An Urban Revenue-Expenditure Forecasting Model" (Unpublished manuscript, Ohio State University, 1979). San Diego County also projects expenditures using econometric techniques. The greater relative importance in a county's budget of health and welfare activities, which are more likely to be sensitive to local economic conditions, adds credence to such an approach. See: County of San Diego, *Six-Year Revenue and Expenditure Forecasts, FY 1979–84,* 1978.

24 For example, the District of Columbia carries out forecasts based on some five hundred "responsibility centers" identical to the units responsible for annual budget preparation, while San Antonio projects expenditures on an agency basis. See: Washington, D.C., *Multi-Year Financial Plan, 1980–1984,* September 1978; San Antonio, Texas, *Long-Range Financial Forecast FY 1979–1984,* January 1979.

25 Productivity is, unfortunately, easier stated than measured. See: John Ross and Jesse Burkhead, *Productivity in the Local Government Sector* (Lexington, Mass.: Lexington Books, 1974).

26 This is the approach that has been used by New York City in *City of New York Four-Year Financial Plan, Fiscal Years 1979–1982* p. II–10. The city has argued (and its various fiscal oversight groups have agreed) that the bargaining strength of the city would be eroded by publishing projections using a particular set of wage rate increase assumptions.

27 For a discussion of estimating the budgetary impacts of inflation, see: David Greytak and Bernard Jump, Jr., "Inflation and Local Government Ex-

penditures and Revenues: Method and Case Studies," *Public Finance Quarterly* 5 (July 1977): 275–302.

28 This approach is used in Washington, D.C., one city with responsibilities for transfer functions. See: Washington, D.C., *Multi-Year Financial Plan, 1980–1984.*

29 For discussions of different methods of cleaning revenue series, see: Roy Bahl, "Alternative Methods for Tax Revenue Forecasting in Developing Countries" (Unpublished paper, International Monetary Fund, Fiscal Affairs Department, 1972); Robert Harris, *Income and Sales Taxes: The 1970 Outlook for States and Localities* (Washington, D.C.: Council of State Governments, 1966); A. R. Prest, "The Sensitivity of the Yield of Personal Income Tax in the United Kingdom," *Economic Journal* 72 (September 1962): 576–96.

30 Regression forecasting techniques provide another method for cleaning revenue series via the use of "dummy" independent variables. Such variables take on the value 0 before a revenue rate (base) is changed and a value of 1 after the change is made. The technique is especially useful when only one or two major administrative changes have been made in a tax source. For discussion of the dummy variable technique, see any of the references cited in footnotes 13 and 16. For examples of the use of dummy variables to clean revenue series, see: Madere, *Municipal Budget Projections.*

31 Each year the Federal Reserve Bank of Richmond, Virginia, publishes a booklet summarizing projections from judgemental and econometric forecasts. For example, *Business Forecasts 1979* presents numerical forecasts from twenty-nine different forecasters or models.

32 *City of New York Four-Year Financial Plan, Fiscal Years 1979–1982,* p. II–10.

5 Budgeting

Budgeting is a public policy process. Almost every decision, activity, and program can be expressed in the financial language of the budget. The service-delivery implications of its dollar and cents are inescapable. The financial distress of local jurisdictions in recent years and the specter of further stringency highlight the importance of the budgetary process, which is, essentially, the rationing of resources representing a multitude of sacrificed alternatives.[1]

The size of the budget and the activities and programs it covers show the dividing line between the public and private sectors. The budget is a major force in determining which goods and services are to be provided by the collective taxing and spending power of government and which goods and services are to be provided by the private market. "Who gets what" is a statement of society's values, preferences, and priorities as expressed and carried out by local governments. The budget lies at the heart of politics; it is a political process conducted in a political arena.

This chapter provides an up-to-date and comprehensive survey of the state of the art of local government budgeting. In spite of the variety of local governmental forms and structures, general descriptions can be offered and analytical patterns can be discerned. The following topics are covered: the budget cycle from initial requests to the postaudit; the budget process, including the interactions of administrators, legislators, interest groups, and others; the many purposes of budgeting, ranging from financial control to management information, efficiency, programming, and performance audits; zero-base budgeting; federal aid; and resource constraints.

The budget cycle

The budget is based each year on a regular set of institutional procedures that encompass a sequence of decisions at interconnected points. In most places budgeting has been structured into a formal cycle of five stages:

Preparation of budget requests

Formulation of recommendations by the budget staff and the chief administrator

Adoption of the budget ordinance by the city council

Implementation of the budget by the executive branch

Audit of the budget by the "auditor."

Each stage is essentially the responsibility of a different actor; thus, there are really five "budgets" in terms of separate and, most often, different spending figures for each formal stage in the budget cycle. The budget adopted into law does not necessarily match the initial submissions of the departments, nor does spending at the end of the year correspond to the budget figures that began the year. The five stages are discussed in detail as follows:

Preparation of budget requests

The first set of budget figures is generated by the departments and represents the funds the departments want for the next year. The preparation of departmental requests varies, depending on the importance attached to budgeting, the size of the department, and the style of the department head. There may be an identifiable departmental budget staff and office, but budget preparation may be the part-time and ad hoc responsibility of the department head and various staff members. Few line managers are involved in the process.

Formulation of recommendations

Departmental budget requests are forwarded to the chief administrative officer for review. This begins the second stage of the budget cycle: the formulation of the executive's own recommended budget, which in turn is submitted for consideration to the legislature.

The authority to compile, combine, and consolidate the individual department requests into a single budget that is matched to available revenues was assigned to the chief executive in the early twentieth century. Today, most municipal governments adhere to the principle of an "executive budget" by giving clear statutory authority to the chief executive (be it the mayor-council or council-manager form of government) to review departmental requests and formulate a budget for the legislature.[2]

Because the executive is generally mandated to submit a balanced budget to the legislature, the revenue estimates are a major part of the second stage. Forecasts of available resources must be on hand when departmental spending requests are reviewed.

The departmental requests are examined by the budget staff for mathematical accuracy and adherence to uniform procedures and technical requirements. With growing computerization, this work can become much more of a routine information processing task.

The chief executive generally relies on the expertise and judgment of the budget staff. The budget staff makes many substantive decisions; by the time the chief executive becomes personally involved with the budget, many routine decisions have already been made. However, because the budget probably is still out of balance, the final decisions—the ones that are the most controversial and have the greatest political significance and program implications—remain for the chief executive. The departments usually have an opportunity to "plead" their cases before the executive's recommendations go to the legislature.

The budget is one of the most important responsibilities of the chief executive—mayor, city manager, or county manager—because it provides institutional focus for planning, programming, and policy. In local government, the organizational location is almost always either in the office of the chief executive or in the finance department.[3]

When the budget is placed with the chief executive, much of the work may be assigned to an administrative assistant or an assistant city manager (a common arrangement in smaller cities). In larger cities and counties, a budget office may be organized such that the budget officer or budget director reports directly to the chief executive. When budgeting clearly and directly is placed with the chief executive, the authority and responsibility are concentrated and its importance as a central decision-making tool is emphasized. When the budgeting responsibility is located in the finance department, it provides greater integration with financial management, especially accounting. Most local governments, in one way or another, provide a strong linkage with the chief executive and his or her staff.[4]

Budget adoption

The third stage of the budget cycle is the legislative review of executive recommendations and the subsequent adoption of the budget by ordinance. The city council or commission that forms the legislative body generally bears little resemblance to its counterparts at the state and national levels. Locally elected council members are mostly part-time politicians. Staff support is minimal. The information, expertise, experience, and skill that enable the United States Congress to conduct a parallel review of the administration's budget is at a minimum.

The council usually reviews the budget in an informal briefing prior to its official submission. As a result, council preferences often have already been incorporated into the formal budget document by the time of its public airing. However, direct legislative contact with department heads is often minimal. The executive and the budget staff answer questions and explain and defend the recommendations. Public hearings, often required by law, are then conducted, after which the budget is voted upon and adopted into law.

Budget execution

The budgetary process does not end with the appropriations ordinance but continues to operate throughout the year as funds are obligated and disbursed. This process of budget execution is the fourth stage of the cycle.[5]

The executive monitors the daily financial transactions. At the same time, he or she reports to the council, to whom he or she is responsible for the implementation of the budget.

Postaudit

The final stage of the budget process is the traditional postaudit. Usually thought of as part of budget execution, it is given special status here to emphasize its growing importance in recent years. In the checks-and-balances of American government, it has long been held that the end-of-the-year verification of accounts and certification of the "books" should be conducted independently of those in charge of the finances during the year. In general, most local governments are required to conduct an external independent audit through a private accounting firm or a state government auditor.[6]

The budget process

Although the budget process is shaped by the formal definitions of duties and authority, the actual expenditure choices are made by individuals operating within an informal structure of roles and influences. These components of the budget process are examined next.[7]

Budget roles

Each of the actors in the budget cycle has a specific role to play as prescribed by his or her formal responsibilities. Each budget role is part of a set of complementary and mutually reinforcing expectations. Roles fit together to define the budgetary division of labor. Departments, which begin the budget cycle, provide the impetus for the decisions of others; they are the spenders. The chief executive pulls the disparate parts together and matches spending with revenue; this is the role of the economizer. The legislature then reviews previous decisions and gives its authoritative stamp of approval to adopt the budget into law; they are the overseers.

Departments are the spenders　In making their requests, departments usually seek more money than was received in the previous year and more than they currently are spending. Rarely do departments voluntarily ask for less. The department head occupies an institutional position that encourages advocacy. It is the responsibility of the department head to promote and defend the department and its program in the competition for the distribution of resources. It is in his or her self-interest to seek a larger budget and more personnel for the power, prestige, and benefits this provides. Furthermore, because departments have few responsibilities to raise money, they are insulated from the resource constraint. Their requests are estimates of need, balanced against the inherent scarcity of resources and the cost of alternative programs.

In the strategy of the budget game, departments are padders. They ask for more than they need or expect to get as a cushion against the reductions that are likely to be imposed by the executive and the legislative reviewers.

This perception of spending is derived from the professionalism of program managers, who are more competent at assessing service needs and wants than at assessing available overall resources. The request for increases often reflects a genuine commitment to goals and objectives and a belief in the importance of the program as a vital community service—all of which translates into an assertive (even aggressive!) budgetary posture.

The executive is the economizer　Whereas the departments provide the upward thrust for increases, the chief executive generally takes the opposing role of the economizer. The chief executive is subject to a wide range of pressures and interests that provide an incentive to hold the line on budget growth. The executive alone is responsible to (and possibly elected by) the entire community. Occupying a position at the center of the budgeting process, the executive sees the disparate and separate interests from a more comprehensive perspective than the other actors.

Furthermore, the executive alone is charged with the formal responsibility of introducing the revenue constraint into the budgetary equation. The executive has to deal directly with the fact that for every dollar spent an equal and offsetting dollar must be collected. Thus tempering the executive's support of any expansion in spending. The chief executive is legally required to submit a balanced budget to the legislature. John Crecine's study of three large cities found that the primary objective of the executive was to balance the budget.[8]

Reductions are imposed, and the result is a budget smaller than that sought by the departments; but the recommendations to the legislature are still likely to be greater than the current level of spending. The economizer role of the chief executive is not translated into opposition to all expansion. Instead, it serves to guide the pace and direction of the increment of annual spending. Until the late 1970s, revenue increases were almost automatic. The executive imposed reductions in initial requests as a means of choosing among competing demands and to make room for his or her preferred programs. In the course of this economizing, the chief executive exercises independent judgment and leadership in the public policy process.

The legislature is the overseer　The part played by the legislature (city council or county board) is one of scrutiny, surveillance, and monitoring of the executive branch of government. The legislature does not assemble and compile the budget but reviews the one that is put together by the executive. The legislature can modify or reject executive recommendations, add to one department or take away from another, change the total, inquire about specific acts of waste and inappropriate use of public funds, make sure that the budget for the previous year was implemented as it was intended originally, and assess the effectiveness of proposed programs. In deciding future spending, the legislature passes judgment on past appropriations. As Jesse Burkhead has written: "The legislature's review of the executive's budget provides a major occasion for examination of the character and quality of administrative actions."[9]

Budgetary influence

Competition and conflict in the budgetary process are endemic, even if muted. Responsibilities and roles differ, and values, preferences, and goals vary. Spenders struggle with the economizers and both are subject to the decisions of the overseers. Who wins and who loses depends on the influence each brings to bear on the decisions of others. The organization called government can be looked on as a coalition of semi-independent units held together by the distribution of material resources—the budget. Power is a major determinant in the resolution of the bargaining for "who gets what." It should come as no surprise that the spending preferences of the strong are most evident in the municipal budget.

Who then holds power? No simple, uniform answer exists. With formal authority concentrated in the chief executive, the prevailing research literature tends to identify the elected mayor or the appointed manager as the central power figure. John Crecine concluded that the "mayor's policies dominate and that the council and department heads have surprisingly little to say about municipal resource allocation on a macro level."[10] Similarly Meltsner and Wildavsky wrote that the city manager of Oakland, California, was, "the key figure in making most of the decisions."[11]

But other researchers have observed different patterns in the structure of influence. Caputo reported that in the four cities he examined, departments, the executive, and the legislature shared equally in determining expenditure outputs.[12] Anton found that in two of the three Illinois cities he studied, the legislature made most budget decisions.[13]

Friedman's study of fourteen mid-size cities reports that the structure of influence is more complex and more varied than reported previously.[14] Influence is comprised of both formal and informal elements. The executive is simply not dominant over both the departments and the legislature.

In some places, the executive is vulnerable to the pressures of the departments. Executive recommendations will emerge as a result of bargaining, negotiation, and compromise. In other places, consultation is at a minimum and unilateral reductions are imposed. Sometimes departments do not even meet with the executive, and do not know what their budgets are before they go to the legislature.

In terms of the relationship between the executive and the legislature, each makes an independent assessment of the pace and direction of spending. They are asserting their formal authority. The legislature does not depend on the executive to make the decisions; and, when disagreements arise and spending preferences are in direct opposition, legislative choices prevail.

A strong executive also is able to limit the contact between the departments and the legislature. Departments should not be able to "go over the executive's head" and appeal to the legislature. Departmental representatives may not even appear at the meeting, and when they do, it is as an agent of the executive and in support of the recommendations made for their department. They are not autonomous and cannot make an "end run" to the council. The legislature may not see the initial spending requests from each department. The legislature is denied an alternative voice, and is compelled to rely on the executive and the information given to them. The council members are prevented from forming a coalition with the departments (and vice versa) as both a resource of and strategy for influence. When they are able to do so, both the department and the legislature have greater influence over the executive and the determination of budget outlays.

Formal budget authority is only one of the "two faces of power." Power is also exercised in a less apparent and less direct fashion. The strong use their informal influence to create barriers to spending proposals they do not favor. They keep budget items from entering the public arena and record; so, the question must not only be asked of what was officially proposed and then eliminated or modified but also what was never public. Overt disagreements are muted. Explicit actions are minimized. The items that are "likely to go" are anticipated with cues and signals being sent and received. Behind-the-scenes communication clears an item before it is formally put forward; thus the choices of others are shaped and limited.

Interest groups and external pressure

Municipal budgeting tends to be isolated from specific, organized community pressure. While constituency support may be a ubiquitous strategy in the political process, when it comes to real participation and influence in the budgetary process interest groups are either uninvolved or uninfluential.[15]

Formal budgeting is relatively autonomous from the specific pressures of organized interest groups in the community. It is an internal, bureaucratic affair, dominated by those occupying administrative offices. Accountability is indirect and ambiguous.

Two mechanisms to enhance the public's influence should be noted: public opinion surveys and decentralized, community-based budgeting. Both have grown out of the movement for greater citizen participation in government. Both seek to provide greater input into the budgetary process to achieve closer correspondence between governmental spending and the public's values, preferences, and priorities. Both, however, can be of but limited use.

Citizen surveys Approaching the public directly through opinion surveys is one way to find out how they want their taxes spent. A scientifically conducted, representative sampling of the entire community has the advantage of recording the attitudes of all residents, not just the voter, the politically active, and the influential.

An interesting approach to these surveys is the notion of budget pies.[16] Respondents are provided with a drawing of a circle—the pie of the whole governmental budget—and are asked about relative program shares. An illustration is offered in Figure 5–1. This pie chart has the advantage of offering a pictorial representation of spending. It examines the intensity of spending preferences relative to limited resources, which correspond to the real world of municipal budgeting. This visual image is a direct and vivid representation of the trade-offs between the total size of the budget and individual programs.

Decentralized budgeting The sequence of budget stages can be restructured to facilitate community access and influence.[17] For example, public hearings could be conducted more often, earlier in the budget cycle (perhaps by the departments themselves), and at various sites throughout the community. An outreach effort could be made to disseminate information and to encourage citizen involvement. On-site workshops could be held to disclose financial information in a clear and understandable fashion and facilitate public access and influence.

Decision-making models

There are two general views of how budget decisions are made: *comprehensive-analytic* and *incremental*.

Comprehensive-analytic decision making has been viewed as being more a

Figure 5–1 Budget pie
questionnaire form.

Assume that you are in charge of deciding how the police should spend their budget dollars on
the following three activities:

A: Patrolling (crime prevention)
B: Detective work (criminal investigation)
C: Administration

Indicate by dividing this budget dollar into three separate sections the way *you* would like to see
the police spend their budget. Identify each section by writing the letter A, B, or C in the corresponding sector.

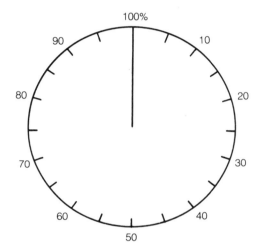

normative (i.e., prescriptive and authoritative) statement of how decisions should
be made rather than an empirical description of how they actually are made.
Several reasons are offered for this view: problem-solving capabilities are limited;
information and time are scarce; analysis has a cost; knowledge is insufficient
to forecast the impact of public programs; goals cannot be isolated; priorities
cannot be clearly set; and social preferences often are overlapping, rapidly changing, and conflicting.

In *incremental budgeting* the first task is to identify and rank goals according
to relative importance. Next is a comprehensive analysis of possible methods
for reaching these goals. The consequences of each are then compared in a
formal, systematic manner, and the selection is made of the single best way to
optimize the desired goal. This model is summarized by Charles Lindblom in
terms of budgeting:

1. Governmental objectives should be as clearly and explicitly defined as
   possible.
2. Alternative policies should be explicitly regarded as alternative means
   toward the achievement of objectives.
3. Specifically, expenditure decisions should be made explicitly and
   deliberately in the light of all objectives they are intended to achieve.
4. In the interests of a rational comparison of alternatives, final expenditure
   decisions should not be made until all claims on the budget can be
   considered.
5. Revenue and expenditure decisions should be deliberately coordinated.

6. For each expenditure, some systematic and deliberate appraisal of benefits and costs should be made.
7. Policy making, including budgetary policy making, should achieve a unified policy.[18]

Incremental analysis defines the existing base of spending and the annual increment. This base, defined as the level of funds appropriated in the current year, is outside the purview of the annual budget cycle. It claims legitimacy as the foundation on which next year's budget is built. Policy commitments of current programs and their spending levels are not reevaluated. Thus, the range of options is limited, and the margins—the narrow range of increases and decreases from one budget year to the next—become the focus of the budgeting process.

The most important factor in the current year's budget is the amount in last year's budget. The future is an extension of the present, as the present is a continuation of the past. The marginal differences in costs from one year to the next are often highlighted by forms that demarcate the dollar or percentage change in spending from one year to another. A sample form is offered in Figure 5–2.

Incremental budgeting also means that the annual review is limited to financial considerations. New policy objectives, options, and impacts are largely excluded.

Figure 5–2   Budget formats that highlight incremental expenditure change, Philadelphia and Rochester, 1979–80.

Philadelphia

Activity	Direct departmental cost detail (3)	Fiscal 1978 actual obligations (4)	Fiscal 1979 estimated obligations (5)	Fiscal 1980 estimates (6)	Increase or (decrease) (7)
Criminal	100	$16,979,515	$18,230,085	$18,893,588	$ 66,503
incident	200	62,948	64,000	67,865	3,865
	300	11,130	11,906	11,906	. . .
	400	. . .	. . .	. . .	. . .
investigations	500	. . .	. . .	379,112	379,112
	800				
	Costs	$17,053,593	$18,305,991	$19,352,471	$1,046,480

Rochester
Major changes/features
For 1979–80, total personnel changes in Patrol activities amounts to a net reduction of 13: a reduction of 16 officer positions and an addition of 3 civilian positions. The civilian positions, consisting of one Senior Support Team Specialist and two Support Team Specialists, represent the institutionalization of the Family Crisis Intervention Team (FACIT) grant.

Transfer to SCIS	− 10 officers	$ − 191,015
Transfer to training	− 1 officer	19,102
Abolishments	− 5 officers	− 95,505
Institutionalization of FACIT program	+ 3 civilians	+ 60,237
Personnel total	− 13 positions	− 245,385
Materials & supplies	. . .	+ 12,200
Services	. . .	− 6,090
TOTAL		$ − 239,275

Spending choices do not emphasize the worth of programs in attaining goals; values and priorities are minimized; and conflict is contained. It is the annual change in the cost of "doing business" that is the issue at hand. Essentially, only dollars and cents data are available, so rules of thumb such as "fair share," across the board percentage adjustments, and balancing-out guide budget making.

Perhaps what is most significant about incremental decision making is the seemingly inexorable increases that occur every year. The cumulative consequences of annual marginal choices are ever growing expenditures. The institutionalism of incrementalism is reflected in the uncontrollable nature of spending. This means that determining the major, long-range pace and direction of spending are outside the formal cycle of budgeting and beyond the effective power of its participants. Little leeway exists to affect the flow of funds in any fiscal year since choices are locked in by past, mandatory, and fixed expenses.

The multiple purposes of budgeting

The purposes of the budget as developed originally by Allen Schick are control, management, and planning.[19] Control is the traditional use of budgeting for financial accountability. Management employs the budget to direct the work toward service delivery. Planning uses budgeting to establish program and financial goals and objectives. The following pages summarize this typology of control, management, and planning, which is both a description of how budgets are used in government and a prescription of how they might and ought to be used.

Budgeting as financial control

Traditionally, the purpose of the budget has been to assure financial compliance and accountability. The budget is necessary to assure the propriety and rectitude of public officials who possess authority over the public purse. Discretion to spend is limited in order to assure that funds are disbursed throughout the year only in the amounts and in accordance with the purposes set forth in the adopted budget. Techniques of "counting and watching" have been developed to monitor and regulate the flow of funds so that at any given time it is known how much is available to be spent, on what, and by whom.

Control budgeting tends to be necessarily negative in its orientation. Its operational objective is to curb governmental spending. By limiting the budget at its inception and by keeping a tight rein throughout the year, the increases are minimized from one year to the next. In this way, the balance between revenues and expenditures can be maintained, tax increases forestalled or lessened, and borrowing costs reduced.

As early as 1920, J. Wilner Sundelsan promulgated a set of principles of budgeting for financial accountability.[20] They are: comprehensiveness, exclusiveness, unity, specification, annual basis, accuracy, clarity, and publicity. They define the characteristics of budgeting for expenditure control and are described briefly in the following paragraphs.

Budgets are detailed Expenditures are authorized line by line, item by item. These form an "object-expense" budget format. As shown in Figure 5–3, each purchase is enumerated and categorized from such major object groupings as personnel and other-than-personnel-services (OTPS, e.g., supplies, materials, equipment, and contractual services) to hundreds, if not thousands, of individual and specific items. The inclusion of personnel position schedules is common. Each account line is coded numerically to identify every transaction. Line items are supposed to limit precisely the amount and narrowly define what can be spent. The greater the detail and the more specific the appropriations, the easier it is to monitor outlays. This is the hallmark of control budgeting.

Budgeting is annual   The time span of the authority to spend, according to this tenet of expenditure control, is restricted and periodically renewed. Each year the regular cycle of budgeting is repeated. Frequent review provides a routine opportunity for close supervision over what has happened to the funds appropriated previously. In this way discretion is limited and autonomy restricted. Almost all local governments adhere to this doctrine of control.

Budgeting is comprehensive   The budget should include a forecast of all financial transactions. Total receipts and outlays should be reviewed together. This includes such special purpose and earmarked revenues as monies to be received from the federal and state governments, all other funds, special districts and authorities, and public benefit corporations that are tied to the general purpose municipality.

001 General fund	Actual expenditures		Current budget,	Projected budget,	Approved budget,
Expenditure detail	1976–77	1977–78	1978–79	1978–79	1979–80
1100 Per ser-executive salaries	$ 0	$ 0	$ 20,400	$ 20,400	$ 33,010
1200 Per ser-fire & police sal & wages	0	0	0	0	8,885,654
1201 Per ser-regular salaries	9,993,568	9,962,617	10,503,068	10,455,049	1,711,002
1202 Per ser-terminal leave	110,247	112,216	148,000	175,000	112,000
1203 Per ser-service awards	237,605	243,903	237,250	237,250	238,050
1206 Per ser-CETA overmatch	0	0	25,364	17,952	0
1210 Per ser-holiday pay F & P	0	0	0	0	286,903
1400 Per ser-overtime	225,636	231,548	227,831	227,831	240,500
1500 Per ser-incentive	421,052	408,435	397,120	398,495	424,960
2200 Per ser-retirement	3,110,228	3,224,546	3,311,117	3,311,299	337,103
Total personal services	14,701,250	15,310,019	16,061,469	16,041,964	16,615,768
3100 OPR exp-professional svs-other emp cost	6,363	65,654	60,699	60,541	70,578
3400 OPR exp-other contractual serv	383	1,200	1,390	1,390	1,880
3401 OPR exp-contractual svs-other	85,236	124,010	165,718	164,354	194,175
4000 OPR exp-travel & per diem	21,053	39,000	44,949	42,550	45,750
4001 OPR exp-travel-motor pool	1,667,751	1,924,192	2,458,827	2,372,826	2,228,556
4100 OPR exp-communication service	105,720	123,189	190,019	171,295	159,649
4201 OPR exp-transportation-freight	140,433	123,347	133,219	132,058	125,000
4203 OPR exp-trans-postage-outside vendors	0	6,000	8,025	8,025	6,200
4300 OPR exp-utility services city	20,505	22,657	31,203	30,440	24,410
4301 OPR exp-utility services other	98,555	105,313	125,756	122,400	131,880
Total operating expenses	2,669,056	3,259,336	4,218,596	4,065,172	3,843,035
8201 GRT & aids contribution	6,008	3,550	4,500	4,500	6,000
Grants-in-aid	6,008	3,550	4,500	4,500	6,000
9100 Nonoperating transfers	0	0	13,618	13,618	0
Nonoperating	0	0	13,618	13,618	0
TOTAL DEPT 150	$17,376,314	$18,572,905	$20,298,183	$20,125,254	$20,464,803

Figure 5–3   Line item budget for Tampa (Florida) Police Department, fiscal year ending 30 September 1980.

The budget is unified   The budget should be organized so that the relationship of the different parts is apparent. All budget items should be treated and presented uniformly, and incorporated as an integral part of a single budget. While the practice of segregating revenues and expenditures is an accepted part of governmental accounting, according to this rule of expenditure control, the budget should make clear the connection between the financial transactions in one part and those in another.

The demarcation of capital expenditures from operating expenses, however, is an example of an exception to the principle of budgetary unity. This means that in most municipalities the financial effects on future annual operating expenses of long-term investments in physical facilities tend to be obscured.

Spending is preaudited   The budget does not constitute a mandate to spend, only the authority to do so. Although legislative action establishes boundaries for expenditures, the actual disbursement of funds is neither automatic nor certain. Departments do not directly write the checks. Many rules and regulations must be followed and many layers of approval must be obtained before any funds are legally obligated and any money is paid out. Bids and quotations must be assembled and reviewed, and requisitions, vouchers, and other documents must be completed by various departments and reviewed by the controller and the purchasing agent before the purchase order can be issued.

The preaudit, or "first instance" review, of the expansionary departments by the economizer is meant to verify that money is available and that it will be used in accordance with accounting standards and legally controlling appropriations. A preaudit is uniform as all agencies are treated alike and are subject to the same rules and regulations. It is comprehensive as it covers all transactions. It is routine as it does not require a special rationale and justification but is built into daily operations.

Budgeting for control focuses on the execution stage of the budget cycle through a process of central regulations, monitoring, and approval.[21] The major components are the following:

1. Personnel, position, and compensation plans are either in the budget or closely linked to it. Filling a position vacancy, a promotion, or any other personnel action involves not only the personnel department but also the budget office. Such financial control helps ensure that the position is legally authorized, that the funds are available, and that the established salary is paid.
2. Purchasing supplies, materials, equipment, and other tangible commodities (even when specifically included in the budget) require special forms and documents and the approval of the budget or accounting office.
3. An apportionment/allottment system times outlays according to the life cycle of the program. The intent is to ensure that appropriations are available for the entire fiscal year.
4. Budget amendments throughout the year are regulated for the most part by the central budget office. Discretion is limited, and rules and procedures govern alterations in line-item amounts within a department or shifts of funds among departments.
5. When a charge is made to an appropriation account, an encumbrance system is used at an early point in the timing of financial transactions and in advance of the completed transaction. An accounting system is used that records the amount when a purchase order is first issued or when bids are accepted on a contract.
6. An internal audit for the actual disbursement of budget monies throughout the fiscal year is designed to ensure that transactions are

recorded accurately and that governmental assets are protected properly. An internal audit is achieved by checks and balances. Authority over funds is shared among a number of individuals; no single person can handle a transaction from beginning to end. When necessary, employees sign for work; other employees may countersign. Forms are numbered in sequence to ensure that all transactions are recorded. Some records are independently confirmed by physical evidence, by inventory, and by external controls. These and other internal audit methods offer a continuous opportunity to prevent misfeasance, malfeasance, and nonfeasance in office.

Generally accepted accounting principles   Although taken for granted in the private sector, adherence to generally accepted accounting principles (GAAP) has often been lacking in local government. These accounting standards were begun by the Municipal Finance Officers Association (MFOA) as early as 1934, through what is now the National Council on Governmental Accounting. The American Institute of Certified Public Accountants and the Financial Accounting Standards Board have now entered the arena.[22] When the accuracy of the numbers is in question, and fiscal sleights of hand obscure a municipality's financial position, the need for consistent and universal accounting principles is underscored. (See Chapter 18 for further discussion of local government accounting.)

Full disclosure   The financial stringency of cities, and the particular inability of a few cities to meet their debt obligations, has focused attention on the need for full disclosure of the financial condition of municipal governments. The notion of the "riskless" status of municipal securities has been shattered. Investors, creditors, and others now are asking for information that presents fairly the financial position of local governments. Unlike corporate instruments of indebtedness, the multibillion-dollar-a-year issuance of municipal bonds and notes is not regulated by the Securities and Exchange Commission (SEC), even though legislation to regulate them has been proposed in Congress several times without adoption. Instead, the preparation of a prospectus is by voluntary compliance with the standards developed by MFOA and the incentives of the marketplace. Whatever form full disclosure takes, it places new requirements on the financial information system to produce valid and reliable information about the financial viability of local government.[23]

Financial reporting   To track funds throughout the fiscal year, a monthly or quarterly projection of spending is developed and actual outlays are then plotted against the projections. This type of financial report shows the rate of spending, which is most relevant for maintaining a balanced budget and preventing unexpected shortages.

Such a report typically includes (1) appropriations adopted at the start of the fiscal year; (2) the amount disbursed for the last month (or quarter); (3) the amount disbursed for the year to date; (4) the amount encumbered (which is separate from the amount disbursed); and (5) the available balance (which is the original appropriation minus the disbursements and encumbrances). A report of this kind may also show comparative information on disbursements for the same month in the previous year, ratios of total expenditures to the available balance and the original appropriation, and the total expenditures to date compared with the prior year to date. The most important item usually is the unencumbered balance. These breakdowns can be shown at any desired level of expenditure detail (e.g., salaries and wages, police pension fund contributions, insurance, and automotive maintenance), depending on the accounting system and account classifications. In addition to this object (or functional) breakdown, reports can be prepared by department or agency programs, geographic districts or neighborhoods, and specific activities.[24]

Postaudit The final component of the budgetary process is the postaudit. Its purpose is to detect and prevent fraud and misuse of funds. Traditionally, audits for financial compliance examine (1) the propriety, legality, and mathematical accuracy of accounts to ensure that receipts have been recorded properly and expenditures made in accordance with authorizations; (2) the fairness and accuracy of accounting statements in presenting a complete financial position of the jurisdiction; and (3) the adherence of financial transactions to generally accepted accounting principles.[25]

Conclusion Unfortunately, the consequences of control budgeting are often a narrow and cumbersome financial management system, characterized by paperwork, detail, duplication, complexity, and inflexibility. Technique ultimately triumphs over purpose and procedures often become counterproductive. In the pursuit of "nickel and dime" savings, outlays are delayed and control is circumvented. For every rule there are various interpretations, and for every procedure there are exceptions.

In an era of increasingly scarce resources, however, the importance of budgeting for expenditure control cannot be undervalued. Despite excesses of red tape and delay, control is a vital part of budgetary and financial management. It helps to ensure legality, public trust, financial responsibility, and the financial solvency of local governments. Good budgeting recognizes these pluses and minuses and builds effective control into the larger framework of operations and planning management. Government exists to provide goods and services to the public and the budget process must serve this end.

Budgeting as operational management

Management budgeting, long known as "performance" budgeting, takes the budget process beyond control to translate the things bought by government into the things done by government.[26] Management budgeting establishes performance goals and objectives and focuses on quantitative indicators of output and achievement. Spending choices then become a vehicle for operational direction and control. Budget review extends beyond the cost of purchases to include the work of the departments and the processes that lead to the completion of programs and tasks.

Expenditures are classified by activity In management budgeting the control format of line items is augmented by the classification of spending activities. Line items by themselves do not indicate the kind and amount of activities undertaken, goods produced, and services rendered. As the Hoover Commission once described performance budgeting, the focus is "upon the general character and relative importance of the work to be done, or upon the service to be rendered."[27]

The end products of government now assume prominence. With the control format, the budget is not only a documentation of past payments, current outlays, and expected purchases; it also shows how dollars are used and what kinds of work are projected.

Narrative statements are provided Narrative statements defining activities are another informational characteristic of management budgeting. These introductory statements relate agency responsibilities and goals to the specific jobs and tasks identified by the classifications of expenditure activity. They help show how appropriations serve the purposes of the agency (see Figure 5–4).

Police administration

This program establishes policies for the administration, direction, and control of the Police Department. It includes costs for the Chief of Police, Assistant Chief, and clerical support for the Chief's office.

Fiscal management

This program is responsible for preparing and implementing the annual Police Department budgets: preparing estimates of revenues from police-regulated business; preparing various required reports such as extended appropriation analyses, annual allotment schedules, etc.; department-wide telephone coordination; and processing of training and travel accounts, direct payment requests, invoices and requisitions, petty cash funds, grant funds, and requests for Council Action.

Research and analysis

This program provides planning support for the Department through its Crime Analysis and Research Support functions. Research Support includes managing all sources of data necessary for planning; producing periodic reports of Department activity; monitoring Department productivity measures; evaluating new products and employee suggestions; grant development; technical research; and disaster preparedness planning. Included in operations support report are: statistical reports, department instructions, suggestions, questionnaires, special studies, resource allocation reports, and miscellaneous reports.

Inspection and control

This program provides continual evaluation of operational policies and procedures to ensure compliance with departmental policies and existing law. Due to the broad spectrum of internal reviews and the need for top management direction, assigned staff report directly to the Chief of Police.

Figure 5–4　Narrative statements for police administration activities, San Diego, California, 1979–80 budget.

Work load is measured　A third feature of management budgeting is work load measurements—quantitative indicators of work actually accomplished. They are a simple counting of the units of work completed, which is intended to correspond to the activity classification of expenditures as displayed in Figure 5–5. As a record is provided of finances, now a record is provided of the goods and services produced.

Efficiency is measured　With the information about costs and services, the efficiency of the programs and tasks can now be measured. Efficiency, usually defined as the ratio of the measurable work done to the measurable resources used in doing that work, often takes the form of the average cost or employee days per unit of work load. Cost accounting is a way to calculate these measures.

Efficiency is also a criterion for spending choices. Just as control budgeting focuses on inputs, management budgeting is the output side of the policy equation. Decisions are not made on the basis of costs without some thought of the end-products; nor are they made in terms of services, divorced from the accompanying costs of providing the services. If two alternatives cost the same, the one that yields the greater return will be selected. Given the same outlay, the one that costs less will be chosen.

Efficiency cannot decide what goals and programs to pursue, nor judge the value and assess the benefits of government. Given the goals of government, efficiency relates services to costs. Once program missions are selected, efficiency is crucial to the assessment of alternate paths to those ends. A management approach to budgeting seeks to pinpoint activities that are not performing well, and to signal the need for corrective action.

Work planning　Budgets can be built around the kind and amount of work to be undertaken in the next fiscal year. These work load targets are the "programming" part of budget preparation and involve scheduling work, developing an organizational structure, and establishing procedures to reach the proposed

Program by account title	Departmental estimate 1980	Appropriation 1979	Expenditures 1978	Increase or decrease, 80 over 79
Criminal investigation				
Cases investigated	12,000.00	12,000.00	13,440.00	. . .
Total investigative manhours	186,200.00	186,200.00	190,000.00	. . .
Total arrests	24,500.00	24,000.00	23,000.00	500.00
Percent of cases cleared	40.00	38.00	33.50	2.00
Regular patrols				
Average no. of units in service per eight (8) hour shift	210.00	209.00	209.00	1.00
Communications				
Calls for service	277,500.00	275,000.00	169,500.00	2,500.00
Records and identification				
No. of requests for records checks	75,000.00	58,000.00	50,800.00	17,000.00
No. of I.D.'s processed	10,000.00	9,000.00	9,150.00	1,000.00
Internal affairs				
Internal affairs complaints	224.00	230.00	260.00	−6.00
No. of complaints handled per staff	32.00	33.00	37.00	−1.00
Police training				
Recruits trained	100.00	80.00	80.00	20.00
Officers trained in service	500.00	1,552.00	1,594.00	−1,052.00
Officers trained in firearms	1,000.00	1,000.00	1,000.00	. . .
Traffic				
Traffic accident reports processed	4,600.00	4,500.00	13,500.00	100.00
Community relations				
Community relations activities	7,000.00	5,000.00	3,650.00	2,000.00
School crossing guards				
No. of crossings staffed	214.00	214.00	214.00	. . .

Figure 5–5   Performance statistics by work program, Pittsburgh Police Department, 1978, 1979, 1980.

plan. Alternative methods to achieve this volume of work should also be considered at this time. Budgeting the work plan is next; the personnel, equipment, materials, and supplies needed to attain the chosen level of work are priced in such terms as money, personnel, and equipment.

Performance projections offer another way to calculate the budget. By linking the input of resources to the output of the activities and work performed, the relationship between a designated level of service and the amount of funds required to achieve that service is established.

Performance reporting   Management budgeting is identified by a systematic performance monitoring system.[28] Feedback is obtained by checking and adjusting specific and measurable productivity targets. Monthly and quarterly estimates of work load and other performance indicators can be established at the beginning of the year and routinely reported as illustrated in Figure 5–6. Actual performance then can be compared with the plan.

Periodic reports on budget execution instill financial sensitivity in day-to-day management. Monthly meetings to review spending against the plan provide an arena for decision making that not only includes those who are spending budget monies but also those who are delivering the service.

Sharp or sudden deviations from expected outlays suggest (1) unrealistic revenue or expenditure estimates; (2) inadequate accounting controls; (3) capricious management decisions that inflate the rate and amount of spending; and (4) unplanned inflationary cost increases. Performance reports make it clear to

Indicator	Fiscal year 1979, annual actual	Fiscal year 1980		
		Annual plan	4-month plan	4-month actual
Agency-wide indicators				
Absence rate (% of scheduled hours)				
Uniformed—paid sick leave	2.5%	2.4%	2.3%	2.4%
Uniformed—line of duty	2.9%	2.6%	2.6%	2.0%
Civilian—paid sick leave (city funded)	3.6%	3.5%	3.4%	3.9%
Civilian—paid sick leave (CETA)	4.4%	3.9%	3.6%	5.4%
Complaints—civilian complaint review board	3,772	3,000	1,000	1,118
Percent of complaints resolved within 90 days	81%	82%	82%	66%
Police officers scheduled daily by chart (average)	10,740	10,343	10,373	10,299
Police officers on patrol per day (average)	6,705	6,636	6,595	6,251
12 midnight to 8am tour	1,191	1,148	1,182	1,097
8am to 4pm tour	2,712	2,674	2,674	2,531
4pm to 12 midnight tour	2,802	2,814	2,739	2,623
Crime complaints (000)	1,301	1,256	419	DNA
Felony complaints (000)	508	509	170	DNA
NYCPD apprehensions (000)	493	432	144	DNA
NYCPD felony arrests (000)	92	94	31	DNA
Summonses issued (department-wide):				
Parking violations (000)	4,508	3,400	1,074	1,195
Moving violations (000)	925	791	252	288
Major mission indicators				
Crime prevention and control				
RMP cars on patrol per day (average)	1,558	1,535	1,534	1,447
One-officer RMP cars on patrol per day (average)	125	122	133	95
911 calls (000)	6,327	6,103	2,094	2,224
Radio runs (000)	2,612	2,563	879	957
Required time to dispatch police unit in response to "crime-in-progress" call (minutes):				
Median	2.6	2.0	2.0	2.3
Mean	4.8	4.0	4.0	5.7
Investigation and apprehension				
Cases investigated	10,323	10,381	3,499	3,772
Percent of investigated cases cleared:				
Homicide	63%	70%	70%	53%
Sex crime	55%	57%	57%	57%
Robbery	27%	30%	30%	16%
Burglary	28%	31%	31%	11%
Warrants outstanding (000)	216	248	227	228
Warrants received (000)	114	122	41	34

Figure 5–6   Management report, New York City, showing agency-wide and mission indicators for the police department.

department heads and other program managers that they must know the budget, the expenses that can be charged to it, and the controls they must exercise over their subordinates.

Modification of preaudit controls   The modification of preaudit controls by the budget office is another feature of a management budget. The once automatic and mandatory requirement for departments to obtain central approval before entering into financial obligations is reduced. Authority over the execution of the budget is decentralized to those who spend the money. The budget office's surveillance and intervention in the many routine expenditure decisions is minimized and departmental discretion is enhanced.

Management budgeting rejects the traditional and still pervasive view that without centralized direction, departments would abuse their spending power and, as a result, overspend. Instead, it contends that internal cost consciousness complements reduced centralized supervision. A condensed focus on performance replaces the tug-of-war over dollars and cents.

As long as aggregate spending totals are maintained and personnel rules and procedures followed, departments have greater latitude in spending. Appropriations are less detailed, line items grouped, forms and procedures simplified. Budget centers are established to hold managers accountable.

Performance auditing The postaudit takes on a new direction toward efficiency and productivity. The U.S. Government Accounting Office has championed this change. As defined, performance audits examine

whether the entity is managing or utilizing its resources (personnel, property, space and so forth) in an economical and efficient manner and the causes of any inefficiencies or uneconomical practices, including inadequacies in management information systems, administrative procedures, or organizational structure.[29]

Performance auditing for management pursues such questions as (1) the need for purchase; (2) the reasonableness of costs incurred, such as those in the purchase of products that have a low price initially but a high maintenance cost and a short life span; (3) the adequacy of safeguards over resources acquired (e.g., inventory control); (4) the adequacy of revenues received for goods and services sold (e.g., franchises); (5) duplication of effort by employees or among organizational units; (6) overstaffing in relation to work to be done; and (7) simplification of forms, procedures, and the flow of paperwork.

Conclusion Most local governments do not have comprehensive productivity improvement programs. Few jurisdictions measure the efficiency of their delivery of services on a regular and continuing basis. And where such measurement systems do exist, they are not employed in the budget process. This is the general conclusion of a recent report by the General Accounting Office.[30] Two-thirds of the cities surveyed indicated that they had made a concerted effort to enhance productivity sometime between 1971 and 1976. Only two-thirds of these places, however, had a measurement system as a component of their effort. The lack of procedures to measure efficiency casts doubt on the usefulness of the endeavor. If the existence of a measurement system is a valid indication of the commitment to productivity, then less than half of the cities surveyed really installed a productivity improvement program.[31]

Budgeting for the purposes of management is not a vital part of the municipal budget process. Although local governments are concerned with productivity and performance, it appears that they are not linked formally and systematically to budgeting.

Budgeting as program and financial planning

Budgeting also serves program and financial planning as a public policy agenda; the budget is an instrument to decide what government should be doing, for whom, why, and with what effects. As Allen Schick wrote, budgeting for planning asks its own set of questions:

What are the long-range goals and policies of the government and how are they related to particular expenditures choices? What criteria should be used in appraising the requests of the agencies? What programs should be initiated or terminated and which expanded or curtailed?[32]

A planning budget has been most closely associated with planning-programming-budgeting (PPB), which gained prominence in the 1960s. Much has been written of the rise and fall of its specific procedures and forms, but this is of less concern than the ideas it fostered.

A budget process that is planning-oriented first plans, then programs, and finally budgets. The initial step is to determine the goals and objectives of spending. These goals and objectives are then translated into operational programs. Finally, the financial requirements of such plans and programs are calculated and shown in the budget. Figure 5–7 shows a schematic diagram of the entire process.

In incremental budgeting, the budget is put together from the bottom up. The budget sequence begins at the lowest level of the organization and successively travels upward to the chief executive and the legislature. Departments usually prepare their initial requests, without specific program guidance from those above. As a result, initial spending figures are unrealistically high.

Consequently, by the time the budget reaches the chief executive, he or she is compelled to cut it in order to achieve the required balance between revenues and expenditures and to implant his or her own program preferences. Nevertheless, any reductions are imposed on the base established previously by the departments. The range of options thus are limited to relatively small modifications in areas of special interest and major political consequence. The same constraints apply to evaluation by the legislature. Once the budget reaches the council members, the momentum of the process compels the legislature to accept it.

Figure 5–7   Planning, programming, and budgeting by process and result.

		Plans	Programs	Budget
Process		Establish spending objectives	Translate objectives into operational programs	Calculate financial requirements
Result		Policy formulation	Management for service delivery	Financial management system

Budgeting for planning seeks to change this pattern to more explicit and formal policy guidance by the executive (and the legislature) during the department's initial preparation of spending requests. The "budget call" includes strategic guidance on what the chief executive thinks is important; program issues that are likely to emerge; fiscal guidance in terms of targets; and general assumptions, constraints, and other factors that need to be taken into account. These instructions go beyond the prevailing vague plea to "hold the line." Thus, setting goals, determining priorities, and planning financial and programmatic implementation are the initial steps in the budget cycle. Issues and controversies are purposefully brought to the surface before the dollars and cents element of budgeting begins.

By first identifying the goals to be achieved and their relative priority, a criterion for spending is established. Because the intent of budgeting for planning is to reexamine past commitments, goals, objectives, and previously adopted programs are reconsidered. Reallocations are made by giving less to what is now less vital.

Furthermore, funds are distributed on the basis of program results. Once the goals have been accepted, a second set of evaluative questions examines the effectiveness of programs in performing their function, satisfying demand, meeting needs, and solving the problems to which they were addressed. The relative success and failure in producing achievements takes its place as a budgetary criterion. Is the program worth the money? What is the ratio of costs to benefits? Are there alternative means to accomplish the same goal?

A program structure is devised   The most visible element that sets a planning budget apart from budgeting for control and management is the rearrangement of line items into a program structure as illustrated in Figure 5–8. This format helps identify and clarify the fundamental purposes of public spending and the priorities among alternative ways to achieve established ends. So, without regard to existing organizational location, complementary activities are grouped by common objectives.

Figure 5–8
Budgetary program structure.

Program: Protection of persons and property

Subcategory
General administration & support
Fire safety & control
Emergency reporting systems
Preventive patrol, traffic control,
  & law enforcement

Element
Administration & support
Technical support
Records & communications
Plans & operations
Identification services
Community relations & training/youth aid
Juvenile investigation
Crime patrol & investigation
Traffic safety
Parking enforcement
Tactical operations
Vice investigations
Police call-box system
Town clerk
Animal shelter

Budgets are planned   While the budget is always a plan in the sense that it is directed toward the next year, it does not necessarily mean that the budget is a product of a planning process. Planning has two meanings in budgeting. One is to assess the consequences of the present upon the future. An explicit and deliberate search for anticipated consequences several years hence is made. A second meaning of planning is to shape the future. Decisions made in one year are meant to bring a desired result in a subsequent year. A series of annual decisions and actions, according to some determinable schedule, may be required to bring about a goal. In this way, each budget is a one-year installment in the implementation of a long-range plan.

Multiyear forecasts of both revenues and expenditures, three to five years hence, represent the future orientation of a planning budget. Revenue projections establish the framework of available resources and highlight the prospect for tax increases and their probable consequences. When coupled with data about general community conditions, a planning budget can contribute to an economic development strategy. Needless to say, available revenues set the

OBJECTIVE	QUALITY CHARACTERISTIC (OR SERVICE ASPECT)	SPECIFIC MEASURE	PRIME DATA SOURCES
Prevention of Crime	Reported crime rates	1. Number of reported crimes per 1,000 population, total and by type of crime.	Incident reports
	Victimization rates	2. Number of reported plus nonreported crimes per 1,000 households (or residents or businesses), by type of crime.	General citizen survey
	Different households and businesses victimized	3. Percentage of (a) households, (b) businesses victimized.	General citizen survey, business survey
	Physical casualties	4. Number and rate of persons (a) physically injured, (b) killed in course of crimes or nontraffic, crime-related police work.	Incident reports
	Property loss	5. Dollar property loss from crimes per 1,000 population (or, for businesses, per $1,000 sales).	Incident reports
	Patrol effectiveness	6. Number of crimes observable from the street per 1,000 population.	Incident reports
	Inspection effectiveness	7. Number of crimes per 1,000 businesses in relation to time since last crime prevention inspection.	Incident reports, inspection records
	Peacekeeping in domestic quarrels and other localized disturbances	8. Percentage of domestic quarrels and other disturbance calls with no arrest and no second call within "x" hours.	Dispatch records, incident reports
Apprehension of Offenders	Crimes "solved" at least in part	9. Percentage of reported crimes cleared, by type of crime and whether cleared by arrest or by "exception."	Incident reports
	Completeness of apprehension	10. Percentage of known "person-crimes" cleared, by type of crime.[1]	Incident reports, arrest reports
	Quality/ effectiveness of arrest	11. Percentage of adult arrests that survive preliminary court hearing (or state attorney's investigation) and percentage dropped for police-related reasons, by type of crime.	Arrest and court records
		12. Percentage of adult arrests resulting in conviction or treatment (a) on at least one charge, (b) on highest initial charge, by type of crime.	Arrest and court records
	Speed of apprehension	13. Percentage of cases cleared in less than "x" days (with "x" selected for each crime category).	Incident reports, arrest reports
	Stolen property recovery	14. Percentage of stolen property that is subsequently recovered: (a) vehicles; (b) vehicle value; (c) other property value.	Incident reports, arrest or special property records
Responsiveness of Police	Response time	15. Percentage of emergency or high-priority calls responded to within "x" minutes and percentage of nonemergency calls responded to within "y" minutes.	Dispatch records
	Perceived responsiveness	16. Percentage of (a) citizens, (b) businesses that feel police come fast enough when called.	General citizen survey, business survey, and complainant survey
Feeling of Security	Citizen perception	17. Percentage of (a) citizens, (b) businesspersons who feel safe (or unsafe) walking in their neighborhoods at night.	Citizen survey, business survey
Honesty,[2] Fairness, Courtesy (and general satisfaction)	Fairness	18. Percentage of (a) citizens, (b) businesses that feel police are generally fair in dealing with them.	General citizen survey, business survey, and complainant survey
	Courtesy	19. Percentage of (a) citizens, (b) businesses who feel police are generally courteous in dealing with them.	General citizen survey, business survey, and complainant survey
	Police behavior	20. Number of reported incidents or complaints of police misbehavior, and the number resulting in judgment against the government or employee (by type of complaint (civil charge, criminal charge other service complaints), per 100 police.	Police and mayor's office records
	Citizen satisfaction with police handling of miscellaneous incidents	21. Percentage of persons requesting assistance for other than serious crimes who are satisfied (or dissatisfied) with police handling of their problems, categorized by reason for dissatisfaction, and by type of call.	Complainant survey
	Citizen satisfaction with overall performance	22. Percentage of (a) citizens, (b) businesses rating police performance as excellent or good (or fair or poor), by reason for satisfaction (or dissatisfaction).	General citizen survey, business survey, and complainant survey

Figure 5–9   Effectiveness measures for crime control (see facing page for notes applicable to Specific Measure 10 and the Objective, Honesty, Fairness, Courtesy").

boundaries for expenditures such that impending imbalances can be identified in advance. The long-range requirements of uncontrollable and fixed costs can be uncovered, as well as the future impact of current commitments.

Multiyear forecasts can show the rapid escalation of spending that sometimes results from program choices. The future financial impact of contracts can be assessed. The forecasting of federal and state payments is also possible; their expiration dates, matching requirements, and possible residual costs can be understood in advance. Cash management and the scheduling of short- and long-range borrowing also depend on multiyear revenue and expenditure projections.

Effectiveness is measured   Budgeting for planning attempts to program effectiveness. Some types of effectiveness indicators are: the improvement and change in conditions that result from programs; client satisfaction; the extent to which needs and demands have been met (i.e., the ratio of actual to potential recipients); the quality of service delivery, which takes into account the degree of excellence; accessibility (i.e., distance travelled); equity of the distribution of services among economic groups, neighborhoods, and any other relevant features; and the cost/effectiveness ratio that determines the expenditure per unit of achieved results. Specific examples of effectiveness measures are displayed in Figure 5–9.

Measures of effectiveness act as feedback on program performance in the same fashion as the financial and management information systems discussed previously. While the reliability and validity of these indicators are difficult to determine, once developed and accepted the indicators can augment the existing performance reporting system.

Program audits   Another element of budgeting for planning is the redefinition of the postaudit to appraise results. This is called program auditing by the Government Accounting Office, because it "determines whether the desired results or benefits are being achieved, whether the objectives established by the legislature or other authorizing bodies are being met, and whether the agency has considered alternatives which might yield desired results at a lower cost."[33]

Conclusion   Although budgeting for financial and program planning has not been a major effort in most cities, PPB, ZBB (discussed in the next section of this chapter), and other management approaches may be used more in the decade of the eighties. The pressures for more productivity, the constraints of tax and expenditure limitations, and the volatile municipal bond market may force cities and other local governments to adopt more precise and diagnostic forms of budgeting and financial planning.

Zero-base budgeting

As with many other heralded reforms, the individual elements of zero-base budgeting (ZBB) are far from unique. In its own particular fashion, ZBB incorporates analytic and evaluative techniques from the past to construct a results-oriented, priority-setting budget process.

1. One person committing four crimes or four persons committing one crime would be four "person-crimes." When the number of offenders involved in a crime is unknown, as may frequently happen with such crimes as burglary, "one" criminal can be assumed for this statistic (or the historical average number of offenders for that type of crime could be used).

2. A satisfactory approach to measuring the degree of corruption, malfeasance, or negligence is lacking. Data on the number of complaints received by the city on these problems should be examined, particularly when their number increases substantially.

ADAM AND BAKER TEAM POLICING

Budget Unit Goal: To protect life and property, prevent crime, respond to all calls for service from citizens, enforce City ordinances, State and Federal laws, investigate and follow-up assigned cases, and improve response time.

Year: 1978
Budget (000): 4,335.1
Positions: 292

1979 Service level options

	Cost (000)		Positions		Dept.	City
S/L	S/L	Cum.	S/L	Cum.	rank	rank
1.	3,878.6	3,878.6	262	262	1/60	2
2.	336.9	4,215.5	28	290	3/60	7
3.	27.2	4,242.7	2	292	16/60	148
4.	148.9	4,391.6	18	310	37/60	PSP
5.	163.4	4,555.0	12	322	45/60	343

Service level narrative

1. *Quality Reduction and Increased Citizen Risk.* Provides service to the citizens in emergency situations and the officers would respond to cases of a less serious nature. Response time will average 12 minutes per call. This level calls for 256 commissioned officers, 6 civilians, 66 marked (blue and white) vehicles, and 27 unmarked vehicles. These officers provide 24-hour police service to the citizenry. Investigative follow-up and crime scene processing is curtailed.

2. *Minimum Preventative Patrol.* Provide twenty-seven commissioned officers and one clerk typist, who are needed to provide beat officers to answer citizen request calls with a 2 minute per call reduction in the response time from 12 minutes to 10 minutes.

3. *Interaction with USD #259.* Provides for the reinstatement of two school liaison police officers who coordinate programs in the schools in two of the team policing areas. At this level, a school liaison officer will be available in each of the six team policing areas.

4. *Adds eighteen police officers to Reduce Response Time.* Adds eighteen police officers to provide coverage in the patrol function for vacations, emergency leave, in-service training, and back-up officers. At this level, response time for calls will be reduced from 10 minutes to 9 minutes per call. Positions are funded effective 1 April 1979 (9 months). Costs include $136,049 for salaries and $12,816 for initial uniforms and equipment.

5. *Improved Supervision and Investigation.* Adds six detectives to ensure more follow-up investigations, to accelerate the investigation process, and to improve clearance percentage; and six lieutenants to provide quality control through supervision and shortened span of control.

Figure 5–10   Decision package format, police operations, zero-base budget, Wichita, Kansas, fiscal 1979.

Much has been written on ZBB. Briefly, it is the identification of decision units, the development of different decision packages for each of these units, and the ranking of the alternative packages.[34]

Decision units are established first by program managers and represent the information aspect of the budget. Decision units can be developed according to such organizational units as programs, activities, and the responsible center. There is no ideal categorization; the major requirement is that decision units be self-contained and susceptible to budget decisions.

Next, decision packages are devised for each decision unit, as illustrated in Figure 5–10. These packages contain all the information necessary for a zero-base budget choice. Each decision package identifies the mission of the decision unit, the activities by which its goals are obtained, the benefits expected (in terms of efficiency and effectiveness measures), alternative means of achieving the objective, and financial and nonmonetary resource information.

Several decision packages are prepared for each decision unit. Each presents alternative levels of expenditure and service outputs. Theoretically at least six packages exist:

1. A zero spending package that describes the consequences of not funding the decision unit
2. A minimum funding package, which presents the legally mandated level, or the point below which it is no longer viable or feasible to continue operations
3. A reduced level, somewhere below current outlays
4. A constant dollar package, which is the same absolute spending level extended into the next year
5. A current service decision package, which is the cost of continuing existing service levels into the next year
6. One or more increased spending and performance levels.

In actual practice, the number of alternative packages tends to be limited to three, either a constant dollar or a current service level (levels 4 or 5) and one above and one below the level chosen. Zero funding levels are hardly ever prepared, and the concept of a minimum package is difficult to establish. Instead, a flat percentage of current funding (e.g., 90 percent) is usually employed to represent the below-the-base package that is so important to the concept of ZBB.

The last step is the ranking of decision packages. This is the priority-setting component of ZBB. The several packages of each decision unit are compared and placed in a hierarchy of preferences. Thus, the total budget is determined by adding the decision packages, beginning with the package with the highest priority ranking and ending with the package ranked lowest, until the cumulative total reaches the predetermined spending limit.

ZBB is primarily an instrument of the executive, to be considered when formulating his or her spending recommendations to the legislature. The form and content of the adopted budget does not have to be recast. However, there is no reason why the legislature cannot take advantage of the ZBB format of decision packages and rankings for its own deliberations.

ZBB does not actually require the preparation and formulation of the budget from scratch each year. It is unrealistic to expect the budget to be put together annually from a zero base. ZBB does not actually challenge the right of existence and the funding base of programs each year; this is unfeasible and unrealistic. It is simplistic to assume that there are no irreversible legal mandates, no history, no past commitments, and no political support. Basic value choices do get reestablished; political coalitions change in strength; alternative service delivery mechanisms are developed; and success or failure is identified. The distance between reviewing everything or nothing is wide. Truth and best practice lie somewhere in between.

ZBB is marginalism with a twist. The focus is still on the annual change in spending levels and where to put the annual increase or decrease in available resources. The battle over the decision packages is fought at the margins, which define the controversies and set the agenda for ZBB.

The marginal analysis in ZBB, however, is significantly different from incremental budgeting. Alternatives below the base of current spending are explicitly formulated. The ranking of decision packages offers the prospect of reallocations among programs and between the incremental expansion of existing programs and the initiation of new ones. This contrasts with incrementalism, where the continuation of existing programs is ranked higher than the initiation of new ones.

Furthermore with ZBB, marginal analysis concerns more than cost; it includes program performance. Alternative levels of expenditures are deliberately and systematically related to different levels of service.

Although ZBB is often viewed as a technique for cutback management, it does not necessarily produce monetary reductions. While ZBB can identify decision units of low priority, ones that are poorly managed and those that do not achieve their missions, expenditure reductions do not follow automatically. Dollars will be saved only if savings decisions are made.

ZBB will not lead to program termination as much as it will lead to the redirection of funds among activities and programs based on considerations of the efficiency and effectiveness of the activities and programs. It is a vehicle to link management and planning to the budget process.

Federal aid

The expansion of national and state government financial support to local government had fundamentally altered the landscape of municipal financing and is a potentially far-reaching breach in the canons of budgetary control, management, and planning.[35] A survey of local government officials conducted by the International City Management Association (ICMA) and the U.S. Advisory Commission on Intergovernmental Relations (ACIR) shows evidence of the impact of these external sources of funds on the spending policy in local governments.[36] Officials who responded to the questionnaire stated that categorical grants, more than block grants, affect local expenditure choices. If the funds from categorical grants were made available for local government to use as they wished, two-thirds of the officials indicated that they would have spent the funds for some other purpose.

Another impact of external monies is the increase in total outlays. Regardless of the amount of federal money received—and the matching funds required—the per capita amount of spending is still higher when federal support is present. The reasons for this include indirect costs associated with enlarged activities, the costs of carrying on the programs dropped by changes in grant laws and policies, and the bureaucratic maladies long associated with federal grants, including accounting, reporting, and auditing mandates.

While few local studies are available, those done for state governments show that federal funds are scrutinized with less care and are subject to less state supervision than those supported by state-generated revenues. There is little reason to believe the situation is any different in municipal governments. The budget process is not comprehensive, nor is it unified. External monies are a major source of the perceived "uncontrollability" of the public purse. Departments are freed from the resource constraint of the local government and supervision by and accountability to local budget officers. As a result, financial accountability is threatened; funds can and are commingled; the audit trail is blurred; and control is reduced.

"Multipocket" budgeting provides an opportunity for departments (sometimes with the concurrence of the executive) to bypass and ignore the intent of legislatively adopted appropriations. Federal funds can be employed to support activities and programs that have previously been turned down by local government councils. The hidden, indirect costs and the implied commitment for future spending are, in most jurisdictions, committed without an explicit decision by the executive and the legislature.

The following budget-making structures and procedures constitute a checklist to assess the degree of local expenditure control over federal (and state) funds:

1. Does the executive budget include federal and state aid? Does it report all of the different forms such aid takes? Or does it report an aggregate city-wide total?
2. Does the city council or county board specifically appropriate federal and state money? If so, is it considered part of the department's total funding or is it delineated as a distinct and self-limiting appropriation?
3. How are outside expenditures categorized? Are they lump sums or line-

items? To what extent do they correspond to the existing budgetary format?

4. Is the intent of these external funds established by the city council or county board in any fashion, such as a report accompanying the budget ordinance, or as part of the appropriation itself?

5. Are the direct and indirect financial impacts estimated?

6. What is the time period of authorization? Is it an annual appropriation or open-ended until all funds are received and spent?

7. Are the amounts of "in-kind" and financial matching requirements specified and appropriated, or are local funds allowed to be transferred or simply counted as the matching requirements by the executive and/or the departments?

8. Are the expenditure controls of budget execution also applied to those funds?

9. How is this money accounted for, reported, and audited?

10. What mechanism exists for the adjustment of shortfalls in the receipt of federal and state money? Is there a reduction in the local share or a reduction in the total amount? Are local funds supplemented or is there no defined procedural response?

11. Similarly, what mechanism exists for the receipt of an increase in outside money? Does the city council or county board have to approve its acceptance and appropriate its use?

12. Is there any legislative mechanism to establish and review criteria for the allocation of federal funds between programs where discretion exists, as in block grant type aid?

Federal and state financial transfers also often impair efficient budgeting. Given the way grants are allocated, formulas written, and rules promulgated, productivity is essentially not rewarded. Money is distributed, for the most part, on the basis of need and tax effort, not on the basis of operational performance.

Seldom are there positive incentives to efficiently manage federal money; any "savings" has to be returned. Compliance with regulations is often more important. The current grant system also inhibits local financial and program planning. Municipalities do not know how much and when they will receive federal and state funds. Payments are often delayed. Uncertainties abound as grant programs come up for reauthorization, as allocation formulas are adjusted, and as funding levels change. Federal monies add an element of unpredictability to the local budget process. The gap in planning, specifically, is evident in the following fashion:

1. The difficulty of estimating the amount and timing of funds to be received exacerbates the inherent complexity of budget forecasting. When there is a matching requirement, it becomes difficult to calculate the amount needed and to provide for it in the local budget. The differences in local government fiscal years only add to the problem. Municipal budgets are often adopted before Congress has acted, and, as a result, may have to be modified during the course of the year.

2. Cash management is more difficult. The mismatch of fiscal years and the uncertainties associated with the amount and timing of such funds play havoc with cash flow projections. Late payments, sometimes in amounts other than anticipated, add a cost to local government in the form of short-term borrowing.

3. Uncertainty hampers program implementation. Often decisions made at the funding level do not allow sufficient time for corresponding decisions and actions to be made by the recipient government. As a result, orderly program delivery is impaired. Short-range projects are emphasized, and expediency becomes the rule. Money is spent in ways other than it would

have been if federal funds were known and available at the time local budget and program decisions were made.

A report by the Congressional Budget Office recognizes these problems and proposes three techniques to deal with the uncertainties of federal aid.[37] *Advance targeting* is the decision to roll five-year spending targets. While such "out-year" projections are certainly available, they are informational and do not represent the recommendations of the President nor the decisions of Congress. The Congressional Budget Office suggests that such advance targets be accepted as statements of policy through their adoption into law. *Advance spending* is appropriating federal funds for a year or more before they can be obligated. This provides an opportunity for early decision making on local funding levels for grants. Finally, *two-year appropriations* is the acceptance of the biennial budget cycle, long evident in many states, for selected federal programs.

Budgeting in a time of constraints

While statements about future public events are hazardous, it appears that local governments are experiencing severe resource constraints. Events of recent years have challenged the continual growth of governmental revenues and spending that have been taken for granted for so long. Budgets are more likely to be made in terms of decrements, rather than increments, to the base of previous spending levels.[38]

Financial stringency has several causes: accelerating expenses; inflation; inelastic revenue sources; rising interest rates; collective bargaining agreements; and rising energy prices. Thus, expenditures increase faster than revenues.

The local economic base may decline. As people and jobs move out of the city, private wealth and public resources decline. There is less revenue available to be collected, but costs do not necessarily drop proportionately. Finally, legal restrictions on taxing and spending represent in some fashion the public's resistance to the continued growth of government. In general, not enough is known about how to budget for decline. Experience provides few lessons about contraction. "Cutback management" is moving into new and uncharted waters.

In some cases, "belt tightening" is all that is required. The operational objective would be to smooth the decline by directing the type and location of the contraction that will take place. However, in other cases, a more fundamental readjustment such as the termination of programs and the lowering of service levels may be required. New programs could not be introduced without redistributing the current budget pie. The scope of municipal government could contract as programs are abandoned or transferred to other levels of government and the nonprofit and private sectors.

Most of those already in government cannot be expected to look favorably toward the approaching stringency. No organization concedes to its own demise with enthusiasm. Strategies and tactics of resistance will be adopted based on the particular survival needs of the individual, the department, and the local government as a whole. Some may choose to stonewall with a plea that "it cannot be done;" austerity will be denied and reductions postponed in the belief that the situation is only short term.

Cuts that will have to be restored later (e.g., deliberate underbudgeting for mandated costs) can be made. Programs that are visible and politically attractive can be reduced so that the resulting hue and cry from the media and affected citizens result in their restoration.

Another way of cutting expenditures is to use the "meat-ax." This has been a traditional approach to balancing the budget, and is, simply, a uniform, across-the-board percentage cut. Be it 5 percent or 10 percent, all departments are treated alike (although exceptions are often made for protective services). This is a simple "aid to calculation" that is easy to understand and implement. It presents few decision-making costs and is politically expedient. Because all departments are treated alike, this type of budget cutting appears to be neutral and fair. In its arbitrariness, all equally share the pain. While it may be feasible in the short term, it has deleterious consequences if followed for the longer term. Because everyone is penalized the same, efficiency, effectiveness, and priorities are ignored.

Spending can be contracted according to the susceptibility of account categories. In this fashion, personnel is likely to be the first item to be cut because it comprises the largest single outlay. A hiring freeze is a convenient and simple action to take. As union contracts generally prevent a decrease in the wages of each employee, the actual result of a cut in personnel is a decrease in the total size of the work force, by both lay-offs and attrition.

A priority ordering of the types of necessary purchases can be identified. Capital outlays can be deferred. Maintenance and repairs can be substituted for new equipment.

In terms of who wins and who loses in the budgetary process, several observations can be noted. First, the chief executive is the one most likely to gain. As the administrative head of government, he or she is the single point of information, contact, and negotiation; he or she possesses certain advantages that the legislature lacks. Second, departments stand to lose the most since their autonomy is challenged by the installation of new systems of expenditure control. In terms of the public, those whose interests are enhanced by limits on government will gain, while obviously those whose interests will be hindered lose. Fourth, and perhaps most important, the local government suffers as its authority is diminished and its discretion to make decisions, establish priorities, and implement policies is undermined. The lack of resources signals a lack of strength. Higher levels of government assume greater importance. State supervision of financial management becomes more rigorous. As state and federal funds become a larger proportion of local resources, the state and federal governments take on new significance. Extra-government bodies are created and the holders of municipal securities assume a new position of influence.

When viewed as a policy-making process, budgeting and the financial crunch reinforces the dominance of traditional, incremental, control budgeting. Accounting principles have regained their ascendancy after years in eclipse. Proactive management and planning approaches are less likely to be installed; they may even be the first to go as a luxury that can no longer be afforded.

A final comment

So where does this leave us? The interests and coalitions that hold the reins of government vary; the demands, needs and financial environment fluctuate; and the techniques and procedures employed to make the budget decisions change. The budget process and its consequent financial policy, however, have to be confronted and understood. This is a constant—as is the political struggle over "who gets what."

1   V. O. Key, Jr., "The Lack of a Budgetary Theory," *American Political Science Review* 36 (1940): 1137–44; B. Lewis Verne, "Towards a Theory of Budgeting," *Public Administration Review* 12 (1952): 42–54; Aaron Wildavsky, *Budgeting: A Comparative Theory of the Budgetary Process* (Boston: Little, Brown & Co., 1975); Naomi Caiden, "Toward a Science of Budgeting: Building Blocks and Patterns" (Paper presented to the annual convention of the American Society for Public Administration, 1977); Royston Greenwood, C. R. Hinnings, and Stewart Ranson, "The Politics of the Budgetary Process in English Local Government," *Political Studies* 25 (1977): 25–47.

2   For the most part, municipal governments adhere to this model. See: Richard E. Winnie, "Local Government Budgeting, Program Planning, and Evaluation," Urban Data Service Reports, vol. 4, no. 5 (Washington, D.C.: International City Management Association, May 1972). Winnie reports

that in three-quarters of 225 cities with populations 50,000 and over, budget preparation was the responsibility of the chief executive. In another 17 percent, it was the responsibility of the director of finance or the director of administration. In only 4 percent of the jurisdictions did the legislature formulate the budget (5 percent answered "Other"). Furthermore, in 81 percent of the council-manager cities, compared with 66 percent of the mayor-council cities, the chief executive officer prepared the budget. Another administrative official, especially a finance director, was more likely responsible for budgeting in mayoral cities. As expected, the city manager form of government represents a more centralized budget system.

At the same time, the chief executive was more likely to be directly responsible for budgeting in smaller cities than in larger ones. In cities with populations of 250,000 and less, the executive was in charge in about 80 percent of the places; above that size, this held true in half the jurisdictions. As the size of the city and the size of the budget increase, a greater differentiation of functions takes place so that a special unit emerges. It would seem that the difference between manager and mayor cities is more a product of the difference in population than anything else. So, overall, it appears that cities of all sizes and forms have adopted the formal tenets of an executive budget.

3   Municipal Finance Officers Association, *An Operating Budget Handbook for Small Cities and Other Governmental Units* (Chicago: Municipal Finance Officers Association, 1978), chapter 2; Lennox L. Moak and Albert M. Hillhouse, "Organization for Financial Administration," in *Concepts and Practices in Local Government Finance* (Chicago: Municipal Finance Officers Association, 1975), chapter 2.

4   The 1971 ICMA survey reported that in one-third of the cities, the office of the manager or administrator was responsible for the budget. In another one-quarter of the places there was a separate budget or budget and research office, and in another one-third of the jurisdictions the budget was prepared by the finance department. In cities of 250,000 and over, two-thirds of the budget offices had separate status, while in places 100,000 and under, less than 10 percent were so organizationally independent. Municipalities 100,000 and under were more likely to locate the budget function within the office of the manager or administrator, but at the same time in these places it was also more likely to be within the finance department. The difference between the manager and other forms of government may account for this seemingly contradictory pattern (but this breakdown is not reported). In any event, it appears once again that size leads to a functional and organizational specialization and differentiation.

5   Louis Fisher, *Presidential Spending Power* (Princeton, N.J.: Princeton University Press, 1975).

6   According to John E. Petersen et al. in *Watching and Counting: A Survey of State Assistance and Supervision of Local Debt and Financial Administration* (Chicago: National Conference of State Legislators and Municipal Finance Officers Association, 1977), pp. 27–33, thirty-five states require that private auditors–certified public accountants or licensed municipal accountants be used to audit all or some of the local governments. In five states most local units are audited by a state agency. In three states audits are conducted by local officials. The remaining states display other patterns.

7   John P. Crecine, *Governmental Problem Solving* (Chicago: Rand McNally, 1969); Lewis Friedman, *Budgeting Municipal Expenditures* (New York: Praeger Publishers, 1975); John E. Jackson, "Politics and the Budgetary Process," *Social Science Research* 1 (1972): 35–60; Thomas J. Anton, *Budgeting in Three Illinois Cities,* Commission Papers of the Institute of Government and Public Affairs, University of Illinois, 1964; Andrew T. Cowart, Tore Hansen, and Karl-Erik Brofoss, "Budgetary Strategies and Success at Multiple Accession Levels in the Norwegian Urban Setting," *American Political Science Review* 69 (1975): 543–58; David A. Caputo, "Normative and Empirical Implications of Budgetary Process" (Paper prepared for the sixty-sixth annual meeting of the American Political Science Association, Los Angeles, 1970).

8   Crecine, *Governmental Problem Solving,* pp. 33–134.

9   Jesse Burkhead, *Governmental Budgeting* (New York: John Wiley & Sons, 1956), pp. 312–13.

10   Crecine, *Governmental Problem Solving,* p. 38.

11   Arnold J. Meltsner and Aaron Wildavsky, "Leave City Budgeting Alone: A Survey, Case Study and Recommendations for Reform," in *Financing the Metropolis: Public Policy in Urban Economics,* ed. John P. Crecine, Urban Affairs Annual Reviews, vol. 4 (Beverly Hills, Calif.: Sage Publications, 1970), p. 344.

12   Caputo, "Normative and Empirical Implications," p. 11.

13   Anton, *Budgeting in Three Illinois Cities,* p. 18.

14   Friedman, *Budgeting Municipal Expenditures,* chapters 5, 6, and 8.

15   Crecine, *Governmental Problem Solving,* p. 189; James Danziger, *Making Budgets: Public Resource Allocation* (Beverly Hills, Calif.: Sage Publications, 1978).

16   Terry N. Clark, "Can You Cut a Budget Pie," *Policy and Politics* 3 (1974): 3–31; John P. McIver and Elinor Ostrom, "Using Budget Pies to Reveal Preferences: Validity of a Survey Instrument," in *Citizens Preferences and Urban Public Policy: Models, Measures, Uses,* ed. Terry N. Clark, Sage Contemporary Social Science Issues (Beverly Hills, Calif.: Sage Publications, 1976); Kenneth Webb and Harry P. Hatry, *Obtaining Citizen Feedback: The Application of Citizen Surveys to Local Governments* (Washington, D.C.: The Urban Institute, 1973).

17   Patricia S. A. Arnaudo and Terry R. Peel, *Citizen Participation in the Executive Budget Process: The Washington, D.C. Experience,* Urban Data Service Reports, vol. 6, no. 6 (Washington, D.C.: International City Management Association, June 1974); State Charter Revision Commission for N.Y.C., *The Expense Budget under Decentralization and Financial Reporting for Decentralized Localities,* N.Y.C. 1973; Jonathan Sunshine, "Decentralization: Fiscal Chimera or Budgetary Boon?" in *Improving the Quality of Urban Management,* ed. Willis Hawley and David Rogers, Urban Affairs Annual Reviews, vol. 8 (Beverly Hills, Calif.: Sage Publications, 1974), pp. 273–302.

18   Charles Lindblom, "Decision Making in Taxation and Expenditures," in National Bureau of Economic Research, *Public Finances: Needs, Sources and Utilization* (Princeton, N.J.: Princeton University Press, 1961), pp. 297–98.

19   Allen Schick, "The Road to PPB: The Stages of Budget Reform," *Public Administration Review* 26 (1966): 243–58; Allen Schick, *Budget Innovation in the States* (Washington, D.C.: Brookings Institution, 1971); Allen Schick, "Contemporary Prob-

lems in Financial Control," *Public Administration Review* 38, no. 6 (November–December 1978): 513–19; Lewis Friedman, "Control, Management and Planning: An Empirical Assessment," *Public Administration Review* 35 (1975): 625–28; Edward A. Lehan, *The Future of the Finance Directorate,* Municipal Finance Officers Association study no. 3 (Chicago: Municipal Finance Officers Association, 1977).

20 J. Wilner Sundelsan, "Budgetary Principles," *Political Science Quarterly* 50 (1935): 236–63.

21 George E. Hale and Scott R. Douglas, "The Politics of Budget Execution: Financial Manipulation of State and Local Government," *Administration and Society* 3 (1977): 367–78; George E. Hale, "State Budget Execution: The Legislature's Role," *National Civic Review* 66, no. 6 (June 1977): 284–90; Allen Schick, "Control Patterns in State Budget Execution," *Public Administration Review* 24 (1964): 97–106.

22 Robert Anthony, *Financial Accounting in Non Business Organizations* (Stamford, Conn.: Financial Accounting Standards Board, 1978); National Council on Governmental Accounting, *Governmental Accounting and Financial Reporting Principles—Statement 1* (Chicago: Municipal Finance Officers Association, 1979); William W. Holder, *A Study of Selected Concepts for Government Financial Accounting and Reporting* (Chicago: National Council on Governmental Accounting, 1980).

23 Municipal Finance Officers Association, *Disclosure Guidelines for Offerings of Securities by State and Local Governments* (Chicago: Municipal Finance Officers Association, 1976).

24 Jan M. Lodal, "Improving Local Government Financial Information Systems," *Duke Law Journal* (1976). 1133–55; The Urban Academy, *An Introduction to "IFMS"* (New York: The Urban Academy, 1976); Roger Mansfield, "The Financial Reporting Practices of Government: A Time for Reflection," *Public Administration Review* 39 (January–February 1979): 157–62; "Financial Reporting by Governmental Units," *Governmental Finance* 7 (May 1978): 2–39.

25 Comptroller General of the U.S., *Standards for Audits of Governmental Organizations, Programs, Activities and Functions* (Washington, D.C.: Government Printing Office, 1972), p. 2.

26 Wayne A. Kimmel, William R. Daugan, and John R. Hall, *Municipal Management and Budget Methods: An Evaluation of Policy Related Research* (Washington, D.C.: The Urban Institute, 1974); Edward A. Lehan, "Programming: The Crucial Preliminary Work of Budgeting," *Governmental Finance* 5 (1976): 6–11; Thomas A. DeCaster and James H. Ryan, *Budgeting for Improved Management,* Urban Observatory Research Report no. 37 (Washington, D.C.: National League of Cities, 1977); Laurence E. Lynn, Jr., and John M. Seidl, " 'Bottom-Line' Management for Public Agencies," *Harvard Business Review* 55, no. 1 (January–February 1977): 144–53.

27 U.S. Commission on the Organization of the Executive Branch of the Government, *Budgeting and Accounting* (Washington, D.C.: Government Printing Office, 1949), p. 8.

28 Stan Altman, "Performance Monitoring Systems for Public Managers," *Public Administration Review* 39, no. 1 (January–February 1979): 31–35; A. Lewin and R. Blanning, "The Urban Government Annual Report," in *Improving Urban Management,* ed. Willis Hawley and David Rogers. Ralph E. Thayer, "The Local Government Annual Report as a Policy Planning Opportunity," *Public Administration Review* 3, no. 4 (July–August 1978): 373–76.

29 Comptroller General of the U.S., *Standards for Audits,* p. 2.

30 Comptroller General of the U.S., *State and Local Government Productivity Improvement: What is the Federal Role?* Report to the Congress (Washington, D.C.: Government Printing Office, 1978).

31 See also Lewis Friedman, "Performance Budgeting in American Cities," *Public Productivity Review* 3 (1979): 50–62.

32 Schick, "The Road to PPB," p. 245.

33 Comptroller General of the U.S., op. cit., p. 2.

34 The literature on ZBB is growing rapidly. For reports on its use, as opposed to general introduction of the how-to-do-it variety, see: Joseph S. Wholey, *Zero-Base Budgeting and Program Evaluation* (Lexington, Mass.: Lexington Books, 1978); John A. Worthley and William G. Ludwin, eds., *Zero-Base Budgeting in State and Local Governments* (New York: Praeger Publishers, 1979); George Bledsoe, ed., Symposium on ZBB, *The Bureaucrat* 7, no. 1 (spring 1978): 3–70; Comptroller General of the U.S., *Streamlining Zero-Base Budgeting Will Benefit Decision Making* (Washington, D.C.: Government Printing Office, 1979).

35 Walter H. Plasila, "State Legislative Involvement in Federal-State Relations," *State Government* 48 (1975): 170–76; National Association of State Budget Officers, *Federal Funds Budgetary and Appropriation Process in State Government* (Washington, D.C.: National Association of State Budget Officers, 1978); Larry Walker, *State Legislative Control of Federal Aid Funds: The Case of Oklahoma,* Legislative Research Series, monograph no. 13 (Bureau of Government Research, University of Oklahoma, 1978); George E. Hale and Marian Lief Palley, "Perceptions of Federal Involvement in Intergovernmental Decision Making" (Paper prepared for the 1977 annual meeting of the Midwest Political Science Association, 1977).

36 U.S., Advisory Commission on Intergovernmental Relations, *The Intergovernmental Grant System as Seen by Local, State, and Federal Officials,* A–54 (Washington, D.C.: Government Printing Office, 1977).

37 Congressional Budget Office, *Advance Budgeting: A Report to the Congress* (Washington, D.C.: Government Printing Office, 1977); *Advance Budgeting: A Report to the Congress: A Compilation of Technical Background Papers* (Washington, D.C.: Government Printing Office, 1977).

38 For analysis of cutback budgeting, see: U.S., Congress, House, Committee on Banking, Finance and Urban Affairs, and Joint Economic Committee, *Local Distress, State Surpluses, Proposition 13: Prelude to Fiscal Crisis or New Opportunities,* Hearings before the Subcommittee on the City?, Hearings before the Subcommittee on the City, 95th Cong., 2d sess., July 25–26, 1978; Selma Mushkin, ed., *Proposition 13 and its Consequences for Public Management* (Cambridge, Mass.: Abt Books, 1979); Anthony H. Pascal et al., *Fiscal Containment of Local and State Governments* (Santa Monica, Calif.: Rand Corp., 1979); Charles Levine, ed., *Managing Fiscal Stress: The Crisis in the Public Sector* (Chatham, N.J.: Chatham House, 1980).

Part two:
Revenue
sources

6 The property tax

The property tax is one of the oldest, and also one of the least honored, ways of raising government revenue. Nevertheless, the tax, which has been evolving since colonial times, is one of the main supports of such local government services as police and fire protection and education. Although some features of the tax—such as those which require intragovernmental uniformity in tax rates and property assessments—represent an attempt to obtain a fair distribution of the tax burden, the tax has always been the subject of substantial controversy. The controversy, however, has intensified on many levels in recent years.[1]

Academic economists, employing different theoretical models, have debated the effects of the tax on income distribution. It has been argued that the property tax is unduly regressive, and concerned legislators in some states have attempted to offset this perceived characteristic by introducing "circuit breaker" provisions and other measures which provide some tax relief for the aged and the poor. The employment of property tax as the basis of local educational expenditure has been attacked on the grounds that the resulting disparities in school spending among local districts are unfair and unconstitutional. Criticism of the tax has been more than academic; use of the tax is being curtailed by taxpayer restrictions such as Proposition 13 in California and similar measures in other states.

Partially as a result of these developments, local government reliance on the property tax has been diminished somewhat. General revenue sharing (GRS) and other aid from the federal government and substantial increases in state funding levels—especially support for education—have reduced the share of total local revenues raised by the property tax. The increased use of other taxes, especially in cities, has added to the percentage of local government tax revenues based on property tax. In spite of these developments, the property tax is, and is likely to remain, the most important source of local government revenues.

Criteria for tax equity, efficiency, and effectiveness

Several criteria may be used to decide whether to impose a tax and to judge its equity, efficiency, effectiveness, and long-range acceptability. These criteria are briefly set forth as essential background for the sections of this chapter that deal with the origin and development of the property tax, the controversial areas affecting the property tax, and the administration of the property tax.

1. *Fairness*. A tax should reflect the ability to pay of those who bear its burden, or the tax burden should be matched by the benefits that taxpayers receive. In general, taxes that take a higher percentage of the income of the poor (regressive taxes) are considered unfair.
2. *Certainty*. The rules of taxation should be clearly stated and evenly applied. In the case of the property tax, appraisal of property should reflect its market value without bias.
3. *Convenience*. A tax should be convenient to pay, with billing dates that coincide with the income streams of taxpayers. However, the opportunity to make monthly escrow payments (under mortgage contracts) and

quarterly payments has made payment of the tax more convenient than a lump sum payment each year.

4. *Efficiency*. Fair administration should be feasible and efficient. The administration and collection costs should not be out of proportion to the revenues. A tax should be appropriate for its geographical jurisdiction; it should neither be easy to avoid nor too costly to enforce.
5. *Productivity*. A tax should produce sufficient, stable revenue.
6. *Neutrality*. A tax should not distort the way a community would otherwise use its resources—unless it is very clear that a change is socially desirable.

Origin and development of the property tax

The property tax is not a tax on *all* wealth; it is a tax on certain types of wealth, that of a person or a firm. Real estate is the main element in the tax base. Many elements of personal property are not taxed, and the property of some owners (other governments and nonprofit institutions) is exempt. The tax rate is applied to the assessed value of a taxable property owned on the assessment date. The assessed value ideally reflects the value of the property involved; no reduction is made in the assessed value because of a mortgage or other debt carried on the property.

In the colonial period, various categories of property were listed as part of the property tax base, with a specific tax rate for each category. Unless a type of property was specifically cited by law, it was not included in the tax base. However, by the middle of the nineteenth century, the tax had evolved into a general property tax. All property was considered part of the tax base unless specifically exempted by law; and a uniform rate, specified by a state law or constitution, must be applied to all property within each district. Property ownership was considered an indicator of the ability to pay taxes, an equity that precluded discrimination among types of property as well as among taxpayers.

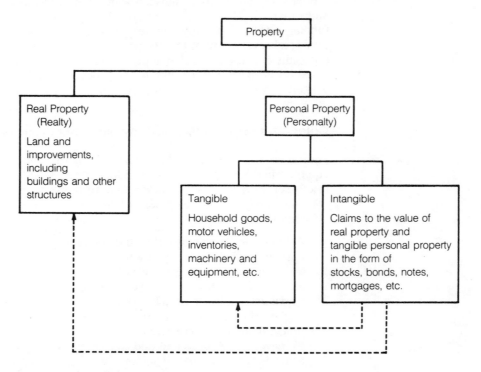

Figure 6–1   Categories of real and personal property.

At the time, the evolution of the tax to a general property tax and the development of uniformity provisions were thought to be reform measures designed to remedy the ills of special property taxes. More recently, some states have introduced property tax classification and provided different rates for different categories of property. These measures, too, are considered reforms. In some cases, different rates are established for residences, farms, and businesses, resulting in different impacts on the distribution of the tax burden. In other cases, different rates on agricultural and open space uses is an attempt to preserve farmland and undeveloped areas.

There are very practical problems with discovering, assessing, and applying a property tax to intangible personal property such as securities, mortgages, and cash. This kind of property generally is exempted from taxation or taxed at lower rates than tangible property. Moreover, a tax on intangibles is easy to avoid and costly to administer fairly. Thus, while some have proposed taxing intangibles at relatively low rates, others argue that it is wisest to eliminate intangible property from the property tax base altogether.[2]

Scope of the property tax

In few places is there a truly general property tax, one that covers and taxes all properties at uniform rates. Although some states have as many as twenty-five classes of property, the tax revenue is primarily derived from real estate that consists of land and improvements and structures on the land. This is clearly shown by the data on property tax collections by source in Table 6–1. Nearly half of the local property tax revenue in 1967 and 1977 was from residential real estate, including farm residences and single-family and multiple-family homes. In 1977, business real estate, exclusive of public utilities, accounted for 18.7 percent of total property tax collections, a decline from the 20.5 percent share in 1967. Real and personal property tax collections from public utilities declined from 7.5 percent of the 1967 total to 5.7 percent of the 1977 total.

Personalty, or tangible and intangible personal property as distinct from real estate, declined in relative importance as a source of tax collections. Where

	1967		1977	
Source	Amount (in millions)	Distribution (%)	Amount (in millions)	Distribution (%)
Households[2]	$13,293	51.0	$32,982	52.7
Realty[3]	11,957	45.9	30,447	48.6
Personalty[4]	1,336	5.1	2,535	4.1
Business firms	10,155	39.0	21,642	34.6
Realty[5]	5,327	20.5	11,672	18.7
Personalty[6]	2,883	11.1	6,405	10.2
Public utilities	1,945	7.5	3,565	5.7
Acreage in farms	2,082	8.0	5,973	9.6
Vacant lots	517	2.0	1,938	3.1
Total	26,047	100.0	62,535	100.0

Table 6–1   Estimated property tax collections by source: 1967 and 1977[1]

Source: U.S. Advisory Commission on Intergovernmental Relations.

1 Includes state property tax collections, estimated at $862 million for 1967 and $2,260 million for 1977. The state taxes were primarily from utilities, railroads, and motor vehicles.
2 Includes farm homes.
3 Includes both single-family dwelling units and apartments; in 1977, about $26 billion, or 41 percent, was from single-family homes and about $5 billion, or 8 percent, from multifamily units.
4 Includes taxes on furniture and other household effects, motor vehicles, and intangibles.
5 Commercial and industrial, other than public utilities.
6 For other than public utilities, includes taxes on merchandise and on manufacturers' inventories, tools, and machinery.

personalty was taxed, it was mostly on the inventories and equipment of merchants and manufacturers and other business firms (except utilities). It declined from an 11.1 percent share in 1967 to a 10.2 percent share in 1977. Taxes on such items of personalty as furniture and other household effects, motor vehicles, and the intangible personal property of households declined from 5.1 percent in 1967 to 4.1 percent in 1977.

The property tax is levied by some state governments as well as by local governments. In fact, in 1902 the states collected $82 million in property taxes, which was 52.6 percent of total state tax revenues. By 1978, however, state property tax revenues, which had risen to $2.3 billion, only represented 2.0 percent of total state tax collections.[3] The states, taxing primarily utilities, railroads, and motor vehicles, make minimal use of property taxes. States have come to rely primarily on sales, income, and other excise taxes, and virtually have left property taxation in the exclusive domain of the local governments. On an overall basis, property tax revenues have declined relative to other taxes. Property taxes accounted for 82.1 percent of the sum of state and local tax revenues in 1902. This ratio declined to 45.9 percent in 1948 and to 34.1 percent in 1978.

Revenue growth

The decline of the importance of the tax on an overall basis does not mean that there has been any decline in the absolute level of property tax collections by local governments. The average yearly rate of increase in local property tax collections was greater than 8 percent through the 1970s. As Table 6–1 shows, collections increased by nearly 150 percent from 1967 to 1977. The property tax still represented 89 percent of local government taxes in both 1902 and 1948, although it had become more than 97 percent of the total in 1932. By 1978 there was an increased use of other local taxes. Nevertheless, the property tax still accounted for more than 80 percent of local government tax collections.

Nationally, the property tax has remained the major source of local financing for local government services. Property tax revenues did not rise as rapidly as total local government revenues or expenditures in the 1970s, largely because of the dramatic increases in federal and state grants and partly because of the increased local government employment of sales and excise taxes. However, the property tax remained important in many communities, especially in particular areas of the nation. In twenty-two states, local governments derived 90 percent or more of their direct tax revenues from the property tax. The New England, Great Lakes, and Rocky Mountain regions relied most heavily on property taxation. In the Southeast there has been less reliance on property taxation and more use of the sales tax. In the Southeast, however, nine local governments derived, on the average, more than two-thirds of their local tax collections from levies on property.

Controversial areas

Although the property tax has remained the major tax of local governments, it has for a long time been one of the least popular sources of public revenue. The tax has been attacked as unfair because the base, unlike that of a net wealth or income tax, does not fully reflect ability to pay and appears to impose unreasonable burdens on the poor. The very nature of the tax has been attacked as one that cannot be administered efficiently or fairly and as one that has encouraged urban blight, suburban sprawl, and unfair disparities in local government services. More recent analyses, however, have challenged the traditional view that the incidence of property taxation rests most heavily on those with lower incomes, and changes in state laws and local practices have reduced some of the regressive pressures.

As a local tax used to support local services, the property tax is a highly visible levy whose costs can be related directly to the benefits of local government programs. This visibility is part of the basis for two developments that originated in California in the 1970s and have had impact over the whole nation. One of these was the problem involved with use of property taxation as the basis for local expenditure on public education; the other was a general move to limit the burden of property taxation and the level of local government spending.

Financing education

In 1971, the California Supreme Court ruled that a local government system to finance public education that discriminates among students on the basis of wealth in the school district is in violation of the equal protection clause in the United States Constitution.[4] In a state school program that relied on local property taxes, the quality of a child's education would depend on the property values of the community. A child in a poor community would receive less of an education than a child in a wealthy community. The Serrano case, and others that followed in other places, made it clear that the wealth or income of the state as a whole should determine the level of spending for every child in the state.

Although the court decisions required the end of any discrimination against any definable group and called for more intrastate equalization of educational spending, the means to accomplish this became the responsibility of the state legislature. The property tax was not discarded as a major source of school support, nor was there any attempt or directive to equalize educational spending on a national (rather than intrastate) basis[5]—even though the reform of the system of financing public education was a matter of national concern.

Among the ways that states could respond to the move for reform was to increase their efforts under equalization and support programs for public schools. During the decade 1962–1972, the national average of state shares for the support of public elementary and secondary school education rose only from 40.5 percent to 42.0 percent of total local school costs. However, by the 1978 school year, the state share had risen to 48.3 percent. State governments now provide the financing for the major share of local expenditures for schools.[6] With the rising contributions from the states and from general revenue sharing in the 1970s, there was a decrease in the pressure on local property taxation for the support of the schools.

The tax limitation movement[7]

From the mid-1970s on, there has been a growing movement to enact restrictions on the growth of taxes. The restrictions that have been used are not uniform across all states. In a number of states, limits have been placed on revenues alone; in other states, limits have been placed on expenditures. Sometimes the limits have come in the form of amendments to state constitutions; sometimes they are simply acts of the legislature. The modern movement to limit governmental activity began in California, with an attack on the property tax spearheaded by Harold Jarvis. The experience in California culminated in voter passage of the famous Proposition 13.

The revolt against the property tax stems from the combination of two developments: the proportionately greater growth of property values relative to income and the increasing employment of such sophisticated devices as the computer to keep assessments up-to-date. The success of the assessor, one who keeps assessment values abreast of rising property values, means that in boom areas such as California, the property tax escalates faster than income and various government units ride a curve of rising revenues.

The essential features of Proposition 13 have been neatly summarized by William Oakland:

The Jarvis-Gann Amendment, or Proposition 13 as it has come to be known: (1) restricts the property tax rate to no more than one percent of assessed value; (2) sets assessed value for a property which has not been transferred since 1975–76 equal to its fair market value in that year plus two percent per year (compounded); in the event that the property has been transferred since 1975–76, the market value at the time of sale is used (plus the two percent growth factor); and (3) requires that new taxes or increases in existing taxes (except property taxes) receive a two-thirds approval of the legislature in the case of state taxes, or of the electorate, in the case of local taxes.[8]

Although the initial voter approval of the Jarvis-Gann Amendment that placed Proposition 13 into the California constitution caused considerable trepidation among local state officials, the actual belt tightening and cutting of programs was less than anticipated because the state government had a considerable surplus, which it parcelled out to the local governments. The initial passage of Proposition 13 has been followed, however, by the passage of Proposition 4, which is essentially an attempt to further restrict increases in governmental activity. Proposition 4 limits increases in governmental spending to increases in population and to the consumer price index (CPI) or state per capita personal income, whichever is lower. Thus, it is worth noting that although the Jarvis movement and Proposition 13 were most heavily directed against the property tax, there is some evidence that the voters in California also have been registering a general protest against the size of the public sector.

The underlying forces leading to Proposition 13 and the potential economic and financial impact of tax limitation legislation were the topics studied at a conference held in 1978 at the University of California, Santa Barbara. The proceedings contain some important insights into the implications of the tax limitation phenomenon.[9]

Shapiro, Puryear, and Ross, for example, suggest that Proposition 13 may be best explained not as a simple reaction against a Leviathan government but rather as "an expression, by the property owner-voter, of dissatisfaction with bearing a growing share of the public financial responsibility."[10] Between 1965 and 1979 the assessed values of single-family housing in California increased at a much faster rate than the assessed values of commercial and industrial property in that state. Shapiro et al. also point to public opinion findings that implied that Californians were generally satisfied with the level of public services received. Legislation that changes the mix of taxes in favor of sales and income taxes may, by favoring these more elastic revenue sources, actually promote a larger rather than a smaller public sector was another point made by Shapiro et al.

In another interesting contribution, Brennan and Buchanan suggest that the taxpayer revolution can be satisfactorily understood only in a public-choice setting they call the nonbenevolent despot model. In such a system, constitutional rather than electoral constraints may be needed to express citizen preferences.[11]

Is the current wave of tax and spending limitation movements a transitory phenomenon? Michael Boskin feels "that nothing could be further from the truth." Boskin's insight is that "the concern over government spending and taxes is primarily a concern over the total tax burden and the aggregate amount of spending at all levels of government."[12] Taxpayer unrest has developed because "all growth in income in the United States since 1973 has been either eaten away by inflation or gone into government spending."[13]

Tables 6–2 and 6–3 contain data compiled by the U.S. Advisory Commission on Intergovernmental Relations (ACIR) that show the extent of the tax limitation

Table 6–2 State limitations on local government taxing and spending powers

Item	Property tax rate limits	Full disclosure laws	Property tax levy limits	Expenditure lids	Assessment constraints
Number of states with such laws *prior to 1970*	40	0	3[1]	1[2]	0
Number of states with such laws *by November 1979*	40[3]	10[4]	20[5]	8[6]	6[7]

Source: ACIR staff compilation based on data prepared by IAAO, CCH, and ACIR.

1 Prior to 1970: Arizona, Colorado, and Oregon.
2 Prior to 1970: Arizona.
3 Due to rapidly rising property values, tax rate limitations have lost most of their effectiveness as a tax control mechanism. As a result, states are now adopting other forms of tax and expenditure controls.
4 Includes only those states that require automatic property tax rate rollback to offset most or all of annual increases in the assessment base in the absence of a rigorous full disclosure procedure, *i.e.*, paid announcement of proposed tax increase and public hearings. States included are as follows: Arizona, Florida, Hawaii, Maryland, Montana, Texas, Virginia, Tennessee, Kentucky, and Rhode Island.
5 By November 1979: Alaska, Arizona, Colorado, Delaware, Indiana, Iowa, Kansas, Kentucky, Louisiana, Minnesota, Ohio, Oregon, South Carolina, Utah, Washington, Wisconsin, Florida, Massachusetts, New Mexico, and Utah.
6 By November 1979: Arizona, Iowa, Kansas, New Jersey, Massachusetts, Nebraska, Nevada, and California.
7 Includes those states placing a limitation on annual assessment increases. States with such limitations by September 1979 include: California, Idaho, Minnesota, Iowa, Maryland, and Oregon. In addition, Nevada will join this list if a ballot measure approved in 1978 receives voter approval again in 1980.

movement. The number of states with levy limits on property tax has increased dramatically since 1970. All of this legislation is bound to have serious effects because all states do not have surpluses to act as a fiscal cushion against the new limits. Since the federal government is itself in a belt tightening mood, it is not likely that the tax limitation pressures will be mitigated by increased state and local reliance on federal aid. State and local governments will be forced, therefore, to increase their productivity, make greater use of fees and charges, and shift some services to the private sector. In her analysis of the tax and expenditure limitation movement, Deborah Matz recognized these forces and concluded:

It seems more likely than not that even if the limitation movement per se has lost some of its momentum, fiscal austerity at all levels of government will prevail. The biggest losers stand to be the poor and lower income families who may not be able to afford new or increased user fees or private service contracts.[14]

Despite the reduction in local cost pressures on education and the property tax reductions resulting from Proposition 13, major efforts also were made in California to limit local expenditure.[15] Other states during the 1970s moved to limit both taxes and expenditures, as illustrated in Tables 6–2 and 6–3.

The requirement to balance budgets in local governments has led some analysts to conclude that the controls of the 1970s went beyond the attempts made in 1930 to limit the burdens of the property tax. The rationale for a balanced budget is to limit local government expenditures and taxes simutaneously and, in some states, to shift the burden from property to other tax sources or to shift some of the financing burden to the state governments.[16] One analyst suggested that rejection of tax increases in the Michigan tax rate referenda, for example, generally indicated that local services had attained or exceeded the level voters considered optimal.[17] In any case, voter initiative provisions on tax rates and other property tax controls were said to have increased because of the rapid growth of local government spending and taxes.[18]

Although some critics of such controls have suggested that simply reducing the property tax would not improve its fairness,[19] ACIR has called for moderation (1.0 percent to 1.5 percent of market value) in the use of the property tax base.

Table 6–3 Recent state and local revenue/expenditure limitations 1 January 1976–1 January 1980.

State	Year	Constitutional or statutory[1]	State limitation	Local limitation[2]	Remarks
New Jersey	1976	S	X	X	State expenditure growth is limited to the increase in state personal income. Municipalities cannot increase their budgets by more than 5% per year. Both limits can be exceeded only by a majority vote on a referendum.
Colorado	1977	S	X		State general fund expenditures are limited to a 7% annual increase. An additional 4% may be allocated to a reserve fund, but amounts over 11% must be refunded to taxpayers.
Michigan	1977	S	X		A Budget Stabilization Fund was established, with provisions for pay-in to the fund during periods of economic growth and pay-out during recessionary periods. It is now used in conjunction with the 1978 state spending limitation.
Rhode Island	1977	S	X		The legislature adopted a non-binding "suggested" 8% cap on the annual growth of budget appropriations.
Tennessee	1978	C	X		Increases in appropriations from state tax revenues are limited to the estimated growth in the state's economy. The lid may be exceeded by majority vote of the legislature.
Arizona	1978	C	X		State spending is limited to 7% of total state personal income. The limit may be exceeded by ⅔ vote of the legislature.
Hawaii	1978	C	X		Increases in state general fund appropriations are limited to the estimated growth in the state's economy. Larger increases must be approved by a ⅔ vote of the legislature.
Michigan	1978	C	X		State tax revenues can increase only as fast as the growth in personal income. If revenues exceed the limit by more than 1%, the excess is refunded through the income tax. If the excess is less than 1%, it is placed in the Budget Stabilization Fund. The limit may be exceeded if the Governor specifies an emergency and ⅔ of the legislature concur.
Texas	1978	C	X		Increases in appropriations from state tax revenues are limited to the estimated growth in the state's economy. The limit may be exceeded by a simple majority of the legislature.
California	1979	C	X	X	Increases in state and local appropriations are limited to population growth and inflation. The limits may be exceeded, but appropriations in the following three years must be reduced to prevent an aggregate increase in expenditures. The limits may be changed by the electorate, but the change is effective only for three years.

Table 6–3 (continued)

State	Year	Constitutional or statutory[1]	State limitation	Local limitation[2]	Remarks
Louisiana	1979	S	X		State tax revenues can grow only as fast as the increase in personal income. Proceeds from severance taxes are not included in the limitation.
Massachusetts	1979	S		X	Increases in local government expenditures are limited to 4%. Override provisions are included. The limitation expires 31 December 1981.
Nebraska	1979	S		X	No political subdivision may adopt a budget in which the anticipated receipts exceed the current year's by more than 7%. Further allowances are included for population growth exceeding 5%. The limit may be exceeded in the event of an emergency or upon voter approval.
Nevada	1979	S	X	X	The state budget is limited to the 1975–77 biennium budget adjusted for population changes and inflation. Local budgets are tied to 1979 fiscal year budgets adjusted for population changes and a partial inflation allowance. The limits may be exceeded "to the extent necessary to meet situations in which there is a threat to life or property."
Oregon	1979	S	X		The increase in state appropriations for general governmental purposes for the 1979–81 biennium is limited to the growth in state personal income in the preceding two years.
Utah	1979	S	X	X	The annual increase in state appropriations is limited to 85% of the percentage increase in state personal income. The increase in local revenues may not exceed 90% of the percentage increase in state personal income, with further adjustments for population growth allowed. The limits may be exceeded by a two-thirds vote of the legislative body of a unit of government.
Washington	1979	S	X		State tax revenues can grow only as fast as the average increase in state personal income over the three previous years. The limit may be exceeded by a ⅔ vote of the legislature.
TOTALS			15	6	

Source: ACIR staff compilations based on: Commerce Clearing House, *State Tax Reporter*; National Conference of State Legislatures, *A Legislator's Guide to State Tax and Spending Limits*, March 1979.

1 C-Constitutional. S-Statutory.
2 Only the six state actions that placed overall limitations on local government revenues and expenditures are included in this table. Since 1970, states have imposed approximately 35 other restrictions on the ability of local authorities to raise property taxes.

"As with any other tax, the heavier it becomes, the less obvious are its virtues and the more glaring its defects,"[20] according to ACIR. Nevertheless, some concern remains for the equity of the tax and the traditional argument that the incidence of the property tax is regressive, falling more heavily on those with low incomes than on those with high incomes.

Tax incidence

The argument that the property tax is regressive relies on several assumptions about the shifting of the tax burden and the spending patterns of different income groups. It is assumed that taxes on owner-occupied homes cannot be shifted, while the taxes on other residential property are shifted to renters in proportion to rents paid. The burdens of taxes on commercial and industrial properties also are assumed to be shifted to consumers through the prices charged for goods and services of these firms.

Statistical studies show that those with lower incomes spend a higher percentage of their incomes for consumption, and specifically for shelter, than do those with higher incomes. If this observation is coupled with the idea that much of the property tax burden is shifted through higher prices for goods and services, including housing, it appears that those people with lower incomes bear a greater tax burden as a percentage of their incomes. Using these assumptions, ACIR has published estimates of the incidence (burden) of the property tax as a percentage of the 1972 incomes of families in various income classes. The property tax burden was greatest on families with incomes of less than $3,000 in 1972, or 13.0 percent of family income. The burden declined to 8.0 percent in families with $3,000 to $4,999 in income. It continued to decline as income rose, to 4.4 percent for the income groups making from $20,000 to $49,999 and to 2.1 percent of those incomes of $1 million or more. While the average burden was 5.0 percent of income, given these assumptions, those with incomes of less than $10,000 were found to carry a greater tax burden.[21]

Henry Aaron and others have challenged the traditional view of the regressivity of property taxation. Aaron suggests an alternative shifting assumption and warns that measuring the burden in relation to current income rather than permanent income may be misleading. Even if property taxation is viewed as an excise tax on housing, Aaron has said, some measures indicate that the effective incidence of the tax shows progression for homeowners and proportionality for renters rather than regressive effects. Aaron views the property tax as a kind of national tax on owners of capital. He concludes that property taxes are thus borne by all owners of capital in the nation in proportion to their ownership of capital. Because ownership of capital and levels of income are correlated he concludes that the incidence of the property tax is, in the long run, progressive.[22]

ACIR also has published estimates of the distribution of the burden of the property tax as a percent of 1972 income, assuming that the tax on improvements is borne only by owners of capital. These estimates show the burden declining from 7.2 percent for those with family incomes under $3,000 to 2.6 percent, for those with incomes from $10,000 to $14,999. However, the burden then rises in stages to 24.5 percent for families with incomes from $500,000 to $1 million, and declines to 18.2 percent of income for those with income levels of $1 million or more.[23] Given the assumptions that relate the tax burden to capital owners, these estimates indicate that the property tax is regressive for lower-income classes and that the burden declines as income rises. Beyond the middle-income range, however, the tax is progressive because the burden rises with increased levels of income. ACIR notes that this progressive effect may be overstated because the implicit income values for the shelter in owner-occupied homes is not included in the definition of income groups or in the estimates of the burden.

The ability of capital owners to shift the burden of the tax to others (in rental fees or in prices charged for products) has been viewed as critical to the determination of whether the property tax is progressive or regressive. Richard Musgrave has noted that different conditions in various markets lead to different conclusions about shifting the tax burdens for rental housing and shifting the burdens for different types of business property. However, he agrees with Aaron's assertion that the use of lifetime income patterns would make the distribution of the property tax burden less regressive; he concludes that the property tax on housing is progressive.[24] Nevertheless, some now believe that the property tax may be less regressive than estimated originally; they feel that the analyses that compare the income and tax rates of local governments are less reliable indicators than studies that compare burdens and incomes of households *within* local governments.[25]

Dick Netzer, an economist who has spent much time studying the property tax, feels that the property tax is not a national tax, nor is it a general tax on capital. He notes that general policies are framed for fifty separate state systems and that separate determinations of rates and assessments are made by some 70,000 local units. As a result, he feels that definitive empirical work must be limited to particular places and times.[26]

Homestead exemptions and circuit breakers

ACIR has noted that homestead exemptions and other programs of property tax relief may not have very significant impacts on the regressive effects of the tax. A homestead exemption excludes a determined amount from the assessed value of a single-family home before the tax rate is applied. The problem, however, is that in many states the amount excluded (sometimes up to $5,000) is the same for all homeowners, regardless of income, age, or property value.

Instead of homestead exemptions, ACIR recommends the use of "circuit breakers," financed by the state government and specifically designed to provide relief for low-income homeowners and renters who may be overburdened by property taxes.[27] Since the adoption of the first circuit breaker by Minnesota in 1964, some twenty-nine states have adopted measures that partially shield low-income families from excessive property tax burdens. Circuit breakers vary substantially among the states. Most states specify income limits that range from $2,500 to $10,000 per couple; the modal level of income ranges from $4,000 to $6,000. In most circuit breaker plans, the amount of relief declines as income rises, and no relief is offered once the income limit is reached. Some states include only homeowners in their programs; others also cover renters. Many programs are restricted to the elderly, with eligibility beginning at sixty-two or sixty-five years of age, and some offer state tax rebates or credits. ACIR has determined that, in general, these special provisions have made the property tax less regressive.[28]

It has been noted, however, that circuit breakers may favor those who are only temporarily poor and those with large amounts of property who may not be poor even if their current amounts of income are low. Moreover, the elderly, who might otherwise liquidate or trade down the value of their homes, may be induced to stay in them if the market values are not fully reflected in the property taxes levied on them as homeowners.[29] A deferral of all or part of tax liabilities until a set future date or until a future sale or transfer of property may be a better alternative to circuit breaker relief provisions for the aged.[30]

Capitalized value of income

The property tax can, as noted above, be viewed as an excise tax on shelter or as a tax stream with a current value that is the equivalent of a sales tax. Another view of the property tax is that of a capitalized tax on property—a view that often cites the property tax as a major cause of urban sprawl.

Both income and property ownership can be viewed as separate bases of ability-to-pay taxation. Income, however, is viewed as a flow over a period of time, while capital, or property, is perceived as a stock of wealth owned on a particular date. These are related concepts because the property is expected to yield income over a future period. One way to determine the value of an asset is to capitalize the value of its expected earnings. For example, assume that a property is expected to yield $500 a year for an indefinite period of time and that the market rate of return to capital is 10 percent a year. The capitalized value of the property is then $5,000, the same as any other asset expected to yield $500 a year given a market rate of return of 10 percent. The owner of that property has levied on his or her account an ability-to-pay tax that is similar to the ability of another person who has an income of $500 from another source. A tax of 1 percent on the property value then imposes an annual burden of $50, the equivalent of a 10 percent tax on the $500 income cited in this example.

Circuit breakers The circuit breaker provision for property taxes is an attempt to relieve persons of tax burdens that are excessive, in relation to their incomes or ability to pay. This provision is analogous to a circuit breaker to prevent electrical overloads. It is designed to protect the poor from a "tax overload" without affecting the property tax revenues from those who are able to pay. This is usually done by providing the relief at the expense of the state, rather than that of the local, governments. The relief, available to the elderly, the poor, or both (depending on the program), phases out gradually as the income of the taxpayer rises, and it is not available for those above stated income levels.

A property tax burden is considered excessive when it exceeds a stated proportion of household income. This varies among the states, from 4 percent to 7 percent. Many states provide ceilings—on incomes, the value of eligible property, and the amount of rebate or relief—and provide relief only for those above 62 or 65 years old. Some states provide relief for renters as well as for homeowners, assuming that a stated proportion of rent (varying among these states from 10 percent to 30 percent) is for property taxes.

The U.S. Advisory Commission on Intergovernmental Relations considers this approach superior to homestead exemptions because the circuit breaker recognizes degrees of need for relief from the property tax. Because it is state financed, the circuit breaker does not burden local governments, especially those where the elderly and poor may be concentrated. However, some object to the provision on several grounds: (1) it fails to recognize fully the ability of the eligible taxpayers to pay with savings, securities, or other assets; (2) it protects the estates of the elderly, whereas permitting deferral of tax payments would not; (3) it permits elderly owners to keep properties off the market, preventing potentially better uses and making property more expensive and more difficult to obtain for the young; and (4) it encourages greater local government spending by making local officials less sensitive to the income pressures of taxpayers. Of course, proponents of the circuit breaker offer responses to each of these arguments.

Source: U.S., Advisory Commission on Intergovernmental Relations, *Financing Schools and Property Tax Relief—A State Responsibility* A–40 (Washington, D.C.: Government Printing Office, 1973), pp. 43-51.

Moreover, whenever there is a change in the tax, the difference may be capitalized and reflected in property value. In the example above, a property yielding $500 in income was valued at $5,000. If, with no other changes, an annual property tax of $100 were levied, the effect would be to reduce the aftertax income to $400. As a result, the value of the property would fall to $4,000, reflecting the capitalization of the tax increase. However, if the tax increase was accompanied by additional services (e.g., improved education or recreation), this could increase the demand for such property and offset the effect of the tax increase. A tax decrease (with no drop in services) could be expected to increase the aftertax income and the capitalized value of the taxed property.

The process of capitalization of the property tax has been cited as a cause of urban sprawl. In some areas, central city tax rates have risen more rapidly and are higher than those in suburban areas. The effects of this are greater tax burdens placed on property owners in the city, and a decline in the value of city property. Although city land and existing structures would have lower values, those planning new construction may nevertheless buy more expensive land in the lower-taxed suburbs—and still receive a lower tax bill and lower overall costs when the improvements and new buildings are counted. This spread of residential and commercial structures to lower-taxed outlying areas has been described as urban sprawl.

Classification by use

Several different approaches have been taken in response to the problems of inner city deterioration and urban sprawl. In nine states and the District of Columbia, property is classified according to its current use.[31] As a result, open land such as that used for agriculture may be taxed at a lower rate. A change to urban uses would result in higher property tax rates, a process that slows the growth of urban sprawl. Tax classification is also used to realign the burden by placing higher rates on business properties than on farms or homes.

Another tax reform provides a lower rate for improvements to deteriorated properties. A 1977 Pennsylvania state law permitted several cities in that state to allow property tax exemptions for a number of years for improvements to deteriorated properties or to properties in deteriorating areas.[32] The purpose of these exemptions is to encourage redevelopment of properties and renovation of neighborhoods.

In California and several other states, special programs have been designed to prevent conversion of agricultural land to other uses. The landowner agrees to maintain the land in agricultural use for ten years; in return, the property tax assessment is based on the capitalized value of the land in agricultural use, rather than on the market value of the land. The owner may incur a substantial tax obligation if he or she cancels the agreement. The criticisms of this arrangement have been that it carries special benefits for the owners and that it is an insufficient inducement to prevent development in the urban-rural fringe areas. Some have suggested land-use zoning instead of differential property tax assessment as a more effective planning tool.[33]

Property tax administration

Some controversy would be present even if the property tax were administered perfectly and uniformly. Because of its inherent features, the property tax has been very difficult to administer. As a result, many criticisms and proposals for reform of property taxation deal with its administration. A prerequisite to evaluation of the criticisms and reform proposals is an understanding of the process of property tax administration.

Property tax relief and reform   The International Association of Assessing Officers believes that the attention being focused on government spending in general and on the property tax in particular is healthy. The property tax, although maligned by many, has several significant attributes, particularly in a federal system of government. As it has evolved, the property tax is the major source of tax revenue directly available to local government and therefore affords local government a strong measure of fiscal independence. Moreover, the tax is a more stable revenue source than either sales or income taxes because property values reflect long-term economic considerations, not short-term economic fluctuations. The property tax captures for local government some of the increases in property value that are partially created by public expenditures. The visibility of the property tax also serves to focus attention on the quality of governance.

Therefore, the International Association of Assessing Officers urges that a thoroughgoing review of each property tax system be performed, that reforms be enacted where they are needed, and that relief be provided when needed in ways that do not violate the ad valorem principles on which the property tax is based.

The International Association of Assessing Officers further believes that property tax systems should adhere to the following general principles.

Assessments should be based on current market values. The property tax is generally conceived to be an *ad valorem* tax, which means that a tax levy is apportioned among taxpayers according to the value of each taxpayer's property.

Assessments should equal estimated market value. Classified property tax systems in which different *tax rates* are applied to uniform, market value assessments are preferable to systems in which uniform rates are applied to nonuniform, fractional assessments.

Assessment systems should be made effective. Methods currently exist that make annual assessments possible at reasonable cost.

Assessors should be shielded from the blame for increasing property tax levies. The popular support for current market value assessment, which is essential to equity in property taxation, is seriously eroded when tax levying bodies ride the coattails of assessors by increasing property tax levies by the percentage increase in assessed valuation following a reappraisal.

Property tax relief should be based on tax abatements or credits, and property tax incentives should be based on use restrictions or on abatements or credits. Property tax relief and/or incentive measures that are based on reductions of assessed value or on other-than-market-value assessment standards have several undesirable attributes. Most significantly, each reduction in the property tax base shifts the obligation to pay property taxes to nonfavored taxpayers.

Exemptions should be kept to an essential minimum, and the rationale for and benefits received by the community from exemptions should be periodically reevaluated. .

Source: Excerpted from International Association of Assessing Officers, "Property Tax Relief and Reform: Statement of the International Association of Assessing Officers," *Assessment Management,* vol. 1, no. 4 (July–August 1979): 29–31.

Discovery

Proper assessment is the keystone of an equitable structure for the property tax. The first step in the administration of the tax is the discovery of the tax base. It is difficult to find intangible assets such as cash, bank deposits outside the assessment district, and other assets for which ownership is not subject to registration and records. Discovery is likely to be limited to the declaration of the owner, plus reliance on other uncertain tax data (e.g., federal income tax returns) or specific legal actions (e.g., probation of an estate) that yield a property listing. The discovery of intangible property may largely depend on the compliance and self-assessment of individuals. Many of these persons may rightly feel that by revealing their assets they incur a tax burden that many others are happy to forgo. Discovery is difficult and uncertain; enforcement costs for full compliance are prohibitive; and high rates of taxation on intangible property invite low rates of compliance. Because the tax on intangible property represents double taxation, the abolition of a tax on intangibles rather than an intensive effort to improve its administration may be the best solution to the administrative problems.

Because the process of discovery of personal property other than automobiles is difficult and incomplete, assessors have tended to be cautious in enforcing this part of the tax. The principal efforts to improve property tax administration are likely to continue to focus on real property.

Discovery of real property is relatively easy. Not only does the property exist *in situ*, and therefore is subject to canvass, but there is also a conventional system for recording both its description (especially the location of land and boundaries) and its ownership.

The initial task of discovery is to record on appropriate forms all of the relevant details about the property. Prerequisites to this task, however, are the establishment of a staff and organization, the selection of a form, and the provision of a system to maintain records and to retrieve information. Not too long ago, the emphasis was on a checklist of data on the location of land and the nature of improvements. Today the emphasis is also on the ability to use computers, specifically to record and retrieve the information.

Inventory

In preparing the property list (inventory), the boundaries as such may not be recorded for the computer. Identification of parcels (tracts or plots of land) will be on the basis of drafting, mapping, and a numbering system designed to permit revisions that could result from consolidation or subdivision of properties. Aerial photographs may be used to confirm the location and to identify parcels and improvements, to establish relationships among different areas, and to check for changes. Such aerial photographs have led to the discovery of land areas that had been omitted from tax rolls for many years.[34]

Assessment

Once discovery and inventory are completed, the property may be appraised. Appraisal and assessment are the heart of the administration of a property tax; in this process, the share of the tax burden is determined for each property owner. The assessor's job is to establish a valuation for each parcel; this determines the total value of the property in the district. Assessment is a complex task. It may not yield to rule-of-thumb appraisal or arbitrary judgment; both equity and law require that each valuation be defensible. The assessor is frequently called on to defend the accuracy of any valuation as well as the uniformity of the method of appraising the value of properties.

The assessor's goal generally is to value the land and improvements of each parcel at the market price (variously characterized as actual, fair, true, cash, or money value) and then set the assessment on each parcel at some uniform percentage of its market value. This is not an easy task. Only a very small proportion of the property on a tax list during any fiscal period is subject to an arm's length market transaction where an actual price would help establish market value. Even when there is direct evidence of a sale price on a parcel, the assessor must be sure that the listed price reflects the market. He or she must be sure that the price listed is not the result of a forced sale or of a transaction between relatives where undervaluation may reflect a gift or other special circumstances.

Annually bringing the assessment of each parcel of taxable property up to market value is highly desirable, even in a relatively static economy. The dynamic nature of the real estate market, especially in metropolitan areas, often prevents assessors' offices from maintaining current market values on the list of properties. In the midst of rapid change and development, many assessors can only hope to do appraisals and reassessments on a fraction of the existing list of taxable property in any given year. Simply making sure that new construction is added to the current tax list may become a major task.[35]

As a result of such pressures, most assessors do not attempt annually to reflect the changes in market price levels. Instead, they try to maintain uniformity in the fraction of current market value at which each parcel is assessed. Even in states where the law specifies that assessments should be at 100 percent of market value, the actual average assessments will vary from this mark.

Some of the differences between assessed and market values reflect administrative problems in reassessing all properties to reflect annual changes in market price levels. Also, many local assessors deliberately use fractional assessments in an attempt to achieve uniformity in the relationship between the assessed value and market value for each property. The rationale for uniformity is that as long as a uniform assessment percentage is applied to all market values, the shares of total property tax revenues borne by each property owner are not distorted. This has been countered by arguments that such underassessment distorts the true tax rate, and that it complicates the administration of state equalization programs that may be related to the assessed property values of the districts. The latter problem, however, is generally solved through sampling techniques. State equalization boards, using the results of their sample surveys, adjust the local assessment ratios for the purposes of state programs.[36]

Where there is an active, competitive market for homogeneous items, market forces will establish a going price that can be used by assessors and other appraisers to formulate the market data approach to assessment. Even when going market prices are subject to frequent change (e.g., the markets for securities, commodities, and livestock), prices are quoted to establish values on a particular day. These market values can be used to impute the value of the units that were not sold on that day. Similarly, current market price data are the most direct evidence of current property market values and should be relatively accurate, even for properties that have not recently changed hands.

Some problems arise, however, because each property is in some way unique. The market values of particular properties, therefore, cannot be directly imputed from transactions on other parcels without accounting for the differences and similarities among them. Nevertheless, it is also clear that even when a small proportion of properties in a particular area is sold during a period of observation, the prices of these transactions provide useful information on the values of other parcels in the area.

Use of sales data   Sales data have been used by assessors and other appraisers for a long time. The simplest way to estimate the market value of a property has been to note the recent sale prices of comparable parcels. Assessors, therefore, note all sales and their characteristics. In some jurisdictions, the sale of a property is a signal for the reassessment of that particular property based on its most recent price; the data in such cases is clear, current, and direct. If there is no revaluation of the properties in the area or district as a whole, however, then the revaluation of recently sold properties will result in higher property tax burdens only on those particular properties. There is a lag in reassessment of unsold parcels and, therefore, in the redistribution of the property tax burden—solely because of the timing of a sale. If a small staff or other constraints preclude annual review and reassessment of *all* properties, it would be more equitable to postpone the reassessment of any properties bought on the market until the number of transactions yields sufficient evidence (and there is enough time) for a general reassessment.

Annual reassessment, at least through the use of traditional methods of viewing and appraising properties, has been beyond the financial capacity of most assessors. Nevertheless, the assessor who has access to a computer may find a reasonable basis for more frequent reassessment. The assessor can code and transfer most of the information on the property records—including property descriptions and assessed values—to computer files. The assessor can, similarly, record all property transactions by noting the price that is stated when the deed is recorded. In places where the full purchase price is not required to be written on the deed or reflected by transfer tax stamps, the information can be obtained by talking with the participants in the transaction.

The sales files may then be listed by the identification number of the parcel (which will also indicate its location), the date of the transaction, the assessed value, and the sale price or adjusted market value. This procedure permits the calculation of an assessment/sales ratio—the ratio between the assessed value and the price. This process has been used not only by local tax bodies, such as counties or school districts, but also by state tax equalization boards and by the surveys made for the 1977 Census of Governments.[37] If the assessment process has been reasonably accurate and the property market stable, the assessment to market price ratio will be close to the official assessment ratio of the jurisdiction.

Separate samplings may be developed for different areas of the district, for different types of property, for each zone, or for any other relevant characteristic. The assessment ratios obtained may serve as the basis for updating assessments in each relevant category of similar properties. Adequate sales data should permit this procedure to be carried out annually at a reasonable cost with a minimum amount of on-site appraisals.[38]

Statistical approaches A somewhat more sophisticated method for bringing assessments up-to-date is multiple regression analysis, which is essentially a statistical method for correlating independent variables with a dependent variable to predict market value.

In appraisal, the characteristics of properties may be used as independent variables in an equation where the dependent variable is the estimate of property values. The coefficients for the independent variables in the regression equation indicate the expected changes in property value from a change in the independent variable (e.g., the nature of improvements).[39]

The employment of market data through various statistical techniques and tests, then, may be used to obtain the assessment values. In some instances, however, properties are not easily or directly comparable to other properties and can make the market data approach unreliable. In these instances, two other methods may be employed for assessment purposes. One of these is to estimate the replacement cost for the improvements on the property. The other approach is to capitalize the net income derived from the property.

Multiple regressions for property values   A multiple regression for assessing property values takes the form of:

$$\hat{y} = a + b_1 x_1 + b_2 x_2 + b_3 x_3 + \ldots + x_n$$

where $\hat{y}$ equals the estimated market value of properties; $x_1, \ldots, x_n$ represent the values of the independent variables; $b_1, \ldots, b_n$ represent the coefficients or parameters for the independent variables; and a represents the intercept value, or the estimated value if zero values were associated with the independent variables.

For this purpose, the independent variables would be the characteristics of the properties in the sample. Examples of such variables would include lot size, location, front footage, type of building, type of construction, number of rooms, and square feet. The data used to estimate the property value would be the market value (dependent variable y) and the property characteristics (independent variables x) for each parcel in the sample of recorded sales.

To see how the equation would be interpreted, let us assume that the equation is related to single-family homes, that x_1 is the independent variable representing the number of bathrooms, and that b_1 (the coefficient for x_1) is $800. On this basis, with all other property characteristics or values for independent variables held constant, the estimated sales price ($\hat{y}$) would increase by $800 for each unit increase in the value of x_1, or for each additional bathroom. If the equation is in logarithmic form, the value for b_1 would be expressed as a percentage change in the value of the estimated sales price for a change in the value of the independent variable. Uses of the equation would include the prediction of different levels of prices associated within different neighborhoods of a community as well as the prediction of different property values within a neighborhood that are associated with differences in lot size, size and type of structure, and other characteristics.

If the capitalization argument is followed, however, the tax rate also has an impact on the property value which, in turn, has an impact on the tax. If these interrelationships are not taken into account, the estimated coefficients will be biased. Multiple regression analysis must be used very carefully.

The replacement value approach involves an estimate of the value of an existing improvement or structure on the property based on the current cost of constructing the structure, less a depreciation allowance for the age of the building. The size, number of rooms, building materials, and similar characteristics of the structure are specifically taken into account. The estimate of replacement cost is made according to current building costs.

The depreciation factors permit the value of the building to be adjusted according to its age and condition. These factors, classified by types of structures, are found in the depreciation tables, which are part of the assessor's manuals. The subtraction of depreciation from the cost of reconstructing the structure yields a net replacement value. This may be roughly checked against available current prices for alternative buildings, even though the buildings may differ somewhat in construction, age, or condition.

The land value of the building site would be estimated separately. This is done by noting sales prices of land that is similar in terms of zoning, general location, size, and any other factors that might affect desirability and price. Both front footage and area of the site may serve as bases for determining the lot value; the values derived may be roughly compared to market transactions for vacant land. Finally, the total of land value plus the depreciated replacement cost of the structure may be compared to the recent sale prices of other properties in order to test the estimate of market value. Although sale prices are used to confirm the estimated assessed value, the other steps are required because no property is exactly similar to another.

When buildings are clustered in housing developments or industrial parks, the adjustments in estimates of property values may be relatively easy. These adjustments are necessary to recognize differences among land values for particular properties. The external checks for market prices may be applied to groups of similar properties to determine the separate assessment valuations for each of the properties involved.[40]

Another method of estimating the market value of property is to capitalize the gross income derived from the property. This is done by discounting the gross income at a weighted average rate of the going rate of interest and the desired rate of return on the equity investment in the property. The approach is seldom used as the sole basis for assessment, but it is useful in checking the values derived by the other approaches.[41] Direct capitalization is particularly helpful when the market for a type of property is imperfect or limited in scope (e.g., hotels and theaters). The success of direct capitalization hinges on the availability of reliable estimates of annual gross income or rent, accurate estimates of operating expenses, and allowances for depreciation. The availability of such estimates permits the calculation of the income for the property. The income or annual rent after operating expenses may then be divided by a current discount rate to estimate the property value. For example, if the net cash flow from a property is $100,000 and the required rate of return is 12.5 percent, then the estimated property value would be $800,000. The sale of similar properties in the estimated price range will confirm the assessor's valuation.

The capitalization method leads to underassessment, however, if the property is not used for its highest possible income—for example a property being held primarily for speculation on future appreciation in value. A case such as this should be revealed in the process of checking the results of the capitalization method with available market data. Any large disparity in estimates of market value—in the absence of specific zoning, classification, or other provisions to the contrary—should be resolved by using the estimate reflecting highest possible returns. The higher value, indicated by sales data, would reflect the market estimate of the capitalized value of the property in its highest, most profitable use.[42]

None of the three methods (market price, depreciated cost, or capitalized value) is likely to be used exclusively. Even when market data are scarce, the available sales transactions are still used to check the values determined by other approaches. The combination of these methods and the existing and developing analytical techniques provide adequate bases on which the assessor can determine reasonable estimates of true values in all but the most extraordinary situations.

Extraordinary cases do exist. For example, such properties as an operating railroad or public utility that serve an area larger than a particular district are not appropriate subjects for local assessment. Estimates of the values of the separate parts of a system may make little sense compared to a valuation of the system as a whole. It is questionable whether a locality that has a portion of the total system—the railroad yards and terminals—in its boundaries should impose a cost on all riders. It is also questionable whether utilities should be required to pay a property tax that is built into the utility rates for all users—especially when there are other taxes on utility revenues. In many states, the state government assumes the responsibility for the assessment of railroad and utility property. In some instances, the states apportion the centrally assessed value among the districts; in others, the states collect the tax for themselves.[43]

For some industries, alternative taxes have been developed in lieu of the property tax. The effects of the property tax could conflict with public policy. For example, property taxes on the value of forests may induce earlier cutting than would otherwise be economically justifiable. In many jurisdictions a severance tax, which is levied on the value of timber when it is cut and sold or used by the owner, has replaced the property tax.[44] The severance tax does not require annual payments, which might force the owners to cut timber prematurely in order to raise cash to pay taxes. The severance tax has also been used in extractive industries.[45]

Periodic reassessment   In a dynamic economy, periodic reassessment is necessary to maintain a reasonable relationship between the assessment base and market values. The problem does not involve just the base but also involves the more important problem of keeping individual properties in line. Although market trends may be clear for real estate prices as a whole, the rate and direction of the trend are not likely to be uniform. There can be many declining neighborhoods in a central city that is surrounded by exuberant suburban developments. During the same period, market values in various neighborhoods could be declining or rising. Periodic reassessment must be frequent enough to reflect these types of situations. In large assessment districts with well-staffed offices, periodic reassessment is a continuing function. Every property is assessed every few years, using a combination of mass appraisal and site-visit techniques and the application of sampling and statistical methods. There may be, of course, some lag in the adjustments for different areas, but the judicious rotation of areas should permit an organized staff to deal with this problem, in spite of the budgetary constraints that may preclude annual reassessment of all areas and parcels.

In the many smaller districts, staff limitations (in both numbers and competence) may preclude the frequent reassessment of existing parcels. The principal effort may be devoted to recording new properties and construction and to noting new prices reflected in transfers. In such cases, the passage of time nurtures inequity. The longer the time between reassessments, the greater the variations between the assessed and market values for particular properties, and the greater the dispersion in the ratios of assessed to market values among properties and neighborhoods.

The most reasonable solution to this problem lies in the consolidation of the smaller assessment districts to achieve economies of scale, which has been occurring to some degree in recent years. There has been a decline in the number of assessment districts and a concomitant increase in the areas served by full-time assessors of greater competence.

A second and perhaps better solution lies in the periodic reassessment of the smaller districts by outside agencies, preferably by professionally qualified consulting firms. A new assessment of all areas and properties in the district is necessary. After giving property owners adequate notice of the new values, a procedure for extensive review and appeal is usually established before the results of the reassessment are used to determine the tax levy. The reassessment should result in a substantial reduction in the coefficient of dispersion for the district, that is, how close the assessed values of different properties are as percentages of their market values.

A general reassessment should be carried out periodically. There are good reasons for doing so. Clearly, a ten-year period is too long to permit dispersion to continue, especially where there is much new construction and where the market is particularly active. The less frequent the reassessment, the more heroic the final adjustments will be and the greater the stress on individual property owners. Sharp changes in value will surely raise opposition to the implementation of reassessment; such opposition is less likely if changing values are accommodated more gradually.

The difficulty individual property owners may have in meeting sharply rising tax levies during a period of rapid value changes may lead to calls for special classification of land for agricultural use, or for a moratorium on the implementation of the new assessments on old holdings. Such measures may be opposed by the owners of new homes who, when old properties are reassessed, benefit from the equalization in the tax burden.[46]

Assessing assessment   How is the quality of assessment itself to be assessed? One way the effectiveness of the assessment process may be tested is by calculating the average coefficient of dispersion or average deviation from the mean. This coefficient reflects the closeness of the range of the ratio of the assessment values to market values for different properties. It therefore estimates how accurately the assessor apportioned the property tax burden among owners on the basis of property values. While more sophisticated statistical techniques can be used, the coefficient of dispersion historically is the accepted measure of uniformity in assessment practice.

The coefficient is calculated in four steps. First, the assessment ratio for each parcel in a sample of recently sold properties is determined. Use of the ratios, instead of the amounts, permits comparisons for different types of properties in different ranges of values. The second step is to determine the mean average or median of the assessment ratios for the sample of transactions. The third step is to compute the average deviation of the individual property assessment ratios from the mean average or median assessment ratio. The final step consists of relating the average deviation to the mean average or median assessment ratio. The result is the coefficient of dispersion.[47]

The four steps are illustrated in Table 6–4. The coefficient of dispersion equalled 17 percent. This measure, if based on a representative sample of different types of property, may be used to grade the effectiveness of the assessment process in a district. A coefficient of dispersion of 10 percent or less is usually considered acceptable because of imperfections in the data and the problems inherent in valuation procedures. The coefficient of dispersion in the example cited would be considered one that would indicate some problems. Many students of property tax administration are concerned with the results of surveys that

Table 6–4   Illustrative table for coefficient of dispersion

Property	Recent price[1]	Assessment value[1]	Assessment ratio[2]	Deviation from average or median[3]
Parcel A	100,000	37,000	37%	55 − 37 = 18
Parcel B	80,000	40,000	50%	55 − 50 = 5
Parcel C	75,000	30,000	40%	55 − 40 = 15
Parcel D	70,000	42,000	60%	55 − 60 = 5
Parcel E	65,000	35,000	63%	55 − 63 = 8
Parcel F	60,000	33,000	55%	55 − 55 = 0
Parcel G	35,000	28,000	80%	55 − 80 = 25
	Mean assessment rate		55%	Avg. deviation 9.4%

$$\text{Coefficient of dispersion} = \frac{\text{Average deviation from mean assessment ratio}}{\text{Average assessment ratio}}$$

$$= \frac{9.4}{55.0} = .17 \text{ or } 17\%$$

1 Hypothetical values are used for this illustration.
2 The assessment ratio is the assessment value as a percentage of the recent price. The average for the seven parcels is calculated at 55%. For this illustration, the mean or average value is equal to the median value associated with Parcel F. Use of the median is an alternative to use of the mean value and, where the values are different, the results may vary.
3 The calculation of the deviation is for the absolute value and disregards the sign, or whether the assessment ratio on a parcel is above or below the average or median.

indicate that 80 percent of the assessment districts have coefficients of dispersion at 20 percent or above.[48]

A problem encountered in some localities is that of the assessor who—despite claims that the same assessment ratio is used for all types of property—tends to favor or to discriminate against industrial, commercial, and rental residential properties. Private dwellings, for example, may be assessed at 60 percent; rental properties, at 50 percent; commercial, at 40 percent; and industrial, at 30 percent. If there are enough representative sales in each category, the assertion of classification bias can be tested objectively. The test is similar to the coefficient of dispersion; the average assessment ratio for each category is substituted for the assessment ratios of the separate properties. This procedure permits the calculation of a coefficient of dispersion relating the average assessment ratios of the different classes of property to the overall ratio for the district.[49] The different assessment ratios, however, may reflect a political view on the tax-bearing capacity of different properties.

Another problem that sometimes appears is overassessment of low-value properties in relation to the assessment of higher-priced properties. Sometimes called regressive assessment, this may occur because the assessor is more familiar with the values of lower-priced properties, which generally are sold more frequently. When the assessment ratios on smaller properties are generally above the average, the ratios for the larger properties tend to fall below the average. Table 6–4 illustrates the problem of regressive assessment. The average assessment is 55 percent. The properties with sales prices of $75,000 or more are assessed below average; those with lower prices are assessed above average.

The problem of regressive assessment may also be exposed by calculating the price-related differential in the assessment ratios. The first step in measuring the price-related differential is to calculate a weighted aggregate assessment ratio (the total value of all assessments divided by the total values of the parcels in the sample). The second step is to calculate the unweighted average of the assessment ratios. The means of the unweighted assessment ratios divided by the aggregate assessment-sales ratio gives the price-related differential. If the two ratios are equal, the price-related differential will be 1, or 100 percent. If the price-related differential is substantially greater than 100 percent, it suggests underassessment of higher-priced properties. A value considerably less than 100 percent would indicate the underassessment of lower-priced properties.

The existence of a price-related differential may be more important for properties in a given category than among categories.[50] Political problems may arise if there is a price-related bias in the assessment ratios of residences in general, or if one section of the city or district is overassessed relative to other districts in the area. A lower assessment of industrial properties as a category (as compared to the assessment ratios for residential or commercial properties), however, may, be the result of a deliberate policy to attract industrial employers and to stimulate economic development.

The coefficient of dispersion may be used to compare the assessment efficiency of different districts. A district is said to be doing work of acceptable quality when the coefficient of dispersion for single-family nonfarm houses in the jurisdiction is less than 20 percent; and yet, 70 percent of the areas sampled as long ago as 1961 failed to meet that standard.[51] The evidence suggests that there is still a need for better property tax administration in a substantial majority of the districts.[52]

Assessment is a complex and often controversial task, and the persons who manage this function carry heavy responsibilities, particularly for the equitable treatment of all taxpayers. The assessment process is facilitated when the components are clearly understood and when the techniques employed make full use of the latest statistical tools and methodologies.

Deriving the tax base

In addition to assessment, the administration of a property tax involves numerous procedures, including establishing rates, billing, enforcing collection. The procedure for determining the tax list is an example. Some properties and owners are eligible for exemptions. These exemptions, which may be partial or complete, are granted under law on the basis of the use of the property (e.g., hospitals, homesteads, and educational, and religious institutions) or on the basis of the status of the owners (e.g., the elderly, veterans, persons with low income, and firms with industrial development incentives). These exemptions vary in their financial impact. In some jurisdictions the impact can be extremely severe if a high proportion of the land is held by large universities, churches, hospitals, public housing authorities, or state and federal government agencies. Even when these organizations make payments in lieu of taxes, the payments seldom equal the amount that would be obtained through property taxes. Of course, the tax exempt entities may return services and economic value to the community in excess of the taxes forgone. In general, though, it may be better to subsidize such activities directly rather than by tax exemption.

Determining the levy

The budget officers usually subtract the estimated amounts of revenues to be derived from sources other than the property tax from the total estimated expenditures. The difference between the two determines the levy to be raised by property taxation. The property tax rate is then determined by dividing the required levy by the total value of taxable property assessments. Adjustments are made for anticipated delinquencies and for estimated tax collections paid

Payments in lieu of taxes
Substantial amounts of property are exempt from local property taxation because of ownership by federal, state, and local governments and by nonprofit, private organizations such as churches, hospitals, and universities. The property tax exemption has the effect of providing a subsidy for those owners and for the activities conducted on those properties. In some cases, however, payments are made in lieu of taxes.

For federal properties exempt from local taxes, these in lieu payments may take the form of a share of the revenues derived from the operation of the properties, such as the royalties or the sale of timber, mineral, or grazing rights. In addition, payments may be made in recognition of local government services, such as school districts, under programs to defray costs resulting from the enrollment of children of federal workers or members

of the armed services at nearby federal installations. Payments in lieu of property taxes may also be made by state governments to compensate localities for revenues lost as the result of state mandated exemptions. Payments may also be made on a voluntary basis by some exempt private organization to compensate for local government services.

In lieu payments, however, usually fail to offset fully property taxes that would have been required in the absence of an exemption. Some argue that the subsidies granted to exempt private properties ought to be voted as appropriations; thus, that the costs would be more explicit than they are under tax exemptions.

Source: Joan E. O'Bannon, "Payments from Tax-Exempt Property," in *Property Taxation USA*, ed. Robert W. Lindholm (Madison: University of Wisconsin Press, 1967), pp. 187–212.

from past delinquencies. The resulting tax rate is expressed in terms of the number of mills per dollar (or the number of tax dollars per thousand dollars) of assessed value.[53]

The amount of tax due on each piece of property is the tax rate times the assessed value of the parcel. Bills reflecting the tax assessment, tax rate, total liability, and terms of payment (dates and discount and penalty rates) are sent to the property owner on record by the tax collector. In some states, billing and collection are centralized by county; in others, the cities, counties, and school districts may all collect these taxes separately. The tax traditionally has been collected in one annual payment in the year after the assessment; but use of quarterly and semiannual installments have become more popular in recent years.

The imposition of penalties and interest charges for late payments is part of the program of enforcing collection. Nevertheless, in many jurisdictions the penalty interest rate is below the market interest rate. This has encouraged delinquencies because it is a way for owners to obtain relatively low-cost loans. Liens against the property are imposed when the tax remains unpaid for a long period. Continued delinquency may lead to seizure and eventually to the forced sale of the property to recover the delinquent taxes. Although the functions of the tax collector and the assessor may be separate, their offices should be well-coordinated. Both should have access to information on the tax roll, and both must be prepared to defend their actions in assessment appeals or enforcement procedures.

State supervision

Some of the responsibility for the improvement of property tax administration has been assigned to state governments. The Advisory Commission on Intergovernmental Relations, for example, once suggested that the states reform the tax laws to remove such elements as intangible personal property, which are impossible to administer; to review exemption laws; to consolidate small assessment districts; to improve assessment personnel standards; and to provide strong state supervision, coordination, and appeal procedures.[54]

The case for more active state supervision is based in part on the feeling that state supervision over local government performance in such activities as education and health is no more important (and is no more a violation of strong local government) than supervision to achieve efficiency and equity in local tax administration.[55]

Improvements in administration have been noted at both the state and local levels of government. Some states, for example, have extended technical and advisory consulting services to local assessment districts in addition to taking over the assessment of some categories of property. The size of some assessment districts has been made larger by designating the county as the assessment unit and by consolidating some of the smaller districts. The use of the computer and the recent development of mass reappraisal techniques have been extended.

Nevertheless, some of the basic problems in property tax administration remain. Research has indicated, for example, that the bias toward a lower rate of assessment on properties with higher values does exist. Although more expensive properties pay more in absolute amounts, the effective tax rate (taxes as a percentage of market value) is lower for those properties in many jurisdictions. The property tax has been made somewhat regressive as a result.[56]

Others contend that the failure to reassess properties frequently enough aggravates the regressivity of the tax. The lag in reassessment generally raises the effective tax rates on those properties where values have declined or risen more slowly than the value of others in the same district. The lag in reassessment also has received part of the blame for the acceleration in urban decay.[57] There is a tendency to delay recording declines in property value, and too much haste in recording increases in assessed values for improvements to property.

The failure to assess the values of property that are exempt from taxation has prevented full knowledge of the costs of those exemptions. There have been calls for assessments of the property, for a repeal of permanent exemptions, for exemptions on a limited basis, and for estimates of the revenues lost by exemption of certain properties (including the exemptions used to attract industry) at a cost to owners of taxable properties.[58] A review of the uses of exempt property, to ensure that such uses are in the public interest, has also been recommended as a way to reduce the controversy surrounding property tax exemptions.[59] As part of a package to aid localities, Connecticut has authorized special grants to "distressed municipalities" for 75 percent of the taxes lost in exempting certain manufacturing properties.[60]

Many states and localities offer industrial exemptions as part of their economic development programs, the principal goal of which is to expand or sustain local levels of employment. This goal appears justified because local taxpayers, by bearing a higher property tax burden to subsidize new industry, have something to gain. Higher employment helps to sustain the demand and prices of local property and, ultimately, it adds to the local tax base. Critics of these inducements note that policies of property tax exemption invite retaliation or imitation; so many areas offer exemptions that there is no longer any competitive advantage in doing so.[61]

There have been many problems in attempting to enforce assessment of properties at full (100 percent) and current market value. However, as has been noted, there is no conflict with equity as long as the assessment percentage is used uniformly in the district. In recognition of this obvious fact, fewer states now have legal or constitutional requirements for full market value assessment. In addition to those states where assessment rates may be varied by use, some twenty-four states now have specific assessment/price ratios below 100 percent.[62]

A problem with the assessment of improvements is couched in the disincentive effect on capital investment. Movements favoring land taxation in the United States began a century ago with Henry George. The arguments for taxing land and exempting improvements are compelling. Proponents note that land values are derived from community investment and development of public facilities (e.g., sewers and roads), so that a land-value tax is an appropriate way to recapture some of that value. A tax on land value is also a neutral tax because it does not discriminate for or against any particular land use; the most profitable use is the same before and after a land tax.

Recent proposals would exempt improvements (partially or wholly) in order to encourage building, to achieve more intensive land use, and to reduce urban decay and housing costs by encouraging the replacement of deteriorated buildings on valuable sites.[63] Such proposals, however, have been seriously questioned on the basis of revenue adequacy; improvements are a major part of the current tax base. There have also been questions about equity in the subsequent shifts of the property tax burden. Current owners of land may be penalized because they paid prices based on a long standing tax system. In addition, the need to alter state laws and constitutions imposes serious political obstacles.[64]

An empirical study of the effects of implementing a site-value or land-value tax has indicated that this would lead to a substantial increase in investment in improvements in the long run.[65] The total exemption of improvements, however, would require very high site-value assessments or high tax rates on land to maintain property tax revenues. Other empirical studies indicate that, on this basis, only partial exemption of improvements would be feasible. Otherwise, it would be necessary to supplement property tax revenues with other nonproperty tax sources.[66]

There is, then, no overall panacea to eliminate the problems of property taxation. Most programs for reform are administrative and give highest priority to "maintaining uniform assessments through frequent and regular revaluation of property" as a way to meet concerns for the poor and for urban decay.[67] ACIR calls for market value appraisal by professionals, under strong state supervision or direct state administration of the assessment system, and with disclosure of assessment ratios so that the fairness of the system can be judged. ACIR also calls for state financing of circuit breaker provisions, and for state payment of some state-mandated local expenditures and in lieu payments for state-mandated property tax exemptions. To avoid further imposition of the severe restrictions required under Proposition 13, ACIR recommends moderation in the use of and reliance on property taxation. Use of alternative tax measures and of state support, as sources of revenue that appear more equitable, would relieve pressures to restrict local government programs.[68]

Conclusion

Past surveys on public attitudes toward taxation have shown the property tax to be the least popular. In a 1978 survey, however, the property tax was favored least by 32 percent of the participants and the federal income tax was favored least by 30 percent. The difference is not very large, which ACIR states, gives "little credence" to the notion that people are getting fed up with property taxes.[69] In its study of school financing, ACIR cites several reasons for the unpopularity of the property tax:

1. No other tax is so harsh on low incomes and so "capriciously" related to ability to pay.
2. The tax appears to be anti-housing when compared to the preferential treatment accorded housing outlays under both the income and sales taxes.
3. The tax is on unrealized capital gains, because increased property values are taxed prior to increases in spendable income.
4. Administration of assessment of the tax base is more difficult and subjective (especially during inflation) than for any other tax, and the shock of reassessment is "without parallel" for other taxes.
5. Less frequent payment (for those who do not pay monthly to escrow accounts) makes the cost more apparent and painful than the current payment of sales and income taxes.[70]

The property tax as an instrument of local government finance requires that we return to an examination of the criteria noted at the beginning of this chapter.

1. *Fairness.* The tax has been criticized as regressive and unfair. Different analyses, based on different assumptions, have reached alternative conclusions concerning the distribution of the burden of the tax. To some extent that distribution has been changed by circuit breaker provisions although, as noted above, such provisions have been subject to criticism. Property tax classification and equalizing grants (especially for school finance) by state governments also have altered the distribution of the tax burden.
2. *Certainty.* Property tax administration has been criticized as biased and costly. Certainly the variations in assessment practices would not be acceptable for other tax bases, such as income. However, improved state supervision, increased professionalism, and new techniques promise improvements in efficiency and equity.
3. *Convenience.* Provisions for more frequent payments, through lending institutions and collection procedures, have made the property tax much more convenient to pay for many people.

4. *Efficiency*. The property tax can be administered efficiently by local governments. This is not generally the case for other major taxes, such as income and sales taxes.
5. *Productivity*. New construction and rising property values in most areas have increased the tax base and provided a fairly stable source of tax revenues despite some fluctuations in income and employment. Local governments require stable, continuing sources of tax revenues to meet the requirements of locally desired levels of expenditure.
6. *Neutrality*. The property tax has been criticized for its adverse effects on housing and for restricting capital investment. A land- or site-value base would be more neutral although difficult to implement.

The property tax is difficult to avoid (as compared to a local sales tax). The clear evidence of the property tax on an annual bill permits the property owner to evaluate the costs of locally provided services. Any limitations on expanding the tax are likely to reflect voter consensus. For these reasons, the property tax has been deemed a stable and acceptable source of local government revenue that is particularly well suited for local administration. Specific criticisms have evoked specific modifications and improvements, and alternative revenue sources have only been used to prevent excessive reliance on property taxation.

The property tax has been justified by ACIR in part for its ability to capture some of the property values created by the community at large. The high visibility of the tax permits greater accountability in local government, and there are substantial problems in finding substitute sources of local government revenue.[71] Therefore, the local property tax provides a substantial basis for local government autonomy.

The property tax has declined as a percentage of total local revenues while federal and state grants have risen. ACIR has concluded that the response to the Serrano decision should not be a massive federal effort to reduce the reliance on property taxes for local school spending, but that the states should bear primary responsibility to deal with intrastate equalization of school spending as well as with any general property tax relief.[72]

None of the highly charged controversy over the property tax has led to calls for its elimination. Property is taxed everywhere in the United States. There is great diversity in the use of the tax. In 1975–76, the tax was $483 per capita in Boston; it was $93 per capita in New Orleans.[73] That diversity has facilitated testing of new policies in different states in an attempt to judge the effectiveness and the costs of proposed changes. New pressures on the property tax may arise, however, if any increased reliance is dictated by declines in intergovernmental grants to local governments or by increases in local government responsibilities.[74]

1 U.S., Advisory Commission on Intergovernmental Relations, *Financing Schools and Property Tax Relief—A State Responsibility*, A-40 (Washington, D.C.: Government Printing Office, 1973), p. 86.

2 J. Richard Aronson, "Intangible Taxes: A Wisely Neglected Revenue Source for States," *National Tax Journal* 19, no. 2 (June 1966): 184–86.

3 U.S., Advisory Commission on Intergovernmental Relations, *Significant Features of Fiscal Federalism, 1978–1979 Edition* (Washington, D.C.: Government Printing Office, 1979). Most of the historical and current data cited in this section are from tables in this publication.

4 Serrano v. Priest, 5 Cal. 3d 584, 487; P. 2d 1241; 96 Cal. Rptr. 601 (1971).

5 U.S., Advisory Commission on Intergovernmental Relations, *Financing Schools and Property Tax Relief*, pp. 3–4.

6 U.S., Advisory Commission on Intergovernmental Relations, *Significant Features of Fiscal Federalism*, p. 20.

7 See: J. Richard Aronson and Eli Schwartz, "Local Government Finance: Some Current Issues" (Workshop, National Science Foundation and Municipal Finance Officers Association, May 1980).

8 William H. Oakland, "Proposition XIII—Genesis and Consequences," *National Tax Journal* 32, no. 2 (June 1979 Supplement):387–409.

9 *National Tax Journal* 32, no. 2 (June 1979 Supplement).

10 P. Shapiro, D. Puryear, and J. Ross, "Tax and Expenditure Limitation in Retrospect and in Prospect," *National Tax Journal* 32, no.2 (June 1979 Supplement):1–10.

11 G. Brennan and J. Buchanan, "The Logic of Tax Limits: Alternative Constitutional Constraints of

the Power To Tax," *National Tax Journal* 32, no. 2 (June 1979 Supplement):11–22.

12 Michael Boskin, "Some Neglected Economic Factors Behind the Recent Tax and Spending Limitation Movement," *National Tax Journal* 32, no. 2 (June 1979 Supplement):37–42.

13 Ibid.

14 Deborah Matz, "The Tax and Expenditure Limitation Movement," in *Urban Government Finances in the 1980's*, ed. Roy Bahl (Beverly Hills, Calif.: Sage Publications, forthcoming).

15 John Shannon and Carol Weissert, "After Jarvis: Tough Questions for Fiscal Policymakers," *Intergovernmental Perspective* 4, no. 3 (summer 1978): 8–12.

16 Helen F. Ladd, "An Economic Evaluation of State Limitations on Local Taxing and Spending Powers," *National Tax Journal* 31, no. 1 (March 1978): 1–18.

17 John Neufeld, "Tax Rate Referenda and the Property Taxpayers' Revolt," *National Tax Journal* 30, no. 4 (December 1977): 441–56.

18 Ladd, "An Economic Evaluation of State Limitations."

19 Anita A. Summers, "Proposition 13 and its Aftermath," *Business Review* (Federal Reserve Bank of Philadelphia), March–April 1979, pp. 5–11.

20 Shannon and Weissert, "After Jarvis," p. 12.

21 U.S., Advisory Commission on Intergovernmental Relations, *Financing Schools and Property Tax Relief,* pp. 31–39.

22 Henry J. Aaron, "A New View of Property Tax Incidence," *American Economic Review* 64, no. 2 (May 1974): 212–21. This view is fully explained and its implications discussed in: Henry J. Aaron, *Who Pays the Property Tax?* (Washington, D.C.: Brookings Institution, 1975).

23 U.S., Advisory Commission on Intergovernmental Relations, *Financing Schools and Property Tax Relief,* p. 34.

24 Richard A. Musgrave, "Is a Property Tax on Housing Regressive?" *American Economic Review* 64, no. 2 (May 1974): 222–29.

25 George E. Peterson, comment, *American Economic Review* 64, no. 2 (May 1974): 234–35.

26 Dick Netzer, comment, *American Economic Review* 64, no. 2 (May 1974): 231.

27 U.S., Advisory Commission on Intergovernmental Relations, *Financing Schools and Property Tax Relief,* pp. 40–41. These are more fully described in: U.S., Advisory Commission on Intergovernmental Relations, *Property Tax Circuit-Breakers: Current Status and Policy Issues* (Washington, D.C.: Government Printing Office, 1975).

28 U.S., Advisory Commission on Intergovernmental Relations, *Significant Features of Fiscal Federalism*, pp. 3, 64–68.

29 Henry Thomassen, "Circuit Breaking and Life Cycle Lock-in," *National Tax Journal* 31, no. 1 (March 1978): 59–65.

30 Summers, "Proposition 13 and its Aftermath," p.11.

31 U.S., Advisory Commission on Intergovernmental Relations, *Significant Features of Fiscal Federalism,* pp. 69–72.

32 *Citizens Business*, no. 2, (Philadelphia: Pennsylvania Economy League, 26 July 1979), p. 497.

33 Hoy F. Carman, "California Landowners' Adoption of a Use-Value Assessment Program," *Land Economics* 53, no. 3 (August 1977): 275–87.

34 Mason Gaffney, "Adequacy of Land as a Tax Base," in *The Assessment of Land Value*, ed. Daniel M. Holland (Madison: University of Wisconsin Press, 1970), pp. 175–76.

35 John Shannon, "Assessment Law and Practice," in *Property Taxation USA*, ed. Richard W. Lindholm (Madison: University of Wisconsin Press, 1967), pp. 39–40.

36 Ibid., pp. 40–61.

37 See, for example: *30th Certification of the Pennsylvania State Tax Equalization Board* (Harrisburg, 30 June 1978); and U.S., Bureau of the Census, 1977 Census of Governments, *Taxable Property Values and Assessment/Sales Price Ratios* (Washington, D.C.: U.S. Department of Commerce, November 1978), vol. 2, pp. 1–35.

38 Ted Givartney, "A Computerized Assessment Program," in *The Assessment of Land Value*, ed. Daniel M. Holland, pp. 125–41.

39 Paul B. Downing, "Estimating Residential Land Value by Multivariate Analysis," in *The Assessment of Land Value*, ed. Daniel M. Holland, pp. 101–23.

40 Kenneth Back, "Land Valuation in Light of Current Assessment Theory and Practice," in *The Assessment of Land Value*, ed. Daniel M. Holland, pp. 38–39.

41 Ibid., p. 38.

42 James M. Buchanan, and Marilyn R. Flowers *The Public Finances*, 5th ed. (Homewood, Ill.: Richard D. Irwin, 1980), pp. 473–76.

43 James A. Maxwell and J. Richard Aronson, *Financing State and Local Governments*, 3d ed. (Washington, D.C.: Brookings Institution, 1977), pp. 134–65.

44 David Klemperer, "An Economic Analysis of the Case against Ad Valorem Property Taxation in Forestry," *National Tax Journal* 30, no. 4 (December 1977): 468.

45 See, for example: Tax Institute of America, *The Property Tax: Problems and Potentials* (Princeton, N. J.: Tax Institute of America, 1967), pp. 143–204.

46 *Philadelphia Evening Bulletin*, 4 August 1972, p. 5. This account describes the activities, including a protest march, of organizations formed in response to a new reassessment in Bucks County, Pennsylvania. Such protests were by no means uncommon in the 1970s.

47 A technical point worth noting here is that the value of the coefficient will differ if the median is used in this calculation rather than the mean in cases where they are not equal, because that inequality results from a skewed distribution.

48 Harold M. Groves and Robert L. Bish, eds., *Financing Government*, 7th ed. (New York: Dryden Press, 1973), pp. 110–11.

49 These issues are discussed extensively in: Karl E. Case, *Property Taxation: The Need for Reform* (Cambridge, Mass.: Ballinger Publishing Co., 1978).

50 Harold F. McClelland, "Property Tax Assessment," in *The American Property Tax: Its History, Administration and Economic Impact*, ed. George C. S. Benson et al. (Claremont, Calif.: Institute for Studies in Federalism, Claremont Men's College, 1965), pp. 109–10.

51 Dick Netzer, *Economics of the Property Tax* (Washington, D.C.: Brookings Institution, 1966), pp. 177–80.

52 U.S., Advisory Commission on Intergovernmental Relations, *Significant Features of Fiscal Federalism*, p. 57.

53 Bernard P. Herber, *Modern Public Finance: The*

Study of Public Sector Economics, 2d ed. (Homewood, Ill.: Richard D. Irwin, 1971), p. 230.

54 U.S., Advisory Commission on Intergovernmental Relations, *The Role of the States in Strengthening the Property Tax*, vol. 1 (Washington, D.C.: Government Printing Office, 1963).

55 Maxwell and Aronson, *Financing State and Local Governments*, pp. 155–56.

56 David E. Black, "Property Tax Incidence: The Excise Tax Effect and Assessment Practices," *National Tax Journal* 30, no. 4 (December 1977): 429–34.

57 Jerome F. Heavey, "Assessment and Property Tax Impacts," *American Journal of Economics and Sociology* 37, no. 4 (October 1978): 431–36.

58 Aaron, *Who Pays the Property Tax?* pp. 84–85.

59 Summers, "Proposition 13 and its Aftermath," p. 11.

60 *Intergovernmental Perspective* 5, no. 1 (winter 1979): 17.

61 Paul E. Alyea, "Property Tax Inducements To Attract Industry," in *Property Taxation USA*, ed. Richard W. Lindholm (Madison: University of Wisconsin Press, 1967), pp. 139–158.

62 U.S., Advisory Commission on Intergovernmental Relations, *Significant Features of Fiscal Federalism*, pp. 69–72.

63 Dick Netzer, *Economics and Urban Problems*, 2d ed. (New York: Basic Books, 1974), pp. 256–58.

64 U.S., Advisory Commission on Intergovernmental Relations, *Financing Schools and Property Tax Relief*, p. 72.

65 Richard L. Pollock and Donald C. Shoup, "The Effect of Shifting the Property Tax Base from Improvement Value to Land Value: An Empirical Estimate," *Land Economics*, 53, no. 1 (February 1977):67–77.

66 Richard W. Douglas, Jr., "Site Value Taxation and Manvel's Land Value Estimates," *American Journal of Economics and Sociology* 37, no. 2 (April 1978):217–23.

67 Summers, "Proposition 13 and its Aftermath," p. 11.

68 Shannon and Weissert, "After Jarvis," p. 12.

69 *Intergovernmental Perspective* 5, no. 1 (winter 1979): 48.

70 U.S., Advisory Commission on Intergovernmental Relations, *Financing Schools and Property Tax Relief*, p. 30.

71 Ibid.

72 Ibid., pp. 4–5.

73 *Monthly Tax Features* 22, no. 6 (August 1978; Tax Foundation, Inc.).

74 David B. Walker, "The New System of Intergovernmental Relations: More Fiscal Relief and More Governmental Intrusions," *Governmental Finance*, (November 1978):17–22.

Sales taxes, income taxes, and other revenues

Because the property tax is regarded as the mainstay of local government finance, it may surprise some readers to learn that local sales, income, and other taxes, along with charges and miscellaneous revenues, generate over 40 percent of the revenues collected by local governments from their own sources. Moreover, nonproperty taxes and nontax sources of revenue assume larger importance in the wake of initiatives to limit property tax revenues, as represented by the Jarvis-Gann Proposition 13 in California. If such initiatives spread to other states, local governments will seek other revenue sources to compensate for restrictions placed on property taxes. Local sales, income, and other taxes, as well as increases in existing fees and impositions of new ones, provide such substitutes, though "tax cut fever" may spill over to these revenue sources as well.[1]

A partial list of objectives sought by local governments in using nonproperty tax revenue sources would include: (1) obtaining additional revenue while avoiding increases in property tax; (2) achieving a wider distribution of the local tax burden among those who benefit from public services; (3) making the tax structure more flexible so it can be tailored to fit peculiar local conditions; (4) obtaining greater responsiveness of local revenues to rising costs and service demands; and (5) reducing the relatively high rates of taxation that can arise in overlapping jurisdictions when all rely on the property tax as their major revenue source.

In what follows, the significance of local nonproperty tax revenues in the overall revenue picture of local governments is described. Then each source—sales taxes, income taxes, and miscellaneous revenues—is discussed in regard to features, extent of use, operational details, and major issues. A brief evaluative conclusion follows each section.

Importance in the revenue structure

The overall importance of nonproperty tax revenue sources as part of the total revenues available to local government, as well as the composition of these sources, is indicated by Table 7–1. In 1967–77 nearly 80,000 local governments (counties, municipalities, townships, school districts, and special districts) received revenue of over $196 billion. Of this, local *general* revenues amounted to over $102 billion, with property tax receipts accounting for over $60 billion. The remainder, which represented over 40 percent of local general revenues, comprises the five categories of local revenues examined in this chapter.

Table 7–2 shows the trend in percentage of local general revenues from each major source from 1957 to 1976–77. Although no striking changes have occurred, there has been a gradual reduction in the proportion of local taxes from 80 percent to 73 percent over the twenty-year period. Also, among the various taxes, the property tax has assumed lesser importance, as have licenses and other taxes, while the shares of both income and sales taxes have grown.

There is considerable diversity in revenue sources by type of local government. Table 7–3 shows the importance of different general revenue sources to each of the five types of local government. Local income and sales taxes, for example, were considerably more important to municipalities than to other types of local government; correspondingly, municipalities relied less on property taxes.

Table 7–4 indicates the share of each revenue source collected by each type of local government. Municipalities collected the largest share of local general revenues from their own sources, followed by school districts, counties, special districts, and townships. Municipalities collected about 36.0 percent of all locally raised general revenue, but levied and received the bulk of local income and sales taxes and 45.2 percent of the miscellaneous revenues. Municipalities, however, received only slightly over one-quarter of local property taxes. School districts received 30.6 percent of all local general revenues, but collected nearly 44.0 percent of all property taxes.

Table 7–1 Local government revenues from all sources, 1976–77

Classification	Revenue (in millions)	% of general revenue
Total	196,458	
Own sources, total	119,626	
General revenue, total	102,214	100.0
Taxes, total	74,852	73.2
Property	60,267	59.0
Sales and gross receipts	8,278	8.1
Income	3,754	3.7
License and other	2,552	2.5
Charges and miscellaneous, total	27,362	26.8
Current charges	19,097	18.7
Miscellaneous	8,265	8.1
Utility	14,299	
Liquor store	306	
Insurance trust	2,808	
Intergovernmental, total	76,831	
From states	60,277	
From federal	16,554	

Source: U.S., Department of Commerce, Bureau of the Census, 1977 Census of Governments, vol. 4: *Governmental Finances*, part 5: *Compendium of Government Finances* (Washington, D.C.: Government Printing Office, 1979), p. 82.

Table 7–2 Percentage of local government general revenues from own sources, selected years, 1957 to 1976–77

Classification	1957	1962–63	1966–67	1971–72	1976–77
General revenue, total	100.0	100.0	100.1	100.0	100.0
Taxes	80.0	78.3	76.4	75.9	73.2
Property	69.3	68.5	66.2	63.5	59.0
Sales and gross receipts	5.8	5.6	5.1	6.5	8.1
Income	1.1	1.1	2.4	3.4	3.7
Licenses and other	3.8	3.1	2.7	2.5	2.5
Charges and miscellaneous	20.0	21.7	23.6	24.1	26.8

Source: U.S., Department of Commerce, Bureau of the Census, 1977 Census of Governments, vol. 6: *Topical Studies*, part 4: *Historical Statistics on Governmental Finances and Employment* (Washington, D.C.: Government Printing Office, 1979), pp. 52–53.

Table 7–3. Percentage of local government general revenues, by type of local government, 1976–77

Classification	Counties	Muni-cipalities	Townships	School districts	Special districts
General revenue, total	100.0	100.0	100.0	100.0	100.0
Taxes	69.8	71.2	88.2	86.8	24.8
Property	56.7	42.7	80.8	84.6	22.7
Sales and gross receipts	8.7	15.8	3.0	0.6	1.9
Income	1.7	8.5	1.6	0.6	. . .
Licenses and other	2.7	4.2	2.7	0.8	0.2
Charges and miscellaneous	30.2	28.8	11.8	13.2	75.2
Charges	22.2	18.6	6.0	8.6	60.9
Miscellaneous	8.0	10.2	5.9	4.6	14.3

Source: U.S., Department of Commerce, Bureau of the Census, 1977 Census of Governments, vol 4: *Governmental Finances*, part 5, *Compendium of Government Finances* (Washington, D.C.: Government Printing Office, 1979), p. 24.

Table 7–4. Percentage distribution of general revenues collected by type of local government, 1976–77

Type of local government	Taxes						Current charges and miscellaneous		
	Total	Total	Property	Sales and gross receipts	Income	License and other	Total	Current charges	Miscellaneous general revenue
All	100.0	100.0	100.0	100.0	100.0	100.0	100.0	100.0	100.0
Counties	22.3	21.2	21.4	23.9	10.3	24.5	25.1	26.5	22.0
Municipalities	35.8	34.8	25.9	70.3	82.6	59.7	38.6	35.7	45.2
Townships	4.5	5.4	6.2	1.7	1.9	4.9	2.0	1.4	3.3
School districts	30.6	36.2	43.9	2.4	5.2	10.1	15.0	14.0	17.4
Special districts	6.9	2.3	2.6	1.6	. . .	0.8	19.3	22.4	12.1

Source: Same as Table 7–3.

The following discussion of the various taxes and charges is based on a sample year in the late 1970s, but the principles involved are likely to have continuing applicability in the 1980s.[2]

Local general sales taxes[3]

The first local general sales taxes were adopted in the 1930s, a time when significant reductions had occurred in local revenues as a result of the Great Depression. New York City adopted a sales tax in 1934, followed by New Orleans in 1938. In 1950 Mississippi adopted a system of state-administered local sales taxes, an innovation that significantly enhanced the feasibility of the tax for a large number of local governments. The most rapid period of expansion in the use of local sales taxes occurred in the 1960s, when the number of states authorizing local sales taxes increased from twelve in 1963 to twenty-five in 1970.

In the mid-1970s general sales taxes were authorized for use by local governments in twenty-nine states and the District of Columbia, although in three states (Kentucky, Oregon, and Wisconsin) none of the local governments authorized to levy a sales tax had chosen to do so. Authorization for the tax may derive from home rule charter powers, general licensing powers, or specific state legislation. The latter is the source of sales tax authority in most localities.

Among the twenty-six states where local governments actually use the local sales tax, the rate ranges from 0.25 percent to 1.0 percent in every state except Alaska, where the local rate can go as high as 5.0 percent (Alaska does not have a state sales tax). The number of governments using the tax ranges from a high of more than thirteen hundred cities and counties in Illinois to one city in Arkansas.[4]

In 1976–77 general sales tax revenue amounted to $5.472 billion, or about two-thirds of the $8.278 billion raised by local governments from all sales and gross receipts taxes. General sales tax receipts represented 5.4 percent of the general revenues for all local governments; however, for municipalities the percentage was almost twice as great, 9.6 percent.

General characteristics

The local sales taxes used in different localities vary greatly in their specific features, but they have in common some general characteristics that distinguish them from other taxes.

Virtually all general sales taxes are *ad valorem* rather than *per unit* taxes— that is, the tax is computed as a percentage of the value of a transaction rather than as a fixed amount per unit of the good exchanged (as is the practice with cigarette and gasoline taxes).

A second common feature is that the tax is levied on purchasers who buy at retail (as opposed to wholesale). Even though vendors are required to collect and pay the tax to the local government, the usual intent of legislative bodies adopting or authorizing the tax is that it be passed on to consumers by the retailer; hence, the tax is often referred to as the "consumers' sales tax." Separate quotation of the tax from the price is required or encouraged in most states having state sales taxes, and this requirement presumably extends to sales taxes levied by localities within states having such laws. At any rate, separate quotation of the tax is the general practice. Almost every state also prohibits sellers from advertising the absorption of state sales taxes, and such prohibitions likewise presumably extend to local sales taxes in those states.

Since sales taxes are intended to be paid at the retail level, sales for resale usually are not taxed. However, while sales of a raw material to be incorporated into a finished product destined for ultimate sale to the consumer are not taxed, sales of such items as tools and coal, which are used or consumed in manufacturing and not incorporated into the product to be sold, usually are taxable. Hence, tax pyramiding does occur; it is more pronounced for some products and services than for others.

Sales taxes are also called "gross proceeds taxes" because the deductions for losses or necessary business expenses permitted under net income taxes, for the most part, are disallowed; the retailer is responsible for collecting and remitting the tax regardless of whether the business shows a positive accounting profit. Similarly, the sales tax does not take account of the personal circumstances of the consumer, as an income tax often does through the use of exemptions and deductions. Thus, a sales tax is sometimes described as an *in rem* rather than a personal levy. Because of this characteristic, the sales tax is frequently criticized for being both horizontally inequitable (failing to treat persons having the same incomes equally) and vertically inequitable (failing to discriminate appropriately between those having unequal incomes). But as will be discussed later, the *in rem* character of sales taxes is not inevitable or necessary.

A sales tax is imposed directly *on* sales and is to be distinguished from the gross proceeds, occupation, or license taxes that are frequently measured *by* sales. Although the sales tax, on the one hand, and license and occupation taxes, on the other, may be directly related to sales, and although they may be completely passed on to the consumer through higher retail prices, the sales tax (as noted above) is expressed separately as part of the total amount of a sale and is tax deductible by consumers who itemize federal income tax returns. The gross receipts, occupation, and business privilege taxes are not expressed separately in transactions, nor are they deductible by consumers.

Except in states where local jurisdictions administer their own taxes, the base of a local general sales tax levied by localities is almost always mandated to be the same as any existing state sales tax base. Although there is considerable diversity in state sales tax bases, all have certain exclusions of goods purchased for business rather than personal use, as well as exemptions of specific consumption goods and services. These exclusions and exemptions generally apply to local sales taxes as well. Localities in about a third of the states exempt food purchased for home consumption; more than half the sales tax states exempt prescription drugs; and several states exempt clothing. Taking these and other exemptions into account, and deducting other categories of consumer expenditures not subject to the retail sales tax (the major item being housing), it has been calculated that only slightly more than two-fifths of all consumer expenditures are subject to a general sales tax.[5] Hence, local general sales taxes (as well as state sales taxes) have a base much narrower than all consumer spending. Nevertheless, the base is still much broader than that of the various *selective* sales or excise taxes on specific categories of goods such as alcoholic beverages and tobacco products.

To deter residents of a local jurisdiction from making purchases in outside areas where there are no sales taxes or taxes with lower rates, the local sales tax often is accompanied by a *use* tax levied on goods bought outside the jurisdiction and used inside it. The use tax is employed by nineteen of the twenty-six states with local sales taxes.

When the use tax is coupled with the assignment of tax liability at the place of delivery (which frees nonresident purchasers from paying the local tax), the effect, in theory, is to insulate local retailers from loss of sales to either residents or nonresidents. In practice, both of these features of local sales taxes have generated difficult enforcement and compliance problems. These will be considered in more detail below.

Frequency of use and diversity   A bewildering variety of local sales taxes exists at any given time. The frequency of use of the tax by local governments varies considerably by state. In Virginia all counties and cities levy a general sales tax, whereas in both Arkansas and Minnesota the tax is used by only one city. Another difference concerns responsibility for administration. In six of the twenty-six states in which local governments actually use the tax, some or all localities administer (i.e., collect and enforce) their own sales tax; in the remainder of the states, local sales taxes are administered by the state government. Finally, use taxes are levied by localities in nineteen of the twenty-six states.

Three other features of local sales taxes deserve brief description at this point: (1) the method of local tax coordination; (2) the location of liability; and (3) the method of distributing collected tax revenues back to localities in states where there is state administration.

The problem of tax coordination arises when sales tax jurisdictions overlap. Three patterns of response to the overlap question exist. In some states only municipalities can levy a sales tax, and in others only counties can do so. Here, the question of overlap has been handled by establishing exclusive jurisdictions. A second response is to allow the tax paid in one jurisdiction to be credited against the amount owed in another. A third response is no response, with full overlap of the sales tax rates levied in each local jurisdiction. However, some states do limit the maximum total rate that can apply, and a local government given first priority can levy the maximum rate and thereby preclude any other unit from using the sales tax. Counties are given this priority in Colorado, Tennessee, and Kansas. A different procedure, followed by the state of New York, gives cities and counties each the right to levy half the maximum rate allowed under state law.

Location of liability establishes whether purchases made in a jurisdiction are subject to the tax in that jurisdiction or whether the tax, if any, is to be levied where the purchased item is to be delivered. In the mid-1970s, liability was at the retailer location in nineteen states and at the point of delivery in seven others. In the former case, a jurisdiction receives the sales tax on all purchases made within it, whether the purchases were made by local residents or by persons residing outside the taxing jurisdiction. Under a point of delivery system, the jurisdiction where merchandise is delivered receives the revenue generated by its own tax on goods delivered there.

Where the local tax is administered by the state, revenues are sent (usually monthly) by the firms collecting them to the state; the state then distributes the revenues back to the localities. In most states where localities levy a sales tax, the state distributes the revenues back to the location where the tax liability was incurred. Hence, there usually is no redistribution of the sales tax revenue among local jurisdictions.

Administrative procedures (or how to set up your own local sales tax) A brief sketch of the steps involved in setting up and operating a local sales tax may be useful. The procedures can be divided into four parts: preparing and updating a list of local vendors, preparing return forms, mailing returns, and auditing returns to ensure compliance.

Establishing a tax roll of sellers liable for the tax is simplified if there is a state sales tax, because the state's tax roll can be used to identify local retailers. Otherwise, local directories, rolls for license taxes, and other sources must be used. Registration forms are then sent to a list of vendors derived from these sources, and a number is assigned to each form as it is returned, establishing the tax roll. Additional field checks may be necessary to determine whether any vendors have been overlooked.

The second and third steps are the preparation and mailing of tax return forms, which the vendors must file with payment of the tax. Most cities levying a sales tax require such returns to be filed monthly. Examples of two such forms are provided in Figures 7–1 and 7–2. Once returns are mailed, it is necessary to make follow-up contacts with delinquents and nonfilers.

The fourth and final part of the procedure is the auditing of returns to ensure compliance. According to a leading authority on sales taxes, "Auditing by trained personnel of vendors' accounts and records is the key to successful retail sales tax administration."[6] While some cities have a large enough staff of trained personnel for auditing, many have too few and some smaller cities have no audit staff at all. Experience of states with sales taxes indicates that one auditor per thousand accounts is the bare minimum for reasonable enforcement and that one per six hundred accounts is more nearly optimum.[7] This issue will be examined later when the question of state versus local administration is considered.

Revenue yield and the local sales tax structure The revenue yield of any tax depends on the tax base and the tax rate applied to this base. For a given tax rate, the yield from a local sales tax will vary as the base (sales subject to the tax) varies. Of considerable importance to municipal managers are the questions of what revenue yields can be expected from a newly imposed local sales tax, how the yield can be expected to grow with the local economy and to fluctuate over the business cycle, and how exemptions, especially for food, will affect the yield.

DUL-T1 (REV. 5/72)

CITY OF DULUTH, MINNESOTA
DEPARTMENT OF FINANCE AND RECORDS

SALES AND USE TAX RETURN

READ INSTRUCTIONS BEFORE COMPLETING RETURN

IF NO TAXABLE TRANSACTIONS WERE MADE DURING THE PERIOD, WRITE "NONE" ON LINES I AND 4, SIGN AND RETURN TO DEPARTMENT OF FINANCE AND RECORDS, DULUTH, MINN. 55802

MAILING ADDRESS

SALES & USE TAX PERMIT NUMBER

PERIOD OF RETURN

DATE DUE:

LOCATION OF THE BUSINESS TO BE REPORTED ON THIS RETURN

I hereby declare under the penalties of criminal liability for willfully making a false return, that this return has been examined by me and to the best of my knowledge and belief is true and complete for the period stated.

SIGNATURE_____

TITLE_____   DATE_____

DO NOT WRITE IN THIS SPACE

IF YOU USE THE ACTUAL TAX METHOD (SEE INSTRUCTIONS) CHECK HERE

I.	GROSS SALES ◆	
2.	DEDUCTIONS (Enter from line 23) ◆	
3.	NET SALES (Line I minus line 2)	
4.	PURCHASES SUBJECT TO USE TAX ◆	
5.	TOTAL TAXABLE AMOUNT (Line 3 plus line 4)	
6.	TOTAL TAX DUE (1% of line 5) ◆	
7.	A PENALTY	
	B INTEREST	
8.	TOTAL AMOUNT DUE (Line 6 plus lines 7A & 7B) ◆	

MAKE CHECKS PAYABLE TO: "CITY OF DULUTH"

MAIL TO: DEPT. OF FINANCE & RECORDS SALES TAX DIVISION 110 CITY HALL DULUTH, MINN. 55802

CHECK ACCOUNTING METHOD USED IN REPORTING GROSS SALES

CASH ☐   ACCRUAL ☐

AVOID PENALTIES

THIS RETURN MUST BE FILED WITHIN 25 DAYS FOLLOWING THE CLOSE OF THE PERIOD.

NEW OWNERS

DO NOT USE PREVIOUS OWNER'S FORM TO FILE YOUR RETURN – ANY CHANGE OF OWNERSHIP ORGANIZATION OR ADDRESS REQUIRES A NEW PERMIT.

(SEE INSTRUCTIONS)

DD-T 17665-OR1

	DEDUCTIONS		
9	SALES FOR PURPOSE OF RESALE		
10	SALES TO CHARITABLE, EDUCATIONAL, RELIGIOUS AND GOVERNMENTAL ORGANIZATIONS		
11	SALES OF MATERIALS FOR USE IN AGRICULTURAL OR INDUSTRIAL PRODUCTION		
12	SALES IN INTERSTATE COMMERCE		
13	SALES OF FOOD PRODUCTS		
14	SALES OF CLOTHING AND WEARING APPAREL		
15	SALES OF GASOLINE		
16	BAD DEBTS (only when on an accrual basis)		
17	SALES OF GOODS DELIVERED OR MAILED OUT OF CITY		
18	RECEIPTS FROM FURNISHING LODGING		
19	OTHER AUTHORIZED DEDUCTIONS (List separately)		
20			
21			
22			
23	TOTAL DEDUCTIONS (Enter on line 2)		

Figure 7–1   Sales and use tax return, Duluth, Minnesota. (Top portion is front side of card; bottom portion is reverse of card.)

In states having a state sales tax, an estimate of the revenue that can be expected from a local sales tax can be made by obtaining information about recent state sales tax receipts in the local government jurisdiction. If there is no state sales tax, a less precise estimate can be made from the experience of other local jurisdictions of similar size, economic characteristics, and retail outlets, allowance being made for differences in tax rates and exemptions. In either case, if the sales tax is to be applied in a locality adjacent to another nontax area to which retail sales may be diverted, the estimates may be excessive. Some actual experience with the tax will be necessary to determine the revenue it can be expected to yield.

Sales tax receipts obviously will vary with fluctuations in business activity and income of the local economy. A considerable number of investigations have been made to estimate how the yields of major state and local taxes are affected by changes in income; the results of these studies have been assembled by the U.S. Advisory Commission on Intergovernmental Relations (ACIR).[8] Estimates

CITY OF NEW ORLEANS
DEPARTMENT OF FINANCE
BUREAU OF REVENUE
ROOM 1W09, CITY HALL, CIVIC CENTER 70112

RETURN POSTAGE GUARANTEED

LOCATION OF BUSINESS

CITY AND SCHOOL
SALES AND USE TAX RETURN OF

	MONTH	YEAR

1. Sales by Cash and Credit			
2. Sales by Food Stamps			
3. Cost of Tangible Property used or consumed			
4. Total (Lines 1, 2 & 3)			
ALLOWABLE DEDUCTIONS			
5. Sales to Registered "W" Wholesalers			
6. Sales for Further Manufacturing			
7. Sales to "M" Multi-Parish Businesses			
8. Sales to State of Louisiana & U. S. Government			
9. Cash Discounts, Sales Returns & Allowances			
10. Sales in Interstate Commerce			
11. Sales of Gasoline			
12. Sales delivered in Jefferson Parish			
13. Sales delivered elsewhere in Louisiana outside of City of New Orleans			
14.			
15. Total Deductions			
16. Amount Taxable (Line 4 less Line 15)			
17. Tax: 3% of Line 16			
18. Excess Tax Collected (Over 3%)			
19. Total (Line 17 plus Line 18)			
20. Less Vendor's Compensation, if not delinquent			
a. 1% of Tax on Retail Sales			
b. 2% of Tax on Wholesale Sales			
c. Total Lines 20a. and 20b.			
21. Amount of Tax Due (Line 19 less Line 20c.)			
22. Less Credit Sales Tax: (New Orleans Advance retail dealers' tax paid to wholesalers on purchases for resale at retail: Amount of Purchases_____)			
23. Net Tax Payable (Line 21, Less Line 22)			
24. Interest - 1% per month from due date until paid.			
25. Penalty - 5% for each 30 days or fraction thereof not to exceed 25%			
26. Total Tax, Interest & Penalty (Lines 23, 24 and 25)			

Gross Business Reported to State _____

	TYPE PAYMENT
FOR OFFICE USE ONLY	CASH
	CHECK

Date | Sign Here | Signature of Preparer Other than Taxpayer

Make Your Remittance
Payable to
CITY OF NEW ORLEANS

To avoid penalties Return must be filed on or before the 20th day of the month following the period covered.
DO NOT use any other taxpayer's return as this will result in improper credit.

WARRANTY

NO RETURNS WILL BE ACCEPTED UNLESS SIGNED BY TAXPAYER OR AUTHORIZED AGENT.

IT IS HEREBY WARRANTED THAT THIS RETURN, INCLUDING THE ACCOMPANYING SCHEDULES AND STATEMENTS (IF ANY) HAS BEEN EXAMINED BY ME, AND TO THE BEST OF MY KNOWLEDGE AND BELIEF, IS A TRUE AND COMPLETE RETURN MADE IN GOOD FAITH, ON THE BASIS OF THE BRACKET SYSTEM, FOR THE TAXABLE PERIOD AS STATED, PURSUANT TO CHAPTER 56 OF THE CODE OF THE CITY OF NEW ORLEANS, AS AMENDED AND RESOLUTION ADOPTED BY ORLEANS PARISH SCHOOL BOARD LEVYING A 1% SALES AND USE TAX.

DID ANYONE PREPARE OR ASSIST IN PREPARING THIS RETURN OR SUPPLY ANY DATA INCLUDED HEREIN?

HENRY G. SIMMONS
DIRECTOR OF FINANCE

YES | NO

ORIGINAL

Figure 7–2   Sales and use tax return, New Orleans, Louisiana. (Form mailed out with postal indicia [not shown here] printed in top right-hand corner.)

are for state rather than local taxes, but they constitute the best proxy evidence available on the question of yield variability of local sales taxes. The studies of state sales taxes reveal that a 1.0 percent change in total income causes a change in sales tax revenue of between 0.8 and 1.27 percent, with the most frequent estimate in nationwide studies being 1.0 percent. Thus, it can be concluded that sales tax receipts both fluctuate with income and grow over time at about the same rate as income grows. This contrasts with personal income taxes, the yields from which are estimated in all studies to fluctuate (or grow) more than proportionately to changes in income. Property tax revenues, on the other hand, are found in most studies to fluctuate less than income. Hence, the sales tax lies somewhere between these other local taxes in the variability of its yield relative to changing economic conditions.

Exemption of food consumed at home significantly reduces the yield of a sales tax, one estimate being a revenue loss of from 15 percent to 20 percent.[9] Thus, a 5 percent sales tax with no food exemption would generate about the same revenue as a 6 percent tax with food exempt. The major reason usually given for exempting food is to make the sales tax more equitable, but there are other methods that can be used to achieve a similar effect without sustaining the increased costs of compliance and administration that the food exemption causes.

Assessment of major issues

The local sales tax has created problems and raised issues in four major areas: administration, revenue allocation, incidence and equity, and locational effects.

Local administration   Problems of administering the sales tax can be divided into those characterizing local administration and those that occur even when the state administers the tax. These two sets of issues are discussed in turn.

In the mid-1970s six states had sales taxes that were both locally levied and locally administered. In Alaska local administration occurred by default since no state sales tax existed. Arizona, Louisiana, and Minnesota had exclusive local administration, duplicating the administrative apparatus at the state level for collecting the state sales tax; and Alabama and Colorado had a dual system in which the state administered the taxes of some local governments and the local government administered them in others.[10]

Experience with local sales tax administration suggests that it results in higher costs of both vendor compliance and governmental administration than would be the case if administration were taken over by the state. With state administration the same amount of revenue can be collected at a lower overall cost (or more revenue can be collected at the same cost). This is especially the case in five of the six states (all but Alaska) where a state sales tax also is collected, duplicating both the tax collection efforts (state and local) and the vendor compliance costs. Other cost and enforcement problems that characterize locally administered sales taxes are the following:

1. Dissimilar state and local sales tax bases bring additional record-keeping, enforcement, and auditing costs.
2. Uncoordinated tax rates within a state add complexity and cost for compliance and enforcement and may bring tax-induced shifts in retail purchases and retail outlet migration from higher to lower tax areas. Although relocation depends on tax rate differentials, not state or local administration, experience suggests that state administration produces greater coordination of rates and makes large rate differentials less likely.
3. Severe enforcement problems are encountered when localities attempt to designate the place of delivery as the point for imposition of the tax. This is an awkward attempt to keep local merchants from losing sales to

persons living outside the taxing jurisdiction. Sellers are required to keep sales records by geographic area, jurisdictional boundaries, or other devices, which they frequently do not do accurately. The place-of-delivery rule almost invites actual or bogus shifts of purchases to destinations outside the jurisdictional boundaries. Use taxes, the natural complement of the delivery rule, also are notoriously difficult to enforce.

4. Low quality is another characteristic of local administration. Lack of enforcement staff in all but the largest cities and counties reduces yield and multiplies inequities and enforcement problems.

5. Finally, local administration means that some local jurisdictions will lose from a revenue point of view. Only state administration can assure redistribution among competing local governments within a county or metropolitan area.

Are there any advantages to local administration? If not, the question is why pockets of local administration still exist.

Since Charles Tiebout's famous paper was published,[11] economists and others have recognized that the existence of many local governments provides individuals with some ability to choose the mix of taxes and local public services they prefer by "voting with their feet." To the extent that state administration of local sales taxes reduces this range of choice, it imposes some costs on citizens. State administration virtually always requires the local tax to have the same tax base as the state tax, and this may necessitate that a locality give up certain exemptions (e.g., for food) or the application of user taxes to intrastate sales, thereby causing a loss of revenue. (This revenue loss may be more than offset, however, by revenue gains arising from more effective enforcement of the tax.) There also may be loss of local control over tax rates, as states with local administration have much wider ranges of local rates than states with state administration. Placed in the context of the many other dimensions of choice not affected by whether a local sales tax is locally or state administered, it seems unlikely that the losses entailed by state administration (if they could be quantified somehow) would be substantial. More to the point, the costs (though also unquantified) identified by actual experience with local administration seem to loom large in relation to its more amorphous benefits. Balanced judgement by several students of the question strongly favors state administration.[12]

There has been a trend toward state administration, either by mandate or, in states where this is not possible, by persuasion through such devices as free state collection.[13] California and New York have had great success, perhaps partly because they learned from the dismal experience California had prior to state administration.[14] On the other hand, localities in some states (notably Colorado and Alabama) that were collecting their own taxes before the beginning of state administration have been unwilling to surrender this task to the state.

Other administrative issues warranting brief discussion are the identification and assignment of vendors to taxing jurisdictions, charges for state collection, and vendor compensation.

Successful sales tax administration necessitates carrying out the prodigious task of continually verifying and updating the location of vendors relative to the jurisdictional boundaries of sales tax localities. This is necessary not only to ensure tax compliance but also to determine, with state administration, how to distribute tax revenues back to localities. Special problems arise when the vendor has multiple outlets, no fixed place of business, more than one place of business, or a place of business outside the state.[15]

Only three states provided free collection of local sales taxes in the mid-1970s: Ohio, Virginia, and Colorado (in the latter case as an inducement to localities to convert to state administration). The rest charged for local collection with the charge being based on cost, on a fixed percentage of the total revenue collected, or on cost up to some maximum percentage of revenue. States charging a fixed percentage of revenue set the charge as low as 1 percent (Nevada) and as high as 4 percent (Illinois). Actual costs of state collection for *state* sales taxes have been estimated by John Due to average just under 1 percent of revenues.[16] Making the reasonable assumption that this same estimate is applicable to state-administered local sales taxes, it appears that most states using a fixed percentage charge apply a rate that exceeds their collection costs.

As for vendor compensation, some states compensate vendors for collecting and remitting both state and local taxes. These payments are all calculated as a percentage of revenue collected (rather than actual cost), though compensation may be greater for early payment and be forfeited if payment is late. Some states also reduce the percentage compensation if revenue exceeds a given amount. Few studies have been made of actual vendor compliance costs and how these costs vary with revenue collected. Yokum's study of Ohio firms found an average compliance cost of almost 4 percent of tax owed.[17]

Revenue allocation   Because local sales tax receipts depend on sales within a jurisdiction and are usually returned to the source of collection, there may be little relation between the revenues collected and the government expenditures that a jurisdiction makes for local public services. Such problems are most acutely apparent in metropolitan areas where some jurisdictions have few residents and many retail stores and others have few shopping areas but many residents. For example, in 1966–67 in Los Angeles County, sales tax collections per capita ranged from $0.04 in the city of Hidden Hills to $12,051.78 in the city of Vernon. The city of Industry, with 826 inhabitants, had such tremendous sales tax receipts ($1,071.77 per capita) that it decided to purchase the old boxcar that carried the remains of Winston Churchill to his grave as the first item for a city museum.[18]

The basic problem with the revenue distribution of a local sales tax to the source of collection is the lack of correlation between sales tax revenues and the expenditures for services, which are generally more closely tied to population. One solution to this problem would be to allocate the tax receipts back to localities by a formula that took account of the economic and social characteristics of various local jurisdictions. Use of such formulas, however, meet with considerable political resistance because of losses of revenue and local autonomy, and they are used in only a handful of the states with local sales taxes.

Incidence, equity, and the food exemption   The traditional view is that sales taxes are shifted to consumers of the taxed goods and services through higher prices, even though the tax is legally imposed on vendors (or vendors are liable for collecting it). The analysis that leads to this conclusion generally takes for granted that retail sales taxes are really more like selective excise taxes than like a general sales tax on all consumer spending. The basis for this conclusion is the following: When the sales tax is imposed, either the taxed products must rise in price or the factors of production used to make these products must accept lower payments. The latter is unlikely since, with 60 percent of the products and services consumers buy (not to mention tax-exempt capital goods) being exempt from the sales tax, these resources generally can find employment in production of these untaxed products if offered lower returns in the taxed industries. Hence, factor prices are unlikely to fall. Instead, it is more likely that prices of the taxed items will rise, and consumers of the taxed products bear the burden of the tax.

This relatively simple story must be complicated by recognition of the limited geographic area in which a local sales tax applies. The added complication is well illustrated by the border tax problem that can arise if sales tax rates vary considerably between neighboring local jurisdictions. Consumers who make purchases in the lower sales tax area can then escape a portion of their sales tax burden. This loss of sales to adjacent areas may alter locational decisions of business firms and have further effects on all sources of local tax revenue.

Aside from such cases in which there is a substantial border tax problem, the general conclusion is that a local sales tax is borne by consumers in proportion to their expenditures on the taxed goods and services. Given this conclusion about incidence, it is possible to apply two basic principles to evaluation of a local sales tax.

The first principle is that the tax paid by an individual should bear a close relation to the benefits received by the individual when tax proceeds are used to provide local public services. Hence, the relevant questions are whether persons who pay more sales tax benefit to a greater extent from local public services than those who pay less, and, if so, what is the closeness of the match between taxes and benefits. Although studies of the relationship between income of the residents of a local jurisdiction and the demand for local public services are primitive, they nevertheless suggest that there is a fairly low responsiveness in the relative demand for major local services (fire, police, sanitation, education, public works) to changes in income.[19] In other words, benefits as measured by willingness to pay (demand) rise with income, but not in proportion to it. Therefore, to comply with the benefit-received principle, taxes should also rise with income, but less than proportionately to it (i.e., the taxes should be somewhat regressive). The ratio of sales tax paid to income falls as income rises (because expenditures on the items subject to sales tax do not rise in proportion to income). Hence, it may be tentatively concluded that a sales tax is broadly consistent with the benefit-received principle.

The second principle rests on ability to pay, and the sales tax does not usually fare as well when evaluated by the ability-to-pay principles of horizontal and vertical equity. Two persons with the same income may spend very different amounts on taxed items and pay different amounts of sales tax. Hence, equals in ability to pay are not taxed equally. Moreover, a sales tax with no exemption or credit for food tends to be regressive, meaning that persons with lower income pay a higher proportion of that income in sales tax than do those with higher incomes. This occurs because the percentage of income spent on items subject to tax falls as income rises.[20] Eliminating this regressivity is perhaps the major reason food consumed at home is sometimes made exempt from sales taxation. Even though exempting food requires a higher tax rate on other covered items to raise the same amount of revenue, the exemption serves to reduce regressivity, making the sales tax paid more or less proportional to income.

Eliminating regressivity by exempting food is achieved at the cost of greater retailer compliance problems and increases in auditing difficulty. Arbitrary decisions must often be made about what is food consumed at home and what is not (e.g., chewable vitamins, candy, soft drinks, and hot food prepared in a store). Grocery clerks must apply the tax correctly by discriminating between food and nonfood items, a source of increased checkout time, nuisance, and errors. The incentive stores are given to overstate the proportion of sales that are food items must be offset by additional auditing effort to prevent retailer evasion of their full tax liability.

What many regard as a better approach to the regressivity problem is allowance of a tax-free amount of food expenditures. The exact size of the allowance may be determined by an estimate (albeit arbitrary) of the cost of a "minimally necessary" amount of food. This allowance can be implemented by either of two procedures. The first is a tax credit against the state income tax, a procedure followed in seven sales tax states. The second is a direct cash rebate, computed as an amount equal to the sales tax that would apply to the amount of food expenditures to be made tax free. This procedure is followed in Boulder, Colorado. It has the additional advantage, not possessed by the tax credit method, of allowing coverage of all persons regardless of whether they pay any income tax. Additional administrative expense is, of course, required to make the direct cash rebates to consumers.

Both of these systems illustrate how a sales tax can be structured to make it more like a personal than an *in rem* levy. Both of these systems also reduce the large revenue loss (or higher tax rates required) and the administrative costs inherent in exempting food.

Locational effects of sales taxes   If a local jurisdiction imposes a sales tax, and there are adjacent nontax areas, the jurisdiction is likely to lose sales of items included in the local sales tax base because of the price differentials faced by shoppers. The important questions concern the size of the loss and the factors that determine how large it will be. As mentioned earlier, a perfectly enforced use tax in conjunction with an assignment of tax liability at the place of delivery would completely neutralize the effect of such a tax on local retail sales. Because such an arrangement is difficult to enforce, however, the local sales tax imposed by a single jurisdiction can be expected to affect shopping decisions. Hence, the first factor influencing the size of the retail sales loss is the extent to which local sales taxes are used by neighboring jurisdictions. In states where local sales taxation is universal and set at uniform rates, as in California, the problem does not arise (except for possible loss of sales to other states). On the other hand, in metropolitan areas where only the municipality imposes the tax, some shoppers are likely to cross municipal borders to escape it. The effect on shopping decisions clearly depends on how much can be saved on purchases by changing purchase locations, compared to the costs incurred (principally in extra travel time and gasoline expenses) to obtain these savings. Where a large savings potential exists, retail shopping centers may be located just beyond the boundaries of a taxing jurisdiction thereby allowing such savings to be realized by consumers.

All such changes in location decisions based on a desire to escape a local sales tax impose what economists call deadweight losses. The loss is called "deadweight" because it is a pure waste. If a shopper were simply refunded the amount that would be saved by changing the purchase location (and thereby induced to make purchases in the taxing jurisdiction), the shopper would be better off (because extra travel time and expense would be avoided) and the local taxing jurisdiction would have no less revenue.

Several studies have been made to determine the magnitude of sales losses due to local sales tax differentials in circumstances where the effects may be most severe. These studies deal with the "border city" problem and examine losses in (1) cities near state borders where purchases may be shifted to avoid a state sales tax, and (2) cases where city-suburban tax rate differentials exist. McAllister's study of three border cities in Washington (Vancouver, Walla Walla, and Pullman) found that, "in every case for the three cities . . ., the trade pattern is different from what would be expected if the sales tax were not a major factor in buying decisions."[21] For New York City, Hamovitch found that an increase of 1 percentage point in the city sales tax rate reduced sales in the city about 6 percent,[22] and Levin found that the city lost sales of taxed goods and gained sales of untaxed goods.[23] Finally, Mikesell conducted a more general study of the effect of city-suburb sales tax differentials and found (with a 95 percent probability) that a 1 percent increase in the ratio of city to suburban sales tax rates caused per capita city retail sales to fall by 1.69 percent to 10.97 percent.[24] (Little or no work has been done to indicate how these induced changes in purchases have affected retailer location decisions.)

These results suggest that local retail sales can be affected significantly by local sales taxes and imply that, to minimize distortion of locational choices, sales tax rates should be uniform throughout as wide an area as possible. Local sales tax systems that create uniformity, as in Illinois, California, and Virginia, serve to minimize such distortions. Uniformity is particularly desirable throughout a county or metropolitan area.

Evaluation and summary

From the foregoing examination of local sales taxes, it is possible to draw some conclusions about what appear, on balance, to be desirable features for such a tax.

First, successful operation of a local sales tax is more likely under state rather than local administration. State administration brings greater efficiency in operation and greater coordination in the tax rates and tax bases in different locations using the tax.

Second, to avoid complicating compliance and auditing, the base of the local tax should be the same as that of the state sales tax (if a state tax exists, as it does in forty-five states).

Third, compliance is greatly facilitated by locating the tax liability with the vendor rather than at the place of delivery and limiting use taxes to out-of-state purchases.

Fourth, the best insurance against adverse locational effects is to prevent sales tax rate differentials among jurisdictions; tax rates should be uniform over as large a geographic area as possible (i.e., countywide is better than citywide).

Fifth, the allocation of local sales tax revenue between counties and municipalities should be sensitive to the division of local government functions (and hence relative expenditures of each), taking account of the revenues available to the respective local governments from other sources.

Even if these conditions were fulfilled, there remains the fundamental question of whether it is wise to use local sales taxes at all. Considered in the context of this chapter, however, local sales taxes are an important revenue source for many localities. They offer localities some extra degree of autonomy in setting local revenue and expenditure levels. In addition, the local sales tax offers a way (albeit imperfect) for localities to collect taxes for services provided to nonresidents; and the local sales tax may be (in the absence of a food exemption or credit) in rough correspondence with the benefit-received principle.

On the negative side, the tax, unless applied uniformly over a wide geographic area, has adverse effects on locational decisions. It also is not in accord with widely held views of horizontal and vertical equity, though this problem could be remedied at least in part by special credits or rebates for taxes paid on food. Finally, tax proceeds are almost always distributed by sales location and hence may not match the demands of constituents for provision of public services. The first and third problems have led some observers to conclude that when additional revenues are to be provided to local government, allowing increases in local sales tax rates would be distinctly inferior to increasing the state sales tax rate and redistributing the extra revenue to localities on the basis of a formula embodying various criteria of local need, such as population and average income. This argument could be carried further to recommend eliminating all local sales taxes and substituting increases in state sales tax rates, or even replacing all state sales taxes with a national sales tax. Such sweeping changes, however, would likely result in a loss in the ability of local governments to satisfy local constituents and an increase in income redistribution among geographic areas and ultimately individuals.

Local income taxes

Local income taxes were levied by over 4,000 cities, counties, and school districts in the late 1970s. Use of the tax, however, was not uniformly distributed over the country. Except for the 1.0 percent employee license tax in Oakland, California, the local income tax was levied only by localities in the eastern half of the United States. Producing about 3.7 percent of overall local general revenues, the income tax ranked just behind the local general sales tax, which generated 5.4 percent. However, as discovered by the man who almost drowned trying to wade across a lake having an average depth of only two feet, averages or aggregate percentages often fail to tell the whole story. Local governments in Kentucky, Maryland, and Pennsylvania derived a sixth or more of all locally raised general revenues from the tax,[25] and for some municipalities (e.g., Philadelphia), it provided well over half of such revenues.[26]

Local income taxes typically have been adopted in response to stringent fiscal circumstances. Most of these taxes, with the exception of those in New York City, Detroit, and Maryland, were not subjected to close scrutiny to assess their equity and revenue implications prior to enactment. Many of their provisions reflect attempts to circumvent legal hurdles or constitutional limitations imposed by state governments rather than to achieve close adherence to widely recognized canons of taxation. Nevertheless, the local income tax potentially has many virtues because of its revenue potential, certainty of incidence, adjustability to the personal circumstances of taxpayers, and ability to achieve a reasonably close correspondence between tax liability and benefits received from local public services.

The following description and assessment of local income taxes has four parts. The first briefly reviews the history of the tax; the second describes the use and features of the tax as of the late 1970s; the third assesses the major issues and problems surrounding local income taxation; and the last is a brief evaluation of the local income tax as an efficient revenue source.

History of the local income tax

The first modern income tax was adopted by the city of Philadelphia in 1938 under authority from the state (the 1932 Sterling Act) permitting the city to tax any nonproperty sources not taxed by the state.[27] In 1939 the Philadelphia tax was declared unconstitutional by the state supreme court for violating the uniformity requirement of the Pennsylvania constitution, which was interpreted to preclude a progressive income tax. The Philadelphia flat-rate tax was progressive because of an exemption of the first $1,000 of income. The following year the city adopted a flat-rate tax on all earned income (i.e., wages, salaries, and net income of professions, partnerships, and unincorporated businesses) within its boundaries, with no personal deductions or exemptions. Major features of this tax—its flat rate, exclusion of property income and capital gains from its base, and lack of personal exemptions and deductions—have been retained, and it has served as the model for localities in Alabama, Kentucky, Missouri, Pennsylvania, and Ohio.

Between 1940 and 1962 the income taxes adopted by localities were all essentially "earned income taxes" of the Philadelphia type. In 1962 Detroit introduced the first change by levying an income tax on all forms of income, including dividends, rental income, interest, and capital gains. Two years later Michigan adopted the Uniform City Income Tax Ordinance incorporating the provisions of the Detroit tax. The tax base was essentially adjusted gross income as defined in the federal Internal Revenue Code.

The next major innovation occurred in 1966 when New York City introduced a personal income tax very similar to the federal levy. Like the tax in Michigan cities, the resident tax base was essentially the same as the federal base and personal exemptions were allowed. In addition, however, income was taxed at graduated rates (ranging from 0.4 percent to 2.0 percent), and the taxpayer was permitted to take personal deductions. (Married couples were allowed to file separately and assign their combined deductions to the spouse with the higher income.)

A final major development occurred in Maryland in 1967, when the state enacted a law under which Baltimore City and each county must levy a local income tax on residents at not less than 20 percent nor more than 50 percent of the state income tax liability. Increases or decreases in rates between these limits had to be in increments of 5 percent. Nonresidents could not be taxed.

Current use and features

If the income tax is defined very broadly to include not only taxes on the income of individuals and corporations but also payroll taxes paid by employers (because this tax is probably shifted to the workers), by the late 1970s local income taxes were authorized for use by localities in fifteen states and were actually being used in thirteen.[28] These taxes ranged from the New York City tax, which closely resembles the federal income taxes on individuals and corporations, to San Francisco's 1.1 percent payroll tax on employers. Because the most important local income tax from a revenue standpoint is the personal or individual tax, the following discussion will be confined to this tax, which is used by local jurisdictions in eleven states.[29]

Like local sales taxes, local income taxes display considerable diversity. Discussion of the characteristics and details of operation is limited to local jurisdictions with a population of 50,000 and over.

Tax rates Localities in all states but Maryland and New York impose income taxes with a flat rate, frequently 1.0 percent. Philadelphia has the highest rate of any locality (4.3125 percent), even when the highest rates of the graduated taxes in Maryland localities and New York City are included in the comparison. Prior to 1980 the highest rate applied to the top bracket ($25,000 and over) in New York City was 4.3 percent; effective in 1980, the New York rates ranged from 0.4 percent to 2.0 percent. In Maryland counties and Baltimore City, which generally apply a tax consisting of 50.0 percent of the state liability, effective rates range from 1.0 percent to 2.5 percent (for taxable incomes of $3,000 and over); the state income tax rates range from 2.0 percent to 5.0 percent.

In most localities, the same rate applies to the taxable income of residents and of nonresidents earning income in the local taxing jurisdiction. However, Indiana counties are permitted to tax nonresidents at a rate of only 0.25 percent, one-quarter of the resident rate. Michigan cities tax nonresidents at half the rate (0.5 percent) applied to residents; localities in Maryland do not tax nonresidents at all.

New York City has a unique structure: nonresidents pay a flat-rate earnings tax (no exemptions or deductions allowed), with a sliding scale of exclusions for the tax base. A nonresident's total tax liability is not permitted to exceed the liability that would be incurred if the nonresident were treated as a resident. The nonresident rates in the late 1970s were 0.45 percent and 0.65 percent of wages and self-employment net earnings, respectively. Beginning in 1980 these rates fell to 0.25 percent and 0.375 percent.

Coordination to prevent double taxation The possibility that the same income will be taxed twice, once at the place of work and once again at the place of residence, cannot arise in Maryland localities, where only residents are taxed. Nor can this happen in the local jurisdictions of Alabama, California, and Kentucky, where income taxes are technically "occupational license" taxes levied only on the economic activity within the taxing unit, residence being irrelevant for determining tax liability. For localities in states where double taxation might otherwise occur, it is virtually always precluded by a provision for crediting the tax paid in one locality to that owed in another. For example, in Pennsylvania (with the notable exception of Philadelphia) residence is given priority; a taxpayer is allowed to credit the tax paid to the place of residence against a tax levied by the jurisdiction of employment. Michigan localities follow the Pennsylvania pattern. In Ohio, however, most jurisdictions credit taxes paid at the place of employment toward the tax owed in the locality of residence.

The situation regarding nonresident taxation in Pennsylvania is sufficiently interesting to merit further discussion. One set of rules covers Philadelphia, and another set covers the entire state. Philadelphia has a prior claim to the earnings taxes it collects from nonresidents, who are permitted to credit this tax against any levied where they live. Philadelphia has no rate limit and has set a rate of 4.3125 percent; other localities, however, are limited by state law to 1.0 percent. Many suburban "bedroom" communities surrounding Philadelphia have chosen not to levy an earnings tax because, effectively, most of the tax base represented by their residents' earnings belongs to Philadelphia.[30]

Precisely the reverse circumstances have arisen in other metropolitan areas of the state (e.g., Pittsburgh, Scranton, Johnstown, and Erie), where localities have a prior claim to earnings tax collections from their residents. Suburban communities around these areas quickly enacted local earnings taxes following the adoption of such taxes in the cities where many suburban residents work. For example, when Pittsburgh enacted a local income tax in March 1954, 130 local jurisdictions within twenty-five miles responded by enacting their own taxes by the end of the year.[31]

Little overlapping of local income taxes has occurred where several jurisdictions overlap because most states limit the use of the tax to one type of local government (counties in Maryland and Indiana, cities in Michigan and Ohio). In Pennsylvania, where overlapping did occur between school districts and either cities, boroughs, or townships, the rate in each jurisdiction (in all areas except Philadelphia, Pittsburgh, Scranton, and a few home rule municipalities) was limited to 0.5 percent (half the maximum permissible rate of 1.0 percent).[32]

Tax base   In most states the tax base for the local income tax differs considerably from that of federal and state income taxes on individuals. The two major differences are that local taxes often (1) exclude property income (rental income, capital gains, dividends, and interest) from the tax base, and (2) disallow personal exemptions, deductions, and employee business expense allowances. These two differences make the income tax in these localities essentially a tax on earned income (wages, salaries, and the net income of unincorporated businesses). The major exceptions to this general pattern are the taxes in Michigan cities, Maryland counties, and New York City, all of which essentially use the federal tax base and therefore include property income. All three also allow personal exemptions, and New York City and Maryland localities permit personal deductions.[33]

Property income has been excluded from the tax base in most localities primarily because of the greater administrative costs of collecting and enforcing a tax on this income source. Whereas the almost universal practice of employer withholding from wages and salaries keeps collection and enforcement costs low, the administrative costs for processing returns for business and professional income (where there is no withholding for salaries and wages) are much higher. The high administrative costs for processing business and professional income returns would seem to indicate similar high administrative costs for other types of nonwithheld property income (rent, dividends, interest, and capital gains).

Administration, collection costs, and procedures   Local income taxes are administered by local taxing bodies (or by coordination among them) in ten of the eleven states where the tax is used. While optional state administration is available in Kentucky and New York, no locality has chosen it. The one exception to this pattern of local administration is Maryland, which mandates state administration of the local "piggyback" income taxes. State and local income taxes are collected using one return, and each county is paid a prorated share of the cost of operating the Maryland Income Tax Division.

In Ohio, Pennsylvania, and Kentucky, local taxing jurisdictions cooperate in administration by combining taxes of local jurisdictions on a single return submitted to a joint collection agency. In Pennsylvania a single return is used to collect the 1 percent earnings tax levied by school districts and coterminous cities, townships, and boroughs. Many of the cost-saving advantages of state administration were achieved in Ohio, where three agencies, located respectively in Cleveland, Columbus, and Dayton, collect income taxes for surrounding localities using a single return and one collection staff.

Collection costs tend to be lower as a percentage of revenues when: (1) a high proportion of the tax is collected by withholding; (2) a high concentration of the locality's employees work for a few large employers; (3) the intensity of tax enforcement is low; and (4) a relatively small number of taxpayers is employed outside the taxing jurisdiction (because employers outside the locality may not voluntarily withhold the tax).

The bulk of all local income tax revenues are collected through employer withholding; monthly remittances usually are required from employers with large work forces and quarterly remittances from others. Quarterly declarations of other taxable income and quarterly payments of the associated taxes are commonly required.

Revenue potential and elasticity   Localities frequently obtain a large share of all their total tax collections from an income tax (in some Ohio localities, as much as 84 percent). The potential revenues from the tax are large and may offset property tax increases.[34]

The revenues collected from a local income tax depend on the tax rate, the income components in its base, the exemptions and deductions allowed, the economic characteristics of the community, and the way the tax is administered. An estimate of the revenue potential of a tax to be used for the first time can best be obtained by examining the size of the relevant income components of the state income tax base in the locality. Applying the proposed tax rate to the proposed income components in the local base (assuming no income types not in the state base are to be taxed locally) produces an estimate, which does not, however, account for local tax revenues collected from nonresidents.

Cities and other local governments in states without a state income tax can make crude revenue estimates by comparing local economic characteristics with those of jurisdictions in other states that have a local income tax or by surveying local employers to get some measure of local wage and salary payrolls. Such estimates, at best, are likely to be inaccurate; they may be seriously awry if local business conditions change substantially in a short period of time or if tax administration is poor and fails to gain the cooperation of local employers in withholding the tax. With experience in collecting the tax, however, projection techniques can be used to forecast revenues.[35]

Automatic changes in local income tax revenues will occur with changes in local economic activity. An important measure of the responsiveness of revenues to such changes is the elasticity of revenues with respect to changes in the gross income of the locality. A flat-rate income tax with a comprehensive base equal to gross income would necessarily have an elasticity equal to 1. A tax with exemptions, deductions, or credits (which do not adjust automatically as gross income changes) will generate revenues that rise more than proportionately to increases in taxable gross income. The same will be true of a tax with graduated rates, since a rise in average incomes pushes taxpayers into higher brackets and raises the effective average tax rate. Hence, the New York City income tax and the Maryland county income taxes, with their exemptions, deductions, and graduated rates, are more elastic than the taxes levied by Pennsylvania and Ohio localities that do not have these features.

Relatively high elasticity of the income tax (as in New York City) is desirable, however, only when local income rises more or less continuously and experiences only mild downward fluctuations—a set of circumstances not within the control of local authorities. Downward fluctuations in income will produce more than proportionate reductions in revenue and can be a source of embarrassment to local officials who may have to cut expenditures. Fortunately (and somewhat paradoxically), the actual experience of income tax cities suggests that the local income tax is a highly reliable and stable revenue source. One study of the revenue fluctuations of Philadelphia, Detroit, and Columbus and Dayton, Ohio, showed that revenues never declined by more than 0.1 percent (between successive years) over the time studied (either since the tax was initiated or since World War II) in spite of recession periods in these cities when the unemployment rate was well above the national average.[36]

Implementation   When localities adopt an income tax, fiscal experts at the Advisory Commission on Intergovernmental Relations recommend state administration to minimize administrative and taxpayer compliance costs and to avoid limitations that characterize local collection.[37] Where a tax is to be administered locally, the local government must establish a tax roll, prepare tax return forms, hire clerical and audit staff, and monitor taxpayers to ensure compliance. Since successful operation of an income tax depends so heavily on employer withholding, a major effort must be made to obtain their cooperation.[38]

Assessment of issues and problems

Major issues in local income taxation arise in five areas: (1) the definition of taxable income and the consequences of alternative definitions on revenues and on distribution of the tax burden by income class; (2) tax incidence; (3) taxation of nonresidents; (4) revenue allocation; and (5) effects on location and the local economy.

Taxable income and equity   In most local tax systems, taxable income is simply gross earned income. Nonbusiness deductions and exemptions are not usually allowed; nor is property income included in the tax base. This definition of income raises two questions. First, should property income be included in the tax base? Second, how does widening the tax base to include property income and allowing personal exemptions and deductions affect the distribution of the income tax burden by income class and the amount of revenues generated?

Equity considerations provide the strongest argument for taxing nonlabor income. Failure to tax this income raises equity problems whether equity is defined by ability to pay or by benefit-received. These problems can be clearly shown by two illustrative situations involving two taxpayers, who shall be called Mutt and Jeff.

In the first situation suppose that in a given year Mutt and Jeff each receive a total income of $10,000. Mutt, however, receives $8,000 in wages and $2,000 in interest income, whereas Jeff receives $3,000 in wages and $7,000 in interest income. If each must pay an earnings tax of 1 percent on wage income, then Mutt has a tax liability of $80 while Jeff owes only $30. Since $10,000 buys the same goods and services regardless of the source of the income, the principle of horizontal equity based on ability to pay would call for both to pay the same tax. In addition, provided that Mutt and Jeff have the same preferences for public services, a concept of equity based on the benefit-received principle also would prescribe equal taxes.

Now, suppose that Jeff receives an income of $20,000—$6,000 in wages and

$14,000 in interest—while Mutt's income remains at $10,000 as before. With the same 1 percent earnings tax levy, Mutt still pays $80 and Jeff now pays $60. Jeff still pays less than Mutt even though he has twice Mutt's total income.

Results like these, which are permitted by exclusion of property income, violate widely held views of vertical equity based on ability to pay. Moreover, since taxpayers with higher incomes probably have higher demands for all types of goods and services, including local public services (i.e., they are willing to pay more dollars per unit of good), failure to tax property income can lead to serious violations of the benefit-received principle as well.

A second advantage of including property income in the tax base is that the same total revenue can be collected with a lower tax rate, and a lower rate is desirable, per se, because taxpayers are given less incentive to modify their behavior solely for the purpose of reducing their tax liabilities. This greater neutrality reduces deadweight losses. Since local income tax rates are typically very low anyway, this advantage may at first seem trivial. Perhaps it is, but one must remember that local income taxpayers are almost always subject to state and federal income and social security taxes as well. By reducing local income tax rates, one is knocking a small chunk off combined federal-plus-state-plus-local marginal tax rate of over 20 percent even for the poorest of taxpayers.

A third advantage of taxing property income is to simplify tax enforcement by making the local tax base identical to the state or federal tax base. Identical tax bases can facilitate the exchange of information on federal, state, and local returns.

The major disadvantage of taxing property income is the higher collection and enforcement costs that must be incurred for effective administration. All local income taxes, except those in Maryland, are locally administered, and the additional local burden of taxing property income (especially for small localities) poses a significant hurdle, because local funds for tax administration are limited. When the income tax is applied only to labor income, the bulk of the collection costs are borne by the employers who withhold the tax; moreover, the incremental withholding costs to employers are small since federal and, in most cases, state income taxes are being withheld already.[39] On the other hand, since property income is not subject to withholding, all the incremental administrative costs of adding property income to the tax base would have to be borne by the local government. The average cost of collecting a dollar of tax on property income is several times as large as that of collecting a dollar of withheld tax on wages. Auditing efforts must be significantly expanded both because there are many more taxpayers than employers and because the greater discretion given to individual taxpayers in reporting, computing, and paying tax on property income implies that this part of the tax must be actively collected rather than just passively received.

The inability or unwillingness of localities to bear the incremental administrative costs that must be incurred to tax property income effectively, taken together with the desirability of taxing property income, provides an argument for state administration of a system like the Maryland "piggyback" tax. Rental income, interest, dividends, and capital gains could then be added to the tax base (since these types of income are included in state tax bases), and the added costs of duplicative local administration and taxpayer compliance (from having to complete a local tax return) would be avoided. Of course, against these advantages must be weighed the losses of local fiscal autonomy.

Tax incidence   Assuming no economic shifting of local income tax, the incidence of a flat-rate earned income tax that allows no personal exemptions exhibits a regressive pattern. Tax liabilities as a percentage of income fall as total income rises. Two factors that contribute to regressivity are the deductibility of the local income tax on federal individual tax returns and the exclusion of property income from the tax base.

Progressive federal rates imply that the higher the taxpayer's income, the more valuable the deduction for local income taxes. Hence, effective rates on local earnings taxes decline as income rises. The exclusion of property income from the local earnings tax base contributes to regressivity because dividends, interest, rental income, and capital gains are heavily concentrated in the upper income groups. Therefore, a tax on earned income only as a percentage of total (labor plus property) income falls as total income rises.

Taxation of nonresidents   Two major unresolved issues in the treatment of nonresidents concern whether they should be taxed and, if so, at what rate, and whether taxes paid in one jurisdiction should be allowed as a credit toward taxes paid in another. In fact, as noted earlier, nonresidents are almost always taxed (Maryland localities being the sole exception) and usually at the same rate as residents. Also, crediting taxes paid to prevent double taxation (really to prevent quadruple taxation from becoming quintuple taxation considering state, federal, and social security taxes) is virtually universal.

If the benefit-received principle is referred to for guidance about these issues, some insights emerge. It is undeniable that commuters who work or shop in a local jurisdiction reap benefits from local government services. Some degree of taxation of nonresident income may therefore be justified by the benefit-received principle, especially if the incremental costs arise mostly from working commuters and if no low-cost system of user charges can be established. The difficult question to answer is what the nonresident tax rate should be. A study by Neenan concluded that Detroit's 0.5 percent tax on nonresident income represented full compensation for benefits received by nonresident commuters.[40] However, benefit estimation is still more a treacherous art than a hard science. One could argue that the total of all taxes levied on resident workers should be greater than that levied either on residents who work elsewhere or on nonresident workers. But since the resident worker is taxed in other ways—via the property tax, for example—it is difficult to justify taxing resident workers at higher income tax rates than nonresidents. Indeed, in localities with relatively heavy property taxation, a lower income tax rate for resident workers might be justified. Moreover, other factors besides the benefit-received principle must be considered. Taxing nonresidents at the same rate as residents, rather than at a lower rate, eliminates the incentive residents would otherwise be given to migrate to neighboring jurisdictions in order to reduce their tax liabilities.

Furthermore, the benefit-received principle does not necessarily support granting tax credits to prevent double taxation. If a commuter receives benefits from a locality (or imposes costs on residents in it), there is no real basis for neutralizing through a credit provision the price paid in income taxes for these benefits. Moreover, the effect of such credits, as clearly demonstrated in Pennsylvania cities other than Philadelphia, is virtually to eliminate the possibility of using the income tax as a means of assessing nonresidents for benefits received. Substitute methods of taxing nonresidents (e.g., sales taxes, amusement taxes) are thereby encouraged, and these methods are likely to be less closely related to the benefits that nonresident employees actually receive.

Revenue allocation   The income tax collections of a jurisdiction depend on the size of its tax base, which in turn depends on the level of economic activity in the locality, the incomes of persons subject to tax, and the assignment of the tax liability to place of residence or employment. Given the tax rate, localities with large tax bases collect large amounts of revenue and those with small tax bases do not. Hence, the income tax does not easily serve as a method of income redistribution between high- and low-income jurisdictions. It should be noted, however, that to the extent one believes that local expenditures should be responsive to local constituents' demands, the revenue distribution among jurisdictions produced by a system of local income taxes is likely to be much more consistent with such demands than the pattern of revenue distribution from a system of local sales taxes. Localities with a large income tax base that is due to a large population will collect relatively large amounts of income tax revenue with which to meet relatively high demands for expenditures, but if such localities have few sales outlets, a sales tax would yield much less revenue to meet the same demand for expenditures.

If one prefers to see more income redistribution from high- to low-income localities, a movement away from all types of local taxation and toward state or federal funding of local expenditures should be advocated. The distribution of state or federally collected revenues back to localities can then be based on a formula that favors poorer localities. In part, controversy over the extent to which local taxation should be used to fund local expenditures is a debate about how much income redistribution among localities is desirable. Also at issue is the question of how much income redistribution to help the poor should be accomplished by giving income transfers to the poor directly and how much should be by transfers to governments in localities where the poor are more heavily concentrated.

Impact on location decisions The impact of local income taxes on choices of individuals of where to live and work and choices of firms of where to locate has not been researched as extensively as the effect of a local sales tax on shopping decisions. Nevertheless, local governments are no doubt influenced by fears of adverse emigration effects resulting from taxation generally, and the local income tax is no exception.

The effect of a local income tax on location decisions is difficult to assess for several reasons. In part, the effect of a given local tax depends on the size of the geographical area in which such a tax is used and the rates applied in neighboring jurisdictions. Differentials among jurisdictions within a given metropolitan area are likely to cause greater locational adjustments than are those between one state or region and another. Also, the effects depend on the other changes (higher local expenditures for services or lower rates for other taxes such as the property tax) that accompany the adoption of a local income tax or a change in the income tax rate. Different persons and businesses may find their respective net advantages from being located in a particular jurisdiction affected in dissimilar ways by the combination of changes accompanying a local income tax levy. The sparse research in the area has found little effect on location decisions.[41] However, since models of locational choice are necessarily quite complex and difficult to test, no firm conclusions have been drawn.

Evaluative summary

The local income tax is a productive and stable revenue source for many localities. Its revenues respond rapidly to rising nominal incomes, a welcome feature in times of rapid inflation when there are large increases in the cost of providing local public services. Despite some early fears, the tax has also proven to be administratively feasible, not only when applied just to earned income and collected in large part through employer withholding, but also when a more nearly comprehensive tax base corresponding to that of the federal income tax is used. Unfortunately, the widespread local administration of the tax has tended to limit the base to earned income; this restriction causes the tax to violate criteria of vertical and horizontal equity, be these criteria grounded in the benefit-received principle or in ability to pay. The treatment of nonresidents is based more on what the law allows and on revenue considerations than on any close adherence to taxation principles. Broadening the tax base to include property income, and implementing state administration to achieve economies in compliance, collection, and enforcement are reforms that have considerable merit.

Other revenues

After the local general sales tax and the local income tax, the remaining non-property sources of local general revenues are (1) selective sales and gross receipts taxes; (2) licenses and other taxes, including occupational and business privilege levies, per capita taxes, occupation taxes, and taxes on real estate transfers; (3) current user charges for such services as education, hospital care, sewage disposal, parking, rental of public housing, parks, and museums (user charges are discussed in detail in Chapter 8); and (4) miscellaneous general revenues from special assessments, sales of property, interest earnings, and fines. In combination, these sources generated almost one-third of local general revenues in 1976–77.

Although economists and other fiscal experts have diverse opinions about the appropriateness of various items in this disparate bundle of revenue sources, some consensus exists. The excise and head taxes in the first two groups have often been criticized as being inefficient, inequitable, or both. A kind word is sometimes uttered, however, for the excise taxes levied on goods that are essential complements of public services, such as local taxes on motor fuels. These taxes resemble user charges because they are linked to the benefits from the use of local streets.

In contrast to many excise and head taxes, direct user charges have been viewed favorably as promoting a more efficient allocation of goods and services and providing closer conformance to the benefit-received principle than general taxes.

The following discussion is limited to *general* revenue sources. Fees, user charges, and other nontax revenues that finance special districts, public authorities, and municipal enterprises are covered in Chapter 8. The data that underlie this discussion are drawn from the 1977 Census of Governments, which provides the only nationwide comparative data on local government finances.[42]

Importance in the revenue structure

The overall significance of miscellaneous sources of local general revenue for all local governments in the late 1970s is revealed by Table 7–5. It is noteworthy that the last two categories, user charges and miscellaneous general revenues, were more important than either the local general sales tax or the local income tax, which provided about 5.4 percent and 3.7 percent of revenues, respectively (see Table 7–2).

A more detailed breakdown of three of these four categories is shown in Table 7–6. (A revenue breakdown of the "License and Other Taxes" category, which contains a disparate collection of items, is not readily available.) This table is largely self-explanatory. The major findings are the following:

1. The bulk of all revenues from selective sales and gross receipts taxes came from taxes on public utilities.
2. Almost one-third of all user charge revenues were derived from hospital services; education and sewerage charges were the next most important sources of user charge revenues.
3. The largest single revenue item obtained from miscellaneous sources was interest from holdings of interest-bearing assets.

The information provided by Tables 7–5 and 7–6, which shows totals for all types and sizes of local governments, can be supplemented by a brief discussion of variations within these broad aggregates. Table 7–3, introduced earlier, shows that municipalities collected a higher percentage of their general revenues from both licenses and other taxes (4.2 percent) and from miscellaneous revenues (10.2 percent) than did either counties or townships, while special districts received over three-fifths of their revenues from user charges. Looking at the

Table 7–5   Importance of miscellaneous sources of general revenue to local government, 1976–77

Classification	Revenue (in millions)	% of total general revenues
Total	$32,721	32.0
Selective sales taxes	2,807	2.7
License and other taxes	2,552	2.5
Current user charges	19,097	18.7
Miscellaneous general revenues	8,265	8.1

Source: Same as Table 7–1.

Table 7–6   Selective sales taxes, user charges, and miscellaneous general revenues of local governments, 1976–77

Classification	Revenue (in millions)	Percentage distribution
Sales taxes, total	$ 2,807	100.0
Motor fuel	75	2.7
Alcoholic beverages	144	5.1
Tobacco products	132	4.7
Public utilities	1,781	63.4
Other	675	24.0
User charges, total	$19,097	100.0
Education	3,468	18.2
School lunch sales	1,609	8.4
Institutions of higher education	1,035	5.4
Other	824	4.3
Hospitals	6,128	32.1
Sewerage	2,446	12.8
Sanitation other than sewerage	646	3.4
Local parks and recreation	633	3.3
Natural resources	156	0.8
Housing and urban renewal	882	4.6
Air transportation	1,113	5.8
Water transport and terminals	413	2.2
Parking facilities	269	1.4
Other	2,941	15.4
Miscellaneous general revenues, total	$ 8,265	100.0
Special assessments	849	10.3
Sale of property	257	3.1
Interest earnings	3,303	40.0
Other (includes fines and forfeits)	3,855	46.6

Source: Same as Table 7–1.

matter from a different perspective in Table 7–4, municipalities collected 59.7 percent of all license and other taxes, 45.2 percent of all miscellaneous general revenue, and over a third of all user charges. Finally, focusing on the effect of city size, reliance by municipalities on user charges and miscellaneous revenues showed some tendency to rise (as a percentage of all general revenues collected from own sources) as city population decreased. Data indicating this inverse relationship for 1976–77 are shown in Table 7–7.

Description and evaluation of miscellaneous local taxes

This section evaluates a number of local taxes using the criteria of equity, efficiency, administrative ease, and revenue potential and elasticity. The taxes examined are per capita (head) taxes; occupation and occupational and business

Table 7–7 Percent of local general revenue raised by municipalities from license and other taxes, user charges, and miscellaneous revenues in 1976–77, by population group

Population group[1]	No. of municipalities	License and other taxes	User charges	Miscellaneous revenue
All municipalities	18,861	4.2	18.6	10.2
7,000,000 or over	1	1.4	13.4	6.7
1,000,000 to 6,999,999	5	7.5	15.5	9.0
500,000 to 999,999	18	5.1	17.1	8.1
300,000 to 499,999	22	3.8	24.0	12.8
100,000 to 299,999	117	4.3	19.1	10.0
50,000 to 99,999	230	3.8	20.5	9.5
25,000 to 49,999	514	4.1	21.5	11.8
10,000 to 24,999	1,212	4.5	22.7	13.4
5,000 to 9,999	1,461	4.7	24.5	12.9
2,500 to 4,999	2,004	5.3	22.3	13.6
Less than 2,500	13,277	4.5	15.5	24.2

Source: U.S., Department of Commerce, Bureau of the Census, 1977 Census of Governments, vol. 4: *Governmental Finances*, part 4: *Finances of Municipalities and Township Governments* (Washington, D.C.: Government Printing Office, 1979), p. 35.
1 Municipalities grouped by 1975 population estimates.

privilege taxes (licenses); real estate transfer taxes; and selective sales (excise) taxes on motor fuel, alcoholic beverages, tobacco products, public utilities, and admissions to amusements.

Per capita taxes   Commonly referred to as a "head tax" (the name being derived from the Latin words *per,* meaning "by," and *capita,* meaning "heads"), the per capita tax (also called a residence or poll tax) was used much less frequently in the late 1970s than in earlier years when many political jurisdictions levied the tax for the privilege of voting.[43] Where the tax was still being used, it was usually levied annually at a fixed amount (typically between one dollar and ten dollars) on all adult residents of the taxing jurisdiction.

The positive and negative aspects of per capita taxes can be summarized briefly. The tax is almost perfectly neutral or efficient because it cannot be avoided by modification of spending, saving, or work choices, and taxpayers are rarely motivated to move out of a taxing jurisdiction to escape a yearly ten dollar tax. The tax guarantees that all adults make a minimum direct contribution to the cost of government; the tax yield exhibits great stability; it is visible, predictable, and simple to report and pay.

The major shortcoming of the tax that has led many localities to abandon it is its low yield relative to administration costs. A tax of one dollar per capita is hardly worth collecting; even a five dollar levy may have collection costs of 25 percent to 30 percent of revenues. The problem grows worse over time if the tax amount is not increased, because collection costs tend to rise with the general level of prices and the cost of government. Were it not for the low tax amount, an additional serious difficulty with the per capita tax would be its regressivity in relation to income. Some localities lessen regressivity by exempting all persons with annual incomes below a certain amount. Finally, the nondeductibility of the tax for federal income tax purposes and the use of the tax by several overlapping jurisdictions (as in Pennsylvania, for example) have been sources of annoyance and confusion to taxpayers and have caused the levy to be labeled a "nuisance tax." Considering all its pluses and minuses, this appears to be an apt description.

Occupation and occupational and business privilege taxes   Historically, taxes on occupations or on the privilege of engaging in an occupation or business were considered property taxes, since in seventeenth century England taxes were levied on the many offices created by grant or letter of appointment (which could sometimes be sold or transferred). Although transferability is no longer typical (seats on the stock and commodity exchanges and taxicab medallions are notable exceptions), many occupations still require membership in a professional association or labor union. Hence, there is still some basis for regarding occupation taxes as taxes on a property right, though the tax now is more often construed as a levy on the privilege of operating a business or practicing an occupation or profession.

Local taxes on occupation and business privileges go by several names, are levied in several forms, and are intended to serve (or are rationalized by) various purposes. The taxes to be examined here are lump sum taxes and taxes on business gross receipts.

Lump sum taxes Lump sum taxes on individuals engaged in occupations and on individual business owners and corporations resemble per capita taxes. The levy is a flat annual amount, invariant to the income or net profit of the taxpayer and thus unrelated to ability to pay. The tax may vary, however, by type of occupation or business.

As with per capita taxes, the major criticisms of lump sum taxes apply with much more force where the tax is sizable. The tax raises equity issues because actual earnings or net profits do not affect the tax liability. Moreover, even though lump sum, the tax would not be neutral because individuals could be induced to shift between differently taxed occupations or out of the taxing jurisdiction to avoid the tax. Where the tax is small (e.g., ten dollars per year), the significance of these negative features is small. If the tax is subject to employer withholding, as is true, for example, of the ten dollar occupational privilege levy in many Pennsylvania localities, the administration costs are considerably lower than for per capita taxes, which require a periodic census to update tax rolls. Flat-rate occupation taxes also can serve as a vehicle (in some cases one of the few available to a jurisdiction) for requiring nonresident workers to make a contribution toward the cost of local public services. Localities having substantial numbers of employees within their boundaries derive large amounts of revenue from these taxes, and the revenue yield is comparatively stable because the tax is paid annually and is not subject to seasonal employment fluctuations.

Gross receipts taxes Local taxes on the gross receipts of incorporated and unincorporated businesses function in most respects either as general sales taxes, if applied uniformly to a wide class of businesses (e.g., all retail and wholesale establishments), or as selective sales (excise) taxes if applied to only one or a few types of businesses (e.g., telephone service). It is highly probable that such taxes are generally shifted to customers of the taxed firms. The major differences between the gross receipts and the explicit sales taxes are that (1) customers may be less resentful of the tax because it is hidden and not calculated as a separate part of the total sales price, and (2) the tax paid by customers is not deductible on federal individual income tax returns.

Most of the issues and problems that arise with general sales taxes also are present with taxes on gross receipts that are applied widely to a locality's businesses. Since the tax is on gross receipts rather than net income, it has been criticized as being inequitable because it discriminates against businesses with a low ratio of net profit to sales. But this criticism is based on the assumption that the incidence of the tax is on the businesses legally liable to pay it. If the tax is shifted to the customers, the true question, as with the general sales tax, concerns the equity of the burden among customers. If the assumption of shifting is correct, the practice in some localities of allowing firms to pay a tax on net income (at ten times the rate applied to gross receipts, for example) in lieu of the gross receipts tax simply causes greater administrative complexity without making the tax any more equitable. Where the tax is imposed on both wholesale and retail businesses, the tax may be discriminatory between vertically integrated and nonintegrated businesses.

The revenue potential of the gross receipts tax depends on its base and the rate applied. Localities with large concentrations of businesses can reap substantial revenues, as with the general sales tax. Assuming the tax is shifted to purchasers, it also may serve to exact a contribution from nonresident shoppers. Where the tax is not levied on all businesses, disputes arise concerning where the line is to be drawn between those that are exempt and those that are not exempt; such disputes may require resolution through court interpretation. Pennsylvania's local mercantile tax on wholesale and retail businesses, for example, has been held to apply to persons who buy and resell but not to persons who sell what they make.[44]

A gross receipts tax has been levied by some localities (e.g., Pittsburgh) on nonprofit institutions that are exempt from other local taxes. Gross receipts taxes also share with sales taxes the problem of allocating sales made within and outside the taxing jurisdiction. Whether a broad-based gross receipts tax should play a role in the financing of local government depends on an assessment similar to that made earlier for a local sales tax.

Real estate transfer taxes   Some types of exchanges are much more visible and easily taxed than others, and this appears to be the major explanation for the existence of the real estate transfer tax. Also referred to as the deed transfer tax, it was used in a sample year in the mid-1970s by local governments in ten states and the District of Columbia.[45] Localities in California and New York taxed only the difference between the sales price and the amount represented by assumed mortgages, or just the equity of the real estate exchanged. All other jurisdictions imposed the tax on the full sales price. The tax rates ranged from 0.05 percent to 1.0 percent. Revenues from the tax were largest in urban areas where there was considerable economic growth and turnover of real estate.

Administrative practices varied greatly in the use of stamps and provisions for recording and transmitting sales prices. Because seven state governments also imposed a transfer tax, there was some tax overlapping.

The real estate transfer tax is an excise tax on the exchange of one type of property. The rationale for such a narrowly based tax, aside from the fact that it permits relatively easy and low-cost collection of revenue, is not apparent. Some users of the tax have justified it as an "initiation fee" for new residents to an area, a kind of user charge imposed for the benefits provided by public capital financed by taxes on older residents. Whatever the merits of this argument, the transfer tax, though modest in size, discriminates against real property transactions and raises their cost relative to transactions of other kinds. The incidence of the tax is not confined to those who actually exchange real estate, since a tax penalizing exchanges usually hurts potential as well as actual buyers and sellers by preventing some mutually advantageous exchanges from ever occurring. Because the tax rate is low, however, the number of exchanges prevented probably is small. (No studies of the effects of this tax on purchase or location decisions appear to have been made.) As for the question of whether the buyer or seller bears the real burden of the tax, in most cases both bear a portion of it regardless of where the legal liability is placed. Hence, there is virtually no validity to the argument sometimes made that, where the tax is imposed by both the state and a local government, duplicate taxation is avoided if one level of government taxes the buyer while the other taxes the seller.

Revenues from the real estate transfer tax tend to be volatile, because they fluctuate with the pace of real estate and construction activity. The tax does have the advantages, however, of providing immediate revenues to finance service demands in rapidly expanding communities and of compensating to some extent for lags that exist in beginning property tax collections on new housing. All things considered, though, this tax has little to recommend it.

Excise taxes   Excise taxes are levied by local governments on a wide variety of individual products and services, but the major taxes are those on alcoholic beverages, tobacco products, and public utilities. Excise taxes may be expressed as a percentage of the sales price or as a given amount per unit of the product or service. The former is called an ad valorem tax, while the latter is called a unit tax.

Because of their narrow base, excise taxes are generally viewed as running afoul of both equity and efficiency criteria. Taxpayers in the same economic circumstances will pay different amounts of the tax if they consume different amounts of the taxed items. Moreover, to the extent that consumption of a taxed good does not rise in proportion to income, the tax is regressive.

In the absence of resource misallocations caused by other factors, excise taxes also distort choices by making the relative prices of taxed and untaxed goods depart from relative costs of production. Consumers are given false signals as to relative costs, and the consequent welfare losses, as mentioned earlier, are referred to as deadweight losses. Additional losses occur if people divert their purchases from one locality to another to avoid paying the tax.

Although excise taxes in general cause equity and efficiency problems, it must be recognized that the excise taxes on alcohol, tobacco, and motor fuel are not necessarily undesirable. Taxes on alcohol and cigarettes could be justified as making an otherwise inefficient allocation of resources less so, taking account of the costs that those who consume these products may impose on third parties. Similarly, congestion and pollution costs resulting from the use of automobiles have sometimes been the (dubious) basis for justifying motor fuel taxes; the argument has also been made that this tax functions as a user charge for the use of local streets. Evaluating the merits of these various arguments would take the discussion too far afield. Suffice it to say that if consumption of a good harms third parties, an excise tax on the good is not always the most appropriate solution to the problem.

Local taxes on alcoholic beverages   A few municipal and county governments tax distilled spirits, beer, and wine, either by excise taxes or by occupational license taxes. Municipal and county governments in eleven states and the District of Columbia used these taxes in 1976–77.[46] Taxation of alcoholic beverages is predominantly a practice of municipalities in southern states. The tax revenues for Georgia municipalities alone accounted for over 40 percent of the nationwide total of such city tax revenues in 1976–77.

Local taxes on tobacco and motor fuels   Localities in seven states and the District of Columbia were taxing tobacco products in the late 1970s, and almost all the revenues were obtained from cigarette taxes. Tax rates on cigarettes ranged from one to thirteen cents per pack. Municipalities in Missouri had the highest average percent of local general revenues from the tax—1.5 percent.

Taxes on various types of motor fuel were levied by localities in nine states and the District of Columbia in the late 1970s.[47] The tax rates on gasoline ranged from 0.75 cents to 3.0 cents per gallon. Based on the sketchy information available, it appears that Hawaii localities led in the percentage of local general revenues obtained from this tax.

Since both gasoline and cigarettes were taxed by higher levels of government, the low per unit rates in most localities (excluding Washington, D.C., which is more like a state than a locality in the context of taxation) is not surprising. It should be noted that the general use of a per unit excise tax for both cigarettes and gasoline causes the revenues from these taxes to vary with physical units sold rather than with the dollar value of sales. Because cigarette consumption for a long time has been actively discouraged by the federal government, the American Heart Association, and other groups, this tax source may decline in relative importance over time. Far more dramatic is the situation with gasoline tax revenues. As constantly rising prices have reduced the total number of gallons consumed, total tax revenues have declined. If revenues from this tax are earmarked for maintenance of local streets, the adequacy of this tax source for road expenses can be expected to be eroded. One change that would alleviate this problem would be to convert the gasoline per unit tax to an ad valorem tax. Revenues then at least would be maintained and probably would increase because the price increases generating the decline in gallons sold are greater in percentage terms than the percentage reductions in the quantity sold. (In economists' terms, the price elasticity of the demand for gasoline is less than 1.) If the tax were ad valorem, the dollar value of tax revenues would rise over time.

Local taxation of cigarettes, alcoholic beverages, and gasoline may cause substantial shifts of purchases out of the taxing jurisdiction, particularly if the locality borders a nontax area. Tax-created price differentials also make organized bootlegging operations profitable, though this is more an interstate than an interlocal problem. The ease with which cigarettes and alcoholic beverages can be obtained outside a local taxing jurisdiction has no doubt been a factor discouraging some communities from levying these taxes.

Some states in which localities initially levied a cigarette tax have switched to a state-imposed, locally subvened[48] tax to reduce administrative costs and to forestall objections of unfair competition when locally different rates are set. California returns a percentage of the state cigarette tax collections to localities based on the percentage of general sales tax revenue distributed back to localities under the Bradley-Burns Uniform Local Sales and Use Tax Law. Nevada, Maryland, and Wyoming subvene part of the state cigarette tax to local jurisdictions on the basis of population.[49] Such systems appear to have much to commend them.

Sales and gross receipts taxes on public utilities In the late 1970s localities in at least forty states derived revenues from either sales or gross receipts taxes on public utilities (mainly electric, natural gas, and telephone companies). Nationwide, municipalities derived slightly more than 4.0 percent of local general revenues, or $1.502 billion, from such taxes. Since the total collected by all local governments was $1.789 billion, it is apparent that municipalities were the predominant users of this tax source. As a percentage of local general revenue of municipalities, the variation was from 0.0 percent in the ten states where no municipality used these taxes to a high of 19.4 percent for municipalities in Florida. Other states where municipalities derived above-average revenues from taxes on utilities were New Jersey (13.7 percent), Washington (11.0 percent), Virginia (9.6 percent), and Illinois (9.2 percent).[50]

From a revenue standpoint, local taxes on public utilities ranked just behind local sales and income taxes in importance and were used by more localities than either of these broad-based taxes. Even in some states with local sales taxes (e.g., Virginia and Kansas), utility tax collections by municipalities exceeded general sales tax collections. Because this tax was no doubt shifted forward and was applied to all utility sales, not just sales to household consumers, the tax was paid by consumers not only when they purchased utility services but also when they bought products and services that required the taxed utility services in their production. Whether the tax has a regressive, proportional, or progressive incidence pattern depends on the relationship between income size and the amount of electricity, natural gas, and telephone service used directly or indirectly.

Because consumption of public utility services is reasonably stable, these taxes provide a fairly predictable source of revenue. At the same time, they distort relative prices and should therefore receive a low score using the criterion of economic efficiency.

Amusement taxes Taxes on admissions to amusements were used widely in the late 1970s only by local governments in Pennsylvania, Ohio, and Washington. These were almost always ad valorem excise taxes, with rates ranging from 1 percent to 10 percent of the admission price. The importance of the amusement tax in local revenue structures is usually quite small except for localities with a race track, sports stadium, or major entertainment facility.

Amusement taxes are generally justified as sumptuary levies, but it is not clear that they are borne disproportionately by the rich, and inequities arise when not all "amusements" are taxed. Some court rulings about what does and does not constitute an amusement are, well . . ., amusing. Various Pennsylvania courts have excluded the admissions to county agricultural fairs from taxation (even though the most congested area of the grounds is often the carnival games and rides), historical museums and forts, and natural caves.[51] The yield from an amusement tax may be relatively unstable because it depends on the entertainment habits and income of those seeking entertainment. The tax may also divert people from taxed sources of entertainment to untaxed ones, causing a competitive handicap for some businesses and deadweight losses to the community at large.

Some firms selling amusement services clearly avoid the bulk of the tax by applying it to only one part of two-part price, one part to gain admission to their facilities (a fee on which the amusement tax is paid), and another for intensity or length of use, on which no tax is paid. Examples of such firms are ski resorts and racquetball clubs.

Despite its shortcomings, however, the tax does provide a means of taxing nonresident users of local services.

Conclusion This section has covered the miscellaneous but by no means minor sources of general revenue to local governments. Although the great diversity and variety of these revenue sources provide localities with greater flexibility in tailoring the local tax structure to local conditions, most of the tax sources included on the revenue menu have serious flaws when judged by traditional canons of taxation. The shortcomings are partially alleviated, however, by the low rates or levels of the taxes. At the same time, a large number of small taxes constitutes a nuisance for taxpayers and entails higher administrative costs than would be the case if just a few broad-based tax sources were used. Resistance to some of the taxes is no doubt low merely because they are applied to narrow groups of taxpayers who pass them on to purchasers who for the most part are largely unaware of their existence. A conclusion one might be tempted to draw is that local miscellaneous revenue sources constitute a "rag-bag" mess. However, there would undoubtedly be considerable resistance to almost any method of replacing the revenues that would be lost if they were eliminated wholesale. In contrast, the local property, income, and general sales taxes all suffer politically from greater visibility. The rag-bag is therefore likely to be with us for years to come.

1 In California, local governments have responded to Proposition 13 by increasing a variety of fees and imposing new ones, especially on builders in the residential construction industry. Business and license fees have also been raised in many California municipalities; charges have been instituted at many museums; fees have been raised at beaches, campgrounds, and parks; and fines for overdue library books have been increased. See: Stephen J. Sansweet, "Catch-13," *Wall Street Journal,* 1 June 1979, pp. 1, 39.

2 Changes in detail are constantly occurring within the myriad local governments. The reader therefore should consult the *Commerce Clearinghouse Reporter* for current information on the revenue sources covered in this chapter.

3   The most important references for the discussion of local sales taxes that follows are: John L. Mikesell, "Local Government Sales Taxes," in *State and Local Sales Taxation,* ed. John F. Due (Chicago: Public Administration Service, 1971); and John F. Due, "Local Sales and Income Taxes," in *Management Policies in Local Government Finance,* ed. J. Richard Aronson and Eli Schwartz (Washington, D.C.: International City Management Association, 1975).

4   For information on rates, administration, and other aspects of local sales taxes, see: U.S., Advisory Commission on Intergovernmental Relations, *Significant Features of Fiscal Federalism: 1976–1977 Edition, Vol. II—Revenue and Debt,* M-110 (Washington, D.C.: Government Printing Office, 1977), pp. 186–89.

5   See: Richard A. Musgrave and Peggy B. Musgrave, *Public Finance in Theory and Practice* 2d ed. (New York: McGraw-Hill Book Co., 1976), p. 327.

6   Due, "Local Sales and Income Taxes," p. 127.

7   See: Due, ed., *State and Local Sales Taxation,* chapter 8, for a discussion of sales tax auditing procedures and experience.

8   See: U.S., Advisory Commission on Intergovernmental Relations, *Significant Features of Fiscal Federalism,* table 139, p. 254.

9   See: Due, ed., *State and Local Sales Taxation,* p. 66.

10 U.S., Advisory Commission on Intergovernmental Relations, *Significant Features of Fiscal Federalism,* tables 101, 102, pp. 186–89.

11 Charles M. Tiebout, "A Pure Theory of Local Expenditure," *Journal of Political Economy* 64 (October 1956):416–24.

12 See: Mikesell, "Local Government Sales Taxes." Also see: John W. Lynch, "Local vs. State Administration of Local-Option Nonproperty Taxes," in *Proceedings of the Sixtieth Annual Conference of the National Tax Association* (1967), pp. 489–504.

13 State administration was mandated in Arkansas, Georgia, Illinois, Kansas, Missouri, Nebraska, Nevada, New Mexico, Ohio, Utah, Virginia, Washington, and Wyoming. Voluntary use of state administration was universal in California, New York, North Carolina, Oklahoma, South Dakota, Tennessee, and Texas. Local sales taxes were authorized but not used in Kentucky, Oregon, and Wisconsin. State administration was mandated if such taxes were used in Kentucky and Wisconsin, while in Oregon there would be local administration. As noted earlier, some but not all local taxes were state administered in Alabama and Colorado.

14 For a discussion of the California experience with local administration, see: *Let's Make Sense Out of Local Sales Taxes* (San Francisco: California Retailers Association, 1955); and California Senate Interim Committee on State and Local Taxation, *State and Local Sales and Use Taxes in California* (Sacramento: State of California, 1953).

15 For a more extensive treatment of these problems as experienced in California, see: Ronald B. Welch, "Two and a Half Years of Progress Toward Integration," *Proceedings of the National Tax Association for 1958,* pp. 128–39.

16 Due, ed., *State and Local Sales Taxation,* p. 311.

17 See: J. C. Yokum, *Retailers' Costs of Sales Tax Collections in Ohio* (Columbus: Bureau of Business Research, Ohio State University, 1961), p. XXI.

18 Lynch, "Local vs. State Administration," p. 493. The figures on per capita revenues are from: Rob-

ert C. Brown, "Some Observations on the Distribution of the California Local Uniform Sales and Use Tax," *Proceedings of the National Tax Association, 1968,* p. 30.

19 See: Robert P. Inman, "Fiscal Performance of Local Governments: An Interpretive Review," in *Current Issues in Urban Economics,* ed. P. Mieszkowski and M. Straszheim (Baltimore: Johns Hopkins University Press, 1979), pp. 285–92.

20 The percentage of income that is consumed falls as income rises (though the rate by which the percentage falls is probably overstated in cross-section data on family budgets). Provided that the 40 percent of consumption that is taxed also does not rise in proportion to income (which appears to be the case), the sales tax is regressive.

21 Harry E. McAllister, "The Border Tax Problem in Washington," *National Tax Journal* 14 (December 1961): 347.

22 William Hamovitch, "Effects of Increases in Sales Tax Rates on Taxable Sales in New York City," in *Financing Government in New York City: Report to the Temporary Commission on City Finances,* ed. Graduate School of Public Administration, New York University (New York: Graduate School of Public Administration, New York University, 1966), pp. 619–34.

23 Harry Levin, "An Analysis of the Economic Effects of the New York City Sales Tax," in *Financing Government in New York City,* ed. New York University, pp. 635–91.

24 John L. Mikesell, "Central Cities and Sales Tax Rate Differentials: The Border City Problem," *National Tax Journal* 23 (June 1970): 206–13.

25 U.S., Department of Commerce, Bureau of the Census, *Governmental Finances in 1976–77* (Washington, D.C.: Government Printing Office, 1978), table 6, pp. 20–22.

26 U.S., Department of Commerce, Bureau of the Census, *City Government Finances in 1976–77* (Washington, D.C.: Government Printing Office, 1978), table 5, p. 55.

27 Charleston, South Carolina, adopted an income tax in the early nineteenth century but abandoned it. New York City enacted a local income tax in 1934, but repealed the ordinance in 1935 before any collections were made.

28 Though authorized under certain conditions to levy income taxes, no local government in Arkansas or Georgia had chosen to do so.

29 Localities in five of these eleven states (Kentucky, Michigan, Missouri, New York, and Ohio) levied a tax on the net income of corporations. With the exception of the New York City tax, localities taxed corporate net income at the same flat rate as the tax applied to individual incomes. In the remaining six states (Alabama, California, Delaware, Indiana, Maryland, and Pennsylvania) localities did not impose this tax.

30 Effective in 1977 for any increases above the current rate of 4.3125 percent, taxes on nonresidents of Philadelphia were limited to 75.0 percent of those levied on residents.

31 William B. Neenan, *Political Economy of Urban Areas* (Chicago: Markham Publishing Co., 1972), pp. 291–92.

32 Municipalities with home rule charters were not limited to a 1 percent rate on residents, and at least thirteen municipalities were applying a higher rate.

33 A recent amendment to Pennsylvania's Local Tax Enabling Act permitted each local taxing authority

to adopt an ordinance granting an earned income tax exemption for any person whose total income from all sources was less than $3,200 per year. How extensively this option was used has not been systematically surveyed, but the impression among local tax officials was that it was granted by many localities. In Indiana, county taxpayers who were allowed the federal credit for the elderly were allowed a credit against the county tax.

34 One study of large cities suggests that the local income tax has been used over the years more as a substitute for property tax increases than as a way to finance higher levels of expenditures. See: Elizabeth Deran, "Tax Structure in Cities Using the Income Tax," *National Tax Journal* 21 (June 1968): 152.

35 A review of these techniques can be found in: Federation of Tax Administrators, *Revenue Estimating: A Study of Techniques for Estimating Tax Revenues* (Chicago: Federation of Tax Administrators, 1956).

36 Neenan, *Political Economy of Urban Areas,* pp. 322–23.

37 U.S., Advisory Commission on Intergovernmental Relations, *1970 Cumulative ACIR State Legislative Program* (Washington, D.C.: Advisory Commission on Intergovernmental Relations, 1969), p. 1 of subject code 33–22–00.

38 A useful guide for local government administration is: Commonwealth of Pennsylvania, Department of Community Affairs, *The Administration of the Local Earned Income Tax* (Harrisburg: Commonwealth of Pennsylvania, 1971).

39 One old estimate of the costs of employer withholding in four Pennsylvania cities found such costs to be between $0.06 and $0.47 per employee-year. See: State of Minnesota, *Report of the Minnesota Interim Commission on Withholding Taxes* (St. Paul: State of Minnesota, 1956), pp. 30–31. Taken from: Neenan, *Political Economy of Urban Areas,* p. 326.

40 Some students of local government finance have questioned the classifications of local revenue sources by the U.S. Bureau of the Census in its quinquennial surveys of governmental finances, especially intergovernmental transfers and current charges. See: Selma Mushkin, ed., *Public Prices for Public Products* (Washington, D.C.: The Urban Institute, 1972), p. 5.

41 Ibid., p. 149.

42 See: John F. Due, "Studies of State-Local Tax Influences on Location of Industry," *National Tax Journal* 14 (June 1961): 163–73; Melvin White and Anne White, "A Personal Income Tax for New York: Equity and Economic Effects," in *Financing Government in New York City,* ed. New York University, pp. 449–91; and Roger W. Schmenner, *City Taxes and Industry Location* (Ph.D. diss., Yale University, 1973).

43 The Twenty-fourth Amendment to the U.S. Constitution outlawed the use of poll taxes in federal elections, and in 1966 the U.S. Supreme Court declared state poll taxes unconstitutional for any government election. See: Bernard P. Herber, *Modern Public Finance: The Study of Public Sector Economics,* 2d ed. (Homewood, Ill.: Richard D. Irwin, 1971), p. 255.

44 School District of Pittsburgh v. Electric Welding Co., 142 A. 2d 433, 186 Pa. Super. 243 (1958).

45 For a compilation of real estate transfer tax provisions in ten states and the District of Columbia, see: U.S., Advisory Commission on Intergovernmental Relations, *Significant Features of Fiscal Federalism,* table 95, pp. 170–71.

46 For a summary of municipal and county revenues from alcoholic beverage taxes, by state, in 1976–77, see: U.S., Department of Commerce, Bureau of the Census, 1977 Census of Governments: *Finances of Municipalities and Township Governments,* vol. 4, no. 4, table 16; *Governmental Finances, Compendium of Governmental Finances,* vol. 4, no. 5, table 47; *Finances of County Governments,* vol. 4, no. 3, table 3 (Washington, D.C.: Government Printing Office, 1979).

47 For information on local excise tax rates on cigarettes and other tobacco products and on gasoline and other motor fuels, see: Tax Foundation, *Facts and Figures on Government Finance,* 20th ed. (Washington, D.C.: Tax Foundation, 1979), table 200, p. 249. For revenue data, see various publications of the 1977 Census of Governments conducted by the U.S. Bureau of the Census with the reports issued by the U.S. Government Printing Office.

48 "Subvene": the state collects the tax and distributes the revenues to local governmental units.

49 Lynch, "Local vs. State Administration," pp. 497–50.

50 All data on local utility taxes are taken from the same source as Table 7–6.

51 Commonwealth of Pennsylvania, Department of Community Affairs, *Taxation Manual* (Harrisburg: Commonwealth of Pennsylvania, 1979), p. 43.

8 User charges and special districts

The mid-1970s have seen a shift in the methods of financing local governments. Property tax revenues increased 31.8 percent during the period from 1973 to 1977. Revenues from user charges increased 57.0 percent, and the revenues from sales and gross receipts taxes increased 62.7 percent. The trend to move away from the property tax and toward other revenue sources, including user charges, is expected to continue during the 1980s.

There are many theoretical and practical criticisms of the general ad valorem property tax; however, it is sufficient to note that the employment of user charges can subdue many of the objections raised against the property tax. User charges can promote efficiency in local government decision making as well as improve the spending decisions of the public. User charges perform the functions attributable to a pricing system. That is, they can ration the supply by allocating the service to those who demand it most. User charges can provide information on the desirability of increasing the supply of the service; they also provide the funds for expansion of that service. If user charges are to achieve their allocation goals, however, they must be carefully designed.

This chapter reviews current practice in the employment of user charges and fees by local governments and the range of items for which user charges and fees are employed. The chapter discusses the issues in the design of optional systems of user charges. The effects of a well designed user charge system will be contrasted to one that is poorly designed. The effects of user charges will also be compared to those of the general property tax—a comparison that will be made in terms of the effects on the location of development, the level of service demanded, and the incidence of the financial burden among income groups. The chapter also contains an outline of the practical considerations in the design and employment of user charges. Finally, the chapter discusses special districts, the various types of special districts, their heavy reliance on user charges for financing, and the effects of special districts on local government efficiency are described.

Current employment of user charges

User charges have been a growing source of local government revenue over the past two decades. The extent of this growth in comparison to that of other sources of revenue is shown in Table 8–1.

Charges, as defined by the U.S. Bureau of the Census, are composed of current charges, utility revenue, and liquor store revenue. Current charges include "amounts received from the public for performance of specific services benefiting the persons charged and from sales of commodities and services. Current charges include fees, toll charges, tuition, and other reimbursements for current services . . . ."[1] Some of the growth in utility charges can be attributed to increased energy costs over the period. Nevertheless, the overall growth in current charges and utility revenues may be partially due to the attempt by local governments to reduce reliance on the property tax. As Table 8–1 shows, property tax revenues have grown more slowly than other major sources of local revenue. In constant dollar terms there has been virtually no growth in property tax revenues, whereas the constant dollars for charge revenues and sales taxes have grown rapidly.

Local government reliance on charge revenues varies among the various types of jurisdictions. As can be seen in Table 8–2, special districts are the most reliant on such charges while school districts are the least dependent. Generally, special districts are formed to provide utility type services and charges to finance these services are readily acceptable. Educational services, on the other hand, traditionally are provided free of direct charges. Counties and municipalities represent general purpose governments that provide such services as education and utilities; consequently, their relative reliance on charge revenues lies between that of special districts and school districts.

Table 8–1 Selected city government revenues, 1972–73 to 1976–77 (dollar amounts in millions)

| | | | | | | % change, 1972–73 to 1976–77 | |
| | | | | | | Current dollars (%) | Constant (1972) dollars (%) |
Source of revenue	1976–77	1975–76	1974–75	1973–74	1972–73	Current dollars (%)	Constant (1972) dollars (%)
Charges, total	$17,766	$15,869	$13,852	$12,167	$11,316	57.0	19.7
Current charges	6,872	6,161	5,443	4,927	4,533	51.6	15.6
Utility revenue	19,682	9,504	8,217	7,067	6,619	61.4	23.0
Liquor store revenue	212	204	192	173	164	29.3	− 1.4
Taxes, total from own sources	26,067	23,336	21,135	19,434	18,477	41.1	7.6
Property taxes	15,653	14,165	13,046	12,244	11,879	31.8	0.5
Sales and gross receipts	5,805	5,109	4,555	3,931	3,567	62.7	24.1

Source: U.S., Department of Commerce, Bureau of the Census, *City Government Finances in 1976–77* (Washington, D.C.: Government Printing Office, 1979), table 1.

Table 8–2 Percentage of revenues from various sources for local governments, 1976–1977

	All local governments	Counties	Municipalities	Townships	Special districts	School districts
Total	100.0	100.0	100.0	100.0	100.0	100.0
Intergovernmental revenue	43.0	45.3	39.6	29.7	39.9	50.4
Tax revenue	41.8	38.3	42.9	62.0	14.1	43.0
Charges and miscellaneous	15.2	16.4	17.5	8.3	46.0	6.6

Source: U.S., Department of Commerce, Bureau of the Census, *Governmental Finances in 1976–77* (Washington, D.C.: Government Printing Office, 1979), table 24.

Types of user charges

The various types of user charges are outlined in Table 8–3. In general, fees are used to compensate the government for expenses incurred when it provides such special services as police and crowd control at private events. The expenses for these services are typically charged to the sponsor. Fees are also charged for administrative paperwork that primarily benefits individuals (e.g., permits for development and filing fees for tract maps). Fees for licenses often are designed to cover the additional expenses to the local government for private activities

Table 8–3   Types of local government fees, charges, and licenses by service areas

Police protection
Special patrol service fees
Parking fees and charges
Fees for fingerprints, copies
Payments for extra police services at
    stadiums, theaters, circuses

Transportation
Subway and bus fares
Bridge tolls
Landing and departure fees
Hangar rentals
Concession rentals
Parking meter receipts

Health and hospitals
Inoculation charges
X-ray charges
Hospital charges, including per diem rates
Ambulance charges
Concessions rentals

Education
Charges for books
Charges for gymnasium uniforms
Concession rentals

Recreation
Green fees
Parking charges
Concession rentals
Admission fees or charges
Permit charges for tennis courts, etc.
Charges for specific recreation services
Picnic stove fees
Stadium gate tickets
Stadium club fees
Park development charges

Sanitation
Domestic and commercial trash collection
    fees
Industrial waste charges

Sewerage
Sewerage system fees

Other public utility operations
Water meter permits
Water services charges
Electricity rates
Telephone booth rentals

**Housing, neighborhood and commercial
    development**
Street tree fees
Tract map filing fees

Street lighting installations
Convention center revenues

Commodity sales
Salvage materials
Sales of maps
Sales of codes

Licenses and fees
Advertising vehicles
Amusements (ferris wheels, etc.)
Billiard and pool halls
Bowling alleys
Circus and carnivals
Coal dealers
Commercial combustion
Dances
Dog tags
Duplicate dog tags
Electrician—first class
Electrician—second class
Film storage
Foot peddlers
Hucksters and itinerant peddlers
Heating equipment contractors
Hotels
Junk dealers
Loading zone permits
Lumber dealers
Pawnbrokers
Plumbers—first class
Plumbers—second class
Pest eradicators
Poultry dealers
Produce dealer—itinerant
Pushcarts
Rooming houses
Secondhand dealers
Sign inspection
Solicitation
Shooting gallery
Taxis
Taxi transfer licenses
Taxi drivers
Theaters
Trees—Christmas
Vending—coin
Vault cleaners
Sound truck
Refuse hauler
Landfill
Sightseeing bus
Wrecking license

Source: Selma J. Mushkin and Charles L. Vehorn, "User Fees
    and Charges," *Governmental Finance*, November 1977,
    p. 48.

(e.g., carnivals). Fees are also charged to oversee the operation of private enterprise. In some cases, license fees are a way for the local government to share the profits of a private enterprise (e.g., a taxi service), in which case, the fees are similar to sales or gross receipts taxes.

User charges are very much like prices charged for privately produced goods. They represent payment for services that would not be provided to the individual if the charge were not paid. For example, an individual may be excluded from playing on a municipal golf course if the required fee is not paid. Individuals or firms, however, are not always given the right to refuse the service and thus to avoid paying the charge. Refuse collection exemplifies this form of user charge. Other user charges, such as those for electricity and water supply, may vary with the amount of the service used. The consumer of these services can avoid some (or all) of the charge by reducing his or her consumption of the good or service.

The degree to which charges are intended to cover the costs of supplying a good or service will vary among services. Services that are considered to be an ordinary function of local government would not be financed by user fees. Educational services are provided free by local governments while the services provided by airports incur user charges. These charges are considered to be appropriate financing devices because they are designed to cover all the costs of producing the service. There are also services for which the charges do not cover full costs.

Some charges are used as a revenue source or as a method of allocating a service among its users. In these cases, the relationship between the fee and current outlays for the service is minimal. Parking fees on existing city streets are fees charged as a revenue source and used as an allocation device.

Table 8–4   Charge revenue as a percentage of expenditures, 1976–77

Parking	128.8
Water terminals	127.5
Airports	96.9
Sewerage	37.7
Hospitals	34.0
Highways	17.6
Parks and recreation	15.6
Sanitation	10.3

Source: U.S., Department of Commerce, Bureau of the Census, *City Government Finances in 1976–77* (Washington, D.C.: Government Printing Office, 1979), table 8.

The data in Table 8–4 show revenues from charges as a percentage of outlays on selected services. It provides some insight into the potential for continued increases in charge revenues. Charges for refuse collection and disposal still are not very common among local governments, nor are charges for sewerage. The highway revenues shown in Table 8–4 are derived primarily from toll bridges, although some toll roads are also included. Given the continuing pressure from federal clean air legislation, it is likely that local highway user charges may be instituted in an attempt to reduce automobile pollution in major cities by curtailing traffic. On the other hand, charges for the use of hospitals, parks, and recreation facilities are not likely to increase substantially.

Principles of user charge design

In order to explain the principles that should be employed in the development of a user charge system for publicly provided services, the form of pricing systems in the private economy should be reviewed.

The price of a soda, for example, reflects the cost to produce and transport that soda from the site of production to the place of purchase. The relevant costs are the increases in the costs of production and transportation (distribution) as the output of sodas is increased by a small amount. Economists refer to this as the marginal costs of production and distribution. Firms will find it most profitable to charge a price equal to the marginal cost; thus, the price charged for a soda will be higher in an area to which the cost of transportation is higher.

A consumer's willingness to pay for a soda depends on the satisfaction he or she expects to receive from drinking it. In general, the soda will be purchased if the consumer expects to enjoy it more than he or she would enjoy another product that costs the same amount of money. More sodas will be demanded if the satisfaction with the product increases, for example, on hot days. More sodas will also be demanded if the price goes down. The relationship between the cost of supplying sodas at the given level of output and the demand for sodas by all consumers determines the price. In equilibrium, the price paid by the consumers covers the cost to the producers to supply the sodas.

These pricing principles have relevance for certain kinds of publicly supplied goods. User charges should reflect the cost of providing additional units of the publicly provided good. This cost often varies by location. For example, it is more costly to collect refuse in low density areas that are far away from the landfill site than to collect refuse in high density areas nearer the landfill. The user charge should be higher for those in the low density area.

User charges can perform the functions of private prices. Charges can allocate demand to those users who most highly value the good or service. For example, by charging for the use of a bridge, those who value highly the services of the bridge would pay the charge and use the bridge; those who did not value the bridge would neither use it nor pay for it.

Variation in costs

Because most user charges should reflect the costs of providing service, the variables affecting these costs are important. There are three cost variables: output, distribution, and demand variation over time. In order to discuss these costs variations a typical water supply utility will be considered. Water is obtained and treated at one location. The cost of producing water at this location depends on how much water is to be supplied to the community. Larger volumes of water require the construction of larger facilities and the use of more operating materials as well as more labor. Thus, there is a positive relationship between long-run costs of the volume of water to be processed and that to be delivered; however, the change in total long-run costs as output may not always increase; it may decline or remain constant. Long-run marginal cost has been shown to decline for movements from small to medium-sized water treatment plants but may remain constant or even increase as larger capacity water treatment plants are constructed.[2]

Once a treatment plant is constructed, a different set of cost relationships is considered. Many costs are fixed during the construction of the plant and these do not change much with the level of usage. The cost of the building, the land, and large equipment are fixed costs; other costs, primarily operating costs, vary with the volume of water produced each day. The change in these costs may be calculated as the volume of water treated in an existing plant is increased. These costs are termed short-run because they reflect the fact that a plant has already been constructed and can be expanded only with a significant delay in time for planning and construction. Short-run marginal costs of treatment (i.e., the incremental cost of treating one more gallon of water at a given level of operation) generally remain constant (or increase only slightly) in the range of the designed capacity of a plant. If designed capacity is significantly exceeded, however, marginal costs may rise appreciably.

Output The relationship between the volume of output and short-run and long-run cost is generally quite clear. Less commonly discussed is the relationship between the location of the customer, the density of development at that location, and the long-run cost of serving the individual. There have been several studies over the past twenty years that have explored the effects of development patterns on the cost of service.[3] Primary emphasis has been on density of development. These studies show that the long-run cost of service declines per household as density of development (number of households per acre) increases. For services like water supply, it is easy to see why this is so. Water pipe is laid down the center of a street and individual service lines extend from the water main to each building. A higher density of development means more dwelling units per mile of water main, which reduces cost and the number of connections as well. Furthermore, the cost of laying a water main increases only in proportion to its diameter, but the volume of water a main can carry increases more than proportionally, according to its square. This means that the average cost per unit of water carried is less in a larger sized main.

Distribution Estimates of the relationship between long-run cost of service and density of development are presented in Table 8–5. These estimates indicate that the variations in cost of service among densities and types of development can be substantial. A low density single-family housing area is five times more expensive to serve than high-rise apartments, the cost falling from $3,311 per household per year for one dwelling unit per acre to $655 per household per year for 60 dwelling units per acre. The relationship between density and costs is less pronounced for water supply and sewerage. Table 8–5 also shows significant variations in operating (short-run) costs as well as in capital costs.

The second component of the distribution cost of supplying various services is the location of the development relative to that of the production site. In water supply, for example, the site of production is usually near a major water course. In order to supply water to households or businesses located at some distance from the treatment plant, water mains are laid from the plant to each location. Clearly, the cost will increase as the distance between the plant and the customer increases. Estimates of this cost of distance for various services is provided in Table 8–6.

Many services are provided at more than one site in a metropolitan area to economize on the cost of transportation and distribution of the service. For example, police and fire stations are located in several neighborhoods. There is, however, a limit to the potential for cost saving. Too many production sites can lead to higher costs of the output. Usually, the increase in the costs of water production at several treatment plants will exceed the savings in the costs of distribution from one plant. Nevertheless, each public service will have a different combination of the number of sites of production and cost of distribution, which will minimize the total costs of supplying all customers.

Demand variation Once decisions have been made on the location and the output capacity of the production facilities and the capacity and location of distribution facilities, the demand for the service becomes important. At some point at or beyond the designed capacity of the facility, the short-run marginal costs of serving additional users increase sharply. If the demand for the service varies significantly over time, the facility may periodically face a capacity constraint. This periodic heavy demand is commonly called *peak load*. If the facility is financed through general revenues or if the same low average-cost price is charged at all times, the result may be an overuse of the facility. Overuse is

Table 8–5 The cost of providing public services by property type and density, 1973

| | Single-family homes (1,000 units) | | | | Multifamily homes (1,000 units) | | | | |
| | | | | | Townhouses, | Walk-up apartments | | High-rise apartments | |
Cost	1 unit/acre	2 units/acre	3 units/acre	5 units/acre	10 units/acre	15 units/acre	30 units/acre	30 units/acre	60 units/acre
Capital cost									
Police	$ 113,852	$ 111,752	$ 109,652	$ 105,452	$ 104,852	$ 104,252	$ 103,652	$ 103,652	$ 103,052
Fire	119,918	108,368	96,818	73,718	52,974	52,974	52,974	52,974	65,474
Sanitation	29,220	27,620	25,220	23,140	21,244	18,140	17,380	15,796	14,820
Schools	5,353,582	5,353,582	5,353,582	5,353,582	4,538,155	4,538,155	4,538,155	1,646,167	1,646,167
Water supply	7,529,720	3,833,744	2,563,857	1,739,362	1,163,154	855,900	485,304	566,792	334,777
Storm drainage	4,835,868	2,420,383	1,595,857	1,068,046	710,649	462,420	231,274	284,552	117,684
Sanitary sewerage	2,963,624	1,586,257	1,121,045	813,398	594,021	438,451	354,678	345,062	274,509
Total capital cost	20,945,784	13,441,706	10,865,360	9,176,693	7,185,049	6,470,292	5,886,917	3,027,495	2,556,483
Yearly capital cost	1,828,203	1,167,283	939,488	788,740	617,607	555,001	494,079	264,018	222,446
Operating cost									
Police	69,817	66,267	62,717	55,617	52,067	49,700	46,150	46,150	42,600
Fire	135,711	116,011	96,311	56,911	41,589	41,589	41,589	54,722	54,722
Sanitation	35,287	33,142	30,315	27,780	25,469	21,686	20,760	18,850	17,640
Schools	1,168,258	1,168,258	1,168,258	1,168,258	988,526	988,526	988,526	269,598	269,598
Water supply	31,821	31,821	31,821	31,821	30,103	30,103	30,103	25,538	25,538
Storm drainage	—	—	—	—	—	—	—	—	—
Sanitary sewerage	41,289	34,401	32,133	30,604	28,022	27,250	26,679	22,825	22,476
Yearly operating cost	1,483,183	1,449,900	1,421,555	1,370,991	1,165,776	1,158,854	1,152,807	437,683	432,574
Total annual cost per dwelling unit	3,311	2,617	2,361	2,160	1,783	1,714	1,647	702	655

Source: Paul B. Downing and Richard D. Gustely, "The Public Service Costs of Alternative Development Patterns: A Review of the Evidence," in Paul B. Downing, ed., *Local Service Pricing Policies and Their Effect on Urban Spacial Structure* (Vancouver, B.C.: University of British Columbia Press, 1977), table 8.

Table 8–6 Annual cost of providing public services per mile distant from public facility site, 1973

Service	Capital or operating costs per mile ($)
Police	438[1]
Fire	216[1]
Sanitation	3,360[2]
Schools	19,845[2]
Water supply	21,560[2]
Storm drainage	6,187[3]
Sanitary sewers	12,179[3]
Total cost	68,498

Source: Paul B. Downing and Richard D. Gustely, "The Public Service Costs of Alternative Development Patterns: A Review of the Evidence," in Paul B. Downing, ed., *Local Service Pricing Policies and Their Effect on Urban Spacial Structure* (Vancouver, B.C.: University of British Columbia Press, 1977), table 9.
1 Includes only operating costs.
2 Includes both capital and operating costs.
3 Includes only capital costs.

generated because the incremental cost of serving one more user or one more unit of use at peak load far exceeds the charge incurred by the consumer. Thus, users compare the value of the service to a price that is below the true cost of their use of the service. At this low price, demand will run high in comparison to the capacity of the facility, and result in the overuse of the facility. This overuse can manifest itself in various ways: in water supply, pressure is lost; in the supply of electricity, brownouts occur; in highway or travel, traffic jams and delays are generated. The social costs of overuse increase and the private costs of lost time and equipment failure rise with the decline in the quality of service. The potential overuse of a service might be eliminated or sharply reduced, however, if at peak demand periods consumers incurred a higher charge to reflect the true cost of peak output.

Design of user charges

The design of user charges should reflect the costs of providing publicly supplied services just as prices for privately produced goods reflect the costs of production and transportation. User charges for most services would have three components.

One part of the user charge would reflect the short-run cost of current output. Generally, this can be done with a single charge per unit that will vary directly with the quantity consumed. When there are significant peak load demands, this quantity charge should be considerably higher during those peak periods. The quantity charge would then reflect the short-run costs of service at the time the service is produced and consumed.

The second part of the user charge would be a payment to cover the difference between the quantity charge and the full cost of production. This difference reflects the outlay for the fixed costs of the service (e.g., plant construction). This capacity charge may be allocated on the basis of each customer's potential use of the designed capacity. Where fixed costs are not very high, the charge may not be levied, because it would be a very small amount or possibly nothing.

The third part of the user charge system would be a location charge that reflects the long-run cost of serving residents at each location and the development density. This charge could be paid monthly or as a connection charge when the area is served initially. A special assessment can be a close approximation to this charge.

The end product of this user charge system is a combination of charges that are higher for those who demand more service, for residents who live in areas that are particularly expensive to serve, and for those who use the service during peak periods. Because this system of charges embodies the costs of service, the charges would provide residents with proper price signals. The response to the charges then provides the local government managers with information on the desirability of increasing the levels of service.

Developers and prospective new residents will decide whether the value of developing a new area is greater than the cost of providing the required public services. The managers of the public facility can observe the quantity demanded during peak times at the peak load prices. If the total revenues generated would cover the total cost of expansion, it is worthwhile to expand the facility. A well designed system of charge has substantial potential for improving the provision of public services because it allocates the available supply to those who value it most, and it provides accurate information on the desirability of expanding service.

Practical considerations

The ideal user charge system would be designed as a three-part user charge. It would consist of the capacity charge, the location charge, and a more sophisticated variation of the quantity charge—the time variable/peak load volume charge (which reflects the costs of servicing various residents). Other costs often alter the ideal form of the user charge system.

Administrative costs   Administrative costs include the cost of collecting data on the individual's consumption of the public services, calculating the costs of serving that resident at that volume of use, and billing for and collecting the user charge. These administrative costs might be relatively large for some services. It is quite difficult and expensive to monitor the volume and noxiousness of sewage put into the treatment system; however, it is relatively easy and inexpensive to install a water meter.

A calculation of the costs to monitor directly individual usage may lead the decision maker to conclude that volume charges are not justified. Indirect methods of measuring volume of use should be considered. For example, volume charges for sewer service often are based on the volume of water consumed. Such indirect measurements can be quite useful if the relationship between that which is measurable and that which is not as easily measured is relatively consistent. These measurements, when used, can retain the advantages of the volume charge without the disadvantages of administrative costs. Nevertheless, there is a quality problem with indirect methods of measurements. Household sewerage may not be as difficult or as costly to treat as industrial waste; consequently, measuring the volume of water used to indicate the volume of sewerage can be misleading. Information on the *quality* of the sewerage may be desirable.

The costs of billing in a user charge system may be substantial. It is possible, but not likely, that the costs would be so high that it would not pay to implement a periodic billing system. In this age of inexpensive computers, however, a municipality that prepares periodic bills for other services may add the cost of processing another item at a minimum of expense.

One last point should be made about the costs of administering user charges. There are many public services for which the use rate among residents is relatively constant. The difference in costs of service among residents such as these may be small. The administrative costs of employing variable charges based on volume for these residents may be higher than the additional revenues collected. The variable charges would not be economical. A similar circumstance may arise when variations in cost of serving residents at different locations are small. The extra administrative costs of instituting a variance in the charge system may outweigh any gains in efficiency.

Acceptance of a user charge system   A second practical consideration is acceptance of the system by the residents, which is based on their understanding of what the user charge is and how it is calculated. When the benefits of the public service are easily identified by those using it, being charged for use is easily understood and readily accepted. Charges for water consumption, fees for use of public golf courses, charges for tennis courts, and tolls for bridges are accepted by most citizens. It is difficult for the benefits of these services to be ignored when their use is obvious to the citizenry. However, charges that cannot be easily related to use will not be easily understood and may be resisted by residents of an area.

Residents faced with a user charge system may consider the federal income tax effect. Whereas local taxes are deductible from taxable income, user charges are not. This means that a dollar paid in user charges is more costly to the local resident than a dollar paid in property taxes. (The difference between the two costs will depend on the individual's marginal income-tax rate.) Thus, the extensive use of charges can make local government services more expensive to residents. This phenomenon will be most significant for high income residents and for high income communities.

Which costs count   The cost of producing public services can be divided into capital costs and operation and maintenance costs. In general, user charges for public services should reflect the full costs of service. The charges should include not only operation and maintenance costs, but also the cost of all the capital employed in the production and distribution of the service. The calculation of these costs may not be easily accomplished because municipal accounting systems are not necessarily designed for this purpose. The current value or the cost of past capital investment may not be available. This is most often the case with long lived assets such as water mains and sewerage. Thus, the costs of service estimates for user charge purposes often do not reflect all the capital costs. This can lead to undercharging and a more rapid expansion of service than is economically justifiable. When the user charge is below the full cost of providing the service, the demand for and the consumption of the service will be relatively high, and will result in an increase in total social costs for everyone.

There are, however, cases where charging the user the full cost of producing the service is not desirable. When the consumption of particular public goods or services by individuals unable to pay user charges is thought to benefit the entire community, the goods and services are called merit goods. A user charge equal to the full cost of production would reduce consumption of the merit good by these individuals. The reduced consumption would lead to the reduced benefits to others in the community; therefore, the user charge to these consumers is reduced or eliminated in order to keep their consumption level high.

Although there is a debate about whether any particular public service is a merit good, local governments continue to implement this concept, particularly in the areas of education and recreation. The implication of a reduced charge for merit goods is that one group, usually the more affluent, subsidizes the consumption of a second group, usually the poor. This is a form of income redistribution, but it differs from other more direct methods (e.g., transfer payments) because it requires consumption of a specific good. The group who provides this form of subsidy recognizes that consumption of these goods by the other group is a benefit to both groups. Recreation improves health and reduces social unrest. Education improves productivity and makes the atmosphere of the community more pleasant. The result is a reduction in long-run costs to the subsidizing group.

User charges for individual services[4]

The production, distribution, and administration costs vary among publicly supplied services such that the charging practices for each should and will vary among services. Practical user charge systems for several services are described in this section. These systems attempt to compromise between the theoretical, the ideal, and the practical realities of the functions of local government finance.

Water supply

The water supply system of a local government closely approximates a privately produced good. In fact, many communities are served by privately owned and operated water utilities. The major arguments for a public system (or a controlled utility) are efficiency, safety, and certainty of supply. The efficiency argument implies that the output of water for a given area (i.e., obtaining it from a source and treating it so that it is fit for human consumption) is subject to decreasing costs as output increases. This makes water a natural candidate for monopoly because output is most often centered with one supplier, particularly when the source of supply is a river or a lake.

All connections should be metered and usage measured and billed periodically. This process is not too expensive and the failure to employ meters and a system of charges based on actual use will greatly increase waste in the consumption of water. The most practical charge is a constant amount per unit of water consumed for all classes of consumers. The exception to this policy is a potentially large volume user whose pattern of use may be random. Major industrial users that exhibit substantial variations in demand can influence total costs. Their demand can only be satisfied by having "excess capacity" or by buying water at higher cost. In these cases, a higher charge per unit would be levied for units consumed significantly above the expected level of demand—or better yet, a capacity charge might be assessed for these users.

The quantity of water demanded by most residential and probably most commercial users is so small relative to the total output that in practice the short-run marginal costs of output can be treated as constant. However, the marginal cost of additional use does increase during peak periods. A higher volume charge should be employed during these times; however, the extra costs involved in metering peak period use may make such a charge unadvisable for all but a few large water users. In this case, in addition to the variable output charge, the average consumer should pay a capacity charge to help cover his or her share of the fixed costs of the treatment plant.[5]

Distribution costs   Distribution costs of water are affected by three variables. They are:

1. The distance from the source of supply or central distribution site (e.g., treatment plant)
2. The density of customers in an area
3. The capacity of service for each customer (usually measured in terms of the size of the lateral pipe from the water main).

It is probably not practical to charge all of the customers on the basis of individual calculations of their cost of service. Instead, service areas can be delineated so that each is relatively homogeneous in terms of distance and density. An estimate of the marginal cost of distribution to each area may then be made; this cost would be allocated to each customer within the area in proportion to his or her expected consumption. A second part of the distribution charge would be based on the number of feet of street frontage each customer occupied. The cost of distributing water increases as the number of feet of pipe between customers increases. A front foot charge based on this cost would be levied on each customer. In those few cases where the capacity to receive water is particularly large, an additional capacity charge may be levied. Such a charge would be most significant for large industrial users in outlying areas.

To summarize, the distribution charge would consist of a flat charge per customer, which would vary with the service area in which he or she is located. The front foot charge also may differ for each customer. Because the physical data on which such charges are based will not change rapidly, the administrative cost of calculating and applying such charges should not be excessive. The sum of these charges for all customers of the water supply service should cover all distribution costs, including expected maintenance costs.

Billing The water charge system suggested here consists of a fixed distribution charge based on service area, capacity to use the system, and front footage. The system also involves a variable charge of a flat amount per gallon for each gallon of water consumed, as measured by the water meter. The total charges could be billed monthly or bimonthly. An alternative billing method is to levy the distribution charge (but not the user charge) as a lump sum or special assessment at the time of development. The lump sum charge has the minor advantage of reducing the complexity of the water billing procedure. On the other hand, having the distribution charge appear explicitly on the monthly bill acts as a continual reminder of the cost of locational choice made by the consumer. It is impossible to say whether this advantage offsets the additional administrative cost without further study.

Although water pricing policies vary substantially among jurisdictions, the most prevalent system has a declining block rate volume charge (i.e., a charge that is lower per unit as more water is used) and, perhaps, a front foot charge. This declining block rate has been justified in the past with the argument that the average cost per unit of water produced and delivered declines as the volume produced increases. An analysis suggests that this may not be the case; thus, there is an argument for a flat volume rate per unit. There are cost savings, however, in delivery of large volumes of water because of savings in pipe, meter, and administrative costs. These savings should be reflected in a proportionately lower capacity charge for large volume users unless usage is erratic. In any case, declining block rates with minimal charges that are below the cost of producing water encourage waste.

The use of front foot charges is a move to cover the costs of distribution. The front foot charge reflects only the density portion of distribution costs; the distance portion of the charge is neglected. Some local governments, notably, Fairfax County, Virginia, have recently recognized this fact. Fairfax County has adjusted its charges for new connections to include at least some of the distance costs. But even these charges include only the capital costs of distribution. Maintenance costs are not included nor are the capacity costs of the treatment facility.

In summary, the current practice in the structure of water charges is not closely related to the cost of service. Users in outlying areas, which are expensive to serve are relatively undercharged whereas users in areas that are less expensive to serve are overcharged. The volume charge, excluding high volume users, usually exceeds the marginal cost of service. These inaccuracies in the pricing system lead to uneconomic growth and demand, and have expensive impacts on many local government water systems.

Sanitary sewerage

The general cost characteristics of the system of collecting and disposing of domestic sewage are similar to those of the water supply system. There are economies of scale in treating sewage; however, it appears that these economies are exhausted in systems that serve 100,000 people.[6] Beyond this population, costs are relatively constant for any given percentage of removal of pollutants. The average costs of collection and transmission increase with a greater distance between the site of production of the sewage and the site of disposal. The costs decrease with increases in the density of the population to be served because a larger system decreases the per capita costs.

The marginal cost of treating sewage is determined by both the strength (or pollution potential) of the sewage and the volume of the sewage. Strength is relatively constant for domestic and commercial customers and need not be included as a variable in their charges. For these users, the volume of sewage is the variable on which to base an output price. Because it is relatively expensive to build meters to measure sewage flows from individual households, a measurement of water consumption might be better. Domestic and ordinary commercial water consumption, exclusive of lawn sprinkling, should reflect a very close approximation of the quantity of sewage discharged. This volume can be estimated by metering water consumption during the winter months. The average of the water meter may be used to determine a monthly charge for the entire year.

The strength of the sewage may be an important variable for industrial customers. This variable may be handled by requiring pretreatment of the sewage to bring it down to the average domestic strength. Another alternative is to impose a strength surcharge on the regular volume charge. Large industrial users also may have significant differences between metered water consumption and sewage flow. Sewage meters, although they are expensive, may be justified in these cases. (It should be noted that the federal Water Pollution Control Act requires major industries that are connected to municipal sewage systems to pay a user charge that covers all costs, including a strength surcharge on the volume of sewage discharged.)

The collection and transmission charge should be calculated in a way similar to that employed for water. Service areas should be defined, and a charge established for service area and front footage. A capacity charge should also be made on the basis of a water meter or water pipe size. The consumption potential of water is a good indicator of the demand for extra sewer capacity. The current practice in charging for sewage sanitation is somewhat more varied than that for water supply. Sewer user charges may simply be a percentage of the water bill. The costs of supplying water, even with a well-designed water user charge, do not necessarily vary with service characteristics in the same way the cost of sewer service may vary.

Another sewer user charge system commonly used is a flat monthly charge that is equal to the average cost of serving all residents. In this case, high cost users (in terms of volume and location) are undercharged. As in the water charge, the marginal cost for more use of the service is zero, which leads to demands for excessive and costly service.

A third charge system currently in use closely reflects the optimal user charge structure. In this simple system, a flat rate is charged per unit of water consumed. This charge may be adjusted for summer lawn watering. A front foot sewer line charge may be employed in conjunction with any of these charge systems.

Storm water sewerage

Storm water will either percolate into the ground or flow across the surface to a surface water body (e.g., lake or stream). Urban development tends to increase surface runoff because buildings, roads, and parking lots are impervious to water. Storm sewerage costs increase with lower density of development and increase with a greater area of paved development. Costs also have a distance component, but this differs from that of sanitary sewers because the collected storm water runoff is released untreated in nearby surface water bodies rather than routed to the treatment plant.

These cost characteristics suggest a storm water user charge system consisting of two parts. Because there is no treatment, no output charge is needed.[7] The collection and transmission costs would be covered by a service area and front foot charge system similar to that suggested for water and sanitary sewers. Note, however, that the service areas will differ from those for sanitary sewers as the location of storm water outfalls is likely to differ from the location of treatment plants. The portion of this charge for service area would be apportioned among land users in the service area on the basis of the surface area of each individual site and on the percentage of that surface area that is covered by impervious materials.

In practice, user charges for storm sewers either are not used or only consist of front foot charges. The charge system would be improved if the potential for generating runoff through development of impervious areas were recognized. Furthermore, distance to a viable outfall site should be reflected in the charge. Omission of these two factors can lead to high cost of service and undesirable locations for development.

Refuse

Refuse (solid waste) collection, like water supply, closely approximates a private service. Disposal costs are a function of the volume of refuse collected. These costs may include environmental damages because disposal sites can contribute to surface and ground water pollution. Marginal costs of collection and transmission are a function of distance and density.[8]

Beyond approximately 500 residents, there appear to be relatively constant returns to scale in collection and transmission costs (per mile). Disposal costs for a sanitary landfill would probably be subject to decreasing costs for a larger population; but because there is no hard evidence on these costs, it seems that for a population beyond 100,000 the economies of scale are exhausted as well. However, costs for marginal collection and transmission and for marginal disposal vary with the volume of refuse collected. The effect of these variations in volume on cost by any one consumer are minor. On the other hand, variations in expected volume among residential consumers, and certainly variations in expected volume between residential and commercial consumers, can be substantial. Consequently, one part of the charge for each group should reflect a capacity charge of a flat price per unit of refuse multiplied by their average volume of refuse.

The cost-of-service characteristics indicate that a two-part charge system would be an optimum method of allocating costs. First, there would be a disposal charge per unit based on actual volume. Second, there would be a charge for collection and transmission based on the varying costs of serving each collection route. This record charge would, therefore, be higher for areas more distant from the disposal site and less densely developed. In contrast to this system, current practice often employs a flat fee that is independent of volume or of location.

There are, however, some practical problems in implementing a two-part charge system. First, the problem of measuring volume must be considered. A seemingly easy method is to count the number of full or partially full thirty gallon (or some other standard size) trash cans collected from each resident. This measure, however, creates a problem of definition: How tightly packed may a "full" trash can be? Moreover, the time the collector would spend to record the number of cans collected from each site would be substantial, and the probability of errors and of consumer complaints is yet another unpleasant aspect of such a measure. Thus, an approximation of the volume charge should be considered. The best collection system for single-family residences may be to collect no more than a certain number of cans per collection day and to charge a flat volume charge. More cans may be collected, but only at an additional charge and with a prior agreement. Special collection charges may be justified for multifamily residential complexes. A number of cans at one location takes substantially less time to collect than the same number of containers at different locations; therefore, the collection charge per can should be less for apartment residences. Multifamily residences and commercial consumers who use special containers and sophisticated handling equipment, such as Dempster Dumpsters, could be charged a lower collection charge per unit. Again, large volumes collected at one stop are less expensive to collect per unit.

Traffic tolls

The costs of providing a road or bridge service have a different character from those of other public services. When a road or bridge is built, it is designed to carry a specific volume of traffic at a specific speed and during a specific time period. If the volume of traffic is below the design capacity, there is no problem of congestion. Thus, with a low volume of traffic, the cost of accommodating one more car is minimal. These costs are mainly the additional wear on the road and the increase in the risks associated with having an accident. When traffic exceeds the design capacity, however, congestion results and speed is decreased. Continued increases in the number of cars attempting to use the facility can cause traffic flow to approach zero.

The costs for heavy traffic include the wear and accident factors plus the losses suffered by travelers due to traffic delays. In order to assure that those using the road or bridge during high demand or peak traffic times consider the costs they impose on other drivers, a user charge may be imposed during peak traffic periods. In practice, there are two options. One option is to operate toll booths with a higher toll during such peak periods as the morning and evening rush hours. The other alternative is to charge no toll during off-peak hours and to operate the booths only during peak traffic hours.[9]

Current practice in charging for roads and bridges usually does not follow this peak load method. Generally, the toll remains constant at all times of the day. In fact, in many cases discount coupons or tokens are sold to frequent users of the facility. These frequent users are commonly peak load users. The discount price may encourage traffic at peak times rather than discourage it. The result is slower traffic and an implied demand for more road or bridge capacity.

The employment of a peak load charge should encourage the use of car pools or divert some of the commuter traffic to public transportation. The bargain price implicit in the flat rate and discount rate structure may not reflect accurately the demand for and the value of expanding the facility. A peak pricing system may give a better reading of total demand for the transportation system as a whole.

Public transit systems

Transit systems also have capacity constraints and wide variations in peak and off-peak demands, which implies that the cost of service during peak periods is high. During off-peak periods, the incremental costs are much lower but they are not zero because the transit system uses fuel and drivers as well as equipment. Another factor that is important to the operating costs of a transit system is trip distance. These cost characteristics suggest a charge that is based on distance traveled on the system. This charge should be higher during peak periods of operation.

The prices now employed for most public transit systems do not adequately reflect the cost structure suggested previously. The price is typically the same during peak and off-peak periods. Also, persons who use the service during peak periods are sometimes sold passes at a discount; thus, peak period prices are actually reduced. Given these circumstances, excess demand during peak hours does not necessarily reflect a true willingness to pay for the expansion of the system. On the other hand, the absence of tolls for cars during peak periods reduces the peak demand for public transit facilities. The mix of incorrect prices provides the policy maker with false information about the desirability to expand both systems.

During off-peak periods, the cost of providing transit service is fairly low. Off-peak users, however, typically are charged the same price as peak users, although the cost of service during these periods is lower than that during peak periods. People consequently underutilize transit systems during off-peak periods. They are unwilling to pay the excessive price.

Because the cost of service increases with distance traveled, it seems appropriate to charge more for longer rides. Several transit services use a practical system of zone fares. The user pays an initial charge but if he or she stays on the vehicle when it crosses a zone, the individual must pay an additional amount. Zones are often coincident with political boundaries. In the absence of zone charges, long distance riders are undercharged and generally overutilize the transit system.

Parks and recreation

The cost characteristics of the park and recreation facilities are largely similar to those of highways or bridges. Once a facility is built, the cost of having one more user at low levels of use is essentially zero. At high levels of use, however, crowding reduces everyone's utility. Tennis courts are a good example of a high use facility. In low use periods, there are always courts available; but at high use times, all of the courts are filled. Some players will not be able to use the courts during the desired time. At such times it is desirable to charge for use of the courts. The charge ensures that those who value the use of the courts most during that time of day can play. Those who may easily rearrange their schedules to play at an off-peak time can avoid the charge. This ensures that the courts will be used to their best advantage.

A system that charges only during peak demands is employed by many park and recreation facilities. Public golf courses commonly charge a higher price on weekends. Often charges are lowered even more for low income groups such as senior citizens; however, these lower prices are generally offered during the off-peak hours of a weekday. These special rates reflect the community's assessment that recreation for these special groups is a merit good.

Development charges

Multipart charges placed directly on users is not the only technique of pricing public services. An alternative approach is for the governmental authority to charge the land developer with a fee that reflects the full capital costs to the municipality of development. This development charge may raise the price of housing in the project, an increase that would be greatest in areas where costs to provide public services were the highest. The higher prices of some projects, however, may not be profitable for the developer because the houses would not sell at the higher price. In other words, the total cost of building the house *and* supplying public services may be greater than the value of the house to potential buyers. A development charge eliminates the development of uneconomical areas.

The administrative costs of levying development charges could be smaller than the multipart user charge. Development charges currently are negotiated between the local government and the developer. Often development charges take the form of in-kind provision of public goods. Park and school facilities are often constructed by the developer. These act as an indirect development charge because they reduce the costs to the local government of supplying services to the area (but may raise the cost of the houses in the development). Development charges, however, are calculated to include those costs that impact on contingent areas or services. These result when incremental costs to the budget for such items as traffic congestion or recreation exceed the regular tax contributions of the new residents. If these outside costs were included, the growing practice of development charges could significantly improve the economic allocation of local government services.

Effects of alternative revenue systems

It is important to note how a user charge system would distribute the costs and influence the decisions of the individual user. There are three major items of interest to local government managers:

1.   The effect of the charges on the location and characteristics of land development
2.   The impact on the quantity demanded of the publicly provided service
3.   The distribution of burden of the financial costs of service among the residents.

Because the property tax is the principal alternative source of revenue for local governments, it is useful to compare its effects with those of a user charge system. In making this comparison, two types of user charges may be discussed: those that take into account the marginal costs of production and distribution (the various multipart charge systems) and those that charge average costs of service to all, regardless of the volume of services consumed or the location of the demand. A charge system that takes account of locational and other service cost differentials is, of course, the ideal system. Such a system employs a marginal-cost user charge. The second system reflects an average-cost user charge. The following discussion compares these two systems to that of the property tax. The practical user charge systems discussed previously were an attempt to develop a practical form of the marginal-cost user charge whereas much of the current practice in user charges resembles the average-cost user charge. Actual practice, however, varies among governments and among services within a given area.

The effects on development[10]

One of the factors that influences the timing and intensity of the development of an area is the amount charged for publicly provided services. A developer who is considering investment in a development project will estimate the cost to construct or improve the homes, offices, or other structures. The developer will also consider the price purchasers are willing to pay for the land and improvements. Included in the construction costs are any development fees to be incurred or in-kind provision of public services to be provided by the developer. Higher fees or service provision require that a higher price be charged for the houses in order to make a profit on the development. Prospective purchasers react to high prices; if the price is too high, they may not purchase the property— in which case the developer may not develop.

In contrast, if user charges are to be levied on the future owner, the maximum amount the potential buyer would be willing to pay for the property will be reduced. In this case, the buyer considers the annual costs of operation, including public-service user charges, when he or she decides how much he or she is willing to pay for a house. Higher user charges for any given level of service reduce the maximum bid for the house. However, when the user charges are levied on the future owner, the developer incurs lower costs, which permits the house to be sold for less. The developer may still make a profit. If the maximum bid of the prospective purchaser is reduced more than the reduction in the price charged by the developer, the property probably will not be developed.

Thus, it appears that land in areas where charges for public services will be high is less likely to be developed. The marginal-cost user charges vary among areas served by the local government. The governments may increase payments and thus lessen the potential profit and the degree of inhibited development in high cost-of-service areas. In lower cost-of-service areas, the marginal-cost user charge will not reduce potential profit as much. Low cost-of-service areas are more likely to be developed, which is exactly what the local government manager wishes because this type of development generates a more efficient service mix.

However, if an average-cost user charge is employed, high-cost areas will pay less for public services than it costs to provide them. The average cost for an entire city will be below the cost of serving these areas. The lower average-cost user charges will increase the probability that these high-cost areas will be developed; potential buyers will bid more for the homes. In contrast, the average-cost user charge in low-cost areas would be above the cost of service. The potential buyer's bid for the house will be less, reducing potential profit to the developer and inhibiting development.

An average-cost user charge can stimulate development in areas where the cost of service is high. The funds to pay for the excess of costs over payments is derived from the residents of low-cost service areas because they pay more than the true cost of service. The marginal-cost user charge does not stimulate inefficient development and does not cause residents of different areas of the city to pay more or less than the cost of serving them.

The locational effect of the general property tax is between the two specific user charge systems. Property taxes are based on the market price of land and improvements. The tax figure is reduced by the amount the purchaser expects to pay for user charges on the public services provided. Charges are reflected in the price of real estate. The property tax will reflect in part the under- or overcharging of the average-cost user charge. Property values will be higher in high cost-of-service areas and lower in low cost-of-service areas than they would be under marginal-cost user charges; however, this relationship will not be perfect.[11] The degree of inaccuracy of the charge will vary among properties although the tax rate will not differ. There are many other factors that cause variations in the value of property, but it is sufficient to note that a property tax helps offset the inaccuracies of an average-cost user charge. The more accurate the user charge design (the more closely it reflects differences in the marginal cost of serving different areas), the less will be the effect on property value. Nevertheless, it is not practical to design a user charge that captures all differences in the marginal cost of service. The resultant errors will be captured in property values. Because the property tax partially captures this change in value, it is advantageous to combine a practical marginal-cost user charge with a property tax. A financing structure such as this is most effective in creating development incentives.

Growth control

The proper design of user charges has implications for the control of growth. A marginal-cost user charge requires the social costs of local growth to be paid for by those causing that growth. An average-cost user charge may promote growth at the expense of existing residents if the cost of serving the new resident is higher than the average cost of serving current residents. These higher costs eventually increase the average cost of the system and result in higher user charges. Because the new residents also pay an average-cost charge, they pay less than the full cost of the services extended to them, and thus are essentially subsidized by the current users. This subsidy actually stimulates demand for new developments. A properly designed marginal system would not provide this stimulus because all new residents would pay for the additional incremental costs of the public services. On the other hand, where the marginal cost of serving new residents is below the average cost of serving existing residents, an average-cost user charge would inhibit the growth of the area.

The property tax method of financing public services has an intermediate effect. It is less growth stimulating than an average-cost user charge, but it still provides some subsidy from existing residents to new residents whenever the cost to serve new residents is higher than that for existing residents.

The effects on demand

The different methods of financing public services also have effects on the demand for the service. The volume charge of a marginal-cost user charge system reflects the full cost of increasing output. Residents will decide how much to consume based on this cost. An average-cost user charge, however, will not be equal to the short-run marginal cost of increasing output. The circumstances will determine whether the charge will be higher or lower than the marginal costs. Therefore, the resident, on adjusting his or her consumption to the price, may over- or underconsume the service. The direction of the effect will depend on the design of the average-cost user charge and the cost characteristics of the public service. In the case of water supply, low volume users often are charged more than the actual costs they impose on the system, an occurrence that inhibits water consumption.

The financing of public services through the property tax implies that the cost to the consumer to use additional units is zero. In most of the cases discussed, the cost to the city of producing more units of a service is positive; thus, the property tax stimulates overconsumption of the service. The effect of this overconsumption is an increase in the cost of local government—which partially explains the movement toward expenditure control observed in California and several other states throughout the country.

It is also true that average-cost user charges and other lump sum methods of financing services lead to excessive demand during peak demand periods. A marginal-cost user charge that is higher during peak periods would help bring about a reduction in the number of people using the facility during peak demand periods. Thus, utilization should spread more evenly during the day. Peak load charges seem appropriate for services such as urban bridges and highways, public transportation, and recreation facilities (e.g., golf courses and tennis courts).

The effects on income distribution

In addition to the effects on development and demand, managers of local governments often express concern for the impacts of alternative financing systems on people in various income classes. Low income people should pay less for public services because their ability to pay is less. But what is meant by paying less? One answer is a comparison of the absolute amount paid by high and low income groups. A more common comparison is the calculation of the payment as a percentage of the person's income. A financing system that requires a payment that is a higher percentage of income for higher income people is called a progressive system. A system that charges lower income groups a higher percentage of their income than it charges high income groups is called a regressive system.

A comparison of user charges and the property tax reveal that both average-cost and marginal-cost user charge systems are relatively more regressive than the property tax.[12] However, a comparison between average-cost and marginal-cost user charges shows that average-cost charges are much more regressive than are marginal-cost charges. The reason for this is that high income people tend to live in larger homes, at lower densities, and in more distant locations; hence, they have higher cost of services and higher marginal-cost user charges. This comparison also suggests that when an average-cost user charge is employed, low income people generally pay more than it costs to serve them. Low income residents may be subsidizing high income residents under these circumstances. With a marginal-cost user charge, this subsidy does not take place.

Special districts

There are various ways to organize the system through which public services will be provided. The municipal government can provide the services, or an organization may provide specific services. The two forms of organization most commonly used in lieu of direct municipal provision are the municipally owned utility (MOU) and the special district. There is often confusion in terminology between these two organizational forms and the public authorities. Public authorities can be either municipally owned utilities or special districts. The range of services provided by special districts includes services previously discussed (i.e., water supply, sewerage, and refuse). Special districts may also be formed for other purposes, including fire protection, housing and urban renewal, and drainage and flood control. The types and numbers of special districts are listed in Table 8–7.

The Census Bureau defines special districts as limited purpose governmental units that exist as separate corporate entities and, theoretically, have fiscal and administrative independence from general purpose governments. Fiscal independence suggests that a special district, as an entity, may determine its budget without review by other local officials or governments, levy taxes for its support, collect charges for its services, and issue debt without review by another local government.[13] Administrative independence, according to the Census Bureau, means that a public agency such as a special district has a popularly elected governing body that represents two or more state or local governments and performs functions that are essentially different from those of its creating governments. Due to the uniqueness of school districts, the definitions here and in subsequent discussion concern only non-school districts.

Many special districts are, by law, agencies subordinate to a parent governmental unit (or units). Those entities are considered to be dependent special districts, and generally possess one or more of the following characteristics:

1. The agency officers are appointed by the chief executive and/or governing body of the parent government(s).
2. The agency controls facilities that supplement or take the place of facilities ordinarily provided by the creating government(s).
3. The agency properties and responsibilities revert to the creating government after the agency's debt has been repaid.
4. The agency plans must be approved by the creating government(s).
5. The parent government(s) specifies the type and location of facilities that the agency is to construct and maintain.[14]

Functional responsibilities of special districts

The Census Bureau groups special districts into single- and multiple-function categories. As Table 8–7 indicates, there were substantial increases in nearly all

Table 8–7 Number of special districts, 1977, 1972, 1967, and 1962, by function

Function	No. of special districts				% change, 1962–1977
	1977	1972	1967	1962	
Single function districts					
Cemeteries	1,615	1,496	1,397	1,283	25.9
School buildings	1,020	1,085	956	915	11.5
Fire protection	4,187	3,872	3,665	3,229	29.7
Highways	652	698	774	786	−17.0
Health	350	257	234	231	51.5
Hospitals	715	655	537	418	71.0
Housing and urban renewal	2,408	2,270	1,565	1,099	119.1
Libraries	586	498	410	349	67.9
Drainage	2.255	2,192	2,193	2,240	0.7
Flood control	681	677	662	500	36.2
Irrigation and water conservation	934	966	904	781	19.6
Soil conservation	2,431	2,564	2,571	2,461	−1.2
Other natural resources	294	231	209	309	−4.8
Parks and recreation	829	749	613	488	69.9
Sewers	1,610	1,406	1,233	937	71.8
Water supply	2,480	2,323	2,140	1,502	65.1
Electric power	82	74	75	76	7.9
Gas supply	46	48	37	30	53.3
Transit	96	33	14	10	860.0
Other	971	889	622	488	99.0
Multiple function districts					
Sewer and water supply	1,065	629	298	138	671.7
Natural resources and water supply	71	67	45	56	26.8
Other	584	207	110	120	386.7

Source: U.S., Department of Commerce, Bureau of the Census, 1977 Census of Governments, vol. 1, *Governmental Organization*, part 1, *Governmental Organization* (Washington, D.C.: Government Printing Office, 1979), table 12.

types of districts between 1962 and 1977. The greatest growth was experienced by transit districts (860.0 percent), followed by sewer and water supply districts (671.7 percent) and housing and urban renewal (119.1 percent). Fire protection districts were the most numerous in all of the years shown in Table 8–7.

Fiscal characteristics

Most special districts in metropolitan areas have the right to levy user charges; they often have significant property taxing powers as well. The property tax is the only form of tax that special districts levy. Reliance on the property tax may exceed 80.0 percent in such categories as fire protection, health services, and libraries. On the other hand, special districts that provide utility services such as sewerage, water, and electricity use little or no property tax revenue. On average, special districts account for only 1.9 percent of the local government taxes in the United States, and in no state did special districts raise as much as 9.0 percent of local taxes.

One of the features that distinguishes special districts from other governmental entities is their heavy use of pricing mechanisms (e.g., user fees, charges, and special assessments). In 1976, 46.0 percent of all special district receipts were derived from charges, compared to 17.5 percent for municipalities and 16.4 percent for counties, townships, and school districts (see Table 8–2). The importance of the use of user fees by special districts lies in the fact that such pricing is a potential means of ensuring a more efficient allocation of public resources. This, however, depends on the design of the charge.

Another financial instrument often employed by special districts is the special assessment. Special assessments are levied on property owners for such public works as pavement improvements, drainage, parking facilities, and other capital improvements. The justification for such levies is that many public works directly enhance the value of nearby land, thereby providing a potential financial benefit to its owners. It is logical to charge part or all of the cost of the works to the landowners. Special assessments are most synonymous to user fees, both in the rationale for their employment and their economic effects.[15] This is because this lump sum charge reflects at least part of the location dependent costs of service. This being the case, the special assessment is equivalent roughly to the present value of future marginal-cost user charges.

In addition to user charges and local taxes, many special districts receive considerable financial aid from federal, state, and other local sources. Table 8–8 outlines the revenue sources, including intergovernmental revenues, for special districts. In fact, the growth in aid monies has been greater than the growth in charges.

Table 8–8 Revenue sources for special districts (amounts in millions)

Revenue source	1966–67	1971–72	1976–77	% change 66–67 to 71–72	% change 71–72 to 76–77
Total revenue	3,778	6,821	14,408	80.6	111.2
Taxes	589	968	1,718	64.4	77.5
Intergovernmental aid	635	1,550	4,332	144.1	179.6
Charges and miscellaneous	1,513	2,672	5,301	76.6	98.4

Source: U.S., Department of Commerce, Bureau of the Census, 1977 Census of Governments, vol. 4, *Governmental Finances*, part 2, *Financing of Special Districts* (Washington, D.C.: Government Printing Office, 1979).

Control of special districts

The officials who control the activities of districts are chosen in a number of different ways. One-half of them are elected and one-half are appointed. Board members are responsible for a variety of district activities, such as the day-to-day administration of district affairs and the employment of the administrative staff. Board members often rely quite heavily on professional consultants and appointed committees to carry out the decision-making processes related to many issues. It is also common for districts to employ a full-time, salaried administrative officer who is responsible to the board and carries out the policies formulated by board members. The tenure of special district board members varies widely.

The creation and the dissolution of special districts may follow a number of procedures, including petitions, public hearings, state action, referenda, and court action. Petitions and public hearings are the most common methods. Following numerous public reports that urged the regulation of special district growth, five states enacted legislation creating "boundary commissions" to control the creation, consolidation, annexation, and dissolution of special districts on a state-wide or county-wide basis. Table 8–9 shows the states that have enacted this legislation as well as the effects of the legislation on the growth of special districts. Each "boundary commission state" appears to have been successful in curtailing district growth.

Table 8–9   Number of special districts (inside and outside SMSAs) in states enacting legislation to control special districts: 1962, 1967, 1972, 1977

State	1962	1967	% change, 1962–67	1972	% change, 1967–72	1977	% change, 1972–77
California	1,962	2,168	10.5	2,223	2.5	2,227	.2
Nevada	85	89	4.7	134	50.6	132	−1.5
New Mexico	102	97	−5.0	99	2.1	100	1.0
Oregon	727	800	10.0	826	3.1	797	−3.5
Washington	867	937	8.1	1,021	9.0	1,060	3.8

Source: U.S., Department of Commerce, Bureau of the Census, Census of Governments, 1962, 1967, 1972, and 1977.

Are special districts desirable?

The number of special districts in the United States has grown steadily over the past several decades (see Table 8–10). One method of evaluating the effects of special district growth is referred to as the "reform tradition." The basic assumption of the reform tradition is that the most logical form of local government is one that is centralized. This assumption is used to deduce the notion that a fragmented local government environment (i.e., one comprising many units of government, including special districts), is ineffective, uncoordinated, and unresponsive. A considerable number of private and public organizations have promoted the reform tradition. They include the U.S. Advisory Commission on Intergovernmental Relations (ACIR), the National Municipal League, and the Committee for Economic Development, which has, in fact, advocated an 80 percent reduction in the number of governmental units in metropolitan areas in the United States.[16]

This view of special districts is exemplified by the following quotation by ACIR on the subject of municipal water supply. "A small number of community water utilities is preferable to a multiplicity of uncoordinated systems. . . . A large number of relatively small water companies or municipal departments is often the result of a lack of coordinated policy for community water resources."[17]

ACIR suggests that districts can "inhibit efforts of district consolidation or annexation that would provide more effective and more efficient service to the whole area."[18]

In evaluating the overall efficiency of special districts in providing municipal services, ACIR has concluded that:

1. Districts frequently provide uneconomical services.
2. Districts distort the political process by competing for scarce public resources.
3. Districts, because of multiplicity, prevent citizens from understanding them and hence controlling them, the result being unresponsive government.
4. Districts increase the costs of government within an area.[19]

The conclusion that special districts are inherently inefficient in comparison to more centrally supplied services is one that must be accepted with caution. For example, one California study has evaluated the economic performance of 153 sewage plants. Some of the plants were operated by municipalities, and others were run by districts. The study found no significant cost differences between the two types of suppliers.[20] The special districts were found to be as efficient as general-purpose units of government in the provision of sewage disposal. The nature of the sewage industry itself implies that special districts can be a mechanism through which efficiency in service provision can be attained.

Table 8–10 Number of special districts in the United States, 1952–1977

Year	No. of special districts	% increase from preceding reported year
1952	12,339	. . .
1962	18,322	48.5
1967	21,264	16.1
1972	23,885	12.3
1977	25,962	8.7

Source: U.S., Department of Commerce, Bureau of the Census, Census of Governments, various volumes.

For example, because many sewage treatment districts operate with increasing returns to economies of scale, smaller communities that desire sewage treatment services often construct their own collection systems and contract with a sewage district for treatment.[21] In this way the smaller jurisdictions can control their own collection system and obtain the advantages of scale economies in treatment costs.[22]

The ability of special districts to attain efficient production of local public services stems from their ability to finance capital expansion. The Metropolitan Water District of Southern California, for example, was formed by a number of municipalities and districts in order to generate necessary funds for investing in facilities to transport water from the Colorado River to the Los Angeles Basin.[23] The economic advantage of this particular institution was cited in 1973 when it was determined that "no single agency could have undertaken such activities without serious diseconomies."[24]

Special districts and consumption efficiency Special districts can be quite conducive to consumption efficiency. Districts provide a mechanism through which diverse collective demands for local public goods and services can be met. A community may consist of five distinct neighborhoods, each one characterized by homogeneous preferences for local public services. Under a consolidated local government organization, it is not likely that the quantities and qualities of the public services provided will match the divergent preferences of each neighborhood.[25] Some individuals will have more public goods and services than they feel necessary at the current tax prices; others will want more publicly provided goods and services but will be unable to obtain them, irrespective of the tax price.

The ability to create or dissolve special districts permits individuals in such a community to create "collective consumption units." These units can provide the quantities and qualities of different types of services that more closely match the preferences of each neighborhood. The desire of comparatively small communities to take initiatives such as this was particularly evident with the popularity of "neighborhood governments" during the 1960s and 1970s.[26]

Another advantage of special districts providing public service is that districts often can operate within more logical geographical boundaries than can general purpose units of government. A flood control district that intersects several local governmental boundaries but services all the residents of a particular floodplain may be more desirable than flood control services that are limited to those areas within legally specified political boundaries.

Special districts and service costs There are two conflicting views regarding the effect of the proliferation of special districts on the cost of producing local public services. One view is that districts do provide an opportunity to lower service costs through the attainment of production and distributional efficiency. The other view is that districts are inefficient and costly modes of service provision.

One study of the effects of special district growth on service costs found that the effective restriction of special district growth, as has been pursued by several states, has led to substantial increases in both local government per capita expenditures and tax shares.[27] These increases in per capita expenditures and tax shares were found to be significantly greater than per capita tax and expenditure growth in a number of states where the growth rate of special districts was the greatest.

The effects of restrictions on special district growth on the cost of providing water supply, sewage disposal, and fire protection (services most frequently provided by special districts) also was studied. In a number of the states that restricted special district growth there were substantial increases in both current operating costs and combined current and capital costs of providing those particular services. ACIR itself recognizes that in cities of over 250,000 population "there are significant diseconomies of scale."[28] Observations such as these have led to the general conclusion that special districts are less efficient than consolidated local governments. The truth may be that the efficiency gains from the organization of special districts differ from district to district and case to case.

The size of special districts   As an indication of some potential consequences of a policy that would restrict district growth, consider the effects of the Swedish local governmental consolidation that has occurred over the past two decades. Sweden has decreased the number of local governmental units by approximately 80 percent, which is, coincidentally, identical to the consolidation proposal put forth by the Committee for Economic Development. The following changes have been noted since the Swedish consolidation plan was implemented:

1. Voter participation in local elections declined appreciably as the local units increased in size.
2. Citizen participation in joining voluntary civic and service organizations declined appreciably as the local units increased in size.
3. As local units became larger, local elected officials differed more markedly from their constituents in such characteristics as income level, social status, and level of education.
4. The resistance of local elected officials to spending programs decreased as the size of the local unit increased.
5. Local elected officials in larger units of local government tended to "follow the dictates of their conscience" rather than the demands of their constituents, probably due to lack of contact with and concern for constituent preferences.[29]

Further research concerning citizen attitudes toward local government has found the following results, which also support the evidence cited previously:

1. The popularity of special district government and its growth away from predominantly rural needs toward more urban services indicate the preference of communities for services tailored to their needs.[30]
2. Nationwide, movements for more centralized local governmental organization are rejected by voters nearly three times as often as they are passed.[31]
3. A 1973 nationwide Harris survey clearly demonstrates that citizen confidence and satisfaction with local government increase as the size of the governmental unit decreases.[32]

The arguments imply that the efficient size and number of special districts depends on many factors. A general decline in their number is not necessarily good, and decisions on expansion or contraction should be made on a case by case basis.

Summary

The increased reliance on user charges as a source of local government revenues is a trend that is expected to continue. In the case of utility type services, the move away from the property tax and toward the user charge is well under way. The reliance on user charges to finance other public services is less extensive, but growing steadily. The extent of employment of user charges is far greater in special districts than in any other form of local government. However, even in special districts, the level of user charge revenue varies significantly among the types of services being provided and among the states using the charge.

The user charge has several potential advantages over the property tax as a source of local revenue. Charges based on the cost of providing public services allow consumer-taxpayers to compare the cost of service with their evaluation of the service. In many cases the charge will allocate use of the publicly provided good to those who value it most. Payment of the charge also provides an indication of the need for expansion of the supply of the service and provides the revenue to finance the expansion.

For a user charge to have these advantages over the property tax, it must be correctly designed. The charge should reflect the full cost of the service. This cost often varies with the area of the city and the density of development. An average-cost user charge, which neglects these variations in cost of service, is likely to be worse than the property tax.

The primary disadvantages of the user charge are its regressive nature and its cost of administration. A marginal-cost user charge is regressive when compared to the property tax; however, it is decidedly less regressive than a poorly designed average-cost user charge. Nevertheless, the cost of administering a marginal-cost user charge may be substantial because it is not likely that the property tax will be completely eliminated. There will probably be no significant savings in the administration of the property tax when more reliance is placed on user charges.

There are several advantages to using special districts to supply public services. Special districts can combine improved efficiency in the production of publicly supplied goods with improved measurement of the demand for those goods and services. On the other hand, special districts can be wasteful and unresponsive to the needs and wants of citizens. Nevertheless, user charges have an important role to play in the future of local government finance. The trend is clearly positive, and growing with citizens' concern for the property tax.

1   U.S., Department of Commerce, Bureau of the Census, 1967 Census of Governments, *Historical Statistics on Governmental Finances and Employment* (Washington, D.C.: Government Printing Office, 1970), p. 135.

2   See: Jack Hirshleifer, James DeHaven, and Jerome Milliman, *Water Supply* (Chicago: University of Chicago Press, 1960).

3   See, for example: Walter Isard and Robert Coughlin, *Municipal Costs and Revenues* (Wellesley, Mass.: Chandler-Davis, 1957); Paul B. Downing, *The Economics of Urban Sewage Disposal* (New York: Praeger Publishers, 1969); Real Estate Research Corporation, *The Costs of Sprawl*, report prepared for the Council on Environmental Quality, Department of Housing and Urban Development, and the U.S. Environmental Protection Agency (Washington, D.C.: Government Printing Office, 1974).

4   See: Paul B. Downing, "Policy Perspectives on User Charges and Urban Spacial Structure," in *Local Service Pricing Policies and Their Effect on Urban Spacial Structure*, ed. Paul B. Downing (Vancouver: University of British Columbia Press,

1977). The reader might find helpful the discussions by various authors in Selma J. Mushkin, ed., *Public Prices for Public Products* (Washington, D.C.: The Urban Institute, 1972).

5   Some cities purposely do not charge high-volume industrial users for the full cost of water and electricity in an attempt to attract more industry to the area.

6   See: Downing, *The Economics of Urban Sewage Disposal.*

7   If an effluent fee were charged for storm water release, then an output charge, and perhaps some treatment, would be appropriate.

8   Paul B. Downing, "Cost and Demand for a Municipal Service" (Unpublished paper, October 1974).

9   Tolls are desirable only if the benefits from controlling use exceed the cost of establishing and operating the system of toll collection.

10   The effects of charges on development are explored by various authors in: Downing, ed., *Local Service Pricing Policies and Their Effect on Urban Spacial Structure.*

11   Paul B. Downing, "User Charges and the Devel-

opment of Urban Land," *National Tax Journal* 26 (December 1973): 631–37.

12 This has been shown in: Paul B. Downing, "The Distributional Effect of User Charges" (Unpublished paper, October 1974).

13 U.S., Department of Commerce, Bureau of the Census, *1972 Census of Governments: Governmental Units in 1972* (Washington, D.C.: Government Printing Office, 1975).

14 U.S., Department of Commerce, Bureau of the Census, 1967 Census of Governments, vol. 1, p. 13.

15 For a more complete discussion, see: Richard M. Bird, *Charging for Public Services: A New Look at an Old Idea* (Toronto: Canadian Tax Foundation, 1976), pp. 105–13.

16 Committee for Economic Development, *Modernizing Local Government* (New York: Committee for Economic Development, 1966).

17 U.S., Advisory Commission on Intergovernmental Relations, *The Problem of Special Districts in American Government* (Washington, D.C.: Government Printing Office, 1964), pp. 74–75.

18 Ibid.

19 Ibid.

20 G. Krohm, *The Production Efficiency of Single vs. General Purpose Government: Findings of the Organizational Structure of Local Government and Cost Effectiveness* (Sacramento, Calif.: Office of Planning and Research, 1973).

21 See: Assembly Interim Committee on Municipal and County Government, *Special Districts in the State of California: Problems in General and the Consolidation of Sewer and Fire Districts Acts, 1957–59* (Sacramento, Calif.: State Printing Office, 1959), vol. 6, no. 12.

22 Downing, *The Economics of Urban Sewage Disposal.*

23 San Diego Water Authority, *Report to the California Council on Intergovernmental Relations, 1973.*

24 Ibid.

25 With a constitutionally imposed majority rule, the level of public goods output will most likely correspond to the preferences of the median voter.

26 See: Howard W. Hallman, *Neighborhood Government in a Metropolitan Setting* (Beverly Hills, Calif.: Sage Publications, 1974).

27 Thomas J. DiLorenzo, "The Role of Special Districts in the Efficient Provision of Local Public Services" (Ph.D. diss., Department of Economics, Virginia Polytechnic Institute and State University, July 1979).

28 U.S., Advisory Commission on Intergovernmental Relations, *Size Can Make a Difference: A Closer Look,* ACIR Bulletin no. 70–8 (Washington, D.C.: Government Printing Office, 1970), p. 2.

29 Jorgen Westerstahl, "Decision-Making Systems" (Paper delivered at the 1973 annual meeting of the American Political Science Association).

30 California Local Government Reform Task Force, *Special District Report,* February 1974.

31 *New County, U.S.A.,* Report, City-County Consolidation Seminar, *The American County,* February 1972, p. 10.

32 U.S., Congress, Senate, Committee on Government Operations, Subcommittee on Intergovernmental Relations, *Confidence and Concern: Citizens View Americans and Government,* vols. I and II (Washington, D.C.: Government Printing Office, 1973).

Part three: Intergovernmental fiscal relations

Fiscal problems of political boundaries

A metropolitan area is a continuous network of interrelated activities. Nevertheless, seemingly arbitrarily drawn boundaries transform this web into discrete cities of varying degrees of governmental affluence and governmental poverty. Underlying this diversity of neighborhoods and cities (and of wealth and squalor), are the highly fluid forces of technological change and the reformulations of social values. The consequences of these dynamic forces become governmental problems when there are inadequate social adaptations to their diversities. Metropolitan problems are rooted in a world of changing demography, social preferences, and technology. All of these problems are exacerbated by the relatively sluggish response of governmental institutions to accommodate changes. The results are a very uneven distribution of the benefits and costs of government.[1]

The most dramatic changes in our metropolitan areas have been the surge of population and economic activity to the cities and then to their suburbs. There has also been a constant regional shifting of people and economic activity throughout the nation. Governmental structures have changed as well, but slowly in comparison to the changing organizational forms in the private sector. Boundaries have shifted, new governments have been created, and functions have been redistributed. In this world of uneven movements the older central cities have suffered more than the suburbs, but, even so, the most fiscally troubled of all the localities have been the poorer suburbs.

Urban places have long lives, and the technology and culture of one period always clash with the technology and culture of past eras. The tendency of fixed capital to stay put aggravates any adjustment process. There are analytical and empirical studies dealing with the economics of the governance of the metropolitan area. The theoretical studies are highly abstract and general; the empirical studies are greatly handicapped, with no usable measure of the output of the local public sector. Despite these shortcomings, the great outpouring of research studies of the past decade has brought an improved understanding of the metropolitan fiscal problem. The sense of crisis has long been endemic for local public finance. There has been no absence of proposals and resulting changes, but too often the unintended consequences seem to dwarf the anticipated results.

The metropolis in historical perspective

The metropolis is encased in its history. Its present condition reflects current objectives and know-how filtered through an obstacle course of previous goals and institutions many decades long. Changing technology, social values, governmental roles, individual preferences, and demographics have all left their mark.

Various metropolitan areas were born and flourished in very different eras. Those urban centers that were founded in the era of the automobile are very different from those that were established during the age of the tall ships. The changes in the technology of production, energy sources and usages, communications, and transportation have forced sharp shifts in the relative advantages of location at different points within the nation and within metropolitan areas.

In old metropolitan areas the changes have called for a massive redistribution of activities over space. This has entailed the use of great resources and has been done at high human costs. Whole neighborhoods vanish or are altered dramatically as streets, utility networks, and buildings, built for an earlier technology, are relocated. The newer metropolitan areas are spared the enormous burdens created by an obsolescent capital stock. Their turn may come, however, as technological change continues to alter relative geographical advantages, and still newer cities are born to compete with the older ones.

Changing technology and values do not dictate the failures of any local government, and, even though fiscal distress is not inevitable, it is possible that there are no ways within the constraints of our federal democracy to avoid local crises. A depressing thought, but the heavenly city may exist only in heaven.

At any given time all metropolitan areas are in the process of adaptation, but for some the burdens of change are much larger than for others. Since all of the metropolitan areas are tied together in a competitive market economy, those with greater adjustment costs will suffer cumulative disadvantages. Obsolescence results in costly production processes, which lead to higher taxes, which discourage business investment, which leads to losses in tax revenues, which inhibit public improvements, which furthers obsolescence. A destructive cycle that ends, finally, in abandonment.

The impact of age

The age of a city has a dramatic impact on its fiscal health. Part of this differential among local governments is due to the fact that younger cities have been able to annex a significant part of their undeveloped hinterlands so that new industries and suburban growth are within the borders of the central city. Equally important is the greater accumulation of urban problems in the older cities.

Nathan and Adams compiled an index of urban health indicators for the central cities of the major metropolitan areas.[2] The index is a composite of ratios of central city social and economic indicators to those of their suburbs. The numbers range from 422 for Newark (in very poor shape) to 67 for Seattle (in great shape). Table 9–1 shows the index number for each city. If the set of cities is divided into three age groups, the unweighted mean index of the oldest group is 209; of the middle group, 143; and of the youngest group, 127. The age of the city is measured from the census year in which the city reached a population of at least 200,000. The population of the oldest group reached that size by 1900, while that of the youngest group reached it in 1930 or later. The contrast is seen most sharply in comparing the oldest group of cities with the younger groups. Only one city in the younger group had an index that was poorer than the mean for the oldest. Aging is not healthy for the local economy nor for the city's treasury.

The phenomenon of costly renewal of old built-up areas and fresh development on clear land is even more dramatically portrayed in a metropolitan area. Even the most decrepit of the central cities has posh suburbs that would be a credit to any metropolitan area. More importantly, the central city of a declining metropolitan area will suffer more grievously the burdens of competitive disadvantage than other parts of the area. The forces of growth and decay strike differentially in a metropolitan area. The costs of relocating among sites within a metropolitan area are small, and movement is relatively frequent; therefore, cumulative processes work more rapidly. All changes, especially the dynamic

Table 9–1   Index of central city disadvantage relative to balance of SMSA, by age group of central cities, 1972

Oldest		Middle age		Younger	
Newark	422	Atlanta	226	Dayton	211
Cleveland	331	Rochester	215	Richmond	209
Baltimore	256	Youngstown	180	San Jose	181
Chicago	245	Columbus	173	Miami	172
St. Louis	231	Akron	152	Fort Worth	149
New York	211	Kansas City	152	Sacramento	135
Detroit	210	Denver	143	Birmingham	131
Philadelphia	205	Jersey City	129	Oklahoma City	128
Boston	198	Indianapolis	124	Grand Rapids	119
Milwaukee	195	Providence	121	Tampa	107
Buffalo	189	Toledo	116	Syracuse	103
New Orleans	168	Los Angeles	105	Omaha	98
Louisville	165	Portland	100	Dallas	97
Cincinnati	148	Seattle	67	Houston	93
Pittsburgh	146			Phoenix	85
Minneapolis	131			Norfolk	82
San Francisco	105			San Diego	77
Mean	209	Mean	143	Mean	127

Sources: Central City Disadvantage index from Richard P. Nathan and Charles F. Adams, Jr., *Revenue Sharing: The Second Round* (Washington, D.C.: Brookings Institution, 1977), p. 86. The index is a composite of city-suburban relationships in regard to unemployment, education, dependent population, income, crowded housing, and poverty. The oldest group of cities reached 200,000 population before 1900, the younger reached that size after 1930, and the middle cities, unsurprisingly, were in between. Population was from various U.S. Censuses of Population.

trends that are advantageous to some of the newer suburbs, are generally magnified by the existence of old boundaries. The advantages to a newer suburb are contained within its boundaries; the losses are contained within the confines of the older city and are not shared by the newly affluent suburb.

The importance of technological change

Technological change, which determines the location and nature of industrial development, has also acted to alter the production processes of government. For example, the communication changes that revolutionized the location of industrial plants have had a similar, but more limited, impact on the optimum distribution of police and the size of a police system. In general, the service industries have been slower in exploiting the new technologies, and government has been still slower. The consequences of the changes have impacted much less on altering boundaries of general governments and much more on encouraging an increasingly complex set of exchange relations among governments and inducing the invention of limited, special-purpose governments. What might have become a single metropolitan service, if only the laws of scale economies were operative, becomes a complex structure of small local services with contractual or service relationships with large units. As a result, the structure of public industries is more complicated than that of their private counterparts.

Technology has also operated on the demand side of government. Two points are of special interest. The decline in transportation and communications costs, which has enlarged the spatial scope of the market for private products, has changed the political marketplace. Concern about policy choices has shifted to broader arenas, and the costs of influencing higher levels of government have declined. The consequence has been a reduction in disparities in local service levels.

The effects of the changes in dynamic technology have been compounded by the changing role of government in our society. The political changes associated with democratization in participation and in policy (which have made the local and national governments more responsive to the demands of the lower income groups) are themselves sufficient to account for the metropolitan problems. Without the political changes, it is more likely that governments would have been able to respond more efficiently to technological change. Urban problems would be less severe. Political constituencies have changed and so has the urban political economy.

Democratization has brought all of society into city hall, and equalization has changed the distributions of services and taxes. The scope of government has been greatly expanded by the growth of welfare services. Given the new political economy, the preferences, wealth, and activities of neighbors—who share in the collective choice—become very important in determining the impact of the government on the individual. The movement of just a few blocks across an "arbitrary" political boundary may put a citizen into a collective choice group of a very different social composition. The results are a mosaic of governments facing citizens who may find it easier to move to a government of their choice rather than to incur the political costs of changing their current government. In particular, the rich must remain mobile to protect themselves.[3]

The growing importance of the federal government

Much of the impact of the federal government on metropolitan governance has been inadvertent. Governments, especially national governments, have grown dramatically since World War I. In recent times, the growth of welfarism has been most dramatic, but the growth of other government services and regulations has extended to almost every sector of society. Federal intervention in transportation, housing, sewerage, and health services has grown rapidly.

Many programs were designed and implemented without any heed to their spatial effects—which did not prevent them from having significant impacts. Other programs, however, have been consciously designed for their regional impacts, perhaps to counteract the unanticipated effects of other programs. That is, federally supported freeways and sewerage systems underwrite new suburban shopping centers, which then compete with the central cities' commercial district, which then obtains funds from the federal government for downtown renewal. Although there is still no consistent federal urban policy, there has been an increasing awareness of the consequences of various programs. There is also a developing conscious effort to consider the effect of a set of programs rather than to consider each program separately.

The significance of political boundaries

Historical forces have changed the uses of space; however, new uses of space have not dictated new distributions among governments. The local boundaries containing these uses are not set by nature and the behavior of the governments is not fixed by fundamental constitutional provisions. The drawing of a boundary is itself a policy decision, influenced by the workings of the political economy. Within that boundary the reshuffling of functions among levels of governments, the transfers of revenues among these levels, and the introduction of new layers of special governments are all policy adaptations to boundary choices. Although boundary drawing and retention are conscious choices, their reconstitution is among the most difficult tasks in the legislative process. To the legislative ear the cries of protest of those injured by change often seem as numerous as the numbers of those to be benefitted by that change.

Boundaries define institutions. Boundaries establish a history and nurture nostalgia and vested interests in such a way that many persons have a stake in their retention. The boundaries, however, are often instances of institutional obsolescence which may be as inhibiting to efficiency as narrow streets, ancient subways, or corroding sewers. Governmental institutions are an act of creation as deliberate as the construction of a fire station. In principle, an organization can be changed more readily; in practice, the bonds that support an institution are usually firmer than concrete and steel. The man-made topography of our metropolitan areas (e.g., road networks and settlement densities) have changed dramatically, whereas the lines defining the political jurisdictions of the region have barely shifted.

The persistence of rigid political boundaries is not solely a case of institutional sluggishness; it also can be an instrument of defense against the high redistributive taxation that can be caused by an influx of impoverished groups into the local government unit. Sharing a community with the poor means paying for services for an unwelcome group and having to consider their preferences in the collective decision process. Thus boundaries become protective barriers when zoning codes are enacted to discourage the entry of the disadvantaged. However, excluding the disadvantaged from some communities means a relative increase in their proportions in other communities. The result is an increasing fiscal disparity among the communities of a metropolitan area. In a period of strong political movement towards equalization, these disparities have led to greater reliance on central taxation and intergovernmental transfers to reduce unequal services and payments for services.

The economics of metropolitan areas

The issues discussed next will be divided into those that affect the demand for public services and those that affect the supply. The private demand factors are concerned with the characteristics of the residents—their preferences, incomes, and collective choice processes. Of less importance are the federal and state programs and mandates, which also influence demand. The supply factors primarily deal with the existence of scale economies, externalities in production and system management and design, and the peculiar decision processes of government. Again, many federal and state actions change the relative costs of different services and for different programs.

This analysis stresses the issues that seem to dominate the thinking of the policy makers and that seem to be the main determinants of changes in the near future. In practice, the structure and behavior of any specific metropolitan political economy is determined by layers of inherited structures and institutions which frustrate the use of any general policies or statements of tendencies.

There is no theory of boundaries, but there is a theory of the size of government, of assignment of functions, and of transfers among governments. Although theory does not explain where boundaries are drawn, it can explain why they are established and maintained and the consequences of their existence. The theory that exists is part of welfare economics, and its spirit is derived from a study of the failures of the market to achieve a social optimum. Policies are built solely around the correction of market shortcomings, not the feasibility of public intervention. The theory is very weak on the discussion of the institutions that would be necessary or useful for the implementation of policy; there is no body of analysis that incorporates decision making about costs and benefits at the legislative and administrative levels into the whole analysis. When this is achieved we may find that government failure will equal or exceed the market failures that programs are supposed to correct.[4]

Individuals and firms can cross local borders easily and, in fact, most economic exchanges do cross local geographic borders. The permanent move of occupants is usually a mixed blessing because while in-migrants increase the volume of taxable resources, they also increase costs. The occupants of a municipality or a school district are a tax-sharing collective; a new member helps to pay the costs of the services, but may also cause the costs to increase. Thus, a new resident imposes external fiscal economies and diseconomies on all current residents. The most desirable in-migrant is wealthy, disdains using public services, and votes with the majority.

The demand for local government services

The analysis of demand for public services is bifurcated, reflecting both the efficient matching of services and tastes found in the world of suburbs and the redistributional response to the deprived found in the world of the central cities. The important point is that the analysis of the demand and the response of local governments deals with efficiency and distribution.

The efficient world of suburbs

The world of suburbs is often viewed by public choice theorists as either the source of the metropolitan fiscal problem or (less commonly) as a model of

---

Urban growth problems in metropolitan areas Data gathered since the Population Census of 1970 substantiate the conclusion that American metropolitan areas continue to face urban growth problems. Most suburban areas continue to grow much faster than their central cities, although for the first time some suburban areas have lost population. Taxable wealth and personal income are growing faster in suburban areas than in their central cities, widening the disparity. As suburbs grow economically, central cities face the problems of population loss, though with increases in the concentrations of poor blacks and Hispanics and a decrease in the proportion of elderly. Compounding the problem is the fact that in some areas of the nation entire metropolitan areas are beginning to show substantial outmigrations with consequences to cities and suburbs alike.

Census data continue to indicate that central cities are faced with rising demands for expenditures which compound their problems. These demands result in increased taxes, high tax rates, and extremely high levels of noneducational expenditures. In all regions except the West, moreover, they have produced a marked increase in central city education expenditures relative to

those in the suburbs. These fiscal trends have been viewed as one factor in the flight of higher and middle income households to suburban areas where taxes are lower and where there is still a greater emphasis on educational rather than noneducational programs.

Suburbs face mounting urban growth problems themselves, although concentrated in certain areas. While not experiencing drastic changes in the socioeconomic character of their population, they confront the need for developing a costly urban infrastructure. Many suburbs can no longer devote an ever-increasing proportion of their budget to educational programs and defer noneducational requirements. Thus, while tax levels and tax rates remain higher in central cities, taxes have increased at a faster rate in the suburbs—particularly in the South and West—narrowing the central city–suburban disparity.

Source: Excerpted from U.S., Advisory Commission on Intergovernmental Relations, *Central City-Suburban Fiscal Disparity and City Distress, 1977*, M–119 (Washington, D.C.: Government Printing Office, 1980), pp. 29–30.

future urban life. Some critics of suburbs see them as draining the central city of its wealth, and their residents as exploiting the central city's infrastructure. Further, these critics maintain that the fragmented governments that serve the suburbs inhibit the development of an orderly and effective policy for the metropolitan area.[5] In contrast, the defenders of the suburbs view them as a competitive market of many governments which give the citizenry an opportunity to choose a package of taxes and services best suited to its needs. Competition among suburbs for shopping centers or more handsome subdivisions is not seen as anarchy but as a healthy spur to make a city more attractive. Both views have some merit; however, the competitive market among governments has, as in many other markets, its failures.

The efficiency analysis of the governance of the metropolitan area, in its simplest form, views the metropolis as a set of competing communities, all of which are similarly located with respect to jobs, shopping, topography, and other features. The analysis focuses on only two of the factors that enter into an individual's residential location: the value of the public services to a resident and the tax price that must be paid by a resident. The simple conclusions of this analysis are that individuals would sort themselves into cities of homogeneous groupings where everyone would be pleased with the public packages they receive. The conclusions are far-fetched if they are considered statements about reality, but the analysis should not be summarily rejected because it does capture some important behavioral characteristics of the suburban world. Its strong conclusions, derived from a few assumptions, have made it an influential force in the discussion of metropolitan policy.

The suburban utopia In the simplest model of a suburban world, it is assumed that there are many suburbs, each offering a different package of public services at a different tax price. If in one community the tax price is the same for all residents, individuals should sort themselves among communities and according to their preferences for such services as police, recreation, and education. The argument is essentially that a commodity bought at any uniform price will be purchased by individuals in amounts sufficient to meet their marginal needs. Therefore, every purchaser would be revealing the same preference. Because preferences are related to levels of education and income, homogeneity should extend to socioeconomic class characteristics as well. For some economists this "club-like" picture of suburbs represents an optimal world.

Three conditions are necessary to approximate this "utopian" world of suburbs. They are summarized as follows:

1. There should not be significant scale economies in production. If they exist, an institutional mechanism has to be created to foster efficiencies in a small city.
2. The ad valorem property tax should be abandoned in favor of a benefits tax or a tax based on the marginal costs of service. This would ensure that everyone pays a uniform tax price.
3. A zoning mechanism is necessary since the market-like sorting out of persons will be unstable. Government controls also are necessary to prevent negative fiscal externalities from in-migration which are the sources of the instability.

Suburban economies of scale The absence of economies of scale in the delivery of public services is a necessary assumption. Governmental boundaries would otherwise grow very large and communities would become fewer in number, in which case, residents would not be able to find a community that would fit their preferred service and tax-price package. The advocates of the competitive local government model suggest that this problem could be bypassed with the adoption of contractual arrangements among governments. If there are significant economies of scale in a service, a county or a large city could produce the service and supply varying amounts to the smaller communities in the area. The charge for the service would be determined by the supplier and each community. This is now being done, but the creation of regional bodies or the use of counties to provide area-wide services, ranging from the complete handling of a function to assisting locals, is a more common practice. In this model, the city or county becomes a cooperative purchasing agency for public services rather than a producer of them. The objective is to achieve efficiency in supply and to provide smaller communities the opportunity to consume only as much as they want or need. Otherwise, these smaller areas would be bound by the collective decision of a large, more heterogeneous population of divergent preferences.

Suburban local finance　A second problem interfering with the achievement of a suburban utopia is the current method of local finance. Everyone does not pay the same tax price to the local government; heavy reliance is placed on the property tax, which is roughly proportional to the value of a house. A person with a more highly valued house would pay a higher tax price than a person with a lower valued house. Both would receive the same amount of street maintenance and educational and recreational services. Thus, the wealthier person may find it to his or her advantage to move to a city which had more wealthy residents to share the cost of public services. For example, two towns may have identical public services which cost a total of $100,000. In the wealthy community there are one hundred families with houses valued at $50,000. In the poor community there are ninety-nine families with $10,000 homes and one family with a $50,000 home. The family with the $50,000 home is paying a tax rate of over 9.5 percent, or almost $5,000. The poorer families are paying the same high tax rate, but due to their low-valued homes their actual payments are only $1,000. If the wealthy family moves to a wealthy community, the tax rate will be 2.0 percent, or $1,000 on a $50,000 house. Thus, the use of an ad valorem property tax might break the expected homogeneity by preference groups in favor of a greater homogeneity by income classes. Residents would sort themselves according to income rather than tastes. Of course, the advocates of the suburban utopia prefer taxing according to benefits received rather than wealth, which, in the case of homogeneous communities, would be a uniform price.

Suburban zoning　Mobility is the third enemy of the suburban utopia. The flight of the middle and upper classes poses a serious problem for the central city. But the poor of the central city have a counter weapon; they can move to the wealthy suburb.[6] A poor person might find that in the city of the rich more public services are purchased than the individual prefers; however, at the lower tax rate, it may be advantageous to live among the rich and to consume more public services than desired because a lower tax rate will be incurred.

Were many of the poor to seek the advantage of living among rich neighbors, the rich would soon lose the advantage of their utopian community. The defense mechanism of the rich is fiscal zoning. The decision rule in fiscal zoning is to authorize land use which has the highest public revenues less the difference of public costs. This would zone out low-valued housing structures. Mobility is not forbidden, but the price of moving into an upper income suburb is increased due to the zoning restrictions.

A consequence of this segregation tendency is the frequently deplored fiscal disparity among communities. Although fiscal disparity is a natural consequence of movement, it is deplored because redistributive objectives have become a prominent part of public policy. Local governments cannot be expected to perform a redistributive role if the poor and the rich are not members of one community. The one exception to this segregation is the central city which extends over a large area and encompasses a large population of all socioeconomic classes. The fiscal resources of its wealthy residents and of its office buildings, factories, and stores were once very large. The central city is not impoverished, but the fiscal role it has assumed has become an intolerable burden. Moreover the city has not been a very successful redistribution agency.

Because there are significant inequalities in the distribution of income, it is not unusual to find inequalities in tax resources among cities.

The theory of the differentiation among suburbs and homogeneity within a suburb is well developed; still, there are few facts to support it. Most studies of a metropolitan area compare all of the suburbs with the central city. When the two are treated separately, however, there are significant differences among suburbs in regard to such factors as average income and educational attainment. Beyond these factors, researchers tend to rely on rather superficial observations in concluding that within the suburb there is a reasonable level of conformity. The one careful study of homogeneity among suburbs found that a sorting of socioeconomic groups does exist, but that it is a far cry from the "club-like" suburbs implied in the model of efficient suburbia. For instance, Pack and Pack found that only 11 percent of suburban towns in Pennsylvania were homogeneous in regard to income. Forty percent of the towns were homogeneous with respect to either occupation, education, or household type.[7] If a "club-like" community is considered homogeneous in regard to at least three of the five qualities of income, education, occupation, age, and household type, then only 15 percent of the Pennsylvania suburbs would qualify. It is interesting to note that the Packs found that the most homogeneous communities are best characterized as family communities with residents who are blue collar workers, poorly educated, and relatively low-incomed; the least homogeneous communities are professional towns, with residents who are well-educated and receiving relatively high incomes.

The redistributive central city and the efficient suburbs

Much of the relative decline of the central city and growth of the suburbs is a result of the fixed boundaries of the older central cities. There have been very few recent annexations achieved by the older central cities. Newer cities in the Sunbelt have grown by the annexation of their peripheries. One hundred and eighty-eight cities considered large in 1950 almost doubled their area by 1970; however, the Northeastern cities increased in area by only 2 percent, the North Central cities by 82 percent, the Southern cities by 224 percent, and the Western cities by 68 percent.[8] In many ways the growth of the suburbs is a political decision not to allow the extension of the city's borders to be coterminous with its economy.

The relative economic decline in the central city can be viewed as a consequence of its trying to carry out one of the other major functions of government, income redistribution, which can be frustrated by a jurisdictional policy of restricting city growth.

The forms of redistribution of income are (1) equality of the provision of government services; (2) an enhancement of services to the poor to correct their inadequate capacity to earn income; and (3) increases in service or cash transfers to the poor to compensate them for their low money incomes. These three forms of redistribution have very different bases in political support and implications for programs, but all of them complicate the governance of the metropolitan area. In all cases, the wealthy pay more in taxes than the value of the public services they receive. Therefore, there is an incentive for them to leave any city which responds to the political mood of redistribution. The out-migration of the wealthy makes it difficult for a typical city to carry on redistribution with its own resources. At one time the central city had adequate fiscal resources. Over time the in-migration of the poor was so large, and the out-migration of the wealthy so extensive, that even with the vast commercial and industrial activity within its borders, the central city foundered under its redistributive tasks.

The equalization of services across neighborhoods is a form of income redistribution. The idea of suburbs as relatively homogeneous segregated communities, where different socioeconomic classes could more closely achieve a balance between their evaluation of the public services and the taxes needed to provide those services, came close to realization in an earlier, pre-redistributional age by a simple choice of neighborhood within the central cities. The streets of the well-to-do were better lighted and cleaned more regularly. Their parks were better maintained. Their schools were better staffed. The wealthy paid more to the community, but they received more from it. Currently, discrimination in services to the rich and poor has been reduced and this has increased the unfavorable spread between tax costs and public services to the wealthy. Of course, some countervailing forces have reduced the fiscal burdens on the wealthy. The property tax has become less significant for central cities, and assessment biases tend to underestimate the assessed values of the more expensive properties.

The equalization of city services across neighborhoods has probably developed at a slower rate than the expansion of the services to the poor.

Health, education, and welfare have become the main areas of public investment in human resources. Much of this activity is a simple transfer of resources in kind. The redistribution objective has been oriented to those services which help the poor lift themselves from poverty. Often these services are provided by the county rather than by the municipality, and the burden remains heaviest on the central county of the metropolis that overlaps the central city.

For the central city, the losses of economic wealth due to equalization forces are compounded by the fact that the costs of equal education, health, and police services are greater for the poor than for the average resident. The central city urban poor are culturally differentiated. The delivery costs of human services are increased because these services bear the extra tasks of integrating the minorities into the dominant culture. If the services to the poor were to be made equal to those of the well-to-do, the budget, and taxes, would have to rise considerably. Otherwise, equality could be achieved only at a lower service level for the entire community and with a significant reallocation of the service budget from wealthy to poor neighborhoods. In reality, costs have risen and the level of services has fallen. The consequence has been further decline in the desirability of the central city as a place of residence for the upper and middle income groups.

The central city has not been impervious to the notion of packaging services to be more responsive to the different groups in the city. There was a period, highlighted by the Model Cities programs, when the goal was to decentralize city hall. It was hoped that a neighborhood political constituency would develop that could influence a decentralized administrative structure to make the public services more responsive to the different needs of the neighborhoods. This movement was politically popular, but it did not achieve much success.

Federal effects on metropolitan services

The federal government has played a confused role in metropolitan development. Much of the federal impact has been indirect, because the federal programs have concerned themselves with solving such problems as water quality or housing. Consequently, the programs have fostered a regional dispersal and a deconcentration of jobs and population.

Population and job dispersal are responses to major changes in technology; suburbanization is a consequence of the stability of big city borders. These trends would have occurred without the federal government; however, the federal government did accelerate them by underwriting local government programs to facilitate the dispersal of jobs and population.

Federal programs have generally been supportive of the suburbanization trends, which have weakened the central city.

The most important influence of the federal government on older metropolitan areas has been its encouragement of new private investment. The tax laws made the building of new capital facilities more advantageous than the maintenance of old ones. This encouraged new construction on the peripheries of the urban area; the underlying motivation was not to move jobs away from the center, although it has had that effect.

Equally destructive of the old urban centers are the regulatory policies that discouraged the use of rail, and highway construction policies that encouraged trucking. The central cities, especially the older ones, are less adaptable to trucking. Moreover, the federally underwritten highway program also encouraged residential dispersal.

Federal Housing Administration (FHA) and Veterans Administration (VA) mortgage guarantees were a major component in the flight to the suburbs. These subsidies to finance housing underwrote the dispersal of the middle classes from the central city. The subsidy was extended by the income tax provision that allowed the deduction of interest and local tax payments. The subsidy to the new areas was increased by federal grants that reduced the local public capital required for new sewage and water treatment facilities.

The above programs are but a sample of those that affect urban problems. Many policies are now being consciously directed toward alleviating the problems. (A Rand Corporation study of the urban impacts of federal policies identified over 130 federal assistance programs directed toward economic development.) In the late 1970s, these efforts involved federal obligations of over $40 billion. Table 9–2 shows the magnitude of these programs, which are classified by type of problem. The major spending programs for urban areas not included in this count are income maintenance, education, and housing. The economic development programs studied were "pro-urban" in the sense that a greater proportion went to cities. Nevertheless, Rand's analysis indicated that the programs were not likely to be effective in counterbalancing the indirect impact of federal programs toward suburbanization.

Supply of services by metropolitan governments

The private market supply of goods is considered to be the various amounts that are produced at different prices. The relationship between the quantity of output and the price is dependent on the costs of input, the technical characteristics of production, the entrepreneurial goal of profit maximization, and the structure of competition among the entrepreneurs. These factors, taken together with the characteristics of demand, will determine the amounts of different commodities produced, the prices of the commodities, and the total distribution of the firms. Many of the same forces of supply and demand apply to the local public sector. It may seem unusual to apply the economic language of private markets to the

Table 9–2   Obligations for federal assistance programs,
by class of urban economic development problem, 1976

Class of problem	Example of program	No. of programs	Obligations (millions)
Places		50	$11,155
	Highway research, planning, and construction		4,532
Jurisdictions		28	17,188
	State and local government fiscal assistance		6,238
People		37	14,298
	CETA—Title II and IV		3,225
Market failures		22	5,301
	Construction grants for wastewater treatment works		4,266

Source: Georges Vernez, Roger J. Vaughan, and Robert K.
Yin, *Federal Activities in Urban Economic Developmment*
(Santa Monica, Calif.: Rand, 1979), pp. 53–6, 59.

supply of goods and services provided by a set of governments that constitute a metropolitan area, but the market metaphor is very useful. Certainly the behavior of local governments depends on input prices, production conditions, and competition among governments. The major difference, a nontrivial one, is that the objective of government decision makers cannot easily be represented as profit-maximization. Furthermore, the demand for public services is not registered by discrete sales, and the maze of legal constraints on government behavior is much greater than that facing the private firm.

The market and games models: suburbs and central city

Two models to explain the decisions of a local government have been proposed: the market and the games.[9] The market model views the government as analogous to a firm, trying to equate the marginal benefit of each service to the marginal cost. The games model views the government as an arena of conflicting groups, each group seeking an allocation of services and costs which would be to its advantage. The test of leadership is to control the conflict and to create a coalition which keeps a party in office. These are extreme statements; in reality, governments will be a mixture of the two models. There is no firm evidence to determine which model is generally applicable, or for which types of government the models are reasonable approximations.[10] However, there is a strong tendency to associate the market model with the suburbs and the games model with the central cities.

The market model has been implicitly discussed earlier in the discussion of suburbs as "club-like" communities. But why should local leadership respond to the market-like forces and the mechanism by which these forces implement their demands? The answer is found in the way citizens express their preferences, which is generally in one of two ways. Citizens will vote for the candidates who are more likely to provide the preferred public-service tax package, or they will move to a jurisdiction which more closely approximates the desired package. Given the great frequency of moving and the low incidence of political participation in the suburbs, it is likely that voting by the feet is the more important mode of expression.[11] Market-like behavior is common, but is it politically effective?

Changing land values is the link between individual mobility and the incentives to the political activists to satisfy the demands of the residents. If the community public-service tax package is attractive, the demand for residences will increase and land values will rise. On the other hand, public services which are not appreciated lead to a decline in demand, a fall in land values, and a loss of residents. This will bring about political activity to change the programs.

Although a rise in land values is a boon to most residents, it can be a bane to others. Bitter conflict between the opposing factions is often the result in the suburban communities. Many suburban municipalities are badly divided between environmentalists (anti-growth) and developers (pro-growth). Improved local services and growth programs lead to increases in land values. If the increases come from higher density and a loss of some amenities, however, there will be local resistance. Zoning codes reduce developmental possibilities and enhance environmental amenities.

Big city politics are characterized by a struggle over the division of the pie rather than over an attempt to increase its size.

The games model is perhaps more applicable to the central city. An increase in jobs—no matter what the source—is the goal in the central city rather than an increase in land values because more jobs satisfy the demands of the numerically superior disadvantaged. In public agencies and political organizations, organizational survival dominates the political agenda, not efficiency. However, the goal of job maximization creates a distorted view of the public fisc and provides an unwise criterion for public actions. Public jobs should be viewed as costs necessary to produce useful outputs, but in the arena of city governmental politics, these expenditures become the "benefits" over which to fight. Costs, instead of being minimized (which would enable the city to become more competitive), are expanded to provide jobs and stability to agencies. In central cities, the defenders of many massive spending programs have not been able to find any benefits other than the employment of minority groups. Nevertheless, these created jobs are sufficient to attract powerful constituencies.

The distinction between the models for suburbs and big cities is so extreme that it may appear to be a caricature. Certainly, suburbanites have their moments of fighting over shares and many urbanites have had a remarkable renaissance as the efficiency of the core of the central city improves. However, the contrast captures the important distinctive features of suburban competitive behavior and the central city's preoccupation with distribution.

Cost considerations

Costs are the value of the resources necessary to produce an output. The choice of an inefficient production process means that given the same resource inputs, more or better products could have been produced. Different production technologies are characterized by how the average costs of output vary with scale of output. Costs are considered decreasing, constant, or increasing if average (or per unit) costs are decreasing, constant, or increasing as output increases. For most production processes it is believed that initially there are sharply decreasing costs followed by a long period of constant costs, and then, as output increases beyond a certain critical point, costs begin to increase. Big cities that grow beyond a certain point will find that their per unit costs will rise as population rises, not decrease as would be expected. On top of the costs of redistribution, the per capita expenditures for regular government services in the big cities have mounted. In 1976–77 the per capita general expenditures of cities over 1,000,000 population were $916 whereas they were only $228 for cities under 50,000.[12]

Even if this shape is typical of most services, there is great variation among services in regard to the scale of operation where constant, decreasing, or increasing cost conditions hold. There would also be differences among services in regard to the particular aspects of the production process which determine different cost conditions. In a world of suburbs decreasing costs have given rise to a complex structure of overlapping special districts, regional authorities, and local offices of state agencies. The many small governments of suburbia are viable only because other non-general service governments have been created to take advantage of scale economies.

Economies of scale   The study of economies of scale in local public services is very inconclusive. Most studies measure expenditures on a per capita basis because city size varies. This measure is incomplete because of quality variation. For instance, low public per capita expenditures on streets may lead to high private costs if congested streets lead to inefficient traffic flows. Without an accurate measure of public output holding everything reasonably constant as the size of a facility or a jurisdiction increases, it is difficult to relate expenditure variation with size of output or even the level of activities. Although it is difficult to define an efficient scale for a service, it is clear that there is often a mismatch between sizes of jurisdictions and efficient units of production. It is not difficult to be aware of the problem, but a solution may be beyond anyone's capacity. For big central cities an increasing per capita (unit) cost implies that there should be a decentralization of production. For the small suburbs it implies there should be a centralization of some services.[13]

The interest in scale economies focuses on a set of related problems: (1) the determination of the optimum-sized jurisdiction; (2) the assignment of functions to levels of government; and (3) the optimum pattern of decentralization. In any case, the consequences of scale economies have affected the actual behavior of metropolitan government.

One set of functions dominated by scale economies are those which can only be effective if they are carried out for an entire system. In these instances, as the number of municipalities entering into a common planning and decision-making unit rises, the quality of output rises per unit of input. For example, the metropolitan area is a highly interrelated network of activities which require consistency in vehicle capacity on and direction of the roads because they go through many cities. In the matter of negative outputs, air pollution controls make little sense if each municipality only monitors its own facilities and pays little attention to the activities of other cities.

A second set of functions that exhibit economies of scale are those with heavy capital investment requirements, especially in distribution systems. Water supply and sewage disposal are classic examples of services few suburban municipalities can perform with reasonable cost effectiveness. The problem has resulted in a proliferation of supramunicipal solutions ranging from the development of multipurpose metropolitan-wide special districts to arrangements where the suburbs contract for the sale of services from the central city.

The more common instances of scale economies are those that exist for some component of a function. For instance, a smaller municipality may purchase its water from a central city's system that is large enough to justify dams and extensive pipelines. Or the local police department may purchase crime analyses from a sophisticated county or state laboratory. If it is possible to contract for the service with some larger government that has been able to achieve scale economies, a smaller city does not have to surrender autonomy because some service components exhibit scale economies. Government services are typically identified with the government's production of services. This need not be so. The municipality can be a retailer, or a cooperative purchaser for its residents. The actual producer can be another government or a private contractor.

Table 9–3 summarizes the results of some historic studies made of scale economies in the local public services. The one clear point that emerged from these studies is that there is no unique size of a community which can be called efficient. Many services are characterized by constant costs; these could be packaged together in municipalities of different sizes without any efficiency losses. Other services can only be produced efficiently by a larger jurisdiction or a jurisdiction which has the capacity to market its excess output. We can anticipate that all services in a central city would have reached at least the lowest point on their average cost curves and some would be in the stage of increasing costs. However, there is likely to be more variety in the suburbs because many cities cannot produce all of the services due to their small size.

Table 9–3 Results of studies of scale economies in local public services

---

Average costs are declining:
  Electricity[1]
  Sewage plants[2]
  Gas[3]

Average costs are about horizontal:
  Elementary schools[4]
  Police protection[5]
  Refuse collection[6]

Average costs are U-shaped with trough at different points:
  High schools[7]
  Fire protection[8]
  Hospitals[9]
  School administration[10]

Source: Adapted from Werner Z. Hirsch, *The Economics of State and Local Government* (New York: McGraw-Hill, 1970), p. 183.

1 Marc Nerlove, *Returns to Scale in Electricity Supply* (Stanford, Calif.: Institute for Mathematical Studies in the Social Sciences, Stanford University, 1961), p. 11; Jack Johnston, *Statistical Cost Analysis* (New York: McGraw-Hill, 1960).

2 Walter Isard and Robert E. Coughlin, *Municipal Costs and Revenues* (Wellesley, Mass.: Chandler-Davis, 1957), p. 76.

3 K. S. Lomax, "Cost Curves for Gas Supply," *Bulletin of the Oxford Institute of Statistics*, vol. 13 (1951).

4 H. J. Kiesling, "Measuring and Local Government Service: A Study of School Districts in New York State," *Review of Economics and Statistics* 49 (August 1967); Werner Z. Hirsch, "Determinants of Public Education Expenditures," *National Tax Journal* (March 1960).

5 H. J. Schmadt and G. R. Stephens, "Measuring Municipal Output," *National Tax Journal* 8 (December 1960); W. Z.

Hirsch, "Expenditure Implications of Metropolitan Growth and Consolidation," *Review of Economics and Statistics* 41 (August 1959).

6 W. Z. Hirsch, "Cost Functions of an Urban Government Service: Refuse Collection," *Review of Economics and Statistics* 47 (February 1965).

7 J. Riew, "Economies of Scale in High School Operation," *Review of Economics and Statistics* 48 (August 1966).

8 R. E. Will, "Scalar Economies and Urban Service Requirements," *Yale Economic Essays*, vol. 5 (spring 1965); W. A. Hirsch, "Expenditure Implications of Metropolitan Growth and Consolidation," *Review of Economics and Statistics* 41 (August 1959).

9 K. K. Ro, "Determinants of Hospital Costs," *Yale Economic Essays*, vol. 8 (fall 1968); H. A. Cohen, "Variations in the Cost among Hospitals of Different Sizes," *Southern Economic Journal* 33 (January 1967).

10 Hirsch in (5) above.

Because of the variation of scale economies, there has been an amazing proliferation of special districts, authorities, commissions, and bureaus functioning in the metropolitan area. These may operate as independent governments or as arms of other governments. They can be fully integrated suppliers of the services or they can be contractors to other governments. The diversity is so great that it is difficult for the Census of Governments to find an adequate definition of government to measure and classify the organizations it surveys. For example, the 1977 Census of Governments has a special volume of regional organizations, which had been ignored in preceding Censuses.[14] The 1,569 organizations surveyed had revenues of $1.3 billion, almost all of which were grants from other governments, especially the federal government. These units are primarily engaged in multijurisdictional planning, coordination, and policy development. There are no figures, however, on the number of local offices of the federal and state governments which function in the metropolitan areas.[15] It is

Table 9–4 Number of local governments inside and outside metropolitan areas, 1977

Types of governments	Inside SMSAs	Outside SMSAs	Total
Counties	594	2,448	3,042
Municipalities	6,444	12,418	18,862
Townships	4,031	12,791	16,822
School districts	5,220	9,954	15,174
Special districts	9,580	16,382	25,962
Total	25,869	53,993	79,862

Source: U.S., Department of Commerce, Bureau of the Census, 1977 Census of Governments, vol. 1, *Governmental Organization*, part 1, *Governmental Organization* (Washington, D.C.: Government Printing Office, 1979), p. 29.

clear that the Census figures underestimate the number of decision-making units in the metropolitan area. Much of this growth is no doubt attributable to the scale shortcomings of suburban governments. Table 9–4 presents the count on the number of "official" local governments inside and outside of metropolitan areas.

In standard metropolitan statistical areas (SMSAs) the single-function districts account for 88 percent of district taxation and 81 percent of district expenditures. The low public visibility of special districts, attributable to their limited functions, is reinforced by their low use of taxes. Only 15 percent of their revenues in the late 1970s was raised by taxes. Over the last decade their use of current charges and miscellaneous revenues has averaged three times more than taxes. Of equal importance, were the intergovernmental grants, which have increased from 23 percent to 38 percent of district general revenues.[16] The limited function and the low reliance on taxes reduce the public attention paid to the behavior of this growing sector of metropolitan government.[17] (Table 9–5 shows the revenues of special districts, single and multipurpose.) Of course the adaptation of a service area to the technical characteristics of production, the insulation from the political hurly-burly, and the use of user charges perhaps implies a more businesslike and efficient service.

Table 9–5 Special district revenue, 1977

Type and source	Amount (in millions)	%
Revenue, total	$14,408	100.0
General revenue, total	11,350	78.8
Intergovernmental	4,332	30.1
Property taxes	1,565	10.9
Charges	4,272	29.7
Other	1,181	8.2
Utility revenue, total	2,893	20.7

Source: U.S., Department of Commerce, Bureau of the Census, 1977 Census of Governments, vol. 4, *Governmental Finances*, part 2, *Finances of Special Districts* (Washington, D.C.: Government Printing Office, 1979), p. 2.

Externalities and spillovers The single-function districts may create external diseconomies for other governmental units because the independent single-purpose governments have no incentive to consider the effects of their behavior on other governments.

As a jurisdiction grows smaller in size or more restricted in functions, its taxes or services are likely to impose costs or generate benefits for persons outside its territory. Whereas externalities in the private market economy are restricted to non-priced benefits or costs, in the public sector, where prices are seldom used, a more general formulation is necessary. When governments adopt programs and policies according to perceived benefits and costs, they are primarily influenced by the costs and benefits which are generated in their jurisdiction, and only slightly influenced by those which appear elsewhere. Nevertheless, if externalities become large, overall inefficiencies will emerge and there will be incentives to reduce them by introducing institutional innovations.

Innovative governmental responses to externalities have taken several forms. Among those forms are compacts among governments, creation of special bodies to plan and influence the behavior of the individual governments, intergovernmental grants, and the reassignment of functions among levels of government. The most common response is an increase in the territorial size of local governments, generally in the form of annexations. Governments rarely merge or create an overall metropolitan government. There have been no systematic studies to evaluate how well these various innovations have succeeded in overcoming externalities, but casual empiricism indicates that it is a mixed story, varying with sources of externality and institutions adopted. The multivolumed report of the U.S. Advisory Commission on Intergovernmental Relations (ACIR), *Substate Regionalism and the Federal System* (1974), is an excellent source of information about practices and proposals, but is unfortunately replete with casual evaluation.

Sources of externalities   The three major sources of externalities are (1) the migration of population; (2) the consumption and production activities of commuters; and (3) the costs and benefits from consumption and production activities which operate within narrow city boundaries. Migration externalities are, for example, the costs to educate youth who then move to another city to work and live. Commuter spillovers are the externalities that cause the greatest concern because they are associated with a generalized feeling that suburbanites "exploit" the central city. It is felt that they use the infrastructure of the central city, although they pay property taxes to their own residential suburb. Nevertheless, the central city gains from the commuters through property taxes on the places where they work and shop and through sales taxes on their purchases. Thus, the direction of gains is uncertain. The externalities caused by the spillovers from the consumption and production activities in the city pose the most difficult problems. Air or water pollution in one city easily spreads to neighboring cities. A vigilant police surveillance in one city can motivate criminals to move on to neighboring cities. An attractive park will attract usage from neighboring cities.

Voluntary agreements among cities to handle externalities are extremely difficult to find. Differences over the amount of contributions and feelings of local pride create very difficult bargaining situations. The more common solution is the creation of commissions with varying degrees of power to encourage or impose overarching solutions in areas where externalities exist. Economists favor open-ended matching grants, which encourage communities to expand their services beyond the level warranted by any perceived internal benefits because there is no limit on the amount contributed. However, because the state or federal agency that grants the funds usually has only a vague idea about the amount of external benefits, the matching ratios often bear little relationship to the division between internal and external benefits. There is no solid research to test how effective these institutions have been; but they have filled in the gaps in the governmental structure of the suburbs.

The special costs of the central city

The central city spends far more per capita than do the suburbs on noneducational activities. The fiscal base of the central cities has been steadily declining relative to that of the suburbs; thus, its tax rate has been growing at a higher rate. This differential persists despite the grants which have supplied relatively more support to the central cities. The sources of this "overspending" by central cities is not clearly understood, which is frustrating because it is difficult to shape a policy to reduce the fiscal disparity without an adequate explanation.

Nevertheless, the central city remains a vital part of the metropolitan area, both in its key downtown services and its function in the absorption of new members of the labor force. The in-migration to the metropolitan area may have been a shock to the older residents, but the new population is there, and it must be housed, educated, doctored, policed, and employed. Although the incremental costs of these functions will not appear explicitly in the local tax bill of the suburban resident, the suburbanite cannot fully escape the costs. The price to the suburbanite is the increase in the state and federal taxes required to support the burdens of the central city.

Policy implications and the future

The current situation is the result of past policy. Critics are prone to characterize the governance of metropolitan areas as balkanized and chaotic, suggesting that the situation grew without rhyme or reason. On the contrary, much of what has happened is a consequence of state and federal legislation. There is a huge body of enabling and mandating legislation directed toward or impinging on the governance of metropolitan areas.

Major policy thrusts have been in three directions.

They deal first of all with the wretched living and working conditions of the poorest members of the population who occupy the central city in disproportionate numbers. Massive programs, using the city as a contractor to supply services for the poverty groups, have been developed to cope with the problem. Categorical grants-in-aid programs have increased the flow of funds to cities (and central cities in particular), but they are designed to satisfy national redistributional policies, not to improve the urban situation.

The grants programs, however, have also reflected the second major thrust, fiscal equity—redistribution to the communities with lesser fiscal resources and greater financial problems, but which make a greater tax effort and still find it necessary to supply poorer services. For example, the countercyclical economic stimulus package, which included such programs as the Comprehensive Employment and Training Act (CETA), was targeted to the hardship cities. The structure of the grants programs have been changing, however, and on balance, fiscal assistance to communities for human service programs seems to be growing.

The third general policy thrust may be loosely characterized as efficiency oriented. Subsidization of those public services that are characterized by externalities and scale economies (e.g., transportation and waste disposal and treatment) was followed by federal support of regional planning and coordinating entities. At a local and state level there was the proliferation of intergovernmental service supply contracts and the creation of special districts to respond to the same needs.

Each of these major policy orientations, although somewhat successful, has exacerbated the problems addressed by the other policies. The anti-poverty programs have often served as little more than income transfer programs keeping the poor inside the central cities and heightening the fiscal imbalance between the central cities and the suburbs. The fiscal support of the central cities has provided some fiscal relief, but it has not improved the competitive position of the central city. The innovations in regional planning and special districts have reduced the pressures to correct the fiscal imbalances. They have not, however, led to the consolidation of services proposed by many reformers. As a result, criticisms of policies and their implementation continue to be voiced.

The governance of metropolitan areas thus is beset with problems and proposed solutions.[18] Too often the patchwork that exists has not solved all the problems and it is assumed that a larger and administratively more tidy entity would do so. Despite the huge outpouring of writing on urban problems, there is no authoritative understanding of how the problems are linked and therefore no foresight into the consequences of new reform policies. Consolidation creates order, but it generates inefficient uniform distribution of services among diverse areas and dilutes the political power of the poor. Is there a partial solution? Can the patchwork of communities be improved to accommodate diverse objectives, not with the hope of eliminating all problems but to do better, which is not an ignoble objective?

The wave of initiatives and constitutional constraints were formulated to restrain specific forms of taxation or to limit the size of government, but the unforeseen consequences are likely to lead to a significant revision in the entire structure of local government.

As the decade of the 1970s came to an end, the tide of the fiscal limitation movement appeared to be swelling. In each state the attack on the fiscal system took a different form, and included a limit on specific taxes (e.g., the property tax); a limit on total taxes, expenditures, or appropriations with many different formulae to define the limits; and the specification of procedures to make it difficult to increase expenditures.[19] It is too early to make general, authoritative statements about the effect of tax limitations, but it is likely that the limitations will be amended so that only a few will remain as originally written. New tendencies are likely to emerge, and local government managers will have to address each of them.

The property tax may be eroded still further. In the smaller suburbs this would mean a weakening of their independent fiscal base. They would find themselves piggybacking on a state sales tax or receiving more state or federal grants. In one way or another they could become increasingly dependent on the outcomes of debates at the state capital and in Washington, D.C. In California, Proposition 13 (which was heralded as a revolt against an unresponsive government) has resulted in a shift of power to the state, an unexpected and unwelcome consequence.

A second major effect of the limitation movement is that government could seek to achieve its objective by regulations rather than by budgetary allocations. This trend is already apparent in land development. Some developers have been ordered to provide streets, parks, and other elements of the infrastructure as a condition for development permission. Instead of the government taxing and providing services, it could demand the services of private parties. In practice, the percentage of local activity attributable to government policy may be greater under regulation than under public provision of services. The public's conservative drive to limit government may result in a much greater scope for government.

The replacement of public production by regulation raises problems far beyond the scope of this chapter. Fortunately, the vast increase in regulation at the federal level has given rise to an intensive analysis of regulatory practices which will benefit local governments. A satisfactory understanding of either the regulatory process, the response of the private sector to regulations, or the best way to design regulations is still in the distant future. The effects of tax limits will be felt slowly and the substitution of regulations will be gradual. There will be time for adjusting local management policies.

Another consequence of the limitations is likely to be an expansion of user charges. In principle and in practice user charges are not taxes because they are voluntary prices paid by users for the amount of the public services they consume. Since user charges are exempt from most of the limitations, they are likely to become an increasingly popular form of local government finance. A shift to user charges will sharply reduce the redistributive effects of a local budget; and therefore, the fiscal advantages of a flight from the central city and the formation of segregated club-like suburbs will lessen.

The trend toward user charges is also likely to lead to a change in government structure. Some limitation formulas may involve the organization of special districts (without taxing powers) and the transfer to some of these districts of functions which had been routinely municipal services. For instance, a parking special district, rich with resources from parking fees, might absorb an unprofitable municipal bus service or street maintenance services.

The important point is to know that changes will become necessary, and that there will be an increasing need to consider innovations and how to facilitate their dispersal. The analysis of user charges for conventional public services is still in its infancy, but there is a large volume of literature on pricing of public enterprises which could help the design of prices for conventional services.

An epilogue on the future

All public policies are deficient because they are designed to deal with future problems and to rely on predicting future behavior. They are, however, based on a study of past behavior. The most serious case of misapplied knowledge is the military policy set by generals who were trained to fight the last war. Firm knowledge is limited to past events, but the future may be dominated by forces that may have been unimportant in the past. This dilemma is as true for metropolitan policy as for any other. Family size has shrunk and working wives are far more evident. The relative costs of energy have changed, the computer revolution rages on, the taxpayer revolt is spreading, and environmental concerns have been cycling. Each of these changes, and the reader can name many more, was much less important in the last three decades, during which time our present metropolitan governance was shaped. Policies, which are necessarily future-oriented, have to evaluate how these changes may affect costs, preferences, objectives, and alternatives for the future. The analysis of the past has to be sufficiently general to plug in these new parameters. The politics of the future will reflect these changes. The education of those who will determine policy should be sufficiently general so that they may absorb the implications of future technology and life style.

1   An undauntingly pessimistic view about the efficacy of solutions is taken by Edward Banfield in *The Unheavenly City Revisited* (Boston: Little, Brown & Co., 1974). The Advisory Commission on Intergovernmental Relations is one of the many organizations that is persistently optimistic in proposing solutions; see: *Improving Urban America: A Challenge to Federalism*, M–107 (Washington, D.C.: Government Printing Office, 1976).

2   Richard P. Nathan and Charles Adams, Jr., *Revenue Sharing: The Second Round* (Washington, D.C.: Brookings Institution, 1977), p. 86.

3   See: J. R. Aronson and E. Schwartz, "Financing Public Goods and the Distribution of Population in a System of Local Governments," *National Tax Journal* 26 (June 1973): 137–60.

4   The new field of public choices aspires to fill the gaps between economic, political, and organizational analysis. See issues of the journal *Public Choice.*

5   Anthony Downs, *Opening Up the Suburbs* (New Haven, Conn.: Yale University Press, 1973).

6   If the poor and the rich are equally mobile, an equilibrium in population distribution between local communities may not exist. For details, see: Aronson and Schwartz, "Financing Public Goods."

7   Howard Pack and Janet Rothenberg Pack, "Metropolitan Fragmentation and Suburban Homogeneity," in *Urban Studies* 14, no. 2 (June 1977): 191–201.

8   Richard L. Forstall, "Annexations and Corporate Changes since the 1970 Census: With Historical Data on Annexation for Larger Cities for 1900–1970," in *The Municipal Year Book 1975* (Washington, D.C.: International City Management Association, 1975), p. 28.

9   Lyle C. Fitch, "Fiscal and Productive Efficiency in Urban Government Systems," in *Metropolitan America,* ed. Amos Hawley and Vincent Rock (New York: Halsted Press, 1975).

10   For a test and review of the arguments, see: Robert P. Inman, "The Fiscal Performance of Local Governments: An Interpretative Review," in *Current Issues in Urban Economics,* ed. Peter Mieszkowski and Mahlon Straszheim (Baltimore, Md.: Johns Hopkins University Press, 1979).

11   On the average less than a third of the adults vote in municipal elections. See: Albert K. Karnig and B. Oliver Walter, "Municipal Elections: Registration, Incumbent Success, and Voter Participation," in *The Municipal Year Book 1977* (Washington, D.C.: International City Management Association, 1977), pp. 65–72.

12   U.S., Bureau of the Census, *City Government Finances in 1976–77* (Washington, D.C.: Government Printing Office, 1979), p. 8.

13   For a summary of these studies, see: U.S., Advisory Commission on Intergovernmental Relations, *Substate Regionalism and the Federal System,* vol. 4: *Governmental Functions and Processes: Local and Areawide* (Washington, D.C.: Government Printing Office, 1974).

14   U.S., Bureau of the Census, 1977 Census of Governments, *Regional Organizations,* vol. 6, no. 6 (Washington, D.C.: Government Printing Office, 1978).

15   Alan Campbell and Roy Bahl guestimate that the number of quasi-governmental and administrative areas or districts may equal the number of governments counted by the Census; see: *State and Local Government: The Political Economy of Reform* (New York: Free Press, 1976), p. 11.

16   U.S., Bureau of the Census, 1977 Census of Governments, *Finances of Special Districts,* vol. 4, no. 2 (Washington, D.C.: Government Printing Office, 1979), p. 9. The design and impact of user charges also are discussed in Chapter 8 of this book.

17   Ninety-four percent of the growth in the number of local governments between 1972 and 1977 within the 1977 SMSAs was due to the increase in special districts. U.S., Bureau of the Census, 1977 Census of Governments, *Governmental Organizations,* vol. 1, (Washington, D.C.: Government Printing Office, 1979), p. 29.

18   For a summary of proposals and arguments, see: U.S., Advisory Commission on Intergovernmental Relations, *Improving Urban America;* Campbell and Bahl, eds., *State and Local Government;* U.S., Advisory Commission on Intergovernmental Relations, *Pragmatic Federalism: The Reassignment of Functional Responsibility* (Washington, D.C.: Government Printing Office, 1976); and the papers by A. Campbell and J. Dollenmayer, Lyle Fitch, and Joseph Zimmerman in *Metropolitan America,* ed. Hawley and Rock.

19   The Advisory Commission on Intergovernmental Relations regularly reports on developments in tax limitation activities in its journal, *Intergovernmental Perspective.*

10 Fiscal structure in the federal system

The public sector in the United States, Canada, and most other federal countries is a highly fragmented system of governmental units functioning within the context of a constitution that defines only very roughly the scope of responsibility and authority at different levels of government. At a conceptual level, a federal model might be constructed consisting of a tidily organized structure in which there exists a clearly recognized *and* constitutionally specified separation of powers among the levels of government; a model in which agencies at the different levels could pursue their activities independently of those at other levels of the hierarchy. Late in the nineteenth century, James Bryce provided just such a conception when he described a federal system as "a great factory wherein two sets of machinery are at work, their revolving wheels apparently intermixed, their bands crossing one another, yet each doing its own work without touching or hampering the other."[1]

The evolution of federal systems, however, has been in sharp contrast to Bryce's metaphor. The activities of levels of government in the modern federal system overlap and intertwine in fundamental and complex ways, so much so that political scientists now tend to characterize our age as one of "cooperative federalism." Some would contend that the assignment of functional responsibility among levels of government is a vacuous issue. As Michael Reagan puts it: "Those things are national and justify grant programs which the Congress *says* are national. The concepts of local and national interest are squishy at best."[2]

In spite of this apparent chaos and absence of principle in the functioning of federal fiscal structures, the economic roles of different levels of government should be considered systematically. This chapter will review the principles of economics in terms of the division of functions among levels of government and examine the structure and development of the intergovernmental fiscal system in the United States and in other federal countries. This will require an extensive examination of intergovernmental grants-in-aid, which probably have played a more central role in the shaping of the modern federal system than any other fiscal instrument.

The division of functions

In economic terms, the functions of government may be defined as supplementing the pricing system to promote an efficient use of society's scarce resources, establishing an equitable distribution of income, and maintaining the economy at high levels of employment with reasonable stability of prices. These functions refer to the public sector as a whole, but the peculiarly federal issue is the proper assignment of these functions to different levels of government.

Economic analysis can provide some insights into this issue. For example, the macroeconomic function of stabilizing the economy at high levels of output and employment without creating excessive inflationary pressures clearly rests with the central government. First, a centralized agency must control the creation and destruction of money. If each local government had access to monetary powers, there would be a powerful incentive to create new money to purchase real goods and services from other jurisdictions, instead of raising money by local taxation. The result would be excessive creation of money with a consequent rapid price inflation. Monetary control, and hence the exercise of monetary policy to stabilize the economy, must be centralized. Additionally local fiscal policy is severely constrained by the scope of local budgetary measures for countercyclical purposes. In particular, the high degree of "openness" of local economies implies very small impacts for strictly local policies. If, for instance, a local authority were to undertake a substantial tax cut to stimulate the local economy, it would find that most of the newly generated spending would flow out of the jurisdiction in payment for goods and services produced elsewhere with little effect on local levels of employment.

In short, the absence of monetary prerogatives and the openness of regional or local economies suggest that the potential for an effective macroeconomic stabilization policy is extremely limited at the local level of government. The stabilization function is the responsibility of the federal government, the monetary and fiscal policies of which can exert a real influence on the course of the economy.

The character of the national economic system also must impose real constraints on the scope of localized redistributive policies. The high degree of mobility of economic units across local jurisdictions implies that one municipality, for example, cannot tax a particular group significantly more heavily than it is taxed elsewhere without creating incentives for movement. If such a municipality were to undertake an aggressive program to reduce inequality in the distribution of local income through, for example, subsidies for the poor and steeply progressive tax rates for the rich, relatively high-income households would tend to leave and settle in jurisdictions where they would obtain more favorable fiscal treatment while poorer families would migrate into the community. A more equal distribution of income may result, but it would be because of the out-migration of the well-to-do and the in-migration of lower income families.

One manifestation of this tendency is the migration from poorer areas of the country to areas with relatively generous income-maintenance programs, a process that has exacerbated the fiscal ills of a number of older central cities. Another consequence of constrained redistributive policies is exemplified by several centuries of the Poor Laws in Great Britain. Under the Elizabethan Poor Laws, the care of the poor was explicitly a local (parish) function to be financed by local taxation, a system which continued into the nineteenth century.[3] The fear that liberal support for the poor would encourage an influx of impoverished people and an increase of local tax rates was a troublesome issue at the local level throughout this period. Writing in the nineteenth century, Edwin Cannan stressed these constraints on local revenue systems:

Local taxation according to ability is impossible except where the localities are very large and divided from each other by strong prejudices. With migration from one place to another as easy as it has long been in England, it is merely ridiculous to expect it to be possible to rate [tax] a millionaire in the parish in which he resides on his whole income. The effect . . . would obviously be to make the wealthy select for their residence the lowest rated places . . . .[4]

This is not to imply that local governments cannot redistribute income to any extent at all; they can and do. Nevertheless, the mobility of households and firms imposes real constraints on the character and level of local taxation. The result of all this is that the central government must not only stabilize the economy but also must assume the primary responsibility for income transfer programs to establish a more equitable distribution of income. Assigning the redistribution function to the central government does not preclude an extensive role for localities in the actual administration and operation of the programs; it simply recognizes that levels of redistribution cannot vary widely across local jurisdictions and that localities cannot be expected to fund the bulk of these programs from their own sources.

It is with regard to the remaining function of the public sector, the direct provision of public goods and services, that decentralized levels of government have their basic economic rationale. Certain public goods, such as national defense, confer benefits on all the members of society; the federal government is unquestionably the appropriate agent for providing such truly national public services. In contrast, many other services with collective characteristics are primarily local in nature. Refuse disposal and sewer systems, fire and police protection, libraries, and recreational resources are but a few examples. In these cases, a compelling argument can be made for the localized provision of services according to local preferences. For reasons of equity, centralized control tends toward uniform levels of output across all jurisdictions, even though such uniformity of output can entail substantial losses in consumer well-being. Wherever possible, levels of consumption of particular services should be adjusted to the tastes of individuals or groups of individuals.[5] Moreover, recent studies suggest that the magnitude of individual losses associated with the uniform provision of public outputs can be quite substantial.[6] By using econometric estimates of demand curves for various local public goods, the potential losses experienced when everyone is required to consume the same level of public output can be seen in contrast to a solution in which each local community provides the output that best satisfies the demands of its own constituency. Given these measures, studies suggest that decentralized provision, as measured by the willingness-to-pay of individual consumers, seems to promise significant gains to consumers relative to those of the "unitary solution" of uniform outputs.

As de Tocqueville noted over a century ago: "In great centralized nations the legislator is obliged to give a character of uniformity to the laws, which does not always suit the diversity of customs and of districts."[7]

The economic literature on local finance over the past twenty years has emphasized the role of consumer mobility in realizing these consumer gains from locally determined service levels. In 1956 Charles Tiebout introduced a model of local finance in which each individual seeks a community that provides the level of public output best suited to his or her tastes.[8] The outcome closely resembles the market solution for private goods.

Just as the consumer may be visualized as walking to a private market place to buy his goods, the prices of which are set, we place him in the position of walking to a community where the prices (taxes) of community services are set. Both trips take the consumer to market. There is no way in which the consumer can avoid revealing his preferences in a spatial economy. Spatial mobility provides the local public-goods counterpart to the private market's shopping trip.[9]

The Tiebout model envisions a system of local finance in which consumers sort themselves out according to their demands for public goods. As in the private market, individual consumers "purchase" their preferred basket of services based on their tastes and the cost of these services.

The Tiebout model does entail a number of heroic assumptions, in particular, one of footloose consumers who move costlessly among localities and choose a community of residence solely on the basis of fiscal considerations. Nevertheless, subsequent research suggests that the mobility model possesses considerable explanatory power. Numerous studies have found, for example, that local property values vary directly with levels of local services. People do appear to pay more for houses of the same size and quality in order to live in communities which provide such amenities as better schools for their children and greater safety from crime.[10]

This should not come as a surprise. Households in the United States do move with considerable frequency. The 1970 census, for example, found that only about one-half of the families sampled were living in the same house as were in 1965. Surely the vast majority of these moves were not motivated primarily by fiscal considerations; they must often reflect a change of location of employment or family status. Whatever the motivation for the move, the process of choosing the new community in which to live is likely to involve serious considerations of local services and taxes. For an individual working in a metropolitan area, perhaps in the central city itself, there typically exists a wide range of choices among suburban communities in which to reside. The quality of such local services as education and safety are likely to be crucial factors in this choice.

In assessing the implications of the local finance literature, it is most important to distinguish between the descriptive and the prescriptive. The mobility model does isolate an important set of forces that have exerted a profound impact on the evolution of metropolitan areas. There has been a strong tendency for families with high demands for public services to live in suburban communities with high levels of amenities; equally, households with lesser demands for public outputs tend to live together in jurisdictions with a lower quality of services. From a descriptive perspective, these models can "explain" the development of metropolitan areas into systems of relatively small suburban communities, each with a relatively homogeneous population when compared to that of the urban area as a whole.

From a prescriptive point of view, however, things are somewhat more complicated. In terms of consumer choice, the Tiebout model has great appeal. Both communities permit each consumer to purchase the quantity of public output that he or she desires at a tax-price equal to its cost. But from a broader social perspective there are some troublesome matters. One can hardly help noticing that, because the demand for services is positively correlated with income, the "sorting-out" process will tend to generate a system segregated by income class. A spectrum of communities ranging from high-income jurisdictions with high levels of services to low-income jurisdictions with low levels of services will emerge. This may not be objectionable, but recent court decisions and other expressions of social concern (busing to achieve racial balance for example), suggest that, for various political and ethical reasons, this outcome may not be acceptable. Whatever conclusions are reached about this apparent tension between local choice and social justice, the mobility model illuminates a powerful set of forces that must be dealt with in the design of social and economic policy.

Intergovernmental grants and revenue sharing

De Tocqueville observed that "the federal system was created with the intention of combining the different advantages which result from the magnitude and the littleness of nations."[11] Economic analysis provides some support for his claim. A centralized authority is necessary to implement macroeconomic stabilization policy, to accomplish socially desirable income redistribution, and to provide, with equality, a pattern of benefits that is national in scope. At the same time, the "littleness" of local fiscal jurisdictions offers compelling advantages in terms of tailoring the provision of certain public services to local tastes. In fact, it is virtually impossible to conceive of a country without certain "federal" elements in the public sector, irrespective of whether the country has a formal federal constitution that guarantees independent tax and expenditure authority to different levels of government. Even in countries with unitary governments, there typically is a considerable extent of de facto budgetary choice at decentralized levels of the public sector. In an economic sense, government sectors in *all* nations are federal because to a greater or lesser degree, discretionary budgetary activity is exercised at several levels of the governmental system.

Although the assignment of functions outlined in the preceding section can provide a framework for thinking about federal fiscal structure, it is a bit too neat and tidy. The macroeconomic and redistribution functions are not *solely* centralized responsibilities. State and local governments do undertake some explicitly countercyclical and redistributive measures.

In particular, some services (e.g., education) are primarily of local interest, although they have important national dimensions or spillover effects. It is unclear how best to structure the provision of such services. As one observer of federal government states:

There is and can be no final solution to the allocation of financial resources in a federal system. There can only be adjustments and reallocations in the light of changing conditions. What a federal government needs, therefore, is machinery adequate to make these adjustments.[12]

The federal system has several levels, and the determination of the appropriate level of government to provide a particular service is often subject to considerable ambiguity.

Federal governments have found intergovernmental grants-in-aid to be a piece of fiscal "machinery" well-suited for dealing with the continuing budgetary tensions among different levels of government. Nearly all federal countries have come to place a growing reliance on these grants. In the United States, for example, William Young contends that "the most powerful engine in the century for reshaping national-state relations has been the grant-in-aid system of national financing of state and local activities."[13] The operations of federal, state, and local governments have come to interact with and overlap one another to such a degree that a basic problem is integrating the budgetary and other decisions of different public units into a coherent and consistent set of policies. From this perspective, intergovernmental grants have proved to be highly flexible fiscal instruments, capable of assuming a number of different forms to promote varied objectives in the public sector. Grants now function as a basic fiscal link among the budgetary structures of the different levels of government.

External effects and intergovernmental grants

Potential distortions in economic decisions exist whenever the choices of one individual (or group of individuals) impinge significantly on the welfare of others outside the market. A classic example is that of the factory spewing forth smoke which imposes external costs on the neighboring laundry. In this case, the decision makers (the factory owners) have no incentive to take into account the costs (the dirty laundry) they generate. Third parties are not considered, so these economic choices fail to incorporate the full range of social costs relevant to the decision. In certain instances where the affected parties are able to come together and negotiate an agreement, voluntary private decisions can yield an efficient outcome.[14] However, this kind of resolution of externalities relies on a number of quite restrictive assumptions such as low transaction costs and an absence of strategic behavior. These considerations suggest that its relevance is limited to cases involving only a very small number of participants.[15] The most likely consequence is a distorted pattern of resource use consisting of excessive levels of activities, which generate external costs and inappropriately low levels of spillover benefits.

External effects are not limited to decisions by private consumers or firms. The programs adopted by one local or state government may have important implications for the well-being of residents of other jurisdictions. A good system of roads in one locality, for example, provides services for travelers from elsewhere. Likewise, medical research funded in one state may produce new treatment or cures of widespread interest. In such instances, we can hardly expect the state or locality to use its own resources to expand its activity to levels for which outsiders would be willing to pay if a payment mechanism existed. From the perspective of the federal government, such myopic decisions by states and localities are a matter of serious concern for programs which have important external effects.

There are nearly always important advantages in enhancing consumer satisfaction by allowing individuals or small groups of individuals to determine their own most appropriate levels of service, instead of having the levels imposed by the central government.

As a representative of the national interest, the federal government could in principle simply take over the whole function and thereby "internalize" all the relevant costs and benefits. Often this response is politically infeasible or simply unconstitutional. But, even if it were a viable alternative, centralization is frequently a cure that may be worse than the disease. The decentralized provision of public services is advantageous in the efficient use of resources because the state or local government is in a position to fashion its programs according to the particular tastes of its constituency.

The federal government does not have to preempt state-local outputs of services that involve external effects across jurisdictions; it may resort to intergovernmental grants to influence state-local choices.

A conditional grant is contingent on some specified behavior on the part of the recipient. In general, there is a requirement that the funds be used for a particular purpose. Unconditional or lump-sum grants have no strings attached; the recipients are free to use the funds however they wish.

Conditional grants The federal government can provide direct fiscal inducements to state and local officials for expansion of specific activities through a properly designed system of grants. The form of these grants is crucial. To encourage expansion of a particular service (e.g., medical research), the use of a *conditional grant* is required. An *unconditional* or lump-sum transfer of funds is unacceptable. The funds must be earmarked for the intended purpose. But more than this, the granting government must ensure that the recipient is not in a position to substitute the grant monies for local revenues. Note that, even if a grant is conditional (in the sense that the recipient is required to use the monies for a prescribed function or program), it does not follow that the grant will induce an increase in spending for the function relative to that which would have been forthcoming in the absence of the grant. For example, a locality which receives a grant to expand local police services might use these funds—especially in periods of rising budgets—to cover *planned* budgetary increments that would otherwise have been financed with locally raised revenues. The grant funds would then, in effect, be available indirectly for use in other programs or, alternatively, for local tax cuts. In short, this "fungibility" of grant funds may allow states and localities to use conditional grants in the same way that they would employ monies with no strings attached, thereby frustrating the intent of the federal grant program. A case in which this is not true is where the state or locality would have expended none of its own funds (or less than the sum of the grant) on the grant-in-aid program. Thus, "demonstration grants" may induce expenditures which would not have taken place without federal assistance.[16]

Matching grants   The proper form of grant when external benefits are present is a matching grant, under which the grantor agees to pay some fraction of the unit cost of the recipient. Under one-to-one matching, for example, the state or locality would receive one dollar in grant monies for each dollar it expended from its own funds. Such a grant effectively cuts in half the cost of the service *to the locality*. Moreover, the only way the locality can increase its grant money is by expanding its own spending. Unlike a fixed sum for some specified purpose, the matching grant reduces the effective price and provides a direct inducement to an expansion of the service. In theory, the matching terms should reflect the magnitude of the spillover effect. If, for example, two dollars of local expenditure generates one dollar of benefits for residents of other jurisdictions, then the granting government's share should be one-third or one-to-two matching. This would effectively induce the recipient to take account of the external benefits. In practice, it may be difficult to determine precisely the exact shares of local and external benefits, but the analysis does provide some guidelines. It suggests that where the purpose of the grant program is to encourage state and local provision of particular services that also are beneficial elsewhere in the nation, the appropriate instrument is the matching grant. Moreover, where the spillover benefits are considered large relative to local benefits, the grant program should offer relatively generous matching terms. These grants, incidentally, should involve "open-end matching"; the matching terms should be available to the recipient at whatever level of spending is selected. If the matching stops at some level of local expenditure on the program, the grant no longer has a price effect and may become equivalent in its effects to an unconditional, lump-sum grant.[17]

The federal government in the United States has made extensive use of matching grants to state and local governments under several programs for which spillover benefits would appear to be quite important. For example, federal matching grants to the states have supported the construction of a national network of highways. Federal agencies also have employed matching grants for various educational programs that are of a clear national interest. The actual evolution of federal systems of intergovernmental grants shall be examined later in this chapter, but these examples suggest that the "economic principles" of grant design can "explain" (or provide a rationale for) the structure of some grant programs.

Equalization of fiscal capacity: a role for unconditional grants

In addition to improved resource allocation, federal systems of government have typically placed an extensive reliance on intergovernmental grants to correct geographical inequities. The basic rationale for these grants stems from perceived geographical differences in fiscal well-being. Some jurisdictions have relatively large tax bases and a population that requires comparatively little in the way of social services. Adequate service levels can be provided with relatively low tax rates in these localities. Other areas often have significantly higher tax rates and a lower level (or quality) of services. Central governments in dozens of countries have responded to these geographical fiscal differentials with equalizing grants with the objective of removing or narrowing the differentials.[18] The stated purposes of the grants usually are to establish a fiscal environment in which each state or locality can provide a satisfactory level of key public services with a fiscal effort that is not discernibly greater than that in other jurisdictions. To achieve this goal, the central government typically bases the allocation of grant funds on the measured "need" and fiscal capacity of the decentralized units of government. In this way, jurisdictions with populations requiring large public expenditures, or with comparatively small tax bases (or with an unfortunate combination of the two) receive proportionately larger sums.

Three points concerning equalizing grants are worthy of special emphasis. First, the proper grant form in this case is an unconditional (lump-sum) grant, the intent of which is to equalize fiscal capability, not to stimulate public spending. From this perspective, it would be inappropriate to employ a matching grant which would effectively lower the cost of services to each jurisdiction and thereby directly encourage increased spending. The implication of fiscal equalization grants is that they vary with a jurisdiction's need and fiscal capacity, but do not change because of the fiscal response of the jurisdiction. Second, although equalizing grants may serve to reduce fiscal differentials *among jurisdictions*, they are not an effective device for achieving the socially desired distribution of income *among individuals*. Such grants will typically channel funds to poorer areas, but they are very clumsy instruments for interpersonal redistributive purposes. Most low-income areas will have some wealthy residents and most high-income areas usually have some poor residents. Transfers from rich to poor *areas* through the medium of equalizing grants are therefore bound to have some unfair redistributive elements. Third, the scope and design of equalizing grants should not overlook the fact that there are powerful market forces that compensate automatically for some of the apparent inequities in a federal fiscal system. The case for equalizing grants is sometimes made in terms of the principle of horizontal equity: people in equal positions should be treated equally. At first glance, it would appear that a system of decentralized finance is likely to violate this principle because the size of the tax base per capita will vary from one jurisdiction to the next. It also appears that different tax rates will be required to raise the same amount of revenue per person. A resident of a locality with a relatively large tax base will thus face a lower tax rate and have a lower tax bill than his or her counterpart in a district with a smaller tax base. This apparent source of inequity was, incidentally, one of the grounds for declaring the system of school finance in the state of New Jersey to be unconstitutional.

Unconditional equalizing grants are not a substitute for a national program to achieve an equitable distribution of income among individuals.

Where there exists a high degree of mobility of households among jurisdictions, however, market forces will themselves tend to eliminate any horizontal inequities. Suppose, for example, that one jurisdiction possesses a notable fiscal advantage over the others (e.g., a relatively large tax base or a lower cost of maintaining clean air in a town located on a hill). In an environment of mobile individuals, the value of such differences will be capitalized into local property values. Consumers will bid for places in the fiscally advantaged community until the increased price of property exactly offsets the fiscal gain. (Sudden changes in the fiscal position of a particular community will generate a once-and-for-all set of windfall gains or losses to reflect the new fiscal circumstances.)[19] Thus, an individual considering the purchase of a residence in a community with a relatively high tax *rate* will find that the high tax liability is approximately offset by the lower price of the property as compared to an equivalent property in a jurisdiction with lower tax rates. Mobility ensures that equals will be treated equally. Whatever fiscal advantages are enjoyed will be paid for in the form of higher actual (or imputed) rent; conversely, higher taxes will be offset by lower prices of property. In the mobility model, horizontal equity is self-policing, which suggests that significant horizontal inequities may be ironed out by market forces within the metropolitan economy. This may not be true, however, at the regional level where the mobility model appears less applicable. Here the obstacles to mobility may permit unequal treatment of equals to persist.

Taxation and revenue sharing

A third important rationale for intergovernmental grants is the establishment of an efficient and fair system of taxation for the public sector as a whole. There exists the sense (and some evidence) that the federal tax system is basically a more just and less distorting structure than the tax systems of state and local governments. The federal income tax, for example, is probably a good deal more progressive than state-local income, sales, and property taxes.[20] Moreover, the taxes at the more decentralized levels of government have a greater potential for distorting the flow of resources in the economy. To take one example, federal taxes cannot be avoided by a change of location within the national economy; therefore, this form of taxation will not create direct incentives for locational distortions in the economy. At state and local levels, however, similar taxes may chase capital from high-tax to low-tax jurisdictions, resulting in real inefficiencies in resource allocation and a subsequent reduction in output. The relatively high mobility of both goods and people across state or local boundaries implies that there may be much more sensitivity to state-local fiscal differentials than to those at the national level.

In addition, states and localities are often able to shift a substantial portion of their tax burden onto residents of other jurisdictions. The taxation of certain production activities in one jurisdiction, for instance, may result in higher prices which are paid largely by outsiders. In the state of Michigan the burden of taxation of the auto industry falls largely on purchasers of new automobiles throughout the nation. Areas which draw heavy tourist populations frequently meet much of their local tax needs through substantial excise taxes on hotel and restaurant bills. But these are not isolated examples. Charles McLure has estimated that, on average, state governments in the United States are able to "export" approximately 20 percent to 25 percent of their taxes to residents of other states.[21]

Thus, it is considerably more difficult to design an efficient and equitable tax system at the state and local levels than at the federal level. Both people and goods can move away from high-tax jurisdictions and thereby introduce serious distortions in the allocation of resources and quite unintended redistribution effects on personal incomes. The federal government, in contrast, has a greater scope for reliance on progressive taxation and can, through a national uniformity of tax rates, avoid the distortions in resource allocation generated by state-local tax differentials. Moreover, a greater reliance on centralized taxation does provide some economies of scale in tax administration. Data for the United States indicate that the cost of administrating the federal individual income tax system amounts to only about 0.5 percent of the revenues received. At the state level, the administrative costs for income or sales taxes are typically 1.0 percent to 2.0 percent of revenues.[22]

It would appear that the equity and efficiency characteristics of the federal-state-local tax system as a whole might be improved by shifting more of the taxation function to the central government. However, there are important reasons for retaining state and local discretion over the size and composition of their expenditures. One way to accomplish these two objectives is through a program of revenue sharing. Revenue sharing is a mechanism through which federal taxation can be substituted for state-local taxes. In a sense, the federal government acts as a tax-collection agent for the states and localities by collecting tax revenues in excess of its own needs and distributing this excess in lump-sum form to state and local treasuries. The appropriate form for these funds is as unconditional grants. If the purpose of these monies is to alter the overall revenue system and *not* to encourage state-local expenditure on particular functions (or spending in general), the revenue sharing grants should have no strings attached. In other words, recipients should not be required to spend the funds as a condition for receiving them.

Although revenue sharing offers a mechanism for the potential improvement of the total tax system, political realities suggest limitations on the extent of its use. An implicit assumption in this discussion is that the central government can function as a tax collector for state and local governments without intruding on state-local expenditure prerogatives. As long as the transfers of funds to state and local officials are truly of an unconditional form, there is no reason *in principle* why the recipient should feel any constraints about how these resources are used. This assumption, however, is naive; if the central government is a major supplier of state-local funds, political pressures and opportunities can be expected to induce central agencies to use this leverage to achieve some of their own objectives. In the United Kingdom, for example, central government grants (primarily of an unconditional form) now account for approximately two-thirds of local authority revenues. Widespread concern over the erosion of local autonomy has resulted and has generated renewed interest in additional sources of tax revenues at the local level. In short, a "modest" revenue sharing program may contribute to the effectiveness of the tax system, but heavy reliance on such programs may, over the long run, undermine the fiscal discretion of decentralized levels of government.

We thus have two potential roles for unconditional grants: fiscal equalization and an improved overall system of taxation. At a pragmatic level, there is no reason why the public sector cannot pursue both of these objectives at the same time through a system of unconditional grants (revenue sharing) in which the size of the per capita grant varies with the fiscal characteristics of the jurisdiction. The United States has attempted to do just this with the general revenue sharing (GRS) program.

The rapid growth of intergovernmental grants

The continuing growth in the size and complexity of the public sector has generated a striking expansion in the use of intergovernmental grants. Such transfers provide a policy tool capable of promoting a number of quite different and important government objectives, a fact that has not gone unnoticed. Table 10–1 provides some aggregate data for the United States that document this striking growth. Federal grants to state and local governments have increased from almost $2.5 billion in 1950 to almost $63 billion in fiscal year 1977. This represents an annual compound rate of expansion of 12.7 percent. Because this rate is well in excess of the rate of growth of federal outlays, these grants have, over time, accounted for an increasingly large percentage of federal spending. About 15.0 percent of federal expenditures now take the form of grants-in-aid to the states and localities.

This rapid expansion in intergovernmental transfers is by no means limited to the United States; it has occurred in most other federal (and nonfederal) countries as well. In a comparative study of fiscal systems, Werner W. Pommerehne found that over the period 1950–1970, large increases in federal transfers were made to other governments in such countries as France, West Germany, Switzerland, the United Kingdom, and Canada. In Canada, for example, central grants to the provinces and local governments grew from only $3 million in 1950 to almost $8 billion by 1975, a compound rate of growth of over 14 percent per annum![23]

The increasing reliance on intergovernmental funds is also apparent from the perspective of the recipients. As Table 10–1 indicates, state governments in the

United States now obtain close to 25 percent of their revenues from federal grants. Local governments that receive aid both from federal sources and from their respective states have also become increasingly reliant on intergovernmental transfers. Table 10–1 shows that, in the aggregate, state grants to local governments have risen from a little more than $4 billion in 1950 to over $60 billion in 1977; similarly, federal grants *directly* to local jurisdictions have grown rapidly, from less than $1 billion in 1950 to over $16 billion in 1977. The relative size of federal and state contributions to the localities is a bit misleading because several grant programs channel funds from the federal government to localities through the states; these monies appear in official figures as state grants to local government. Regardless of the specific source, local governments now depend on intergovernmental grants for almost 40 percent of their total revenues.

Table 10–1 Growth in intergovernmental grants in the United States for selected years (amounts in millions)

Year	Federal grants to state and local governments	Federal grants as % of total federal outlay[1]	Federal grants to states as % of total state revenues	State aid to local government[2]	Direct federal grants to local government	Grants received by local government as % of total local revenue[3]
1950	$ 2,486	5.8	16.4	$ 4,217	$ 211	27.5
1960	6,974	7.6	19.4	9,522	592	27.2
1965	11,029	9.3	20.2	14,010	1,155	28.4
1970	21,857	11.1	21.6	26,920	2,605	33.1
1971	26,146	12.4	23.4	31,081	3,391	34.1
1972	31,253	13.5	23.8	35,143	4,551	34.0
1973	39,256	15.9	24.2	39,963	7,903	37.1
1974	41,820	15.5	22.5	44,553	10,199	38.2
1975	47,054	14.4	23.4	51,068	10,906	38.8
1976	55,589	15.2	22.7	56,169	13,576	39.1
1977	62,575	15.2	22.5	60,311	16,637	39.2

Source: The data (either presented directly or used to calculate percentages) for years prior to 1976 are from Tax Foundation, Inc., *Facts and Figures on Government Finance*, 19th Biennial Edition (New York, 1977), tables 57, 110, 134, 147, 185; for 1976 and 1977, data are from U.S. Bureau of the Census, *Governmental Finances in 1975–76*, table 5, and *Governmental Finances in 1976–77*, table 5.

1 Total federal outlays as measured under the Unified Budget.
2 State aid includes substantial amount of federal aid that is channeled through state governments to localities.
3 Grant revenues include payments from both the federal and state governments.

These transfers support a wide variety of public programs. Table 10–2 indicates the breakdown of federal grants by categories of aid for fiscal year 1977. Note, in particular, the diversity of purposes for grant funds. A substantial chunk (27 percent) of federal intergovernmental transfers is for public welfare. There is a sound rationale for this because it is extremely difficult for states, and especially for localities, to engage in aggressive redistributive programs to help lower income households. As a result, the federal government has used intergovernmental transfers extensively for redistributive purposes. Some critics would advocate that the current system of federal support for state and locally administered welfare programs be abolished, and that a uniform national system of transfer payments to the poor be established—with sole responsibility for this particular function resting with the central government.

It was noted earlier how these grants provide a stimulus for state-local programs that confer benefits on residents of other areas. Federal grants for highways and for various educational activities are good examples of such grants; the population of the United States has an important interest both in a good system

Table 10–2 Federal intergovernmental expenditures, 1976–77 (in millions)

Program	Amount
Education	$10,205
Grants-in-aid	8,339
Elementary and secondary education	2,302
School lunch and school milk program	2,144
Human development	1,564
Maintenance and operation of schools	696
Occupational, vocational, and adult education	660
Emergency school assistance	238
Education for the handicapped	118
Work incentive training	99
Other grants-in-aid	518
Payments for services	1,866
Scientific research and development	1,840
Tuition payments	26
Public welfare	19,250
Medical assistance (Medicaid)	9,829
Maintenance assistance	6,337
Social services, NEC	2,405
Special supplemental food programs (WIC)	279
Food stamp program	250
Work incentives, NEC	242
Other	178
Health and hospitals	2,353
Health Services Administration	720
Alcohol, drug abuse, and mental health administration	471
Health Resources Administration, NEC	410
National Institutes of Health	294
Environmental pollution abatement and control	191
Other	267
General revenue sharing	6,764
Highways	6,173
Natural resources	969
Housing and urban renewal	2,914
Air transportation	381
Social insurance administration	1,532
Other and combined	22,238
Unemployment compensation for federal employees, ex-servicemen, and temporary extended benefits	5,213
Labor and manpower, NEC	4,747
Waste treatment facilities	4,052
Community planning and development	2,207
Urban mass transportation	1,891
Antirecession fiscal assistance	1,694
Law Enforcement Assistance Administration	684
Civil defense and disaster relief	287
Federal contribution to District of Columbia	281
Programs for the aging	203
Promotion of science, research, libraries, and museums	177
Payments in lieu of taxes	168
Other	634
Total federal intergovernmental expenditure	73,045

Source: U.S., Department of Commerce, Bureau of the Census, *Governmental Finances in 1976–77* (Washington, D.C.: Government Printing Office, 1979), tables 10, 12.

Note: Federal intergovernmental expenditure includes, in addition to pure grants, federal payments for certain services from state and local government so that the total of these expenditures exceeds somewhat the figure for federal grants-in-aid for fiscal year 1977 that appears in Table 10–1.

of national roadways and in an educated electorate. Conditional intergovernmental grants provide a mechanism for higher level governments to represent the broader concern of the citizenry through budgetary incentives.

In contrast to some other countries (e.g., Canada), the federal government in the United States has relied almost exclusively on conditional grants. These grants typically involve some kind of cost-sharing between the federal agency and the recipient state or locality such that the effective price at which the recipient purchases the aided good or service is lowered. This is accomplished in one of two ways: through an explicit grant formula that specifies the respective shares of the grantor and recipient, or through an application and negotiation procedure for a "project grant" under which the state or local share is determined in the process itself. In both instances, the federal government has typically included equalizing elements by providing more generous matching terms to jurisdictions with lesser fiscal capacity. This is accomplished by using "variable matching grants" in which the fiscal circumstances of the jurisdictions enter into a formula that determines the federal matching share. The federal administrator of project grants takes local fiscal capacity into consideration in determining the local contribution. Formula grants, according to one study, are the major grant instrument in the federal intergovernmental transfer system in the United States, accounting for about 66 percent of the dollar total of federal grants to state and local governments. These grants are given primarily to the states. In contrast, project grants by the federal government are mainly for transfers to local governments. They make up about 20 percent of the dollar total of federal intergovernmental transfers.[24]

In addition to its extensive system of conditional grants, in 1972 the United States instituted a program of general revenue sharing with state and local governments. The accepted view of revenue sharing as a purely unconditional form of intergovernmental transfers is not quite accurate in this case. There is a House formula and a Senate formula, and each state is allowed to select the formula under which its entitlement is determined. The two revenue sharing formulas are rather complicated and allocate these monies on the basis of a number of criteria.[25] For example, a state's entitlement to revenue sharing funds depends not only on its population but also on its level of per capita income, its fiscal effort (measured by total state-local taxes as a percentage of aggregate personal income), and its level of income-tax collections. As a result of these special provisions, revenue sharing disbursements on a per capita basis ranged in fiscal year 1976 from a low of $21.51 in Illinois to a high of $39.24 in Mississippi. The revenue sharing program in the United States is modest in size and its political future is, at this juncture, certain at least until 1983. If it should continue over the longer run, it will result in a shift in the tax structure of the United States that will raise the federal share of tax receipts.

The design and effects of intergovernmental grants

The previous discussion suggests that the economic principles of grant design provide some basic insights into the existing structure of the intergovernmental transfer system. However, because the treatment has been a broad one, a closer examination of federal transfers to state and local governments will reveal a number of anomalies. This should not be too surprising because the design and enactment of grant programs is, in part, the result of an interaction of governors, local government officials, and various special interest groups with federal legislators. Such interaction is frequently characterized by a tension resulting from the grant administrator's desire to restrict the use of funds to realize his or her own objectives and the recipient's efforts to minimize any strings attached to the monies. The form of the grant program that finally emerges must reflect, to some extent, the nature of their compromise.

It is interesting to explore a bit further the extent to which this structure appears consistent with our economic criteria for grant design. A primary justification for intergovernmental grants is the existence of external benefits across governmental jurisdictions for a range of state and local services, including such things as highways and educational programs. For such programs, a system of matching grants, where the respective matching shares would roughly reflect the extent of the spillover benefits, would be desirable. From this perspective, certain characteristics of the federal grant system are quite puzzling. Under most of these matching grants, federal matching ceases at some modest level of transfers (the major exceptions being federal grants for public assistance and Medicaid). This implies that the states and localities that have reached maximum funding are receiving no inducement to take into account the spillover benefits their fiscal decisions generate. Matching grants should, in principle, be open-ended. Matching should not be cut off at some specified level; the provisions must apply to any potential *extensions* of budgetary programs if these provisions are to induce state and local officials to take into consideration the spillover effects associated with the program.

Moreover, it would appear very difficult to justify the actual matching shares under a number of programs by the extent of external benefits. For example, the federal share for interstate highway construction has been 90 percent of cost, although it would seem very unlikely that 90 percent of the value of the interstate highways passing through a particular state would accrue to out-of-state drivers. To an even greater degree, the benefits from sewage waste-treatment systems are largely local. There may, in some instances, exist significant external effects involving neighboring jurisdictions, but hardly enough to rationalize the existing federal share of 75 percent of construction costs. More generally, a study by the Advisory Commission on Intergovernmental Relations reveals that most federal grant programs require either a low (less than 50 percent) or *no* matching on the part of the recipient state or local government. Only about 5 percent of federal grant monies are in programs requiring high matching (over 50 percent from the recipient).[26] For many programs, external benefits themselves appear inadequate to justify the magnitude of the federal share.

In addition to the issue of the matching share itself, other elements in grant design can have a profound impact upon the effectiveness of a particular grant program. One important illustration is the federal subsidy program for waste treatment plants to reduce water pollution, under which the federal government has provided several billion dollars for the construction of new waste treatment facilities. As various studies have shown, the failure to link the grants directly to their intended purpose—the reduction of water pollution—has seriously undercut their efficacy. In particular, the subsidies support only a specific technology—waste treatment—even where a less costly and more effective alternative exists. Moreover, by subsidizing only the *construction* of treatment plants, the program has provided no incentive for the efficient *operation* of these facilities. One study found that in over half of the plants studied, services were substandard either because of poor operating procedures or because the plants were not designed to treat the waste load delivered to them.[27]

The tendency over the past decades has been toward the consolidation of specific programs into larger "block grants" to the states and localities with the funds distributed by formula. This movement to consolidate grants has much appeal. In particular, it has served to simplify the federal grant system by replacing a maze of overlapping, and sometimes conflicting, individual programs with a single grant of funds to support a fairly wide range of state or local services. Such block grants permit the recipient much greater discretion in the use of the monies enabling state and local officials to allocate their resources more closely in line with their own local priorities. At the same time, it must be recognized that block grants provide virtually no economic incentives for the use of funds for particular services or functions. Because they entail no matching requirements, these grants do not affect the cost to the respective state or locality of providing additional units of public services. As noted earlier, the fungibility of grant funds makes conditional block grants, in principle, equivalent to purely unconditional transfers of funds. For this reason, they are not a suitable policy instrument for resolving distortions in the provision of public services associated with external benefits or costs.

In evaluating federal grant programs, we must, in addition to considering general principles, actually observe, and attempt to measure, the impact of the programs on the decisions, budgetary and otherwise, of state and local officials. There has been some effort in this direction, although our understanding of the effects of federal grants is quite spotty. Despite the considerable variation in the particular estimates from one study to the next, most research findings suggest that federal grants have had a substantial stimulative impact on state and local expenditure. Grant monies have not been used simply to substitute for state-local tax revenues.[28] Moreover, the evidence supports the expectation that conditional grants generate a larger expenditure response (dollar for dollar) than do purely unconditional transfers, with high federal matching providing a greater stimulus than that of low matching.

Although these general results are consistent with our theoretical expectations, another aspect of the findings that is somewhat more intriguing is the extent to which budgetary expansion appears, in some instances, to be surprisingly large. Consider, for example, the case of a purely unconditional grant to a local community. Because such grants contain no explicit incentives for budgetary expansion, the members of the community may be expected to treat these monies as a kind of windfall, a supplement to their wealth or income. In principle, it should not really matter that the monies flow into the local government treasury; if local officials are really responsive to the preferences of their constituencies, it should make little difference whether the grant goes to the local government or directly into the pockets of the local residents. From this perspective, an unconditional intergovernmental grant is simply a veil for a federal tax cut directly to individuals.[29] The implication of the "veil hypothesis" is that the additional local public spending generated by a dollar of lump-sum grants to the local government should be approximately the same as the increment to public expenditure resulting from a one-dollar increase in private income in the jurisdiction. In both cases, aggregate income in the jurisdiction has risen by a dollar so that the desired increase in public spending should be about the same. However, existing empirical work suggests that this is not the case. In particular, if the present size of the state and local sector is any guide to desired marginal adjustments, increases in private income to induce additional state-local expenditure on the order of ten to fifteen cents per dollar of additional income might be expected. The evidence indicates, however, that the stimulative effect of unconditional intergovernmental transfers is much larger than this; it is closer to a figure of fifty cents on the dollar. The evidence on the apparently large stimulative impact of unconditional grants comes from a number of sources including various econometric studies and an actual "monitoring" of the general revenue sharing program. There are, however, important qualifications attached to these results and they should not be regarded as the last word on the subject.[30]

Although an understanding of the workings of intergovernmental grants is far from complete, economic analysis does provide a number of important insights. In particular, the federal government in the United States has found these grants an attractive policy tool to encourage state-local programs that also serve the broader national interest (the promotion of an improved distribution of income and the establishment of a more efficient and equitable tax system). However, to accomplish their intended objectives at the least cost to society, individual grant programs must take the proper form and they must provide the appropriate incentives for state and local decision makers. The careful evaluation of grant programs in terms of the economic principles of grant design, with evidence on the response to particular types of fiscal incentives, can make a valuable contribution to the evolution of a structure of intergovernmental transfers that more effectively promotes the objectives of public policy.

Historical tendencies in federal fiscal structure

Fiscal systems have moved in the direction of an increasing reliance on intergovernmental transfers from the central government to decentralized levels of the public sector. This trend raises the somewhat broader question of whether the expansion of these grants is a symptom of a continuing tendency over time toward the centralization of fiscal structure. Over a century ago, de Tocqueville predicted that "in the democratic ages which are opening upon us, . . . centralization will be the natural government."[31] With reference to the federal form of government in particular, Edward McWhinney cites Bryce's Law, the proposition that "federalism is simply a transitory step on the way to governmental unity."[32] The thesis, more generally, is that a public sector characterized by a substantial reliance on decentralized budgetary choice is an *unstable* structure. It will, over time, move toward more reliance on a central government.

A case can, in fact, be made for the centralization thesis in terms of rising incomes, improved transportation, and new modes of communication that tie the regions and localities in the modern nation-state much more closely together. These developments have fostered a growing mobility and interdependence that make decisions in one part of the country of increasing significance elsewhere in the country. In a society characterized by such mobility, the services provided in one jurisdiction have an "option value" to people who currently reside in other areas, people who *may*, at some future date, choose to move to another jurisdiction.[33] The thrust of this line of argument is that certain basic features of economic growth serve to promote an increased centralization of government. As Michael Reagan writes: "Many more problems today than in the past are national in the sense of being affected by developments elsewhere in the nation or having their own impact upon other parts of the nation."[34]

However, the case for the centralization thesis is far from ironclad. As noted, the mobility model of local finance suggests that individuals seek out communities that provide the public services they want. From this perspective, improved urban transportation and mobility may permit the local public sector to perform its functions more effectively. The point here is that economic growth can, in important ways, facilitate the congregation of individuals with similar demands for local public goods and, in this way, generate potentially powerful forces (both in economic and political terms) for a continued substantial reliance on local budgetary choice.

To the extent that diverse local jurisdictions can each cater to the particular demands of their own relatively homogeneous populations, there will exist strong support for a major role for local government within the public sector.

The net effect of growing affluence on the extent of centralization in the government sector is not altogether clear. Some forces seem to promote a heavier reliance on the central government, but there are opposing tendencies as well. An examination of some fiscal indices of public-sector concentration may suggest which of the two sets of forces appears to have been the stronger. Before looking at the actual data, however, the ambiguities inherent in any measure of centralization of government should be acknowledged.[35] There is no single, satisfactory measure of the "quantity" of decision-making power at different levels of government; even if there were, certain inherent index number problems would emerge in an attempt to weight the roles of the federal, state, and many local governments to produce a single index of fiscal centralization. Nevertheless, certain summary measures may at least suggest the sorts of tendencies (if any) in the hierarchical structure of the fiscal system.

Table 10–3 presents an historical profile of public expenditure in the twentieth century by level of government in the United States. The first four columns are absolute spending; the last three columns indicate percentage shares. The federal share of total public expenditure may be regarded as a kind of "centralization ratio" that reflects the extent of fiscal centralization in the United States.

A cursory examination of Table 10–3 provides strong support for the centralization thesis. The federal share of total spending rose from about one-third to two-thirds from 1902 to 1978. The state government share of total spending roughly doubled from about 11 percent to 20 percent. These increases in the federal and state shares came, by definition, at the expense of local governments, whose relative share in public expenditure fell from over 50 percent to only 16 percent. Increasing fiscal centralization of a substantial magnitude would appear to characterize the twentieth century in the United States.

Table 10–3 Public expenditure by level of government for selected fiscal years (billions of dollars)

Year	Total public expenditure	Federal	State	Local	Percentage shares Federal	State	Local
1902	$ 1.6	$ .6	$ .2	$ .9	34.5	10.8	54.8
1913	3.2	1.0	.4	1.9	30.2	11.6	58.3
1922	9.3	3.8	1.3	4.3	40.5	13.6	46.0
1932	12.4	4.3	2.6	5.6	34.3	20.6	45.1
1940	20.4	10.1	4.5	5.8	49.3	22.3	28.5
1950	70.3	44.8	12.8	12.8	63.7	18.2	18.1
1955	110.7	73.4	17.4	19.9	66.3	15.7	18.0
1960	151.3	97.3	25.0	29.0	64.3	16.5	19.1
1965	205.7	130.1	35.7	39.9	63.3	17.4	19.4
1970	333.0	208.2	64.7	60.1	62.5	19.4	18.1
1975	560.1	340.5	122.2	97.4	60.8	21.8	17.4
1976	625.8	389.9	127.7	107.5	62.4	20.4	17.2
1977	680.3	430.6	137.7	112.1	63.2	20.3	16.5
1978	759.7	483.3	153.9	122.5	63.6	20.3	16.1

Source: Tax Foundation, *Facts and Figures on Government Finance*, 20th Biennial Edition (Washington, D.C.: Tax Foundation, Inc., 1979), tables 5 and 6, pp. 17–18.
Note: Intergovernmental grants-in-aid are treated as expenditures by the first disbursing unit (not by the recipient).

However, a closer study of Table 10–3 suggests some important qualifications to this finding. In particular, after 1950, the federal share levels off and federal spending in 1978 as a percentage of total public expenditure was almost exactly the same as in 1950. State and local shares likewise changed little. The conclusion is that, although a strong tendency toward fiscal centralization characterized the first half of this century, it seems to have weakened in the last thirty years.

It is important to note that Table 10–3 attributes intergovernmental transfers to the grantor so that the dramatic growth in federal grants shows up as expansion of federal spending. It is not clear how these funds should be allocated to measure the extent of fiscal centralization. They should, perhaps, be attributed to the government units that actually spend the funds for goods and services (partic-

Table 10–4   Percentage shares of expenditure
with intergovernmental transfers attributed
to recipient level of government

Year	Federal	State	Local
1902	34.0%	8.2%	57.8%
1913	29.8	9.2	61.0
1922	39.2	11.7	49.1
1932	32.4	16.3	51.3
1940	45.0	17.4	37.6
1950	60.4	15.4	24.2
1960	59.7	14.6	25.7
1965	57.9	15.3	26.8
1970	55.5	16.9	27.6
1975	52.4	18.7	28.9
1976	51.5	19.8	28.7
1977	52.8	18.9	28.3

Source: Data for fiscal year 1975 and prior years are calculated from figures in *Facts and Figures* . . ., 1977, tables
5, 134, and 185; data for 1976 and 1977 are from same
sources as Table 10–1.

ularly for unconditional or block grants). If, in fact, intergovernmental transfers
are attributed to the recipient (see Table 10–4), the centralizing tendencies in
the fiscal structure of the United States are a good deal less pronounced. Since
1950 the federal share has actually declined, while state and local shares have
both risen. These data would suggest that the centralizing tendencies that characterized the first half of the century have actually reversed themselves since
1950.

Fiscal data from other countries reveal similar trends. As shown in Table 10–5,
the share of the central government in Canada has declined noticeably since
1950. In a study of fiscal patterns in several countries over the period 1950–70,
Werner Pommerehne found that the central share had declined in every instance.
As seen in Table 10–6, this was not a sudden or dramatic shake-up in fiscal

Table 10–5   Canadian
shares of public
expenditure by
level of government

Year	Federal	Provincial	Local
1900	57.1	NA	NA
1910	50.0	27.6	22.4
1920	59.2	17.0	23.8
1930	32.1	24.6	43.3
1938	34.3	36.1	29.6
1950	52.2	25.2	22.6
1960	50.5	24.1	25.4
1965	43.1	28.7	28.2
1971	37.1	37.9	25.0
1975	40.4	38.6	21.0

Source: Werner W. Pommerehne, "Quantitative Aspects of
Federalism: A Study of Six Countries," in *The Political
Economy of Fiscal Federalism*, ed. W. E. Oates (Lexington,
Mass.: Lexington Books, 1977), p. 311, for figures shown
for 1971 and earlier years. Data for 1975 were calculated
from Canada, Ministry of Industry, Trade, and Commerce,
Canada Year Book 1978–9 (Ottawa, Ont.: Ministry of In-
dustry, Trade, and Commerce, 1978), chapter 20.
Note: Intergovernmental transfers are treated as expenditures
by the recipient government.

Table 10–6   Central government expenditure as percentage of total government expenditure for four countries since 1950

Year	France	Germany	Switzerland	United Kingdom
1950	85.6	48.4	32.9	76.6
1955	80.5	44.3	33.4	75.0
1960	83.2	39.9	30.7	68.0
1965	81.7	40.3	26.9	60.6
1970	79.3	37.9	26.2	60.0

Source: Werner W. Pommerehne, "Quantitative Aspects of Federalism: A Study of Six Countries," in *The Political Economy of Fiscal Federalism*, ed. W. E. Oates (Lexington, Mass.: Lexington Books, 1977), p. 311.

structure, but rather a gradual and continuing shift away from centralization over the entire twenty-year period.

The picture that emerges from the fiscal data is a fairly complex one, but one that does not support any sweeping hypothesis of a pervasive and continuing tendency toward a more centralized fiscal structure. On the contrary, over the past three decades the trends would seem to be in the opposite direction, an indication that local government is alive and well. This really should not be too surprising because the local provision of certain services offers such important advantages that it would seem quite unlikely that the local sector would simply wither away.

While a simplistic version of the centralization thesis does not seem tenable in light of the evidence, the evolution of the public sector both in the United States and elsewhere exhibits some intriguing elements. In particular, with the absolute growth in the public sector as a whole, there seems to be a tendency toward the formation of new sorts of units and jurisdictions for public decision making. The government sector, in brief, seems to be evolving into a more complex and highly specialized set of institutions. This is taking different forms in different countries. In the United States its most dramatic manifestation is the rise of special districts, which more than tripled during the period from 1942 to 1977. This reflects an increasing specialization in the public sector, for most of these districts are single function entities. Moreover, the range of services provided by special districts is quite wide and diverse, and includes highways, sewers, housing, libraries, fire protection, natural resources, hospitals, and cemeteries. There has, however, been a large reduction in the total number of governmental units. This is the result primarily of the consolidation of smaller school districts and some small townships.

The creation of new jurisdictions and units has not, however, been limited to single-purpose public agencies. In fact, when looking across the public sectors in the western industrialized economies, we see repeatedly the establishment of "new" levels of government to cope with new demands on the public sector. Metropolitan governments have been created in some urban areas in the United States, in Toronto, and in several European urban centers. They were created in an attempt to integrate fiscal decision making between suburban residential communities and the central cities that serve them. At the same time, the inability of a central government to adequately meet certain "regional needs" has led to the establishment of a regional government in Italy and a proposal for Scottish and Welsh assemblies in Great Britain. In Britain, Alan Peacock contends that the "deviation in individual and group preferences from those reflected in the existing amount and pattern of government services has become more marked [and has resulted in] the growing demand for devolution. . . ."[36]

Moreover, the formation of new governments has not been restricted to the lower tiers. We are in the process of watching the emergence in Europe of a wholly new level of government whose jurisdiction will be the entire membership of the European Economic Community (EEC). It is not yet clear what the precise range of responsibilities and powers of the new government will be, but the contrast between a newly created European level of government and the move toward devolution in certain member countries does suggest the diversity of pressures operating on the public sector.

The implications of these historical changes on the trends and future of federal fiscal structure are not wholly clear. However, any simplistic notion of a continuing centralization of government that leads to the eventual extinction of local government seems highly unlikely on a priori grounds and inconsistent with recent fiscal trends. Local government will continue to make an essential contribution to the functioning of the public sector. This by no means implies a static view of local structure and its role in the federal system. Local government has shown itself quite capable of taking new forms in response to the changing demands on the government sector of the economy. It is interesting to speculate on the growing specialization that these new forms represent. The general growth of the public sector has no doubt made it feasible to increase the degree of specialization in the government sphere. Here may be a principle for the public sector that parallels Adam Smith's famous dictum for the private sector: "The division of labour is limited by the extent of the market."

1   James Bryce, *The American Commonwealth* (New York: Macmillan, 1896), p. 325.

2   Michael Reagan, *The New Federalism* (New York: Oxford University Press, 1972), p. 81.

3   Geoffrey W. Oxley, *Poor Relief in England and Wales, 1601–1834* (North Pomfret, Vt.: David & Charles, 1974).

4   Edwin Cannan, *The History of Local Rates in England* (London: Longmans, 1896).

5   See the discussion of the "Decentralization Theorem" in Wallace E. Oates, *Fiscal Federalism* (New York: Harcourt Brace Jovanovich, 1972), pp. 33–38, 54–63.

6   See, for example: David Bradford and Wallace Oates, "Suburban Exploitation of Central Cities and Governmental Structure," in *Redistribution Through Public Choice*, ed. Harold Hochman and George Peterson (New York: Columbia University Press, 1974), pp. 43–90; and Michael Boss, "Economic Theory of Democracy: An Empirical Test," *Public Choice* 19 (1974): 111–15.

7   Alexis de Tocqueville, *Democracy in America*, the Henry Reeve text as revised by Francis Bowen, further corrected and edited by Phillips Bradley (New York: Vintage Books, Random House, 1945), vol. 1, p. 169

8   Charles Tiebout, "A Pure Theory of Local Expenditures," *Journal of Political Economy* 64 (October 1956): 416–24.

9   Ibid., p. 422.

10 See, for example: Wallace Oates, "The Effects of Property Taxes and Local Public Spending on Property Values: An Empirical Study of Tax Capitalization and the Tiebout Hypothesis," *Journal of Political Economy* 77 (1969): 957–71; and Gerald S. McDougall, "Local Public Goods and Residential Property Values: Some Insights and Extensions," *National Tax Journal* 29 (December 1976): 436–47. For an alternative approach involving the study of fiscally induced patterns of migration, see: J. Richard Aronson and Eli Schwartz, "Financing Public Goods and the Distribution of Population in a System of Local Governments," *National Tax Journal* 26 (June 1973): 137–60.

11 De Tocqueville, *Democracy in America*, vol. 1, p. 168.

12 Kenneth C. Wheare, *Federal Government*, 4th ed. (London: Oxford University Press, 1963), p. 117.

13 William H. Young, *Ogg and Ray's Introduction to American Government*, 13th ed. (New York: Appleton-Century-Crofts, 1966), p. 62.

14 Ronald Coase, "The Problem of Social Cost," *Journal of Law and Economics* 3 (October 1960): 1–44.

15 William Baumol and Wallace Oates, *The Theory of Environmental Policy* (Englewood Cliffs, N.J.: Prentice-Hall, 1975), chapter 2.

16 See: Oates, *Fiscal Federalism*, chapter 3.

17 Ibid.

18 For a careful examination of equalizing grants and their use in federal countries, see: Russell L. Mathews, ed., *Fiscal Equalization in a Federal System* (Canberra: Centre for Research in Federal Financial Relations, 1974).

19 For some findings on the capitalization of fiscal differentials into local property values, see the papers cited in note 10.

20 For a good summary of the evidence on the incidence of various taxes in the United States, see: Joseph A. Pechman and Benjamin A. Okner, *Who Bears the Tax Burden?* (Washington, D.C.: Brookings Institution, 1974). As Pechman and Okner make clear, any conclusions on overall tax incidence must be hedged by a number of important qualifications.

21 Charles McLure, "The Interstate Exporting of State and Local Taxes: Estimates for 1962," *National Tax Journal* 20 (March 1967): 49–77.

22 Joseph Pechman, *Federal Tax Policy*, rev. ed. (Washington, D.C.: Brookings Institution, 1971), p. 53; James Maxwell, *Financing State and Local Governments*, rev. ed. (Washington, D.C.: Brookings Institution, 1969), p. 102.

23 Werner W. Pommerehne, "Quantitative Aspects

of Federalism: A Study of Six Countries," in *The Political Economy of Fiscal Federalism*, ed. W. E. Oates (Lexington, Mass.: Lexington Books, 1977), pp. 336–37.

24 See: U.S., Advisory Commission on Intergovernmental Relations, *Federal Grants: Their Effects on State-Local Expenditures, Employment Levels, and Wage Rates*, A–61 (Washington, D.C.: Government Printing Office, 1977). This study uses data for 1972.

25 For a careful analysis of these formulae, see: Robert Reischauer, "General Revenue Sharing: The Program's Incentives," in *Financing the New Federalism*, ed. W. E. Oates (Baltimore: Johns Hopkins University Press for Resources for the Future, 1975), pp. 40–87.

26 U.S., Advisory Commission on Intergovernmental Relations, *Federal Grants*, pp. 26–28.

27 V. Kneese and Charles L. Schultze, *Pollution, Prices, and Public Policy* (Washington, D.C.: Brookings Institution, 1975), chapter 3.

28 For useful surveys of the empirical work on the budgetary impact of intergovernmental grants, see: Edward M. Gramlich, "Intergovernmental Grants: A Review of the Empirical Literature," in *The Political Economy of Fiscal Federalism*, ed. W. E. Oates, pp. 219–40; and U.S., Advisory Commission on Intergovernmental Relations, *Federal Grants*.

29 For a formal presentation of the veil hypothesis, see: David F. Bradford and Wallace E. Oates, "The Analysis of Revenue Sharing in a New Approach to Collective Fiscal Decisions," *Quarterly Journal of Economics* 85 (August 1971): 416–39.

30 See: Gramlich, "Intergovernmental Grants"; and Richard P. Nathan and Charles F. Adams, Jr., *Revenue Sharing: The Second Round* (Washington, D.C.: Brookings Institution, 1977). For a useful collection of papers exploring this whole issue, see: Peter Mieszkowski and William Oakland, eds., *Fiscal Federalism and Grants-in-Aid* (Washington, D.C.: The Urban Institute, 1979).

31 De Tocqueville, *Democracy in America*, vol. 2, p. 313.

32 McWhinney, *Comparative Federalism*, 2d ed. (Toronto: University of Toronto Press, 1965), p. 105.

33 On option value in local finance, see: Burton Weisbrod, *External Benefits of Public Education* (Princeton, N.J.: Industrial Relations Section, Princeton University, 1964).

34 Reagan, *The New Federalism*, p. 77.

35 On this issue, see: Oates, *Fiscal Federalism*, chapter 5.

36 "The Political Economy of Devolution: The British Case," in *The Political Economy of Fiscal Federalism*," ed. W. E. Oates, p. 51.

Fiscal structure of local authorities in Britain

The object of this chapter is to analyze the fiscal and management problems of local government (referred to as local authorities) in Britain.[1] It is hoped that American readers will gain some insight into their own institutions by comparing them with the British counterparts.

This analysis consists of four main parts, beginning with a description of the institutional structure of local government in Britain. The next section examines how local governments budget their income and expenditures and describes the service functions of each set of local government bodies. It also reviews the proposed reforms of the financial structure of local authorities, examines the debate about new sources of local authority revenues, and looks at how the central government circumscribes the autonomy of local authorities.

The third section examines how efficiently local authority revenues are used. The primary purpose here is to illustrate the comparative lack of evaluative research and how this lack of evidence has led to a general uneasiness about local authority expenditures. The last section of this chapter deals with the evolution of developed (federal) forms of government in Britain and how they have affected local problems. For example, what are the results of greater autonomy for Scotland and Wales and how has the development of the European Economic Community (EEC) influenced local government in Britain?

Finally, we see that the degree of local autonomy in Britain is quite limited. Local government is so circumscribed by both micro- and macroeconomic controls that some view it as little more than "a local office of the central government." It would appear that many United Kingdom citizens would prefer to increase local autonomy and that some ways of achieving it are, and will continue to be, widely discussed.

The institutional structure of local government in Britain

In 1974 the structure of local government in Britain was significantly altered. Prior to this time, the system had not been changed since the 1888 Local Government Act. The structure of local government in England and Wales prior to 1974 is summarized in Figure 11–1. Local government in London was organized on a two-tier system. The upper tier was the Greater London Council, and the lower tier consisted of the City of London and the London boroughs. Outside of London, eighty-three large towns had been given the county borough status. Their councils were single-tier authorities that had control over all functions. The rest of England and Wales was divided into administrative counties with boundaries generally similar to the geographical counties (e.g., Surrey, Lancashire, and Devon).[2] The county councils were upper-tier authorities; the second tier consisted of municipal boroughs (the larger towns), urban district councils (the smaller towns), and rural district councils. In the rural district council areas, there were two tiers, the lower being the parish. The large cities (e.g., Manchester, Liverpool, and Birmingham) had county borough status and were independent of the often rural county councils.

Figure 11–1   Local authority structure in England and Wales before 1974 (E = England, W = Wales).

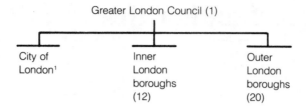

Greater London Council (1)

| City of London[1] | Inner London boroughs (12) | Outer London boroughs (20) |

County boroughs (E79 + W4 = 83 total)

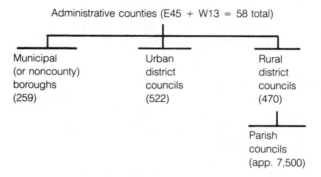

Administrative counties (E45 + W13 = 58 total)

| Municipal (or noncounty) boroughs (259) | Urban district councils (522) | Rural district councils (470) |

Parish councils (app. 7,500)

[1] Technically the city is not part of the Greater London Council.

The structure of local government in Scotland was similar to that of Britain; it is summarized in Figure 11–2. In Scotland prior to 1974, there were four cities with jurisdiction over their areas, and thirty-one county authorities.

The characteristics of these structures remain important in the contemporary debate about what should be the definition of the geographical areas of local authorities and the allocation of functions between these authorities. The governmental structure introduced in 1974 may be further reformed, and the structure prior to 1974 may be influential in this reformation.

The organization of local government introduced on 1 April 1974 was a radical departure from the previous structure.[3] The new organization was the result of a royal commission and was introduced by a Conservative government.[4] The organizational structure of the Greater London Council, however, was unaffected by the reforms of 1974 and remains as shown in Figure 11–1.

Figure 11–2   Local authority structure in Scotland before 1974.

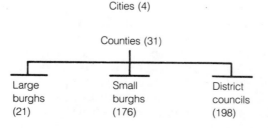

Cities (4)

Counties (31)

| Large burghs (21) | Small burghs (176) | District councils (198) |

Figure 11–3 Local government structure in England since 1974.

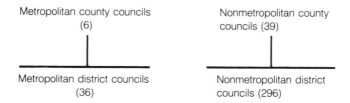

Metropolitan county councils (6)

Nonmetropolitan county councils (39)

Metropolitan district councils (36)

Nonmetropolitan district councils (296)

The reform abolished county boroughs and redrew the boundaries of many county councils. In England, six metropolitan county councils and thirty-nine nonmetropolitan county councils were established. These new county councils are made up of second-tier authorities, respectively 36 in the metropolitan district councils, and 296 in the nonmetropolitan district councils. The 6 metropolitan county councils cover areas with population densities similar to that of the Greater London Council.[5]

Since 1974 there have been eight nonmetropolitan county councils and thirty-seven second-tier nonmetropolitan district councils in Wales.

Figure 11–4 Local government structure in Wales since 1974.

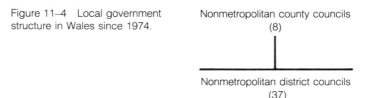

Nonmetropolitan county councils (8)

Nonmetropolitan district councils (37)

The new Scottish structure of local government is composed of nine regional councils and fifty-three second-tier district councils. The post-1974 institutional structure of local government in Britain consists of fewer and larger authorities than before, but the new structure is in a state of uneasy equilibrium. Strong pressure groups and the political parties appear to favor some new reformation (particularly with regard to the allocation of education, social services, and library functions among the authorities). Nevertheless, because the 1974 reforms were expensive and disruptive, it is unlikely that the 1974 structure will undergo a major reformation for many years to come.

Figure 11–5 Local government structure in Scotland since 1974.

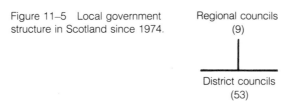

Regional councils (9)

District councils (53)

The budget and service functions of local government in Britain

The radical changes in the structure of British local government were accompanied by a significant reallocation of service functions.

Local government expenditure

The largest current expenditure of British local government is education, £7,457 million or 38.5 percent of the total (see Figure 11–6). The next three largest items of expenditure in 1977 were debt interest, social services, and police. The education outlays and the expenditures under these other three service heads accounted for over 67 percent of total local authority expenditure in 1977.

Another view of these expenditure flows is set forth in the summary to Table 11–1. This shows that 68.5 percent of local government expenditure is on final consumption, 15.5 percent is on debt interest, 4.4 percent is on private sector grants, and the rest is primarily private sector subsidies.

The evolution of local authority expenditure over the last decade will be examined briefly. If the 1968 data of all education expenditures (£1,587 million or 36.7 percent) are aggregated, debt interest payments (£791 million or 18.3 percent), personal social services (£116 million or 2.7 percent), and police expenditure (£261 million or 6.0 percent), these items amount to £2,755 million or 63.7 percent of current expenditure. The primary cause of the difference in the 1968 and 1978 total percentage figures is due to the rapid expansion of the social services.

In Table 11–2 the details of the capital account of local government are shown. As with the current account, a small number of items dominate the expenditures. Capital expenditure on housing in 1978 was £1,542 million or 46.3 percent of total capital expenditure. Another substantial capital outlay was in the education sector where £492 million or 14.8 percent of total capital expenditure was spent in 1978. The aggregate of housing and education expenses accounted for 61.1 percent of total expenditure in 1978 (£2,034 million). The same items in 1968 accounted for £1,047 million or 60 percent of total capital expenditure.

The overall level of local authority expenditure in relation to total government expenditure and gross national product (GNP) has remained relatively static during the decade from 1968 to 1978, as shown in the data in Table 11–3. The overall size of the total public sector grew from 48.3 percent of GNP in 1967 to 49.9 percent in 1978. The share of local government in the total activity of the public sector remained at approximately the same level, falling slightly from 33.2 percent of public expenditures in 1968, to 31.8 percent in 1978. Local government expenditures as a portion of GNP declined slightly from 16.0 percent in 1968, to 15.9 percent in 1978.

Figure 11–6   Local authority current expenditure, 1977 (£ million).

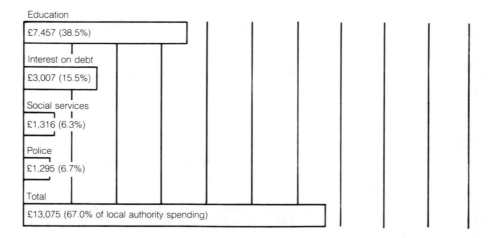

From a financial point of view, it appears that one in three pounds spent by the state in Britain is spent by local government. However, much of this local expenditure is controlled or mandated by the central government. The form of these controls is both fiscal (i.e., control of budgets and spending) and nonfiscal (i.e., the imposition of centrally legislated "norms" and "standards" for the provision of services). The simplest way of elaborating the nature and extent of these controls is to discuss them within the context of the major expenditure categories, especially education and housing.

In 1978 total local authority expenditure on housing amounted to £2,038 million.[6] This expenditure was used to service and expand the stock of council (local government owned) houses, to improve the quality of the private stock by a program of grants and loans to private owners, and to reduce the price of council housing for poor tenants by providing them with rent rebates.

The government's role in the housing market expanded rapidly after the first world war. Since 1919, there have been numerous pieces of legislation that have encouraged local governments to expand and maintain the publicly owned housing stocks. The principal way this legislation works is by central government subsidies that reduce the cost of housing construction to local authorities. As a consequence, local governments have significantly expanded their housing stocks. Approximately 30 percent of the housing stock in Great Britain is now owned and operated by local government. This form of housing is popular not only because it is subsidized but also because antiquated accountancy practices link rent levels to historic, rather than to replacement, costs.

The extent of these subsidies is augmented by rent rebates. In addition to rental fees that are below the market rate, the low income household can, subject to an income test, receive a rebate on the subsidized rent. In 1976–77, the average subsidy to council house tenants was £232 per annum. The average subsidy to poor tenants in receipt of rent rebates was £377 per year, and the average subsidy to nonpoor tenants was £186 per annum. This admittedly poor distributional and allocational system is difficult to change because council house tenants are not likely to support politicians who would reduce their income by instituting a more rational policy. All these subsidies, whether they subsidize the cost of house construction or lower rent through rebates, are the result of national legislation. The local authorities have little discretion in their implementation.

Not only does central government manipulate local government through financial means, but it also uses nonmonetary controls. Thus, in the housing sector, local governments are obliged to submit all of their plans for new construction to the Department of Environment for approval. All council houses have to meet national criteria (the Parker Morris standards) that determine ceiling height, food storage capacity, electricity service standards, and a variety of other aspects of local authority housing. These quality criteria generally are adjudged to be quite high, particularly since many private sector houses are built to lower standards. The public housing standards increase costs and reduce the number of new units that can be constructed out of the housing budget.

Similar controls are used by central government to regulate local government education activities. Control of finances, control of school building programs, and control of the curricula are powers available to Whitehall. A good example of this power is the use by central government of laws to force local authorities to organize their schools in line with the state's comprehensive (mixed ability and nonselective) schooling policies, which are in some ways contrary to the wishes of many local politicians, teachers, and parents. This policy was implemented vigorously by the Labour government; however, the Conservative administration has reversed this policy and prevented some Labour party local governments from implementing comprehensive schooling policies.

The education budget is labor intensive, and thus the outcomes of the wage bargaining process have important implications for the budget. Almost all of the

Table 11–1 Local government current expenditure, 1968 and 1978 (£ million)

Current expenditure, final consumption	1968	1978
Civil defense	4	4
Roads and public lighting	232	791
Employment services	8	40
Housing	6	74
Environmental services:		
Sewerage and sewerage disposal	46	22
Refuse collection and disposal	86	395
Public health	37	177
Land drainage and coastal protection	14	53
Parks, pleasure grounds, etc.	63	331
Town and country planning	19	166
Libraries, museums, and arts	48	222
Police	261	1,251
Administration of justice	32	126
Fire service	59	278
Social services:		
Education	1,342	6,344
National Health Service[1]	153	. . .
Personal social services[2]	116	1,316
School meals and milk[3]	112	439
Rate collection[4]	21	91
Records, registrations, and surveys	6	22
Cemeteries	8	24
General administration	71	394
Subtotal	2,744	12,560
Nontrading capital consumption	159	710
Subtotal	2,903	13,270
Subsidies		
Housing	78	242
Passenger transport	1	211
Other trading	15	59
Current grants to personal sector:		
Scholarships and grants for higher education[5]	133	674
Rent rebates and allowances[6]	. . .	180
Debt interest		
On loans from central government	237	1,326
Other	554	1,681
Subtotal, current expenditure	3,921	17,643
Balance: current surplus before providing for depreciation and stock appreciation	402	1,732
Total	4,323	19,375
Summary (percentages)		
Final consumption	67.1	68.5
Subsidies	2.2	2.6
Current grants to personal sector	3.1	4.4
Debt interest	18.3	15.5
Balance	9.3	8.9
Total	100.0	100.0

Source: Central Statistical Office, *National Income and Expenditure 1968–78* (London: HMSO, 1979), Table 8.1, p. 59.

(see facing page for notes to Table 11–1)

labor contracts of local government employees are negotiated at the national level. As a result, deviations from national pay rates are relatively small among localities. For example, school teachers and garbage disposal men in Newcastle have the same pay scales as similar personnel in Devon and Kent.

The central government also controls the supply of many professionals employed by local governments. Thus, the central government, by reducing the financing and facilities for training teachers and social workers, has been able to control the number of professionals trained in these fields. This has resulted in larger class sizes in schools (over thirty students on average) and heavier workloads for social workers.

In examining the expenditure patterns of local governments in Britain, it appears that these governments are responsible for spending nearly 15 percent of the gross national product and about 29 percent of the total public expenditure. This local government expenditure pattern is dominated by a few major service items—education, personal social services, police, housing, and debt interest. These, and all the other expenditure items, are closely regulated by central government by manipulation of the "purse strings" and through the use of hundreds of central controls, which impose centrally determined policies on the local government units of Britain. Some local authority discretion does remain, and it is perhaps unfair to view local government in Britain solely as "the local office of Whitehall (or central) government," it is important to remember that the autonomy of local government is circumscribed severely in many areas of activity.

Local government finance

Although the structure of British local government was reorganized in 1974, the pattern of finance has not changed significantly since that time.

As shown in Table 11–4, the primary source of local government current account income is central government grants, amounting to £10,147 million in 1978 or 52.4 percent of local authority income. Most of these grants are not specific and are allocated to local governments according to a formula known as the Rate Support Grant (RSG). The rates are the revenues derived from a property tax, first introduced during the time of Queen Elizabeth I, and which account for 29.4 percent of local government current revenue. The income from trading and rental of council houses accounts for 15.6 percent of revenue. The remaining 9.7 percent of income comes from interest payments.

The reliance of local government on central government grants has increased steadily. Since 1968, such grants have increased 8.5 percent and rates for local property taxes have decreased by 6.4 percent of current expenditure. This increased dependence of local government on the central government in London has led to discussions about the possibility of introducing independent forms of local taxation.

The role of central government finance is also significant in the expenditures of local governments on capital account. During the last ten years the sources of local government capital expenditures have oscillated between borrowing

1 NHS functions (e.g., the ambulance service) provided by local government prior to 1974 are now provided by the National Health Service itself.

2 Part of the increase in PSS expenditure between 1968 and 1978 was caused by the transfer of some functions from the NHS to local authority PSS in 1969.

3 One third of a pint of milk is provided free of charge to all school children under the age of nine years. School meals are financed partly out of charges (30 pence per day) and partly out of subsidies (about one half of the cost of an average meal).

4 The rate is a local property tax.

5 Means tested grants are given to most students in full time higher education (universities, polytechnics, and colleges). These grants meet tuition charges and maintenance costs in the case of a full grant.

6 Rent rebates to poor residents of local authority (commonly called council) houses were introduced in 1972 and are means tested.

from the central government and borrowing from the open market. The factors affecting this movement have been (1) the level of the interest rates and (2) the control exercised by the central government through its refusal to sanction local government borrowing in the open market. The central government has kept a tight control of local authority finance and capital expenditure in order to stabilize the economy—its macroeconomic goal.[7]

The magnitude of the swings in central government loans is sometimes quite large. For instance, central government capital loans to local government in the 1976–78 period fluctuated widely, as shown in Figure 11–7. When "squeezed" by central government, local governments increased their capital market activities

Table 11–2   Local government capital expenditure, 1968 and 1978 (£ million)

Capital expenditure	1968	1978
Gross domestic fixed capital formation		
Roads and public lighting	195	329
Trading services		
Road and rail passenger transport	12	32
Harbors, docks, and airports	34	25
Other	20	89
Housing	784	1,542
Environmental services		
Water	68	33
Sewerage and sewage disposal	115	39
Refuse collection and disposal	14	38
Public health services	2	8
Land drainage and coast protection	13	61
Parks, pleasure grounds, etc.	18	78
Town and country planning	53	118
Libraries, museums, and arts	7	18
Police	22	42
Fire services	7	21
Social services:		
Education[1]	263	492
National Health Service[2]	15	. . .
Personal social services	24	60
Other	47	134
Subtotal	1,713	3,159
Capital grants to personal sector	22	94
Capital grants to public corporations	. . .	93
Net lending to private sector:		
For house purchase	9	−13
Other	1	2
Total	1,745	3,335
Summary (percentages)		
Housing	44.9	46.3
Education	15.1	14.8
Roads and lighting	11.2	9.9
Sewerage	6.6	1.2
Other	22.2	27.8
Total	100.0	100.0

Source: Central Statistical Office, *National Income and Expenditure 1968–78* (London: HMSO, 1979), Table 8.2, p. 61.

1 Some education capital expenditure (e.g., universities) is financed by the central government.

2 National Health Service functions carried out by local government prior to 1974 have, since that date, been carried out by NHS itself.

Table 11–3 Total government expenditure and local government expenditure, 1968 and 1978 (£ million)

Expenditure	1968	1978
Total government expenditure, central and local	18,289	71,351
Local authority total current expenditure	4,323	19,375
Local authority total capital expenditure	1,745	3,332
Gross national product (GNP)	37,890	142,835
Total government expenditure as a percentage of GNP	48.3	49.9
Local authority total expenditure as a percentage of total government expenditure	33.2	31.8
Local authority total expenditure as a percentage of GNP	16.0	15.9

Source: Central Statistical Office, *National Income and Expenditure 1968–78* (London: HMSO, 1979), Tables 1.1, 9.1; pp. 3, 63.

by borrowing. It is unfortunate for local government capital programming that the central government, in seeking to cut aggregate demand in the economy, uses local capital expenditures as a tool to achieve this end.

The preceding overview of local authority revenues gives an indication of recent magnitudes and trends. The complexity of these can be seen only after a more detailed examination of the principal components of these accounts.

Central government grants for current expenditure   Over 50 percent of local authority current revenue comes from central government grants. The expanding role of central government support for current finance consists largely of nonspecific grants paid under the Rate Support Grant (RSG) program. The size of the grant to a local authority is determined by relative local needs, local resources, and domestic elements. The element of need is related to the size of the local population and such items as housing density, housing quality, and the number of retirees and single parent households in the locality.[8] The local resources element is payable to a local authority if its local tax base is low (i.e., less than "the national standard rateable value per head" prescribed by the central government for the year). In 1976–77, the tax base was £176. The size of the payment

Table 11–4 Local government revenue, 1968 and 1978 (£ million)

Revenue source	1968	1978
Current account		
Current grants from central government		
Grants not allocated for specific services	1,706	8,415
Grants allocated for specific services	192	1,732
Rates	1,548	5,693
Gross trading surplus and rent	781	3,015
Other (interest, etc.)	96	520
Total	4,323	19,375
Capital account		
Capital grants from central government	144	263
Borrowing requirement		
Net loans from central government	589	362
Borrowing from other sources	548	638
Current surplus before providing for depreciation and stock appreciation	402	1,732
Other	62	337
Total	1,745	3,332

Source: Central Statistical Office, *National Income and Expenditure 1968–78* (London: HMSO, 1979), Tables 8.1, 8.2; pp. 58, 60.

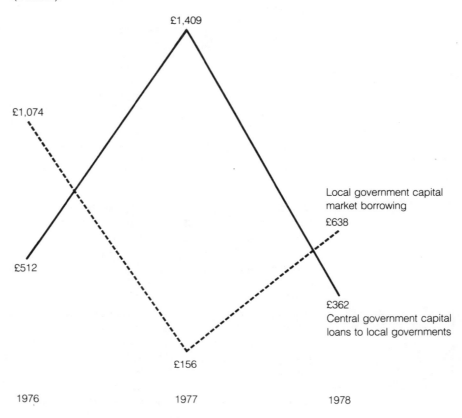

Figure 11–7 Local government borrowing and central government lending, 1976–78 (£ million).

of the resources element is equal to the size of the deficiency per head multiplied by the authority's population. The third component of the grant is the domestic element. This is designed to compensate local authorities for the imposition by the central government of lower rate percentages on domestic hereditaments (private houses). Since 1967, the rental values on which the taxes or rates are based have been fixed at a lower level for private houses than for industrial properties, largely because the central government fears the possible consequences of imposing full rates on private dwellings.

The element of need generates the largest expenditure in the central government equalizing grants, consisting of about £3,500 million in 1977–78. The calculation of "needs" by central government bureaucrats along with the actual expenditure experiences of local authorities are analyzed annually in documents that are covered by the Official Secrets Act and, as such, are not available for public analysis. In 1978, the 1977–78 analyses were "leaked" and they showed that many local authorities controlled by the Labour party spent at levels above central government "need norms," while many local authorities controlled by the Conservative party provided service levels below the need norms.[9]

In analyzing the impact of the British centralized system, it is important to recognize that although the center legislates for "norms" and "standards," its ability to implement its complex and often ill-understood objectives is not absolute. Local autonomy survives perhaps in reaction to the over-regulation of the central government. Despite central government intervention, local benefit-tax margins can diverge by significant amounts and these differences may affect the geographical distribution of people.[10]

Capital finance   The chief source of local authority capital finance is the Public Works Loan Board (see Table 11–5) which raises money from central government loans. The interest rate on its loans to local authorities is fixed by the central government treasury. This rate is generally equivalent to the rate at which the treasury can borrow on the open market, and also is a rate usually below that which local authorities would incur if they floated their own loans. Local government debt issues must have prior consent of the Department of the Environment. Thus, the central government can regulate the volume and amount of loans to assist its macroeconomic policy. The second main source of local government capital finance is marketed mortgages or bonds. These are trustee securities secured by the full taxing ability of the local authority. Market interest rates are charged, and this debt has a wide range of possible maturity options. This source of capital finance is limited by the amount of local rates and other revenues available for security.

One other form of borrowing is the temporary loan of capital, which is supposed to finance capital formation prior to a more permanent loan. Generally, this money is raised in the market over a very short period and at slow market interest rates. The use of such instruments is clearly dependent on the availability of long-term financing. When long-term financing is affected by economic conditions, temporary loan financing is also affected.

Table 11–5   Percentage sources of local government capital finance (total debt and percent of total)[1]

Finance source	1966–67	1976–77
Public Works Loan Board loans	34	37
Stock issues	8	5
Bonds/mortgages	32	32
Temporary loans	16	13
Internal advances	4	2
Other	6	11
Total	100	100

Source: Institute of Municipal Treasurers and Accountants, *Return on Outstanding Debt 1966–67*, London, 1967; Chartered Institute of Public Finance and Accountancy, *Return on Outstanding Debt at 31st March, 1977*, Statistical Information Services, London, 1977.
1 The total outstanding net debt in 1966–67 was £7,987 million; in 1976–77 it was £31,023 million.

Tax rates   The only independent source of local tax revenues is the tax (or rate) paid by those who occupy land and buildings. Agricultural property and most charities are exempt. Each property or hereditament is given a rateable value (RV), which is theoretically equal to the annual rental value it would have if it were on the free market. The amount of tax a person (or firm) pays is equal to the RV multiplied by the poundage (the tax rate set by the local authorities).[11] The RVs of all properties are determined and reassessed periodically by the Inland Revenue. There are, however, very few rented properties in the free market to use as a guide for setting RVs.[12] Thus, the RVs currently are only approximations of true rental values.

New forms of local taxation   The inaccurate assessments, the regressive nature (despite an income related rate rebate scheme) of rates, and the increased dependence of local governments on government grants has led to two decades of protracted and, so far, largely ineffectual discussions of new sources of local tax revenue. At least seventeen possible new local tax sources have been debated: an alcohol tax, a corporation profits tax, death duties and inheritance taxes, income taxes paid in the area of residence, income taxes paid in the area of work, a value added tax, a petrol (gasoline) tax, automobile license duties, a payroll tax, a poll tax, a purchase tax, road congestion charges, a sales tax, a selective employment tax, a tobacco tax, a turnover tax, and revenues from the nationalization of development land. However, it appears unlikely that any of these taxes will be adopted in the early 1980s because of the current political climate.

The reasons for this conclusion are two-fold. First, the central government does not seem to have any wish to increase local autonomy by introducing new local sources of taxation. The current view of the treasury is that financial and planning controls over the local authorities are necessary to attain equity and efficiency. Second, all the tax instruments proposed for use in the reform of local authority taxation seem to have problems which generate opposition.[13] For example, the turnover tax is rejected because it discriminates against firms that are not vertically integrated. The poll tax is rejected because of its regressivity. The difficulties of allocating the profits of multi-area companies among the competing authorities in which they are located are an obstacle to the use of a local corporation profits tax. Road congestion charges would generate local revenues only in congested urban areas; they also might act as a disincentive to road improvements if such programs reduced congestion and, subsequently, revenue. Few anticipate the transfer of death duties and inheritance taxes to the local authorities, and the nationalization of development land has been unsuccessful (little land was marketed) in generating much income.[14]

The transfer of tobacco and alcohol taxation revenues to local authorities has attracted some support, but this type of tax instrument can affect regional sales patterns because people will go to low tax areas to make their purchases. This effect is more likely if the tax is a high percentage of cost and applies to only a few goods. Local authorities would prefer a low rate local sales tax to a high rate excise tax.

The use of local payroll and income taxes is not supported by central government. These taxes raise problems associated with a possible increase in administrative costs due to overlapping assessment and collection authorities. There also is the problem of whether the tax should be related to residence or work place.

Another proposal from advocates of increased local taxation is automobile taxes. With the decision to phase out automobile license duties because of their high administrative costs, a tax on gasoline has been proposed. Clearly, the costs of collecting increased local tax revenues from petrol taxation could be fixed at acceptable levels. However, the political will to move in this direction appears absent, despite many local lobbies favoring increased autonomy.

User charges   As with the debate about new forms of local government tax revenue, the discussion of an increase in user charges has been quite detailed. It has, however, led to only minor policy changes. This discussion must be set in a theoretical context.

The theory of public goods   The theoretical concepts of jointness of supply and interrelated utilities set forth a theory of public goods. Public goods are those with such characteristics that private markets fail to provide them efficiently, and that their efficient allocation requires collection of one form or another. It has been argued that, although corrective measures to ensure the efficient allocation of resources in the face of private market "failure" may be best carried out at the national level, public action or the provision of the public good at the local level may be preferable.

Jointness of supply   Certain aspects of the traditional economic analysis merit careful consideration. The problems of jointness of supply and nonexcludability are relative rather than absolute features of markets, although these problems may change as technology changes. For example, a lighthouse will warn several individuals of navigation hazards. A single individual's use of the light will not reduce the supply of the light to another (i.e., the light is in joint supply). No one may be excluded from viewing the light as it is there for all to see (i.e., the light exhibits the nonexcludability characteristic). However, the jointness in supply in this case is not necessarily perfect. An historical analysis of the lighthouse example shows that efficient production of this "public good" is possible in private markets—some English lighthouses were run privately for profit, financed by harbor dues in neighboring ports, in the eighteenth century.[15] Furthermore, advances in nautical technology (e.g., shipboard radar) have made the problem of market failure in this area less important. In fact, modern navigation equipment has made the lighthouses redundant for all but the most humble of craft. Such edifices remain partly because of the lack of flexibility in decision making and partly because manned lighthouses can serve other functions, one of the most important of which is to inform investigators about the state of mariners who run aground near the lights.

Market failure   Thus, theory and historical evidence indicate that the problems faced by communities wishing to supply an efficient level of public goods are relative and change over time. Indeed, the theoretical analysis is concerned solely with market failures on the demand side of the market. The theory of public goods attempts to cover little about the relative efficiency of public versus private production of these goods and services. Market failures (which call for intervention in markets for goods with public attributes) might be rectified by financial intervention of the state, but do not necessarily require public production of the goods and services.

Education, for example, is an important function of local government, but the involvement of the state in the production of education can be questioned. If the provision of education by the private market is inefficient because of market failures, the publicness of education, or perhaps income inequalities, one solution is to provide financial support to the disadvantaged groups. The redistribution of income, via taxes and subsidies, may be a better method of overcoming the market failures of providing an efficient level of education. (However, this may not hold if we are interested in providing only education, and not a general mix of educational goods.)

This conclusion is important because it indicates that the state's involvement in the production of public goods, or goods with some degree of publicness, might be relatively small. The crucial information required to determine the extent of state involvement in the production of any good or service, is whether production by the government is more efficient than production by nongovernment bodies.

Efficient resource allocation requires that goods and services be produced by whichever bodies, public or private, consume fewer resources in the production process.

Efficiency   The best educational policy then may be for the government, local or central, to redistribute resources to attain efficiency and equity, and to leave the production of goods and services to the most efficient institutions. Thus, state or private bodies, whichever are the more efficient, should provide the education service. An economic price should be levied on service users. If it is determined that some of the users require more of the service, they could be subsidized by the state. Thus, those users would consume what the state considered to be the "required" amount of the service.

The production of goods and services by local government (and central government) should be questioned. Public production should be advocated only when it is demonstrably more efficient than private production. Many publicly provided services might be financed by user charges.

It is possible that user charges would be an efficient means of financing many aspects of local government in Britain. Services provided by such facilities as airports, libraries, art galleries and museums, and cemeteries and crematoria may be funded by user charges. Traffic and transport functions, refuse disposal, and many aspects of social work and housing could be paid for with user charges also.

One area in which user charges are feasible is education, especially if they are associated with the use of vouchers. The issue of tied purchasing power (vouchers) to parents with school-age children might channel school finance to those types of education favored most by the consumers. There are many variants of a voucher for education. These variants serve to demonstrate that the mechanism is a feasible policy instrument which can be molded to suit the societal objectives. The variant used in Alum Rock, California, was a relatively conservative model; more flexible methods are available. User charges could be extended to schools.[16]

One British county council, Kent, is about to introduce a trial scheme for education vouchers. The Kent innovation, too, is of a conservative nature. Its redistributive effects are small and the efficiency effects will be muted because of the particular voucher plan being discussed, but it is indicative of a more flexible response by local councilors to the question of financing and producing local authority services.

The primary advantage of user charges is that consumer response to them gives decision makers information about consumers' preferences for particular quantities and qualities of goods and services. Furthermore, the direct financial sacrifice involved in consumption may increase the monitoring of product quality by consumers, and increase their demand for "value for money."

The relative costs of user charges are not known because generally there has been little experimentation with alternative models of finance and production. Where there has been experimentation, its evaluation has often been imperfect. Clearly, user charges might be difficult to apply (i.e., inefficient) to police and fire service protection, but equally clear are the possibilities that education, housing, and trading services could be financed partially or entirely by user charges.

The attractiveness of user charges is that they are an alternative to taxation for financing publicly provided goods and services. In the United Kingdom there is increasing pressure to reduce the burden of direct taxation. If taxation is reduced, current levels of publicly provided services may be maintained by raising user charges in areas where they already exist and introducing them where they have never before existed. The price of services would be more explicit to consumers, which may generate incentives for more effective use of society's scarce resources.

The principal problem of the user charge mechanism is that it creates burdens for the disadvantaged (i.e., the poor's ability to pay is less than that of the rich). This problem can only be overcome satisfactorily if the state is prepared to redistribute cash (e.g., by a negative income tax scheme or a voucher) to the least advantaged groups in society. The potential gains in efficiency of the user charge system make this method of financing publicly provided goods and services very attractive.

Summary

Local government relies heavily on central government finance, both on the current account where over 52 percent of revenue is derived from central government grants, and on the capital account where nearly 43 percent of revenue is derived from central government loans and grants. The mechanisms through which this support is derived from central government are mainly the Rate Support Grant and the Public Works Loan Board.

The main local revenue source is the rates (property taxation). Protracted and detailed discussions of new forms of local taxation and user charges recently have taken place in Britain. The objective of these changes would be to increase local autonomy. Despite the slow implementation of policy changes, it may be that user charges offer some attractive benefits, specifically, more efficiency in local government activity. Furthermore, the central government may have to permit changes in the structure of local finance if demands for a reduced tax burden are to be met.

It may be that current levels of publicly provided services can only be maintained if unpopular taxes are replaced by user charges.

The organization of local government

The organizational structure in which local governments expend their budgets is quite complex. The service obligations of various local authorities in England and Wales are as follows:

1. *Metropolitan county council* functions are strategic planning, national parks and countryside, traffic and transport, Passenger Transport Authority (PTA), highways, caravan sites, housing (reserve powers), police and fire service, food and drugs, weights and measures (consumer protection), museums and art galleries, and refuse (garbage disposal).
2. *Metropolitan district* functions are airports, baths and pools, off-street car parking, libraries, museums and art galleries, education, planning, social services, cemeteries and crematoria, food and drugs, markets and fairs, parks and open spaces, housing, and refuse.
3. *Nonmetropolitan county council* functions are education, social services, public libraries, and all metropolitan county council functions, except Passenger Transport Authority.
4. *Nonmetropolitan district* functions are the same as metropolitan district functions (excluding education, social services, libraries) and public transport.

The functions of the Scottish local authorities[17] are as follows:

1. *Regional councils* feature strategic planning (including the use of resources), transport and roads, industrial development, police, fire, education, and social work.
2. *District councils* feature local planning, housing, local health and amenity controls, building control, and libraries.[18]

Although each of these authorities is eligible to receive central government grants and subsidies, not all of them are permitted to levy local property tax rates. The district local governments have the power to collect rates. The counties and the metropolitan areas have the power to require the districts to collect rate tax revenue on their behalf, but have no independent authority to collect such revenues themselves. (This is called the power of precepting.) Thus, each year the ratepayer's tax bill is made up of two parts: one set of monies that directly finances district local authority activity; and one set of incomes, precepted by the counties and the metropolitan areas, to finance their services. All of the revenue is collected by the district authority which, after deducting the rates to finance its activity, passes the money on to the counties.

Any reform of local government tax sources or service functions might lead to the reform of this organizational structure. However, the problems following local government reorganization in 1974 were considerable. Any more significant changes in the next decade seem unlikely.

Efficiency in local government

We now turn to the control of local government expenditure and the mechanisms that provide decision makers with incentives to strive for efficient resource allocation in the local government sector. In particular, the process by which the central government reviews local government functions via the Public Expenditure Survey Committee (PESC) mechanism, and the use of such evaluative techniques as cost-benefit analysis will be reviewed.

Public Expenditure Survey Committee

The work of the Public Expenditure Survey Committee (PESC) is an annual exercise of the central government aimed at evaluating all government programs and rationing the available resources among the competing departments. The Committee receives detailed requests from all of the departments of government. Since the early 1970s departmental bids for funds have been prepared with the help of local authority representatives. The result is that local authority expenditure discretion is constrained by Whitehall's view of the forecasted total costs and expenditures on the one hand, and the reluctance of local government to exercise discretion and face the cost of increased rates (taxes) and political discontent on the other hand. These constraints are reinforced by Whitehall statements about the "necessary" rate increases needed to fulfill forecast expenditure plans. If the local electorate observe that the rate increases in their area exceed the guidelines, they have a longer stick with which to beat their local politicians.

Thus, local authorities are integrated into the public expenditure planning process—which can be frustrating. For example, the local authorities working with the Department of Education may decide on program expansion. Such an expansion, however, may be frustrated by the Department of Environment's refusal to increase the Rate Support Grant. The frustration usually is treated in the following manner:

"[Local authority representatives] come to me and complain about this but you can't stop ministers talking. My answer is to tell the local authorities that they can do what they want. But they've got their Rate Support Grant and any more spending they want to do has to fall entirely on the local rates. It's cold comfort to them, but it does help control total spending."

PESC government negotiator[19]

The PESC exercise makes the financial constraints very explicit and encourages the careful reappraisal of policy in central and local government. This PESC appraisal takes place annually, culminating each year in November or December with the announcement of the level of the Rate Support Grant. One part of the appraisal, the five-year rolling program, involves the critical examination of policy over a longer period and clearly sets out the Committee's view of the role of local government over a five-year period. Although imperfect in some ways, it has received approval from such outside observers as Heclo and Wildavsky.

Program evaluation

The PESC exercise is essentially a macroeconomic system of appraising public spending. The central government planners attempt to integrate local government expenditures into the macroeconomic forecasting model and constrain such expenditures to ensure that policies and planning targets are consistent. This process involves but little detailed economic evaluation of micro-policy options.

The theoretical methods of carrying out detailed evaluation programs and projects—cost-benefit analysis and cost-effectiveness analysis—are well established.[20] Although their application in local government in Britain is spasmodic, there is some use made of these concepts. For example, the Gloucester County Council applies cost-benefit analysis to select the best road projects. This involves the application of a methodology developed by central government (the Road Research Laboratory) which gives values for hidden costs and benefits such as time, injuries, and death. These assigned values enable decision makers to establish a list of priorities for road work.

The use of such techniques is inhibited in many areas by the lack of data about many of the indirect costs and benefits of the projects under consideration (i.e., by the lack of output or outcome measures). As a result, such areas of local government activity as education and social work have not been appraised using these techniques.

Policy appraisal could be developed further in at least two ways. First, proxies for the output of social services can be evolved and used to appraise the activities of this labor intensive and expensive portion of local expenditure.[21] Such proxies are the subjects of increasing research activity in some local authorities in Britain. Second, a less ambitious technique, cost-effectiveness analysis, can be applied to appraise the costs of alternative methods to achieve a given policy objective.

In education, for example, simple numeracy, literacy, and intelligence goals can be established as given objectives. Then such alternative teaching regimes as "traditional" vis-à-vis "liberal" could be appraised. Thus, it is possible to analyze the costs of alternative methods of achieving given education goals. These devices, unfortunately, have not been used very widely in the United Kingdom or elsewhere.

The lack of application of evaluative techniques to local authority services is unfortunate because it compounds the existing ignorance about the efficiency of these services and encourages the maintenance of such technologies as "chalk and talk" in education, which have doubtful efficacy and are labor intensive. The possibility of substituting capital for labor in the local authority sector is relatively unexplored territory. More careful evaluation may reveal significant possibilities for such substitution and cost reductions. If the professions are prepared to permit evaluation and to alter the once labor intensive technologies of education and other services, there could be important changes in the activities of local government in the decades to come.

Perhaps the major managerial challenge in British local government during the next decade will be the extension of economic evaluation of programs and their performance. At the macroeconomic (aggregate) and central government level, the PESC exercise exerts considerable pressure on local bureaucrats to carry out appraisals of their activities. At the microeconomic (individual firm or consumer) level, this pressure has resulted in the rigorous application of techniques of economic evaluation in some sectors (e.g., road construction and improvement), and relatively little application in others (e.g., social services and education). In all cases these local outcomes reflect the departmental activity or inactivity of the central government. The spread of such techniques of appraisal is likely to be significant, and will be encouraged by poor economic performance and continued pressure on public resources.

Devolution, the autonomy debate, and the future of local government

The recurrent theme of the preceding sections has been that the central government control of local government in Britain is extensive and detailed. Despite, or because of, the limited nature of local autonomy, public pressure for the devolution of power to Scottish and Welsh assemblies resulted in referenda in 1979. Although the decision then was to avoid moves toward federalization in the United Kingdom, the commitments to the European Economic Community (EEC) are such that a federal European State may yet evolve.

Devolution and federalism

Although the English and Scottish crowns were amalgamated early in the eighteenth century, Scotland has maintained a separate but related legal system and a certain degree of devolved power in Edinburgh (embodied in its Secretary of State, a member of the British Cabinet). The Welsh crown was amalgamated with that of England many hundreds of years ago, but Wales, nevertheless, has maintained to some extent a separate culture. During the last decade, growing nationalist movements in Scotland and Wales have resulted in legislation that could have devolved governmental functions from Whitehall to Edinburgh and Cardiff. Some of these functions (e.g., education) are primary spheres of local authority activity; consequently, if devolution had been agreed to by the citizens of Wales and Scotland, the nature of the debate about resource support would have become complicated. The assemblies of each country would have essentially received grants from Whitehall, and the local authorities then would have to bargain with the assemblies. Instead of having to bargain with Whitehall alone, local authorities in Wales and Scotland would have to debate about policies and resources with their national assemblies as well.

Despite the decision by the Scottish and Welsh electorates to reject devolution (i.e., the decentralization of power), these issues may re-emerge in the years to come if political preferences shift and the minority favoring devolution becomes a majority. The domestic devolution debate has been accompanied by a debate about the possible creation of a federal Europe. The Treaty of Rome (1957), which established the European Economic Community (EEC), set forth the framework for economic and political integration. So far, progress on political integration has been limited. In June 1979, the first direct elections for the European Parliament took place; the powers of this Parliament are limited.

Nevertheless, the EEC Commission is becoming increasingly active in implementing policies of economic integration that may affect the behavior of local authorities in Britain. The scope of the Commission's activity is determined by the Rome Treaty. The possible ways in which the Commission may implement this Treaty and affect local government seem extensive. The harmonization of taxation systems and tax rates across the EEC is a long-range goal of the Commission. Local tax systems and tax rates currently diverge enormously; the adoption of uniform tax systems and tax rates across the EEC could bring radical changes to the pattern of local government finance in Britain. The implementation of the Rome Treaty may also affect the quantity and quality of local authority services. The potential effects of the EEC on British local government appear to be substantial, but the exact nature of the implementation of the Rome Treaty will only become apparent in the next decade.

The outlook for local government in Britain

Local government in Britain is characterized by apparent discretion but actually it has very limited autonomy in any real sense. The central government in Whitehall controls the constituent bodies of the local government structure with extensive financial and nonfinancial policy instruments. For instance, if a local authority wishes to build an apartment house its capacity to raise capital is carefully appraised, its building standards are centrally determined, and its rental policies are highly circumscribed.

Popular interest in local government is limited. Despite the large budgets spent by these bodies and the seemingly ubiquitous nature of their activities at a local level, the local government electoral turnouts are typically below 30 percent. The low voter turnout is perhaps not surprising, given the limited nature of local autonomy.

The extensive erosion of local autonomy that has arisen from the pursuit of macroeconomic stability and redistribution goals is criticized by many in Britain. The efficiency of the government in pursuing macro- and microeconomic objectives is being questioned. This questioning of service efficiency has been accompanied by a discussion of alternative forms of finance. Only time will tell whether this critical outlook of central government policy will restore some local autonomy. The outlook at the beginning of the 1980s is for increased centralization—despite some pious political statements to the contrary.

1   Thus the concern of this chapter is the local governments of England, Scotland, and Wales. Northern Ireland is excluded from the analysis.

2   The exceptions to this general rule were Lincolnshire and Yorkshire, which were divided into three administrative counties; Suffolk and Sussex, each divided into two; Cambridge and the Isle of Ely, amalgamated into one unit; and Huntingdon and the Soke of Peterborough, also amalgamated into one.

3   The organization of the National Health Service was reformed at the same time the structure of local government was changed. The National Health Service is run not by local government but by a separate regional/area structure. In 1974 this structure took over several functions, such as ambulance services, that previously were the responsibility of the local authorities.

4   For a summary of these proposals, see: Alan K. Maynard and David N. King, *Rates or Prices?* (London: Institute of Economic Affairs, 1972).

5   The six metropolitan county councils are Greater Manchester, Merseyside, South Yorkshire, Tyne and Wear, West Midlands, and West Yorkshire.

6   This is the sum of current and capital expenditure, subsidies for housing, and rent rebates and allowances.

7   Curiously, central government has often chosen to regulate the economy by manipulating capital rather than current account budget items; i.e., the brunt of reflation and deflation often falls on the construction industry. This policy also has political attractions: it is apparently "dynamic" but affects no one's consumption in the short run. See: Alan Maynard and Arthur Walker, "Cutting Public Expenditure," *New Society*, 5 December 1975.

8   All these factors and their weightings are set out in: "Local Government Finance (England and Wales): The Rate Support Grant 1975," House of Commons Paper no. 31 (London: Her Majesty's Stationery Office), pp. 16–19.

9   This information was leaked in a report of the *Guardian* newspaper: "The Mystery of the Miscalculated £3500 mn," *Guardian*, 23 November 1978, p. 3.

10 For an interesting elaboration of this point, see: J. Richard Aronson, "Financing Public Goods and the Distribution of Population in Metropolitan Areas: An Analysis of Fiscal Migration in the United States and England," in *Economic Policies and Social Goals*, ed. A. J. Culyer (London: Martin Robertson, 1974).

11 If the poundage is 50 pence in the pound, then the rates payable on a hereditament with an RV of £250 would be £125 (i.e., £250 × 50/100). Since 1967, domestic hereditaments (private houses) have paid a lower rate than industrial hereditaments (factories, offices, etc.).

12 There is little evidence about free market rents in the housing sector because over 50 percent of properties are owner occupied, a further 30 percent are council houses, and the remaining private rented houses (15 percent of the total housing stock) are subject to rent control legislation.

13 For a more detailed debate of these taxes, see: Maynard and King, *Rates or Prices?*, pp. 55–62.

14 For a discussion of this legislation, see: Alan Maynard, "An Economic Analysis of the Land Act," *Local Government Studies*, July 1976.

15 For an analysis of this, see: R. H. Coase, "The Lighthouse in Economics," *Journal of Law and Economics* 17 (October 1974): 357–76.

16 For further details of alternative voucher schemes and their advantages and disadvantages, see: A. Maynard, *Experience with Choice in Education* (London: Institute of Economic Affairs, 1975).

17 Because of their separate identity and remoteness, Orkney, Shetland, and the Western Isles have their own single-tier authorities which carry out all local authority functions.

18 In the Highlands, Borders, and South West Regional Council areas, library services are provided by the regional authorities and not by the districts.

19 H. Heclo and A. Wildavsky, *The Private Government of Public Money* (London: Macmillan & Co., 1974), p. 350.

20 For instance, see: A. Williams and R. Anderson, *Efficiency in the Social Services* (Oxford: Blackwells, 1975); and R. Sugden and A. Williams, *The Principles of Practical Cost Benefit Analysis* (Oxford: Oxford University Press, 1975) and Chapters 2 and 3 of this volume.

21 For instance, see: K. G. Wright, "Output Measurement in Practice," in *Economic Aspects of Health Services*, ed. A. J. Culyer and K. G. Wright (London: Martin Robertson, 1978).

Part four: Financial management

12 Managing financial condition

During the 1970s, governments at all levels began to experience an increasing number of financial problems. These problems were related to increased demand for services, unionization of public employees, structural changes in the economy, shifts in population, double-digit inflation, and significant changes in intergovernmental relationships. The financial crisis in New York City in 1975 and the inability of other cities to secure long-term financing brought these issues to national attention. California's Proposition 13 and similar revenue and expenditure limitations in other states placed even greater attention on the financial health of local governments. As a result, officials at all levels have been forced to place a high priority on financial problems.[1]

Most financial problems do not develop suddenly. They build over time. Financial problems generally can be traced to one or more of the following circumstances:

1. A decline in revenues
2. An increase in expenditure pressures
3. A decrease in cash and budgetary surpluses
4. A growing debt burden
5. An accumulation of unfunded liabilities
6. An erosion of capital plant
7. A decline in the tax base or an increase in the need for public services
8. An increase in intergovernmental constraints and mandates and an overdependence on intergovernmental funding
9. The emergence of adverse external economic conditions, such as increasing inflation or unemployment
10. The occurrence of natural disasters and emergencies
11. The influence of local political pressures
12. The lack of effective legislative policies and management practices.

Some of these circumstances (e.g., a growing debt burden) are in the control of a local government. Others (e.g., the emergence of adverse external conditions) may not be. Nevertheless, with enough time a local government may be able to take actions to mitigate their effects. For example, in the short run, a local government may not be able to turn around a decline in its tax base, but it may be able to reduce its expenditure levels to adjust for reduced revenues.[2]

The purpose of this chapter is to provide tools a local government can use to identify problems and provide time to take corrective action.

Evaluating financial condition

The term "financial condition" has many meanings. In a narrow accounting sense, it can refer to whether a government can generate enough cash (or liquidity) over thirty or sixty days to pay its bills. This is referred to as *cash solvency*.

Financial condition may also mean *budgetary solvency*. Can a local government generate enough revenues over its normal budgetary period to meet its expenditure obligations and not incur deficits?

In a broader sense, financial condition may refer to the *long-range* ability of a government to pay *all* the costs of doing business, including expenditure obligations that appear in each annual budget and those that appear only in the years in which they must be paid. Examples of these latter expenditure obligations are pension costs; payments for accrued employment leave; deferred maintenance; and replacement of capital assets such as streets, equipment, and buildings. Although these costs will eventually show up in a budget, an analysis of one to five years may not reveal them. Thus, the long-range balance between revenues and costs warrants separate attention and may be referred to as *long-range solvency.*

Finally, financial condition may determine whether a government can provide the level and quality of services required for the general health and welfare of a community. Does the local government have *service level solvency?* For example, a local government that is unable to support an adequate level of police and fire services will suffer with problems of service level solvency. It would also suffer from cash, budgetary, or long-range solvency problems if it did provide the police and fire services.

Few local governments face such severe and immediate financial problems that they are likely to default on loans or fail to meet payrolls and other current obligations. Therefore, this chapter will adopt a broad definition of financial condition to encompass the four types of solvency described previously. By using this broad definition, we hope to deal with the concerns of the many local governments that find themselves in one or more of the following situations:

1. Seeking a way to put a few identifiable problems in a broader perspective
2. Sensing the emergence of problems, but having difficulty pinpointing them
3. Searching for a systematic way to monitor changes and anticipate future problems, although currently in good financial condition.

Therefore, financial condition is broadly defined as the ability of a local government to pay its way on a continuing basis. Specifically, it refers to a local government's ability to (1) maintain existing service levels, (2) withstand local and regional economic disruptions, and (3) meet the demands of natural growth, decline, and change.

Ability to maintain existing service levels

Maintaining existing service levels means the local government can afford to pay for the services it is currently providing. In addition to the services funded by local revenues, the ability to maintain programs that are currently funded by external sources (e.g., federal grants) where the aid is scheduled or likely to diminish and where the service cannot practically be eliminated when the aid does disappear must also be considered. The ability to maintain such capital facilities as streets and buildings in a manner that protects the initial investment in them and keeps them in usable condition, and the ability to provide funds for future liabilities which may currently be unfunded (e.g., pension, employee leave, debt, and lease purchase commitments) also are of significant importance.

Ability to withstand economic disruption

Financial condition is the ability to withstand local and regional economic disruption. For example, a major employer's decision to move a manufacturing plant out of town would take away many of the community's jobs and a large part of the tax base. A surge of national inflation that affects expenditures more heavily than revenues, and leaves local governments with more dollars but less purchasing power is another example.

Ability to meet future demands of growth and decline

Finally, financial condition is the ability of a community to meet the future demands of change. As time passes, local governments grow, shrink, or remain the same size. Each condition has its own set of financial pressures. Growth can force a community to assume rapidly new debt to finance streets and utility lines, or it can cause a sudden increase in the operating budget to provide necessary services. Shrinkage, on the other hand, leaves a community with the same number of streets and utilities to maintain but with fewer people to pay for them. Even an area that remains stable in size can experience financial pressure. For example, if population remains stable but undergoes changes in composition, the government often must respond with new programs. This necessitates expensive start-up costs, and possibly programs that themselves may be more expensive. New programs are necessary, for example, if a population becomes poorer or older.

The basic questions, therefore, are (1) Can the local government continue to pay for what it is currently doing? (2) Are there reserves or other vehicles for financing economic and financial emergencies? and (3) Is there enough financial flexibility to allow the local government to adjust to the normal process of change? If a community can meet these challenges, it is in good financial condition. If it cannot, it is probably experiencing or can anticipate problems.

Obstacles to measuring financial condition

To determine whether a local government is in good financial condition, officials first need to be able to measure it. If a definition of financial condition that considered only cash and budgetary solvency had been chosen, the range of measurement issues to be discussed would have been narrow. By including long-range and service level solvency, however, a host of problems is encountered. These problems are related to (1) the nature of a public entity, (2) the current state of the art in municipal financial analysis, and (3) the current character of municipal accounting practices.

The social nature of a public entity   Private firms can determine easily whether they are sound financially. The basic test is dollar profit, which roughly translates into efficiency. For the public entity, profit is not a motive, and efficiency is only one of many objectives. The primary objectives are health and welfare, political satisfaction, and other issues that can be measured only subjectively. Therefore, by including the concept of service level solvency in the definition of financial condition, we have to settle for something less than precise measurement.

The state of the art   Until recently, practitioners and researchers in the field of public finance have concerned themselves primarily with the issues of cash and budgetary solvency. They have not paid as much attention to the issues of long-range and service level solvency. The exception has been the investment community, which has more specifically concerned itself with debt-carrying capacity. During the last few years, local governments as well as other institutions have broadened their concerns; however, neither has yet developed a comprehensive and practical way to evaluate the financial condition of an individual local government.[3]

This can be attributed to a number of factors. First, the growth-oriented environment of local government prior to the 1970s did not always demand close attention to the broad range of issues that affect financial condition. Second, data on economic and demographic events are difficult and sometimes impossible to obtain. Third, the data that are available do not always permit comparisons of one locality to another because each is unique in size, function, geography, revenue structure, and other significant characteristics. Fourth, there is no accepted theory to explain the links between economic base and local government revenues. How and to what extent, for example, does a decline in employment or a shift from manufacturing to retail specifically affect the revenues of a local government?[4] Lastly, the state of the art does not provide normative standards for what the financial characteristics of a local government should be. What, for example, is a healthy per capita expenditure rate, level of reserves, or amount of debt? The credit rating industry has many benchmarks for evaluating local governments, but these benchmarks have to be considered in combination with the more subjective criteria (e.g., the diversity of the city's tax base or its proximity to regional markets).[5] Some attempts have been made to develop standards by averaging various municipalities or otherwise comparing one to another, but, because of the uniqueness of each and the lack of sufficient objective data, these comparisons have fallen short of gaining authoritative acceptance.

The state of municipal accounting systems   During the early 1900s, local government accounting systems grew with an emphasis on auditing and on providing high visibility to the dollars which passed through the government accounts. The accounting systems stressed legal compliance and the ability to track the path of each dollar that passes in and out of the local treasury. Thus, the concepts of fund accounting and flow of funds—that is, segregating current revenues and expenditures into very small, auditable pieces—were developed with little attention given to cost accounting and measuring long-range financial health.

The result is that most local governments do produce budgets showing revenues and expenditures, and most states require these budgets to be balanced in one fashion or another. In addition, most local governments produce year-end financial statements, including balance sheets and operating statements.

These reports show the flow of dollars in and out of the local government during a particular year, but they do not provide all the information needed to evaluate long-range financial condition. They do not show in detail the costs of each service provided. They do not show on an annual basis all costs that are being postponed to future periods. They do not necessarily show the accumulation of unfunded pension liabilities or employee benefit liabilities. They do not show reductions in purchasing power caused by inflation. They do not show decreasing flexibility in the use of funds—the result of an increase in the number of state and federal mandates. In addition, the reports do not show the erosion of streets, buildings, and other fixed assets that are not being maintained; nor do they relate changes in the economic and demographic conditions to changes in revenue and expenditure rates. Finally, the reports are prepared only for a one-year period and do not reflect a multiyear perspective that shows the emergence of favorable or unfavorable conditions.[6]

The Financial Trend Monitoring System

Evaluating a jurisdiction's financial condition can be complex. It is a process of sorting through a large number of pieces, including the national economy, the population level and composition, the local business climate, the actions of the state and local government, and the character of the internal finances of the local government itself. Not only are there a large number of these factors to evaluate, but also many of the factors are difficult to isolate and to quantify.

In addition, no single piece tells the whole story. Some are more important than others, although usually this is not known until all of the pieces have been assembled. For example, revenues may be higher than ever in absolute amounts. They may be exceeding expenditure levels by a comfortable margin. However, if a local government does not consider that a 5 percent annual inflation rate during the past ten years has cut its purchasing power by well over half, and that it has had to make the adjustment by deferring street maintenance, it may be lulled into thinking that its financial condition remains quite healthy.

In the face of this complexity, of the lack of complete accounting data, and of the lack of accepted theories and normative standards, is it possible to rationalize the process of evaluating financial condition?

The answer is yes. Regardless of the obstacles, a local government can still collect a great deal of useful information, even if this information is only part of all there is to know. Medical science has learned little about the human body compared with what remains to be learned. This lack of total knowledge, however, does not prevent doctors from using what they do know to prevent diseases and from diagnosing problems before they become serious.

The Financial Trend Monitoring System (FTMS) is a system that identifies the factors that affect financial condition and arranges them in a rational order so that they can be more easily analyzed and, to the extent possible, more easily measured. It is a management tool that pulls together the pertinent information from a community's budgetary and financial reports, mixes it with the appropriate economic and demographic data, and creates a series of local government financial indicators that, when plotted over a period of time, can be used to monitor changes in financial condition. The indicators deal with thirty-six separate issues, including cash liquidity, level of business activity, changes in fund balances, emergence of unfunded liabilities, and development of external revenue dependencies.

Use of the system does not provide specific answers to why a problem is occurring, nor does it provide a single number or index to measure financial health. It does provide (1) flags for identifying problems, (2) clues to their causes, and (3) time to take anticipatory action.

It also provides a convenient tool for describing the financial strengths and weaknesses of a municipality to a city council or county board, a credit rating firm, or others who need to know. It can provide a rational means for organizing internal staff priorities or it can provide a vehicle a council may use to set long-range policy priorities. Finally, if used prior to budget time, it can provide a logical way of introducing long-range considerations into the annual budget process.

How does FTMS work?

The Financial Trend Monitoring System (FTMS) is built on twelve "factors" which represent the primary forces that influence financial condition. These financial condition factors are then associated with thirty-six "indicators" that measure different aspects of seven of these factors. Once developed, these indicators can be used to monitor changes in the factors, or more generally, to monitor changes in financial condition. The twelve factors together with the thirty-six indicators make up FTMS. The factors will be discussed first, and then the indicators.

The financial condition factors   The twelve financial condition factors are shown in Figure 12–1. They are described more fully by the items shown in the brackets.

Figure 12–1   Financial condition factors—environmental, organizational, and financial—with definitional and descriptive elements.

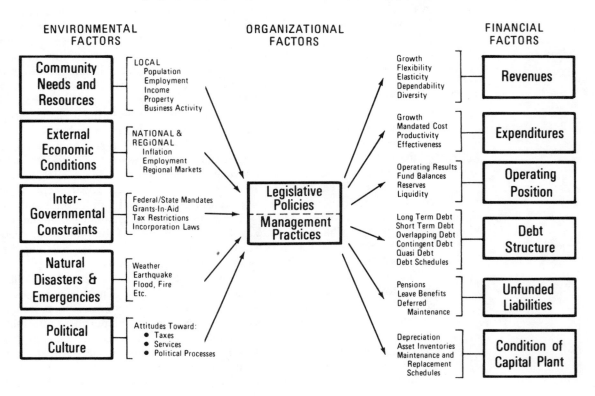

Each factor is classified as an environmental factor, an organizational factor, or a financial factor. They are closely associated and derived from the causes of financial problems listed earlier. Taken together, they represent an inventory of considerations and can be used as a guide to organize and assemble the varied and elusive issues that must be considered when financial condition is being evaluated.

Figure 12–1 arranges the factors as if they were inputs to and outputs from each other. This type of relationship is not the only one that exists. For example, many factors at times feed back into themselves and other factors. In addition, the arrangement of the factors suggests that there is a clear cause-and-effect relationship between the environmental factors and financial factors, although this is not always true. The relationships shown here, however, are the primary ones and will be the focus for this system.

In short, the environmental factors representing the external influences on a local government are filtered through a set of organizational factors. The result is a series of financial factors that describe the internal financial structure of the governmental unit. Each factor is discussed individually in this chapter. The following discussion considers them in their broad context and discusses only the groups of three factors.

The environmental factors affect a local government in two ways. First, they create demands. For example, a population increase may force the community to add police, and the acceptance of a new grant may require new audit procedures. Second, the environmental factors provide resources. For example, the increase in population that created the need for additional police services also increases community wealth and tax revenues. The new grant that required new audit procedures also provides funds to build a new city hall.

One way or another, environmental factors create demands, provide resources, establish limits, or do all three. Underlying an analysis of the effect environmental factors have on financial condition is the question of whether they provide enough resources to pay for the demands they make.

The organizational factors are the responses the government makes to changes in the environmental factors. In theory, any government can remain in good financial condition if it makes the proper organizational response to adverse conditions. It may reduce services, increase efficiency, raise taxes, or take some other appropriate action. This assumes that public officials have enough notice of the problem, understand its nature and magnitude, know what to do, and are willing to do it.

These are optimistic assumptions, especially in light of the political constraints, the deficiencies in the state of the art, and the limitations in municipal accounting as discussed earlier.

The question to consider in an analysis of the effects the organizational factors have on financial condition is whether the legislative policies and management practices of the local government provide the opportunity to make the appropriate response to changes in the environment.

The financial factors reflect the condition of the government's internal finances. In some respects they are a result of the influence of the environmental and organizational factors. If the environment makes greater demands than resources provided and if the organization is not effective in making a balancing response, the financial factors would eventually show signs of cash, budgetary, or long-range insolvency. In this respect the financial factors are where untreated problems will eventually become visible. In analyzing the effect financial factors have on financial condition, the question of whether the governmental unit is paying the full cost of operating without postponing costs to a future period (when revenues may not be available) is of major importance.

The financial condition indicators The indicators are the primary tools of the system. They represent a way to quantify changes in the factors discussed above. Figure 12–2 shows the thirty-six indicators along with the factors with which they are associated. Next to each indicator is an arrow pointing either up or down. These arrows should be read as "increasing" or "decreasing." If a city finds that an indicator is moving in the direction shown, it should be considered a potential problem requiring further analysis.

Indicators are shown for only seven of the twelve factors. This is for two reasons. First, not all the factors are quantifiable in a meaningful management sense, so some, such as Political Culture, and Natural Disasters and Emergencies, show no indicators. Second, some indicators apply to more than one factor but are shown in only one place. For example, Percentage of Intergovernmental Revenues, shown under Revenues, could also be considered an indicator under Intergovernmental Constraints, insofar as it measures the dependence a local government may be developing on grant revenues. Likewise, Operating Deficits, shown under Operating Position, could be considered an indicator under Legislative Policies and Management Practices. The indicators have been grouped under the factors into which they fit most logically or conveniently.

Conclusion

Many aspects of financial condition cannot be measured explicitly, but there is much that can be done. By quantifying the thirty-six indicators and plotting them over a period of at least five years, local government officials may begin to monitor their government's financial performance. They can observe such things as increases in unfunded liabilities, decreases in business activity, and decreases in property tax collection rates. They can carefully watch the liquidity position,

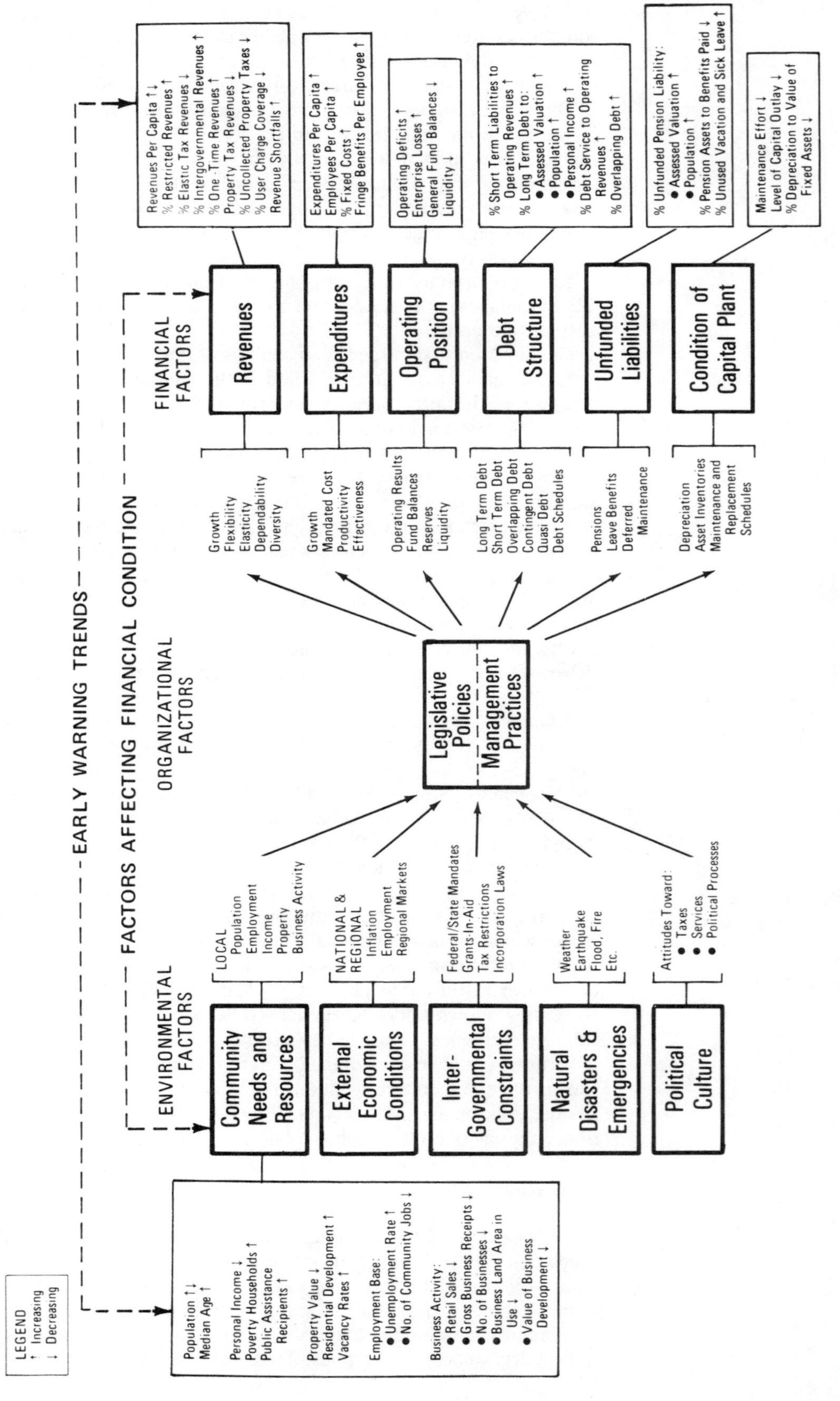

Figure 12–2 Financial Trend Monitoring System showing 12 financial condition factors, definitional and descriptive elements, and 36 financial indicators.

— — — — EARLY WARNING TRENDS — — — — FACTORS AFFECTING FINANCIAL CONDITION — — —

LEGEND
↑ Increasing
↓ Decreasing

FINANCIAL FACTORS

Revenues
Revenues Per Capita ↑↓
% Restricted Revenues ↑
% Elastic Tax Revenues ↓
% Intergovernmental Revenues ↑
% One-Time Revenues ↑
Property Tax Revenues ↓
% Uncollected Property Taxes ↓
% User Charge Coverage ↓
Revenue Shortfalls ↑

Growth
Flexibility
Elasticity
Dependability
Diversity

Expenditures
Expenditures Per Capita ↑
Employees Per Capita ↑
% Fixed Costs ↑
Fringe Benefits Per Employee ↑

Growth
Mandated Cost
Productivity
Effectiveness

Operating Position
Operating Deficits ↑
Enterprise Losses ↑
General Fund Balances ↓
Liquidity ↓

Operating Results
Fund Balances
Reserves
Liquidity

Debt Structure
% Short Term Liabilities to Operating Revenues ↑
% Long Term Debt to:
• Assessed Valuation ↑
• Population ↑
• Personal Income ↑
% Debt Service to Operating Revenues ↑
% Overlapping Debt ↑

Long Term Debt
Short Term Debt
Overlapping Debt
Contingent Debt
Quasi Debt
Debt Schedules

Unfunded Liabilities
% Unfunded Pension Liability:
• Assessed Valuation ↑
• Population ↑
% Pension Assets to Benefits Paid ↓
% Unused Vacation and Sick Leave ↑

Pensions
Leave Benefits
Deferred Maintenance

Condition of Capital Plant
Maintenance Effort ↓
Level of Capital Outlay ↓
% Depreciation to Value of Fixed Assets ↓

Depreciation
Asset Inventories
Maintenance and Replacement Schedules

Legislative Policies Management Practices

ORGANIZATIONAL FACTORS

ENVIRONMENTAL FACTORS

Community Needs and Resources
LOCAL
Population
Employment
Income
Property
Business Activity

Population ↑↓
Median Age ↑
Personal Income ↑
Poverty Households ↑
Public Assistance Recipients ↑
Property Value ↓
Residential Development ↑
Vacancy Rates ↑
Employment Base:
• Unemployment Rate ↑
• No. of Community Jobs ↓
Business Activity:
• Retail Sales ↓
• Gross Business Receipts ↓
• No. of Businesses ↓
• Business Land Area in Use ↓
• Value of Business Development ↓

External Economic Conditions
NATIONAL & REGIONAL
Inflation
Employment
Regional Markets

Inter-Governmental Constraints
Federal/State Mandates
Grants-In-Aid
Tax Restrictions
Incorporation Laws

Natural Disasters & Emergencies
Weather
Earthquake
Flood, Fire
Etc.

Political Culture
Attitudes Toward:
• Taxes
• Services
• Political Processes

calculate the effect of postponing capital facility maintenance, identify an increasing dependence on external revenues, or anticipate the effects of previously hidden budget deficits.

The use of these indicators will not provide answers to why a problem is occurring or what the appropriate solution is, but it may provide the opportunity to make an informed managerial response.

The financial condition factors

This section of Chapter 12 briefly describes each of the twelve financial condition factors and shows the applicability of the thirty-six financial indicators to these factors. The financial indicators, grouped by financial factors, are shown in Figure 12–3.

Figure 12–3   Financial Trend Monitoring System showing
36 financial indicators grouped by 7 financial condition factors.

Financial condition factor	Financial indicator
Revenues	1 Revenues per capita 2 Restricted revenues 3 Intergovernmental revenues 4 Elastic tax revenues 5 One-time revenues 6 Property tax revenues 7 Uncollected property taxes 8 User charge coverage 9 Revenue shortfalls
Expenditures	10 Expenditures per capita 11 Employees per capita 12 Fixed costs 13 Fringe benefits
Operating position	14 Operating deficits 15 Enterprise losses 16 General fund balances 17 Liquidity
Debt structure	18 Current liabilities 19 Long-term debt 20 Debt service 21 Overlapping debt
Unfunded liabilities	22 Unfunded pension liability 23 Pension assets 24 Accumulated employee leave liability
Condition of capital plant	25 Maintenance effort 26 Level of capital outlay 27 Depreciation
Community needs and resources	28 Population 29 Median age 30 Personal income 31 Poverty households or public assistance recipients 32 Property value 33 Residential development 34 Vacancy rates 35 Employment base 36 Business activity

Revenues

Revenues determine the capacity of a local government to provide services. Important issues to consider are growth, diversity, reliability, flexibility, and administration. Under ideal conditions, revenues would be growing at a rate equal to or greater than the combined effects of inflation and expenditure pressures. They would be sufficiently flexible (free from spending restrictions) to allow necessary adjustments to changing conditions. They would be balanced between elastic and inelastic with respect to economic base and inflation—that is, some would grow with the economic base and with inflation, and others would remain relatively constant.[7] They would be diversified by source to reduce overdependence on residential, commercial, or industrial land uses, or on such external funding sources as federal grants or discretionary state aid. User fees would be reevaluated regularly to cover the full costs of services.

Analyzing a revenue structure will help to identify the following types of problems:

Deterioration in revenue base

Internal procedures or legislative policies that may adversely affect revenue yields

Overdependence on obsolete or external revenue sources

User fees that do not cover the cost of services

Changes in tax burden

Lack of cost controls and poor revenue estimating practices

Inefficiency in the collection and administration of revenues.

Changes in revenues can be monitored by using the indicators listed below. (The following indicators are numbered to correspond to the numbering in Figure 12–3.)

1. Revenues per capita
2. Restricted revenues
3. Intergovernmental revenues
4. Elastic tax revenues
5. One-time revenues
6. Property tax revenues
7. Uncollected property taxes
8. User charge coverage
9. Revenue shortfalls.

Expenditures

Expenditures are an estimate of local government service output. Generally, the more a government spends in constant dollars, the more service it provides. This reasoning does not take into account how effective the services are or how efficiently they are delivered. The first issue to consider to determine whether a local government is living within its revenues is expenditure growth rate.

Because most local governments are required to have a balanced budget, it is not likely that expenditure growth would exceed revenue growth. Nevertheless, there are a number of subtle ways for a municipality to balance its annual budget and create a long-range imbalance in which expenditure outlays and commitments grow faster than revenues. Some of the more common ways are to use bond proceeds for operations, siphon small amounts from intergovernmental grants, borrow, or use reserves. Another way is to defer maintenance on streets, buildings, and other capital stock. A local government also may defer funding of a future liability (e.g., a pension plan). In each of these cases, the annual budget remains balanced, but the long-range budget develops a deficit. Although long-range deficits can be funded through windfalls (e.g., federal grants) or surges in revenue due to inflation, there is a risk in allowing deficits to develop.

A second issue to consider is the level of mandatory or "fixed" costs. This is also referred to as expenditure flexibility. It is a measure of how much freedom a local government has to adjust its service levels to changing economic, political, and social conditions. A city, county, or borough with a growing percentage of mandatory costs will be proportionately less able to make adjustments. As the percentage of debt service, matching requirements, pension benefits, state and federal mandates, contractual agreements, and commitments to existing capital plant increases, the flexibility of spending decisions decreases.

Ideally, a municipality will have an expenditure growth rate that does not exceed its revenue growth rate. It also will have maximum spending flexibility to adjust to changing conditions.

Analyzing a local government expenditure profile will help identify the following types of problems:

Excessive growth of overall expenditures as compared to revenue growth or growth in community wealth (personal and business income)

An undesirable increase in fixed costs

Ineffective budgetary controls

A decline in personnel productivity

Excessive growth in programs which create future expenditure liabilities.

Changes in expenditures can be monitored by using the indicators listed below.

10. Expenditures per capita
11. Employees per capita
12. Fixed costs
13. Fringe benefits.

Operating position

Operating position refers to the ability of a local government to balance its budget on a *current* basis, maintain reserves for emergencies, and maintain sufficient cash to pay its bills on a timely basis.

Balancing the current budget During a typical year a local government will usually generate either an operating surplus or an operating deficit. An operating surplus develops when current revenues exceed current expenditures. An operating deficit develops when the reverse occurs. In rare instances, revenues and expenditures may balance exactly. An operating surplus or deficit may be created intentionally as a result of a conscious policy decision. It also may be created unintentionally, because it is difficult to predict precisely revenues and expenditures. When deficits occur they are funded usually from accumulated fund balances; when surpluses occur they are dedicated usually to building prior years' fund balances or to funding future years' operations.

Reserves Reserves are built through the accumulation of operating surpluses. They are maintained for the purpose of providing a financial cushion in the event of a loss of a revenue source; an economic downturn; an unanticipated expenditure demand due to natural disasters, insurance loss and the like; the need for large-scale capital expenditures or other non-recurring expenses; or an uneven cash flow.

Reserves may be budgeted in a contingency account or carried as a part of one or more fund balances. They can be highly visible in the financial statements or buried in balance sheets and operating statement transactions. If carried as an unappropriated part of fund balance, the resources may never appear in a municipal budget—nor be discussed during budget deliberations.

Liquidity   Liquidity refers to the flow of cash in and out of the government treasury. Cities often receive their revenues in large installments at infrequent intervals during the year. If revenues are received before they need to be spent, the city will have a positive liquidity or cash flow position. It is advantageous to a city to have some excess liquidity or "cash reserves" as a cushion in the event of an unexpected delay in receipt of revenues, an unexpected decline or loss of a revenue source, or an unanticipated large expenditure. For whatever reason, if a city has a negative cash flow and has no cash reserves, it must borrow or put off paying its bills.

An analysis of operating position can help identify the following situations:

Emergence of operating deficits

Decline in reserves

Decline in liquidity

Ineffective revenue forecasting techniques

Ineffective budgetary controls

Inefficiencies in management of enterprise operations.

Changes in operating position can be monitored by using the indicators below.

14. Operating deficits
15. Enterprise losses
16. General fund balances
17. Liquidity.

Debt structure

Debt structure is important to analyze because debt is an explicit expenditure obligation which must be satisfied when due. Debt is an effective way to finance capital improvements and to even out short-term revenue flows, but its misuse can cause serious financial problems. Even temporary inability to repay can result in loss of credit rating, increased cost of future borrowing, and loss of autonomy to state and other regulatory bodies.

Cities usually use short-term debt to even out cash flows. At times they may find they are unable to repay short-term debt during the year in which it was borrowed because of revenue shortfalls or overexpenditures. In this event, they may choose to repay the loan and then reborrow the money. In effect the original loan is repaid from the proceeds of the new loan. This is called "rolling over" the debt and has the net effect of turning short-term debt into long-term debt. If this continues over a number of years and the amount of outstanding debt increases each year, it is a sign that the debt is being used to finance operating deficits—a sure indication of problems.

The most common forms of long-term debt are general obligation, assessment, and revenue bonds. Even when these types of debts are used exclusively for capital projects, local governments need to be careful that their outstanding debt does not exceed their ability to repay as measured by the wealth of the community in the form of property value or personal and business income. Another way to evaluate ability to repay is to consider the amount of principal and interest or "debt service" that the municipality is obligated to repay each year. Also to be considered are "overlapping debt" and debt of other jurisdictions against which the local government has pledged its "full faith and credit."

Under the most favorable circumstances, debt would be proportionate in size and growth to the tax base of the local government, would not extend past the useful life of the facilities which it finances, would not be used to balance the operating budget, would not require repayment schedules which would put excessive burdens on operating expenditures, and would not be so high as to jeopardize a locality's credit rating.

An examination of a debt structure can reveal:

Inadequacies in cash management procedures

Inadequacies in expenditure controls

Increasing reliance on long-term debt

Decreases in expenditure flexibility due to increased fixed costs in the form of debt service

Use of short-term debt to finance current operations

Existence of sudden large increases or decreases in future debt service

The amount of additional debt that the community can absorb.

Changes in debt structure can be monitored by using the indicators shown below.

18. Current liabilities
19. Long-term debt
20. Debt service
21. Overlapping debt.

Unfunded liabilities

An unfunded liability is one that is incurred during the current or a prior year but that does not have to be paid until a future year, and for which reserves have not been set aside. It is similar to debt in that it represents a legal commitment to pay some time in the future. Due to their potential magnitude, if these types of obligations are permitted to grow over a long period of time, they can have a substantial effect on a locality's financial condition. There are two types of unfunded liabilities which are considered here: pension liabilities and employee leave liabilities.

Both have significant potential because (1) they do not appear in the ordinary financial records in a way that makes it easy to assess their impact; and (2) they build up gradually over time, so it is easy not to notice them until a severe problem has developed.

An analysis of a local government's unfunded liabilities can answer the following questions:

Is the locality's pension liability increasing?

How fast is it growing?

How much is unfunded?

Are pension contributions, pension system assets, and investment earnings keeping pace with the growth in benefits?

Is the amount of unused vacation and sick leave per employee increasing?

Are policies for payment of unused vacation and sick leave realistic compared to the locality's ability to pay?

Changes in unfunded liabilities can be monitored using the indicators listed.

22. Unfunded pension liability
23. Pension assets
24. Accumulated employee leave liability.

Condition of capital plant

The bulk of a municipality's wealth is invested in its physical assets or capital plant—its streets, buildings, utility networks, and equipment. If these assets are not well maintained, or if they are allowed to become obsolete, the result is often a decrease in the usefulness of the assets, an increase in the cost of maintaining and replacing them, and a decrease in the attractiveness of the area as a place to live or do business.

Cities often defer maintenance and replacement because it is a relatively painless way to reduce expenditures and ease financial strain. If deferral is continued, however, it can create serious problems which become exaggerated because of the huge sums of money invested in the facilities. Some of the problems associated with continued deferred maintenance are:

The creation of safety hazards and other liability exposures that may result, for example, from a potholed street

A reduction in the residential and business value of the area as the result of, for example, neighborhoods with broken curbs, cracked sidewalks, damaged street signs, and unmowed medians

A decrease in the efficiency of equipment, for example, from an obsolete truck that spends more time in the garage than on the street

An increase in the cost of bringing the facility up to acceptable levels as would occur if the capping of a street were delayed so long that the street had to be reconstructed completely

The potential for creating a huge unfunded liability in the form of a backlog in maintenance that may result during accelerated deterioration.

The condition of capital plant is especially difficult to monitor because few local governments maintain comprehensive records of their fixed assets outside of their enterprise funds. No state requires its municipalities to maintain accounting records of fixed assets. Despite these difficulties, changes in the condition of capital plant can be monitored to a limited extent through the use of the indicators listed below.

25. Maintenance effort
26. Level of capital outlay
27. Depreciation.

Community needs and resources

Community needs and resources encompass the economic and demographic characteristics of population, employment, personal income, property value, and business activity. This is an umbrella category that treats "tax base" and "economic and demographic characteristics" as different sides of the same coin. On one hand, these describe a community's wealth and its ability to generate revenues (i.e., the level of personal, commercial, and industrial income). On the other hand, they constitute the demands that the community will make on its government (e.g., public safety, capital improvements, and social services).

Of particular importance is the fact that community needs and resources are all closely interrelated and affect each other in a continuous cycle of cause and effect. Increases in population cause an increase in business activity, which creates additional jobs and increases the level of retail sales. A loss of jobs causes people to leave the community to look for new jobs, the result of which is a decrease in the level of retail sales and a decrease in the demand for homes. The decrease in the demand for homes causes housing prices to fall and results in a decrease of property tax revenues. These are only some of the possible scenarios; there are countless others.

In addition, changes in these characteristics tend to be cumulative. On the down side, for example, a decrease in population lowers the demand for housing and causes a corresponding decline in the market value of housing. This, in turn, reduces the revenues generated by property tax. Further, the initial population decline has a negative effect on retail sales and personal income; city revenues drop even further. The government, however, cannot always balance the revenue loss with a proportionate reduction in expenditures. Fixed costs in its expenditure structure remain regardless of population loss or decline in business activity. In fact, it may be forced to raise taxes to make up for the lost revenues, a move that places a heavier burden on the remaining population. As economic conditions decline and as taxes rise, the community becomes a less attractive place to live and the population may decline even further. The cycle continues.[8]

These characteristics are the most difficult to formulate into indicators because the data are not easy to gather. The eleven indicators shown at the end of this section represent only those for which reasonable data are available. Even so, some local governments will have difficulty gathering some of the information.[9]

In addition to analyzing these indicators, a local government also may want to look at such subjective issues as its economic geography, locational advantages, and land-use characteristics, especially as they relate to the locality's ability to generate revenue. Also important are its plans and potential for future development. The diversification of the commercial and industrial base should be considered for its revenue-generating ability, employment-generating ability, vulnerability to economic cycles, and relationships to the larger economic region. An important issue in terms of the economic region is the balance between the community's exports and imports. Also to be considered are the occupational characteristics, the skill and educational levels of the population, the age and condition of its housing, and the prognosis for new construction and redevelopment. This type of information is difficult to formulate in precise mathematical indicators, but the information is useful in evaluating financial condition.

An examination of local economic and demographic characteristics can identify the following types of situations:

A decline in the tax base in terms of population, property values, employment, or business activity

A need to shift public service priorities because of a change in the density, age, income, or type of physical development in the community

A need to shift public policies because of a loss in competitive advantage of the locality's businesses to surrounding communities or because of a surge in inflation or other changes in national or regional economic conditions.

Changes in economic and demographic characteristics can be monitored by using the indicators shown below.

28. Population
29. Median age

30. Personal income
31. Poverty households or public assistance recipients
32. Property value
33. Residential development
34. Vacancy rates
35. Employment base
36. Business activity.

External economic conditions[10]

External economic conditions include such things as trends in inflation, employment, economic wealth, and business activity. By and large, these conditions are beyond the control of a local government, and usually local governments can only react to them. The best tool available for adjusting to changes in external economic conditions is anticipation.

In the long term, this means building a local economic base that is protected from sudden downturns in the business cycle but that can take advantage of upturns. This task is easy to prescribe, but difficult to practice. It requires enough capital spending and service delivery to encourage business owners to stay and expand. It requires a stable, revenue-producing commercial and industrial community with markets that will not diminish during national recessions. Likewise, it requires careful use of land-use and taxing policies. Taxes should be low enough to prohibit other communities from drawing business away, and land-use policies need to be permissive enough to permit businesses to adapt to changing conditions.

The prescription also requires enough public services to meet the needs of the business community and to create an economically stable residential community. Finally, it requires the proximity of labor and such resources as rivers, forests, mineral deposits, and business markets.

In the short term, a local government is much more immediately vulnerable to changes in economic conditions than it is in the long term. Thus, it must be prepared to make dramatic and often painful adjustments. The way these adjustments are made will depend on such factors as:

The composition of the local government's tax base and its sensitivity to the external economy

The structure of its tax rates and its ability to maintain revenue yields in the face of economic downturns

The level of revenues from intergovernmental sources

The mix of services it is required by law or practice to provide

The level of fixed costs and the concurrent ability to adjust spending levels downward in the face of economic downturns

The flexibility and willingness of public officials to make appropriate budget decisions during economic change.

External economic conditions and their impacts are hard to measure at the local level because of lack of data and deficiencies in the state of the art. Most of the techniques currently used are costly to implement and require expertise not usually available to the average local government. With the exception of providing directions for making inflation adjustments for some of the thirty-six indicators, the FTMS presents no indicators for explicitly measuring external economic conditions at the local level. However, many of the indicators presented under the factor Community Needs and Resources are closely related to the issues that affect external economic conditions, especially those indicators relating to employment, business activity, population, and other regional concerns.

Intergovernmental constraints[11]

By virtue of state and federal constitutions, local governments are "creatures" of the state in which they are incorporated. Even in states where they can incorporate by charter, the state often dictates the form of charter. In addition to incorporation laws, local governments are affected by a host of other intergovernmental constraints ranging from cooperative, inter-local agreements to restrictions mandated by the federal government. These constraints can be classified as relating to local government structure, local government service responsibilities, financing powers, and intergovernmental mandates.

Local governments have in recent years expanded their powers by means of expanded service delivery and expanded influence with the state and federal governments, but the controls placed on local governments by these and other agencies have also increased. Intergovernmental service mandates, annexation laws, revenue and spending limitations, reporting requirements, and "tag-along" restrictions of federal funds have created situations in which local governments find themselves with less flexibility.

Because of the highly subjective nature of intergovernmental constraints, only a few indicators can be developed to measure them. They include measures relating to tax or debt ceilings as established by law, the level of intergovernmental revenues, the level of expenditures for mandated programs, and the level of local "matching funds" used to support grants. For the purpose of measuring financial condition, the above indicators under the factors for Revenues, Expenditures, and Debt Structure may be used.

Natural disasters and emergencies

Natural disasters include fire, flood, blizzards, tornadoes, and similar events which require significant expenditure outlays as a response. To the extent that they can be anticipated, natural disasters can be budgeted for and, therefore, have less impact on financial condition. When they occur unexpectedly and require large unplanned expenditures, their impact can be significant. Much of the burden can be absorbed by federal and other intergovernmental assistance, but the local government still may have to bear much of it.

Natural disasters and emergencies cause harm in several ways. First, they may destroy municipal equipment and property. Second, their aftermath may require the locality to provide emergency services in police, fire, and general welfare. Third, the community at large may need help to replace lost private property. Fourth, the natural disaster may undermine the health of the local business community. If this results in decreased business activity and employment, local government revenues may drop.

In addition to receiving advance notice of and preparing physically for natural disasters, a local government can also try to maintain financial reserves to lessen the immediate impact and to provide flexibility in responding to the situation.

Political culture[12]

Of all the factors that affect financial condition, political culture is perhaps the most difficult to analyze, explain, and predict. This is because it is influenced by the interaction of individual people and their varying economic, ethnic, and religious backgrounds.

Political culture is important to consider because it influences local attitudes toward taxes and services. This, in turn, affects the legislative body of the local government.

In addition to social and demographic characteristics, other issues to be considered are:

The manner of political representation

The extent of citizen participation

The structure of the government organization

The process of decision making

The content of political issues

The age, size, and density of the community

The character of the geographic region.

Because of the highly subjective nature of political culture, no indicators for measuring it are presented.

Legislative policies and management practices

Conventional wisdom holds that management practices and legislative policies are the most critical aspects affecting financial condition. Theoretically, a local government can adjust to adverse or beneficial environmental changes by changing its pattern of expenditures. That is, if the environment provides less revenues, the local government can reduce its service levels. Underlying this belief are the assumptions that the governmental unit will have enough notice of problems, that it has the ability to understand the nature and extent of the problem, that it knows what to do, and that it is willing to do it. In light of normal political constraints, deficiencies in the state of the art, and the limitations in municipal accounting as discussed above, the aforementioned assumptions are optimistic. Nevertheless, practices and policies are the factors over which a local government does have control. It is through them that a government can exert leverage when wrestling with financial problems.

A recent study by the Advisory Commission on Intergovernmental Relations (ACIR) found that management practices and policies are extremely important and that "unsound financial management stands out as one of the most important potential causes of financial emergencies in local governments."[13] This study defines "financial emergency" as a situation in which a municipality can no longer provide existing levels of services because it cannot meet payrolls, pay current bills, pay money due other government agencies, or pay debt service on bonds and maturing short-term notes. This situation may arise because the municipality lacks either cash or appropriation authority.

The ACIR study found that changes in the environment—such as a decrease in the tax base or increases in expenditure requirements—contributed to emergencies. But the *management practices and legislative policies* of the local government were what permitted small operating problems to grow until they reached emergency proportions. Nearly every locality in the study that had faced an emergency had maintained an excess of expenditures over revenues, and usually over a number of years.

For example, one city in Michigan used police and fire employee pension contributions for general city purposes, collected property taxes in advance of the year due, and deferred its obligations and bills for eight years. Finally, the city could not pay its employees, its pensions, or its creditors. It had to turn to the state for help in solving its financial problems.

Another city in Pennsylvania piled up a huge operating deficit by using cash from restricted funds to cover a cash deficit in the general fund. Many other cities got into trouble when they used short-term debt (usually tax-anticipation notes) to borrow more than they could repay the next year.

Credit rating firms evaluate the financial condition of cities for the purpose of providing bond ratings. Management practices and legislative policies are a very important consideration.[14] In deciding what rating to give local government bonds, these firms look closely at how the local government administers its money. For example, they assess the "professionalism" of its management by looking at the quality of financial reporting and capital planning,[15] and whether the city uses any financial gimmickry.[16] They also consider how responsive the legislative body is by looking at whether elected officials have been willing to raise tax rates when necessary.[17]

In short, sound financial practices and policies enable a local government to maintain good financial condition and to avoid financial emergencies.

The balance of this chapter highlights the importance of the factor Legislative Policies and Management Practices by reviewing nine practices commonly used by local governments, all of which can jeopardize a local government's financial health.

Practices that can jeopardize financial health

A good accounting and reporting system (see Chapter 18) is the essential ingredient for sound management practices. Without good numbers, a local government cannot be sure whether any but the most obvious problems exist and how big those problems are.

Accounting and reporting, however, are only part of the picture. Even if it has a satisfactory accounting and reporting system, a local government may be relying on practices and policies that can jeopardize its financial condition if used for too long. These dangerous practices fall into three categories:

Practices that allow a local government to balance its budget by repeatedly using one-time sources of revenues (e.g., the reserves or proceeds from assets sold in previous years)

Practices that allow a local government to defer a large amount of current costs to the future (e.g., postponing expenditures for maintenance and replacement of capital assets or deferring pension liabilities)

Practices that allow a local government to ignore the long-range or full-life costs of a liability (e.g., deciding to build or purchase a capital asset without calculating the full-life costs of owning, operating, and maintaining that asset).

Most local governments recognize the problems inherent in the practices noted, and in normal circumstances would not engage in them. In times of stress caused by financial problems or political pressures, however, a locality may find itself tempted or even forced to use them.

As an interim strategy, these practices can give the local government the time it needs to find long-range solutions to its financial troubles or to resolve temporary problems. For example, deferring maintenance costs for one year may allow the government to institute new cost-cutting programs or to adjust levels in a service. But using these practices and policies all of the time can harm the financial condition of a local government in three ways.

First, they can *create* problems. A community may have few financial problems, but if it does not take into account the full-life costs of a new program or project, it may commit itself to future liabilities that cannot be met. This can happen, for example, when additional employee fringe benefits are granted without costing them out in dollars and projecting their impact on future budgets.

Similarly, a local government may accept a grant without considering how local resources will replace grant dollars when the grant runs out.

Second, these practices may *compound* existing problems. For example, when a local government defers a current expenditure by postponing maintenance on capital equipment, effectiveness and efficiency may go down and service delivery costs may go up. Moreover, the equipment may deteriorate to the point where it becomes more expensive to repair than to maintain regularly.

Finally, these practices may *delay recognition* of existing problems. This is the most dangerous result, because it may permit problems to persist and grow to serious proportions. If this occurs, the steps required to solve the problem may be much more costly and difficult than if the problem had been dealt with early. For example, if over several years a local government does not fund accrued pension liabilities, pension costs eventually can become an extremely large percentage of fixed costs at a time when revenues are no longer growing or are decreasing. This can force an ill-timed and disruptive reduction in services.

It is not always easy to perceive how or to what extent these practices may be jeopardizing a city's financial health. To evaluate whether or not the use of such practices may be harming your city's ability to keep in good financial condition, read the description of the practices and policies that follows. *After* reviewing the practices and policies, ask the questions listed below. These questions are patterned after the ones used by credit rating firms when they evaluate the financial health of a local government.

1.   Has the practice been used for two or more consecutive years during the last five years, or for at least three of the last five years?
2.   Has more than one practice been used in any one of the last three years? Is there a pattern of use of these practices?
3.   Have any plans been made to deal with problems created or compounded by use of the practice? Does the local government have the long-term financial resources to respond to these problems?

Practices that sustain an operating deficit

An operating deficit occurs when current expenditures exceed current revenues. This may occur even though the annual budget is balanced because a balanced budget can be achieved by using one-time sources of revenues (e.g., a surplus from a previous year or proceeds from the sale of an asset) to supplement current revenues.

An operating deficit in any one year may not be cause for concern, but frequent and increasing deficits can be a warning signal. If an operating deficit is allowed to continue or grow, three questions should be asked: Is the local government continuing a level of services and expenditures that it may not be able to afford in the long run? Is the local government ignoring the underlying cause of the deficit (e.g., a declining revenue base or decreased productivity)? Is the problem compounding itself?

Local government officials may have trouble spotting an operating deficit because most municipal accounting systems do not provide information that makes the existence of an operating deficit obvious. The lack of cost accounting or full accrual of revenues and expenditure denies a local government precise information on its operating position. Nevertheless, there are telltale signs that point to the existence of an operating deficit. These signs are the repeated use of the following practices:

Using reserves (fund balances) from prior years

Using short-term borrowing

Using internal borrowing

Selling assets

Using accounting gimmickry.

Continual use of reserves Surpluses from prior years are a "cushion" for most local governments. They allow the locality to meet current cash flow requirements, temporary shortfalls in revenues, or unexpected expenditure demands without suddenly adjusting tax rates or cutting expenditures during the budget year. Also, fund balances can help municipalities avoid short-term borrowing, thereby saving interest costs (although the municipality also forgoes the opportunity to earn interest on a fund balance).

If reserves from prior years are consistently declining over several years, this is one indication that the governmental unit may be sustaining an operating deficit. Relying on reserves to sustain the deficit can be damaging to the unit because it is left with fewer resources to face a financial emergency, and reliance on reserves may affect the unit's credit rating when credit rating firms examine its history of fund balances.

Continual use of short-term borrowing In short-term borrowing, the local government incurs a debt that it must pay back within one year. When revenues and surpluses do not provide enough cash to meet expenditures during the fiscal year, tax anticipation notes (TANs) can be issued to obtain cash during this period. When revenues begin to exceed cash requirements, these notes are redeemed. Similarly, bond anticipation notes (BANs) can be issued in anticipation of bond revenues.

Lending institutions and the community generally regard such borrowing as an acceptable fiscal procedure—so long as it is temporary in nature and expected revenue flows are clearly large enough to repay amounts borrowed within the fiscal year. At times, however, a community may find itself unable to repay short-term borrowing within this time period because of revenue shortfalls or overexpenditures. In this event, it may choose to repay the loan and then reborrow the money, or simply pay only the interest on the loan and not the principal. This practice is called "rolling over" short-term debt. In effect, it can turn short-term debt into long-term debt. Several analysts spot local governments with financial troubles by looking at the level of short-term debt outstanding at the end of the fiscal year as a percentage of revenues.[18] Rolling over short-term debt can create several problems for a local government:

The local government must pay added interest cost for the time the debt remains outstanding.

The credit rating of the local government may be affected because investors and bond rating firms look closely at short-term debt when assessing the investment worthiness of a municipality.

Unless revenues are increasing or the debt is rolled over yet another year, the local government is forced to reduce service levels in the next fiscal year to pay off the debt.

Continual use of internal borrowing Internal borrowing occurs when one fund runs out of money and the municipality "borrows" from other funds, rather than from an outside source. Municipal accounting is fund accounting. In a private business, the entire business is treated as a single entity. In municipal accounting, however, revenues and expenditures are recorded into different funds, each with its own balance sheet and operating statement. In this situation, money can be transferred from one fund to another.

Not all internal transfers are "borrowing." Some internal transfers occur regularly as a matter of explicit policy. For example, if an enterprise activity is generating a surplus, the surplus may be transferred periodically to the general fund to subsidize other city expenses. There is no intention of repaying the money later. Similarly, a municipality may shift money into an intragovernmental service fund to reflect the value of services provided by one department of the local government to another.

Internal "borrowing" occurs when money is transferred from funds that have been accumulating for a special purpose (e.g., a capital improvements fund or a sinking fund) with the intention of repayment at a later date.

The use of internal borrowing to meet a short-term revenue shortage can save a local government money because it is usually less expensive to borrow internally than externally. Borrowing internally also can be easier and quicker because fewer actors are involved in the process.

To use internal borrowing repeatedly, however, can create a future liability which the local government may not have the resources to meet. This can force a disruptive reduction in services or cause a problem in the fund from which the money was borrowed. For example, if money is borrowed from a capital improvement fund and cannot be repaid, improvements may have to be delayed or forgone. If money is borrowed from a self-insurance fund, the local government is risking its ability to absorb large losses from liabilities.

Selling assets　Most local governments own property or facilities that are also of value to other local governments or private interests (e.g., utilities, golf courses, and vacant parcels of land). Selling one or more of these can bring in one-time revenue to a local government. For example, the city of Cleveland sold the city sewers in 1974 to a new independent authority and used most of the proceeds for general city operating expenses that year.[19] When these one-time revenues are used for current operating expenditures instead of one-time needs, they are sustaining an operating deficit. Aside from sustaining the operating deficit, selling an asset may harm the long-range financial condition of a local government in the following ways:

It may deprive the municipality of some flexibility in service delivery capacity because it no longer has control of how the service is provided.

By selling under pressure caused by the need to raise revenues, the municipality may be forced to accept a lower price than it would have accepted otherwise for the property.

If the local government decides to reacquire the asset, it may be more expensive at a future date.

The sale of a utility or recreational facilities may make the community and citizens more dependent on others for prices and availability.

Accounting gimmickry　Finally, a local government may manipulate accounting methods to make a budget appear balanced. For example, if a payroll day fell on the last day of a fiscal year, the municipality could wait one day to record that expense, and thus make the current year's expenses appear to be smaller. This could make an end-of-year surplus look larger or a deficit appear smaller or disappear altogether.

Three commonly used accounting gimmicks are postponing current obligations to future periods; accruing revenues from a future fiscal year to the current fiscal year to make current revenues appear higher; and extending the length of the fiscal year—for example, from twelve to thirteen months—so that revenues in the thirteenth month can be counted as revenues for the current year.

Many of the local governments that have had financial problems have relied on these gimmicks to balance their budgets.[20] These gimmicks do nothing to solve the underlying problems; they only disguise them. Credit rating firms and other municipal analysts look unfavorably on such gimmicks. These gimmicks should be considered unsound practices because, even if they do not violate the word of the accounting standards and state laws regarding accounting practices, they almost always violate the intent of those laws and standards.

Practices that defer current costs

A municipality is deferring current costs when it does not meet all its expenditure needs in the current budget. Two examples of the kinds of costs that can be postponed are contributions to employee pension funds and expenditures for maintenance of streets, buildings, and equipment.

Deferring current costs has several general drawbacks for local governments:

It sustains a level of services and expenditures the municipality may not be able to afford in the long run.

It can affect a municipality's bond rating. Credit rating organizations consider unfunded liabilities to be an unfavorable sign.[21]

Because these costs do not ordinarily show up on municipal financial records, their impact may not be recognized until the problem is serious.

Two kinds of deferred costs are discussed here: deferred pension liabilities and deferred maintenance of capital assets.

Deferring pension liabilities A pension liability is a legal commitment a local government made to pay benefits to its employees at some point in the future.

There are two basic ways to fund this liability. One way is to set up a special fund and fully fund benefits as they are accrued ("full funding"). The other way is known as "pay-as-you-go" (pay-as-you-acquire). This method involves making only current pension payments from the general fund as they become due.

Many local governments choose the pay-as-you-go method because it involves less spending from the current budget. This method may seem successful as long as the money is available when needed. Deferral, however, may create a more serious problem than the problem it avoids—especially if accrued benefits are rapidly increasing while revenues are stagnant or dropping. As more employees become entitled to benefits, and as the cost of benefits grows with inflation, pension costs can become a large fixed cost to the operating budget.

Deferring maintenance expenditures The capital assets of a local government include its streets, buildings, utility networks, and equipment. If these assets are not well maintained, or if they are allowed to become obsolete, efficiency will go down, costs of maintenance and replacement will go up, and the area will become less attractive to residents and business owners.

In times of financial strain, communities often see deferred maintenance and replacement as a relatively painless short-run way to reduce expenditures. Continued deferral, however, can create serious problems because of the huge sums of money invested in capital facilities.

Practices that ignore full-life costs

A local government that fails to consider the long-range costs of a liability can jeopardize its own financial condition by building in a future imbalance between revenues and expenditures. Many municipalities do this by granting labor agreements without costing out nonsalary benefits, or by arranging to construct or purchase a capital asset without calculating the full-life costs.

Ignoring the full costs of nonsalary employee benefits Nonsalary benefits include pensions; holiday, sick, and vacation leave; and educational provisions. Local government officials have a difficult time assessing whether the locality can afford these benefits, or how much to budget for them, because the value of benefits often varies from one employee or group of employees to another. Benefits depend on such variables as occupation or length of employment. A special analysis needs to be done to translate the costs into budget dollars. If nonsalary benefits are not calculated, a local government may face the following problems:

It may not be able to accurately budget enough money for benefit costs in the current budget.

It may have trouble making long-range expenditure forecasts, and thus will be unable to prepare for increases as they occur.

It may find itself in a weak position in negotiating with labor unions because, without good information on the exact cost of a proposal, it is difficult to negotiate and make "trade-off" judgments among competing proposals.

It may not be able to predict the budget impact of increases or decreases in personnel.

Ignoring the full-life costs of capital assets   The capital assets of a local government are long-term investments. The initial costs of these assets are high, and during the capital planning and budgeting process the locality usually carefully considers how to finance the asset.

Often overlooked, however, are the long-range costs of owning and maintaining the asset—the "full-life" costs. The capital and operating budgets are developed separately, and the operating impact of owning and using the asset is not generally part of the process. These costs also may change over time, and the cost of using an older asset may be much less than the cost of using its replacement. New costs may not be considered when the asset is replaced. For example, a new building may require air conditioning, elevators for the handicapped, or other features that require more maintenance and more energy to operate.

Some disadvantages of not knowing total costs are:

The municipality may not be able to accurately budget the operating costs of the asset.

The municipality may have incomplete information when choosing which capital asset to obtain. As an example, because maintenance and ownership costs are significant for a fleet of garbage trucks, the locality may find it cheaper to contract for solid waste services.

The municipality may have trouble making long-range forecasts of expenditures.

Conclusion

This chapter has outlined the Financial Trend Monitoring System, an applied, practical approach for monitoring the financial condition of a local government through the use of financial indicators. These thirty-six indicators are organized around the framework shown in Figures 12–1, 12–2, and 12–3. The broad purposes of the FTMS are to help a city or other local government make sense of the many factors that affect its financial condition, develop quantifiable indicators, and provide a process for using the indicators to show early warning signals of trouble spots in specific areas of revenues, expenditures, and debt. In addition, a brief summary has been included on nine clearly identifiable practices that can jeopardize financial health.

1   This chapter is excerpted from: Sanford M. Groves and W. Maureen Godsey, *Evaluating Financial Condition,* 5 handbooks (Washington, D.C.: International City Management Association, 1980): Handbook 1, *Evaluating Financial Condition,* pp. 1–19, and Handbook 3, *Financial Jeopardy! Policies and Practices That Can Affect Financial Health,* pp. 2–10.

2   For a discussion and case studies of cities that have had financial problems, see: U.S., Advisory Commission on Intergovernmental Relations, *City Financial Emergencies: The Intergovernmental Dimension* (Washington, D.C.: Government Printing Office, 1973).

3   For a comprehensive review of work done to date on evaluating financial condition, see: J. Richard Aronson, *Municipal Fiscal Indicators,* Information Bulletin of the Management, Finance and Personnel Task Force of the Urban Consortium (Washington, D.C.: U.S. Department of Housing and Urban Development, 1979); and Robert Berne and Richard Schramm, "The Financial Solvency of Local Governments: A Conceptual Approach" (Report prepared for the International City Management Association, March 1978). Individual works of particular interest include: Muncipal Finance Officers Association, *Is Your City Heading for Financial Difficulty?: A Guidebook for Small Cities and Other Governmental Units* (Chicago: Municipal Finance Officers Association, 1979); Philip M. Dearborn, *Elements of Municipal Financial Analysis,* special report, parts 1–4 (Boston: First Boston Corp., 1977); George Peterson et al., *Urban Fiscal Monitoring* (Washington, D.C.: The Urban Institute, 1978); Terry N. Clark et al., *How Many New Yorks?,* Comparative Study of Community Decision-Making, report no. 72 (Chicago: University of Chicago, April 22, 1976); J. Richard Aronson and Eli Schwartz, *Determining Debt's Danger Signals,* Management Information Service Reports, vol. 8, no. 12 (Washington, D.C.: International City Management Association, December 1976).

4   See, for example: Roy W. Bahl, Alan K. Campbell, and David Greytak, *Taxes, Expenditures, and the Economic Base: Case Study of New York City* (New York: Praeger Publishers, 1974).

5   For a discussion on how credit rating firms rate local government bonds, see: Wade S. Smith, *The Appraisal of Municipal Credit Risks* (New York: Moody's Investors Service, 1979); Hugh Sherwood, *How Corporate and Municipal Debt is Rated: An Inside Look at Standard and Poor's Rating System* (New York: John Wiley & Sons, 1976); Moody's Investors Service, Inc., *Pitfalls in Issuing Municipal Bonds* (New York: Moody's Investors

Service, 1977); John E. Petersen, *The Rating Game* (New York: Twentieth Century Fund, 1974).

6   For a more in-depth discussion of some of the problems associated with current municipal accounting systems, see: Roger Mansfield, "The Financial Reporting Practices of Government: A Time for Reflection," *Public Administration Review* 39, no. 2 (March–April 1979): 157–62; and Coopers & Lybrand, *Financial Disclosure Practices of the American Cities: Closing the Communications Gap* (Boston and New York: Coopers & Lybrand, 1978).

7   In this sense, an elastic revenue is one that directly responds to changes in economic base and inflation. As economic base and inflation go up, elastic revenues would go up in roughly the same proportion; if the economic base were to shrink or inflation were to decline, revenues also would drop in proportion.

8   For a discussion of the impact population and economic decline can have on a large central city, see: George Peterson, "Finance," in *The Urban Predicament,* ed. William Gorham and Nathan Glazer (Washington, D.C.: The Urban Institute, 1976), pp. 38–58; and George Peterson, *The Economic and Fiscal Accompaniments of Population Change* (Syracuse, N.Y.: Metropolitan Studies Program, Syracuse University, 1979).

9   For example, cities with their own income or occupation tax will be able to monitor personal income easily. Those without these taxes will find the information almost impossible to get other than from their ten-year federal census unless their state makes the information available.

10 Excerpted from an unpublished report prepared for the International City Management Association by Astrid E. Merget, Associate Professor, The George Washington University, 1979.

11 Ibid.

12 Ibid.

13 U.S., Advisory Commission on Intergovernmental Relations, *City Financial Emergencies.*

14 Sherwood, *How Corporate and Municipal Debt is Rated,* p. 119.

15 Ibid., p. 9.

16 Ibid., p. 121.

17 Ibid., p. 127.

18 David T. Stanley, *Cities in Trouble* (Columbus, Ohio: Academy for Contemporary Problems, 1976), p. 7.

19 Ibid., p. 9.

20 Ibid.

21 Sherwood, *How Corporate and Municipal Debt is Rated,* p. 119.

13 Debt management

This chapter concentrates on managing the sale of long-term debt, which, if practiced poorly, can result not only in higher interest costs but also in the bankruptcy of the issuing local government. The sale of debt, particularly for smaller local governments, is not an everyday event, and most finance officers are not as familiar with the procedures for the efficient and prudent management of debt as they are with their other responsibilities.

Both the chief administrative officer and the finance officer of the local government need an overall understanding of the subjects covered in this chapter, including the types of debt, the unique characteristics of municipal bonds, the ways bonds are bid and sold, and the nature of the bond market. Those financial managers and specialists who are directly involved in municipal debt may well find it profitable to make a detailed study of the section in this chapter headed "Basis of Award," which defines and compares net interest cost (NIC) and true interest cost (TIC). State and local governments raise funds to finance their expenditures principally by taxation, by grants-in-aid from other governmental units, and by incurring short-term debt or selling bonds. The method or combination of methods used to finance an activity depends on a number of factors, including the purpose and magnitude of the expenditure, the timing of the benefits, population and income trends, the political environment, and legal constraints. On a more specific level, expenditures of state and local governments are generally classified as either *current* or *capital* depending primarily on whether the goods and services purchased are consumed in more or less than one year. Purchases of services and short-life goods are generally classified as current expenditures or operating expenses, and purchases of longer-life goods as capital expenditures.

Almost all state and local governments are prohibited by law from financing current expenditures through long-term debt instruments where payments are not levied until long after the expenditures have been made and the benefits have been received. Local governments are not supposed to incur fiscal year deficits in their current budgets, although many do borrow for periods no longer than the end of the same fiscal year in order to finance expenditures that must be made before the scheduled receipt of tax and grant revenues. These are called *tax-anticipation loans* (occasionally termed *revenue-anticipation loans)*. On the other hand, most state and local governments may finance capital expenditures by long-term debt.

Financing capital expenditures

Capital expenditures generally are defined as expenditures used to purchase the physical goods that will add to the purchaser's capital stock and that will be retained for more than one year. Public capital expenditures are typically the construction of schools, highways, utility plants, airports, housing, and office buildings. The timing of the outlays for such projects cannot be synchronized with the timing of the benefits derived. The expenditures are made over a short period of time; and the goods are consumed and the benefits received over a longer period. Who should pay for the expenditures? Should it be the residents of the community at the time the expenditure is made (*pay-as-you-acquire*), the residents of the community at the time the benefits are received (*pay-as-you-use*), or those who use and benefit directly from the services provided (*pay-as-you-use*) whether residents or not. A number of arguments are made for and against either strategy. An argument in favor of *pay-as-you-acquire* (often termed *pay-as-you-go*) is that because the choice of the expenditure is made by the current residents, the cost should not be imposed on future residents who have had no say in the decision. It is also believed that the expenditure will not restrict future borrowing for other projects, and that the interest cost of future borrowing is not increased by an increase in the amount of debt outstanding.

Proponents of *pay-as-you-use* argue that the payment of the cost (the amortization of the bonds) can be synchronized to time with the enjoyment of the benefits, and that as the number of beneficiaries using the facility increases (creating a broader tax base), the cost per capita decreases. Continued inflation is likely to bring higher per capita income; the higher per capita income, in turn, will bring another decrease in the per capita burden.

Except for smaller capital projects, governmental units generally find that the arguments for pay-as-you-use tend to outweight those for pay-as-you-acquire. The burden of pay-as-you-acquire is usually much too heavy for large capital projects to be borne. Thus, local governments prefer to finance the majority of their large capital projects through debt. Whether they can do so depends on legal and political constraints—governmental units must have statutory permission to borrow for specific purposes. A bond issue may not be floated before obtaining a legal opinion which states that the borrowing may be undertaken for the intended purpose, and that the coupon interest is exempt from federal income taxes, if the bonds are to find buyers.

Types of debt

The method by which funds are to be raised to pay the coupon and maturing amounts of the bonds (the debt service) affects the type of bond to be issued. The debt service payments may be financed by the taxpayers in the community as a whole, by the specific users of the services generated by the project, or by both. Bonds whose payments are to be financed by all taxpayers of the issuing governmental units are termed *general obligation* (GO) bonds. GO bonds are secured unconditionally by the full faith, credit, and taxing powers of the issuing government. If the taxes levied initially are insufficient to meet the debt service payments in any period, the issuer is legally obligated to either raise the tax rate or to broaden the tax base to obtain the necessary funds. Some other bonds, however, are secured by designated special taxes and only by general taxes if the special taxes are insufficient. These bonds also are considered general obligation bonds. Although the issuers of general obligation bonds are legally obligated to raise tax revenues to meet shortfalls in scheduled debt service payments, they may sometimes find that obtaining increased revenues is economically impossible or rejected by the electorate. If the scheduled debt service payments are not made in full, the bonds go into default.

Bonds whose debt service payments are to be financed by charges placed exclusively on users of the publicly provided services are termed *revenue bonds*. These charges are referred to as *user charges* and may include service charges, tolls, special taxes, admissions fees, leases, and rents. If revenues from user charges are insufficient to meet the debt service payments, the issuer generally is not legally obligated to levy taxes to avoid default. Revenue bonds are similar to bonds issued by private enterprises. Some revenue bonds, however, are hybrids, secured first by user charges and, if these are insufficient, backed by the

Debt management terminology

Coupon amount. The stipulated dollar interest amount to be paid periodically, generally semiannually, per $1,000 par value bond.

Maturing amount. The dollar principal or face (par) value of the bonds that is promised to be repaid at each maturity.

Debt service payments. The sum of all the coupon payments in a period plus the dollar amounts of any bonds scheduled to mature in the period.

Callable bonds. Bonds that may be repurchased (the call price) at the option of the issuer after a stipulated deferment period (the call date) and before maturity at no more than a stipulated price. If the called bonds are repurchased with the proceeds of other newly sold bonds, generally at a lower interest cost, the bonds are said to be *refunded.*

Pollution control bonds. Bonds sold by a special government pollution control district to finance the installation of pollution control equipment in a private

enterprise within its jurisdiction. The equipment is leased to the private enterprise and the debt service payments are financed by these proceeds.

Industrial development bonds. Bonds sold by a special government industrial district to finance plant and equipment for a private enterprise within its jurisdiction. The plant and equipment are leased to the enterprise and the debt service payments are financed by these proceeds.

Sinking fund. A fund established by bond issuers, generally required in the bond indenture, that is increased through time for the purpose of either retiring some of the outstanding bonds before their maturity or reducing the risk of default of the bonds. The fund is generally restricted to investment in liquid securities.

Spread. The difference between the underwriter's bid on a bond issue and the resale price; includes bid preparation expenses, selling commissions, underwriter's fee, management fee, and profit.

---

full faith, credit, and taxing powers of the issuing or some other governmental unit. These bonds are referred to as *indirect general obligation bonds.*

Which type of bond the issuer uses depends on a number of factors, including the nature and magnitude of the project and the legal authority and constraints of the issuer. If the benefits of the services generated by a project accrue in significant amounts to members of the community who do not use the services directly as well as to the direct users, the project is termed a *public good.* Examples of public goods are law enforcement, fire protection, schooling, and public health facilities. Because the benefits of projects that create public goods are enjoyed by almost all members of the community, the cost of the capital facility for these activities should be borne by the community as a whole. This can be achieved by the sale of general obligation bonds.

If the benefits of the project accrue almost entirely to a group of readily identifiable purchasers, the project is more a private or merit good than a public good. Examples of such goods include municipally owned electric and water systems, athletic stadiums, auditoriums, and limited access highways and bridges. For the sake of equity, the costs of these projects should be borne primarily by the users. Such projects are best financed by revenue bonds.

The dividing line between public and private goods, however, often is not clear. Many public goods provide greater benefits to some members of the community than to others, and many private goods provide some benefits to non-purchasers. Highways and bridges may be free or toll, and schools can be free or they can charge partial or full tuition. Thus the type of charge to be imposed is not always clear, and the type of bond to be issued to finance a particular project most equitably and efficiently is not always obvious.

There also are political and legal considerations that play an important part in the decision to impose a charge or issue a bond. For example, in most states, general obligation bond issues have to be approved by the voters; revenue bonds do not usually need such approval. Therefore, projects that may not have a sufficiently large political appeal may be financed by revenue bonds even though they may be principally public goods. Revenue bonds also are exempt from most of the debt ceilings applicable to general obligation bonds. As a result, revenue bonds may be favored if the issuer is close to the debt ceiling or expects to issue large amounts of general obligation bonds to finance projects with a higher priority.

On the other hand, some projects—for which revenue bond financing appears most appropriate because the users are readily identifiable as the primary bene- ficiaries—may not with reasonable user charges generate sufficient revenues to meet the debt service payments. Such projects may include municipal performing arts centers and sports arenas. These projects can be financed only by general obligation bonds or lease back bonds of a joint powers authority or by a non- profit corporation. In a more general context, GO bonds may also be preferred because the more secure backing and smaller risk of default permit them to be sold at lower interest costs than comparable revenue bonds.

Clearly, the decision to finance a particular project by general obligation or by revenue bonds is complex and involves careful analysis of economic, financial, legal, and political considerations.

Trends in municipal debt

The use of debt by state and local governments has increased rapidly in the post- World War II period. As shown in Table 13–1, $48.6 billion of new long-term debt was sold in 1978, more than twice the dollar amount in 1973 and twelve times the dollar amount in 1950. The growth rate, however, has been relatively consistent with the other major sources of municipal receipts and revenues. The sharp jump in new bond issues since 1975 reflects, in large part, a sharp increase in the refunding of outstanding issues—in particular, *advance refunding*, which is the repurchase of the bond before the issue's earliest call date—to take ad- vantage of the lower market interest rates in this period and the favorable arbitrage opportunities with respect to taxable U.S. Treasury issues. Refundings totalled $10 billion in 1977, up from less than $1 billion in 1975 and only $3 billion in 1976. (In mid-1978, the U.S. Treasury tightened its regulations against arbitrage bonds in general; this made advance refundings less profitable and their volume dropped sharply.)

Arbitrage is the practice of purchasing something in one market for immediate sale in another at a higher price—in this case, the practice of buying bonds with high interest rates and simultaneously selling tax-exempt bonds with low interest rates.

The use of short-term debt also increased sharply in this period and, in some of these years, exceeded the sale of long-term debt. The abrupt decline in short- term borrowing in 1976 reflects the withdrawal of New York City from this market. In the early and mid-1970s, New York City accounted for almost 25 percent of the total amount of short-term bonds issued in each year.

The amount of revenue bonds has increased much faster in dollar value than

Table 13–1 Trend in amounts of municipal debt sold, 1950–1978 ($ billions)

	Long-term debt			Short-term debt
Year	General obligation bonds	Revenue bonds	Total	
1950	3.1	0.6	3.7	1.6
1955	4.3	1.7	6.0	2.6
1960	5.2	2.1	7.3	4.0
1965	7.8	3.5	11.3	6.5
1970	12.1	6.1	18.2	17.9
1971	16.3	8.7	25.0	26.3
1972	14.4	9.3	23.7	25.2
1973	13.4	10.6	24.0	24.7
1974	14.1	10.2	24.3	29.0
1975	16.1	14.5	30.6	29.0
1976	18.2	17.1	35.3	21.9
1977	18.1	28.7	46.8	21.3
1978	17.9	30.7	48.6	21.6

Source: Board of Governors of the Federal Reserve System, *Federal Reserve Bulletin*; and *Municipal Finance Statistics*, published by the *Daily Bond Buyer*.

has the amount of general obligation bonds. In 1950, revenue bonds accounted for less than 20 percent of all long-term municipal bonds sold. By 1970, this percentage had increased to 33 percent and to over 60 percent by 1978. The increased sale of revenue bonds may be attributed to four primary factors:

1. The growing tendency of state and local governments to use debt to finance facilities that traditionally are not considered to be pure public goods
2. The political pressures that have made it more difficult to obtain a favorable vote to issue general obligation bonds
3. The legal restrictions on general tax increases
4. The brief fall in interest rates after 1974 encouraged an increase in the advance refunding of outstanding issues (primarily revenue issues), which originally sold at higher interest rates.

Table 13–2 shows how municipal bonds are employed. Between 1968 and 1977 the proportion of bonds sold to finance school and highway construction declined sharply, whereas the proportion for gas and electric, hospitals, and pollution control increased equally sharply. These changes reflect the extensive use of revenue bond financing. Schools and highways are public goods for which user charges are more difficult to apply. However, utilities, hospitals, and pollution control projects readily lend themselves to user charges and financing by revenue bonds. The increase in bonds to finance pollution control projects offset almost all of the decline in industrial development bonds. Both are generally financed by revenue bonds.

Unique aspects of municipal bonds

Municipal bonds are different from bonds issued by other issuers because the income received by investors from coupon payments on municipal bonds is free from any taxing authority. A few states, however, tax the interest on bonds issued within those states. Income earned by the appreciation in the price of municipal bonds between the time they are bought and sold is taxed by federal, state, and local taxing units, but these gains are taxed at the capital gains rate, which is generally lower than the rate applied to other income.

Table 13–2 Municipal bond sales, by purpose

Purpose	1977 ($ billions)		1968 ($ billions)	
	$	% of total	$	% of total
Total	45.1	100.0	16.4	100.0
Schools	5.1	11.3	4.7	28.6
Water and sewer	4.5	10.0	1.9	11.6
Highway and bridges	1.4	3.1	1.6	9.8
Gas and electric	5.8	12.8	. . .	. . .
Hospital	4.7	10.4	. . .	. . .
Industrial aid	0.5	1.1	1.6	9.8
Pollution control	3.9	8.6	. . .	. . .
Public housing	. . .	. . .	0.5	3.0
Veterans aid	0.6	1.3	0.2	1.2
Other	18.7	41.4	5.9	36.0

Source: *Municipal Finance Statistics*, published by the *Daily Bond Buyer*.
Note: Leaders (. . .) indicate data not available.

The tax exemption of the coupon interest significantly affects the market for municipal bonds. Investors are concerned usually with after-tax income. The higher an investor's marginal income tax bracket, the greater the value of the tax exemption. For example, although a tax-exempt municipal investor would favor a comparable 8 percent Treasury bond trading at par value over a hypothetical 6 percent municipal bond also trading at par value, a private investor who is in a marginal tax bracket of 25 percent would see no difference between the two, because both would yield him or her the same 6 percent after-tax return. If the private investor were in the 50 percent marginal tax bracket, the 6 percent municipal bond would yield the same after-tax return as a hypothetical 12 percent Treasury bond. Thus, the municipal bond buyer is generally in the higher tax brackets.

Institutional investors also are subject to different marginal income tax rates. The net income of commercial banks and casualty and property insurance companies is subject to the full corporate tax rate of 46 percent above $100,000. (The net income of pension funds and life insurance companies, however, is taxed at considerably lower rates.) As a result and in contrast to taxable coupon securities, the demand for municipal bonds is restricted to wealthy individuals, commercial banks, and casualty and property insurance companies. At the year end of 1977, commercial banks held 42 percent of all municipal securities (including short-term debt) outstanding, individuals (including trusts) held 30 percent, and casualty and property insurance companies held 18 percent. Thus, these three groups accounted for 90 percent of all holdings of municipal securities.

Moreover, not only is the tax-free municipal bond market narrower than the market for most other securities, but also it is more volatile. The asset size of commercial banks tends to move cyclically against the trend as a result of U.S. Federal Reserve stabilization policies. Bank assets tend to grow compared to the rest of the economy, expanding rapidly when the economy is in the doldrums and more slowly when inflationary pressures intensify. The impact of this cyclical pattern on the demand for municipal bonds is reinforced by cyclical demands for business loans from banks. The demand for business loans picks up when the economy is strong and the growth of bank assets is slow. This trend reverses itself when the economy contracts. Given this cycle (and given that municipal bonds generally are viewed as less profitable than business loans), commercial bank demand for municipal securities is strong during and immediately after recessions and weak during periods of economic boom. This contra-cyclical pattern in demand is readily evident in available data. Banks increased their holdings of municipal securities by only 1 percent in 1969 and by only 6 percent in 1973 and 1974, years of relatively low unemployment, inflationary pressures, and monetary restraint. In contrast, the banks increased their holdings of municipals by almost 20 percent in 1968, 1970, and 1971 and by 10 percent in 1972 and 1977, years of relative economic slack and relatively mild price pressures and monetary expansion. This volatility in bank demand for municipal bonds is reflected in the great volatility of interest rates on municipal bonds. This is particularly true in the market for short-term municipals in which the banks play the most important role.

Unlike most other new bond issues, which are sold one maturity at a time, new municipal bonds are usually sold in serial form. Serial bonds are a package of individual bonds with more than one term to maturity. Municipal serial bonds typically contain a large number of individual maturities ranging annually from one year to more than twenty years. The dollar par value of each maturity may be the same or it may vary. The winning underwriter breaks out the serial package and resells the bonds individually to investors. Because the bond issue matures over time rather than all at once, the serial form often relieves the need for the issuer to establish a sinking fund. General obligation bond issues are usually entirely in serial form. Revenue issues are either entirely in serial form or in serial form up to a date followed by one or more larger "term" bonds, which are balloon payments that mature on single dates some years after the last serial maturity. The balloon payment term bonds generally are subject to mandatory call in equal amounts in each year between the maturity of the term bond and the last preceding maturity. This effectively transforms them into serial bonds. As will be discussed later in this chapter, the serial nature of new municipal bonds has complicated the process by which issuers competively sell new bonds at the lowest possible interest cost.

Planning a bond issue

The first step in planning a bond issue is to determine the precise cost of the project to be financed. (Underestimating the cost may be expensive because the sale of supplementary bonds later may be more difficult and costly.) Estimating the cost of large projects often requires the assistance of cost engineers. The next consideration is whether to sell general obligation bonds or revenue bonds. As noted earlier, this decision involves identifying and evaluating:

1. The direct and indirect beneficiaries of the project
2. The time pattern of the stream of benefits generated by the project
3. The revenues that may be raised by alternative types of user charges
4. The cost-effectiveness of user charges (the relation of revenues collected through user charges to the cost of collection)
5. The legal authority of the municipality to issue general obligation bonds
6. The probability of voter approval of these bonds
7. The legal ability to raise general taxes
8. The projected need to finance other projects of equal or higher priority by general obligation bonds and the impact of this issue on the interest cost of those bonds
9. The interest costs of each type of bond.

Maturity structure

Revenue bonds, which do not require voter approval, are generally easier to plan than general obligation (GO) bonds. However, they generally carry a higher interest rate because they are not secured by the full faith and credit of the issuer. They also require careful estimates of the user charges to be applied and the revenues to be derived. After the selection of the appropriate type of bond, the more specific planning starts. A proper maturity structure must be designed. This structure depends on whether the issue is a GO or a revenue bond. For revenue bonds, the estimated annual revenues should cover the debt service payments by some accepted multiple called the *coverage ratio*. This ratio should be checked against those prevailing for similar projects in other jurisdictions. Thus, if the average coverage ratio is 150 percent, the debt service payments in any year should total only two-thirds of the net revenues estimated for that year. The longest maturity should not exceed the estimated useable life of the project or the last year for which significant net revenues are estimated.

In contrast, the maturity and debt service structure of new general obligation bonds depends on the estimated annual overall tax revenues of the issuer and the maturity and debt service structure of all current outstanding general obligation bonds. Tax revenue must finance the debt service payments of all GO bonds. Thus, the scheduled debt service payments for all GO bonds should never be greater than the projected current revenues of the issuer in any year, less the estimated other current expenditures in that year. (The projection may include reasonable increases in the tax rates.) The greater the debt service payments on current outstanding bonds in any one year relative to the estimated tax revenues for the year less other current expenditures, the smaller should be the amount of new bonds scheduled to mature in that year. To keep debt service payments relatively stable from year to year, new maturities should be structured to meet these constraints based on the pattern of the maturity structure of the outstanding bonds. The maximum length of time to maturity of general obligation bonds generally is prescribed by state statute.

When a project is to be financed by general obligation bonds, it is important that the new bonds neither cause the statutory debt ceiling to be exceeded nor move the issuer to a position where necessary future debt financed expenditures would be restrained. The restrictions on total debt frequently include liabilities other than bonds (e.g., contingent liabilities and bank loans).

At this stage of the planning, if not earlier, the issuer should contact a financial advisor and an independent municipal bond counsel. No bond issue should be marketed without the assistance of an independent bond counsel, who will provide an independent evaluation of the legality of the issue and determine whether it complies with various applicable state and local statutes and qualifies for exemption from federal income taxes. The use of financial advisors is more discretionary with the issuer and depends, in part, on the availability of qualified in-house personnel. This is particularly desirable for larger projects, or if the issuer does not regularly sell bonds.

Call provisions   A call provision permits the issuer to repurchase the bonds before maturity at a predetermined maximum price. Thus, for the purchaser, bonds with call provisions have more than one possible maturity date. Call provisions provide flexibility to the issuer because (1) the bonds can be refinanced if, at some time in the future, interest rates should decline; (2) they can be retired ahead of schedule if funds become available; and (3) existing bonds with overly restrictive covenants can be retired.

Of the factors noted above, the first is the most common for exercising the call provision on municipal bonds. The second does not generally affect municipal bonds because municipalities may invest funds in taxable securities (without paying income taxes on earnings) and borrow at tax-exempt rates. It generally is not profitable for municipalities to retire bonds before maturity; it is more advantageous for them to invest excess funds. The third factor generally applies only to revenue bonds.

Once the bonds are issued, their prices vary inversely with the market interest

Services provided by municipal bond counsel

Determines whether the legal authority for the issuance of the bonds is consistent with constitutional requirements and limitations

Ensures that the statutory or charter authority for the issuance of the bonds is consistent with constitutional requirements and limitations

Prepares the legal documents for the issuance of the bonds, including the legal instruments necessary to authorize the issuance of the bonds and to describe the bonds and their security

Ensures that the bonds are within the applicable debt limitations

Ensures that any applicable tax limitation as to rate or amount is observed

Ensures that any required elections regarding the bonds are called and held in conformity with law

Reviews the official statement to make certain that the legal information is correct and that no material information has been omitted

Examines the proceedings of the authorizing body providing for the sale of the bonds to ensure that the bonds will be sold legally

Ensures that a competitive sale is advertised properly or that an underwriter in a negotiated sale is selected properly

Determines whether the bid accepted is legally acceptable in a competitive sale

Is prepared to answer inquiries from rating services, investors, underwriters, trustees, paying agents, and others prior to the delivery of the bonds

Prepares an unqualified opinion as to the tax-exempt status of the bonds.

Source: Adapted from Center for Capital Market Research, *Planning, Designing, and Selling General Obligation Bonds in Oregon: A Guide to Local Issuers* (Eugene, Oregon: University of Oregon, 1978).

---

rate. The advantage of the call provision is that it permits the issuer to repurchase bonds at a price below their market value if interest rates should decline. This, of course, benefits the issuer at the expense of the buyer. To compensate for this potential loss in market value or in interest income, investors will charge a higher initial interest rate for callable than for non-callable bonds. This higher interest rate is referred to as the *call yield premium*. The price at which the bonds may be repurchased is termed the *call price* and is set somewhat above par. The difference between the call price of a bond and its par value is referred to as the *call price premium*. The magnitude of the call yield premium on a particular issue varies with a number of characteristics of the bond issue and the state of the market at the time the issue is sold initially. Call provisions typically also provide for a period of time during which the bonds may not be called. This period is termed the *deferment period*. In general, the call yield premium will be greater with (1) higher current interest rates; (2) lower call price premiums; and (3) shorter deferment periods.

Issuers must weigh the potential benefits of a call provision against the initial higher interest costs. As a compromise, issuers frequently choose call provisions that are economical to exercise only when interest rates decline significantly. This generally has little effect on the initial interest cost of the issue. Also, the initial interest rate may not be much affected if the issue carries a call price well above par value and has a deferment period of at least ten years. (This, of

Services provided by financial advisor

Surveys issuer's debt structure and financial resources to determine borrowing capacity for current and future capital financing requirements

Gathers all pertinent financial statistics and economic data, such as debt requirement schedule, tax rates, and overlapping debt that would affect or reflect on the issuer's ability and willingness to repay its general obligation bonds

Determines appropriate user charges and estimates revenue flows for projects to be financed by revenue bonds

Advises on the time and method of marketing, terms of bond issue (including maturity schedule), interest payment dates, and call features

Reviews bidding procedures for competitive sales and the securing of an appropriate underwriter for negotiated sales

Prepares, in cooperation with bond counsel, an official statement, notice of sale, and bid form and distributes them to all prospective underwriters and investors

Evaluates the benefits of obtaining one or more credit ratings and contacts the rating services to ensure that they have all the information and data they require to properly evaluate the issuer's credit worthiness

Is present when sealed bids are opened and stands ready to advise on acceptability of bids

Helps coordinate the printing, signing, and delivery of the bonds.

Source: Adapted from Center for Capital Market Research, *Planning, Designing, and Selling General Obligation Bonds in Oregon: A Guide to Local Issuers* (Eugene, Oregon; University of Oregon, 1978).

course, implies that the call provisions will be applicable only to bonds in the serial package that have a minimum of ten years to maturity.)

Almost all municipal revenue bonds have call provisions, but only about one-half of all general obligation bond issues are callable. Call provisions in issues sold in recent years have increased as interest rates have increased since World War II. One study of bonds with call provisions issued in 1960 indicated that approximately 45 percent of the revenue bonds and 35 percent of the GO bonds were called before maturity. The higher call rate for revenue bonds occurred because revenue bonds often have mandatory call provisions that require the issuer periodically to retire a fixed portion of the bond issue.

Advance refunding As noted, most callable bond issues have a deferment period before which the bond cannot be refinanced through call. However, should interest rates drop sharply after the date of sale, but before the end of the deferment period, the issuer may sell new bonds at the lower rates. The proceeds of this issue then are placed in an escrow account and invested in interest bearing securities, most often those of the U.S. Treasury. The outstanding bonds are either retired at the first call date (a *crossover refunding*) or legally annulled (a *defeasance refunding*). Unlike a regular refunding, at which time the refunded bonds are retired immediately, an advance refunding simultaneously will have old and new refunding bonds outstanding, which increases the total volume of municipal debt. The net debt of the municipality, however, remains about the same if the amount of assets invested in the bond escrow account is factored out.

The profitability of advance refunding depends not only on the steepness of the decline in interest rates, but also on the amount of profit the Treasury permits between the tax-exempt borrowing rate and the rate earned on the investment of the escrow funds in taxable securities. Until 1978, the profits realized from selling and buying the same thing (arbitrage) were sufficiently high to encourage the use of advance refunding even when the present value of the saving, derived from the fall in the market interest rates, was not very great. The concern for both the proper use of the tax exemption privilege and the increases in interest rates caused by sharp increases in the volume of outstanding municipal securities led the Treasury to minimize the profits that could be obtained from arbitrage. As a result, the volume of advance refunding slowed greatly.

Credit rating

The greater the perceived risk of default, the greater the interest rate required by investors. The risk of default depends on the type of security. Revenue bonds are secured by the net revenues accruing from user charges on the project financed (e.g., a bridge, a water plant, or a turnpike). Thus, the credit quality of revenue bonds is related to the potential earnings of the enterprise. The greater the debt coverage ratio (the ratio of annual net operating revenues over debt service charges), the smaller the probability of default. On occasion, the minimum permissible debt coverage ratio is deliberately written into the covenant to provide assurance that the issuer will charge fees high enough to meet its debt obligations. In making investment decisions, investors compare the debt coverage ratio on a particular revenue bond with the ratios on similar bonds of other issuers. Debt coverage ratios differ among different types of projects, but they generally range from 120 percent to 200 percent. In evaluating credit quality, the investor also will examine such factors as the past performance of the issuer, the quality of management, the financial experience of similar projects elsewhere, the appropriateness of user charges, and the projected population and income growth trends in the service area.

Evaluating credit quality   General obligation bonds are secured by the full faith, credit, and taxing powers of the issuer. For most issuers, available tax income includes some combination of income, sales, and property taxes. Credit quality depends on the ability of the appropriate tax base to generate the required debt service payments and to finance regular current expenditure. This ability depends on economic, financial, debt, and administrative factors. Important economic factors include the level and growth of the aggregate and per capita income of the area; the population growth trends in the area; the diversity of the income base; the age distribution of the population; the diversity of industry and employment; the diversity of the tax base; the characteristics of the largest tax payers; the sensitivity of the tax base to economic fluctuations; and the characteristics of the housing stock and building activity.

Financial factors include the composition of the issuer's budget; the sources of revenue; the ability of revenues to meet current expenditures; the stability of the revenue/expense ratio; the past relationship of the projected and realized budgets; the budget trends; the necessity for short-term financing; the quality of financial reporting, auditing, and control systems; and, more recently, the requirements of pension funds. Debt factors include such measures of debt burden as debt per capita; the ratio of debt outstanding to total household and business income in the issuer's jurisdiction; the ratio of debt outstanding to the market value of taxable property; the debt service payments as a percentage of estimated tax revenues; the unused debt margins; and the history of voters' approval of tax increases and bond issuance. Because many political subdivisions overlap, the debt factors must be analyzed not only for the particular governmental unit issuing the bonds, but also for all units that may levy taxes in the jurisdiction of the bond issuer (e.g., the state). These data are termed *overlapping debt* factors and measure the total debt burden on the taxpayers. The greater the overlapping debt, regardless of the debt of any particular unit, the greater the debt burden on the taxpayer.

Acquiring the necessary information on the credit quality of municipal bonds is costly to investors in terms of both money and time. Much of the costs of search and analysis will remain constant or increase slowly with investment size. Thus, the costs of analysis are proportionately greater for smaller investors. Until recently, much of the necessary financial data was not readily available from the issuer; and the high costs of analyzing credit quality priced many smaller investors out of the market and increased interest costs.

Assigning the credit rating   A number of financial advisory services now undertake credit evaluations to reduce the costs of search and analysis to smaller investors. These evaluations are based on analyses of the various ratios and factors already noted. The evaluation is summarized in credit rating symbols. The two major municipal bond credit rating agencies are Moody's Investor Service and Standard and Poor's. The rating symbols of the two agencies are similar (see Table 13–3). Ratings for new municipal securities are requested by the issuer. The costs of making the ratings are paid by the issuer, and the ratings are provided free to all investors. The cost of the analysis varies depending on population size for general obligation bonds and complexity of the evaluation for revenue bonds. The ratings are reviewed annually at no additional charge. Despite the cost of obtaining a rating, the issuer will benefit considerably if the availability of the rating broadens the market for the issue and increases its marketability enough to lower interest costs. As shown in Table 13–4, the lower the interest rate, the higher the credit rating. This does not indicate by itself that the lower interest rate is attributable to the rating; it may be attributed to the basic credit quality of the issue. Nevertheless, it appears that the cost of the rating is more than offset by the reduction in interest cost. Unrated bonds, on average, trade at the same interest rate as Baa rated bonds, although there is a wide dispersion.

Checklist: rules of thumb for sound credit rating

Total all local debt (including debt of overlapping governments) as a percentage of the market value of the property tax base:
 less than 5% is very good;
 over 10% signals possible trouble.

Growth rate of total debt
 should not rise excessively over the growth rate of the tax base and the growth rate of local personal incomes.

Total debt per capita:
 less than $550 is low;
 over $1,300 signals possible trouble.

Short-term debt:
 should all be retired each fiscal year;
 carry-over or "rollover" between years signals trouble.

Debt service (annual retirement of long-term debt plus all interest) as a percentage of total revenue from own sources:
 should be less than 20% to 25%;
 total of short-term debt plus debt service should be less than 40% of own-source revenue.

Table 13–3　Moody's and Standard and Poor's credit ratings for municipal bonds

Rating		
Moody's[1]	Standard and Poor's[2]	Description
Aaa	AAA	Best quality, extremely strong capacity to pay principal and interest
Aa	AA	High quality, very strong capacity to pay principal and interest
A-1 A	A	Upper medium quality, strong capacity to pay principal and interest
Baa-1 Baa	BBB	Medium grade quality, adequate capacity to pay principal and interest
Ba and lower	BB and lower	Speculative quality, low capacity to pay principal and interest

1　Strongest bonds in A and Baa groups are designated as A-1 and Baa-1, respectively.
2　Plus (+) and minus (−) signs may be added to show relative standing within major rating categories.

The ratings also are used by larger investors. Some investors (e.g., commercial banks) are restricted by law, or by regulations, from purchasing lower quality securities, often considered those rated Baa or below. Other larger investors use the ratings as a yardstick against which to compare their own in-house evaluations.

In addition to the two national rating agencies, a number of large commercial and investment banks, which serve as underwriters, prepare in-house evaluations of credit quality in the process of preparing a bid. Many of the firms will make these evaluations available to investors if the firm wins the bid.

To obtain the best possible rating, the issuing locality should make as much relevant information as possible available to potential underwriters and investors.

Table 13–4　Interest rates on long-term municipal bonds with different credit ratings, December 1977

Moody's rating	%
Aaa	5.07
Aa	5.23
A	5.46
Baa	5.79
Average	5.39

Source: *Moody's Municipal and Government Manual* (New York: Moody's Investor's Service, 1978), p. a10.

Municipal bond insurance　In recent years, a number of private insurance firms have offered to insure municipal bonds so that, in the event of a default by the issuer, the insurance company assumes the prompt payment of all coupon and maturity amounts to the investors.[1] The cost of the insurance is charged to the issuer and varies from 0.5 percent to 3.0 percent of the amount of the original principal and interest, both of which depend on the insurance company's evaluation of the risk of default. The insurance decreases the investors' losses in case of default and reduces the interest rate required on the bonds. Standard and Poor's rates all insured bonds as either AAA or AA. Moody's does not change the rating on insured bonds, arguing that to do so would be to rate the insurance company rather than the issuer. Whether an issuer should obtain insurance depends on the issuer's evaluation of the cost of the insurance relative to an estimation of the savings to be gained by the reduction in the interest payments over the life of the bond issue.

Official statement and disclosure

About one month before the scheduled sale of the bonds, the issuer should publish a preliminary *official statement* or *prospectus*. This statement should describe the provisions of the bond issue and provide enough information to permit investors to price the bonds properly. Once the bonds are sold to the winning underwriter, the final official statement is prepared and includes the details of the issue and the coupon rates. Unlike the official statements of private issuers, the official statements of state and local governments need not comply with the regulations of the Securities and Exchange Commission (SEC) or any other federal government agency.[2]

Prior to 1974, the content of official statements varied greatly. This was particularly so for general obligation bonds. The statements ranged from one mimeographed sheet—even for large issues—to highly professional booklets of detailed information. Most statements, however, compared poorly with the prospectuses required of private issuers.

In 1975, the near default of both the New York State Urban Development Corporation and New York City and the threatened default of a number of other older East Coast cities focused attention on the bonds of municipal issuers. It was believed that the general lack of relevant information and, in some instances, the inclusion of misleading information (intentional and unintentional) contributed to keeping the true financial condition of the issuers hidden from the public and investors. In response to the paucity of information, a number of bills were introduced in Congress to establish minimum standards for official statements and to have bond issuance supervised by a federal agency. None of the bills were enacted. Nevertheless, issuers became more aware of the importance of proper disclosure and of the potential for legal liability in case of inaccurate or omitted information. In addition to the attempts made in Congress, a number of states adopted legislation stipulating minimum disclosure requirements. In Oregon, for example, a statute requires the following requirements for general obligation issues:

1. The issuer shall prepare and make available upon request to bidders and investors a preliminary official statement that includes the following:
   a. Past and current financing and estimated future financing of the issuer;
   b. Brief description of the financial administration and organization of the issuer;
   c. Brief description of the economic and social characteristics of the issuer which will permit bidders and investors to appraise the issuer's ability to assume and service adequately the debt obligation;
   d. Any other information the issuer may provide or which the Oregon Municipal Debt Advisory Commission may require by rule.
2. The preliminary official statement described in subsection (1) of this section shall be available not later than the date of first publication of the notice of bond sale.
3. The preliminary official statement shall contain the best available information which shall be accurate to the best knowledge of the issuer. However, any errors or omissions in the preliminary official statement shall not affect the validity of the bond issue.[3]

The Oregon Municipal Debt Advisory Commission also has prepared detailed guidelines for official statements for issuers of different sizes.

In 1976, the Municipal Finance Officers Association (MFOA) published *Disclosure Guidelines for Offerings of Securities by State and Local Governments*. These guidelines were followed in 1978 by *Guidelines for the Use By State and Local Governments in the Preparation of Yearly Information Statements and Other Current Information*. Both sets of guidelines were the work of a large number of individuals representing issuers, underwriters, and bond counsels. The MFOA guidelines have been widely accepted among issuers and have reduced the pressures for federal government supervision. It is important for issuers not only to prepare a complete and accurate official statement but also to make it available early enough for potential underwriters and investors to study and analyze the contents. The preliminary official statement should be made available some twenty to thirty days before the date of sale. More complete and timely information should broaden the market and lower the effective interest cost to the issuer.

Two recent surveys have shed light on the types of data underwriters and investors consider the most useful in evaluating the credit quality of general obligation bonds. In Table 13–5, the items that the MFOA guidelines recommend for disclosure are ranked according to the importance assigned to them by twenty-five major underwriters. Similarly, Table 13–6 shows the importance of information about the issue and the issuer according to the weight assigned to each by forty-five large commercial banks serving as underwriters and investors. Both surveys indicate that factors such as total debt outstanding, debt per capita, and sources of revenues to repay the debt are viewed as the most important information items for analyzing the credit quality of an issue.

Financial control systems have been improved and greater emphasis placed on gathering, compiling, reporting, and verifying financial data.

The increased emphasis on complete and timely disclosure has had an unexpected, but beneficial, side effect. Many issuers discovered that the information they were receiving on their own financial position was incomplete and, on occasion, inaccurate. As a result, the governmental units often were not able to make the best financial decisions nor to undertake corrective action in time to prevent more serious difficulties. It is less likely now that any financial difficulties experienced by issuers will catch the public, the investors, and the issuers themselves unaware again.

Table 13–5   MFOA disclosure items ranked in importance by underwriters

Rank	Disclosure item	Average[1]
1	Financing current obligations with long-term debt	3.88
2	Repayment of long-term debt by issuing additional obligations	3.87
3	Receipts used to repay debt	3.84
4	Accounting practices and deviations	3.80
5–6	Fund trends and changes	3.72
5–6	Retirement plan funding	3.72
7–8	Comparison of operations	3.64
7–8	Changes in tax assessments and collections	3.64
9	Audit reports	3.60
10	Cash flows	3.59
11	Taxation procedures	3.52
12	Budgetary practices	3.50
13	Assessed value of taxable property	3.48
14	Ten largest taxpayers	3.44
15	Emergency funds	3.29
16	Financial statements	3.17

Source: Robert W. Ingram, "A Review of the MFOA Disclosure Guidelines," *Governmental Finance* 7, no. 2 (May 1978):38.
1 Maximum score is 4.0.

Table 13–6 Disclosure information ranked in importance by large commercial banks

Rank	Information item	Average[1]	Standard deviation
1	Total debt outstanding	3.833	0.377
2	Debt to actual value ratio	3.745	0.488
3	Overlapping debt outstanding	3.638	0.529
4	Debt per capita	3.630	0.532
5	Tax collection history	3.625	0.570
6	Changes in financial position	3.596	0.614
7–8	Population trends, income, etc.	3.563	0.542
7–8	Actual value of property in tax jurisdiction	3.563	0.649
9	Operating revenues	3.479	0.618
10	Assessed valuation	3.447	0.746
11	Tax rate limits	3.435	0.620
12	Operating expenditures	3.417	0.679
13	Debt to assessed value ratio	3.386	0.895
14	Accounting policies used	3.277	0.772
15	Principal taxpayers	3.250	0.601
16	Portion of tax rates applicable to debt	3.213	0.690
17	Tax rate history	3.087	0.661
18	Sinking funds applicable to outstanding debt	3.021	0.737
19	Bond rating	2.958	0.771
20	Current assets and liabilities	2.957	0.806
21	Fixed assets	2.333	0.853

Source: Arthur S. Boyett and Gary A. Giroux, "The Relevance of Municipal Financial Reporting to Municipal Security Decisions," *Governmental Finance* 7, no. 2 (May 1978):30.
1 Maximum score is 4.0.

Method of sale

Municipal bonds are sold by issuers to investors through underwriters. Underwriters, individually for smaller issues or as part of a syndicate for larger issues, buy the entire bond issue (generally in serial form) from the issuer and resell the component individual bonds to investors. Thus, underwriters assume the burden of distributing the bonds. If they miscalculate, they risk having to sell the bonds at a price below the purchase price and incurring a loss. Issuers may sell the bond issue to underwriters by competitive (public) sale or by negotiation. In a competitive sale, the issuer announces the particulars of the issue, details the basis on which the bonds will be awarded to a bidder, and solicits bids. In a negotiated sale, the issuer chooses a particular underwriter (or, for large issues, a syndicate of underwriters) in advance of the sale date. The price and some other particulars of the issue are negotiated between the two parties.

Frequently, the method of sale is stipulated by state statute. Most states require that general obligation bonds be awarded by competitive sale. Revenue bonds usually may be sold by either method. Because of the sharp increase in revenue bonds issued in recent years, the proportion of bonds sold by negotiation has increased. In 1978, more than 50 percent of the dollar value of municipal bonds was sold by negotiation. Five years earlier, this proportion was only 25 percent. Except for small issues, on which bids may be received from private parties, underwriters are either commercial banks or investment banks (securities dealers). Investment banks may bid on all types of municipal securities. Commercial banks are restricted by federal law to bid only on general obligation bonds and on a limited number of revenue bonds, primarily those issued for housing or university purposes.

The role of the underwriter differs greatly in the two sales methods. In a competitive sale, the underwriter becomes involved only after the public notice of sale has been published, generally two to four weeks before the scheduled date of sale. The design of the issue is fully completed at that time and has been prepared without formal assistance from any bidding underwriter. To avoid conflicts of interest, underwriters who provide formal advice to the issuer in the design of the bond issue often exclude themselves from bidding on the issue.

Underwriters will decide whether to prepare a bid once the notice of sale has been published. Most larger issues are too risky and too costly for a single underwriter to purchase and distribute. More than one underwriter will join to form a syndicate. One or more of the larger underwriters, or a regional underwriter on a smaller issue, serves as manager of the syndicate and assumes the major responsibility for preparing the bid. The decision of an underwriter or underwriting syndicate to prepare a bid on an issue is based on the financial conditions in the market, the kind of reception the underwriter receives from traditional bond buyers about the issue, and the past bond experience of the same issuer. Some underwriters have bid on bonds of particular issuers for many years and have developed a file both on the issuer's credit quality and on the customers who prefer these bonds. This kind of preliminary analysis is important because the unusually large number of issues and issuers makes the municipal bond market more segmented than most other security markets. In 1978, more than five thousand new bond issues were marketed, most of which were sold by different issuers.

If an underwriter decides to prepare a bid, additional work is required to determine the yields each maturity needs to attract investors, to find potential investors, and to prepare a bid that will have a chance of winning the bond issue and yielding a profit when the bonds are reoffered for sale. If the underwriter misgauges the market and prepares a bid based on an expectation to resell the bonds at yields that turn out to be too low, the bond prices will have to be lowered. This would reduce, possibly eliminate, the underwriter's expected profit. Underwriters plan to resell the bonds within a few days of the sale, although physical delivery of the bonds by the municipal issuer is generally thirty to sixty days after the date of sale. Because payment to the issuer occurs only on delivery of the bonds, underwriters rarely have funds tied up in the issue prior to delivery—except for a small "good faith" check on deposit with the issuer. However, the costs involved in searching the market and preparing the bid are recovered only if the underwriter wins the bids with a spread that is large enough to recover costs and profits when the bonds are resold. Losing underwriters must charge these costs to profits on the issues for which they are the winning bidder. The risk of not recovering preparation costs restricts the effort underwriters put into a competitive bid preparation.

In a negotiated sale, the underwriter enters the process at a much earlier stage. Once the decision has been made to sell a new bond issue by negotiation, the issuer will contact one or more underwriters to acquaint them with the particulars of the issue and to solicit information on the approximate interest costs, the *spread* (profit) the underwriter intends to charge, and the services that the underwriter will perform. Often issuers will first contact the underwriters used in previous sales and with whose services they have been satisfied. The underwriter selected will usually assist the issuer in such matters as designing the issue in terms of maturity dates, maturity amounts, and call provisions; preparing the official statement; obtaining a credit rating; selecting the appropriate time to market the issue; meeting with major potential investors; and complying with the legal requirements.

The underwriters can engage in a longer and more intensive search process for bonds sold by negotiation than for those sold competitively, because they are involved at an earlier stage in the process. This process also may reveal that the issue could be sold at a lower interest cost if it were redesigned to meet the demands of an investor who wishes to buy a larger amount of bonds with a maturity different from those planned or who wants a particular coupon rate.

The issue can be modified to meet these demands before the sale. Additionally, a competitive sale date cannot be easily changed; a negotiated underwriting date can be. Thus, if the underwriter believes that the market is particularly unsettled or that an unusually large number of similar bond issues are scheduled to be sold on the same day, the sale date can be changed. This increased flexibility can reduce interest costs somewhat.

The type of bond sale that is best for the issuer depends on the particular characteristics of the issuer and the issue. Studies have shown that, on the average, bond issues sold by competitive bid have lower interest costs to the issuer than comparable bonds sold by negotiation—even after adjustment for the additional services provided. But wide differences exist. The interest cost savings on competitive sales are usually largest for well-known, high credit quality issues; they become smaller as the credit quality of the issuer decreases, and turn negative for low credit quality issues of little known issuers. For the last group, interest costs appear lower, on average, on negotiated sales. Because of these differences, each finance officer should make a careful determination of which method is best for the issuer, basing the opinion on credit quality, national or regional visibility, size of issue, frequency with which issues have been marketed, any special complicating features of the issue, and conditions in the securities market at the time. Because underwriters perform greater services in negotiated sales at no apparent "out-of-pocket" costs, some finance officers may have elected to use this easier method without sufficient cost-benefit analysis.

Notice of sale

The notice of sale is the issuer's official statement announcing the intention to sell a bond issue by competitive sale. The notice of sale provides summary information about the issue, describes the method by which the bonds will be awarded to the winner, and solicits bids. At minimum, the notice of sale should include:

1. The total par amount
2. The par amounts in each maturity
3. The maturity dates
4. The call provisions, if any
5. The maximum interest cost permitted
6. The minimum dollar bid permitted
7. The time, date, and place where the bids will be accepted
8. The basis on which the issue will be awarded
9. The constraints placed on the bid
10. The size of the good faith check, if required
11. The name of the bond counsel
12. The name of the person who may be contacted for additional information.

The notice of sale should be advertised early and widely to attract the largest number of bidders. Often, advertising requirements are mandated by state law. Advertisement in local and major state newspapers may be sufficient for smaller issues. Larger issues, or any issues that have regional or larger visibility, should also be advertised in the *Daily Bond Buyer*. The complete notice or a summary of sale should appear at least once in these newspapers twenty to thirty days before the scheduled sale. Studies show that the larger the number of competitive bidders on an issue, the lower the interest cost.[4]

In addition to the publicity given to the sale, the number of bids received on a competitively sold issue is a function of a number of characteristics of the issue and market conditions. On the average, the number of bids increases with the quality of the credit, the degree of stability in the financial markets, and, to some extent, the dollar amount of the issue. Beyond a certain par size, the number of bids declines as underwriters join progressively larger syndicates to finance and market the issue. Thus, both very small and very large municipal bond issues tend to receive fewer bids than do comparable medium size issues.

Basis of award

Bids received in competitive sales are awarded according to the criteria specified in the official notice of sale. Generally, the issue is awarded to the lowest interest cost bid, although on occasion the determining factor may be the highest bid on the price of the bonds. The coupon rates on each of the maturities in the serial issue are determined by the bidders. Although the lowest interest cost criterion appears straightforward, the method by which it has been used historically in the sale of municipal serial bonds to underwriters has resulted frequently in the acceptance of an interest cost bid that is higher than necessary to the issuer.

In the market, bonds are traded or priced on the basis of their yield to maturity or, more technically, the internal rate of return. The internal rate of return is the rate that discounts the contractual stream of future coupon payments and the final payment at maturity to the current price. The price of the bond is thus the present value of all the future payments. The concept of present value places a lower value on each dollar for every future year in which it is paid. If the market interest rate is 10 percent, the present value of one dollar paid one year from now is 90.9 cents; paid two years from now, 82.6 cents; and paid ten years from now, 38.6 cents. The higher the market rate of interest, the lower the present value of a given future payment.

Prior to the introduction of electronic computers, the calculation of the yield to maturity on a bond was a time-consuming process. Most participants in the bond market relied on prepared bond tables which were precomputed so that, given the coupon rate, the par value, the number of years to maturity, and the market price, the yield to maturity could be determined. Conversely, given the going market yield, the market price could be determined. For an issue of serial bonds, the computation of the overall yield to maturity is much more complex and time-consuming than for individual bonds, and, in this case, bond tables are not practical. As a result, yield to maturity was not a feasible criterion by which to award the underwriting of municipal bonds. Thus a simplified interest rate concept was used—*net interest cost* (NIC). NIC in percent is the aggregate dollar coupon payments scheduled over the life of all bonds in the serial issue, plus any discount below the par value of the issue that the underwriter bids (or less any premium bid over par), divided by the sum of the product of the par values of each bond and the number of years to its maturity. The last term is referred to as the *number of bond year dollars*. In equation form

$$NIC = \frac{Total\ coupon\ interest\ payments\ +\ bid\ discount\ (or\ -\ bid\ premium)}{Number\ of\ bond\ year\ dollars}$$

NIC is quick and easy to compute. An example of a NIC computation is shown in Table 13–7, and covers a three year serial issue with a par value of $3,000. One thousand dollars is scheduled to mature each year. Coupons are assumed to be paid annually, rather than semiannually. The underwriter places 5 percent coupon rates on each maturity and bids par value for the bonds. The NIC is 5 percent.

Although NIC is relatively easy to compute and to understand, it has two serious drawbacks when used to award municipal bonds to a bidder. Unlike the yield to maturity, NIC is not based on present value. Ten dollars in coupon interest payments in the first year is valued the same as five dollars paid in the first and second years, and the same as one dollar paid in each of the first ten years. If these were bids, all three alternatives would have equal NICs. The taxpayers, however, would benefit if they paid the ten dollars in one dollar annual installments, rather than as a lump sum in the first year; they would gain in present value terms. As a result, a ranking of bids by NIC may not be the same as a ranking by an interest computation employing present value, which gives a more accurate measure of the cost of funds to the community.

The yield to maturity for a serial issue is referred to as *true interest cost* (TIC) or the Canadian method. TIC is the weighted average of the yields to maturities of the individual bonds in a serial package with an adjustment for the underwriter's spread.

The NICs and TICs of the bids received may be compared. If the accepted low NIC bid is not also the low TIC bid, the issuer is not obtaining a meaningful lowest cost bid. Legally, it is the correct bid, but economically, it is not. Accepting such a bid implies that the present value of the coupon interest payments scheduled to be made over the life of the bonds is higher than on another bid.

Table 13–7 Computation of net interest cost (NIC)

Number of years to maturity (A)	Total par value ($) (B)	Coupon rate (%) (C)	Bond year dollars (A × B) (D)	Coupon payments (C × D) (E) ($)
1	1,000	5	1,000	50
2	1,000	5	2,000	100
3	1,000	5	3,000	150
Total	3,000		6,000	300

Bid discount = 0

$$\text{NIC} = \frac{\text{total coupon payments} + \text{bid discount}}{\text{total bond year dollars}}$$

$$= \frac{\text{column (E)} + 0}{\text{column (D)}} = \frac{300 + 0}{6,000} = .05$$

$$= 5\%$$

The second major drawback to the NIC method is that it affects the way bidders construct their bids and causes them to prepare higher interest cost bids. Underwriters are middlemen who buy the entire serial bond issue as a package and sell the individual composite bonds separately. In order to prepare winning bids, underwriters first estimate the lowest yields to maturity that will still enable them to resell the individual bonds to investors (*reoffering yields*) and establish the underwriting spread needed to cover preparation and marketing costs and provide a net profit. They place coupon rates on the individual bonds in a pattern that will produce the lowest possible NIC consistent with reselling the bonds at the estimated reoffering yields. If correctly computed, the underwriter will obtain aggregate revenues (*production*) from the sale equal to his price bid on the issue plus the desired spread. Because the NIC formula does not value dollars paid early any higher than those paid later, it is possible for the underwriter to reduce the NIC of the bid for a given TIC by placing high coupons on the early bonds in the serial issue and low coupons on the later bonds.

The relationship between net interest cost and true interest cost as the coupons are changed is presented in Table 13–8 for the hypothetical three year serial bond issue described in Table 13–7. TIC is computed on the basis of annual compounding; the underwriter's spread is neglected. The coupons on the bonds are such that the NIC is always $300, or 5.0 percent. Thus, if NIC were used to award the issue, the issuer would be indifferent among these bids. In Bid A, all three bonds have 5.0 percent coupons. Both the NIC and TIC of this bid are 5.0 percent. The computation of NIC is shown in the top panel of Table 13–8. Bid B is "frontloaded" so that it has a 30.0 percent coupon on the first bond

Table 13–8　Comparisons of hypothetical bids with net interest cost (NIC) and true interest cost (TIC) constant

Bid and years to maturity[1]	Coupon rate, NIC, TIC (%)	Annual debt service ($)	Bid and years to maturity[1]	Coupon rate, NIC, TIC (%)	Annual debt service ($)
NIC constant[2]			**TIC constant**		
Bid A			Bid G		
1 year	5.00	1,150.00	1 year	5.00	1,150.00
2 years	5.00	1,100.00	2 years	5.00	1,100.00
3 years	5.00	1,050.00	3 years	5.00	1,050.00
Total	. . .	3,300.00	Total	. . .	3,300.00
NIC	5.00	. . .	NIC	5.00	. . .
TIC[3]	5.00	. . .	TIC[3]	5.00	. . .
Bid B			Bid H		
1 year	30.00	1,300.00	1 year	29.05	1,290.50
2 years	0.00	1,000.00	2 years	0.00	1,000.00
3 years	0.00	1,000.00	3 years	0.00	1,000.00
Total	. . .	3,300.00	Total	. . .	3,290.50
NIC	5.00	. . .	NIC	4.84	. . .
TIC[3]	5.17	. . .	TIC[3]	5.00	. . .
Bid C			Bid I		
1 year	12.00	1,190.00	1 year	11.75	1,187.50
2 years	3.00	1,070.00	2 years	3.00	1,070.00
3 years	4.00	1,040.00	3 years	4.00	1,040.00
Total	. . .	3,300.00	Total	. . .	3,297.50
NIC	5.00	. . .	NIC	4.96	. . .
TIC[3]	5.04	. . .	TIC[3]	5.00	. . .
Bid D			Bid J		
1 year	6.50	1,160.00	1 year	6.45	1,159.50
2 years	5.00	1,095.00	2 years	5.00	1,095.00
3 years	4.50	1,045.00	3 years	4.50	1,045.00
Total	. . .	3,300.00	Total	. . .	3,299.50
NIC	5.00	. . .	NIC	4.98	. . .
TIC[3]	5.01	. . .	TIC[3]	5.00	. . .
Bid E			Bid K		
1 year	2.00	1,130.00	1 year	2.00	1,130.50
2 years	5.00	1,110.00	2 years	5.00	1,110.50
3 years	6.00	1,060.00	3 years	6.05	1,060.50
Total	. . .	3,300.00	Total	. . .	3,301.50
NIC	5.00	. . .	NIC	5.02	. . .
TIC[3]	4.98	. . .	TIC[3]	5.00	. . .
Bid F			Bid L		
1 year	0.00	1,100.00	1 year	0.00	1,101.50
2 years	0.00	1,100.00	2 years	0.00	1,101.50
3 years	10.00	1,100.00	3 years	10.15	1,101.50
Total	. . .	3,300.00	Total	. . .	3,304.50
NIC	5.00	. . .	NIC	5.08	. . .
TIC[3]	4.92	. . .	TIC[3]	5.00	. . .

Source: Center for Capital Market Research, *Improving Bidding Rules to Reduce Interest Costs in the Competitive Sale of Municipal Bonds*. (Eugene: College of Business Administration, University of Oregon, 1977).

Note: Leaders (. . .) indicate not applicable.

1 All bids in this table are predicated on the par amount of $1,000 for each of the years to maturity, totaling $3,000.

2 The amount bid in each case equals total par value ($3,000).

3 Interest is compounded annually.

and 0.0 percent coupons on the other two bonds. Because market yields on these maturities are not likely to follow the same pattern as the coupons, the underwriter would reoffer the first bond to investors at a premium considerably above par value and reoffer the last two bonds at large discounts below par value. These premiums and discounts are between the investor and the underwriter and differ from those between the underwriter and the issuer, which affect directly the NIC or TIC. All of the $300 interest payments are made in the first year. The NIC remains at 5.0 percent but the TIC increases to 5.17 percent. Bids C through F frontload progressively less. Bid F is the ultimate in "backloading" because interest is paid only on the three-year bonds. Its coupon is 10.0 percent, and the one- and two-year bonds have 0.0 percent coupons. Thus, $100 is paid in each of the three years the bond issue is outstanding. Again the NIC is unchanged at 5.0 percent, but, because the payments are made later, the TIC declines to 4.92 percent. It follows that for a given TIC, the NIC will decrease as the frontloading of the coupons increases; and the issuer should not be indifferent among these bids. Underwriters can lower the NIC bid on an issue for a TIC that is determined by reoffering yields. An example of this is shown in the bottom panel of Table 13–8 for the same three year serial bond issue. This time, the TIC is constant at 5.0 percent and the coupons on the individual bonds change from extreme frontloading in Bid H to extreme backloading in Bid L. The corresponding NICs increase from 4.84 percent to 5.08 percent.

When a bond issue is frontloaded, the early bonds will have coupon rates that generally are greater than their reoffering yields. These bonds will be resold by the underwriter to investors at a premium above par values. Conversely, the later bonds will have coupon rates less than their reoffering yields and will be resold at a discount below their par values.

It is likely that premium and discount bonds may have to be sold at higher "penalty" yields than bonds with coupons close to their reoffering yields (which will be priced at or near par value). The penalty yield is best illustrated with discount bonds. As discussed earlier, income from coupon payments on municipal bonds is exempt from federal income taxes. However, profits realized from increases between the buying price and the price at sale of municipal securities are subject to capital gains taxes. Low coupon bonds sold at initial discounts are subject to a federal capital gains tax on the difference between the original selling price and the maturity par value. They are no longer completely tax-exempt. Investors will purchase these bonds only if they receive yields higher than those on comparable par or completely tax-exempt bonds to compensate for the present value of the capital gains tax at maturity.

Very high coupon bonds that force the bond to be sold at a price factored at 108 or higher also trade at higher yields than comparable par bonds. Investors require penalty yields on these bonds to compensate them for the higher risk and the costs of having to reinvest the coupon payments at favorable interest rates. The higher penalty yields on either discount or premium bonds reduce the revenues of the underwriters on the resale of the bond issue to investors. To generate enough revenues to pay the issuer the price bid on the overall issue (par value plus a bid premium or minus a bid discount), the underwriter will increase the coupons on some bonds. This raises the NIC on the issue, but by less than the frontloading initially decreased the NIC. Thus the discounts and premiums charged investors by the underwriter indirectly affect the NIC and TIC of a bid.

Because TIC is an average of the yields on the individual bonds, the existence of penalty yields increases the TIC of an issue, even if the coupon structure is designed to lower NIC. The higher yields demanded by investors on the discount and premium bonds created by the underwriters are "passed through" to the issuer in terms of higher TICs. Moreover, because all bidders under NIC are confronted with the same incentives, all bids on an issue may have some penalty yields. Thus, even the low TIC bid received under NIC bidding is likely to be higher than the low TIC bid that may have been received had the issuer used a different award criterion. The source of the higher interest costs is the bidding rules used by the issuer (these rules stipulate NIC), not the underwriter. The latter only attempts to win the bid and earn a profit within the rules established by the issuer.

If individual bonds need to be reoffered at penalty yields to lower NIC and win the bid, they will be produced.

The existence and costs of penalty yields when bonds are awarded by NIC can be seen clearly from an issue sold by the state of Minnesota in 1972. This is not a representative issue, but it is useful for purposes of illustration. The issue had a par value of $25 million maturing in equal amounts over twenty years. Seven bids were received. The coupons and reoffering yields of the winning low NIC bidder are shown in Table 13–9. Also shown are the coupons and reoffering yields of the low TIC bidder and estimates of the reoffering yields at which the bonds could have been sold successfully had the coupon rates been at or near their par values. These yields are estimated from the market yields on comparable bonds on the same date.

On a TIC basis, the low NIC bid was the highest of the seven bids submitted. The low TIC bid was the fourth lowest NIC bid. The penalty yields associated with the 50 percent coupons on the first four maturities relative to the 10 percent

Table 13–9 Coupon rates and reoffering yields of winning and low TIC bidders and estimated efficient reoffering yields on sample bond issue[1]

Years to maturity	Winning bidder (low NIC)		Low TIC bidder		Estimated efficient reoffering yield
	Coupon rate	Reoffering yield (%)	Coupon rate	Reoffering yield (%)	
1	50.0	3.65	10.0	3.10	3.10
2	50.0	3.75	10.0	3.40	3.35
3	50.0	4.00	10.0	3.70	3.55
4	50.0	4.20	10.0	3.85	3.75
5	10.0	4.10	10.0	4.00	3.95
6	10.0	4.25	10.0	4.15	4.10
7	5.0	4.25	10.0	4.30	4.20
8	5.0	4.35	4.7	4.30	4.30
9	4.75	4.45	4.7	4.35	4.35
10	4.75	4.55	4.7	4.45	4.45
11	4.75	4.65	4.7	4.55	4.55
12	4.75	4.75	4.7	4.65	4.65
13	5.0	4.85	4.8	4.75	4.75
14	0.1	6.30[2]	4.8	4.85	4.85
15	0.1	6.30[2]	5.0	4.90	4.90
16	0.1	6.30[2]	5.0	4.95	4.95
17	0.1	6.30[2]	5.0	5.00	5.00
18	0.1	6.30[2]	5.0	5.00	5.00
19	0.1	6.30[2]	0.1	6.70	5.05
20	0.1	6.30[2]	0.1	6.70	5.05
NIC (%)		4.58		4.66	. . .[3]
TIC (%)		5.51		4.90	4.75

1 State of Minnesota bond issue sold 26 September 1972.
2 Estimated from price data in fincancial press.
3 Not applicable.

coupons of the low TIC bids range from 30 to 55 basis points (one-hundredth of a percentage point). But even the 10 percent coupons would have caused the bonds to sell at premiums priced to require penalty yields. Note how much higher the reoffering yields were on the 10 percent coupon bonds than the estimated yields on the par bonds of the maturity.

The effect of large discounts below par on reoffering yields is also evident. Reoffering yields jump by 145 basis points from 4.8 percent to 6.30 percent on the winning bid when the coupon declines from 5.0 percent to 0.1 percent between the thirteenth and fourteenth maturity. The penalty yields on these bonds is in excess of one percentage point. Note that even the low bid from the TIC criterion placed 0.1 percent coupons on the last two maturities so that these bonds also sold at penalty yields. However, if a more efficient award criterion, say TIC, had been specified from the inception, then all of the bids would have been lower. At any rate, the combined present value cost of the selection of the "wrong" bid, which resulted in penalty reoffering yields, was estimated to be about $1.25 million higher than necessary interest payments over the life of the bonds. This amount would not have been expended had more efficient bidding procedures been used.

As noted, this is not a representative example. Many issuers and underwriters have been aware of the potential for excessive interest costs when using NIC. To minimize the effects, constraints are often placed on the value of the coupons to be used by bidders. But often these constraints are not as efficient as possible and, on occasion, none are imposed. The example of the Minnesota sale specified no coupon constraints whatsoever. A survey of municipal bonds sold in 1972 and 1973 indicated that the excess cost in terms of the overall present value of higher interest costs paid over the life of the bonds sold competitively by NIC was between $20 million and $40 million in each of these years. This was only a fraction of one percent of the par value of all bonds sold competitively, but it is a large dollar amount that could be avoided at virtually no cost to the issuer.

Bidding procedures that would avoid these excess interest costs have been developed by the Center for Capital Market Research at the University of Oregon. The Center recommends that all but the smallest issuers use TIC criteria to award their bonds. The widespread use of computers, and readily available TIC computer programs, no longer makes the computation of TIC difficult or time-consuming. Almost all underwriters now have had experience with TIC bidding so that there should not be a reduction in the number of bids received.

Nevertheless, some issuers are restricted by law to use NIC, and other issuers may feel that the issue size is so small that all the bidders may not have TIC capability. For them, the Center recommends limiting the range of values of the coupons that underwriters may place on the individual bonds; thus, no coupon on a bond would be smaller than that on the preceding maturity. This constraint is termed *nondescending order* (NDO), and reduces the probability that the individual bonds will be reoffered at large discounts on premiums that require costly penalty yields. Because each bond issue is different, however, it is important for finance officers to select the constraints most appropriate for their particular issue.[5] Conditions are improving. In 1978, about 40 percent of the dollar volume of all bonds sold competitively was awarded on the basis of efficient bidding criteria. This is an increase from approximately 5 percent in 1972, and has resulted in significant cost savings to issuers.

Broadening the market

As discussed earlier in this chapter, the tax-exemption feature effectively narrows the market for municipal securities to investors in high marginal federal income tax brackets (e.g., wealthy individuals, commercial banks, and property and casualty insurance companies). The feature tends to exclude such important buyers as endowment funds, foundations, and pension funds. The relatively narrow market may cause interest rates on municipal securities to be higher after tax adjustment than they might be otherwise. In addition, the cyclical instability of bank demand for municipal securities has made interest rates on municipal bonds more volatile than on most other securities.

In periods of heavy business loan demands, banks reduce their purchases of municipal bonds, the market for municipal securities shrinks significantly, and the interest cost on new securities rises sharply.

For some time, the Treasury has contended that the current form of tax exemption represents an inefficient and costly subsidy to state and local government issuers. It is inefficient because the interest cost savings to issuers is less than the income tax loss to the Treasury. This occurs because high quality, long-term municipal bonds sell at almost 70 percent of the interest rate on Treasury securities with the same term to maturity. Thus, the cost savings to the tax-exempt issuers is about 30 percent. However, a large number of municipal bonds is purchased by investors whose marginal tax brackets are substantially higher than 30 percent. The loss to the Treasury from the reduction of income tax revenues from these investors is greater than the 30 percent interest savings to the local issuers. For example, if the average purchaser of municipal bonds were in the 50 percent federal income-tax bracket, the interest rate to municipal issuers would have to be 50 percent of the interest rate on comparable Treasury securities in order for the gain to the issuer to be equal to the loss to the Treasury.

To increase the efficiency of the subsidy, the Treasury has proposed a *taxable bond option* (TBO) for issuers. Under this proposal, issuers could sell taxable municipal bonds instead of tax-exempt bonds. This would, of course, increase the interest cost of the bonds. The Treasury, however, would make a direct payment to the issuer to compensate for the higher cost. The Treasury also would collect the full tax revenues from investors. The desirability of the TBO to state and local governments depends on the ratio of the Treasury compensation to the interest costs. The larger the ratio of payment, the more attractive the program. In addition to the compensation, the Treasury argues that issuers would benefit from the lower and more stable interest costs resulting from the demand for the securities by a larger number and a wider range of investors. The higher pretax interest rates would make municipal bonds attractive to individual and institutional investors in lower marginal tax brackets (e.g., moderate income households, endowment funds, pension funds, and life insurance companies). Moreover, when commercial banks reduce their demand for municipal securities, these new investors are likely to increase their demand to absorb at least part of the shortfall.

In spite of its appeal, a proposal for a taxable bond option has not been enacted by Congress. This may be attributed primarily to the facts that (1) economically, state and local governments have not found that the payment the Treasury would make to offset the higher interest costs is high enough, in spite of the fact that the proposals have called for payments ranging from 30 percent to 40 percent of the market interest rate; and (2) politically, state and local governments are fearful of more intervention by the Treasury in their debt management decisions. Thus, the TBO has remained an idea whose time has not yet come.

---

1   Three firms currently offer such insurance: American Municipal Bond Assurance Corporation (AMBAC), MGIC Indemnity Corporation, and Municipal Bond Insurance Corporation. The first two are subsidiaries of the Mortgage Guaranty Insurance Corporation and the third is a joint venture by four large property and casualty insurance companies.

2   The Municipal Securities Rule Making Commission was organized in 1975 as an independent, self-regulatory agency to supervise and monitor the activities of firms and individuals engaged in the trading of municipal securities for the protection of investors. It cannot, however, require the issuers to furnish information to investors or underwriters, as does the SEC for private issues.

3   Oregon Revised Statute 287.018.

4   See, for example: Michael H. Hopewell and George G. Kaufman, "Costs to Municipalities of Selling Bonds by NIC," *National Tax Journal* (December 1974):531–41.

5   Center for Capital Market Research, *Improving Bidding Rules to Reduce Interest Costs in the Competitive Sale of Municipal Bonds: A Handbook for Municipal Finance Officers* (Eugene: University of Oregon, 1977).

14 Cash management

A number of studies have shown that many local governments carry cash balances in excess of those necessary for immediate transactions. There is a cost involved in carrying excess cash funds: the loss of earnings forgone on the investment of idle funds in marketable securities. The purpose of this chapter is to explore methods for improving the management of cash in order to obtain additional revenue from investing temporary excess funds in marketable securities.

The discussion begins with a treatment of cash budgeting and the constraints that shape the cash balance position. Two models for determining optimal cash and security positions are then analyzed. Adaptations of the economic ordering quantity (EOQ) model are useful in cases where cash inflows and outflows are relatively predictable. The Miller-Orr control model may fit those situations where the cash flows are more volatile.

The chapter moves on to a discussion of effective methods of investing in marketable securities, gives an outline of the general principles of such investment, the types of marketable securities involved, and the role of the securities portfolio. Lastly, the chapter briefly touches on the problem of investment policy for pension funds.

Procedures for cash management

The actual cash position of a city, county, or other local government and the constraints that shape that position will be discussed shortly. First, however, it is necessary to outline the role played by cash budgeting—a vital initial step in cash management.

Cash budgeting

In order to forecast the need for cash balances, the finance officer must prepare a series of periodic cash budgets. Although these budgets can be drawn up for almost any interval, monthly forecasts are the most common. It should be emphasized at the outset that a cash budget differs from operating and capital budgets in that it is much less detailed. The cash budget needs only show the aggregate of forecasted cash expenditures and cash inflows for the period. If proper care has been taken in the preparation of the operating and the capital budgets, if control is exercised over expenditures, and if revenues are stable and relatively predictable, the cash budget is likely to be quite accurate. Because of the greater predictability of the receipts and expenditures of governments as compared to business, cash budgets for municipal governments are usually more accurate than those for business corporations.

The principal sources of revenue for the local government are the property tax and various state and federal grants-in-aid. Because the property tax remains the main source of local revenue, the bulk of cash receipts are concentrated in one or two relatively short periods of time in the local tax calendar. Other tax receipts may be spread more evenly over the year. For purposes of cash management, it is essential to forecast when the taxes will actually be collected in cash. In most cases, predictions based on the analysis of past experience are quite accurate. However, the cash receipts of municipally operated utilities also must be projected according to their seasonal fluctuations, if any.

After the timing of projected receipts is forecast, the finance officer should forecast cash disbursements. *General expenses,* which include wages and other operating expenses, can be projected with a considerable degree of accuracy on the basis of past experience and the adopted budget plan. The outlays on capital expenditures also can be projected from a budget, although the timing of these expenditures during the budget period is not entirely certain. The timing of debt servicing, a contractual obligation, is quite certain.

The forecasts of receipts and disbursements are combined to determine the net impact on the cash position for any given time period. A sample cash budget for the hypothetical city of Anytown is shown in Figure 14–1. The purpose of the cash budget is to determine the timing and magnitude of projected cash needs as well as that of any projected cash surpluses. According to Figure 14–1, the city of Anytown forecasts an operating cash deficit in January, February, and March. The finance officer can plan to meet these deficits either by floating tax-anticipation loans or by selling marketable securities purchased during previous surplus periods. In April, the city receives payment of the semiannual property tax and thus has surplus funds. The financial officer may then repay the tax-anticipation loans or invest cash in excess of transaction needs in short-term marketable securities. By proper planning, the efficiency of cash management can be improved resulting in income from interest or a minimization of interest payments on short-term notes. The cash budget is an all important tool for achieving these objectives.

Fiscal item	January	February	March	April	May	June
Expected receipts	$480	$513	$718	$3461	$ 487	$496
Expected disbursements	891	902	907	905	1341	904
Receipts less disbursements	(411)	(389)	(189)	2556	(854)	(408)
Cash at beginning of month	181	(230)	(619)	(808)	1748	894
Cumulative cash position at end of month	(230)	(619)	(808)	1748	894	486

Figure 14–1   City of Anytown, cash budget, January–June, 19___ ($000).

Cash position

The transaction cash balance maintained by a municipality should be determined with reference to two constraints. The first constraint is the minimum compensating balance requirement imposed by commercial banks. The second, self-imposed, constraint consists of the determination of the optimal cash balance held considering transaction costs, cash out risks, and current interest rates. The minimum cash balance a municipality holds should be the larger of these two amounts.

Commercial bank services

Commercial banks provide a wide array of services for which they expect compensation in the form of imputed return on the deposits held with them, or in the form of explicit fees. Most banks prefer the former. The principal services performed by the banks include the clearing of check deposits, the acceptance of cash deposits, and the accounting for checks and warrants drawn against the account. As most checks deposited by a municipal government are drawn on local banks, there is generally little need—or even the possibility—to accelerate collections through such special arrangements as lock boxes, concentration banking, and the wire transfer of funds.[1] In most cases, deposit activity in the account is straightforward and does not call for any special arrangements with the banks.

Although collections generally cannot be accelerated, municipal governments do have the ability to slow payments through the use of warrants. A warrant is a draft payable through a bank. When a warrant is presented for payment, the bank does not pay it until it is accepted by the municipality. The use of warrants reduces the amount of funds the municipality must have on deposit at any given time. Banks, however, do impose higher service charges for warrants than they do for checks because of the greater amount of clerical work involved. Therefore, these increased costs must be balanced against the earnings available to the municipality on the funds retained by their use.

Cost of services

The bank determines the cost of servicing an account on the basis of the account's activity and then decides on the average daily balance needed for the bank's compensation (the balance that must be carried by the depositor if there are to be no additional charges). In analyzing an account, a bank calculates the actual average collected balances over some period of time. From the average collected balance, the bank subtracts the required reserve percentage—about 16 percent currently for demand deposits of larger banks, and this residual becomes part of the earning base on which the bank's income is generated. The imputed total income obtainable from the account is determined by multiplying the earnings base by the average rate earned by the bank on its loans and investments. Naturally, the basic earnings rate fluctuates with interest rate levels in the money market, an important factor in today's dramatically fluctuating money markets.

The income from an account is offset by the estimated cost of servicing the account's activity. Most banks have a schedule of costs on a per item basis for such transactions as processing deposited checks, paying checks drawn on the account, and paying warrants. The account is analyzed for a typical month, during which the sample transactions are multiplied by the per item costs and totalled. If total income exceeds total costs, the account returns some profit to the bank. There is a minimum average level of cash balances at which a given account breaks even. This becomes the required cash balance or compensating cash balance.

Because banks differ in their earnings rate as well as in their costs and methods of account analysis, the determination of compensating balances varies. Thus, a municipality would be wise to "shop around" to find the bank requiring the lowest compensating balances for a given level of activity. Some municipalities make a practice of periodically placing their banking business up for bids. In this way, banking is treated like any other purchase subject to competitive bidding. However, various state statutory rules and requirements limit the freedom of a locality to make depository arrangements. Some of these require that a local government use only banks located in the state or even in the same city. Some require that deposits be divided proportionately among the local banks. Other state regulations may bar the local government from carrying its funds in thrift institutions (savings banks and savings and loan associations [SLAs]) instead of commercial banks. Most common are the restrictions on volume, which limit the amount that can be carried with any bank. Sometimes the limit is the Federal Deposit Insurance Corporation (FDIC) insured amount (currently $100,000). More often the limit amount is determined by some ratio of the deposit to the bank's capital accounts or a ratio of the deposit to the bank's total assets.[2] These various requirements may reduce the flexibility of the municipality in achieving optimal cash management, especially the advantages that may be derived from economies of scale in pooling deposits.

In recent years there has been a trend toward paying fees for services rendered in lieu of maintaining a compensating balance. The advantage to the municipality in this arrangement is that it may be able to earn more on the funds released from the compensating balance than the fees it pays for the services rendered. The higher the interest rates obtainable in the money markets, the greater the possible earnings vis-à-vis the cost of service charges. To determine if the municipality would do better to pay the service charges rather than to maintain the full required compensating balance, the charges may be compared with the estimated earnings to be made on the funds released. In spite of the fact that many banks in the past resisted placing normal services (e.g., the clearing of checks) on a fee schedule, an increasing number of bank services are being offered on a fee basis.

The balances maintained at a bank and the services performed by the bank should be analyzed carefully. If the municipality's average deposits are in excess of the required compensating balance, funds may be tied up unnecessarily. However, the problem of determining the optimum transaction cash balance must be solved before it can be decided whether excess cash is being carried. It may well be that the local government would do best by maintaining a cash balance in excess of the minimum required by the bank if the optimum transaction balance is in fact larger.

Models for determining cash and security positions

How is the optimum cash balance determined independently of the compensating balance requirement imposed by the bank? Assume that the municipality's holdings of total liquid funds, which comprise both cash and marketable securities, have been set. This total amount consists of funds appropriated for capital improvements and not yet spent; funds set aside for debt servicing and other special purposes; and funds that have accumulated through the seasonal collections of taxes or through the flotation of tax anticipation loans. If the total amount of liquid assets (cash and marketable securities) is established, the next step is to decide how much of each of these assets to hold. A number of guidelines are available.

The simplest guidelines are certain "rules of thumb" which are still used by many municipalities. One rule is to hold a certain number of days' expenditures as the cash balance. For example, the cash balance might be expenditures for one week. If weekly expenditures average $125,000, this amount would be the cash balance maintained, with residual liquid funds being invested in marketable securities. Whenever the cash balances fell below $125,000, securities would be sold to restore the cash balance to that amount. Other rules based on expenditure patterns can be easily devised. In most municipalities, forecasts of cash needs are quite accurate and the prospect of unexpectedly running out of cash is not likely; consequently, rules of thumb can provide useful operating procedures for cash management. The additional effort and expense of the more sophisticated models may not be justified, particularly for the smaller municipality, because the administrative costs may exceed possible benefits. One important factor entering into the decision to use a more complex model would be the height of the prevailing interest rates as compared to the extra costs of administering the model.

Analytical models that permit accurate measurement of the optimum cash balance have been developed. The use of the computer has resulted in some fairly complex systems. However, the relatively simple models (e.g., the economic ordering quantity [EOQ] formula and the Miller-Orr model) illuminate most of the variables contained in the more complex programs.

Economic ordering quantity

One common cash model is derived from the economic ordering quantity (EOQ) formula used in inventory management.[3] Here, the carrying cost of holding cash (the interest earnings forgone on the cash balance) is balanced against the estimated fixed cost per transaction of transferring funds from the marketable securities portfolio to cash or vice versa. The costs of carrying cash are directly proportional to the average cash balance held (i.e., the greater the cash balance maintained, the greater the possible earnings forgone on the investment of these funds in marketable securities). On the other hand, the total transaction costs vary directly with the number of transactions, and these will be lower if a higher average cash balance is maintained. Thus, there is a trade-off between the total carrying costs and the total transaction costs over a given period for various levels of cash.

Figure 14–2 illustrates this trade-off. Assume that the time period *OT*, measured on the horizontal axis, is the duration between property tax payments and that the municipality receives a large amount of cash at the outset of a period. There are no other receipts during the period, although new receipts will be received at the end of the period. Assume also that expenditures are steady and that total expenditures expected are just equal to the cash receipts at the outset of the period. The municipality must decide on the optimal average cash balance. One strategy might be initially to hold *X* dollars in cash; when this is expended, replenish it by selling *X* dollars worth of marketable securities. This transfer of funds would be undertaken whenever cash levels reached zero; thus, there would be four transactions in total, including the original transfer of cash to marketable securities in order to get the cash balance down to *X*. (Initial cash receipts would be multiplied by four.) The average cash balances are *X*/2 in Figure 14–2. The opportunity cost is this average balance multiplied by the rate of interest available on marketable securities (*X*/2 multiplied by *i*).

Another strategy is to have maximum cash of *Y* and to transfer *Y* dollars from marketable securities when the cash balance reaches zero. The number of transactions is eight—twice as many as cited previously—but the average cash balance

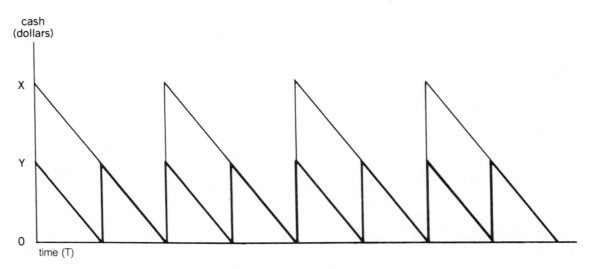

Figure 14–2   Inventory model applied to cash management.

is less, namely, *Y*/2. Thus, the average cash balance can be lowered only if we have more transactions from marketable securities to cash over the period. On the one hand, a lower cash balance reduces the total earnings forgone on the investment (this is equivalent to the carrying cost), but it increases the total transfer or transaction costs. The determination of an optimal average cash balance involves a trade-off between these two types of costs, which move in opposite directions. The optimal size cash balance *minimizes* the total of both transaction costs and the opportunity cost of interest earnings forgone for the period.

The total costs of carrying cash can be expressed in the following equation:

$$P = b\left(\frac{T}{C}\right) + vT + i\left(\frac{C}{2}\right) \tag{1}$$

where *P* equals the total cost of cash management; *b* equals the fixed cost per transaction of transferring funds from marketable securities to cash or vice versa; *T* is the total amount of cash payments or expenditures over the period involved; *C* is the size of the transfer, which is the maximum amount of cash; *v* is the variable cost per dollar of funds transferred; and *i* equals the interest rate on marketable securities for the period involved.

Two parts of the equation (*b* and *v*) reflect the two types of costs (fixed and variable) involved in transferring funds between marketable securities and cash, or vice versa. Included in *b*, the fixed costs per transaction, are such items as the time it takes the finance officer or other officials to place an order with an investment banker; the time the official uses to record the transaction; the cost of the secretarial time needed to type the transaction and the purchase orders; the time devoted to recording the transaction in the controller's office; and the time needed to record the safe-keeping notification. These costs are the same regardless of the size of the transaction and are incurred each time a transaction takes place. A cost study should be undertaken to estimate their magnitude. Because costs vary with the office efficiency and the wage rates of a municipality, no one transaction cost figure is appropriate for all municipal governments. In the equation, *T*/*C* represents the number of transfers during the period, *b(T/C)* (transaction costs multiplied by the number of transfers) is the total of the transaction costs for the period.

The major part of the variable cost, *v*, are such costs as brokerage fees, which are proportional to the size of the transfer. In the equation, *vT* represents total brokerage fees over the period. The brokerage fees vary with the given volume of dollars transferred over the period, and not with the number of individual transactions. These costs are the same regardless of the number of transfers so they are not a factor in the determination of *C*, the optimum withdrawal, or of *C*/2, the optimum average balance.

The last term in the equation represents the total earnings forgone by holding a positive cash balance during the period. (If the cash balance is borrowed from the banks, *i* represents the interest paid to the lending institution.) As *C*/2 represents the average cash balance, the total interest forgone is obtained by multiplying *C*/2 by *i* (the current interest rate on marketable securities). The appropriate rate of interest is that associated with the securities that would have to be sold to replenish the cash. Generally, this is the rate on short-term market instruments and not the average rate of return on all marketable securities. If the initial cash balance and size of transfer (*C*) is set at a higher level, the number of transfers between marketable securities and cash (*T/C*) decreases, as will the total costs. However, an increase in *C* results in a greater average cash balance (*C*/2), which then results in a higher opportunity cost of interest income forgone. When these two costs are balanced at the margin, total costs are minimized.

The equation used to solve for the value of *C* that results in minimum costs is the well-known economic ordering quantity (EOQ) formula, where C^* is the optimal transfer size and initial cash balance. Equation (1), which represents total costs, is differentiated with respect to C and the derivative set to equal zero, obtaining:

$$\frac{dP}{dC} = \frac{i}{2} - \frac{bT}{C^2}$$

$$\frac{i}{2} = \frac{bT}{C^2}$$

$$C^2 = \frac{2bT}{i} \tag{2}$$

$$C^* = \sqrt{\frac{2bT}{i}}$$

The size of *average* cash balance, $C^*/2$, varies with the square root of the level of cash payments, T. This implies that as the *level* of total cash expenditures increases, the amount of cash the municipality needs to hold increases less than proportionally. In other words, economies of scale are possible in cash management. This argues against the proliferation of special cash funds because the combined transactions of two activities can be handled by a smaller balance than the sum of two separate funds. To be sure, the segregation of funds is often a requirement of outdated laws. Municipal officers should strive to change such laws where possible, as cash management efficiency can be improved if separate accounts can be consolidated. By transacting all banking business through a single account, or through as few accounts as possible, it is possible to release extra funds for portfolio investment.

The ACIR has suggested several methods for improving cash management. One is a lock box system that speeds the deposit of receipts (taxpayer payments) to the bank. Another possibility is the use of zero balance accounts, which is one general account and separate clearing accounts for different departments. These clearing accounts are maintained at zero balance, but the bank automatically transfers funds from the master account when checks are presented for payment. This method gives the finance officer control over the individual accounts, but it still permits a consolidation of cash and economizes the size of the cash balance.[4]

To illustrate the application of the EOQ formula, a sample problem is offered for solution.[5] Consider a municipal government with estimated total cash payments (T) of $6 million for a three-month period. These payments are expected to be at a steady rate over the period. The cost per transaction (b) is $50, and the interest rate on marketable securities (i) is approximately 12 percent per annum or 3 percent for the quarter. Therefore,

$$C = \sqrt{\frac{2bT}{i}} = \sqrt{\frac{2(50)(6,000,000)}{.03}} = \$141,421. \tag{3}$$

Thus, the optimal initial cash balance and transfer size is $141,421, and the average cash balance is one-half of $141,421 or $70,710. This means the municipality should make approximately forty-two transfers from marketable securities to cash for the period ($6,000,000/141,421 = 42+$).

The optimum number of transactions will be larger if transfer costs are relatively low and interests rates relatively high. On the other hand, the higher the cost per transfer and the lower the interest rate, the higher the starting cash balance for each period and the smaller the number of transfer transactions.

In this illustration, the total cost of cash management for the period under the optimum solution is:

$$P = \$50 \left(\frac{\$6,000,000}{\$141,421} \right) + .005 \, (\$6,000,000)$$
$$+ .03 \left(\frac{\$141,421}{2} \right) = \$7,242. \tag{4}$$

If an initial cash balance and transfer amount of \$200,000 had been used instead of \$141,421, the equation would be:

$$P = \$50 \left(\frac{\$6,000,000}{\$200,000} \right) + .005 \, (\$6,000,000)$$
$$+ .03 \left(\frac{\$200,000}{2} \right) = \$7,500. \tag{5}$$

Here the lower transaction costs do not offset the greater amount of interest forgone on the cash holdings. If the initial cash balance and transfer size had been set at \$50,000, however, the equation is:

$$P = \$50 \left(\frac{\$6,000,000}{\$50,000} \right) + .005 \, (\$6,000,000)$$
$$+ .03 \left(\frac{\$50,000}{2} \right) = \$9,750. \tag{6}$$

In this case, the amount of interest earnings lost is reduced, but there are now too many transfers within a more-than-offsetting increase in transaction costs.

For most municipal governments, the assumption that cash payments are steady over a specified period of time is true with respect to operating expenditures. Of course, capital improvements may sometimes fluctuate, making for some irregularity in the total expenditure stream, but these can be forecast. Capital expenditures tend to involve single payments and are highly predictable; they need not be part of the operating cash balance at all.

Municipal government expenditures usually are predictable enough to make the EOQ approach feasible, yet the flow of cash payments is seldom completely certain. To cover a modest degree of uncertainty, however, a precautionary balance may be added to the transaction balance so that the transfer from marketable securities to cash is triggered before the cash balance reaches zero. (Such use of precautionary balances in the amount of Z is illustrated in Figure 14–3.) Nevertheless, in general, the EOQ model gives the finance officer a fairly good benchmark for judging the optimal cash balance. The model does not have to be used as a precise rule; it merely suggests the optimal balance under a given set of assumptions. The actual cash balance may be somewhat larger if the assumptions do not hold together entirely.

The Miller-Orr model

In those cases where there is significant uncertainty in the stream of cash payments, the EOQ model may not be applicable—a situation that would be the exception rather than the rule. If conditions vary, other models can be devised to determine optimal behavior. For example, if cash balances fluctuate randomly, a control theory may be applied to the problem. Assume that the demand for cash is not known. The idea is to set control limits so that when cash reaches an upper limit, a transfer of cash to marketable securities is effected; and when cash balances touch the lower limit, it triggers a transfer from marketable securities to cash. As long as cash balances stay between these two limits, no transactions take place.

In the Miller-Orr model, the levels at which the control limits are set depend

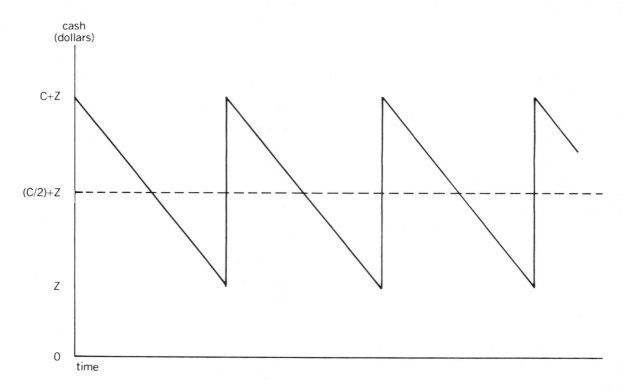

Figure 14–3   Inventory model applied to cash management with precautionary balance of *Z*.

on the fixed costs associated with each security transaction and the opportunity cost of holding cash.[6] As before, assume these two types of costs are known or can be estimated and that the transaction cost of selling a marketable security is the same as that for buying a security. In essence, the demand for cash must be satisfied at the lowest possible total cost. Although there are a number of different applications of control theory, a simple illustration suffices here. The Miller-Orr model specifies two control limits—*h* dollars as an upper bound and zero dollars as a lower bound. The model is illustrated in Figure 14–4. When the cash balance touches the upper bound, *h* minus *z* dollars of marketable securities are purchased, and the new balance becomes *z* dollars. When the cash balance touches zero, *z* dollars of marketable securities are sold and the new balance again becomes *z*. If there are possible delays before a transfer can be completed, the minimum bound could be set at some amount higher than zero, and *h* and *z* would move up in Figure 14–4. However, zero will be used as the lower bound for purposes of illustration. The control limits are determined in keeping with the transactions and opportunity costs as well as the degree of likely fluctuations in cash balances. The greater the likely fluctuations, the greater the control limits. The Miller-Orr model is applicable only if cash balances fluctuate randomly.

The optimal value of *z*, the return-to-point for security transactions, is

$$z = \sqrt[3]{\frac{3b\sigma^2}{4i}} \qquad (7)$$

where *b* equals fixed cost per security transaction; σ^2 equals variance of daily net cash flows (measure of dispersion); *i* equals interest rate per day on marketable securities. The optimal value of *h* is simply 3*z*. With these control limits set, the model minimizes the total costs (fixed and opportunity) of cash management. Again, the critical assumption is that cash flows are random. The average cash balance cannot be determined exactly in advance, but it is approximately $z + h/3$. As experience increases, however, it can be calculated easily.

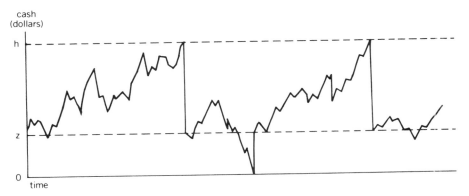

Figure 14–4   Miller–Orr model for cash management using control limits for the purchase and sale of marketable securities.

Optimal cash balances

Two models for determining an optimal level of cash balances have been presented. The EOQ model assumes that cash payments and inflows are predictable, whereas the control limit model assumes that inflows and outflows are random. In most municipalities the cash flow is essentially predictable, so the simple EOQ model is more applicable than the Miller-Orr model. If there is only moderate uncertainty, the EOQ model can be modified to incorporate precautionary balances. On the other hand, the Miller-Orr model can serve as the benchmark for determining cash balances where there is a strong element of uncertainty. Generally, the average cash balance will be considerably higher when this model is used than if the EOQ model is used. In tests of these two models run with data for the city and county of Honolulu, it was found that the Miller-Orr model resulted in an average cash balance four times as high as that which resulted from the use of the EOQ model.[7] Thus, when the balances of a municipality are higher than those dictated, even by the Miller-Orr model, and cash payments are relatively predictable, it is certain that the cash balance is too high.

The optimal average cash balance will be the higher of the compensating balance requirement of the bank and that suggested by a cash inventory/marketable securities model. In many cases the compensating balance requirement may exceed the self-imposed constraint of the cash inventory model. On the other hand, if the costs of security transactions are high or the cost of holding cash is low (because the interest rate is low), it is possible that an average balance in excess of the compensating balance requirement should be maintained.

Investment in marketable securities

Once a municipality has decided on an optimal cash balance, the rest of its treasury funds may be invested in a portfolio of marketable securities. For most municipalities the portfolio will come to 70 percent or more of its total liquid assets; for municipalities more efficient in cash management, the portfolio may be more than 90 percent. The choice of securities for the portfolio is somewhat limited because most states have set up legal restrictions on the securities in which a municipality may invest. However, the legal list still permits some flexibility. The legal lists usually permit investment in U.S. Treasury securities, U.S. agency securities, obligations of other municipal governments within the state, and bank certificates of deposit (CDs). The yield, maturity, safety, and other characteristics of each of these securities will be examined. First, the reasons why different securities carry different market yields need to be explored.

Different market yields

Market yield differences on securities exist because of variations in (1) the length of time to maturity; (2) the degree of default risk; (3) the ease of marketability; (4) the call provisions; and (5) the tax status. In the following discussion, the influence of each of these factors on market rates of interest will be examined.

Maturity The relationship between yield and maturity can be studied graphically. The yield and maturity for securities may be plotted such that they differ only in length of time to maturity and such that the degree of default risk is presumably held constant. The yield-maturity relationship usually is presented for default-free Treasury securities. Examples of yield curves (or term structures) are shown in Figures 14–5 and 14–6. Maturity is plotted on the horizontal axis and the market yields plotted on the vertical axis; the relationship between market yields and the time to maturity of the security is described by the yield curve.

In October 1976 and January 1977, the yield curve was sloped upward. However, in the middle of the money market halt by the U.S. Federal Reserve in March of 1980, the curve had a strong downward slope.

The direction of the term structure has considerable significance for participants in the market. Normally, when the market consensus is balanced, whether

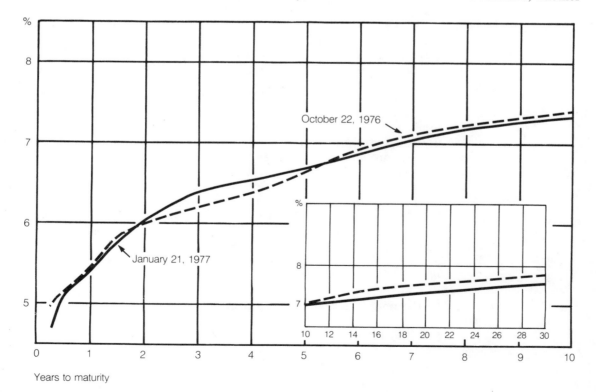

Figure 14–5   Market yields on government bonds for thirty years, issues of 22 October 1976 and 21 January 1977.

the future course of the general interest rate will be upward or downward, the curve will slope slightly upward because long-term instruments will carry a higher yield than the short-term instruments. This indicates net risk aversion (or liquidity preference) on the part of the market. If the market interest rate changes, the price of long-term instruments will show a considerably greater fluctuation than the price for shorter-term securities. Because some part of the portfolio is designed for turnover (short-term uses) and because there is a desire to avoid changes in values (the utility of possible gains does not offset the disutility of possible losses), short-term financial investments generally have a lower yield than longer-term investments of the same class.

The yield curve will show a more pronounced upward slope when there is a market expectation that the level of general interest rates will rise in the future. The explanation of this phenomenon is simple. Under these conditions, the long-term borrower is willing to contract to pay a somewhat higher rate because it is probable that the rate will go up still higher in the future. The short-term borrower pays a lower rate presently, but is likely to pay a higher rate when he or she rolls over or renews his or her borrowings in the future. In contrast, the lender may decide to lend short because after cashing in the short-term instruments, there are likely to be higher yields available in the market.

If the market expects a decline in the prevailing interest rates, there will be a "reversal" in the term structure and a downward sloping yield curve will result, as shown in Figure 14–6. (The yields on short-term securities in the winter of 1979 and early spring of 1980 were higher than on long terms.) The reasons for this downward slope are the reverse of those presented for the pronounced upward sloping yield curve. In this situation, investors may shift some of their funds to the longer end of the market to lock into the attractive current yields.

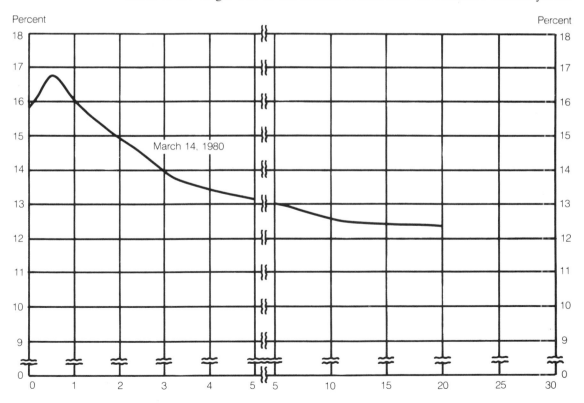

Figure 14–6 Yield on U.S. government securities,
issue of 14 March 1980.

Some normal long-term borrowers may pay temporarily the high rates prevailing on the shorter maturities, expecting that they will be able to refund at lower rates in the future.

It behooves the city finance officer, whether arranging borrowing or the placing of funds for investment, to understand what the market's current yield curve is saying about the future of the interest rate.

Default risk   The second factor that contributes to differences in yields is related to the possibility that the borrower will default on principal or interest payments. Investors will demand a risk premium (a higher interest rate) as an inducement for them to invest in securities that are not default-free. All other factors constant, the greater the possibility of default, the higher the interest rate. Because Treasury securities are regarded as default-free, other securities may be judged in relation to them. (U.S. agency issues are almost rated equally to Treasury securities in credit worthiness.) Municipals are judged on the basis of security ratings published by Moody's Investors Service or Standard & Poor's Index. If the municipality is able to accept the risk, it can achieve somewhat higher returns by investing in riskier securities.

Marketability   Marketability, the third factor in yield differentials, relates to the ability of the owner of a security to sell the security. Marketability has two dimensions: the price realized and the amount of time required to sell the asset. The two are interrelated in that it is often possible to sell an asset in a short period of time, given a sufficient price concession. For financial instruments, marketability is judged in relation to the ability to execute the sale of a significant volume of securities without offering a significant price concession. The more marketable the security, the greater the ability of its owner to execute a large transaction near the present quoted price. With all other factors equal, the more marketable securities will carry lower yields.

Call provisions   A call feature on a financial instrument allows the borrower to buy it back at a predetermined price before maturity. The call privilege works to the benefit of the borrower, providing the individual with the flexibility of refunding the issue before maturity if interest rates move significantly lower. Because an issue is usually called at a time when interest rates are low, the investor has to place the funds in other securities, often a sacrifice of yield to maturity. The call provision, therefore, works to the disadvantage of the investor. Investors consequently will demand a yield inducement to invest in a callable security. Virtually all corporate bonds have a call feature; however, many municipal bonds do not. Some U.S. Treasury bonds are callable; these usually are deferred call features that cannot be exercised until approximately five years before maturity. Because municipalities usually do not put funds into corporate bonds, the effect of the call feature is relatively unimportant to them as investors.

Tax status   Another factor affecting observed differences in market yields is the impact of taxes. The most important effect is that of the federal income tax. Interest income from state and local government securities is tax-exempt, although capital gains on municipal bonds are taxable. Because of the tax exemption, local government securities sell in the market at lower yields than do Treasury or corporate securities of the same maturity. Local governments do not pay federal income taxes on their investment income so the tax-exempt feature is of no use to them, and they should not invest in state and local government securities. They should invest in Treasury, or other high grade securities, where higher yields are available. All other things being the same, municipalities (as well as tax-exempt endowment funds) should invest in the securities that show the highest pretax return.

Deep discount bonds bearing low coupon rates may have lower market yields because the eventual recovery of the discount is taxed at the lower capital gains rate. To offset this advantage, high coupon bonds often offer a better pretax yield. When possible, local governemnts should take advantage of the "bargain yields" on high coupon bonds selling at par or above.

Comparisons and trade-offs   Five factors have been presented that explain yield differentials on securities: time to maturity, default risk, marketability, callability, and taxability.[8] By analyzing securities on the basis of these factors, the finance officer can assess what must be given up with respect to the first four factors in order to achieve higher yields. Treating the yield on a very short-term Treasury bill as the basic yield, the market in terms of a structure of yields may be analyzed. Differences in yields are illustrated in Table 14–1 for instruments which differ in maturity, default risk, and marketability.

Table 14–1   Representative yields to maturity of various financial instruments, May 1980

Instrument	Yield (%)
3-month Treasury bill	8.58
3-month commercial paper	9.49
6-month certificate of deposit	9.78
Long-term Treasury bond (10-year)	10.18
Long-term corporate bond (industrial)	11.91
Long-term municipal bond (mixed quality, tax-free, 20-year)	7.59

Source: *Federal Reserve Bulletin*, June 1980.

Types of marketable securities[9]

In the section that follows, the more prominent marketable securities available for municipal investment are described and then the question of how investment decisions might be made is considered. It should be noted that various rules and laws may limit the municipality to a range of investments it can make. The U.S. Advisory Commission on Intergovernmental Relations (ACIR), citing the experience of the Oregon Local Government Investment Pool, suggests that in many cases (if the state so legislates) smaller municipalities might pool their funds and achieve larger yields than possible individually.[10]

Treasury bills   U.S. Treasury obligations constitute the largest segment of the fixed-income securities market. Treasury securities are classified as bills, notes, and bonds. Treasury bills (with maturities of 91 days and 182 days) are auctioned weekly by the Treasury, with one-year bills sold periodically. Treasury bills are sold on a discount basis and are extremely popular as short-term investments. A large number of them are outstanding; they have a high degree of marketability, and are default-free. The market in Treasury bills is very active and transaction costs involved in the purchase or sale of the bills in the secondary market are quite small.

Treasury notes and bonds   Treasury notes and bonds carry stated interest rates or coupons. Notes are issued for maturities of one to seven years. Treasury bonds are issued for terms of seven years or more. As notes or bonds approach their due dates, however, they can be bought on the market to serve the needs of short-term investors. In general, Treasury securities are the safest and most marketable investments, but, with the exception of tax exempts, they yield the lowest return for a given maturity of all investment instruments.

Agency securities Obligations of various agencies and corporations chartered by the federal government (agency securities) are guaranteed by the agency issuing the security. The principal agencies issuing securities are the federal land banks, the federal home loan banks, the federal intermediate credit banks, the Federal National Mortgage Association (Fannie Mae), the Government National Mortgage Association (Ginnie Mae), and the banks for cooperatives. These securities are sold in the secondary market through the same security dealers that handle Treasury securities. With the increase in the floating supply caused by the sharp increase in agency financing, marketability has been enhanced considerably. Although agency issues are considered highly acceptable by the investment community, they nevertheless still provide a small yield advantage over Treasury securities of the same maturity. Maturities of these issues range upward from a month to approximately fifteen years with about two-thirds of the existing securities maturing in less than a year.

Repurchase agreements In an effort to tap new sources of financing, government security dealers offer repurchase agreements (Repos), which provide for the sale of short-term securities by the dealer to the investor, provided that the dealer agrees to repurchase the securities at a specified price on a specified future date. The investor receives a given yield while holding the security, with the length of the holding period tailored to the investor's needs. Thus, repurchase agreements can give a municipality a great deal of flexibility with respect to maturity. Rates are tied to the rates on Treasury bills, the federal fund rate, and the loans to government security dealers by commercial banks. There is little marketability, but the usual time to maturity is only a few days. Because the instrument involved is a U.S. Treasury security, there is little risk; ordinarily the purchaser will retain the security if the dealer defaults on the repurchase agreement.

Negotiable certificates of deposit Another short-term investment that may fit the needs of municipal portfolios is the negotiable certificate of deposit (CD). A CD is simply the deposit of funds at a commercial bank for a specified period of time and at a specified rate of interest. These short-term investments, which originated in 1961, have become quite popular. Money market banks quote rates on CDs, which change periodically in keeping with changes in other money market rates. Regular CDs have a given term, with an interest penalty if they are cashed before maturity. They carry deposit insurance and are used by many cities, especially smaller ones. Negotiable CDs differ from regular CDs in that they can be sold on the open market at any time without paying an interest penalty. Currently, *negotiable* CDs cannot be sold below $100,000 face value, nor do they carry deposit insurance. But their yields tend to be greater than those on Treasury bills of comparable maturity.

Original maturities of CDs range from 30 to 360 days. A sizable secondary market has developed for CDs from the large money market banks. (The CDs of smaller banks have no marketability, so the municipal investor usually must wait until final maturity before funds can be realized.) Default risk here involves the possibility of bank failure—in most cases a low risk, but a risk still greater than that of other instruments. Some municipalities make a practice of investing only in the CDs of the local banks that do business within the locality, and frequently, the allocation of CDs among banks is determined on the basis of relative deposits or check clearances in the municipality. The idea is to support local banks, which benefits the municipality in a number of ways.

Portfolio of marketable securities

The municipal investor should choose from the legal list those securities that maximize earnings in keeping with the needs of the municipality. Typically, these needs are expressed in terms of maturity—that is, when the funds are likely to be needed—and in terms of a precautionary balance that may be needed for unexpected cash drains. Although the cash budget is used to determine planned cash needs over the near future, the finance officer must be ready for greater cash needs arising from unexpected cash drains or poor outcomes of revenue levies. These negative possibilities should be expressed in terms of the possible effects on the cash position. The costs (and embarrassment) of a possible shortfall in funds in relation to other uses for the monies determines the size of the precautionary balance.

Because the securities in the legal list are high quality, *default risk* is not a problem for the typical municipal investor. Reviewing the other four factors that cause yield differentials, it is apparent that municipalities do not face *call risk* because they do not invest in long-term corporate bonds, nor is *taxability* a direct factor for the municipal investor. The city should simply seek safe securities that provide the greatest pretax return—securities whose market value is near par or above. Having determined that three of the five factors affecting yields are relatively unimportant, the municipal investor can concentrate on the last two, namely, *maturity* and *marketability*. The municipality should try to spread maturities so that due dates generally coincide with the need for funds. Short-term needs can be satisfied by Treasury bills, repurchase agreements (Repos), and certificates of deposit; but, because negotiable CDs are not marketable, and must, in general, be held to maturity, a significant portion of the funds held for liquidity or emergency purposes should be in the form of Treasury bills and short-term Repos.

The municipality should arrange to have a steady flow of securities coming due. The concept of the even spacing of maturities can be extended to the intermediate-term period. For example, if spacing is properly achieved so that securities come due every quarter, a municipality is able to plan for future needs and to provide the flexibility to make adjustments with minimum dislocation. Treasury notes and bonds and U.S. agency securities can be used for intermediate-term needs. Due to the irregular timing of the issuance of U.S. agency securities, it is not always possible to achieve efficient spacing with them, but these securities do provide a yield advantage with only a slight sacrifice in marketability.

Generally, some portion of the cash funds of a municipality is unencumbered in that it is not attached to a specific short-term need. Accordingly, the finance officer can invest some of these funds in long-term Treasury and agency securities. However, when making long-term investments, the most important consideration is the expectation of the future course of interest rates. If a municipality invests in long-term securities, and if the interest rates subsequently rise, the municipality will suffer a considerable decline in the market price of its investment. In general, the finance officer should resist the temptation to reach for the higher yields available on long-term securities unless the city has to eventually meet a long-term obligation of about the same maturity.

Another source of funds often arises from the flotation of construction bonds, when the outlays on the project are not due for a considerable period of time. In general, these funds should be invested in short- and intermediate-term securities to avoid possible unfavorable price fluctuations.

In summary, the municipality should space maturities of its marketable securities in short- and intermediate-term areas of up to three years. This is particularly important for the first year, during which time maturities should be closely matched with cash needs. In addition, the municipality should hold Treasury bills and Repos for emergency use, as determined by any cash drains. Investment in longer-term securities should be made with particular attention to timing, when possible, in order to avoid buying at the trough of an interest rate cycle.

The discussion of portfolio considerations has been purposely general. Each municipality will have different amounts of funds available for investment and different needs for funds. The larger the securities portfolios, of course, the greater the potential for specialization and economies of operation. The more time devoted to researching, spacing maturities, keeping abreast of market conditions, and analyzing and improving the portfolio, the higher the return that may be achieved and the more consistently the return will meet the cash needs of the municipality.

Pension fund investments

Virtually all municipalities have some form of retirement, disability, and death benefit plans for their employees. These plans involve contributions by the employee and the employer which are invested in a special fund. The initial contributions, dividends, interest and capital gains accrue to pay ultimate benefits, the size of which depends on the return on investment for a given level of contributions. There is, consequently, an incentive to achieve high returns. Safety is of the utmost importance, however, and laws have been enacted by states to protect the principal invested. Unfortunately, these laws may place too much emphasis on safety so that the local government is handicapped in achieving a reasonable return on investment.

The investment management of a pension fund may be handled by the municipality itself, by an outside organization, or by a professional money manager. Many states have statewide retirement plans in which the municipalities may join. In California, for example, the State Public Employees Retirement System handles the pension funds for most of the municipalities in the state. Once a municipality joins the system, it has no control over the investment of funds short of withdrawing from the plan. Instead of joining a statewide retirement plan, some municipalities use private insurance companies or bank trust departments for their pension plans and use social security as a base retirement benefit plan, supplementing it with other arrangements to achieve a higher level of benefits. In most cases, the municipality gives the chosen institution complete discretion over the investment of funds because most municipalities lack the expertise to handle the investment of their pension funds. When a municipality manages its own pension fund, it frequently faces pressure to buy certain securities that are not in keeping with its objective. For example, it might buy a state or local bond of its own or of some other municipality as a favor. It was noted earlier that there is an opportunity loss associated with such an investment, because higher pretax yields are available on other types of securities. The municipality's decision to manage its own pension fund portfolio or to avail itself of professional management entails comparing the differences in likely performance with the differences in cost. Professional management usually has an annual cost of some fraction of a percent of the total asset value of the portfolio. One way to reach a decision is for the municipality to determine the cost of internally duplicating the basic services and expertise provided by the professional. Because the professional is in the business of managing a number of portfolios, economies of scale as well as special services (e.g., research) are possible. For these reasons, only the largest municipalities are usually able to justify managing their own pension funds.

If the decision is made to commission a money manager, the municipality frequently invites a number of money managers to make presentations. On the basis of these presentations and an analysis of the past performance of the managers, the municipality must choose the one who is likely to give it the best performance. After the investment manager has managed the fund for a period of time, the municipality should evaluate the manager's performance, not only in terms of rate of return but also in terms of risk. Risk, usually defined as the possibility that actual returns will deviate from expected returns, may be measured in terms of past fluctuations from an established norm. The idea is to maximize the rate of return for a given level of risk or risk class.

It is not the purpose of this brief sketch to provide a definitive treatment of performance; rather, it is to acquaint the reader with the factors and standards that are important in judging the performance of investment managers. More detailed works specifying how to measure performance are available elsewhere.[11]

Summary

A well-managed cash flow system enables cities, counties, and other local governments to release funds for profitable investment in marketable securities. This chapter has discussed both the methods and procedures that can be used in organizing cash flows and positions, and has also analyzed various aspects of the securities market from a managerial perspective.

The importance of cash budgets has been demonstrated in forecasting the actual needs for cash balances, which permits the finance officer to plan ahead. The actual cash position carried is influenced by the minimum deposit requirements of commercial banks, but it may be calculated alternatively by the use of models for determining cash and security positions. These models range from simple rules of thumb (e.g., holding a certain number of days' expenditure as the cash balance) to sophisticated mathematical models (e.g., the economic ordering quantity [EOQ] formula or the Miller-Orr model).

Once an optimal cash balance has been determined by the use of such methods, any extra municipal treasury funds may be invested in a marketable securities portfolio. The finance officer should be aware of the factors influencing market yield such as maturity, default risks, marketability, call provisions, and tax status. The officer should understand the various types of marketable securities available and the nature of pension fund investments.

1 For a discussion of these arrangements, see: James C. Van Horne, *Financial Management of Policy*, 5th ed. (Englewood Cliffs, N.J.: Prentice-Hall, 1980), chapter 16.

2 For a more detailed coverage of these rules, see: U.S., Advisory Commission on Intergovernmental Relations, *Understanding State and Local Cash Management* (Washington, D.C.: Government Printing Office, 1977).

3 This model was first applied to the problem of cash management by William J. Baumol. See: "The Transactions Demand for Cash: An Inventory Theoretic Approach," *Quarterly Journal of Economics* 66 (November 1951):543. It has been further refined and developed by a number of other analysts.

4 U.S., Advisory Commission on Intergovernmental Relations, *Understanding State and Local Cash Management*, p. 19.

5 See: J. Richard Aronson and Eli Schwartz, *Improving Cash Management in Municipal Government*, Management Information Service Reports, vol. 1, no. LS-6 (Washington, D.C.: International City Management Association, 1969). This article builds on a previous article by Aronson: "The Idle Cash Balances of State and Local Governments: An Economic Problem of National Concern,"

Journal of Finance 23 (June 1968):499–508.

6 See: Merton H. Miller and Daniel Orr, "A Model of the Demand for Money by Firms," *Quarterly Journal of Economics* 80 (August 1966):413–35.

7 Rita M. Maldonado and Lawrence S. Ritter, "Optimal Municipal Cash Management: A Case Study," *Review of Economics and Statistics* 47 (November 1971):384–88.

8 Further analysis of these factors is found in: James C. Van Horne, *Financial Market Rates and Flows* (Englewood Cliffs, N.J.: Prentice-Hall, 1978).

9 For a more detailed discussion of these and other instruments, see: Federal Reserve Bank of Cleveland, *Money Market Instruments* (Cleveland: Federal Reserve Bank of Cleveland, 1970).

10 U.S., Advisory Commission on Intergovernmental Relations, *Understanding State and Local Cash Management*.

11 See, for example: Bank Administration Institute, *Measuring the Investment Performance of Pension Funds* (Park Ridge, Ill.: Bank Administration Institute, 1968); Peter O. Dietz, *Pension Funds: Measuring Investment Performance* (New York: Free Press, 1966); and *The Institutional Investor* 5 (August 1971), special issue on pension funds.

15

Collective bargaining, wages, and local government finance

One of the most significant developments in the area of municipal government since the early 1960s has been the explosive growth of public employee unionism. With unionization, in turn, has come demands for collective bargaining and increasingly aggressive and militant behavior on the part of organizations of public employees. As a result, many municipalities already burdened with serious fiscal problems have begun to experience more stresses from this new quarter.

The growth of public sector unionism

As of the late 1970s, total union membership in the United States was approximately 20 million and included roughly 20 percent of the total national labor force. Although total union membership has been increasing over the past several decades, it has not grown as rapidly as the labor force. In contrast to the rather sluggish growth of unionism as a whole is the extremely rapid recent growth of unionism in public employment, especially in the local government sector. As Table 15–1 shows, currently about 54 percent of all full-time employees of local government are members of labor unions or employee associations. This figure is nearly three times larger than the corresponding percentage of all private sector employees belonging to labor organizations.

Organizations of public employees in the United States are not a new phenomenon. Some public employee unions (e.g., police and teacher organizations) may trace their origins back to the nineteenth century. To a great extent, public employee unions originated and grew in response to the same forces to which unions in the private sector responded. Inflation is a major determinant of union growth,[1] and during past periods of severe inflation (e.g., the years following

Table 15–1 Full-time employment in local governments, by function, October 1976

Local government function	Total full-time employees (000)	Organized full-time employees (000)	Organized employees as % of total
All local governments	6,919	3,745	54
Education	3,698	2,400	65
Highways	285	103	36
Public welfare	178	77	43
Hospitals	428	130	30
Police protection	463	253	55
Fire protection	210	151	72
Sanitation (other than sewerage)	119	59	49
All other functions	1,507	574	37

Source: U.S., Department of Commerce, and U.S., Department of Labor, *Labor-Management Relations in State and Local Governments: 1976*, Special Studies no. 88 (Washington, D.C.: Government Printing Office, 1978), p. 18.

World War I and World War II), police, firefighters, teachers, and other public employees turned to unions. Some of the reasons for the slow early growth of public employee unionism are the job security traditionally enjoyed by public employees, fringe benefits, and other working conditions superior to those of most private sector workers. Of equal importance was the fact that unionism and demands for collective bargaining usually were strongly resisted by the local government employers. Such resistance was possible because there was *no* statutory right for public employees at any level (local, state, or federal) to bargain collectively until recently.[2]

Around 1960, the traditional resistance of public employers to unionism weakened. This changing climate was precipitated by several developments; among them was Executive Order 49 issued in 1958 by New York City Mayor Robert Wagner. The order was the first to grant collective bargaining rights to employees of a municipality. The signing of Executive Order 10988 by President John Kennedy in 1962, which granted limited representational and bargaining rights to employees of the Federal Government, should also be noted as a significant step toward unionism. Although it did not directly affect organized public employee groups at the local level, this executive order did help break down the longstanding atmosphere of the public employer's reluctance to deal with unions.

More impetus was given to the growth of public unions, when in 1959, Wisconsin enacted legislation that gave municipal workers the right to organize and bargain collectively. This was soon followed by similar legislation in other states. As of the late 1970s, thirty-nine states had enacted some form of labor relations laws covering all or some categories of public sector employees. However, these laws vary greatly in substance and in scope from state to state.

The tremendous growth in the need for social services of all kinds—education, health care, public welfare, job training, for example—and the subsequent rise in the demand for public workers to deliver these services have provided a very favorable climate for organizing public employees into unions.

There is another growth factor underlying this recent expansion that should be noted, and that is the very rapid rise of government employment since 1957. Since that time, government civilian employment has doubled in size, with about 90 percent of the expansion occurring at the state and local levels. So rapid has this growth been that, of the roughly 29 million jobs created in the United States from 1957 to 1977, about one in every four has been in state or local government employment.[3] Unions generally mount drives to organize new jurisdictions where the potential membership gains are greatest whether in the public or private sector.[4] The push to unionize public employees came precisely at a time when the fortunes of private sector unionizing were at a low ebb, when union organizers saw public employees as attractive new targets to help bolster the sagging general membership levels. On the other hand, employer resistance to unionism traditionally has been softer during a time of growth in the demand for labor.

Unions and associations of public employees

The organizational structures that characterize unions of public employees today are more heterogeneous than those of unions in the private sector. Some organizations are active at only one level of government—local, state, or federal—while others are active at all three levels. Some organizations are quite restrictive in their recruiting efforts, desiring to represent public employees in specific occupations; others will organize public employees of any type. A few organizations even actively recruit workers in both the private and the public sectors.[5]

Traditionally, a distinction has been made between unions and professional associations. Unions in the public sector have been much more concerned with such matters as wages, benefits, and working conditions. Associations, on the other hand, tended to focus their efforts largely on professional matters and the quality of the services delivered. Today, the difference between the two is less distinct because the professional associations have become much more conscious of matters pertaining to the economic well-being of their membership.

In the paragraphs below, the characteristics of the major organizations of local government employees will be examined briefly. These organizations are listed in Table 15–2.

Table 15–2   Major unions and associations representing local government employees

Organization	Type	Estimated public employee membership (000)[1]
American Federation of State, County, and Municipal Employees (AFSCME)	Union (AFL–CIO)	957
American Nurses Association (ANA)	Association	200
American Federation of Teachers (AFT)	Union (AFL–CIO)	446
National Education Association (NEA)	Association	1,887
International Association of Fire Fighters (IAFF)	Union (AFL–CIO)	174
Fraternal Order of Police (FOP)	Association	135
International Conference of Police Associations (ICPA)	Association	200
International Union of Police Associations (IUPA)	Union (AFL–CIO)	31
Service Employees International Union (SEIU)	Union (AFL–CIO)	200
Laborers' International Union (LIU)	Union (AFL–CIO)	75
International Brotherhood of Teamsters (IBT)	Union	75

1 Except where noted below, membership figures are based on information supplied by the U.S. Bureau of Labor Statistics for 1976. For AFSCME, IUPA, and SEIU, the membership figures represent each organization's own membership count for the year 1978. The LIU and IBT figures are rough approximations for the mid-1970s. In the case of the ANA, AFT, and NEA, the membership counts include an unascertainable number of private sector employees, but only for the ANA is the number of such employees substantial.

AFSCME

The American Federation of State, County, and Municipal Employees (AFSCME) is one of the most rapidly growing unions of public employees. The growth of its membership followed a major policy shift in the mid-1960s, when the union firmly committed itself to the collective bargaining process and espoused the right to strike. AFSCME is the largest union comprised almost exclusively of public employees. Its membership in the late 1970s totalled approximately 957,000, about half of whom were employees of local governments. Among its ranks are employees of almost all types (except firefighters and teachers) in local and state governments.

Police and firefighter organizations

Police and firefighter organizations represent the uniformed services among public employees. Together, these organization have memberships of over 500,000 public employees.

Three major organizations currently represent the majority of organized police officers. The Fraternal Order of Police (FOP) is the oldest body, and it includes both police officers and supervisors in its constituency. In the past, the FOP attempted to disassociate itself from the image of a labor organization, but in recent years it has espoused collective bargaining for its members.[6] The Order's constitution still prohibits strikes, but this ban has not prevented its locals from striking. By the late 1970s, the FOP included approximately 135,000 members.

In contrast to the FOP, the International Conference of Police Associations (ICPA) is a confederation of independent organizations, rather than of individual members. The body was founded in the mid-1950s and currently numbers about 200,000 members. Like the FOP, the ICPA forbids strikes (a policy that has not always been followed by its locals).[7]

The International Union of Police Associations (IUPA) is a fledging group that broke away from the ICPA in early 1979. This group, too, is a confederation of locals, and is affiliated with the AFL-CIO. The group now numbers approximately 31,000 members. As is the case with the other two major police organizations, the ICPA does not endorse the strike weapon. It prefers legislation with binding arbitration. Most of its membership are rank-and-file police officers, but the union has also chartered command officer associations.

Although none of the police and firefighters unions and associations endorse walkouts as a part of the collective bargaining process, many of their locals have gone out on strike.

Although the FOP, ICPA, and IUPA represent the bulk of organized police personnel, several other organizations (among them AFSCME, the Service Employees International Union, and the International Brotherhood of Teamsters) represent a small number of police locals scattered throughout the country.[8]

The major organization of firefighters is the International Association of Firefighters. The IAFF is affiliated with the AFL-CIO and has a membership of 174,000, which includes both uniformed firefighters and management (officers). Unlike the police associations and other groups of public employees, IAFF is the only public employee union that is virtually without competition in the organization of firefighters. Through the IAFF, locals of firefighters have increasingly turned to collective bargaining to achieve economic benefits. By the late 1970s, however, the IAFF had not openly espoused strikes, although its members have not been deterred from doing so.

Nurses and teachers organizations

The American Nurses' Association (ANA) currently boasts almost 200,000 members. It represents about 100,000 nurses in collective bargaining and several years ago rescinded its long-standing no-strike policy. The ANA also believes in the right of supervisors to organize and bargain collectively; consequently, some ANA locals include both supervisors and nonsupervisors in the same unit. Recently, the American Federation of Teachers (AFT) launched a drive to organize nurses and other workers in the health care industry, a move that placed it in direct competition with the ANA.

The bulk of the nation's teaching labor force are part of two major organizations. The National Education Association (NEA) membership includes over 1,880,000 teachers and the membership of the American Federation of Teachers (AFT) numbers approximately 446,000. The NEA traditionally had been concerned primarily with professional and educational matters, but faced with the growing competition from the AFT, it recently has taken an active role in promoting collective negotiations. Moreover, the long-standing NEA ban on strikes was dropped in the late 1960s.

The AFT, on the other hand, is a teachers' union that is affiliated with the AFL-CIO. The AFT for some time has endorsed both collective bargaining and the strike weapon. In recent years, there have been movements to merge the two national teachers organizations and, in fact, several local and state AFT and NEA affiliates work together (e.g., New York State, Los Angeles, New Orleans, and Miami). However, the AFT's affiliation with the AFL-CIO has proved to be a major obstacle in this regard.

Both the ANA and AFT are considered to be representative of the professional groups of public service employees.

Mixed unions

In contrast to the groups described above, there are a number of organizations with memberships that include both public sector and private sector employees. The three unions with the largest number of employees in local government are the Service Employees International Union (SEIU), the International Brotherhood of Teamsters (IBT), and the Laborers' International Union (LIU).

The Service Employees International Union (SEIU) currently has a membership of approximately 625,000. Of these, some 200,000 are public employees, and the majority of them are at the city and county levels. The SEIU has been most successful in recruiting employees of hospitals, schools, and social service agencies.[9] The Teamsters, as of the mid-1970s, included about 75,000 workers in county and municipal employment in its overall membership of 2 million.[10] Most of the organizational success of the Teamsters has been among employees in street and sanitation departments, but it has also succeeded in organizing other groups of public employees (e.g., police officers). The Laborers' International Union (LIU) is an AFL-CIO affiliate with a membership of public employees who number approximately 75,000, most of whom are in unskilled and semi-skilled construction work.[11]

All local government workers unions, with the exception of the police and firefighters, approve of and use the strike weapon.

The legal issues affecting municipal bargaining

Employees of government were specifically excluded from the right to form unions and to bargain collectively, rights that were bestowed on private sector employees by the National Labor Relations Act (NLRA) of 1935 and the Labor Management Relations Act (LMRA) of 1947. According to section 2 (2) of the LMRA, "the term employer . . . shall not include the United States or any wholly owned Government corporation, or any Federal Reserve Bank, or any state or political subdivision thereof . . . ."[12] Thus, unions of local government employees have had to depend on state laws, executive orders, or other avenues to exercise legally their collective bargaining activities.

Public employee bargaining legislation

In 1959 Wisconsin became the first state to grant collective bargaining rights to local government employees. A surge of legislation in other states soon followed, and as a result, there are now thirty-nine states with laws granting bargaining rights to certain groups of government employees. In addition, four other states, either by the opinion of the attorney general, the executive orders of the governor, or the decisions of state personnel boards have issued orders authorizing such bargaining.[13] Currently, only a handful of states still have no legal or executive basis for authorizing collective bargaining for public employees.[14]

Despite the near universality of legal authorization for collective bargaining, state laws are extremely varied. It is not possible to present here a detailed state-by-state examination of the various laws; however, brief comparisons can be presented of several major legislative features that have implications on the state of municipal finance in local governments.

Coverage and duty to bargain

There are considerable differences among the state statutes concerning the type of public employees covered by the law. Some laws (those in Michigan and New York, for example) are comprehensive and cover virtually all local public employees. Other states have restricted their coverage to such specific groups as teachers or firefighters.

The type of negotiations required by the statutes also varies among the states. Some states (e.g., Florida and Kansas) only require that the public employer *meet and confer* with employees; other states (e.g., Michigan) mandate that *collective bargaining* take place. The difference between the terms is more than semantic. *Meet and confer* discussions generally refer to a type of negotiations in which the public employer agrees to discuss terms and conditions of employment. Whatever agreement is reached, however, is written as a memorandum of understanding rather than a collective bargaining contract. Moreover, in most *meet and confer* situations, the employer is not bound legally to negotiate or to abide by the terms of the agreement. *Collective bargaining*, in contrast, refers to a situation in which both the public employer and the public employee representatives are equal parties in the negotiating process, the result of which is a mutually binding collective bargaining contract.[15]

Scope of bargaining

The scope of bargaining defines the topics that are subject to negotiations. The scope of collective bargaining is itself a very important aspect of the bargaining process. From the union's perspective, if the scope is quite narrow, the potential impact of collective bargaining is reduced. On the other hand, if the scope is extremely broad, management may find that its operating flexibility is weakened.

The National Labor Relations Act (as amended) defined the scope of bargaining for employees in the private sector as "wages, hours, and other terms and conditions of employment."[16] Although the above terms may seem sufficiently specific and unambiguous, much controversy has arisen over the years about which items are mandatory items for bargaining purposes. As one observer has noted: "Mandatory topics . . ., those judged to be within the purview of 'wages, hours, and other terms and conditions of employment', . . . [have been] continually stretched to accommodate a wider variety of topics. Students today are astounded to learn that the subject of pensions became a mandatory subject of collective bargaining only after a Supreme Court decision."[17]

Many of the state laws have borrowed NLRA language in mandating bargaining over "wages, hours, and other terms and conditions of employment" for public employees. However, widely different interpretations of essentially identical language have been offered from state to state.[18] Thus, the scope of public sector bargaining with respect to wages, hours, and other terms and conditions of employment often has been more limited than is the case in the private sector. For example, although wages are typically the single most important subject of public sector bargaining, some wage-related items (e.g., pensions) are not subject to bargaining in certain states. Instead, these items may be decided by legislative bodies. Where such matters are not subject to negotiation, unions most frequently resort to lobbying and similar tactics to achieve their demands.

Discussions of employee work hours in collective bargaining are sometimes more limited in the public sector. The laws of some states establish the maximum number of hours of work for some specific groups, such as firefighters. In terms of education, most states have set a minimum number of days for instruction, which, in effect, determines the work year for teachers.[19]

Finally, in matters pertaining to "other terms and conditions of employment," the scope of public sector bargaining again has been more limited than it is in the private sector. Assignments, transfers, promotions, and layoffs are frequently the subjects of negotiations in private employment; this is less likely to be the case in the public sector. In some states, however, certain groups of public employees have been striving to include manning requirements and other traditional "managerial prerogatives" within the scope of collective bargaining. Police and firefighters in Wisconsin, for example, have succeeded in bringing the personnel practices of police and fire chiefs to the bargaining table.[20] Teachers in Michigan also have successfully bargained for class size limitations, provisions for instruction and curriculum councils, and student disciplinary procedures.[21]

Strikes and dispute settlements

There has been an historical ban on the use of the strikes by state and local public employees. In states where strikes are mentioned in the state statutes, they usually have been flatly prohibited. Where no specific statutory mention is made, common law usually has determined that strikes are illegal. Despite prohibitions, local public employee strikes have occurred with growing frequency over the past fifteen years.

More recently, these traditional bans against strikes have weakened somewhat. As of the late 1970s, at least seven states permitted certain groups of public employees to strike under a given set of circumstances.[22] Again, the specific provisions of these laws vary widely across the states. In Oregon, for example, some groups of public employees may strike after specific procedures for resolution of the dispute are exhausted and following notification of strike intent. However, if the health, safety, or welfare of the public is endangered, such strikes may be enjoined. Montana will permit public nurses to strike, but only if no other hospital within a 150 mile radius participates in the action. No state law currently gives its state or local employees unlimited strike rights; and, in those states with statutory bans on public employee strikes, severe penalties (which may include forfeiture of tenure and loss of pay) are often prescribed.

As an alternative to permitting the resolution of public sector disputes via the strike, nineteen states had enacted compulsory binding arbitration laws for certain groups of state or local government employees by the end of 1978. In most statutes, arbitration is preceded by mediation and represents the final step in the bargaining process. Conventional arbitration, in which the decision-making authority of the arbitrator is not restricted, must be imposed in nine of the nineteen states. In the others, some form of "final offer" arbitration is used for which the arbitrator may accept the terms (item-by-item or entire package only) of one of the parties.[23]

Unionism and earnings of municipal employees

Municipal wages have been rising quite rapidly over the past twenty years and, in some cases, now exceed the levels paid for comparable private sector jobs. However, to attribute the wage increases to unions alone would be a mistake, because there is reason to suppose that the process of public sector wage determination is likely to lead to relatively high wage levels even in the absence of collective bargaining.

Wage trends in the public and private sectors

It is possible to construct from the national income and product accounts of the United States a comparative series on average annual wages and salaries paid in the public and private sectors.[24] Such a series is presented in Table 15–3, along with wage and salary ratios and rates of change for selected time periods. It should be noted that the wage and salary series for the government employees includes both local *and* state employees. (It is not possible to construct a separate series for local government employees from national income accounts.)

Table 15–3   Average annual wages and salaries per full-time equivalent employee, private sector and state and local governments, 1952–1977

Year	Wage or salary, private sector		Wage or salary, government		
	$	Average annual change (%)[1]	$	% of private sector	Average annual change (%)[1]
1952	3,485	. . .	3,177	91.	. . .
1955	3,954	4.3	3,600	91.	4.3
1960	4,856	4.2	4,544	94.	4.8
1965	5,840	3.8	5,581	96.	4.2
1970	7,649	5.6	7,804	102.	6.9
1975	10,674	6.9	10,865	102.	6.8
1977	12,239	7.1	12,230	100.	6.1

Source: U.S., Department of Commerce, Bureau of Economic Analysis, *National Income and Product Accounts of the U.S., 1929–74* (Washington, D.C.: Government Printing Office, 1974); and *Survey of Current Business* (various issues, 1975–80).
Note: Leaders (. . .) indicate not applicable.
1 Average annual rate of change from last listed year.

Several interesting trends should be noted in Table 15–3. First, the ratio of average state and local government wages to average private sector wages has risen over the past twenty-five years from .91 in the early 1950s to approximate unity today. This should not necessarily be interpreted as an indication that government employees were once underpaid and that recently their wages have been brought into line with those in the private sector. The mix of occupations in the public and private sectors is quite different; thus, there is no reason to suppose that the "ideal" relative wage ratio ought to equal one. Table 15–3 simply indicates that wages have been rising considerably faster for local and state government employees, especially during the period from 1960 to 1970.

A more narrow view of the trends in municipal and private sector wages is shown in Table 15–4. As can be clearly seen in Table 15–4, wages rose at a faster rate for municipal employees than for nonsupervisory private employees during much of the period 1960–70. The differences in the rates of change of municipal and private earnings from 1960 to 1975 are especially pronounced.

Although Tables 15–3 and 15–4 indicate that wages of municipal employees have been rising at a faster rate than wages of private sector employees, they do not indicate how relative wage levels compare across specific job categories. Indeed, such a comparison is subject to limitations because it is only recently that the U.S. Bureau of Labor Statistics (BLS) has begun to collect data on

Table 15–4   Average annual rate of change in earnings of selected municipal employees and nonsupervisory workers on private nonagricultural payrolls

Years	Full-time noneducational municipal employees (%)[1]	Firefighters (%)[2]	Police (%)[2]	Nonsupervisory workers on private nonagricultural payrolls (%)[3]
1952–55	3.8	4.3	4.4	3.7
1955–60	4.2	4.4	4.4	3.6
1960–65	4.4	4.3	4.3	3.4
1965–70	7.2	7.3	7.5	4.7
1970–75	7.4	7.2	7.1	6.4
1975–77	5.9	6.4	5.7	7.5

Source: U.S., Bureau of the Census, *City Employment* (Washington, D.C.: Government Printing Office, various years); and U.S., Bureau of Labor Statistics, *Employment and Earnings* (Washington, D.C.: Government Printing Office, various years).

1 Based on average monthly earnings.
2 Based on maximum salary scales.
3 Based on average weekly earnings.

municipal and comparable private wage levels. Moreover, the BLS sample of municipalities is rather small, so any conclusions must be made with caution.

In the first BLS survey report (undertaken during 1970–71), information was reported for only eleven cities.[25] Municipal salary levels were compared with average salaries of local private industry for a number of comparable job categories—office clerical, data processing, and maintenance and custodial jobs. As a group, office clerical workers in nine of the eleven local governments received higher salaries than their private sector counterparts, and in four cities the differences were in excess of 15 percent.[26] Municipal data processers earned more than comparable private sector workers in six of the eleven cities, and city maintenance and custodial employees earned comparatively more in seven of the eleven cities. It should be noted that these figures represent broad group averages only; there is considerable variation among the rates of pay for more detailed occupations within each of the categories. Nevertheless, in most of the eleven large cities studied, local government workers held pay advantages over workers in private industry.[27]

The BLS has repeated its earlier survey, somewhat broadening both the number of occupations and the number of municipalities studied. The findings of the latest such survey (1976–77) for twenty-five cities show that municipal wages exceeded private sector wages for most of the occupations analyzed.[28] Only in the case of helpers (in the maintenance trades) and truckdrivers was the intercity average public-to-private pay ratio less than unity, and then by just a few percentage points. However, because only about one-half of the municipalities surveyed were able to provide information on public pay for these two occupations, the results may not be fully representative.

The available information on the trends and levels of wages and salaries in the municipal sector leads to the following conclusions. First, wages and salaries in the public sector grew at a faster rate than did wages and salaries in the private sector from the period 1957 to 1977. Second, this faster growth has led to a situation in which municipal pay scales exceed those of similar private sector jobs in some large cities today. Because this period of wage and salary growth corresponds closely with that of the advent of widespread collective bargaining for municipal employees, the relationship between the two bears consideration. However, to analyze fully the question of union influence on public sector pay scales, the process of wage determination in the public sector first must be examined.

Prevailing wages

Nearly all major levels of government in the United States are required to pay their employees wages and salaries comparable to those paid workers doing similar work in the private sector. This practice is usually known as the *prevailing wage principle* and seems reasonable both in terms of equity for public employees and in terms of efficiency for the government employer who is assured workers of acceptable quality.[29] Adherence to the prevailing wage principle, however, is very likely to lead to public sector pay levels that are, in fact, *higher* than those in the private sector.[30]

There are several reasons for this upward bias in public sector pay. First, often medium- and large-size private firms only are surveyed by government employers in an attempt to ascertain the prevailing wage. Smaller-size firms (which usually pay lower wages) are systematically excluded simply because the procurement of such information is costly. Nevertheless, the magnitude of the subsequent bias caused by excluding smaller firms from comparison may be quite large. The portion of all nonagricultural employees in the private sector who work in establishments that employ fewer than 250 employees—and who are likely to be excluded from salary comparison surveys—is approximately 60 percent.[31] These workers, it is estimated, are paid approximately 15 percent to 20 percent less than employees in firms with at least 1,000 employees.[32]

In adhering to prevailing wage principles, public employers often react in an uneven fashion to the private sector wages, which may be "out of line" as a result of unusual market forces. To be more specific, it is not uncommon to see government employers match high private pay levels which have been raised through the pressures of private union power. On the other hand, it is *not* generally the case for a government employer to match private pay scales that are unusually *low* because only one—or a very few—firms employ the bulk of the area's labor force (employer monopsony). The government employer will generally pay higher wages than necessary. The result of this type of assymetrical reaction to market forces that affect the prevailing wage principle is a second factor in the upward bias to public sector wages.[33]

A situation of employer monopsony (literally, "one buyer") will generally lead to wage levels below those that would exist in a competitive labor market with large numbers of buyers and sellers of labor.

Finally, government policy in setting wages for certain "unique" public sector jobs (jobs for which no private sector equivalents exist) often has the result of imparting more upward bias to public sector pay. The most obvious examples of such unique public sector job categories are those of police and fire service personnel. In most municipalities a system of pay *parity* exists for these two occupations whereby the salaries of the two groups are tied by some sort of fixed formula.[34] Because of the differences in the attractiveness of the two occupations and the dissimilar labor markets that each serves, the parity pay principle generally has resulted in the overpayment of firefighters, as evidenced by the presence of substantial queues and waiting lists for firefighter positions in many of the nation's cities.[35] In some municipalities, sanitation workers also are considered part of the uniformed services group, which has resulted in pressure to narrow the gap between the pay of sanitation workers and that of police and firefighters.[36]

Thus, adherence to the prevailing wage principle as currently administered is a potential cause for public sector pay levels to exceed those of the private sector—even in the absence of unionism. This potential, it should be added, seems to be present for all public sector occupations in which public employees in management and professional jobs tend to be more visible to a public that is largely skeptical of the value of highly paid employees.[37]

The economic issues in municipal bargaining

One of the major arguments supporting the rights of all workers to organize and to bargain collectively through unions of their own choosing hinges on the concept of "bargaining power."[38] What is meant by bargaining power? Neil Chamberlain has suggested a simple, yet useful, definition which is applicable to situations involving labor-management relations. According to Chamberlain, bargaining power is an individual's ability to secure the agreement of another party on his or her own terms. This ability (or power) of a worker to secure an employer's agreement is dependent on the cost of the agreement to the employer relative to the cost of disagreeing with the worker's demands.[39] Among the costs of disagreement to management, for example, would be the cost of incurring (or prolonging) a strike. The costs of agreement include the opportunity to attain a lower-cost settlement should management hold out longer than the employees. Quite obviously, the higher the ratio of the relative costs of disagreement and agreement, the higher the bargaining power of the party in question.[40]

A worker who faces management alone, it is argued, may be at a substantial disadvantage in negotiating the terms of his or her employment relationship. Acting in a collective fashion, however, may result in a more equal distribution of bargaining power for the employee.

The relevance of Chamberlain's notion of bargaining power to the situation of collective bargaining in public employment is straightforward. If collective bargaining is a viable method of determining wages and other terms of employment for workers in the public sector, then it is important that the resultant bargaining power of unions (or of management) not be excessive. Most economists would define excessive bargaining power to be a level of power that is substantially greater than is the norm in the private sector.

Are the characteristics of municipal employment such that the bargaining power of public employee unions is potentially excessive? Several features of public employment appear to support this contention. The elasticity of demand for most groups of public employees is small.

Because the fear of job loss ordinarily serves as a brake on union wage demands, it follows that some public sector unions are able to raise wages to higher levels without the fear of job loss. The argument that the demand for public employees is highly inelastic rests on the fact that many of the services performed by public employees are both essential and without close substitutes. In other words, the public usually has neither the desire nor the option to demand fewer such services should they become more expensive as a result of higher taxes. Thus, according to the Chamberlain bargaining power model, many public sector unions can make it costly for the public employer to disagree with a given set of demands—and these costs may not be confined solely to the municipal budget. A transit strike, for example, may so inconvenience the local citizenry that enormous political pressure to settle the dispute may be brought to bear on municipal officials. Other examples of essential, non-substitutable services are those provided by police officers, firefighters, and sanitation workers.

The trends do not all go one way, however. Local government layoffs do take place as a result of tax limitations and drastic expenditure reductions. In addition, there is more competition for local government jobs than there has been for a generation. Two of the reasons are falling demand (school teachers, for example) and the demographic curve (more young people competing for a static or falling level of jobs).

It is important to note that most goods and services provided by the private sector are not as essential as those provided by the public sector. Consequently, the cost of a high wage settlement in private industry may not always be passed on to the consumer. To the extent that this is true, a greater degree of restraint in union wage demands in the private sector is necessary.

The elasticity of demand for labor can be defined as the percent change in quantity demanded given a unit percent change in the wage.

The fact that many public services are both essential and without close substitutes alone raises the bargaining power of public sector unions by making the cost of disagreement to the public employer high. But there are also forces operating in the public sector that seem to make the immediate cost of agreement to a union's demands lower than might be the case in the private sector. This is likely to occur when the full budgetary consequences of a union demand (e.g., a multiyear contract) might not be felt until several years into the future when a change in the municipal pension plan might have occurred. By that time, the political leadership will have changed, and the full costs of the agreement will be borne by another generation.

The wage impact of public employee unions

Recently, there have been numerous attempts to measure the wage effects of unions at the municipal level. The studies have looked at different occupations over varying periods of time and have utilized diverse statistical techniques. The results, which are summarized in Table 15–5, lead to several tentative generalizations.

First, it is clear that the effects of unions on wages of local government employees vary by occupation. The observed differential for teachers has been rather small—generally under 5 percent. For police and firefighters, the effects have been somewhat larger, reflecting perhaps the greater bargaining power possessed by these two groups. On the average, however, the findings summarized in Table 15–5 all indicate that public sector unions generally have had a positive impact on wages, although the impact has not been extraordinarily large. This finding, of course, flies against the fear that the effects of unionization and collective activity would be ruinous to municipal governments. On the contrary, the wage effects attributed to public sector unionism have been (on the average) relatively smaller than the effects of unions in the private sector— where the most reliable evidence suggests that the long-run average union/non-union wage differential is about 10 percent to 15 percent.[41]

This evidence suggests that the effective bargaining power of municipal employee unions may not be as great as previously thought. Several reasons might account for this, among them, the constraints that the collective bargaining statutes have imposed on strike activity. Although it is true that illegal public employee strikes continue to occur, there is good reason to suppose that their incidence is still lower than they would be if legalized. There also is the possibility that political pressures and shifting public sentiment may work to limit the bargaining power of public employee groups. In San Francisco, for instance, a citizenry annoyed by "highly paid" municipal employees (e.g., street sweepers with a 1975 base pay of $17,300), passed charter amendments in 1975 that revised the prevailing wage-setting procedures. The following year, wage cuts averaging $2,000 were put into effect for certain groups of city employees.[42]

Table 15–5   Wage effects of unions at local government level according to major studies

Occupational group	Time period	Sample	Findings
Firefighters[1]	1961–66	100 cities	Unionization raised average hourly wage by 2%–10%.
Firefighters[2]	1969	270 cities	Unionization raised average hourly wage by 2%–18%.
Municipal employees[3]	1965–71	245 cities of 50,000 or more population	Union/nonunion differential less than 1%.
Hospital employees[4]	1966–72	21 metropolitan areas	Union influence about 4%.
Municipal employees[5]	1962–70	11 large cities	Union/nonunion differentials ranged from 0%–15%.
Noneducational municipal employees[6]	1967	478 cities	Union/nonunion differentials varied from 2%–16%.
Teachers[7]	1968	50 states	Union/nonunion differential no more than 4%.
Teachers[8]	1970	83 large cities	Union/nonunion differential was 3.7% for beginning salary level.

1 Source: Orley Ashenfelter, "The Effect of Unionization on Wages in the Public Sector: The Case of Firefighters," *Industrial and Labor Relations Review* 24 (January 1971): 191–202.
2 Source: Ronald G. Ehrenberg, "Municipal Government Structure Unionization and the Wages of Firefighters," *Industrial and Labor Relations Review* 27 (October 1973): 36–48.
3 Source: James L. Freund, "Market and Union Influences on Municipal Employee Wages," *Industrial and Labor Relations Review* 27 (April 1974): 391–404.
4 Source: Myron Fottler, "The Union Influence on Hospital Wages," *Industrial and Labor Relations Review* 30 (April 1977): 342–355.
5 Employees covered in this study included teachers, police, firefighters, and common-function employees. Source: Roger W. Schmenner, "The Determination of Municipal Employee Wages," *Review of Economics and Statistics* 55 (February 1973): 83–90.
6 Employees covered in this study included police, firefighters, streets and highways employees, and others. Source: Ronald G. Ehrenberg and Gerald S. Goldstein, "A Model of Public Sector Wage Determination," *Journal of Urban Economics* 2 (July 1975): 223–245.
7 Source: Hirschel Kasper, "The Effects of Collective Bargaining on Public School Teachers' Salaries," *Industrial and Labor Relations Review* 24 (October 1970): 57–72.
8 Source: Robert J. Thornton, "The Effects of Collective Negotiations on Teachers' Salaries," *Quarterly Review of Economics and Business* 11 (winter 1971): 37–46.

Employee benefit levels and public sector bargaining

Compared to the number of studies that have been undertaken to ascertain the wage impacts of municipal employee unions, the number of studies on the non-wage impact of unions is fairly small. Before reviewing these, it would be useful to examine first how employee benefit levels compare in the public and private sectors today.

Comparative public-private employee benefit levels

Data on fringe benefits in the public sector are generally not as abundant as data on wage levels in the public sector. Since 1970, however, the Labor Management Relations Service (LMRS) of the National League of Cities (NLC) has conducted several surveys of benefits paid to municipal employees.[43]

Based on the first LMRS survey in 1970, sworn municipal personnel (e.g., police) were found to have received benefits equal to 33.8 percent of pay for hours worked. The benefits included pensions, social security, vacations, holidays, paid sick leave, health benefits, workman's compensation, uniforms, death benefits, non-production bonuses, and educational expenses. General personnel in municipal employment, on the other hand, received benefits equal to 28.2 percent of pay for hours worked. The average for all sworn and non-sworn personnel was about 31.0 percent for year 1970. In contrast to this percentage, benefits as a portion of pay for hours worked amounted to approximately 27.4 percent for employees in the private sector.[44]

In the LMRS survey undertaken, the findings showed that the rate of growth in fringe benefits for both public and private sector personnel was very rapid over the first half of the 1970s and continued at a reduced rate from 1975 to 1977.[45] Most importantly, however, the survey pointed out that cities continued to spend a larger percentage of pay for fringe benefits than did private industry. Sworn municipal personnel (police officers and firefighters) received fringe benefits that were equivalent to 46.0 percent of total on-the-job pay; for the general municipal personnel the ratio was 42.7 percent. This meant, for example, that every police officer and firefighter (on the average) received $46.00 in fringe benefits for every $100.00 in salary. Corresponding industry ratios were 41.0 percent for nonmanufacturing industry personnel and 41.9 percent for all industry personnel. The report further noted that 42.0 percent of fringe benefit expenditures cover time-off pay (primarily vacations, holidays, and sick leave) and 34.0 percent cover pensions and social security payments.[46]

Other than the LMRS reports, there are few comprehensive studies of municipal fringe benefit levels. In a study undertaken for the state of Illinois in 1976, Norman Walzer and David Beveridge analyzed one hundred communities of varying sizes. They discovered that firefighters received benefits equal to 45 percent of pay, compared to 42 percent and 39 percent received by police and public works employees, respectively. In all three cases, the percentages were again greater than the percentage for the costs of benefits in private industry.[47]

The fact that the average level of fringe benefits paid to municipal employees exceeds that paid to private sector employees is not in itself surprising. Even before wide scale unionization, local governments were relatively generous with fringe benefits.[48] However, higher fringe benefit levels (and greater job security) usually were considered to be trade-offs for the generally lower pay levels characteristic of the public sector—pay levels that, for some occupations, have now begun to surpass those in the private sector.

Pensions

Pensions, traditionally included in the compensation packages of public employees, account for the largest share of total non-wage benefit expenditures for local government employees. More recently, public employee unions have shown great interest in bargaining for more generous pension systems, with respect to both eligibility for retirement and the size of annuities. However, changes in public pension schemes usually require more effort on the part of unions and management than do other fringes. Retirement provisions for municipal personnel are subject to the law in some states (e.g., New York), with the result that changes must be effected through the state legislatures; and, in some cities (e.g., San Francisco), retirement provisions are outlined in the city charters and may be amended only by a vote of the citizenry. There is also the fact that the complexity of retirement plans often necessitates costly and time-consuming studies of actuarial soundness and fiscal impact before changes can be made.[49]

The total membership in state and local employee retirement systems has been increasing rapidly in recent years—from 7.1 million in 1966–67 to 11.0

million in 1976–77.[50] This rate of growth, which exceeds the rate of growth in state and local employment, indicates that the coverage rate has expanded. In fact, it is estimated that the current coverage of state and local employees in pension systems today is close to universal. This is to be contrasted with the situation in the private sector where only about one-half of the workers in commerce and industry have been enrolled in pension plans in recent years.[51]

A growing number of state and local pension plans now make some provision for adjusting postretirement benefits. Some states have enacted legislation that results in automatic increases in benefit levels given changes in the consumer price index (CPI); these adjustments reflect a system that is similar to the civil service retirement scheme for employees of the federal government. In other states, there are provisions for other types of automatic adjustments which are not triggered by changes in the CPI.[52] The significance of such automatic adjustments is that they are virtually unknown in private sector pension plans.

Another major difference between public and private pension plans concerns the formulas of earnings used to calculate benefits. Private plans generally use an "all career average" earnings formula for calculating benefits, but most municipal retirement systems use formulas based only on the average earnings levels during the years preceeding retirement. The LMRS survey of municipal employee benefits for 1975 found, for example, that over 40 percent of all municipal personnel were covered by plans that based retirement benefits on the final three-year average pay. In fact, for 18 percent of sworn municipal personnel, pay during the final year before retirement is the only consideration.[53] In periods of rapid inflation, of course, it is advantageous to the employee to have retirement pay based on the fewest number of years as possible. Because the latest years of earnings generally will also be the highest years of earnings, yearly pension benefits are much higher than they would be otherwise.

Despite the differences noted, the paucity of studies makes it difficult to compare the differential magnitude of benefit levels for municipal and private pension plans. However, Bernard Jump has made an interesting sample comparison of eleven retirement plans—eight of them in municipalities and three in private industry.[54] Although a substantial range of benefits is provided by the various cities, he notes that the benefits paid by each of the eight public plans were superior to those provided by any of the three private plans. Furthermore, for employees of ages sixty-two and sixty-five earning $15,000 at retirement, net replacement rates for three cities that provided social security coverage were above 100 percent! (Replacement rates equal the percentage of retirement benefits to salary at retirement.) For the three private plans, replacement rates were considerably lower.[55]

Other benefits

It is difficult to generalize about the exact magnitude of the influence of unions on other fringe benefits, although it appears that such benefits are being liberalized under union pressure.

In his study of nineteen local governments, David Stanley noted that most municipalities have been liberalizing overtime rates and certain other special pay arrangements (e.g., differentials for night shifts). Interestingly, some of these pay arrangements have led to unforeseen difficulties. In one municipality, it was suspected that sewer workers had requested their friends to call for emergency service at night so that the workers could take advantage of the generous overtime pay provisions.[56] All in all, it is difficult to say to what extent the liberalization of special pay arrangements is due to union demands because such liberalization has been occurring in the private sector also.

In terms of other fringe benefits, Stanley found that shorter hours of work rarely were mentioned in the lists of union demands for the governments that he studied—the sole exception being those of firefighters. In many of the municipalities that were studied, union pressure was able to reduce significantly firefighter hours, which averaged considerably more than forty hours per week in some instances. Whether the apparent lack of concern in bargaining for shorter hours reflects an already shorter average work week for municipal employees is impossible to ascertain because (surprisingly) no comprehensive statistical information is available. Stanley's study shows further that annual vacation policies in the local governments studied appeared to be fairly consistent with those granted in the private sector.[57]

Collective bargaining and the budget-making process

Whatever the magnitudes of the effects unions have had on municipal wage and fringe benefit levels, it is generally agreed that unions have created additional pressure on the already difficult budgetary situations faced by many local governments. This pressure has been felt not only with respect to the size of budgets required to finance higher wage and benefit levels, but also with respect to the budget-making process itself.

When the budget is being formulated for the forthcoming fiscal year, it is important that enough time be allotted to permit the various municipal departments and agencies to calculate their budgetary requirements, submit them for review, and have them adopted or amended by the city council or other appropriate body. To accommodate these procedures, budgetary preparation in most local governments is undertaken six to eight months before the start of the new fiscal year. For the most part, both the timing and the general procedures followed in the budget formulation process were developed when the public employer exercised sole control over the determination of employee compensation. Thus, the traditional practices are not always compatible with the new restraints imposed by collective bargaining.[58] The budget schedule has become "less controllable" from the perspective of the public employer.[59] The major reasons for this, of course, are the unpredictability and time-consuming nature of the bargaining process, which may make it difficult for the public employer to settle with the union before final budget approval. Therefore, it is sometimes suggested that the public employer initiate collective bargaining as early as nine months prior to the beginning of the new fiscal year.[60] Should bargaining begin late in the budget-making process and continue after the adoption of the new budget, such serious problems as the need for a re-ordering of funding allocations, a search for additional revenue sources, or a possible budget deficit may result.[61] Indeed, unions sometime follow the strategy of timing collective bargaining (and the threat of a strike) to coincide with the budget submission deadline.[62] The exertion of union pressure at this time is designed to force the public employer to yield to union demands—which might otherwise be rejected—as the price to be paid for completing the budget on schedule.

It is important for the public employer to have at hand mechanisms for coping with union demands and for producing a minimal adverse impact on the budget and budgetary process.

It is clear that municipal collective bargaining should be closely attuned to the budget-making process, especially since the revenue-raising powers of most municipalities are limited. Nevertheless, the most careful planning efforts do not mean that negotiations will always run smoothly and impasses not occur.

In some states, provisions of public employee bargaining statutes have been enacted to help ensure that the negotiations process and the budgetary process occur simultaneously. The Massachusetts statute, for instance, stipulates that in the event that a municipality and a union fail to reach agreement sixty days prior to the final date for setting the municipal budget, either party—union or management—may initiate factfinding procedures to increase the likelihood of settlement. The Rhode Island statute requires that organizations of public employees give written notice requesting collective bargaining at least 120 days before the final date on which the municipality may appropriate funds.[63] Legislation in both New York and Connecticut requires that municipal bargaining be completed before the date on which the chief administrator is required to submit a budget to the legislature.[64]

In states where no such legislation exists or where problems of synchronization occur despite the legislation, public employers have resorted to other devices. One such mechanism is the adoption of budgets with estimates of the wage and salary increases still to be negotiated. In a survey of bargaining practices in Illinois public institutions, Milton Derber found this practice to be fairly common.[65] Of course, in the event that the estimated wage allowance proves to be too low, additional funds may have to be provided. The local governments in Illinois surveyed by Derber normally provided such additional funds by transfers among or between budget funds, supplemental appropriations, borrowing, or higher taxes.[66] Regarding the practice of adopting a budget that contains estimated future wage settlements, the question of "overbudgeting" or "padding" is often raised. These terms refer to the practice of hiding funds in various budget categories, which can be used to finance a wage settlement that is higher than anticipated. Although overbudgeting is used on occasion, the practice is marked by disadvantages that limit its usefulness as a management tactic. Many public employers feel that padded items usually can be detected by skillful union negotiators during the budget-search process.[67] Indeed, the tactic sometimes may even backfire if union negotiators discover the overbudgeted amount and make it a target for additional bargaining demands.[68]

Two additional devices that help to minimize the extent to which collective bargaining might clash with the budget schedule are the retroactive pay practice and the long-term contract. The retroactive pay practice allows the terms of the settlement to be backdated to the expiration date of the original contract. Although public managers do not universally approve of the retroactive pay practice as a bargaining device, Derber found it to be commonly used in his survey of Illinois municipalities.[69] On the other hand, long-term contracts (i.e., contracts of two or three years duration) owe their attractiveness to the fact that they reduce the number of opportunities for impasses in negotiations to interfere with the budgetary process. Another advantage to long-term contracts is that they can save the public employer the additional time and expenses of yearly contract negotiations.[70]

The preceding discussion has indicated that unions have created new pressures on municipal budgets by assuming a more important role in matters regarding both the budgetary process and the size of the budget. At the same time, it is clear that both bargaining and budget making are fairly flexible processes that can be adjusted to some extent in the event that the two processes do not mesh initially.[71] It should be emphasized that most of these mechanisms are designed to reduce the severity of the problems that result when negotiations proceed beyond the budget adoption date.

For successful negotiations, it is important that the public employer make every effort to have an informed and well-planned negotiations strategy. Such a strategy requires that detailed costing of all union demands be undertaken during the negotiations process. Careful costing is a *sine qua non* for the public employer in the negotiations process, not only for the purpose of preventing later budget overruns, but also for the purpose of informing the union negotiators, who may be unaware of the true costs of a certain proposal to the municipality.[72] In addition, effective negotiations require a public employer to have a positive set of proposals regarding wages, salaries, and fringe benefits. This set of proposals should have as a frame of reference the budget proposed for the coming year and should be based on such information as changes in the consumer price index, local labor market conditions, and pay levels in other communities. Such a well-planned negotiations strategy will also do much to increase the probability of successful negotiations.

Public employer responses to the unions

The increased personnel costs that result from bargaining have evoked a variety of responses from local governments, ranging from tax increases to expenditure cutbacks, from employee layoffs, delays and cancellations of capital construction to efforts to improve employee productivity. Several of these managerial responses are discussed in the following paragraphs.

There is evidence to suggest that responses to the higher wage costs brought about by unionism have varied according to the size of the municipality. In his analysis of more than 700 cities, Stanley Benecki found that the response to the higher compensation levels negotiated by unions has been employment cutbacks in large cities and increased government spending in smaller cities.[73]

Several explanations might be offered for the differential response by cities of different sizes. Generally, larger cities provide more numerous and varied services than do smaller cities. The latter are, instead, more likely to provide the core of essential municipal services (police and fire services and education). Consequently, the possibility of employee lay-offs may constitute a type of emergency option for larger cities that is not generally available to smaller cities. On the other hand, the difference in municipal response may also reflect the fact that the collective bargaining relationships tend to be older and more established in the larger cities. If so, the expenditure adjustments to collective bargaining which seem to characterize the smaller cities may well represent the short-term impact, while disemployment adjustments constitute a long-term impact.[74]

Another managerial response to higher labor costs associated with bargaining is productivity bargaining. Productivity bargaining refers to situations in which labor agrees to alter inefficient work methods in return for added compensation. The compensation increase is, in effect, paid for by the presumed cost savings associated with the elimination of the uneconomic work rule. Britain has experimented with productivity bargaining with some success, and the interest has recently spread to the United States, where several local governments also have tested it. In Detroit, for example, municipal sanitation workers have agreed to changes in work procedures in return for a share in the cost savings.[75] Orange, California, has utilized productivity bargaining with its police force by granting bonuses for reductions in the incidence of crimes that involve rape, robbery, and burglary.[76]

Despite the acclaim that productivity bargaining has received in some areas, it is important to realize that it is not a panacea for all of the financial woes faced by local governments. Although output per hour of labor may be increased to the extent that public management is able to "buy out" the former work practice, the unit cost saving may be neutralized (or even overwhelmed) by the compensation *quid pro quo*. This is very likely to be a problem in situations where it is difficult to accurately measure productivity.[77]

Some concluding observations

The central focus of this chapter has been to describe the phenomenon of collective bargaining in the municipal government sector and to analyze some of the major impacts on wage levels, fringe benefits, and public management. The statistical data and arguments presented have indicated that municipal wages have risen over the past fifteen years at a rate faster than the wage growth of most non-government employees. Municipal wages now are often higher (and, in some cases, considerably so) than wages of comparable private sector employees.

It is not clear, however, whether unionism has been the dominant factor behind this municipal wage growth. The union wage-impact studies cited in this chapter are unanimous in their conclusions that the effect of unions on municipal wage levels has been modest and generally less than the impact of most private sector unions on their wages. The principal factors underlying municipal wage growth appear to be the rising demand for public services and the biases inherent in the use of the prevailing wage principle. In terms of fringe benefits, the impact of the union is more uncertain. Although the existing evidence shows that fringe benefits (pensions, in particular) of municipal employees are higher than those in the private sector, it is generally believed that public employers traditionally have been more generous in this area—even before the advent of collective bargaining.

The logical conclusion then, is that unions are not the major culprits behind the rash of urban fiscal crises in the late 1970s—contrary to public opinion. It is true that unions have created additional strains on municipal budgets, but to charge them with primary responsibility simply does not correspond with the available evidence.

On the other hand, it is clear that the assertion of greater job security and more generous fringes in public employment is a trade-off for lower pay scales is no longer valid. In many cases, local government employees enjoy higher earnings, higher fringe benefits, and greater job security. It is also interesting to note that the level of government employment continued to grow during the recession of 1974–75. Although virtually all manufacturing and nonmanufacturing industries reported declines in employment over the period from September 1974 to April 1975, employment in the state and local government sector grew by about 408,000 employees. Of course, the job security traditionally associated with public employment is not and has never been absolute. In times of municipal fiscal crunches, employee lay-offs do occur. Public employment, however, still appears to be much more "recession-proof" than any industry in the private sector, and a strong case can be made for public compensation levels to reflect this fact.[78]

1   Albert Blum, "Why Unions Grow," *Labor History* 9, no. 1 (winter 1968); 48–49; Orley Ashenfelter and John Pencavel, "American Trade Union Growth: 1900–1960," *Quarterly Journal of Economics*, August 1969, p. 441.

2   Hervey A. Juris and Peter Feuille, *Police Unionism* (Lexington, Mass.: Lexington Books, 1973), p. 11.

3   Barbara Cottman Job, "More Public Services Spur Growth in Government Employment," *Monthly Labor Review* 101, no. 9 (September 1978): 3.

4   Ashenfelter and Pencavel, "American Trade Union Growth," p. 437.

5   Jack Stieber, *Public Employee Unionism* (Washington, D.C.: Brookings Institution, 1973), p. 1.

6   Juris and Feuille, *Police Unionism*, p. 29.

7   Alan E. Bent and T. Zane Reeves, *Collective Bargaining in the Public Sector* (Menlo Park, Calif.: Benjamin-Cummings Publishing Co., 1978), p. 19.

8   Juris and Feuille, *Police Unionism*, p. 29.

9   Stieber, *Public Employee Unionism*, p. 3.

10   Bent and Reeves, *Collective Bargaining*, p.20.

11   Ibid.

12   Labor Management Relations Act, 1947, title 1, sec. 2 (2).

13   Arkansas, Illinois, New Mexico, and Virginia.

14   At the time of this writing, only the following eleven states had not passed permissive legislation of some type regarding public employee bargaining: Arizona, Arkansas, Illinois, Louisiana, Mississippi, New Mexico, North Carolina, Ohio, South Carolina, Virginia, and West Virginia.

15   U.S., Department of Commerce, Bureau of the Census, *Labor-Management Relations in State and Local Governments: 1976*, State and Local Government Special Studies, no. 88 (Washington, D.C.: Government Printing Office, 1978), p. 2.

16   Labor Management Relations Act, 1947, title 1, sec. 8 (d).

17   Walter Gershenfeld, "An Introduction to the Scope of Bargaining in the Public Sector," in *Scope of Public Sector Bargaining*, ed. Walter Gershenfeld (Lexington, Mass.: Lexington Books, 1977),

p. 2. The Supreme Court decision alluded to is *Inland Steel Company v. United Steelworkers of America*, 336 U.S. 960 (1949).

18 Ibid., p. 4.

19 Michael H. Moskow et al., *Collective Bargaining in Public Employment* (New York: Random House, 1970), pp. 241–42.

20 James Stern, "The Scope of Bargaining in the Public Sector in Wisconsin," in *Scope of Public Sector Bargaining*, ed. Walter Gershenfeld, p. 199.

21 Charles Rehmus, "The Scope of Bargaining in the Public Sector in Michigan," in *Scope of Public Sector Bargaining*, ed. Walter Gershenfeld, pp. 21–22.

22 Pennsylvania, Hawaii, Alaska, Oregon, Montana, Vermont, and Minnesota.

23 Kevin Corcoran and Diane Kutell, "Binding Arbitration Laws for State and Municipal Workers," *Monthly Labor Review* 101, no. 10 (October 1978): 36.

24 U.S., Department of Commerce, Bureau of Economic Analysis, *National Income and Product Accounts of the U.S., 1929–74* (Washington, D.C.: Government Printing Office, 1974).

25 Stephen H. Perloff, "Comparing Municipal Salaries with Industry and Federal Pay," *Monthly Labor Review* 94, no. 10 (October 1971): 46–50.

26 Ibid., pp. 46–48.

27 Ibid., p. 46.

28 U.S., Department of Labor, Bureau of Labor Statistics, *Wage Differences among Large City Governments and Comparisons with Industry and Federal Pay, 1976–77*, report 549 (November 1978), p. 4.

29 Walter Fogel and David Lewin, "Wage Determination in the Public Sector," *Industrial and Labor Relations Review* 27, no. 3 (April 1974): 411.

30 Ibid., pp. 413–14.

31 U.S., Department of Commerce, Bureau of the Census, *County Business Patterns: 1970* (Washington, D.C.: Government Printing Office, 1971), p. 29.

32 Richard Lester, "Pay Differentials by Size of Establishment," *Industrial Relations* 7, no. 1 (October 1967): 57–67.

33 Fogel and Lewin, "Wage Determination," pp. 417–23.

34 Juris and Feuille, *Police Unionism*, pp. 121–22.

35 Fogel and Lewin, "Wage Determination," p. 427.

36 Ibid.

37 Ibid., p. 416.

38 For example, according to the Labor Management Relations Act of 1947, the "inequality of bargaining power between employees . . . and (certain) employers" was held to be one of the justifications for implementing the policies of the act (title I, sec. 1).

39 Neil Chamberlain and James Kuhn, *Collective Bargaining*, 2d ed. (New York: McGraw-Hill Book Co., 1965).

40 Ibid.

41 H. Gregg Lewis, *Unionism and Relative Wages in the United States* (Chicago: University of Chicago Press, 1963), p. 5.

42 For a descriptive account of the San Francisco pay determination changes, see: Harry C. Katz, "Municipal Pay Determination: The Case of San Francisco," *Industrial Relations* 18, no. 1 (winter 1979): 44–58.

43 U.S. Conference of Mayors, Labor-Management Relations Service, *National Survey of Employee Benefits for Full-Time Personnel of U.S. Municipalities* (Washington, D.C.: Labor-Management

Relations Service, 1970, 1973, and 1975).

44 Results of the 1970 LMRS survey as reported in: Stanley M. Wolfson, "Survey/Fringe Benefits in the Public Sector," *Public Management* 55, no. 10 (October 1973): 6.

45 U.S. Conference of Mayors, Labor-Management Relations Service, *Fourth National Survey of Employee Benefits for Full-time Personnel of U.S. Municipalities* (Washington, D.C.: Labor-Management Relations Service, 1979).

46 Ibid., p. 8.

47 Norman Walzer and David Beveridge, "Municipal Employee Benefits: The Intergovernmental Dimension," *National Tax Journal* 30 (June 1977): 135–42.

48 David Stanley, *Managing Local Government Under Union Pressure* (Washington, D.C.: Brookings Institution, 1972), p. 83.

49 Ibid., p. 85.

50 U.S., Department of Commerce, Bureau of the Census, 1977 Census of Governments, *Employee-Retirement Systems of State and Local Governments*, vol. 6, no. 1 (Washington, D.C.: Government Printing Office, 1978), p. 1.

51 *Employee Pension Systems in State and Local Government* (New York: Tax Foundation, 1976), p. 4.

52 Ibid., pp. 16–17.

53 U.S. Conference of Mayors, Labor-Management Relations Service, *Third National Survey of Employee Benefits for Full-time Personnel of U.S. Municipalities* (Washington, D.C.: Labor-Management Relations Service, 1977).

54 Bernard Jump, Jr., "Compensating City Government Employees: Pension Benefit Objectives, Cost Measurement, and Financing," *National Tax Journal* 29, no. 3 (September 1976): 240–56. The cities were Atlanta, Chicago, Dallas, Detroit, Los Angeles, New York City, Philadelphia, and Washington, D.C. The private plans were those of Eastman Kodak, IBM, and New York Telephone.

55 Ibid., p. 244.

56 Stanley, *Managing Local Government*, p. 81.

57 Ibid., p. 83.

58 Milton Derber et al., "Bargaining and Budget Making in Illinois Public Institutions," *Industrial and Labor Relations Review* 27, no. 1 (October 1973): 79.

59 Stanley, *Managing Local Government*, p. 118.

60 Bent and Reeves, *Collective Bargaining*, p. 128.

61 Ibid.

62 Stanley, *Managing Local Government*, p. 116.

63 Derber et al., "Bargaining and Budget Making," p. 79.

64 Neil Chamberlain and Donald Cullen, *The Labor Sector*, 2d ed. (New York: McGraw-Hill Book Co., 1971), p. 153.

65 Derber et al., "Bargaining and Budget Making," p. 57.

66 Ibid.

67 Ibid.

68 Stanley, *Managing Local Government*, p. 119.

69 Derber et al., "Bargaining and Budget Making," p. 57.

70 Joseph Domritz, "Collective Bargaining and Public Administration: The Role of Long-Term Contracts," in *Collective Bargaining and Public Administration* (Chicago: Public Personnel Association, 1971), pp. 16–17.

71 Derber et al., "Bargaining and Budget Making," p. 61.

72 Bent and Reeves, *Collective Bargaining*, p. 135.

73 Stanley Benecki, "Municipal Expenditure Levels and Collective Bargaining," *Industrial Relations* 17, no. 2 (May 1978): 227.

74 Ibid., p. 228.

75 National Commission on Productivity, *Improving Municipal Productivity: The Detroit Refuse Collective Incentive Plan* (Washington, D. C.: Government Printing Office, 1975).

76 John Greiner, *Tying City Pay to Performance* (Washington, D.C.: Labor Management Relations Service, 1974), p. 20.

77 See, for example: Raymond D. Horton, "Productivity and Productivity Bargaining in Government: A Critical Analysis," *Public Administration Review* 36, no. 4 (July–August 1976): 412.

78 See: Robert Bednarzik, "The Plunge of Employment During the Recent Recession," *Monthly Labor Review* 98, no. 12 (December 1975): 3–4.

16 Pension fund management

In recent years there has been a growing concern for the conduct and condition of state and local employee retirement programs. Questions about public pension plans are from several areas of concern: Are pension promises made to employees secure? Will the benefits be adequate? Are the programs being managed in the most efficient and economical manner? And—most crucial to all concerned—will benefits promised today be affordable by the contributing governments tomorrow?

Public pensions have moved to the front of the stage in public financial administration, primarily because they affect so many people and involve so much money. As of the late 1970s, almost all of the 12 million state and local employees were covered by some form or another of a pension plan, and well over 2 million retirees and survivors depended on benefit payments for all or part of their livelihood.

State and local governments pay nearly $14 billion a year in contributions, accounting for about seven cents out of every tax dollar collected. In addition, employees belonging to contributory plans were contributing an average of 5 percent of their wages to help finance their retirement plans. Even at this high rate of contribution, however, public pension systems have been falling behind in accumulating sufficient resources to meet their future obligations. As the growth in public sector employment levels off, the number of beneficiaries and the amount of benefit payments will grow more rapidly than the current public payroll and total tax collections. Unless more can be set aside today, or the terms and conditions of pensions can be modified, the public sector will increasingly feel the burden of meeting underfunded pension obligations. This discouraging prospect has undoubtedly increased the emphasis placed on the management of state and local retirement programs.

The problem of unfunded pension liabilities and the financial burdens that will be involved in meeting them recently has been the subject of much study. Less well advertised, but perhaps of greater consequence in the long run, is the corrosive influence of inflation on the orderly financing of pension obligations. The financial soundness of most pension plans and the real worth of the benefits to be paid depend heavily on the ability of pension managers to earn returns on their investments and to stay ahead of the rising cost of living. Failure to do so will mean either a reduction in the real worth of benefits, increased contributions to meet retirement goals, or some combination of both. Unfortunately, the recent performance of the economy and financial markets has made pensions increasingly difficult to fund, and the balance between what is equitable to workers and what is affordable by governments is increasingly difficult to find.

The rapidly mounting costs of pensions are in part caused by the prevailing lack of policy concerning their design, financing, and administration. Reforming pension practices in the future will be made even more difficult because the very nature of the obligations and oversights will leave a legacy of financial and administrative problems for the future.

The universe of public pensions

Like most aspects of state and local government, public employee retirement systems come in many forms and in many sizes, and are often separately administered systems. A special survey made in 1975 by the Pension Task Force of the United States House of Representatives counted nearly 5,788 separate systems, covering more than 12.5 million employees.[1] It should be noted that the Pension Task Force study included as a plan any arrangement that provided postretirement income (e.g., deferred compensation plans and life insurance contracts), whether administered by a governmental entity or in the public sector.

However, for purposes of describing the pension universe that falls under the heading of financial management, the definitions used by the U.S. Bureau of the Census and the corresponding accounts may be useful. The Census Bureau excludes from its count of retirement systems those systems that forward contributions to private insurance companies as premiums paid for the purchase of annuity policies, make direct payments of benefits from annual appropriations of general funds, and have members who belong to the Teacher's Insurance and Annuity Association (TIAA) without any state or local supplemental coverage. As a result, only systems administered by a sponsoring state and local government and subject to the accounting and auditing controls of the government are contained in the Census numbers.[2] According to the 1977 Census of Governments information, there were a total of 3,075 systems with a combined membership of 11 million employees and more than 2 million current beneficiaries.[3]

Membership and level of administration

Retirement systems for state and local governments are administered at both the state and local levels. As shown in Table 16–1, 86 percent of the covered employees belong to state administered systems, which also account for 77 percent of the financial assets. On the other hand, local government systems make up 94 percent of the total number of the systems, although they account for only 14 percent of the employee membership. It has been estimated, however, that approximately 6.5 million of the 9.4 million members of the state administered systems are local government employees.

Table 16–1   Key measures of state and local retirement systems, 1977

Classification	No. of systems	Total membership (millions)	Beneficiaries (millions)	Receipts ($ billions)	Payments ($ billions)	Assets ($ billions)
Total	3,075	10.95	2.27	25.35	9.77	123.48
State	197	9.41	1.66	19.29	7.06	94.91
Local	2,878	1.54	0.61	6.06	2.71	28.57

Source: U.S., Bureau of the Census, 1977 Census of Governments, *Employee-Retirement Systems of State and Local Governments*, vol. 6, no. 1 (Washington, D.C.: Government Printing Office, 1978).

Table 16–2 gives an indication of the growth in the coverage of employees by pension plans over the last twenty years. Comparing the number of full-time equivalent employees to active pension plan members, the ratio of coverage had increased to an estimated 92 percent. In view of the already wide coverage and the slowing down of growth in government employment, it is unlikely that active membership in plans will grow very rapidly in the future. The number of beneficiaries will continue to grow, however, as the membership matures.

Table 16–2   State and local pension membership and full-time employment, 1950–1977

Year	No. of full-time government employees (millions) (A)	Active pension members	
		No. (millions)	% of (A)
1950	3.8	2.6	68.0
1960	5.5	4.5	82.0
1970	8.5	7.3	86.0
1977	10.6	9.7	92.0

Source: U.S., Congress, House, Committee on Education and Labor, *Task Force Report on Public Employee Retirement Systems* (Washington, D.C.: Government Printing Office, 1978), p. 174; and for 1977 data: U.S., Bureau of the Census, *Public Employment in 1978* (Washington, D.C.: Government Printing Office, 1979), p. 9, and U.S., Bureau of the Census, 1977 Census of Governments, *Employee-Retirement Systems of State and Local Governments*, vol. 6, no. 1 (Washington, D.C.: Government Printing Office, 1978), p. 11.

Most of the employees belong to a relatively small number of the plans. Of the 3,075 plans, 120 of them have a membership of 9,974,000. Thus, there are only 977,000 members for the remaining 2,996 plans, of which nearly 2,200 have fewer than 100 members—only 0.5 percent of all membership. These very small systems predominate at the local level.

The contrasts in the number of systems among the individual states are great, ranging from one plan in the state of Hawaii to cover all state and local employees to 480 plans in the state of Pennsylvania (which is evidently understated).[4] The contrast in the size of individual systems is particularly great when the very largest systems are considered. Two statewide systems—one in California and one in New York—include more than 500,000 members each, and the largest five systems involve 17 percent of all state and local employees who belong to retirement systems.

At the local government level, 84 percent of all systems were administered by municipalities; 7 percent, by townships; 6 percent, by counties; and the remainder, by school districts and special districts. Membership in the county government systems tended to be considerably larger, on average (2,200 members), than in the systems administered by cities (425 members).[5]

Despite the continuing large number of local plans, there has been a tendency to concentrate membership in the largest systems. The portion of employees covered by systems in excess of 100,000 members grew from 50 percent to 60 percent between 1972 and 1977. The trend toward this type of employee concentration has many advantages in terms of administrating and rationalizing plans, especially among potentially competing jurisdictions and groups of employees. On the other hand, concentration can lead to political problems and diminish the power of individual employing governments to control their personnel policies and pension costs.[6]

Coverage by class of employee

Most jurisdictions have separate plans for different categories of employees. As Table 16–3 shows, retirement administration tends to be diffused among employee types, especially at the local level. The general employee coverage systems represent only 19.5 percent of the number of all plans, but include 53.6 percent of all covered employees. Public employee retirement systems (PERS) are those

Table 16–3 Classes of employees covered by state and local retirement plans, 1977

Employee class	% of retirement plans			% of retirement plan members		
	Total	State	Local	Total	State	Local
Total	100.0	100.0	100.0	100.0	100.0	100.0
General employees	19.5	31.5	18.7	53.6	58.0	49.9
Education	2.2	22.3	0.8	19.5	22.9	16.6
Police	32.0	10.7	33.5	6.7	4.4	8.5
Fire	31.6	4.1	33.6	4.8	3.3	6.1
Police and fire	7.7	3.0	8.1	6.8	7.2	6.5
Other	7.0	28.4	5.3	8.6	4.2	12.4

Source: U.S., Bureau of the Census, 1977 Census of Governments, *Employee-Retirement Systems of State and Local Governments*, vol. 6, no. 1 (Washington, D.C.: Government Printing Office, 1978), p. 11.

not restricted to any particular type of employee. Frequently, however, fire and police employees belong to separate small, locally administered retirement systems that often feature plans with relatively liberal age and service requirements and superior benefits. On the other hand, teachers and other school employees have tended to be brought together in plans administered at the state level. Similarly, legislators and judges tend to form special plans that appear relatively preferential in benefits, with short periods of service requirements and rapid vesting. To what extent this recognizes the peculiarities of uncertain and difficult jobs or is simply a convenient way of increasing compensation to levels beyond the public's view is a matter of occasional debate.

Financial flows and assets

Table 16–4 provides an overview of the financial operations of state and local retirement systems, and includes the rates of growth during 1967–1977. As shown, retirement funds are financed by a combination of three sources—government employer contributions, employee contributions, and investment earnings. The state and local retirement sector is unique in its traditional reliance on employee contributions (such plans are called contributory plans). However, this source of funds is of diminishing importance. In contrast, the role of earnings on the financial assets of the funds is of rapidly increasing importance. In 1977, this source accounted for almost 31 percent of all receipts, a sign of the growing maturity of the funds as their assets accumulate.

Another indicator of the growing maturity of the pension systems is the growth of outpayments to employees retiring or withdrawing, or to other beneficiaries of the plans. Although payments in 1977 amounted to only 8 percent of the assets, this growth is greater than the growth of the financial assets. Barring a resurgence in the rapid growth of the public sector, benefits paid out should continue to grow, as should investment income, but long-term projections are difficult to make. Benefit payments could accelerate and investment earnings could decrease; consequently, employer and employee contributions may need to be increased in order to prevent the level of assets (and future earnings) from eroding.

What is not shown in Table 16–4 is the present value of future benefits that will need to be paid and their relationship to the existing amount of assets and the level of contributions. The current lack of sufficient assets to offset these forecasted liabilities (i.e., the future benefits) and the insufficiency of current

> **The present value of future payments is the value of those payments discounted back to the present time through the use of a compound interest (or discount factor). The discount formula for any period is $PV = FV(1 + i)^n$ where PV = Present Value, FV = Future Value, i = interest rate, and n = number of periods.**

contribution rates to accumulate the needed reserves are of major concern in determining the financial viability of funds and their long-term costs to governments.

Most public pension plans provide *defined benefits,* which are a certain level of benefits (as defined by the term of the plan) to which the government's contribution is committed. This type of benefit covers virtually all public employees. Conversely, a few employees are in pension programs that have *defined contributions,* for which the participant's benefits are based only on the amount contributed by the employee and any income earned from those contributions. Only about 2 percent of all public employees are covered solely by defined contributions plans, and some 16 percent are covered by combination plans that have both defined benefit and defined contribution elements.[7]

Table 16–4 also presents a different perspective on the financing of public pension systems and their importance in the overall government budget. In 1967, government contributions to pension systems represented less than 7.0 percent of payroll costs and 4.0 percent of tax receipts. By 1977, the respective figures were 9.0 percent of payroll and almost 7.0 percent of taxes. It should be borne

Table 16–4   Financial data on state and local employee retirement systems, 1967–1977

Classification	1967	1977
Receipts ($ billions)	6.58	25.35
Annual growth rate (%)[1]	. . .	14.5
Government contributions ($ billions)	3.05	12.40
Annual growth rate (%)[1]	. . .	15.0
% of receipts	46.4	48.8
% of tax collections	4.0	7.0
% of payroll	6.9	9.9
Employee contributions ($ billions)	1.96	5.23
Annual growth rate (%)[1]	. . .	10.3
% of receipts	29.8	20.6
Investment earnings ($ billions)	1.56	7.44
Annual growth rate (%)[1]	. . .	17.3
% of receipts	23.8	30.6
Payments (benefits and withdrawals; $ billions)	2.68	9.77
Annual growth rate (%)[1]	. . .	13.8
% of receipts	40.8	38.5
% of assets	6.8	7.9
Financial assets ($ billions)	39.26	123.48
Annual growth rate (%)[1]	. . .	12.1

Source: U.S., Bureau of the Census, 1977 Census of Governments, *Employee-Retirement Systems of State and Local Governments* (Washington, D.C.: Government Printing Office, 1978); and U.S., Bureau of the Census, 1967 Census of Governments, *Employee-Retirement Systems of State and Local Governments* (Washington, D.C.: Government Printing Office, 1968).
Note: Leaders (. . .) indicate not applicable.
1 Annual growth rate, 1967–1977.

in mind that approximately two-thirds of state and local government employees belong to plans that also include social security coverage, the contribution rates of which are not included in the figures above. The social security rates have climbed from 4.4 percent (maximum base of $6,600 in 1967) to 5.85 percent (taxable base of $16,500 in 1977) and are projected to rise further, increasing the overall retirement related costs of government employers and employees.

A recent survey of the employee benefits of municipalities estimates that the combined pension contribution and social security payments amounted to approximately 13 percent of payroll in 1975.[8]

History and legal setting

An understanding of the public employee pension universe as it exists today is facilitated by knowledge of how it has developed over time. Public pensions began when some cities established limited benefit programs for firefighters, police officers, and teachers in the late nineteenth century. The number of plans accelerated rapidly in the 1930s and 1940s (particularly during the fourteen-year period following 1937, when public servants were not eligible for social security coverage), with approximately one-half of the largest state and local systems being founded between 1931 and 1950. In contrast, the smaller local plans burgeoned later, with two-thirds of them being established after 1950.[9]

The creation of the various plans over a long period of time—moving ahead in different states at different times under different pressures—has resulted in a heterogeneous mixture of administrative structures, benefit provisions, and funding techniques. Generally, changes have come about without benefit of any consistent policy or legal framework at either the state or the local level. As a result, attempts to rationalize or restructure the plans frequently are bogged down in a maze of legal and moral conflicts. Few attributes of public pensions are commonly shared among the states, and this is a source of difficulty both in operating such systems and in analyzing the results of those operations. Often pension provisions of great substantive importance are tucked away in nooks and crannies of obscure laws and then shaped by various judicial interpretations.

Provisions regarding benefit levels, contribution formulas, eligibility, funding requirements, and allowable investments are often spelled out at length in a multitude of state statutes. Home rule cities may establish their own systems as they please; cities subject to "bracket laws" (specialized legislation that pertains to only one or a few jurisdictions) may be hemmed into antiquated and conflicting requirements. Frequently, common law interpretations of particular issues are relied on instead of having each issue specifically addressed by a legislative body. The resulting patchwork of laws leads to much uncertainty and confusion about what exactly the pension obligations mean to the employee and employer. For example, some states have constitutional provisions that treat conferred pension rights as a fundamental matter of contract that cannot be impaired except through amendment. Other states view such rights as statements of policy rather than matters of legal contract. Still others view the pension in almost the same way as a gratuity, giving little comfort to the employee as to the security of his or her pension.[10]

Laws governing pension provisions and their financing are technically complex and have long-range cost impacts. This means that state and local legislative bodies carry a heavy burden in assessing the implications of pension-related decisions and the condition of retirement funds. In an effort to develop expertise in these matters, many states have created permanent legislative bodies to screen bills and to recommend reform measures. Other states have attempted (with varying degrees of success) to provide formal state supervision of local government pension systems.

According to the recommendations of the U.S. Advisory Commission on

Intergovernmental Relations (ACIR), such regulatory entities should have the power to provide technical assistance, maintain information, and have the authority to require reviews and comments on proposed changes in state and local retirement systems.[11]

Public retirement system organization

Establishing retirement policies, administering contributions and benefits, and managing the plan's investments are all part of a pension program. But, like many other aspects of state and local government, form does not necessarily follow function. The relationships the various functions of a pension plan have to one another are so varied that they defy easy generalization. Public employee retirement plans were established at different times by governmental entities to provide primarily for postretirement payments to employees. Beyond that simple observation, the details of any particular plan's relationship to the contributing government, to its employees, and to a host of other public and private entities are subject to great variation.

How retirement systems are structured

The prototypical state or local retirement system is a special trust fund created under the laws of the state or of a municipality to provide pensions and other employment-related benefits to government employees. Usually, such laws state that the administration of the system shall be the responsibility of a retirement board, a board of trustees, or a particular department or office in the sponsoring government. However, within any common statutory framework, the responsibilities and details of practice can vary greatly from one jurisdiction to another.

Some statutes spell out the operations in great detail; others let the retirement board or responsible department work out the particulars in the form of bylaws and regulations. Moreover, the governing board or responsible department usually (in the case of larger systems) delegates much responsibility to a chief administrator or plan executive, who oversees the day-to-day operations of the system.[12]

Retirement boards can have either broadly or narrowly defined power and can be either aggressive or passive in setting policy. In some large systems, retirement boards make legislative recommendations, set investment policy, establish rules of benefit entitlement, review and approve the budget, and hire inside staff and outside consultants to carry on daily operations. At the other extreme, retirement boards may be left with relatively little to do, spending most of their time reviewing disability and retirement claims. For example, the legislative bodies of the parent government may retain close control over the plan's administrative budget through an appropriation process and may also delegate investment and other administrative functions to government departments and offices that are independent of the retirement board.

Among the various retirement system structures, three broad categories can be identified in terms of how independent the retirement fund is from the sponsoring or contributing government unit or units.

The most prevalent structure is the separate retirement board that—within the limits of its legal authority—sets policies, issues regulations, and oversees pension practices. The statutory powers of the board may be broadly or tightly defined, but the ultimate authority to make operating decisions is retained by the board, either for its (or its staff's) direct exercise or for delegation to private agents acting on its behalf.

In other cases, a separate retirement board exists, but some aspects of the system's operation may be entirely beyond the retirement board's control. For example, the investment function may be assigned to a government official (e.g., a comptroller, treasurer, or finance officer) or the investment responsibility may reside in a separate investment board that invests the pension fund's money along with that of other state or municipal agencies.[13]

A third variant is found where city departments or public officials carry out the administrative duties of the pension system and the power to set policy is retained by the governing body. In these cases, the administration of the retirement plan is part of a government's internal activity and separate retirement boards to oversee pension activities do not exist. This third variety is frequently found in smaller systems. Often, however, the responsibility for execution of investment policy is given to an outside private trustee (e.g., a bank or insurance company). Not infrequently, other services relating to the payment of pension benefits may also be assumed by a private trustee.

Many public pension plans are multi-employer systems with several local governments (and sometimes state agencies) joining together in the plan's sponsorship and financing. Such plans are usually set up under an umbrella of special state authority, and the contributing governments share in the policymaking through representation on a board of trustees. Members of such boards are statutorily defined, appointed, or elected in such a way as to be representative of the various types of government and, not infrequently, of active employees and retirees who are members of the system.[14]

Retirement board membership

Retirement boards usually consist of seven or more members who are specified under enabling legislation. Generally, they are officials serving ex officio, officials appointed by the chief executive or controlling legislative body, representatives of non-governmental interests, or representatives elected by plan members. At least 80 percent of retirement boards have elected or appointed officials serving on them, 70 percent have employee representatives (usually elected by members of the system), and 40 percent have members from the public at large.[15]

Normally the qualification for board membership is ex officio in the case of government officials and general popularity in the case of elected employee representatives. Professional knowledge of pensions, personnel policies, or finance is not a prerequisite. Most pension boards—and probably most elected officials who find themselves responsible for the retirement system's administration—must rely heavily on inside administrators and outside advisors to help set policy and to carry on day-to-day operations.

Pension administrators

Day-to-day administration of a retirement plan may be lodged in several different places and entail a variety of duties. Larger systems with broad powers usually hire a full-time plan administrator to provide leadership, deal with professional services and the public, and oversee the activities of a staff. In smaller systems, city clerks, finance officers, town managers, and police and fire chiefs may find themselves serving as a part-time administrator of a plan and its investment officer. In many cases all or a major part of those responsibilities may be carried out by consultants and insurance companies.

Generally speaking, the plan's chief executive officer's duties will include overseeing compliance with the laws that control the plan, hiring staff, maintaining records, executing transactions, and carrying out the retirement board's policy directives.[16]

A major part of the administrator's activities will be dealing with the various technical advisors who typically are used to support various pension activities. Particularly important to most funds are actuaries, investment advisors, and accountants, whose specialized services are of greatest value when rendered on an independent basis.

The duties of investment advisors and actuaries will be discussed later, but at this juncture it is important to stress the need for a strong accounting and reporting system within the fund. The accounting and financial reporting practices of public pension systems have been the subject of considerable concern, because of both a lack of widely followed standards and a general lack of timely and useful disclosure. Several organizations in both the private and public sectors are examining how pension accounting and reporting practices can be improved. A stimulus to these efforts is provided by the recurring proposal that federal standards regarding plan disclosures—akin to those enacted for the private sector under the Employee Retirement Income Security Act (ERISA) of 1973—be enacted for the state and local sector.[17]

Benefits design and adequacy

The primary purpose of a pension plan is to provide an income for employees who have retired. This is normally done through monthly payments of an annuity that commences when the employee becomes eligible on leaving the job covered by the pension. Most pension plans are designed to take effect when the employee goes into normal retirement, having completed a certain number of years' service or having reached a specified age. In the state and local sector, the prevailing requirements for retirement are that employees have attained an age of between sixty-two and sixty-five and that they have served for at least five to ten years. However, there are a large number of variations on the basic theme that alter both eligibility for retirement and the size of the benefit payments. Because of the variety of factors and formulas used to calculate the level of benefits, it is only after the characteristics of a particular plan are examined that anything can be said about the adequacy of any given pension.

Types of benefits

Retirement benefits typically are defined by a formula that takes into consideration an employee's salary and years of service. This is a major feature of a defined benefit plan. In the case of the defined contribution plan, there is no benefit formula (aside from basic eligibility rules) because the employer is obligated only to contribute to the plan and the level of benefits will depend only on the total amount contributed and the investment performance of the fund during the years of contribution and retirement.

Benefit formulas are grouped into two classes: flat benefits and unit benefits. Flat benefits express the level of benefits to be paid out as either a fixed dollar sum or as a percentage of a salary base. The number of years of service does not enter into the calculation under a flat benefit plan. Flat benefit plans are of diminishing importance in the state and local sector and usually are found in such small local plans as fire and police service pension plans.

Unit benefit plans tie benefits to length of service and accumulate units of benefit credit for each year of the employee's service. The units of service typically are expressed as a percentage of the employees' compensation. For example, an employee who attains retirement age after working for thirty years would receive 60 percent of his or her base compensation as calculated at the time of his or her retirement.

Two factors are of particular importance in the unit of benefit calculation: the compensation base and the percentage of service credit used in the formula. The question of compensation, in turn, involves two subsidiary questions regarding employee compensation and the time period over which it is measured. Most retirement plans use the employee's base pay as the basis for the calculation of the pension, but a large number also include overtime pay, sick pay, and longevity pay as part of the base—all of which will increase the monthly benefit payments for any given percentage calculation of unit service.

The other important variable is the time period of compensation used for the calculation of the benefits. The majority of state and local workers are members of plans that take the average compensation for the last three to five years. However, a large percentage of plans are based on one year or less (either the last year of employment or the year of highest salary). Furthermore, a large percentage of local fire and police systems base retirement benefits on pay received during the *last day* of employment.[18]

When a very short time interval is used for the formula (e.g., the last day of employment) and the compensation base is expanded to include such factors as overtime pay, there is the possibility of abuse. Retiring workers may be given last minute promotions or large doses of overtime to enlarge their compensation base and thus increase monthly retirement benefits.

Most employee retirement plans include benefits other than those associated with normal retirement, including disability benefits, death benefits, and survivor benefits. By far the most controversial—and in many ways, the most difficult— benefits to administer are those related to disability. Again, locally administered systems, especially those for fire and police service personnel, have been subject to abuses in this area. To cite the findings of the Public Pension Task Force report:

On a national basis the number of disability retirees in the police and fire category as a percentage of all retirees is about 23 percent. Yet for large, similarly situated police and fire plans this ratio ranges from less than 10 to over 80 percent. A large share of such variations which cannot be attributed to different definitions, environment, etc. result in varying degrees in what might be described as administrative largesse. Administrative laxity in the disability area has forced at least one plan in the past into court appointed receivership. Small plans can be particularly vulnerable to abuse in this area.[19]

Cost-of-living adjustments

The need to keep pension benefits in line with the cost of living has received increasing attention over the years. In an inflationary environment, retirees' benefits can be eroded quickly by the rise in consumer prices. Most state and local employees are covered by plans that make some sort of adjustment in an effort to keep pace with inflation, although few attempt to match fully rising prices. These adjustments can take several forms.

Ad hoc adjustments may be legislated from time to time, as determined by the legislative body controlling the benefits. Other plans have formal requirements to increase benefits at a constant percentage over time or have them geared in some way to increase as the consumer price index increases. In most cases, however, the amount of increase in any given year is limited to a certain percentage (e.g., a maximum of a 3 percent increase). A fairly large number of plans also gear benefits to the level of investment earnings.[20]

The importance of cost-of-living adjustments to the preservation of purchasing power and benefits is illustrated in Table 16–5. At a 6 percent rate of inflation, a fixed-dollar pension benefit would have only 75 percent of its original purchasing power at the end of five years and only 31 percent in twenty years in the absence of adjustments for inflation. There are other ways to protect purchasing power. Some plans tie benefits to the salary levels of the positions held by the retiree at the time of retirement. Thus, as salaries increase, so do benefits. Other plans place part of the pension funds in a variable annuity, whereby benefits will rely partially on investment earnings. This approach helps if investment earnings keep pace with inflation, but this outcome is by no means assured.

Cost-of-living adjustments that keep benefits up with the cost of living can be prohibitively expensive (which is the reason that many such provisions carry a cap). For example, the benefits of a typical plan may be 140 percent greater if the rate of inflation is 4 percent (and 170 percent greater if it is 6 percent) than the benefits not adjusted to the cost of living.[21]

Table 16–5 Purchasing power of a fixed-dollar amount of benefit after periods of time under various rates of price inflation as a percentage of first-year purchasing power

Time period (years)	Annual rate of inflation			
	0%	4%	6%	8%
5	100	82	75	68
10	100	68	56	46
20	100	46	31	21
30	100	31	17	10

Source: Howard Winklevoss and Dan McGill, *Public Pension Plans* (Homewood, Ill.: Dow Jones–Irwin, 1979), p. 140.

Early retirement

Most retirement plans permit employees to retire with reduced benefits before the normal retirement age. Early retirement eligibility is expressed in terms of age and of length of service (i.e., age fifty-five with at least twenty years of service). The cost of early retirement can be considerable, not only because benefits need to be paid out over a longer period of time but also because the income from the assets that would otherwise have been set aside is reduced and has less time to accumulate.

Benefits under early retirement often are reduced by some rule of thumb that permits the retiree to receive a percentage of the benefit that would have been paid at normal retirement (typically benefits are reduced by 0.5 percent for each month before the normal retirement age). However, such rough guides usually result in understating the true cost of providing early retirement to the employer. Thus, early benefits should be computed actuarially to be equal to the cost of providing unreduced benefits at a later age.

Early retirement may not be simply a nice fringe benefit. It may also serve certain personnel policies, such as encouraging employees to leave service when their skills are no longer needed or when they are not capable of doing the required work.

Income replacement levels

The ultimate objective of retirement benefits should be to give the retiree a level of income sufficient to maintain a reasonable postretirement standard of living. Unfortunately, this objective has not been scientifically designed and retirement benefits have tended to grow in a crazy quilt fashion, with various employee groups alternately trying to get ahead or catch up with one another.

If maintaining a satisfactory standard of living is a desirable pension objective, then pension adequacy can be described as a relationship between an employee's income at time of retirement and the benefits received on retirement. Determining this relationship calls for a complex set of calculations, which need to take into consideration the retiree's changing circumstances and his or her need for discretionary income. For example, a retired person who no longer pays social security taxes (and who usually will be receiving social security benefits) has a different tax status, has completed his or her savings program, and no longer has work-related expenses. There may be offsetting costs in medical and other expenses associated with old age, but usually the expenses of maintaining an equivalent standard of living are less on retirement. Therefore, the amount of replacement income needed to gain equivalency can be considerably less than the gross income the worker received prior to retirement.[22]

To compute the benefit income needed to meet the standard-of-living equivalency objective, federal, state and local taxes, social security taxes, employee contributions, employee contributions to the pension plan, and certain work-related expenses and personnel savings are deducted from the preretirement gross income. Those employees eligible for social security will, in addition to their retirement income from the pension plan, receive benefits from social security that should be taken into account.

The results of a study of benefit levels that are needed to meet a standard of living equivalency are shown in Table 16–6. As may be seen, subtraction of those factors that consumed income prior to retirement, but that no longer do after retirement, represent different and increasing percentage of income as income rises. To summarize the results, replacement income (under the assumed conditions) is calculated to range between 50 percent and 80 percent for workers not covered by social security and 45 percent to 73 percent for workers covered by social security.

Higher income replacement rates are needed for those not covered by social security not only because they do not receive social security payments but also because they must pay higher taxes on the retirement benefits, which, unlike social security payments, are subject to federal as well as some state and local taxes.

Using somewhat different definitions of replacement income, the Pension Fund Task Force study found that as of the mid-1970s, state and local pension plans were providing (on average) net income replacement ratios of 100 percent to employees retiring at age sixty-five with thirty years or more of service. Replacement rates were definitely higher, on average, for lower income employees. Those employees who received social security did better, with approximately 75 percent enjoying net income replacement ratios in excess of 100 percent.[23]

Table 16–6 Retirement incomes needed at various levels of gross earnings at retirement

Gross earnings at retirement ($)	Employees not covered by social security		Employees covered by social security	
	Retirement income needed for equivalence ($)[1]	% of gross	Retirement income needed for equivalence ($)[1]	% of gross
7,500	5,982	79.8	5,483	73.1
10,000	7,688	76.9	7,023	70.2
15,000	9,941	66.3	8,944	59.6
20,000	11,378	56.9	10,048	50.2
30,000	13,735	53.1	13,945	46.5
40,000	19,885	49.7	17,910	44.8

Source: Howard Winklevoss and Dan McGill, *Public Pension Plans* (Homewood, Ill.: Dow Jones–Irwin, 1979), pp. 30, 32.
1 For a discussion of how standard of living equivalence is determined, see Winklevoss and McGill, chapter 2.

Integration with social security

A major deterrent to the growth of public pension systems was that public employees were originally excluded from social security coverage. In the 1950s, a series of amendments made it possible for public employees to join social security, and a steadily growing number of plans elected to do so. By 1977, approximately 70 percent of all workers belonged to retirement systems where some or all of the active members were covered by social security.[24]

Social security benefits have a significant impact on overall postretirement income, and they reduce the amount of pension payments needed to reach a given level of replacement income. On the other hand, with employer and employee contribution rates steadily rising, belonging to social security also presents significant costs for both parties.

Unfortunately, social security benefits generally have not been taken into consideration in the design of retirement plans. Only about 16 percent of all public employee plans use some formal method of integrating pension and social security benefits to arrive at a total retirement income package.[25] Moreover, many of the existing integration methods are out of date and have failed to keep up with the increases in social security benefits. Generally, the lack of an effective method of integration has led to relatively high rates of replacement income for covered retirees, especially for those in the lower income brackets.[26]

State and local employees can voluntarily join the social security system and they can also elect to terminate their participation. Recently, in a desire to avoid high employer and employee contributions, several systems—mainly smaller ones—have withdrawn from social security. It is usually felt that contributions earn more benefits if retained for investment by the local retirement system.

Estimations of the costs and benefits of staying in social security are extremely difficult to make. Usually, some employees gain and other employees lose. Congress, nonetheless, is concerned about the financial and equitable consequences of having a large segment of the work force outside the social security system and has been actively considering making universal coverage mandatory. Whatever its other benefits, such a move would cause dramatic increases in existing employee retirement systems in which benefits currently are not integrated with social security.

Pension costs and financing techniques

How pension costs are determined and how they are financed present some of the more difficult and controversial topics in the policy formulation and management of retirement systems. Financing practices in the state and local sector have been slow to recognize the full, multiyear cost consequences of granting benefit promises; frequently the burden of paying for the costs has been left to future generations of taxpayers. This places the promised benefits in jeopardy because future generations may be unwilling or unable to bear the burden.

It also should be noted that the selection of funding techniques is primarily a problem for defined benefit plans, for which there is a fixed commitment by the fund to pay benefits—whether the fund has sufficient assets or not. In the case of a defined contribution plan, the government, once having made its contribution, is free of future liability—the risk being borne by the employee, who depends only on how much has accumulated in his or her account and how productively the pension fund assets have been invested.

The great divide in financing defined benefit pensions and determining their costs is between those systems that recognize the cost when the worker *earns* an increment of his or her future payment and those systems where the pension benefit is recognized when the worker *collects* his or her benefit. The former approach, which recognizes accrued liabilities, falls under the general heading of the advance or reserve funding method. The pay-as-you-acquire (pay-as-you-go) method does not recognize costs and liabilities when they are created. Liabilities accumulate that are not offset by employer contributions set aside to help pay for the promised future benefits. The decision to set aside funds pertains only to the employer's share. In contributory plans, the employee's contributions are always set aside in a reserve and credited to his or her account.

Over the years there has been a debate as to the advantages of reserve funding versus pay-as-you-acquire, but the preponderance of opinion (and practice) is that employers should set aside funds to match benefits as they accrue.[27] When properly done, this requires making contributions based on actuarial methods that project what benefit payments will be needed in the future, given the plan's characteristics.[28] It is important to remember that the present value of the benefits does not depend on the techniques chosen to finance the plan. The cost of the plan to the community as a whole is the same no matter what financing scheme is adopted.

There are variations on the themes of advanced funding and pay-as-you-acquire, and the particular financing method employed by a system may be a combination of each. For example, a technique popular at one time, is that of terminal funding. Under this approach, the retiring employee has a lump sum set aside, which, with the earnings it will make, will provide benefit payments throughout retirement. In this case some assets (unlike pay-as-you-acquire) are set aside, but not nearly as much as would be in the advanced fund techniques to be discussed below.

In terms of current practices, the bulk of public employee systems use some form of advanced funding to finance all or a major part of their defined benefit retirement plans. Based on a recent survey, only about 17 percent of all plans (and covered employees) rely entirely on pay-as-you-acquire financing techniques. A larger proportion—25 percent—employ advanced funding methods not actuarially based. Even among the 58 percent of the plans that are actuarially based, the contribution formulas are often inadequate to recognize full costs and to accumulate sufficient assets.[29]

Actuarial funding

The objectives of an actuarially funded plan are relatively clear, but the applications require a skilled actuary. To allocate what will be an uncertain future outflow of benefit payments back to present values, the actuary typically needs to assume the future behavior of investment earnings, salary rates, death rates, and terminations (decrements). On the basis of these assumptions, which have probabilities associated with them, a stream of future benefit payments is projected and then converted into present values. Correspondingly, a scheme is devised to determine the amount and timing of funds needed to be set aside in order to ensure the system's ability to meet future payments.

The actuary has a variety of ways to accomplish this complicated exercise, and a variety of specialized terminologies are used to describe what is being done.[30] Unfortunately, a rigorous discussion of these terms is beyond the scope of this chapter, although some fundamental explanations may be useful in understanding the main concepts.

Typically, the actuary is concerned with determining two types of costs that need to be established and funded. First is the *normal cost,* the present value cost of those obligations incurred as a result of employee services rendered in the current period. Second, there may be costs as a result of unfunded *past service* or *supplemental* liabilities that also need to be met. This second type of liability can be caused when a new plan is begun or when an existing plan is modified (for which contributions were not received at earlier dates). Changes in actuarial assumptions resulting from the failure of previous assumptions can also change liabilities. These costs also must be amortized over a period of time (thirty or forty years) if a plan is to be fully funded.

Both the normal and the supplemental costs are not absolute concepts. Each depends on the particular cost or benefit allocation method being used by the actuary.[31]

There are a variety of ways in which pension costs can be allocated, but the two major methods are the accrued benefit and the projected benefit methods. In the first case, the normal cost is the value of benefits accruing in the current year, and the actuarial liability is equal to all benefits accrued to date. This method tends to have low initial costs for young entrants (and immature pension funds) because the interest factor has a longer time to work, but it has relatively high costs for older workers and older plans.[32]

The projected benefit method gives a normal cost that remains constant over an employee's career (usually as a constant percentage of wages) if the assumptions hold. To project benefits, future salary levels must be assumed. Under the entry age normal method (a variant of the projected benefit method), the constant amount (or percentage of payroll) that must be set aside to accumulate the desired amount by retirement may be determined.

Pension liability and condition

There is no single way to determine the required contribution rates or the costs of a public pension plan. As a result, there is much confusion over what is the liability, unfunded liability, and general financial status of plans.

Both liability and unfunded liability are basically matters of definition and depend on the actuarial methods used to determine costs (or allocate benefits).[39] Thus, the liability or unfunded liability, given assets on hand, of a particular fund can vary greatly and can be noncomparable among funds. Other complications need to be borne in mind. Whatever the definition being used, it will usually be some ratio of assets to liabilities (the degree of funding), and the trend in that ratio will be more important than the actual dollar amount. In other words, some notion of relative magnitude is needed. Second, whatever the particular methods being employed, the credibility and timeliness of the actuarial assumptions are of utmost importance because they, in fact, determine the final value under all methods.

Still, the popular need for a "hard" number has focused attention on the intuitively appealing—but technically troublesome—concept of unfunded liability as a representation of a debt not covered by assets. Despite the above difficulties, these concerns about pension plan condition are not misplaced. A host of studies that attempted to make as rigorous comparisons as possible, given the paucity and noncomparability of data, has shown large unfunded liabilities in state and local pension plans, which could imperil the security of promises to plan members or the fiscal condition of the underlying sponsors.

It has been recently estimated that there was $150 billion to $170 billion in unfunded liabilities in state and local pensions as of 1975.[33] Another detailed study of seventy such plans undertaken by the U.S. General Accounting Office reported that forty of the plans (56 percent) were not contributing enough to restrain the growth in refunded liabilities, much less to amortize them in an orderly fashion.[34] It was found that to place the seventy funds on a funding standard similar to that required of private pensions under federal regulation would require an increase of $1.4 billion in annual employer contributions, which is 60 percent above their current annual level of $2.4 billion.

Understandably, the varieties of actuarial methods and associated concepts of liability have not only caused anxiety and confusion among experts and lay people alike but also have made analysis of plan condition (and its implications for members and contributors) difficult. Experts, for example, do not agree on the level of funding considered to be satisfactory (ratio of assets to liability). But there does appear to be agreement that the ratio should be increasing over time and that the assets should be sufficient to cover the obligations owed to those already retired. In the absence of uniform definitions and consistent applications, the analyst will need to depend on a series of indicators of condition rather than a single absolute measure of it.[35]

Actuarial assumptions

Whatever methods are used to determine and pay for pension costs and liabilities, the underlying actuarial assumptions and their plausibility are extremely important in judging the condition of a pension system. Furthermore, because of the long time periods involved in actuarial analysis, slight changes in assumptions can cause great variation in liability and associated normal costs and required contribution rates.

Different cost allocation methods and definitions of liability use different assumptions; thus the impact of a change in any one assumption is not always evident immediately. Moreover, the design of a plan's benefit package may dictate the importance of a particular assumption in the determination of costs and liabilities and the degree to which the system must be funded. Generally, assumptions dealing with economic trends, interest rates or earnings (used to discount future benefits to present values), future salary levels (because most plans use an average of final salary as the basis for benefits), and rates of inflation (for plans with cost-of-living escalators built into benefits) are most important. However, certain assumptions concerning a particular plan's population characteristics (decrements) can also be important. For example, high rates of early retirement and disability retirement can have severe consequences for plan finances if the assumptions used do not reflect actual plan experience. Other assumptions, regarding such things as employee turnover and mortality, appear to be less critical in the determination of pension costs.[36]

An important point is that each significant assumption used in actuarial calculations should be a realistic estimate of what the plan's future experience will be. This is contrary to present practice in many cases. For example, assumptions, because of infrequent re-evaluations, may be allowed to go out of date. Assumptions also have been allowed to offset one another; a low interest rate assumption may be used to adjust for the fact that there also has been a low assumption (or none at all) regarding future salary increases. Actuarial calculations, excluding the particular methodology used, are extremely dependent on the credibility of the actuarial assumptions, and these assumptions need to be explicit and to comport with the "real world" in order to interpret accurately the plan condition.[37]

Investment of pension fund assets

The meteoric rise in assets has made public pension fund managers increasingly active and sophisticated investors. The trend in both the public and private sectors has been toward expanding the types of eligible investments. Investment portfolios reflect growing diversification into new investment areas. Public pensions have been spurred by a desire to generate greater earnings on investments as more plans were created, benefits enriched, and defined benefit packages adopted. Use of new investment media often required the relaxation of legal impediments that traditionally had limited pension investments to high-grade corporate bonds and to federal, state, and local government securities.

A basic cleavage in pension investment policies typically has been the choice between debt instruments—fixed income obligations that return a steady stream of interest payments, barring default—and equity securities that are evidences of ownership, which may pay variable dividends and for which the primary attraction has been potential growth in dividends and appreciation in capital value. Within the broad classifications of debt and equity instruments are many varieties of securities, which may vary by the nature of the issuer, the maturity of the obligation, or the specifics of the security (e.g., priority of payments and ability to convert from one form of obligation or ownership to another).

Table 16–7 shows the growth and composition of investment assets held by state and local pension funds. The detail of the types of investments and the changing pattern of their investments is discussed later. The relative concentration on debt securities, particularly corporate bonds, that make up more than 50 percent of assets is to be noted. The second most important asset is the corporate equity, which has shown dramatic growth in the last two decades. Corporate stocks and bonds combined represented nearly 80 percent of total assets in 1977. Broadly speaking, these securities in post-World War II years have come to supplant United States government and state and local government debt obligations, which reigned supreme in 1950.[38]

Table 16–7   Assets of state and local retirement systems, by type of investment, 1950–1977 ($ billions)

Type of investment	1950	1960	1970	1975	1977
Total[1]	4.9	19.7	60.3	106.0	133.0
Deposits and currency	0.1	0.2	0.6	1.7	2.3
Corporate equity	. . .[2]	0.6	10.0	25.8	31.4
U.S. governments	2.5	5.9	6.6	6.8	14.7
Short-term	0.1[3]	0.3	0.8	0.5 ⎫	7.6
Long-term	2.4	5.4	4.3	1.7 ⎭	
Agencies	0.0	0.2	1.5	4.6	7.1
State and local obligations	1.5	4.4	2.0	2.5	3.0
Corporate bonds	0.6	7.1	35.0	60.9	72.6
Mortgages	0.1	1.5	5.9	8.2	9.0

Source: Board of Governors of the Federal Reserve System,
  Flow of Funds Accounts 1946–1975 (December 1976); and
  Flow of Funds Accounts 4th Quarter 1977 (February 1978).
1 Items may not sum to totals because of rounding.
2 Less than $50 million.
3 Estimated on basis of distribution of U.S. government obligations in 1951.

State and local pension assets traditionally were invested heavily in the obligations of the federal government or those of their own state or the sponsoring local governments. The rationale for such investments was conservatism—the federal government's debt representing the premiere security in terms of safety and liquidity, but only offering a low rate of return. As may be seen in Table 16–7, in 1950 state and local government pension systems held more than one-half of their assets in United States securities, most of which were concentrated in long-term obligations. Since that time, there has been a steady erosion in holdings of United States government long-term bonds. However, as in the 1975–77 period, United States government short-term obligations became important investment vehicles for pension fund managers who wanted to preserve liquidity while waiting for other investment markets to change.

A new investment form, but one that is still relatively unimportant in state and local pension portfolios, is found in the obligations of United States agencies. These securities serve to provide long-term investments of the highest quality at good yields and to provide a source of liquidity as short-term notes. Several of the federal agency securities represent what might be considered investments that support such socially useful activities as housing, small business, and rural development.

State and local government obligations

State and local obligations constitute a controversial form of state and local pension investment. State and local pensions were heavily invested in such securities. There were several reasons for this. State and local securities were typically one of the few allowable forms of investment for public pension funds. Also, public funds were used to support local markets for such securities, especially when credit markets were unreceptive.

State and local obligations, however, are not typically an attractive investment for pension funds. Because the funds themselves are tax-exempt, they receive no benefit from the tax-exempt nature of the interest income paid on the securities. When freed from investment constraints, state and local pension plans were quite willing to allow their investments of state and local securities to dwindle through the 1960s and 1970s.

The crisis in New York City and the resulting rescue efforts brought a heavy investment in the "big MAC" bonds by the New York City Employee Pension Fund. However, outside of the investment by these plans in state and local securities, there recently has been very little investment by state and local pension plans in state and local government securities.

Corporate bonds

In the 1950s, state and local pensions shifted from government securities to corporate bonds, which rose from 12 percent to nearly 60 percent of total assets between 1950 and 1970. During this period, the corporate debt security replaced United States government and state and local obligations as the premiere fixed-income obligation of the pension funds.

Corporate bonds have attributes that are especially appealing to state and local pensions. By and large, the chosen securities are part of larger listed issues that give relatively high rates of return (in comparison to those available on government securities). The post–World War II period had dissolved many of the fears about credit quality in private debt, and an abundance of high-grade industrial and utility debt was available. Simultaneously, secondary markets were listed for such obligations, thereby easing trading and pricing and making the market value of the securities easy to follow. The extensive use of bond ratings and the fact that the market is under the regulation of the Securities and Exchange Commission (SEC) gives a certain confidence and reliability to these securities.

State and local pension activity in the fixed-income securities of corporations had just begun when yet another investment frontier presented itself—the common stock.

Corporate equities

Starting in the 1960s, state and local pensions began to be major purchasers of corporate equities. Pension fund managers and trustees knew that the entry into the common stock market presented new problems and greater uncertainty; yet, the pressure of the times—the need to cope with inflation and to maximize the earnings on assets—dictated a prudent investment approach to the long-term growth potential offered by equities to offset the lackluster performance of fixed-income assets. Studies during the 1960s indicated that over the longer pull (1926–1960), investments in equities outperformed all other investment forms in terms of total return, and that these returns appeared to be increasing.[39]

The move to common stocks could not be accomplished without a further revamping and liberalization of the many restrictions under which state and local governments operated in making eligible investments. In the early 1960s public pensions that did permit equity investments generally allowed such investments of 10 percent or less of total assets. However, investment restrictions on equities were relaxed substantially and, in some cases, totally scrapped.[40]

The entry into the stock market by state and local pension plans has not been accompanied by speculative excesses. The systems generally are partial to blue-chip securities, which have proven dividend records. Nevertheless, the recent performance of the stock market has been disappointing. After doubling in value during the 1960s, the market averages slumped badly by the mid-1970s, with volatile stops and starts replacing their once robust growth.

Real estate

The last major category of public pension investment to be reviewed is real estate. Such investments by pension funds, although important in some funds, have never been a major factor in the aggregate. Investment usually has taken place in the form of mortgages; some equity interests have been acquired, however. As Table 16–8 shows, holdings of mortgages have grown slowly during the last twenty-five years, representing less than 10 percent of total investment in recent years.

Table 16–8 Percentage composition of assets of state and local retirement systems, by type of investment, 1950–1977

Type of investment	1950	1960	1970	1975	1977
Total	100.0	100.0	100.0	100.0	100.0
Deposits and currency	2.0	0.8	1.0	1.6	1.7
Corporate equity	1.5	2.5	16.8	24.4	23.5
U.S. governments	52.0	24.3	11.0	6.4	11.1
Short-term	2.0	1.2	1.3	0.5	5.7
Long-term	50.0	22.2	7.1	1.6 }	5.3
Agencies	0.0	0.8	2.5	4.3 }	
State and local obligations	31.3	18.1	3.3	2.4	2.3
Corporate bonds	12.2	29.2	58.1	57.5	54.6
Mortgages	2.0	6.2	9.8	7.7	6.8

Source: Board of Governors of the Federal Reserve System,
Flow of Funds Accounts 1946–1975 (December 1976); and
Flow of Funds Accounts 4th Quarter 1977 (February 1978).

Mortgages have not been a favored investment because of their illiquidity and the difficulties of servicing them. Also, pension managers have not been eager to select among mortgage purchases or to foreclose on the home of someone in default. Still, several states and some local systems did make a positive effort to acquire mortgages, usually showing a definite preference for in-state and in-town properties.

Public pension interest in the mortgage market has been given a considerable boost by the creation of several new capital market instruments, either backed directly with government guarantees or representing highly protected pools of conventional mortgages.[41] Also, special pools of mortgages have been formed using the mortgages of one state to appeal to those who wish to invest in-state.

Investment has not been confined to residential real estate. Comparisons among commercial mortgage yields, especially among equity interests in real estate, and yields available on common stocks have shown the real estate market to be a consistent winner over the past ten years. Some of the larger pension systems have begun to explore more sophisticated investments in real estate, often taking positions in syndicates and "selling off" depreciation rights to private investors who can use the tax shelter.

Investment management

Faced with a broad range of potential investment instruments and changing markets—not to mention greater exposure to official and public scrutiny—the management of the typical pension system often turns to professional help.[42]

Many forms of investment advice are available to the pension administrator or board. For example, a large system may elect to develop its own internal staff capability, not only to manage day-to-day operations of investments but also to serve as advisors to the board of trustees. Another option is for the board to delegate its investment responsibilities to an investment committee or to another government entity (e.g., a state investment board) that has such capability.

The third and most widely used option is for the fund to employ outside investment professionals to manage and advise it on investment decisions. The relationship between the fund and private parties varies greatly and usually is the basis of a carefully drawn contract. Thus, professional management may entail a broad delegation of responsibility and decision-making power, not only over the general composition of the portfolio but also over the day-to-day selection and sale of specific securities. Or, the private professional might act in a consultative role, helping to set policy but having no responsibility in making particular investment decisions. Another important advisory role is that of monitoring the investment performance of the fund.

Investment managers and counselors are typically separated into three types: bank trustees, insurance companies, and independent firms of investment counselors, many of whom specialize in retirement system investments. The services rendered can vary greatly among any one of the three types. For example, a bank trustee may act as the administrator of an individual fund, established solely for the client, or it may take the client's investments and mix them with those of other investors in a commingled fund. Likewise, insurance companies offer a variety of annuity packages.

The particular relationship between the private investment advisors and the board of trustees often is controlled by statutes that designate allowable investments for the fund and the degree to which and to whom the fund may delegate investment responsibilities. The Pension Task Force Report has criticized the consequences of tight restrictions, created both by statute and by policy, on investment expenses and portfolio composition, noting that "first rate investment management and advice may be foreclosed to the pension plans having such restrictions."[43]

Investment restrictions   State and local retirement systems, as creatures of state and local government laws and ordinances, operate in an atmosphere in which most of their activities—including pension fund investments—are subject to some form of direct or indirect legal constraint.

Legal restrictions on state and local pension fund investments fall into two major categories. The first category concerns specific statutory and constitutional restrictions that detail the kinds and composition of investment that may be made by pensions. The second level of restriction is found in the particular guidelines and limits that apply to pension fiduciaries or their agents (investment counselors), which deal with more general legal doctrines regarding the prudence of their actions. Over the past two decades there has been a move away from an extensive list of requirements for the types of investments that pensions could make toward a more expansive notion of discretion, the *prudent man* rule.

Placing the fiduciary responsibilities of managing public pension fund investments under a *prudent man* rule has been an avenue for diminishing the detailed constraints often found in state law. But the flexibility actually afforded investment managers depends heavily on how the prudent man rule is interpreted in a particular state. The rule under state and common law is basically that a trustee must, in administering a trust, exercise such skill as a person of ordinary prudence would exercise when dealing with his or her own property, and to do such with a view toward preservation of the estate and the amount and regularity of the income to be derived. However, there have been different interpretations of the prudent man rule in state courts.

Some states adopted what came to be known as legal lists, which allow only a percentage of the assets to be invested according to the prudent man standard. Such legal lists may apply to fiduciaries in general, including pension fund trustees, and can accomplish the same level of restriction (and perhaps even more difficulties of interpretation) as a legal list drawn specifically with public employee pension systems in mind.[44]

Risk and return measures   For the most part, it may be safely presumed that retirement systems exemplify the classic long-term investor who works in an environment of well-defined inflows and predictable outflows. Such stability and long-term horizons should give the systems a low preference for liquidity and an ability to withstand substantial short-term risk. Because pension funds can wait a long time for returns and can tolerate risk, a wise portfolio policy and sufficient diversification should enable the funds to be invested long-term and to weather the storms of short-term market fluctuations.

The extrapolations in the earnings used to plan pension fund investment strategies entail such long periods of time and necessarily involve uncertainty about future levels of prices and interest rates. The standard analysis used to assess risk and return in the pension area has taken the long view and relied heavily on historical trends in rates of return.

A common approach in the examination of long-term investment returns is to rely heavily on extrapolating long-range historical trends in rates of return on broad aggregates of investments. One set of general benchmarks (based on studies of long-term rates of return for the past 50 years) is that common stocks on average have returned a compounded annual rate of 9.0 percent; long-term corporate bonds, 3.8 percent; long-term United States government bonds, 3.3 percent; and United States short-term notes, 2.3 percent.[45] It is, of course, realized that the historically higher rates of return on stocks have not been without risks. Maintaining any portfolio involves risk—the risks of both security price fluctuations and of possible default. The long-term record, however, shows that the biggest risk is the loss of purchasing power caused by inflation. During the fifty-year period, 1925–1975, the annual rate of inflation averaged 2.3 percent.

Portfolio management is much more difficult today because of a persistent, and seemingly incurable, high inflation rate.

Appeals can be made to look at historical trends in rates and to examine periods of several years to judge the adequacy and value of investment counsel. Still, there remains the impulse—if not the responsibility of pension trustees and managers—to keep close track of results in order to see how well investments are performing in comparison to similarly situated systems, and also to determine how well they are meeting the system's investment objectives. Many private services produce performance measures that often compare the performance of a particular fund to that of a widely used market index, such as that of Standard & Poor's or Moody's Investors Service. Such comparisons can be troublesome for the unwary, primarily because market indexes do not face the day-to-day problem of managing a portfolio under a particular set of constraints and investment objectives.[46]

1   U.S., Congress, House, Committee on Education and Labor, *Task Force Report on Public Employee Retirement Systems* (Washington, D.C.: Government Printing Office, 1978), pp. 51–97 (hereafter cited as *Pension Task Force Report*).

2   For an explanation of the Census definitions and how they differ from those used in the *Pension Task Force Report*, see: U.S., Bureau of the Census, 1977 Census of Governments, *Employee-Retirement Systems of State and Local Governments*, vol. 6, no. 1 (Washington, D.C.: Government Printing Office, 1978), pp. 5–6.

3   Ibid., p. 3.

4   According to the *Pension Task Force Report*, p. 55 (using different definitions), there were 1,413 plans in Pennsylvania.

5   U.S., Bureau of the Census, *Employee-Retirement Systems*, p. 13.

6   See: Thomas P. Bleakney, *Retirement Systems for Public Employees* (Philadelphia: University of Pennsylvania Press, 1972), pp. 20–23.

7   *Pension Task Force Report*, pp. 53–54.

8   U.S. Conference of Mayors, Labor-Management Relations Service, *Third National Survey of Employee Benefits for Full-time Personnel of U.S. Municipalities* (Washington, D.C.: Labor-Management Relations Service, 1977), p. 6.

9   *Pension Task Force Report*, pp. 61–62.

10 For a comprehensive treatment of participants' rights, see: Robert Kalman and Michael Leiby, *The Public Pension Crisis: Myth, Reality, Reform* (Washington, D.C.: American Federation of State, County, and Municipal Employees, 1972), chapter 5.

11 U.S., Advisory Commission on Intergovernmental Relations, *Information Bulletin: State and Local Government Pension Reforms* (Washington, D.C.: Government Printing Office, 1979).

12 *Pension Task Force Report*, p. 65.

13 See, for example: Comptroller General of the United States, *The Investment Decisionmaking Process in New Jersey Public Employee Retirement Plans* (Washington, D.C.: Government Printing Office, 1977), appendix I.

14 *Pension Task Force Report*, pp. 205–6.

15 Ibid., p. 207.

16 For a discussion, see: Municipal Finance Officers Association Committee on Public Employee Retirement Administration, *Public Employee Retirement Administration* (Chicago: Municipal Finance Officers Association, 1977).

17 An extensive examination of issues surrounding retirement system accounting and reporting. For issues, see: John E. Petersen, *State and Local Pension Financial Disclosure* (Washington, D.C.: Government Finance Research Center, Municipal Finance Officers Association, 1979).

18 According to the Pension Task Force survey, nearly 33 percent of police and fire service plans used final day's rate or year's pay to calculate pension benefits. *Pension Task Force Report*, p. 112.

19 Ibid., p. 67.

20 Ibid., p. 168.

21 Howard Winklevoss and Dan McGill, *Public Pension Plans* (Homewood, Ill.: Dow Jones–Irwin, 1979), p. 144.

22 Ibid.; see chapter 2 for a detailed discussion.

23 *Pension Task Force Report*, pp. 124–25.

24 U.S., Bureau of the Census, *Employee-Retirement Systems*, p. 11.

25 *Pension Task Force Report*, p. 111.

26 See: Sidney T. Kaufman, "Pension Funding Problems," in *1978 Public Employee Conference Proceedings* (Brookfield, Wis.: International Foundation of Employee Benefit Plans, 1979), p. 25.

27 For more discussion of the debate on advanced versus pay-as-you-acquire financing, see: Robert Tilove, *Public Employee Pension Funds* (New York: Columbia University Press, 1976), pp. 131–41.

28 See: David J. Ott et al., *State and Local Finances in the Last Half of the Seventies* (Washington, D.C.: American Enterprise Institute for Public Policy Research, 1975), pp. 65–69.

29 *Pension Task Force Report*, pp. 150–51.

30 Ibid., pp. 158–163.

31 The interested reader is referred to Winklevoss and McGill, *Public Pension Plans*, part II, for an extended discussion of pension funding techniques and associated actuarial concepts.

32 Ibid., chapter 6.

33 *Pension Task Force Report*, pp. 163–66.

34 U.S., General Accounting Office, Comptroller General of the United States, *Funding of State and Local Pension Plans: A National Problem* (Washington, D.C.: Government Printing Office, 1979).

35 *Pension Task Force Report*, pp. 166–72. See also Winklevoss and McGill, *Public Pension Plans*, chapters 14 and 15.

36 For a nonrigorous discussion of the relative importance of actuarial assumptions, see: John S. Perreca, "How to Understand Your Actuary—Almost," *Pension World*, October 1979, pp. 35–42. For more rigor, see: Howard Winklevoss, *Pension Mathematics* (Philadelphia: Pension Research Council, 1978), chapter 17.

37 *Pension Task Force Report*, pp. 158–62.

38 For a more complete analysis of state and local pension investment practices, see: John E. Petersen, *State and Local Government Pension Fund Investments* (Washington, D.C.: Government Finance Research Center, Municipal Finance Officers Association, 1979).

39 One influential study of the period showed that the average yield on a "buy-and-hold" portfolio made up of all New York Stock Exchange listed stocks for the period 1926 to 1960 was 9 percent. For bonds, the total return was more on the order of 3 percent for the period. Lawrence Fisher and James Lorie, "Rates of Return on Investments in Common Stock," *Journal of Business* (January 1968): 1–26.

40 *Pension Task Force Report*, p. 132.

41 Ronald Struck, "Mortgage Backed Securities: A Primer," *Pension World*, February 1978, pp. 17–21.

42 Tilove, *Public Employee Pension Funds*, pp. 214–20.

43 *Pension Task Force Report*, p. 196.

44 James D. Hutchinson, "The Compleat Fiduciary," *Pension World*, April 1978, p. 53.

45 Although many have performed long-term rates of return, a commonly cited recent study in the area is: Roger Ibbotson and Rex Sinquefield, "Stocks, Bonds, Bills, and Inflation: Year-by-Year Historical Returns (1926–1974)," *Journal of Business* (January 1976): 11–47. The returns include both current payments (interest and dividends) and changes in prices.

46 See: Robert Levy, "Common Sense in Comparative Performance," *Pension World* (April 1978): 8–11.

17 Inventory, purchasing, and risk management

The main concerns of the local government financial manager are to keep the municipality's economy viable, to maintain a manageable financial structure, and to avoid undue debt and fiscal crises. Under current conditions of high demands for government aid and services and static sources of revenue, the overall problems of structuring and administering the budget, maintaining an adequate cash flow, and preserving the municipality's credit constitute a formidable task. Nevertheless within these broader duties, the financial manager may be called on to help administer or to advise on more operational activities such as purchasing, inventory control, and insurance and risk management. These activities are not to be dismissed lightly, for when these problems are handled efficiently, they save considerable funds—which may be used for other functions or to lower tax needs.

It is not necessary that the financial manager be versed in all the details, computer programs, and mathematics involved in these areas of management science. It is enough that the financial manager understand the general nature of the problem and the form of the solution so that he or she can evaluate the reasonableness of the policies that are implemented. The manager must also understand that the latest or most sophisticated program may not necessarily be the most desirable. A very sophisticated program may cost more to implement or to administer than it produces in additional or incremental savings. (Moreover, sophisticated programs often have more "bugs" and experience more failure than some of the adequate, simpler procedures.)

There is, however, one element in most of these programs for which the input or knowledge of the financial manager is directly needed—the cost of funds (i.e., a reasonable discount rate or interest rate). The financial manager is the one most likely to give a reasonable estimate of the true cost of funds to be used for the current problem.

Inventory management

In the past, inventory management consisted primarily of making a list of the municipality's land, buildings, and equipment; determining the location of each item; assigning a value to the item; and, on occasion, seeing that each item was adequately protected by insurance. It was recognized that the purchasing agent had to deal with inventory problems when he or she set the appropriate quantity for purchases and worked at assuring timely deliveries. The procedures used, however, were not always sufficient to attain optimum efficiency; the basis of inventory control was not always completely understood.

Inventory may be considered in very broad terms. The usual inventory is thought of simply as a stockpile which may consist of paper supplies, books, food, chemicals, or hardware. But, in a broader sense, the cash in the municipal treasury is an inventory; the number of machines owned is an inventory; operating space is an inventory; the number of employees in a department is an inventory. The number of people standing in line at some bureau counter or the number of cars waiting to pay a toll on a superhighway may be thought of as a type of negative inventory. In these cases, it is called a queue and may be considered a detriment rather than a store of value. Queuing theory—an offshoot of inventory management theory—offers an analytical solution to such problems as the optimum number of toll booths compared with the potential length of the waiting line.

An overview

As a beginning, consider the problem of setting the optimum inventory for commodities that may be purchased from regular suppliers. If one or more completely reliable suppliers were near by and were willing to provide instantaneous delivery and there were no fixed order or check-in costs, the user would not need to carry an inventory. If such circumstances are not prevailing, the optimum inventory is designed to (1) minimize the total of ordering and holding costs, and (2) control the frequency of stockouts or shortages relative to holding and storing costs.

The major categories of costs entering into the various inventory models are the ordering costs, the holding costs, and the expected probable stockout costs.

1. Ordering costs include the cost of preparing specifications, obtaining competitive bids, negotiating, and receiving the item into stock, as well as the clerical and correspondence costs of actually placing the order.
2. Holding costs (also called carrying costs) include the costs associated with deterioration, possible obsolescence, storage space, unexplained losses, insurance, and imputed financing costs. Generally a percentage of the cost of inventory is estimated as the carrying cost. Thus, 20 percent to 30 percent per year of the purchased cost of the inventory would probably be adequate to reflect deterioration, potential obsolescence, insurance, and finance costs (i.e., the implicit opportunity cost of funds tied up in inventory).
3. Stockout or shortage costs arise from any inconvenience to users, the costs of delays, or the losses that might occur if, for example, determining there is a power outage. These costs may be quite difficult to estimate—for example, determining the extra expenses of restarting a project. They also may be as simple to determine as the costs of the emergency efforts to acquire the needed item.

For a municipality, the estimated cost of a stockout that involves the failure to provide some service includes the resentment that may develop among the citizens due to the loss of service. There is an implicit political or social cost for such resentment. The importance of each inventory item should be analyzed, and a rough dollar amount (including an implicit payment for citizen inconvenience) should be established as the cost of a stockout.

Although there are some sophisticated operation activity models, the two common basic inventory models are the economic ordering quantity model and the safety stock model.[1] The economic ordering quantity (EOQ) handles the optimum size and the frequency of orders; the safety stock model deals with the optimum inventory to minimize the costs of stockouts relative to carrying costs. These two models are not competitive but complementary. In fact, there exist various dynamic or tracking models that may be used to combine the factors into one model.

In practice, "rules of thumb" have been developed for handling these problems; some of the better rules probably approximate the more precise solutions obtained by the relatively sophisticated and more expensive computer techniques.

Determining safety stocks

Let us first look at the problem of determining the optimum level of the safety stock to reduce the occurrence of shortages to a reasonable number. Safety stocks are carried because the patterns of supply and demand can be somewhat erratic and because these patterns do not run in phase. Obviously, the closer supply and demand flows can be synchronized, the lower the need for safety stocks.

The function of the safety stock is, as far as it is economically feasible, to avoid the loss caused by stockouts when supplies are not available or a shortage of raw materials causes a slowdown or shutdown in operations or in the construction of a project. A stockout entails the loss to citizens from an interruption of service and their resulting dissatisfaction. A shortage of supplies can reduce the level of a particular operation (snow removal, for example). There are usually extra costs associated both with slowdowns or shutdowns and with restoration of full service. In general, operating costs usually are minimized if service can be kept to a standard level.

The solution to the safety stock problem first involves a careful analysis of activity patterns—that is, how erratic and in what size do orders come; how dependable are the suppliers; and how long does it take to receive a new shipment? Then estimates have to be made of the cost of stockouts. What is the cost in lost citizen service and in shutdowns and startups? The answers to these questions are combined into a stockout loss probability function. This function relates the various sizes of inventories the city might carry to the probability of stockouts occurring in a given time period, multiplied by the estimated cost of a stockout loss. Clearly, the larger the inventory the local government carries relative to its normal use level, the smaller the probability of stockout losses. A smaller inventory increases the probability of stockouts occurring. A very large inventory may reduce the probability of stockouts to almost zero. A graph of the stockout loss function looks something like Figure 17–1.

Figure 17–1 Expected stockout loss as a function of inventory size.

Part of the safety stockout analysis includes the establishment of a reorder point. The reorder point is set to trigger an order when the existing inventory reaches a certain level. This level is established on the basis of expected use patterns and average delivery times.

A large inventory is desirable to avoid stockouts, but the costs associated with carrying an inventory increase directly with inventory size. These are the holding costs, insurance, storage costs, possible costs for spoilage and obsolescence, and

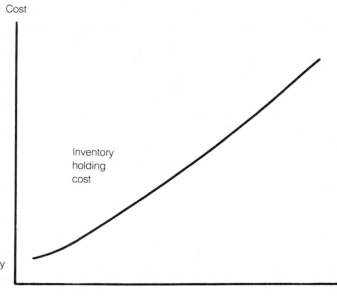

Figure 17–2   Inventory holding cost as a function of inventory size.

the cost of the funds tied up in the inventory. The last item is very important and is, of course, of direct concern to the finance officer. Because all these costs can be converted into percentages and are directly related to the size of the inventory carried, they can be converted into an inventory holding cost function. This function would look something like Figure 17–2.

The optimum safety stock inventory is set at the point where the total of the two kinds of costs is at a minimum. Figure 17–3 illustrates a graphical solution of the problem. The optimum inventory size in the example is shown at point *E*. (It should be noted that this is not the same as setting the probability of stockout losses at a minimum. What we have done is to determine an "acceptable" stockout loss level.)

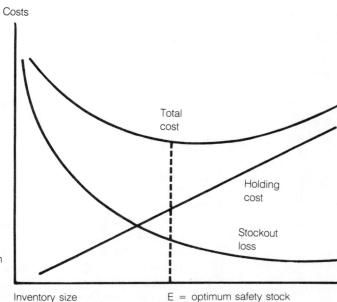

Figure 17–3   Optimum inventory as a function of stockout loss and holding cost.

The solution *also* can be obtained by marginal analysis. The minimum cost is the point where the first derivative of the holding costs equals the derivative of the stockout loss function (i.e., where the marginal costs of the two functions are equal).[2] This would be expressed as:

$$\frac{\partial SO}{\partial X} = \frac{\partial HC}{\partial X} \tag{1}$$

where ∂SO represents stockout loses; HC, holding costs; and X, inventory size. It might be noted that since the cost of capital is an important part of the holding cost function, a rise in the cost of capital should move managers to economize on inventory holdings.

Of course, what has been illustrated is the theoretical model underlying inventory policy. In practice, rules of thumb have been developed which presumably closely approximate the ideal solution. These rules have been developed for different kinds of operations and are stated in *such terms*, as for example: (1) inventories should cover about fifteen days' usages; (2) raw material stocks should cover thirty days of normal service; or (3) inventories should be turned over at least four times a year.

Since inventories absorb funds (i.e., they must be financed), and since inventories are generally ordered in advance of needs, the efficiency with which inventories are controlled has considerable effect on the operations of the financial manager, who has to make sure that funds are available to pay the suppliers and to take advantage of the best possible credit terms.

The optimum ordering quantity

Another part of the inventory problem is concerned with the optimum amount per order once the safety stock has been determined. The economic ordering quantity problem arises because there is a set of expenses known as ordering costs involved in handling supplies. These costs consist of the cost of preparing an order, the clerical and correspondence costs of placing the order, and the costs of checking the order once it is received. It is generally assumed that part of the ordering costs are a fixed cost per order—that is, they do not vary significantly with the size of the order. Therefore, if orders are placed in larger quantities, there is a decrease in the ordering costs per unit. On the other hand, with any given rate of use, the average inventory carried goes up when orders are placed in larger quantities. The basic EOQ model may be used to determine the amount of the order and how often goods should be ordered.

The economic order quantity (EOQ) model

The family of inventory models known as the economic ordering quantity models are employed to deal with the optimum lot size of the order for the purpose of minimizing the amount and frequency of ordering costs. The EOQ model can be used alone to determine the whole inventory problem if there is an assured supply nearby and/or if usage rates are very stable, whereby there are no likely stockout losses and the safety stock may be zero. Because these conditions are not likely, the EOQ model generally is combined in some manner with the safety stock models.

The solution of the EOQ model essentially uses three variables:

1. A predicted demand or usage function for the applicable planning period
2. The holding cost variable related to the size of the inventory
3. The ordering or transaction costs—the costs of placing an order, checking it in, and getting it into stock. In general, it is assumed that ordering costs are approximately the same regardless of the size of the order.

Thus, there are economies of scale achievable by ordering larger quantitites.

The idea is to set the size of orders so that total holding and ordering costs are minimized for the given period. If, given the rate of usage (or demand), smaller orders are placed, the average inventory will be low and holding costs will be held down. On the other hand, a policy of small orders makes it necessary to order more frequently and raises the total of ordering costs. (The problem is also depicted in Chapter 13, "Cash Management.")

In simple situations the EOQ is often superimposed on the safety stock. This relation has been graphically depicted in Figure 17–4, which shows the relation of order size and the average inventory over time. Under Policy A with larger order sizes, the average inventory in excess of the safety stock is twice that of Policy B; however, in any given time period, there will be twice as many orders.

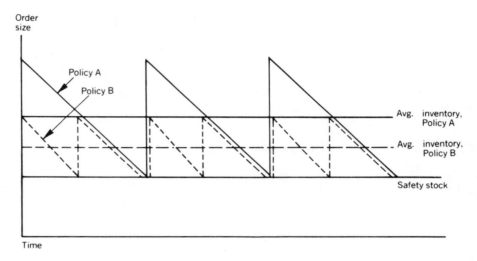

Figure 17–4   Relationship of order size and average inventory by two inventory policies over time.

The problem of the optimum ordering quantity is one that lends itself to solution by use of the computer. However, in terms of graphics the solution looks something like Figure 17–5. The optimum inventory order size is where the total of ordering costs and carrying costs for the period is minimized.

Although we have graphically depicted the EOQ solution in the form of totals, it is clear that the operational solution would be done marginally. The optimum EOQ is obtained where marginal holding costs and the marginal ordering costs are equal. The solution has been worked out where the functions are linear and yields the following mathematical formula:

$$EOQ = \sqrt{\frac{2SO}{HU}} \qquad (2)$$

where S equals estimated demand or usage in dollar terms for the pertinent period; O is ordering costs per order; H equals holding costs as a rate for the given period (e.g., the total cost of funds and insurance as 24 percent for a year or 12 percent for six months); and U is costs per unit.

The formula as given will solve the optimum EOQ in terms of units.[3] If U is dropped out of the equation, EOQ will give the optimum dollar amounts of the order; however, it is useful to have a unit cost when quantity discounts are

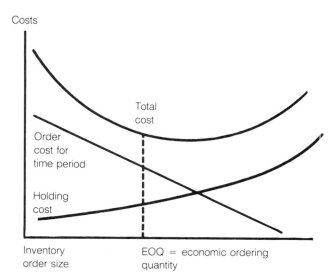

Figure 17–5   Optimum ordering quantity in relation to holding costs and ordering costs.

offered, and when it is desirable to compare the optimum order sizes as unit costs are varied.

In this simple analysis, the problem of the safety stock and the ordering quantity have been treated separately. The inventory resulting from the economic ordering quantity (one-half on the average of the EOQ) has been solved independently and presumably placed on top of the safety stock. In theory, at least, the two should be solved simultaneously because a larger EOQ policy results in higher *average* inventories and reduces the probability of being out of stock. There are more complex computer models that do solve the EOQ and safety stock simultaneously. One such probabilistic model is the Newsboy model, which assumes a strong need for the time period and embodies a penalty or loss for carrying inventory past the use period.[4] This model may be especially appropriate for solving the inventory for seasonal needs such as the amount of road salt for the winter season. In general, however, it is a managerial decision whether the additional precision of the more refined models are worth the extra cost, time, and effort.

Whatever inventory system is adopted, it should be audited regularly to see if the program is operating efficiently. Where the inventory appears to be excessive, it should be checked to make certain that it falls within the established guidelines. Particular attention should be paid to determine whether there is any collusion with suppliers to overbuy particular items.

Where the municipality is small and where it does not seem efficient to develop a computer program, certain rules of thumb may be practiced which help approximate the optimum inventory. These rules of thumb generally are stated in terms of the number of days of normal usage. The advantage of rules of thumb are that they are easily understood and relatively simple to put into practice. Nevertheless, it is often worthwhile to prepare a one-time solution by use of one of the more sophisticated methods to ascertain whether the rule of thumb produces a reasonable approximation to the optimum solution.

The financial manager may not have direct responsibility for inventory management. The management science and computer science specialists will find these problems more central to their areas of expertise. As can be seen from this discussion, however, a vital part of inventory holding cost is the cost of the funds absorbed in carrying the inventory. The financial manager should note when *real* interest costs rise and make sure that the inventory managers make the proper adjustment (i.e., reduce the average inventory carried). Of course, the cost may decrease if holding costs drop.

Stockout probability approach

Another approach to the safety stock problem avoids the difficulty of making an explicit dollar cost estimate of a stockout. A study of past levels of operations is made to develop the probability of sustaining a shortage at different levels of inventory holdings. The manager is given an analysis that is in this form. If inventory is carried at average holding costs of $100,000 a year, there will probably be three stockouts a year. However, by raising the inventory size by 10 percent—giving a carrying cost of approximately $110,000 per year—probable stockouts can be reduced to two per year. Which is preferable? If the decision maker makes the second choice, he or she has decided that avoiding all the costs and inconveniences of a probable additional stockout is worth $10,000 a year. Although this seems roundabout, it is nevertheless a perfectly valid approach to solving the problem in a nonprofit organization where some of the costs are not precise or explicit.

Speculative inventories

It is sometimes recommended that inventories be purchased in advance of need to avoid price rises, but this is easier said than done. This tactic only yields a gain when the rise in prices exceeds the inventory carrying costs. Thus, if carrying costs are 20 percent a year, the price of the inventory item has to rise by over 20 percent during the year to justify carrying excess stock. Moreover, interest rates, which are an important part of the holding costs, have a disconcerting way of rising with the expected rate of inflation. Thus, a rise in interest rates (and holding costs) during periods of expected inflation is likely to be encountered. In general, municipalities should avoid speculating on inventories, although it is sometimes prudent to negotiate advance purchasing contracts with suppliers for future deliveries at definite prices during periods of uncertainty.

Queuing theory

The English pride themselves on their ability to stand patiently in line, or queue, without exhibiting undignified behavior. (Americans, on the other hand, do not seem to be so tolerant.) Queuing theory deals with the solutions to waiting line situations. All of the problems require the balancing of the same two elements: the costs and disutility of those waiting in line and the costs of investing in the additional facilities to move the line faster. Some well-known waiting situations are lines at ticket booths and cashier windows, golfers waiting to tee-off, and skiers at the lifts. Other waiting situations are more subtle—for example, prospective patients relative to the number of beds in a hospital, processing time versus the number of clerks in an office, and traffic flow versus the width of streets. The queuing problem is complicated further because the rate of arrivals is usually not constant; instead it shows "peaks" and "valleys." Providing enough facilities to cover all the peaks can require a large investment, one which will lie idle most of the time.

The costs of providing service facilities should be analyzed carefully. The municipal executive who states that no citizen will have to wait for attention any longer than five minutes on the average has specified a service level policy. Inherent in this policy statement are assumptions about the department's obligations to the citizens, notions about courtesy, and knowledge of the costs of maintaining this service level.

Suppose, for example, that the municipal swimming pool is concerned with selecting the number of ticket sellers it wishes to have during the summer season. Each seller is to be paid a salary and provided with a change making machine, a basic change fund, space, and a counter. The management of the municipality will have to decide the varying operating costs and service levels that will be acceptable in light of the imputed costs or inconveniences to the patrons waiting in line.

Queuing analysis customarily deals with the probability distributions associated with the rates of arrival of people or items to be processed. Arrivals may be sparse at some times and concentrated at others; there is no way of storing idle service time. Unfortunately, the queue discipline that governs most waiting lines is "first-in, first-out" (FIFO), although those of "most vocal" and "very important person" (VIP) frequently prevail. The length of the waiting line thus is a probability problem. The probable length and implicit costs of the waiting lines, which might be expected for different levels of service facilities, can be compared to the costs of maintaining varying amounts of facilities. The problem is analagous to the safety stock inventory models that balance the costs of the line (stockout costs) to the amount of facilities (carrying costs). The solution to the problem usually can be obtained by the use of computer programs.

Summary

General features of inventory management can be illustrated by the problem of the optimum inventory and its determination. This involves a knowledge of the costs of ordering, of carrying, and of being short of items.

The choice of an inventory system should be based on its service performance in addition to its explicit money costs; the implicit costs of shortages should be considered also. Many factors not quantifiable in explicit dollars impinge on inventory decisions. For example, the decision makers should have a feeling for what can be expected or what will be tolerated by the citizens. They may try to express this feeling in equivalent money terms. For example, they must try to calculate the costs of having a team of men stand idle waiting for pipe, meter, and valves to hook up a home to the water supply; they must also make the more difficult estimate of the cost of losing the good will of the homeowner/citizen who is impatient and loud and waiting for water.

In contemporary inventory management (and in the related problem of queuing theory), many mathematical techniques can be applied alongside the traditional common sense or rule-of-thumb judgments to maximize managerial efficiency.

Purchasing

In many communities, the purchasing department falls within the purview of the financial manager. In any case, it is important for the financial manager to be cognizant of the purchasing department's activities, because many of these activities impinge directly on the budget, and because the careful use of purchasing techniques can significantly reduce expenditures.

The central purchasing offices have the difficult task of organizing the purchases of many departments. The staff must be diplomatic and skillful because their department's function often runs counter to the natural urge of the line department managers and supervisors to organize a self-sufficient operation—even when such organization would lead to a potentially more costly system of decentralized purchasing. Obviously, the activities of most departments cannot keep a full-time purchasing staff busy; centralized purchasing can use a full-time staff and prevent an unnecessary duplication of facilities. Moreover, it can obtain quantity discounts by buying items common to several departments in larger lots.

The basic purchasing functions

The functions of the purchasing agent are:

1. To be familiar with the sources of supply
2. To understand pricing, business practices, and market conditions
3. To know the statutes and ordinances that control bidding
4. To establish a system that ensures that discounts are taken, that quality is tested, that ordered items are properly received and stored, and that deliveries are prompt
5. To deal effectively with salesmen and contractors as well as with municipal service departments
6. To have authority to obtain bids based on the precise specifications that the agent has helped formulate.

Often it is advisable to have the purchasing agent control such central services as duplicating, mailing, and operating the municipality's storage facilities.

The purchasing agent circulates notices to suppliers and advertises for bids. Agents should be aware that the lowest selling price is attractive only if the quality of the item and the bidding company's reputation for reliability in meeting delivery dates and quantities are acceptable. Purchasing agents should be able to expedite shipments and reduce transportation costs. They need to know how to get supplies in emergencies; at the same time, they should encourage departments to acquaint them with their needs far enough in advance to reduce the incidence of emergency shortages.

Purchasing agents ease the brunt of bureaucracy for suppliers by providing them with simple but complete order forms. By arranging for quality testing at vendor plants, they can help avoid the costs involved in returning inferior items. When deliveries are spread over a long period of time or when budgetary restrictions prevent immediate payment, purchasing agents can obtain appropriate terms of credit. They do not accept quantity overruns (i.e., when the manufacturer offsets any damaged units by including extra units in the order) unless the need is clear and a reduced price is offered. They participate in the various phases of budgetary planning to anticipate new supply needs and to locate new suppliers in advance. They may anticipate price inflation by using inventory models that balance carrying costs against the potential savings in future purchase prices (where this is clearly appropriate and not too risky); otherwise, they try to safeguard the budget by ordering at advance prices.

Purchasing agents should also systematize significant parts of their functions. For example, they may use prenumbered multipart forms with copies for the supplier (whose copy is the purchase order), the purchasing department files, the accounting department, and the receiving facility. By accounting for and matching the numbers on these copies, it is easy to determine proper authorizations, agreement with the order, and physical receipt of the goods. Purchasing officers should develop and supervise the operation of inventory ordering systems. They must maintain up-to-date records which are regularly audited. Their task, in short, is both complex and responsible.

Group purchasing versus individual replacement

Should a group of particular items be replaced all at once (group replacement) or replaced as each fails in operation (individual replacement)? This general question originated with the replacement of light bulbs as part of a preventive maintenance program. It was discovered that replacing all the lights as a group was less expensive than individual replacement, because of quantity price discounts and the efficiency in scheduling labor. A similar situation occurs with the acquisition and maintenance of fleets of cars or of "fleets" of typewriters and adding machines. In general, the decision is not only to undertake group or individual replacement but also to choose the best replacement cycle if group replacement is more economical. To solve the problem, a minimum standard of service performance for the items under consideration should be established. Then, account must be taken of the price discount on the items purchased in bulk, the expected length of life of each item, and the local government's cost of capital. This type of problem is well suited to computer application.

Total-cost purchasing

Total-cost purchasing, often referred to as least-cost versus low-bid purchasing, is useful in analyzing bids for the supply of heavy equipment. It is sometimes considered appropriate to have suppliers include in their bids not just the purchase price of the equipment but also their guaranteed maximum maintenance costs and a minimum repurchase price for the used machine at the end of the period. Sometimes a better arrangement is to hold the personnel of the municipal public works department responsible for maintenance, with the proviso that if costs exceed the guaranteed maximum, the seller reimburses the municipality for the difference.

An illustration of selecting least-cost bids where three suppliers bid on a piece of heavy equipment is as follows:

Supplier	Purchase price	Total 5-year guaranteed maintenance cost	Repurchase price at end of five years
A	$23,000	$11,000	$ 2,000
B	$30,000	$ 5,000	$15,000
C	$26,000	$12,000	$10,000

The specifics of the guarantee are that Supplier C has specified that his five-year guarantee is $800, multiplied by the age of the machine each year. A and B have agreed to apportion their guarantees evenly over the five years (i.e., $2,200 per annum for A and $1,000 per annum for B). Suppose the municipality uses a 20 percent discount rate in analyzing such decisions. To obtain the solution, the total cost of each bid should be calculated in present value terms using the following formula:

$$K = P + \left[\sum_{i=1}^{5} R_i \left(\frac{1}{1.2} \right)^i \right] - T \left(\frac{1}{1.2} \right)^5 \tag{3}$$

where K equals net present value; P equals purchase price; R_i equals maintenance cost for each year; and T equals repurchase price. Therefore,

Supplier	Purchase price	Plus present value of maintenance costs	Minus present value of purchase price	Equals net present value
A	$23,000	$6,579	$ 804	$28,775
B	$30,000	$2,991	$6,029	$26,962
C	$26,000	$6,318	$4,019	$28,299

The least expensive total cost bid is B; this bid would not have been selected had only purchase price been considered. One of the advantages of total-cost purchasing is that suppliers of high quality equipment, whose product enjoys lower maintenance costs and higher repurchase prices, may submit bids that are highly competitive.[5]

Getting help

Administrators of a very small municipality may consider joining other local governments and sharing the costs and benefits of a common purchasing agent. Under such sharing arrangements—called horizontal cooperation—costs often have been greatly reduced and service levels have been improved.

Cooperative arrangements involve many factors, each of which may influence a decision to join. Some of the more important questions to be considered are:

1. Will the level of service be comparable to the one the city or county currently enjoys?
2. Will the municipality be able to control the service by controlling the planning, the formulation of acceptable common specifications, and the availability of service?
3. Can problems such as labor disputes be avoided?
4. Can a suitable basis for sharing costs be found?

Many local governments report that citizens dislike cooperative endeavors because they fear relinquishing autonomy. Too much autonomy can, however, lead to uneconomical, fragmented services.

However, it has been found that municipalities willing to cooperate in purchasing functions often have great difficulty agreeing on uniform item specifications. To begin on a sound footing, it may be wise to select initially only three or four commodities for cooperative purchasing. This will act as a pilot run for the system. Once the initial items have been handled satisfactorily, other items can be added. Some equitable base for allocating shared costs should be determined. Detailed records should be maintained to show costs applicable to the different partners.

One great advantage of cooperative programs lies in the interchange of ideas and personnel. Alternative approaches to problems are widely discussed in such programs; and an opportunity is provided for personnel to gain experience and training by working with experts in the field from other local governments.

Cooperative efforts do not have to be horizontal, as in the case of cooperative contracts for shared services. It may be preferable to pursue vertical cooperative efforts with the county, for example. This is usually done on a fee basis. The advantage to this effort is that because the county is larger and can attract several municipalities to the group, the economies of scale in the training and use of staff are more evident to the cooperating municipalities.

Cities of varying sizes may contract with private industry or with a county or special district for the supply of various services. Important services that may be obtained on a fee basis from either industry or from the county or special district include:

1. Street lighting (including design, installation, and maintenance)
2. Garbage disposal and sanitation services
3. Health services, including exchange of information and the maintenance of ambulances, hospitals, and health departments
4. Tax assessment and collection
5. Water supply
6. Law enforcement
7. Street and highway maintenance (including repairs, cleaning, and snow removal).

Summary

Central purchasing departments have the difficult task of balancing the advantages of central organization with the varied needs of individual departments. The purchasing officers have a number of clearly defined functions, ranging from familiarity with sources of supply to possession of the authority to obtain bids based on precise specifications. They also have a multiplicity of specific tasks, ranging from ascertaining the reputation of a bidding company to obtaining appropriate credit terms for long-term deliveries. Purchasing departments need to pay particular attention to cost factors during periods of inflation. Specific problems purchasing officers must handle are group purchasing as opposed to individual replacement of items, the use of total-cost purchasing, and cooperative arrangements with other local governments.

Risk management and insurance planning

The problems of maintaining an adequate insurance and risk management program generally fall under the rubric of financial management. Because there has been a significant increase in vandalism, arson, the cost of automotive repairs, and governmental liability in recent years, the price of insurance has increased dramatically. Thus, the importance of risk management programs has also increased.

Risk management is a broad field, requiring managers to have an understanding of the probabilities of losses that can occur from property damage and adverse liability claims, the differences between optimum and maximum insurance coverage, and the costs and benefits of protection (i.e., insurance) and prevention programs in economic terms. Although the municipality may carry insurance, there is still reason to initiate an acceptable safety program. At the very least, such programs reduce the level of premiums.

The municipality's risk manager has access to expert advice about preventive and safety programs. Fire department personnel are familiar with causes of fires and how to minimize their outbreak; the police constantly deal with burglaries and vandalism; the local government accountant knows how to prevent defalcations; public works personnel know about the construction of buildings and the proper care of public facilities; and building custodians know about dangerous conditions and practices. Local government lawyers can provide information about the kinds of incidents that have resulted in legal claims. Informing all employees that risk prevention should be the concern of all and an intrinsic part of their jobs goes a long way toward establishing a proper safety atmosphere. The formation of employee safety committees is highly recommended.

No matter how much care is taken to avoid accidents, some mishaps are bound to occur. Therefore, provisions need to be made for restoring matters to an acceptable state should a loss occur. This can be done by adopting a balanced insurance program; however, it should be understood that the basic theory of insurance implies that the expected value of the premiums paid will exceed the value of the probable or expected losses. The insurance company must pay its salesmen, its agents, its administrative expenses; it must cover losses out of premiums received; and, finally, it is in business to earn a net return on its invested capital. From a purely monetary perspective, insurance is a "bad bet;" the policyholders, nevertheless, have rational reasons for carrying insurance. By doing so, the policyholder exchanges a small current loss (the premium) for a very much larger, possible loss. The psychological disutility (or unhappiness) caused by such a large loss, outweighs the disutility of the money expended in small payments on the premium. In short, all municipal insurance programs must weigh the "regrets" of suffering a possible heavy loss against the costs of the premiums. In theoretical terms, a rational insurance policy is designed to minimize net regrets.

Risk management planning[6]

Local governments are subject to four basic kinds of risks that should be isolated, identified, and inventoried to provide the information base for risk management planning. They are: (1) damage to real and personal property; (2) property loss; (3) loss of income or increased costs that ensue from property losses; and (4) liability. These risks can be identified and classified by reviewing contracts, leases, property inventory records, and other documents; by inspecting buildings and other properties; by locating major areas of potential loss through risk discovery questionnaires; and by diagramming highly programmed operations and activities to locate possible high risk points.

After risks have been identified, potential losses should be reviewed and evaluated for potential frequency and severity. Frequency refers to the number of losses. Severity refers to the cost or size of losses. This evaluation then leads to consideration of the four basic ways of controlling risk, which are elimination, reduction, assumption, and transfer.

Risk elimination   The elimination of risk obviously is the best way to handle potential losses. It can be done by changing work methods and equipment. A more drastic approach is to stop performing a particular service, activity, or task. Examples include installation of safety equipment, major changes in solid waste collection methods, abandonment of an unsupervised playground, and transfer of fire protection from an all-volunteer department to another public or private agency.

Risk reduction   Safety programs are the best known and often the most effective ways to reduce the incidence of accidents and other losses. An effective safety program involves far more than equipment safeguards. It also includes management policies and surveillance, employee training, employee involvement through committees and other means, appropriate records, and a continuing safety process.

Many other methods are available for effective risk control. Some random examples include: separating the individual responsibility of reconciling bank statements from the responsibilities of writing checks and making deposits; inventorying physical equipment, stock items, and other physical assets as part of an annual postaudit; conducting frequent and unannounced safety inspections; enforcing safety rules for hard hats, special shoes, and goggles; reviewing personnel rules for grievance and appeal procedures on safety questions; providing for regular motor vehicle inspections and preventive maintenance; and checking state-determined experience modification factors for application to workers' compensation insurance coverage.

Risk assumption   After taking all feasible steps to eliminate or reduce risk, the next step is to explore methods of risk assumption and transfer. The major methods for full and partial assumption are to charge the loss to the departmental budget (no problem if the loss is small); to use a variety of deductibles as part of insurance policies; to set up a funded reserve to cover larger losses; to assume workers' compensation losses; and to assume physical damage losses to city-owned automobiles and other motor equipment.

Risk transfer   The last step in risk control is to transfer risk by hold-harmless agreements, insurance, and pooling. Hold-harmless agreements have only limited application, but they can be used, by contract or purchase order, to transfer liability for losses to another organization doing business with the local government. They are worthless, however, unless they are legally enforceable and the contracting person or firm has enough capital or other resources to make financial restitution. The other methods of transfer—buying insurance and insurance pools—are covered in the subsequent sections of this chapter. The Appendix "Risk management in a small city" shows the steps that were taken in Kirksville, Missouri, in insurance planning, evaluation of coverage, and ongoing reporting and evaluation of insurance management.

Insurance coverage

There are two main rules of effective insurance management. First, although there should be protection against catastrophic losses, there is no requirement for insuring against minor recurrent losses. Second, where the risks are recurrent and inherent in many eventualities, self-insurance may be used. Roos and Gerber advise that only potential *major* losses be covered: "Only those exposures which could financially cripple the city should be insured, making the best use of deductibles and excess coverage as is financially feasible."[7] In bluntest terms, if the municipality gets stuck for a few $500, $1,000, or $5,000 claims, the losses should be taken in stride. This is petty cash, annoying, but of no consequence except for possibly indicating flaws in the prevention program.

The wise coverage for an individual is not necessarily the wisest coverage for a local government. The municipality has more resources to cover a loss, including:

Federal disaster assistance

Funded reserves established for that purpose

The ability to spread judgments over a longer period

Bond issues

Special tax levies

Citizen or group donations

Other sources special to each municipality (e.g., pooling risks with other communities).

Moreover, the larger city has a multitude of buildings and cars, not just one or two, so that it can count on a reasonably stable statistical dispersion of losses. But, what are the consequences in terms of insurance of owning a multitude of buildings and cars? If the local government paid no fire insurance premiums on fifty buildings, the amount saved on the annual premiums might pay for a fire loss in any one of them. Similar analysis applies to automobile collision insurance. If the municipality uses fifty cars, it obtains a risk exposure equivalent to fifty years of driving experience for a single car. If the annual premiums are well in excess of the annual expected losses, the locality avoids the need to carry collision insurance on its vehicles.

The local government enjoys a position in the aggregate not available to the individual. The municipality may find that where the losses on single occurrences are relatively small, self-insurance is likely to be advantageous. Commercial insurance premiums include a loading charge for the expenses of administration and sales equal to 30 percent to 50 percent of the total payment. Thus, the municipality may have a lower cost for administration and not pay a sales commission on self-insurance.

The rule of carrying insurance policies against catastrophes and of self-insuring infrequent minor losses can be carried out in a number of ways:

1. Do not insure park shelters, bleachers, swimming pools, small tool sheds, comfort stations, and other such facilities against property damage.
2. Do not carry collision insurance on automotive equipment.
3. Write insurance contracts that contain significant deductible clauses.
4. Carry excess coverage property insurance to cover disastrous losses.

Because a municipality has large properties, too much risk should not be placed on a single company. A loss that would be catastrophic for a moderate-size community might also be large enough to exhaust the financial reserves of many moderate-sized companies.[8] In this case, the municipality should investigate the asset size of the company and make sure that the company uses a reinsurer.

Insurance costs

Local governments have limited resources. Taxes can be raised only so much before outraged citizens become militant. Budgets consequently, should reflect economically sound policies and procedures. Bearing this in mind, what then can be done to reduce the cost of insurance programs? A listing of the important steps, most of which will be reviewed in subsequent paragraphs, includes the following:

1. Maintaining effective prevention programs
2. Writing deductible clauses into policies
3. Writing fire policies subject to coinsurance clauses
4. Using excess coverage insurance
5. Creating self-insurance funded reserves
6. Eliminating duplicate coverage
7. Determining how fire insurance rates on commercial and industrial properties are established.[9]
8. Keeping complete loss experience records to support arguments for better ratings
9. Working with insurers on property inspections, coverage inventories, and safety programs
10. Using blanket coverage policies
11. Obtaining bids from competing insurers
12. Setting up an insurance pool.

Coinsurance   Coinsurance clauses reduce the total insurance premium, but they must be used cautiously to avoid undercoverage. Such clauses call for the municipality to carry a stipulated percentage of the insurable value of an asset as the face amount of insurance if it wishes to be fully reimbursed for partial losses.

Partial losses are reimbursed according to the ratio of the face value of the policy to the stipulated percentage. Thus, suppose City A carries a policy with an 80 percent minimum coinsurance clause on a given property. The property has a value of $100,000 and the face value policy is indeed $80,000. A partial loss of $20,000 now occurs. City A will be reimbursed according to the formula:

$$\left(\frac{\text{Insurance carried}}{\text{Coverage agreed}} \right) \text{Amount of loss} = \text{Limit of recovery}$$

In this case,

$$\left(\frac{\$80,000}{\$100,000[.80]} \right) \$20,000 = \$20,000$$

Suppose that City B carries the same type of policy. Suppose also that the value of the property has risen to $125,000, but the city has not increased its coverage. Then

$$\left(\frac{\$80,000}{\$100,000[.80]}\right) 20,000 = \left(\frac{80}{100}\right) \$20,000 = \$16,000$$

and City B will only recover $16,000, or 80 percent of the loss.

Excess coverage   Excess coverage policies that separate the basic policy from other policy coverages may result in overall premium savings. Excess property insurance policies (i.e., those insuring losses of between $50,000 and $100,000) are more available today than they were some years ago. Substantial savings in premiums are sometimes possible with such policies. Realizing the maximum savings from excess coverages, however, requires more than a mere comparison of current premiums on standard full coverage policies with policies that have different excess limits.[10] The writing of such policies and comparing of costs may be complicated, and insurance experts should be used to evaluate the policies.

Blanket insurance   Blanket insurance covers a multitude of perils in a single policy, thereby eliminating duplication of coverage and avoiding the cost of holding many separate policies. Blanket policies may be written on particular locations or on all locations collectively. If a blanket policy is carried on all locations, however, there is the chance that a coinsurance deficiency in one building could operate to reduce the total face amount of insurance below the stipulated coinsurance percentage.

Competitive bids   Many cities achieve significant savings in premium costs by calling for competitive bids. Without competitive bidding, some insurers may not bid for the policies, because they fear favoritism has already directed the contract, and other insurers may exert political pressure on the risk managers. Bidding discourages this activity. Bidding also compels the risk manager to prepare careful specifications and to become more familiar with the hazards that require insurance.

Nevertheless, bidding may have its shortcomings. Under a negotiated policy, an insurer who settles a claim (pays off) during a period of losses hopes that his or her efforts will be rewarded by continuation of the business. Bidders have no such assurance, however, and therefore may not do their best to give complete service and cover all claims. They may even contemplate cancelling the policy. Moreover, the process of preparing detailed specifications for bidding is itself a costly activity.[11]

Agents' associations   An alternative to competitive bidding is the use of the services of an agents' association. This arrangement has proved very successful for the city and county of Denver, Colorado. First, a committee, in conjunction with the Denver Insurers' Association, conducted an inspection and made a survey of all exposures. It found the following:

Prior to the introduction of the producer association program each department handled its own insurance. No system plan had ever existed for discovering the exposures of the municipality, nor had a risk management plan been utilized. Fire insurance on buildings and contents was found to be woefully inadequate; in some cases, the city could not have collected more than 10% to 25% of loss. There were frequent duplications of insurance policies, under and over insurance of buildings, and even insurance on buildings that no longer existed.[12]

With the formation of the association, policies were then written by agents on a randomly determined rotating basis. No agent could receive more than a fifty dollar commission on any policy; all commissions beyond that amount went into the association's bank account. Favoritism was eliminated and a vastly improved risk and insurance program resulted.

If an agents' association is used, the local government should insist on certain standards with respect to adherence to specifications and the establishment of premiums. Otherwise, there is the risk of the business being passed around from year to year on a noncompetitive basis, perhaps resulting in higher costs to the municipality.

Placing insurance by public bidding

Arguments for public bidding

1. All agents and brokers have an equal opportunity to bid.
2. Public officials have less pressure put on them regarding the placement of business.
3. Public officials must take a more active interest in the government's insurance program because of the need to draft specifications.
4. There *may* be a lower premium cost, but often this is not the case and the direct negotiation method is cheaper.

Arguments against public bidding

1. Sometimes bidding occurs every year, and this can drastically limit the number of insurers bidding.
2. Some qualified companies may not bid due to the time and expense of preparing bid forms.
3. Most local governments are not capable of preparing bid specifications or evaluating bid responses without independent, professional assistance.
4. The lowest priced policy may not be the best because the claims and safety engineering services of a higher bidder may be worth more than a small reduction in cost.
5. If specifications are too rigidly fixed, creative approaches to meet the government's needs will be inhibited.

Source: Charles K. Coe, *Understanding Risk Management: A Guide for Governments* (Athens: Institute of Government, University of Georgia, 1980), p. 34.

Deductible clause and self-insurance   How should the risk manager decide on the optimum size of the deductible clause? The local government should weigh the possible total losses (i.e., the explicit financial loss and, most important, the psychological loss) of the uninsured risk of the deductible feature against the savings in premiums. If possible losses are small and independent, the economics favor the deductible clause. The insurance manager should note the possibility, however, that a single or related mishap—a fire in the city garage, for example— could cause all the noninsured losses to fall together and lead to a larger overall loss than the manager could sustain at one time.

Leaving small recurrent losses uninsured is a form of self-insurance. However, a formal self-insurance policy involves the creation of funded reserves to cover significant uninsured losses.

If the municipality does not carry a commercial insurance policy and if there is no reserve, the municipality is pursuing a "no insurance" program. No insurance can be quite dangerous, unless excess coverage insurance is carried.

Self-insurance can also be dangerous if excess coverage is not carried. The Roos and Gerber questionnaire cited an impressive list of cities that did not carry such coverage. Two or more fires would have eliminated the self-insurance funds of those communities.

How should a funded reserve be established? W. G. Brockmeier offers the following suggestion:

Reserves may be built up in a number of ways. Where large amounts are involved, it is frequently not feasible to initiate a self-insurance fund by the immediate setting up of full reserves out of available cash. Therefore, in initiating self-insurance, it is often advantageous to begin with a moderate retention of risk and set aside the insurance premiums saved thereby for the creation of the reserve. As the reserve grows, additional exposure can be retained on the same basis and the plan expanded to its full scope over a period of years. On the other hand, if adequate reserves for full-scale operation of the contemplated plan can be set up immediately, the advantage of self-insurance can be more promptly realized.[13]

A funded reserve is similar to a bond sinking fund. Total size for the fund is decided in advance of a given number of years, and annuity calculations are used to arrive at the required annual deposit needed to reach the desired fund size. A funded reserve, however, is unlike a bond sinking fund in that the sinking fund must be a set amount; the reserve, which depends on the value of the underlying properties, may have to grow over time. Under conditions of inflation, a target reserve of $1 million to be created within five years may prove inadequate once it reaches its desired level. If a level payment into the fund suits budget design, the inflation factor can be estimated and subtracted from the interest rate (in the annuity formula). Alternatively, the sinking fund payment may be adjusted each fiscal period to reflect the inflation that has occurred in the preceding period. Once the appropriate size is attained, the interest earnings of the fund should be sufficient to provide for a large share of yearly demands on the fund.

There is no single answer to the question of what is the proper size for a sound self-insurance fund, but a knowledge of past experience and of "clustering" of risks is helpful in determining the size of the self-insurance fund. If exposures in property are widely separated, risk is diminished and a smaller fund might suffice. Some sort of fund, however, should be carried to shield the local government from such unusual and difficult-to-insure risks as earthquakes, floods, and ecological contamination.

In the past, excess loss insurance policies—those covering claims of between $50,000 and $100,000 or more—were used mainly in the liability field. Since the mid-1960s, such policies have become available in the property field. These policies can provide a substantial savings in premiums and still offer a significant amount of protection for a catastrophic loss when combined with a self-insurance program or with commercial policies with less than full coverage.

Can self-insurance programs (increasingly referred to as "risk retention" policies) work? The following example is excerpted from a pamphlet published by the Insurance Company of North America:

One example of a large city that self-insures is Newark, N.J., which has retained all its insurance risks since May, 1977. Workers' compensation and property coverages had been self-insured prior to that time, but the city had purchased its other coverages from commercial carriers. Newark's budget office estimated that to insure the city's risk commercially in 1978 would cost in excess of $5.5 million for self-insurance, including administration charges.

Newark has established a self-insurance trust fund for liability exposures that is administered by the city's insurance commission, which had previously been responsible for buying its commercial insurance.

The trust is funded from surplus above budget allocations for claims payments and from other city contributions. By 1979 the trust stood at close to $2 million with the city's goal ultimately to increase it to $10 million, at which time Newark intends to purchase a $10 million umbrella liability policy that, combined with the fund, should enable the city to respond to catastrophic losses.

As a means of controlling the cost of its self-insurance program, Newark places considerable emphasis on efficient claims settlements. Liability losses generally cost the city between $250,000 and $300,000 annually, with workers' compensation claims and administration expenses running $1.8 million in 1977. This compares favorably with insurance studies prepared for Newark which show that an experience-rated workers' compensation policy would have cost the city $2.7 million, and a manual-rated one $3.6 million.[14]

Liability insurance

Many difficult issues arise in the area of liability insurance for accidents caused by municipal employees. The general precept of carrying insurance for catastrophes while paying insignificant claims remains valid, nevertheless.

A starting point for deciding on liability coverage would be for the municipality's insurance agent to join the local government's attorney in a study of recent local court cases to review (1) the type of liability claims being made; (2) the frequency of each type of claim; and (3) the level of awards for various cases. It is also important to ascertain whether the municipality has any special immunity from damages arising from wrongs or injuries to others as a result of the activities of its personnel. The extent of this responsibility has been the subject of many court cases. Although there used to be considerable immunity against damages arising from "governmental" functions, there is no immunity against general liability for damages arising from the "proprietary" functions.

The case of *Russell* v. *Men of Devon* (1788), which set a precedent, granted municipalities immunity from liability for the conduct of their employees on the basis "that it is better that an individual should sustain an injury than that the public should suffer an inconvenience." In interpreting this principle, immunity from liability was extended to the operations of such governmental functions as police and fire protection, public health education, and welfare. It was, however, withheld from the conduct of such proprietary functions as providing water and other utility services, maintaining streets, and operating swimming pools. In recent years, most states have set aside the principle of immunity; the question of whether a municipality is liable for the torts of its servants (employees) depends on state law. If an insured municipality wants to protect possible injured citizens, it should require its insurer to waive any subrogated rights the municipality might have under the immunity laws.

Recently, there has been a marked trend toward narrowing governmental immunity, both by statute and by court decision. The result has been that cities and other local governments are held liable for a much wider range of activities and services; the line between governmental and proprietary functions is much less clear-cut. Thus more liability insurance for most cities and other local governments is necessary; managers and finance officers should take greater care than they have formerly in surveying areas of potential liability to assure that coverage is carried where needed.

The Insurance Company of North America, commenting on the *Rex peccare non protest* doctrine, wrote: "Now sovereign immunity has been partially or totally abolished in more than 40 states, leaving many government bodies vulnerable to suits for negligence on the part of their employees."[15]

Moreover, the city can become embroiled in the law of agency and resulting liabilities when it commissions independent contractors to construct buildings and roads. The usual comprehensive general liability policy often excludes liability for property damage caused by:

1. Blasting or explosion other than explosion of air or steam vessels, machinery, and power transmitting equipment
2. Collapse of or structural damage to a building or other structure resulting from grading, excavating, pile driving, demolition, and the like
3. Damage to wires, conduits, pipes, mains, sewers, and other subterranean installations where the damage is caused by mechanical equipment while grading, paving, excavating, or drilling.

Presumably, the contractor is the one most responsible for such mishaps; however, because the municipality might be named as a codefendant for damages in such cases, it would be well to carry an umbrella liability policy. This policy (which is the equivalent of the excess coverage policy used in the property field) covers all of the possible hazards that may not be mentioned in the regular policies and, in addition, provides much higher maximum coverage. Given the tremendous rise in the claims for damages that modern juries are willing to award, such umbrella policies are advantageous to municipalities—particularly since damages for the loss of lifetime income for workers injured on the job may amount to many millions of dollars. A description of umbrella policies follows:

The umbrella liability policy is a very broad contract written to apply only after coverage under other policies has been exhausted. If a claim is covered under both an umbrella liability policy and a comprehensive general liability policy, the umbrella policy will not pay until the limits under the comprehensive general policy have been exhausted. If a claim is covered only under the umbrella, it will pay after the insured has paid a large deductible amount specified in the policy. The deductible amount frequently is $25,000, though larger and smaller deductibles are available.

Umbrella policies are not standardized; they vary rather widely from company to company. The limit of liability under most of these policies is $1,000,000 or a multiple of $1,000,000. Policies with limits of $50,000,000 or more are relatively common. The policy usually includes automobile liability, all of the general liability coverages, personal injury liability, and employers liability coverage, though they are not specifically listed in the policy.[16]

In general, most local governments do not carry separate automobile liability policies; instead, they cover themselves in their general liability policies. The coverage limits for auto accidents vary, but commonly cover bodily injury to a maximum of $500,000 per person, $1,000,000 per accident, and $100,000 for property damage.

It is important, in drawing the policies, that the limits chosen apply per occurrence and that there be no aggregate limit during the term of the policy. It would be wise to provide for the automatic inclusion of vehicles, streets, buildings, grounds, or other property added or constructed subsequent to the issuance of the liability policy. In this way, absence of explicit notification to the insurer does not interfere with protection.

A clause also should be inserted stating that any errors or omissions will not operate to the prejudice of the municipality and that any such property inadvertently omitted or erroneously described shall be included under the policy from its date of inception.

Liability policies should cover not only the municipality but also its appointed officials, agents, employees, and authorized representatives when acting in these capacities for the municipality. Liability policies should rigorously avoid making the local government responsible—via guarantee or warranty—for the information it has provided. It is up to the company to verify the information provided by the local government. One of the benefits of entering into an insurance contract is that the company's experts review the risks and make recommendations for prevention as well as assess the extent of existing hazards.

Protection against dishonesty

Bonding municipal employees is the customary method of protecting against employee dishonesty. Various types of bonds are available. In the absence of contrary statutory regulations, it is often recommended that the amount of coverage on an individual basis (when a blanket bond is not used) equal the largest amount of negotiable funds (cash, checks, and securities) under the control of the employee at any time. Nevertheless, this coverage can prove inadequate. Many grand thefts are perpetuated over long periods of time and not committed in a single day.

Protection against dishonesty should not rely solely on bonding. Prevention of defalcations should be the main objective, and much of the responsibility for this rests on the finance officers. Prevention is based on the development of an effective system of internal control—a system of checks and balances in the handling of assets. For example, the person who acts as cashier should not act also as bookkeeper. Disbursement and receipt forms should be prenumbered and numbers checked. In the case of disbursements, the purchase orders should be reviewed for authorization, the receiving slips should be matched against purchase orders, the invoices should be checked for agreement with both the purchase order and the receiving slip, and all supporting documents should accompany the check so that the local government's treasurer may review them before signing the disbursement. Spot checks of inventory, equipment, and properties should be made to ascertain agreement with municipal records, and audits of all offices and procedures should be planned on a frequent but irregular basis. Probably no system is foolproof, but a good system can be a very effective deterrent to theft.

Workers' compensation insurance

The local government is liable if any of its employees are injured in the course of work. Thus, a state-imposed statutory obligation to insure such risks has occurred in several places. As of the early 1970s, six states required their municipalities to insure with the state fund; a dozen states allowed the option of using either the state fund, private insurers, or self-insurance; and municipalities in the remaining states used commercial insurance or self-insurance. Because workers' compensation claims usually are relatively small or may be spread over time, the use of self-insurance should be encouraged.

Losses for activity interruption

Although local governments are not subject to the same business interruption risks as commercial enterprises, the municipal insurance program should take into account the fact that certain activities yield significant on-going revenues. A water pumping station may represent a $200,000 investment but, more important, it may be vital to the income of the entire water system. An airport costing $20,000,000 conceivably could lose gross revenues of $1,000,000 each day that it is closed following a disaster.[17]

The local government should protect itself against interruption of activities by such preventive measures as backup equipment and alternate facilities. It also should consider carrying regular or self-insurance to cover losses when these measures fail. J. D. Todd warns:

Another important step in effective risk management is the identification of those exposures the direct loss of which would not prove too expensive, but which could cause serious repercussions and further losses to the city. For example, the loss of a fire station would not be catastrophic, but if it is the only fire station within many miles and it is destroyed, any fire in town would probably result in a total loss. . . .

The potential size of ultimate losses resulting from the destruction of a single exposure must be measured to decide on the appropriate means of controlling the losses.[18]

In addition to the direct losses to the local government, administrators should consider coverage for liability for the contingent losses to the citizens where the contributory negligence of the municipality's operations can be proved.

Insurance pools

An increasingly popular approach to restraining the rising costs of risk coverage is the municipal insurance pool. Such pools enable a group of smaller local governments to self-insure (at least for smaller risks) and reduce administrative costs, thus obtaining better terms on broad-based commercial policies. However, it is necessary to make sure that the state laws permit such combinations before a pool can be formed.

Although municipal insurance pools originally concentrated on workers' compensation coverage, many now have broadened the coverage to include comprehensive and automotive liability and, in some cases, property insurance. The pools now in existence operate under the following guidelines (see Figure 17–6):

1. The local governments generally pay a premium to the pool in proportion to their payrolls.
2. The localities agree to cover small losses on their own, perhaps to a maximum of $1,000 per loss.

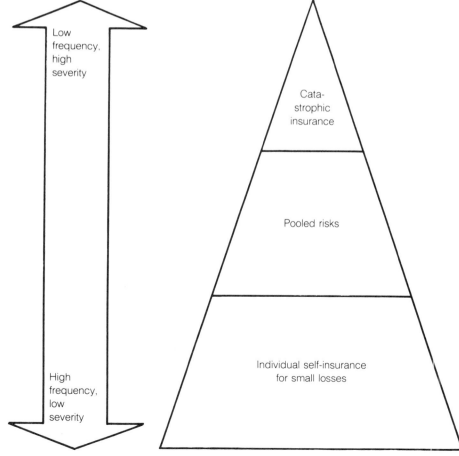

Figure 17–6 Progression of frequency and severity in municipal insurance pools.

3.   Losses of up to some amount (e.g., $50,000) will be covered by the pool.
4.   The pool will obtain excess risk insurance to cover losses in excess of $50,000, or the localities will each carry their own excess risk insurance.

Some legal problems result in those states where the pool has to be constructed as an independent, nonprofit corporation. If the pool initially experiences a surplus in operations, a fund is built up. After the fund reaches a particular amount, the surplus is returned to the participating members.

The pool essentially has the potential to reduce insurance costs because it enables smaller communities that do not have sufficient diversification of risk to engage in self-insurance. Moreover, because the pool reduces administrative costs, it enables the combined units to obtain lower rates on the excess risk policies. At any rate, recent experience shows a considerable number of successfully functioning pools that have returned considerable savings to their members.[19]

Summary

Risk management is a broad field. Knowledge of both the law and the results of losses occasioned by property damage or liability claims is essential. Good information for municipal departmental experts helps prevent losses, but a balanced insurance program can help restore a municipality to an acceptable state of affairs if a loss does occur. Although the municipality should carry insurance against catastrophic events, self-insurance may be used for minor recurrent risks. A number of guidelines and statistical techniques may be used to ascertain the proper size of the self-insurance fund, and a number of practical steps can be taken to reduce premium costs. Coinsurance, blanket insurance, and competitive bids are methods that help to cut insurance costs. The services of an agents' association can also be used.

The risk manager should note the role of liability insurance under the current conditions of broader definitions of governmental liability. The risk manager also is given the responsibility of protecting against employee dishonesty. Finally, he or she may note the increasing attention being paid to the formation of municipal insurance pools as a method of restraining escalating premium costs.

1   If supplies are easily replenished without penalty, then the safety stock can be zero, and the inventory problem is essentially solved by the EOQ model.

2   It may not really be correct to speak of two costs in this context. The stockout loss function is actually the return from holding an inventory; it is a measure of stockout losses *avoided*. Thus, we are really equating the marginal return from the inventory to the marginal costs of carrying the inventory.

3   The number of times orders should be placed during a given period is also solved by the economic ordering quantity—that is, the usage or sales during the period divided by the EOQ gives the number of times orders will be placed.

4   For further modifications of the Newsboy model and greater depth on the subject of inventories generally, see: A. W. Corcoran, *Costs: Accounting, Analysis, and Control* (New York: John Wiley & Sons, 1978), chapter 14.

5   Further discussion of this subject may be found in: J. Peter Braun, *Total-Cost Purchasing*, Management Information Service Reports, vol. 3, no. S–4 (Washington, D.C.: International City Management Association, 1971).

6   This discussion of risk management planning is based on: Charles K. Coe, *Understanding Risk Management: A Guide for Governments* (Athens: Institute of Government, University of Georgia, 1980), especially the three-step process of risk identification, risk control, and risk management evaluation. This publication includes a concise review of major types of risk and insurance coverage.

7   Nester R. Roos and Joseph S. Gerber, "Insurance and Risk Management," *The Municipal Year Book 1973* (Washington, D.C.: International City Management Association, 1973), p. 113.

8   Acceptable insurance companies may be determined in part by using *Best's Insurance Guide* (Alfred M. Best Co., Inc., 75 Fulton Street, New York, N.Y.), which gives a financial and a management rating for all stock companies. An A:BBB rating is considered the lowest acceptable rating as far as cities are concerned. Of course, many factors other than financial conditions are important. Many companies reinsure larger policies.

9   For a concise description of the fire insurance industry, including methods of setting rates, the application of the grading schedule, and areas of coverage, see: Harry C. Bigglestone et al., "Other Organizations and the Fire Service," in *Managing*

Fire Services, John L. Bryan and Raymond C. Picard, ed., (Washington, D.C.: International City Management Association, 1979), pp. 92–108, 130–32.

10 J. D. Todd, "Management Techniques Applicable to City Insurance Programs," *Municipal Finance* 44 (August 1971):12.

11 Further discussion of both the benefits and the hazards of bidding may be found in: Georgia Chapter, Society of Chartered Property and Casualty Underwriters, *Municipal Risk Management* (Cincinnati: National Underwriters Company, 1971), pp. 95–96.

12 Ibid., p. 91.

13 W. G. Brockmeier, "Self-insurance vs. Insurance for Large Cities," *Municipal Finance* 44 (August 1971): 20.

14 *Insurance Decisions: Rising Government Liability* (Insurance Company of North America, 1980). Risk retention is discussed on pages 4 and 5.

15 Ibid., pp. 1–2.

16 Georgia Chapter, Society of Chartered Property and Casualty Underwriters, *Municipal Risk Management,* p. 107. This is an informative book that the risk manager should have at hand.

17 Lost income is a very difficult figure to measure reliably. Certainly, income is lost from flights that are canceled, but business in the city also may be deprived of customers as a consequence. Some of the loss undoubtedly is made up by substitute means of transportation.

18 J. D. Todd, *Effective Risk and Insurance Management in Municipal Government* (Austin: Institute of Public Affairs, University of Texas, 1970), p. 61.

19 New York State Legislature, Assembly Ways and Means Committee, *Municipal Insurance Pools,* (Albany, N.Y.: State of New York, January 1980) and *Insurance Decisions: Rising Government Liabilities,* pp. 8–10.

18

Local government accounting

Financial accounting and reporting by local governments have assumed positions of substantially increased significance during recent years because of the near financial failure of several of the nation's largest cities and heightened constituent interest in the cost, quantity, and quality of various government services. In response, modern public administrators have recognized the need to develop adequate accounting systems that possess multiple reporting capabilities to communicate with constituents and other interested parties, to plan and control operations, and to discharge certain stewardship responsibilities.

Government accounting systems must provide data to many users and the varied information needs of those users should be anticipated to the fullest extent possible. Another important function of an accounting system is to provide assurance to managers, constituents, and investors that adequate internal accounting controls exist for safeguarding assets.

The users of accounting information

In discussing financial accounting and reporting systems, several methods of categorization are possible and each is subject to the criticism of being somewhat arbitrary. However, a classification process does enhance a logical process of development, and for that purpose the following section of this chapter is divided into a discussion of the necessary capabilities of the accounting and reporting system from three distinct financial report user perspectives.

Reporting to external users

This function involves reporting primarily to those institutions and individuals external to the governmental unit. Such users normally lack either implicit or explicit authority to prescribe the nature, timing, content, and extent of the financial information they receive. The users include constituents, creditors, suppliers, and any others transacting business with the governmental unit. Many of these users have an intense need for financial information, because they frequently have or contemplate having a direct investment or business interest in the operations and financing of the governmental unit.

Because external users of financial information do not possess the authority to specify for themselves the characteristics of the external reports, rules and practices have been developed and adopted by the accounting profession. These practices, referred to technically as generally accepted accounting principles (GAAP), are necessary so that external users may be sure that similar economic events are accorded similar accounting treatments both among many reporting entities and through different reporting periods. Furthermore, such users are put on notice, through GAAP, that accountable events will be shown in the financial statements in a specified way.

Reporting to the internal manager

This function involves reporting to the members of the management and administration of a governmental unit who are responsible for guiding the government toward the accomplishment of its objectives. Among the many responsibilities of these users are the management functions of planning, organizing, executing, and reviewing the operational and strategic endeavors of the governmental unit. As such, most of these users possess the ability to acquire a large amount of financial information. Although some of this information may be in the form of published external financial statements, much of the needed data are not available from the usual external reports. The accounting and reporting system must provide additional information for the internal users.

If the most efficient and effective use is to be made of the limited tax revenues of the local governments, financial information is needed to facilitate the application of cost-benefit analysis to various programs and activities. Although the reports to decision makers and managers may be prepared on a recurring basis, the system must possess flexibility to meet unique, unusual, or nonrecurring reporting demands. These types of managerial accounting and analysis techniques have only recently assumed a significant position in many governmental operations and are not as robust and advanced in their application as might be desirable.

Financial information used in planning, performance evaluation, and other financial analyses must be timely, reliable, relevant, and understandable.

Reporting for compliance

This function requires the provision of information to those who, although not directly involved in day-to-day operations, possess significant authority over the governmental entity. Granting authorities, governing boards, legislative bodies, closely related governmental units, and other significant providers of funds or revenue may require compliance reports to show that funds were properly used. Users of compliance reports are capable of specifying the characteristics of the information they desire but these reports, once established, tend to remain formalized and constant for a relatively long period of time.

Standards of financial reporting

Remote users, lacking the authority to specify the type of information they desire, depend on generally accepted accounting principles for useful, well-understood financial reports. Fortunately, the concept of financial statements prepared in conformity with GAAP is relatively well developed in the accounting profession. One particularly useful definition, formulated by a subcommittee of the Financial Accounting Standards Board, states:

Generally accepted accounting principles are primarily conventional in nature. They are the result of decisions, they represent the consensus at any time as to how the financial accounting process should operate and how financial statements should be prepared from the information made available through the financial accounting process.

Inasmuch as generally accepted accounting principles embody a consensus, they depend heavily on notions such as "general acceptance" and "substantial authoritative support," which have not been and probably cannot be precisely defined. There is concurrence, however, that the notions of "general acceptance" and "substantial authoritative support" relate to the propriety of the practices, as viewed by informed, intelligent, and experienced accountants in the light of the purposes and limitations of the financial accounting process.[1]

The accounting profession in the United States has followed this rationale in creating bodies capable of establishing GAAP. Standards and practices representing GAAP for state and local governments have been developed since the 1930s by the National Council on Governmental Accounting (NCGA) and the predecessor committees sponsored by the Municipal Finance Officers Association (MFOA). An audit guide dealing with state and local government financial practices was issued in 1974 by the American Institute of Certified Public Accountants (AICPA), which has also been active in this process since 1974. Financial accounting standards for the preparation of financial statements in accordance with GAAP are presently described by two separate documents: (1) *Government Accounting, Auditing, and Financial Reporting* (GAAFR), promulgated by the NCGA in 1968; and (2) *Audits of State and Local Governmental Units* (ASLGU), issued by the AICPA in 1974.[2]

Since their issuance, respectively, in 1968 and 1974, both of these documents have been interpreted and amended to clarify and revise certain practices. In particular, substantial modifications have been made in GAAFR by two statements issued in 1979 by the National Council on Governmental Accounting: NCGA Statement 1, *Governmental Accounting and Financial Reporting Principles* (GAFRP), and NCGA Statement 2, *Grant, Entitlement, and Shared Revenue Accounting and Reporting by State and Local Governments*.[3] As the American Institute of Certified Public Accountants has noted:

GAAFR's principles do not represent a complete and separate body of accounting principles, but rather are part of the whole body of generally accepted accounting principles which deal specifically with governmental units.[4]

The structure and authority for setting accounting and reporting standards for state and local governments have been contentious. As of early 1981, the NCGA was involved in a collective project with several other professional organizations, including the AICPA and the Financial Accounting Standards Board, to restructure the manner under which governmental accounting principles are established. Envisioned is a Governmental Accounting Standards Board made up of five full-time board members who are expert in governmental accounting and finance, and who would be supported by adequate research and administrative staffs. Under this structure, emerging issues can be addressed more quickly, due process established, and research conducted in a more efficient and direct manner than is presently possible.

Financial reporting is a complex communication form, related primarily to the transmission of economic data about an organization to concerned individuals and institutions.

The overriding criterion of success for the financial communication process is the usefulness of the information provided, not the reporting process itself. Financial accounting and reporting should be tailored to the goals and objectives of different receiving organizations and should reflect those differences in the financial statements. GAFRP and ASLGU recognize this concept in specifying the types of reports to be prepared by governments.

The fund basis of accounting and reporting

To a person familiar only with business financial accounting and reporting practices, governmental accounting represents a radical change. Business enterprises

Sources of state and local government accounting principles

Three organizations are primarily responsible for establishing, reviewing, and changing accounting standards for state and local governments. The standards issued by these groups help provide uniform accounting and financial reporting for citizens, the bond market, state and federal granting agencies, and public accounting companies.

The National Council on Governmental Accounting (NCGA) is a group of twenty-one volunteer members from local, state, and federal governments and the academic and private sectors; the group operates with the financial support of the Municipal Finance Officers Association (MFOA). NCGA has been operating since 1934, originally as the National Committee on Municipal Accounting. Generally accepted accounting principles (GAAP) were established by NCGA in its 1968 publication, *Governmental Accounting, Auditing, and Financial Reporting.* This publication has been superseded by NCGA Statement 1, *Governmental Accounting and Financial Reporting Principles,* and by NCGA Statement 2, *Grant, Entitlement, and Shared Revenue Accounting and Reporting by State and Local Governments,* both published in 1979. In 1980, MFOA published *Governmental Accounting, Auditing, and Financial Reporting,* not as an authoritative statement but as an interpretation of NCGA Statement 1.

The American Institute of Certified Public Accountants (AICPA) influences accounting principles for state and local governments, particularly through its *Audits of State and Local Governmental Units,* an industry audit guide published in 1974 by the AICPA Committee on Governmental Accounting and Auditing. The AICPA audit guide was modified recently through the issuance of Statement of Position 80–2 to make the guide consistent with NCGA Statement 1.

The Financial Accounting Standards Board (FASB), a standard setting body for the private sector, also influences state and local governments and their independent auditors as a source of generally accepted accounting principles (GAAP). NCGA Statement 1, for example, requires that governmental enterprise funds follow GAAP that are applicable to business enterprises. In addition, *Audits of State and Local Governmental Units* identifies certain FASB and AICPA pronouncements as those to be followed by state and local governments.

In addition, state and local government accounting practices are heavily influenced by federal government accounting and reporting requirements for grant programs, which often mandate accounting requirements, and by state laws covering financial reporting for state and local governments.

The Governmental Accounting Standards Board (GASB) has been recommended by a special committee composed of representatives of the above groups and the National Association of State Auditors, Comptrollers, and Treasurers and the United States General Accounting Office. The GASB proposal would set up a separate and independent accounting standards board to set standards. The agency would have full-time staff and financial backing and would represent a broad range of groups in public and private sectors concerned with state and local government accounting standards. In addition the special committee has proposed establishment of two other entities: the Governmental Accounting Foundation, to provide oversight and fund raising for GASB; and the Governmental Accounting Standards Advisory Council, a group of twenty or more persons to advise on a wide range of problems and issues.

prepare GAAP-based reports for the total organization, which is defined in terms of the overall organization, not the separate parts. However, the accounting and reporting entity for state and local governments has been defined as the *fund* or *fund type* activities. GAFRP defines a fund as:

. . . a fiscal and accounting entity with a self-balancing set of accounts recording cash and other financial resources together with all related liabilities and residual equities or balances, and changes therein, which are reported for the purpose of carrying on specific activities or attaining certain objectives in accordance with special regulations, restrictions, or limitations.[5]

The fund basis of accounting recognizes that (1) most governmental assets are not fungible, and (2) data on budgetary compliance are an exceptionally important part of the stewardship responsibility of government. Government activities must be accounted for through a series of distinct *fund* accounting and reporting entities in order to control resources and to demonstrate compliance with the various legal and budgeting constraints affecting government. Information on the flow and use of financial resources represents the most significant economic phenomenon of government reports. The primary operating statement must be designed to reflect the in-flow and the related out-flow of financial resources.

Most local governmental activities (e.g., police and fire protection) are financed by taxes and other fixed or restricted revenue sources, and expenditures are controlled through various budgetary processes. Certain "business-type" activities of governments (e.g., airports, utilities, and golf courses) are operated so that the costs incurred can be recovered by charging fees to the specific users of those services. These activities are controlled by matching revenues to expenses in order to ensure that the user charges are adequate to maintain the service. Because of the different aspects of their supporting revenues and operating and financing objectives, the accounting and reporting practices for the proprietary activities differ from those for standard governmental activities.

GAFRP has established eight generic fund types divided into three separate fund categories (i.e., governmental, proprietary, and fiduciary).

Governmental funds

1. *The general fund* is normally the most important fund of a municipality. It accounts for all resources not otherwise devoted to specific activities and finances many of the basic municipal functions, such as general administration and police.
2. *Special revenue funds* account for the receipts from revenue sources that have been earmarked for specific activities. For example, a city with a special property tax levy for parks might have a park fund.
3. *Capital projects funds* account for the acquisition of capital facilities, which may be financed out of bond issues, grants-in-aid, or transfers from other funds. This type of fund, which is most closely related to the capital budgeting process, is limited to accounting for the receipts and the expenditures on capital projects. Any bond issues involved will be serviced and repaid by the debt service funds.
4. *Debt service funds* account for the financing of the interest and the retirement of the principal of general long-term debt. Where sinking fund term bonds have been issued, a debt service fund accounts for the sinking fund set up to retire the bonds.
5. *Special assessment funds* account for the financing and construction of those public improvements that benefit a specific group of properties. For example, the costs of a street-paving project or a sewer extension may be assessed against the abutting properties rather than charged against the taxpayers as a whole. These funds are a special type of capital projects

fund that handles both the financing and the expenditure. Special assessments are often paid by abutting property owners in installments over a number of years. In order to finance the immediate construction, the funds often issue bonds that are paid off by the proceeds of these assessments. Use of special assessment funds will be more limited in the future as a result of recent consideration of special assessment accounting by the National Council on Governmental Accounting. In essence, the activity accounted for by special assessments funds will be spread among several other types of governmental funds. Specifically, the resources used for construction and the related construction activity will be accounted for in a capital project fund. The accumulation of monies to pay interest and principal on any special assessment bonds will be recorded in a debt service fund. Finally, long-term special assessment bonds payable will be reflected as liabilities in the long-term debt group of accounts in a manner consistent with the general obligation long-term debt of the municipality.

Proprietary funds

6. *Enterprise funds* account for business-type activities. Municipal utilities, golf courses, swimming pools, toll bridges, and other activities supported largely by user charges are accounted for by this type of fund.
7. *Internal service funds* are similar to enterprise funds except that the services are not rendered to the general public but are for other governmental organizational units within the same governmental jurisdiction. For example, if a central photocopying machine is financed out of one budgetary line-item and is available free to all departments, there is little incentive for the department heads to economize on its use. This is not true, however, if a central duplicating service department charges each department on the basis of use. The operations of such departments as municipal garages, central purchasing offices, and even municipal office buildings have been placed under this type of fund to account for the costs of services they provide and to encourage economy in their use.

Fiduciary funds

8. *Trust and agency funds* account for assets held for others or for nontax resources held by the government under specific trust instructions. Taxes collected for (and to be forwarded to) other governmental units are accounted for in agency funds. The most important municipal trust funds are those associated with retirement systems. Another example of a trust fund is the money donated to the local government to buy park equipment as a commemoration. Such a donation would be accounted for as a trust fund although it partakes of the nature of a special revenue fund.

Budgetary accounting

The budget plays an extremely important role in the administration of public resources. GAFRP states that an annual budget should be adopted by every governmental unit, that the accounting system should provide the basis of appropriate budgetary control, and that a budget-to-actual expense comparison should be included as part of the appropriate financial statements. The budget itself frequently is made part of the formal accounting system by entry into the general ledger. Governmental budgets represent a mandate for requiring as well as limiting expenditures; however, expenditures are subject to revision as economic or operating circumstances change. Budgeted revenues are referred to as *estimated revenues,* the budgeted expenditures are termed *appropriations.* Estimated revenues may be characterized as anticipatory assets; appropriations may be referred to as anticipatory liabilities. Formal budgets exist for almost all funds and fund types, but usually the budget-to-actual comparison reports are prepared only for the general and special revenue funds.

Because budgetary compliance is of such significance in managing governmental activities, and because expenditure overages may represent civil or even criminal wrongs, techniques have been adopted to ensure conformance with budget specifications. One such technique is encumbrance accounting.

Encumbrance accounting Administrators must know how much of an available appropriation has not yet been expended or otherwise committed to the acquisition of any particular good or service. As in commercial accounting, an expenditure and its related liability should be recognized only when the governmental unit incurs an obligation that must be paid or otherwise satisfied. However, once a government manager reports an intent to purchase a particular object, an encumbrance of funds should be recorded even prior to the time a definite liability is recorded. Prior to the time liability exists, the managerial commitment to expend resources is reflected as an encumbrance.

The use of an encumbrance system of accounting is especially desirable for governmental funds in which a maximum budget limit is set for each period (usually a year). When expenditure maximums are approached, accounting provides an early warning system; it also helps to ensure that no unexpected liabilities emerge after the end of the year that must be paid from the current year's budget. In such a case, a reported encumbrance would provide notice of a lingering commitment.

Encumbrances can only be recorded as estimates based on quotes from manufacturers. Expenditures reflect the actual amounts paid out. Encumbrances should not be reported in the financial statements as expenditures or liabilities, even though they appear in the accounting records. The encumbrance should be treated as a direct reduction of the unreserved fund balance; the reserve for the encumbrances account should be reported as a reservation of the fund equity that has been committed to a particular future expenditure. This is, of course, consistent with the nature of encumbrances and enhances the representational faithfulness of the financial statements. Finally, if an encumbrance lapses (i.e., the proposed expenditure is never completed), the amount in the reserve for the encumbrances account should be returned to the unencumbered portion of the fund's account.

The importance of a proper encumbrance system cannot be overemphasized. If encumbrances are not recorded for orders and commitments, administrators may appear to stay within their budget by encouraging suppliers to delay tendering their bills until the next budget period. These bills, however, become a burden on the next period, and thus that period's appropriation is exhausted prematurely. The payments due on later bills may be delayed again and again, and eventually the deferred payments would constitute a large and not fully recognized floating debt. When the municipality finally converts to an encumbrance system, this accumulated debt must either be funded or an extra tax assessment implemented to put the municipality on a current basis.

Nevertheless, one of the problems of budgetary control is that most governmental units are eager to use up their unencumbered balances at the end of the fiscal year. Otherwise, the unused appropriation may expire at the end of the budgetary period. This eagerness can lead to a rush of purchase orders in the last days of a fiscal period. Where this practice is abused, the local government manager should closely examine the outstanding encumbrances at the end of the year and, if necessary, cancel them.

Other equity reserves The unreserved fund balance of a governmental fund should reflect its residual equity in assets that are free and available for future commitment and expenditure. The reserve for the encumbrances portion of the equity section of a fund's balance sheet is not available for expenditure; it reflects the estimate of the resources that have been committed to a particular expenditure's objective. Other reserve accounts are often necessary to achieve the goal of reporting the appropriate uncommitted fund balance. For example, when a fund expends cash to acquire supplies, any unused supplies are shown as assets in the financial statements even though they are not, as such, expendable assets. Therefore, it is necessary to reduce the unreserved equity of the fund in expendable assets by establishing a balancing "reserve for inventory." Other equity reservations include reserves for contingencies, non-current repayable advances to other funds, and future expenditure limitations. An example of the reporting for fund equity is provided in Figure 18–2 as part of the balance sheet for a governmental fund.

Accounting for proprietary funds

The financial accounting and reporting for funds of the proprietary type parallel that found in business enterprises that operate to provide goods and services on a fee-for-service basis. Because the objectives of proprietary funds must cover all operating costs through user charges of the service, an income determination/capital maintenance accounting model is employed. In such an accounting model, expenses as well as expenditures are measured. Therefore, a statement of changes in financial position that reflects the sources and application of resources is employed, just as it is for governmental funds. However, proprietary funds also prepare an income statement matching revenues and expenses. An expenditure essentially reflects the cost of acquiring a good or service. An expense may also represent the expiration in use of the good or service. Governmental funds reflect only expenditures, whereas proprietary funds report expenses as well.

Since recognition of all expenses is mandated for proprietary funds, accounting for fixed assets and their related depreciation is necessary also. The cost of fixed assets (which represent an expenditure of resources at the time of acquisition), must be allocated over time to include operations for the estimated life of the asset, which must then match the use cost of the asset and the revenue it generates.

A balance sheet must also be prepared to communicate information about the resources and obligations of the fund at a particular point in time. The balance sheets of proprietary funds differ from those of other governmental funds in at least two significant practices. First, the fixed assets employed in rendering the proprietary service net of an allowance for accumulated depreciation are reported as assets of the fund. Second, the long-term debt incurred by a proprietary fund is reflected as a liability of that fund.

The use of something resembling the proprietary type of account is especially recommended for service funds that render services to other elements or units of government. One objective of those funds should be to "break even," to cover the costs from the revenues charged for services. This objective places many of the profit-oriented incentives for efficiency and effectiveness into the conduct of governmental operations.

Fiduciary funds

Accounting and reporting for fiduciary trust and agency funds should follow either governmental or proprietary practices as appropriate in the circumstances. For example, if a tax agency fund is used to collect and remit sales taxes for several different levels of government, then the operating and reporting emphasis is on the strict accountability for in-flow and out-flow of monies. However, if the operation of a fiduciary fund is designed to break even, then the income determination/capital maintenance accounting and reporting model of proprietary funds should be employed.

Fixed assets and long-term debt

In contrast to the proprietary type of funds, the fixed assets acquired by regular governmental funds are reported in the general fixed assets group of accounts. Long-term debts incurred by governmental funds are accounted for in the general long-term debt group with one exception. The special assessment funds, however, must account for their own long-term debt as the debt will be serviced from revenue derived from the special assessments made on the users of the improvement. Those resources are not provided by general taxpayers in the same manner as are other revenues. Thus, two groups of accounts are employed to provide control over, and stewardship information on, the fixed assets acquired and the long-term debt financing incurred on their behalf by governmental funds. Because the reporting focus of governmental assets is reflected as an application of resources and not as assets, the incurrence of long-term debt is treated as a source of revenue and not as a liability of the fund in question. The two groups of the debt and asset accounts are employed to complete the stewardship story and to provide accounting control over those assets and liabilities that are excluded from the reporting components of the individual governmental funds.

Financial reporting

Two types of financial statement packages are recognized by GAFRP: (1) general purpose financial statements that provide an overview of the financial position and the results of operations of all fund types; and (2) comprehensive annual financial reports that contain the general purpose financial statements, an introductory section, supporting statements, and a statistical section.

Figure 18–1, reproduced from GAFRP, shows the relationships of the elements in the financial accounting and reporting system and the degree of fund and fund type aggregation deemed necessary for the two types of financial reports.

Examples of simplified summary financial statements are presented in Figures 18–2 and 18–3. These are designed to reflect the account reports required for general purpose financial statements for a single governmental fund or fund type.[6] In regard to the summary statements shown in Figures 18–2 and 18–3, such reports present detailed information about fiscal and budgetary compliance, funds flow, and current liquidity adequacy. The operating statement is prepared on a functional or program basis rather than on an object of expenditure basis. That is, expenditures are classified by activity (e.g., public safety or education) rather than by nature (e.g., salaries or supplies). The statement of revenues and expenditures compared with budgeted amounts provides the users of the financial statement with necessary information on the government's resources and the application of these resources to specific programs or activities. Users are in a position to make their own judgments and form their own conclusions about the manner in which the government collects monies and how it allocates expenditures. Furthermore, the degree of budgetary compliance is also made evident by this statement. Footnotes to the statement (not presented here) provide additional information that assists statement users in assessing the financial condition of the entity. However, although this type of reporting is deemed adequate for external users, a need clearly exists for the more detailed kinds of information that are contained in the special reports prepared for internal management.

Figure 18–1
The financial
reporting pyramid.

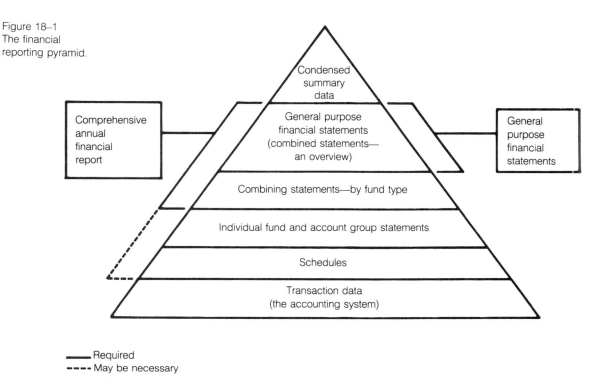

Condensed
summary
data

General purpose
financial statements
(combined statements—
an overview)

Comprehensive
annual
financial
report

General
purpose
financial
statements

Combining statements—by fund type

Individual fund and account group statements

Schedules

Transaction data
(the accounting system)

── Required
---- May be necessary

Management reporting

Managerial accounting and reporting are concerned with the capture, retention, summary, and display of information that will assist municipal administrators in planning, controlling, and evaluating those operations under their control. The heart of such a system is a concept referred to as *responsibility accounting*. In essence, responsibility accounting recognizes that individuals and programs should be held accountable only for those events that are within their ability to influence or control.

Therefore, in establishing a system of responsibility accounting, it is important to determine the costs that are associated with various programs, activities, or work units. Such costs may then be compared with those of prior periods, with estimated or standard costs, or with alternative costs.

Assets			Liabilities and fund equity	
Cash		$ 15,000	Liabilities	
Short-term investment (at cost;			Accounts payable	$10,000
market value $123,000)		120,000	Payroll taxes payable	2,000
Property taxes receivable	35,000		Total liabilities	12,000
Less: allowance for				
uncollectable taxes	3,000	32,000	Fund equity	
			Reserve for encumbrances	7,000
Due from other funds		1,500	Reserve for inventory of	
			supplies	10,000
Inventory of supplies		10,000	Undesignated fund balance	149,500
			Total fund equity	166,500
Total assets		$178,500	Total liabilities and equity	$178,500

Figure 18–2 General fund balance sheet, Trojan City, 31 December 198__.

Classification	Budget	Actual	Actual over-(under-)estimated
Revenues			
Taxes	$240,000	$290,000	$50,000
Licenses and permits	30,000	36,000	6,000
Intergovernmental revenue	120,000	90,000	(30,000)
Charges for services	40,000	45,000	5,000
Fines and forfeitures	6,000	9,000	3,000
Miscellaneous	4,000	10,000	6,000
Total revenues	440,000	480,000	40,000
Expenditures (current)			
General government	45,000	41,000	4,000
Public safety	100,000	98,000	2,000
Highways and streets	60,000	60,000	–0–
Sanitation	40,000	39,000	1,000
Health	20,000	18,000	2,000
Welfare	30,000	25,000	5,000
Culture—recreation	16,000	13,200	2,800
Education	14,000	12,600	1,400
Capital outlay	75,000	75,000	–0–
Debt service	25,000	25,000	–0–
Total expenditures	425,000	406,800	18,200
Excess of revenues over expenditures	15,000	73,200	58,200
Fund balance (beginning of year, 1 Jan.)	76,300	76,300	–0–
Undesignated fund balance (end of year, 31 Dec.)	$ 91,300	$149,500	$58,200

Figure 18–3   General fund statement of revenues, expenditures, and changes in fund balance, budget and actual, Trojan City, year ended 31 December 198__.

Cost determination

Cost determination is central to measuring the economic endeavor needed to deliver a given service or perform a certain function. The following discussion divides cost determination into two separate functions:

1. Cost accounting, which is the continuous and routine process of analyzing, classifying, capturing, and summarizing cost data within the confines and control of a single accounting system and reporting results to users on a regular basis. NCGA, in defining cost accounting, adds that cost accounting assembles and records ". . . all the elements of cost incurred to accomplish a purpose, to carry on an activity or operation, or to complete a unit of work or a specific job."[7]
2. Cost finding is a less formal method of program or activity cost determination that is done on an irregular basis for special purposes.

Cost determination for most of the business-type activities of local governments (e.g., utilities and airports) is relatively straightforward and primarily involves reclassification of existing expense (expired cost) data which have been generated routinely for financial reporting. This reclassification generally involves transferring costs from a general responsibility center to a function or activity center that provides direct services to constituents. This process may be accomplished manually using relatively simple work sheet procedures or electronically through the use of computer routines.

Cost determination for activities contained within a general fund is more difficult and requires additional procedures. Specifically, to determine the cost of operating any particular responsibility center of the general government, it is necessary to convert data prepared for financial reporting purposes on an expenditure basis to expense or cost data in a form useful for managerial reporting purposes and to reclassify the expense or cost data to the functional areas benefited. Data from several funds may need to be considered, because a single government function may be financed and accounted for through several funds. For example, the cost of maintaining public roads and streets may be financed partly from a special gasoline tax revenue fund and partly through general fund expenditures.

Cost accounting, cost finding, and cost evaluation are useful for allocating resources in a rational manner and in assisting the evaluation of the efficiency and economy of particular government functions. At least four specific steps are necessary in this process. They are as follows:

1. Activity identification, the selection of a meaningful measure of productivity for a project
2. Cost determination, the isolation of costs incident to conducting the activity identified in (1)
3. Cost and activity data accumulation, the capture, retention, and reporting of information specified in (1) and (2)
4. Evaluation, the analysis of the data to uncover the relationship of outputs as measured in (1) and inputs as measured in (2).

Components of cost determination   In regard to step 2, cost determination, it is widely recognized that there are three components of the total cost of any product or service. They are:

1. Direct materials, the cost of items used directly in the production of a good or service (e.g., asphalt in a street-paving project)
2. Direct labor, the salaries and other costs of employees related directly to a product or service (e.g., wages of employees working in a street-paving project)
3. Overhead, the indirect costs that are associated with the production of a good or service (e.g., employee benefits).

Accounting records frequently exist for the determination of the first two costs, although, as previously mentioned, the data may be contained in several funds. The determination of overhead costs may involve substantially greater effort. There are at least two major problems in attempting to allocate overhead costs to particular projects or services. The first concerns the availability of the cost or financial data. For example, the cost of machinery used to pave a street may be unknown, and surrogates for depreciation (e.g., use allowances) must be adopted. Second, some costs benefit more than one project, and sophisticated allocation techniques may be required. For example, the cost of a personnel department operated by the general fund benefits every department of the government that hires employees. Therefore, the cost of the personnel function should be allocated to the various service or production departments on a rational basis whereby each benefiting department is charged an appropriate share of the costs. Cost finding techniques are useful in these situations.

Some costs involved in rendering a service, although material in amount, are not readily apparent and require careful study to detect and allocate properly. For example, fringe benefits (e.g., the pension costs of employees) may be paid from the general fund; and, if such expenses are not considered, the full cost of a particular activity may be understated. Care must be exercised to ensure that all costs relating to a given project or service are, in fact, allocated to that service.

There are several methods of resolving each of these problems,[8] but one particular technique has received a great amount of attention in recent years. Internal Service Funds (ISF) are used by state and local governments to account for the provision of goods and services by one department (the provider) to other departments (the consumers) of government. These service activities are set up as though they are business enterprises, although they are operated by one government office for other government entities on a fee-for-service basis.

For ISF operations, most professional literature confines discussions to the effects on the department providing the service. Most writers deal with the problems of matching revenues with expired costs to determine income and to measure capital. Many articles and other documents have pointed out the management incentives created for the providing department when an independent service department fund is established.

However, the impact on the consuming department frequently is not considered in detail. The use of space in a municipal building provides a good illustration. If a municipal building is accounted for through the general fixed assets group of accounts, and building expenses such as utilities and maintenance are paid through the general fund, then no vehicle exists to charge departments for the building space occupied. The total or full costs of operating the various departments that occupy the building are understated consequently. Building space is essentially treated as a "free good." This provides a disincentive for efficient operation because the user departments tend to ask for additional space without consideration of costs.

On the other hand, if the provision of building space is accounted for through a service department, the total cost of operating the building is captured in the routine of ISF general ledger accounting, thus obviating the need for cost finding. A determination of the real cost of operating each department, including space, is facilitated. Finally, the goals of responsibility accounting are achieved by holding the property manager accountable for the quality and financial success of building operations. Note that an important by-product of ISF operation is that full cost information by each user department is generated as a routine bookkeeping function.

With full cost accounting, space-consuming departments are charged for space occupied, encouraging departments to use only as much space as is efficient for operations.

Regardless of the manner by which cost information is accumulated, program cost determination is only a beginning in understanding the operating and financial characteristics of various activities. Careful cost evaluation is a necessary corollary to cost determination.

Cost evaluation   Whenever a set of costs can be related to an activity, it is possible to assess the activity from the perspective of efficiency and economy. In evaluating any given activity, it is necessary to establish certain acceptable standards of performance and levels of activity. Because activity forecasts underlie most resource allocation decisions, the actual performance of a function may be assessed according to standards of performance or volume of activity established during the planning phase.

In traditional line-item budgets, the expenditure lines are prepared for a single level of activity, although revisions may be effected when necessary throughout the budgetary period. Nevertheless, a specified maximum expenditure level is established and operating results and expenditures are compared with this budget, regardless of any differences between actual activity levels and estimates underlying the original budget. Thus, this method of static budgeting is acceptable for controlling expenditure levels, but it is unsatisfactory for evaluating programs and management control.

An improvement on traditional budgeting is reflected in the flexible budget, which modifies static budgeting by recognizing the financial impact of fluctuations in the actual activity levels. Expenses under flexible budgets may vary according to service levels attained. Flexible budgets are designed for many levels of activity rather than for a single level. This facilitates the evaluation of the financial aspects of an operation by comparing what the estimated costs should have been at a given activity level with the costs actually incurred.

The determination of cost must be based on a careful analysis of performance characteristics. Costs usually are classified as either fixed or variable. Fixed costs remain constant in total over a relevant range of activity levels, whereas variable costs change with changes in the activity level. An example of a fixed cost is building rental, which remains constant with the lease regardless of the activity taking place in the building. An example of a variable cost is the cost of fuel to run the city's vehicles; this changes with the amount of vehicle use.

Variable costs tend to remain constant per unit of activity over a given activity range, but the fixed costs per unit of activity change as activity levels change. Fixed costs per unit decrease over a given range as output increases, and increase as output decreases. However, production cannot be expanded indefinitely because of the limited capacities of any facility. This acts to establish the range of activity levels to be considered.

Three separate and distinct steps are necessary to set up flexible budgeting procedures.

1. A static budget is prepared based on a relevant measure of activity, which is deemed reasonable on the basis of expected future activity. This is accomplished *prior* to the operating period.
2. A flexible budget is developed based on the actual activity level achieved during the operating period. The differing cost behavior of fixed and variable cost characteristics must be considered when tailoring the original static budget to a flexible budget for the actual activity level experienced. This step is accomplished *after* the operating period.
3. Actual expenses incurred are compared to the amounts allowed in the flexible budget. Any significant variance from the flexible budget levels should be analyzed to facilitate any needed corrective, executive action.

Variance analysis

Variance analysis is the process of evaluating what caused a deviation between the flexible budget and the actual costs incurred. The combination of flexible budgeting and detailed variance analysis provides a powerful tool for the evaluation of efficiency.

Variance analysis can take many forms and the type suggested here should not be viewed as necessarily the right one for all situations. In general, overall variances determined by comparing the flexible budget with actual costs should be subdivided into at least three component subvariances:

1. *Spending.* The analysis of spending variance compares actual costs incurred with those predicted in the flexible budget for the activity level achieved. Fixed costs included in this variance are the same as those in the static budget because they are not, by definition, expected to change with activity. The spending variance reveals only the impact of differences between costs expected and costs incurred at the activity level encountered.
2. *Usage.* Volume variances in costs are affected by fixed costs only. This

variance reflects the economies (or diseconomies) of use resulting from spreading the same total fixed costs over greater (fewer) units of activity. For example, if the activity level achieved exceeds that planned in the static budget, then each productive unit of activity absorbs a smaller fixed cost per unit. Volume variance summarizes the economic impact of using a facility more or less intensively than was anticipated originally.

3. *Efficiency.* The time variance relates to how many hours were required to accomplish the total activity relative to how many hours should have been required according to the flexible budget. For example, if the flexible budget indicates that it should take 100 hours for each one million gallons of sewage processed, but experience indicates that 120 hours are required, then an unfavorable time variance will be evident. This variance should then be translated into dollars to understand its economic impact.

Even when detailed variance analyses are conducted, management will typically be required to make additional studies in order to determine the underlying causes of the variances. Variances may contain hidden meanings. Spending variances, for example, may be due to a rate of inflation that is faster than expected and thus represent a forecasting deficiency, not an operational shortcoming. Efficiency variances may be the result of activities that are more severe or complicated than anticipated and indicate a need to allocate additional resources, not to initiate punitive action. At times, a careful analysis of unfavorable variances will show a level of performance that was higher than anticipated.

Variances demonstrate only the degree of departure from management plans. They are "attention getters" or "red flags" that require further study.

Managerial accounting techniques provide a dynamic basis for predicting, understanding, and controlling operations. Employed intelligently, such controls can provide an early warning system against adverse economic and operational events. Budgets, prepared on a static basis, cannot provide the data necessary for an adequate evaluation of just how efficiently and effectively a government is being run. The management practices recommended here are designed, not as substitutes but as supplements to standard budgeting. They are designed to provide legal control of expenditures and financial reporting in accordance with GAAP.

Compliance reporting

The accounting and reporting systems of local governments should be capable of providing specified information to a variety of regulatory or granting authorities. Such reporting capabilities should be considered and anticipated during the development of an accounting system so that all financial, managerial, and compliance reporting requirements can be met by a single accounting system.

Accounting reports to granting or regulatory authorities generally are concerned with the application of specific and restricted resources to the performance of some specified functions or activities. Many of the general aspects of financial and managerial reporting may be applicable to compliance reporting as well. However, there are several notable differences in the reporting objectives to granting authorities.

For example, granting agencies frequently reimburse the recipient governments for the costs incurred in administering the grant program, but the costs that are refundable under the terms of the grant may be defined in a manner that requires the application of special cost finding techniques. An allowable or refundable cost generally is expressed as a necessary cost of administering a particular program. It is necessary to determine carefully all of the costs related to a grant program and to establish a cost accounting system capable of capturing data in conformity with the grant provisions.

Frequently, grant provisions require a recipient government to provide matching contributions to the grant program. Whereas cash, supplies, or services are easily recognized in determining the municipal contribution, other contributions—especially those made in kind—are more difficult to trace. For example, the depreciation of equipment used in a program may represent a matching contribution. The labor effort expended on the program may qualify as a matching contribution even in situations where employees do not devote all their time to the grant program. Carefully documented accounting records and sound allocation practices will help assure the reimbursement of all allowable costs for matching contributions.

The provisions of the particular grant document and standardized references such as Office of Management and Budget (OMB) circulars A–87 and A–102 provide recipient governments with guidance in establishing adequate accounting systems for meeting the compliance reporting requirements.[9] Municipal administrators should consult the relevant technical sources for specific provisions covering each grant or contract. Normally, the grant will refer to the relevant OMB circular or include specific additional requirements as part of the grant instrument.

Auditing

Auditing in state and local government traditionally has not been utilized to the degree desirable. Auditing activities have been concerned primarily with financial and compliance issues. It is now quite clear that the audit function holds substantial promise for municipal managers attempting to improve the levels of operational efficiency and program effectiveness. In fact, the concept of auditing with a broader scope is particularly useful in environments such as governments where a direct profit motive is, by necessity, lacking.

The General Accounting Office (GAO) of the federal government has been active in developing standards for auditing the economy and effectiveness of programs. Specifically, the GAO recognizes three necessary elements in a full scope audit.

Financial and compliance. Determines whether financial operations are properly conducted, whether the financial reports of an audited entity are presented fairly, and whether the entity has complied with applicable laws and regulations.

Economy and efficiency. Determines whether the entity is managing or utilizing its resources (personnel, property, space, and so forth) in an economical and efficient manner and determines the causes of any inefficiencies or uneconomical practices, including inadequacies in management information systems, administrative procedures, or organizational structure.

Program results. Determines whether the desired results or benefits are being achieved, whether the objectives established by the legislature or other authorizing body are being met, and whether the agency has considered alternatives that might yield desired results at a lower cost.[10]

Modern auditing techniques are capable of addressing these elements and providing valuable management tools for both asset control and project evaluation. Although independent external auditors are available to provide evaluation services on a contract basis, it is frequently desirable to maintain fully capable internal auditing departments. On the other hand, because internal auditors are employees of the governmental unit and are not subject to external professional standards of conduct, it is important to establish controls to assure the independence and competency of the internal audit department and the adequacy and quality of the audits it conducts. Figure 18–4 summarizes the provisions of an internal audit, acts as a self-evaluation guide, and suggests certain standards that must be considered when establishing an internal audit function.[11]

The use of performance auditing techniques is increasing rapidly, but generally accepted standards for conducting broad-scope audits have not yet been established at the level that exists for financial and compliance audits. The limitations as well as the potential of performance auditing should be considered carefully by municipal managers before establishing audit programs and objectives.

Figure 18–4
Audit standards.

General standards

Audit scope
1. Authority to conduct audits
2. Fulfillment of audit responsibilities
3. Consideration of user needs

Staff qualifications
1. Audit staff education requirements
2. Professional achievements of audit staff
3. Continuing education programs for audit staff
4. Appraisal systems
5. Use of consultants

Independence
1. Organizational placement of the head of internal audit
2. Organizational independence of internal audit staff
3. Freedom to audit
4. Level of management reported to
5. Audit report availability

Professional care
1. Clear definitions of authority and responsibility
2. Written policies for planning, conducting, and reviewing audits, and other quality control measures

Examination and evaluation standards

Audit planning
1. Isolate problems
2. Avoid redundancies
3. Determine personnel needs
4. Develop audit programs
5. Establish detailed steps
6. Review procedures

Staff supervision
1. Level of supervision required
2. Supervisor availability
3. Supervisory reviews
4. Preparation of time budgets
5. Evaluation of performance

Internal control, evidence, and compliance
1. Adequacy of description, documentation, and evaluation of internal control
2. Appropriateness of audit evidence procured
3. Procedures based on evaluation of internal control
4. Compliance with operating policies
5. Restrictive-regulation-related evidence gathered for the above steps

Audit conduct
1. Procedures associated specifically with each of three audit types: (a) financial and compliance, (b) economy and efficiency, and (c) program results audits
2. Weaknesses detected in each of aforementioned areas
3. Adequacy of work papers as to form, content, clarity, and relevance

Reporting standards

Form and distribution
1. Medium used (written, oral, etc.)
2. Formats employed
3. Distribution policies

Timeliness
1. Meeting reporting deadlines
2. Other general considerations of frequency and timing of reporting

Content
1. Clarity, convenience, objectivity, tone, and scope of the report
2. Adequacy of supporting evidence offered in report
3. Adequacy of underlying audit evidence not cited in report

Financial reports
1. Whether financial statements present what they purport to present
2. Whether all disclosures are included
3. Appropriateness of auditors' opinion or disclaimer

Summary

Accounting and reporting systems for state and local governments, like the information systems in commerce and industry, must be capable of meeting many diverse requirements. The systems capabilities should be designed to meet diverse operational reporting objectives. Included in these objectives are reporting in conformity with GAAP to assist external decision making; providing operational information management; and demonstrating financial and fiscal compliance with various laws, regulations, and granting instruments. The usefulness of accounting data is limited only by the imagination and creativity of the information users and the reporting capabilities of the system. It is worthwhile in constructing the system to devote substantial funds to determine the information needs of the user and to plan and design the system. For example, electronic data processing (EDP) would seem to offer considerable advantages to local government managers. Employment of EDP may be more costly than a manual system and should be made only after careful analysis of the volume of reporting objectives, the volume of transactions, and the organizational complexity of the entity.

Budgetary accounting practices strengthen the controls over governmental fund expenditures. Encumbrance accounting and the use of equity reserves support other budgetary control measures to help assure compliance with the budget, laws, and regulations.

Cost accounting and cost finding represent valuable tools for government managers attempting to evaluate performance and program effectiveness. The use of such accounting control tools as flexible budgeting, standard unit costing, and detailed variance analysis are being adopted by increasing numbers of local government units.

The rise of intergovernmental financial activity has required more sophisticated reporting systems. Intergovernmental grants, contracts, and other resource transfers necessitate special purpose compliance reports and have also resulted in higher professional accountability standards.

Finally, the increased use of operational auditing has complemented traditional financial and compliance auditing to make the audit function more valuable to local government managers. Audits that report on the efficiency and economy of operations, as well as on program effectiveness, have begun to spread as government officials respond to tighter budgetary constraints. Broad-scope audits provide evidence and support for decisions on resource allocations and program funding levels. The results of such audits are useful in communicating the quality of management to the taxpayer and bond holders.

1   Marshall S. Armstrong, "Some Thoughts on Substantial Authoritative Support," *Journal of Accountancy*, April 1969, p. 50.

2   The citation for each document is: National Council on Governmental Accounting, *Governmental Accounting, Auditing, and Financial Reporting* (Chicago: Municipal Finance Officers Association, 1968); and Committee on Governmental Accounting and Auditing, American Institute of Certified Public Accountants, *Audits of State and Local Governmental Units* (New York: American Institute of Certified Public Accountants, 1974).

3   The citation for each statement is: National Council on Governmental Accounting, Statement 1, *Governmental Accounting and Financial Reporting Principles* (Chicago: Municipal Finance Officers Association, 1979), subsequently referred to in this chapter as GAFRP, and National Council on Governmental Accounting, Statement 2, *Grant, Entitlement, and Shared Revenue Accounting and Reporting by State and Local Governments* (Chicago: Municipal Finance Officers Association, 1979).

4   Committee on Governmental Accounting and Auditing, *Audits of State and Local Governmental Units*, p. 9.

5   National Council on Governmental Accounting, Statement 1, *Governmental Accounting and Financial Reporting Principles*, p. 6.

6   Ibid., Appendix A. This appendix shows more detail for these summary financial statements.

7   National Council on Governmental Accounting, *Governmental Accounting, Auditing, and Financial Reporting*, p. 157.

8   For example, see: Robert J. Freeman, Harold H. Hensold, and William W. Holder, "Cost Accounting and Analysis in State and Local Governments," in *The Managerial and Cost Accountant's Handbook*, ed. Homer A. Black and James D. Edwards

(Homewood, Ill.: Dow Jones–Irwin, 1979), pp. 794–839.

9   U.S., Executive Office of the President, Office of Management and Budget, *Principles for Determining Costs Applicable to Grants and Contracts with State and Local Governments,* Circular A–87 (Washington, D.C.: Government Printing Office, 1968); and U.S., Executive Office of the President, Office of Management and Budget, *Uniform Administrative Requirements for Grants-in-Aid to State and Local Governments,* Circular A–102 (Washington, D.C.: Government Printing Office, 1972).

10 U.S., General Accounting Office, Comptroller General of the United States, *Standards for Audit of Governmental Organizations, Programs, Activities, and Functions* (Washington, D.C.: Government Printing Office, 1972), p. 2.

11 U.S., General Accounting Office, Comptroller General of the United States, *Self-Evaluation Guide for Government Audit Organizations,* Audit Standards Supplement Service, no. 9 (Washington, D.C.: Government Printing Office, 1976); summarized in: William W. Holder and Raymond J. Clay, "Criteria for Internal Auditing," *Hospital Progress,* January 1979, p. 52.

19 Capital budgeting

The capital budget is concerned with the selection of capital expenditure projects, the timing of the expenditures on the projects selected, and the estimates of the impact on the regular operating budget of the various plans that might be used to finance the capital expenditures. This chapter analyzes the local government capital budget within this framework. It thus complements Chapters 4 and 5, to which the reader is referred for discussions of forecasting and modeling procedures and the formulation of the regular operating budget. This chapter also helps conclude the discussions of debt management, cash management, financial management, and municipal accounting contained in the preceding chapters.

The following discussion progresses in logical sequence from an analysis of the methods of selection and evaluation of capital projects to the use of studies of the economic base, land use, and population data in the formulation of the capital budget. The estimating of fiscal resources and the specific analysis and forecasting of revenues and operating expenditures for the fiscal plan are then discussed. The remainder of the chapter is a detailed examination of the construction of a hypothetical fiscal resource study.

Selection and evaluation of capital projects

A capital expenditure may be defined as one used to construct or purchase a facility that is expected to provide services over a considerable period of time. In contrast, a current or operating expenditure is for an item or service that is used for a short time. Moreover, a capital expenditure usually is relatively large compared with items in the regular budget. Thus, in a small locality, expenditures on police patrol cars might be part of the capital budget, whereas in a larger city patrol cars may be purchased annually under a regular budgetary appropriation. Even in the large city, however, the operating budget should distinguish between (1) regular operating expenses and (2) recurrent or small capital items. The purchase of recurrent capital items such as typewriters should be given special attention even though the appropriation is usually part of the regular operating budget rather than the capital budget.

Because the capital budget involves relatively large items meant to serve the municipality for some time, its components should be analyzed carefully. Although requests for the consideration of capital projects may originate with diverse groups—the operating departments, the administrative officers, the planning commission, or interested citizens—the responsibility for analysis and evaluation of capital expenditure requests should be centralized in one department. Decisions on capital projects should be given to the planning department or agency under the direction of the city or county chief administrator. Partially on the basis of the information supplied by the economic base, land use, and population studies, the planning agency—with the direct aid and input of the finance department—should make an economic and financial evaluation of the requested projects. The planning group should determine which projects should be included in the capital budget to be submitted to the appropriate local legislative body. The priorities, timing, and listing of the projects in the capital improvement program are not the sole responsibility of the finance officers, but the officers should be instrumental in providing some quantification of the economic desirability of the proposed projects.

Determining worthwhile projects

In theory, the determination of worthwhile public capital investments is straightforward. A public investment is desirable when the present value of its estimated flow of benefits, discounted at the community's cost of capital (or time preference rate), exceeds or equals its cost. If the project meets this criterion, it is considered profitable because it earns more than the community's "interest rate." On a more formal level, the theoretical criterion may be applied. The stream of net future benefits, which includes all the gains to the community, must be quantified: each year's return is discounted to obtain its present value; the sum of the present values is compared to the immediate outlay on the project; if the sum of present values exceeds the outlay, the project should be accepted.

The mathematical formula for obtaining the net present value (NPV) of a project is, generally,

$$PV = \frac{B_1}{(1+i)} + \frac{B_2}{(1+i)^2} + \cdots + \frac{B_n}{(1+i)^n} + \frac{S_n}{(1+i)^n} \qquad (1)$$

$$NPV = PV - I$$

where PV is the present value of the annual flow of the benefits (B_1, B_2, ... B_n) over time to n years; S_n is the scrap value or the remaining value of the project at the end of its economic life in year n; and i is the applicable discount or interest of the community. NPV equals the net present value or the present value of the benefit stream minus I, the investment cost of the project.

The equation for the internal rate of return is formally similar to that for present value:

$$I = \frac{B}{(1+r)} + \frac{B_1}{(1+r)^1} + \cdots + \frac{B_n}{(1+r)^n} + \frac{S_n}{(1+r)_n}$$

However, in this case, I (the cost of the project) is given and r (the rate of discount that brings the PV of the benefits equal to the outlay, I) must be solved. When $r > i$ (the cost of capital), the project is acceptable.

Table 19–1 shows an example of the simple mechanics of the capital evaluation problem. The project illustrated would be accepted because at a community social cost of capital of 10 percent, the present value of the estimated stream of benefits is $7,156,700, which is $1,156,700 in excess of the project's cost of $6,000,000. Thus the projected rate of return on the project is higher than the 10 percent discount rate—the estimated time preference rate or cost of capital for the community. The discount factors for different interest rates may be found readily in books of interest rate tables. In addition, many computer programs have been developed which handle present value problems.

Quantifying benefits and costs

Although simple in theory, public investment decision making is not very simple in practice. For one thing, the benefits of a project are not always readily quantifiable. Many of the benefits are of an intangible nature; their value is common or social, involving the whole municipality, and not easily ascertainable

Table 19–1   Net present value of capital project

Year	Investment cost of project (1)	Estimated net annual undiscounted benefits	Discount factor (social cost of capital = 10%)	Present value of benefits
0	$6,000,000		$\dfrac{1}{(1.10)^n}$	
1		$1,000,000	.9091	$ 909,100
2		2,500,000	.8264	2,066,000
3		3,000,000	.7513	2,253,900
4		1,500,000	.6830	1,024,500
5		1,000,000	.6209	620,900
6		500,000	.5645	282,300
Total	$6,000,000	$9,500,000		$7,156,700

in money terms. (Of course, this factor of common value is the very reason that many activities are assigned to the public sector.)

Although a public park provides recreation, fresh air, light to adjoining properties, and beauty to the traveler and visitor in the town, a money value for these benefits is difficult to determine. Nevertheless, there are some indicators that allow for some estimate of the benefits. How much will people pay to use private lakes, parks, and preserves? What is the private outlay for vacations, scenic trips, and other pleasures among the population of the town? What are the outlays on private lawns, landscaping, gardens? Surely a park provides benefits similar in nature to these other activities; thus, some estimates of its value can be made, even though the problem of accounting for all the benefits of fresh air and open space is quite difficult. Of course, estimating benefits becomes somewhat easier when public services are sold to the public rather than distributed free of charge. By paying for a service, the consumer indicates how much he or she values the service. Even under these conditions, however, some benefits are not easily captured in the price for the service.

Accounting for the spillover or neighborhood effects of a project is a complex problem. If the municipality puts in a sewage treatment plant, part of the benefits of stream improvement may accrue to other communities in the same area. If these external benefits could be measured, should some of their value be included in the accounting? There are some pleasures in being a good neighbor; the residents of any given town obtain the spillover effects from the beneficial activities of other towns. In financially tight times, however, it is difficult to be purely altruistic. Thus, one argument in favor of grants-in-aid from higher levels of government is that the grants compensate the community that undertakes projects for those benefits that spill over to citizens of other localities.

Even where a monetary quantification of benefits is difficult to obtain, the investment criteria analysis can still be used in a counterpart context. The question may be posed: Given the cost of a proposed project and the community's discount rate, what flow of annual benefits would justify the cost of this project? Does this flow of annual benefits, even though not exactly measurable, appear reasonable or attainable? If so, the project is desirable.

A difficult problem is estimating the community's cost of capital (or time preference rate). What rate of interest should be used in discounting the stream of benefits from a public project? It might appear that the borrowing rate of the municipality would be the appropriate rate. Because the interest on municipal debt is exempt from federal income taxation and because payment generally is backed by the taxable wealth of the entire community, the explicit rate on municipal issues is the lowest of all market interest rates. However, this low explicit rate is probably not the true "social cost of capital" to the community.

Because governmental debt is a "prior charge" on the community's wealth that ranks potentially above all other obligations in the area, an increase in debt imposes a "risk charge" on all the income streams or wealth in the community. The burden of this risk charge must raise the cost of capital (i.e., the necessary rate of return) required on all new and renewable capital investments made in the area. The decision makers have to account for this additional imputed burden when analyzing the economic desirability of investing in public projects, and they should raise the presumptive social discount rate accordingly. An approximation of the true social discount rate might be a rough weighted average of the interest on municipal bonds and the yields on such other claims as bonds, stocks, and mortgages held in the community.[1]

Inflation and real interest rates

The problems of forecasted inflation, a persistent rising trend in prices and costs, complicate capital planning programs because, by their very nature, capital outlays are forward looking. Forecasted inflation raises the expected dollar value of the future benefits, which should apparently increase the present value of the projects and lead to a more expansive program. On the other hand, a rise in the expected inflation rates leads to a rise in the current nominal rate of interest in the money and capital markets. The rate of interest is highest during an inflationary period. This increase in the social discount rate acts to reduce future benefits. Under equilibrium conditions (if all estimations are accurate), these factors cancel out and the real value of any project remains unchanged.

Unfortunately inflation may also act to weaken the economic fiber of the community and make it difficult to find the resources to support public programs into the future.

Conflicting criteria

There has been much discussion of the problem of selecting projects when (1) there are more projects that pass the economic test and appear socially desirable than a fixed capital budget will allow, and (2) there are "mutually exclusive alternative" projects—where only one out of a number of projects is to be selected because all of the projects serve the same function. Two standard criteria are used for selecting desirable projects.

1. *Net present value method.* As explained previously, the net present value (NPV) is obtained by subtracting the initial outlays from the gross present value of the benefits calculated by discounting at the community time preference rate. A project is acceptable if the NPV is positive.
2. *Internal rate of return method.* The internal rate of return is the rate that brings the present value (PV) of the benefit flow into equality with the initial outlay. If the internal rate of return exceeds the community's discount rate (time preference rate), the project is economically desirable.

Both these criteria will indicate whether a single project is acceptable. If a project's net present value is positive, it necessarily follows that its internal rate exceeds the community's cost of capital. Nevertheless, the two criteria can give conflicting signals. Thus under the constraint of a limited budget or when mutually exclusive alternative projects are ranked, some projects that show higher rates of return may rank lower in terms of the amount of net present value.

It should be noted before proceeding that the arbitrary constraint of a fixed budget may be irrational. An overly tight budget can result in uneconomic behavior by forcing the substitution of less efficient projects or by delaying the implementation of worthwhile improvements. If economically desirable projects exist that cannot be undertaken because of a limited budget, the public officials must persuade the community to accept a larger budget. This should be done, however, with some circumspection; before pressing for the acceptance of additional capital projects, the evaluator must be certain that all the costs and benefits have been counted and that the discount rate to be used is not too low. Of course, enlarging the budget to accommodate all worthwhile noncompeting projects is the ideal or long-run solution; in the interim, the second best solution is to make sure that the group of projects selected within the budget limit shows the highest combined net present value.

In the case of mutually exclusive alternative (or substitutable) projects, however, the two criteria of the largest internal rate of return or the largest net present value may give different rankings to the projects. In this case, selecting the best project is a true economic problem. Projects may show up with conflicting rankings because of the existence of three (not necessarily mutually exclusive) conditions:

1. The shapes of the benefit flows over time differ.
2. The investment sizes of the projects differ.
3. The durations of the benefit flows differ.

A case where the shape of the benefit flows differs (condition 1) is illustrated in Table 19–2. Project A has a higher internal rate of return than Project B (11.7 percent for A against 10.0 percent for B), but if the cost of capital was 6.0 percent, Project B's net present value would be higher than that for A ($113,532 for B against $85,510 for A). As always, where this type of conflict in rating appears, the project with the higher internal rate of return has the higher earlier benefit flow; the rival project with the higher net present value has a relatively higher benefit flow in later periods. If the decision between the projects was made on the basis of the rate of return, earlier returns would be at the cost of greater returns later and this trade would be at a higher rate than the community's time preference. The most desirable project is the one with the greatest net value of total benefit flows as determined by the community's time preference or discount rate. This is determined by the net present value criterion.

Table 19–2 Comparison of projects when shape of cash flow differs

Project A

Years	(1) Outlay	Benefits	Discount rate (6%)	Present value of benefits
0	$1,000,000			
1		$ 700,000	.9434	$ 660,380
2		200,000	.8900	178,000
3		200,000	.8396	167,920
4		100,000	.7921	79,210
	$1,000,000	$1,200,000		$1,085,510

Project A has a net present value of $85,510. Its internal rate of return is 11.7%.

Project B

Years	(1) Outlay	Benefits	Discount rate (6%)	Present value of benefits
0	$1,000,000			
1		$ 100,000	.9434	$ 94,340
2		200,000	.8900	178,000
3		700,000	.8396	587,720
4		320,000	.7921	253,472
	$1,000,000	$1,320,000		$1,113,532

Project B has a net present value of $113,532. Its internal rate of return is 10.0%.

It might be noted that the net present value depends heavily on the estimate of the appropriate discount rate. At higher discount rates, the advantage of Project B over Project A begins to disappear. At 10 percent Project B just qualifies as feasible with a zero net present value, whereas Project A would still have a positive net present value and would therefore be the more desirable project. This simply means that in times of high *real* interest rates (i.e., when there is a tight supply of capital), the financial managers must try for projects with returns that will come in the near term rather than in the distant future.

The case when the size of two projects differs (condition 2) is illustrated in Table 19–3. Here the smaller project, A, has the greater rate of return, but the larger project, B, has the higher net present value. This means that the size increment in Project B earns benefits at a rate higher than the community's cost of capital even though there is an "averaging down" of the internal rate. If the bigger project is conceived in two parts, one of which is an increment to the smaller project, it becomes clear that the criterion of net present value gives an unambiguous, correct answer.

In addition to its service as a planning tool, another function of the capital budget is its use in public relations. Thus, in many jurisdictions the capital budget will contain maps, attractive sketches, and pictures of proposed capital projects.

The case of differing durations of the benefit flows (condition 3) cannot be resolved simply. The problem is that not only may internal rates of return differ but also that a net present value of, for example, $100,000 for a stream of benefits lasting five years cannot be directly compared to the net present value of $120,000 for an alternate project which lasts seven years. Actually what is involved is a comparison of different strategies carried out over time and not merely a comparison of two projects. The comparison of strategies may not be too difficult if it can be assumed that each project can be renewed at the end of its life and at the same costs and benefits as the current project. In this case, the net present values of each project can be annualized (reconverted into an equivalent flat annual amount over the life of each project).

These amounts can be compared directly. Table 19–4 illustrates such a problem. Although the net present value (NPV) of Project B is larger, the equivalent annuity of Project A (at 10 percent) is $18,450 per annum and the equivalent annuity of B is $17,040 per annum. Thus a series of A projects is preferred to one of B projects because the former results in a higher stream of net benefits over time.

However, in the case when the future renewal costs and benefits of each

Table 19–3 Comparison of projects when size differs

Project	A	B	Difference between A and B as independent Project B-A
Cost	$1,000,000	$1,200,000	$200,000
Present value of benefits at 10.0%	$1,500,000	$1,770,000	$270,000
Internal rate of return	12.50%	12.25%	11.00%
Benefit cost ratio	1.50X	1.48X	1.35
Net present value	$ 500,000	$ 570,000	$ 70,000

Table 19–4 Comparison of projects when duration differs (using method of annualization)

Project A

Year	Outlay	Returns	Discount factor (at 10%)	Present value
0	$80,000			
1		$ 60,000	.909	$ 54,540
2		50,000	.826	41,300
3		40,000	.751	30,040
	$80,000	$150,000		$125,880

NPV = $125,880 − 80,000 = $45,880.
Equivalent annual stream of return for three years at 10% = $18,450.

Project B

Year	Outlay	Returns	Discount factor (at 10%)	Present value
0	$170,000			
1		$ 80,000	.909	$ 72,720
2		70,000	.826	57,820
3		60,000	.751	45,060
4		50,000	.683	34,150
5		40,000	.621	24,840
	$170,000	$300,000		$234,590

NPV = $234,590 − $170,000 = $64,590
Equivalent annual stream of return for five years at 10% = $17,040.

project may not be an exact reduplications of the present projects, annualization will not work. The solution must be obtained by comparing the net present value of a series of linked, shorter-lived projects to the net present value of an alternate series of longer projects, both ending at a reasonable common time. Thus if capital Project A lasts four years and rival Project B lasts six years, a comparison of the net present value of three A-type projects with forecasted costs and benefits renewed at the end of four years and eight years should be made with the net present value of two linked B-type projects. The forecast aspect is difficult, but the calculation itself is not as difficult. Thus, if I equals the project cost at each renewal period, B equals benefits for each time period, i equals community discount rate, and NPV equals net present value, then:

$$NPV_A = I_{A_1} + \frac{B_1}{(1+i)} + \dots$$
$$+ \frac{B_4}{(1+i)^4} - \frac{I_{A_4}}{(1+i)^4} + \frac{B_5}{(1+i)^5} + \dots \quad (2)$$
$$+ \frac{B_8}{(1+i)^8} - \frac{I_{A_8}}{(1+i)^8} + \frac{B_9}{(1+i)^9} + \dots$$
$$+ \frac{B_{12}}{(1+i)^{12}}$$

$$NPV_B = I_{B_1} + \frac{B_1}{(1+i)} + \dots$$
$$+ \frac{B_6}{(1+i)^6} - \frac{I_{B_6}}{(1+i)^6} + \frac{B_7}{(1+i)^7} + \dots \quad (3)$$
$$+ \frac{B_{12}}{(1+i)^{12}}$$

The forecasted costs of renewing each project when the time comes and the estimate of the extended benefits must be made specific. Then NPV_A may be compared with NPV_B to see which is larger.

The problems of present value analysis for capital investment programming appear to be quite complicated, but it is the estimation of benefits and not the actual calculations that is difficult. It appears that an attempt to make present value analyses of projects is worthwhile even if some estimates of the benefit flow are necessary. The exercise, in any case, should improve the evaluation of the economic desirability of many capital projects.

One tendency of capital planning that should be avoided is the temptation to place funds in new projects and to delay the repair and renovation of existing facilities. "Cities often defer maintenance and replacement because it is a relatively painless short-run way to reduce expenditures and ease financial strain."[2] Such deferrals, however, can cause all sorts of community hazards and costs in the present and may lead to much larger capital expenditures in the future. Maintenance and repair should not be ignored in the formulation of the capital budget. In many instances, such activities may show the highest net value of benefits.

In constructing the capital budget there is one proviso that should be kept in mind. The object of the capital planner is to increase the general wealth and welfare of the city, not just to better the position of the public treasury. Only over time, and perhaps in an imprecise manner, will an improvement with diffuse benefits eventually bring about increased revenues; in the meantime, the impact of the expenditures on the municipality's budget is quite direct. Nevertheless, the capital planner must not ignore the wider benefits of a project because of undue concentration on one-sided counting of explicit costs. The final effect of the community's expenditures is a municipality with a richer, happier, healthier, and wiser population.

Using economic base, land use, and population studies

An effective capital budgeting program rests on a foundation of economic base studies, land use reports and maps, and population and migration studies. Often, such studies have already been made by the local planning commission, but perhaps too often, the documents are forgotten and are left to gather dust in a back room. In any case, these studies can provide underlying information for projecting fiscal resources, measuring need, and indicating the best location for capital projects.

The economic base study, the land use study, and the population and migration studies overlap. The economic base study should contain data (e.g., size, employment, and location) on existing industries. It should contain an economic history of the municipality, an analysis of trends in economic development, and forecasts of employment, wages, construction, and the locations of economic activity in the area.

Land use studies show population density and contain an inventory of industrial, residential, recreational, commercial, and vacant land. These studies can be used to determine the amount of land available for various sorts of future development. Population and migration studies contain data on present population characteristics, income, talents, and human resources. They indicate where people currently live and where they are likely to move in the future. The population study should give data on age classes so that projections can be made for such items as the size of the future labor force, schooling needs, and facilities needed for older people.

Capital budget makers should be involved in the original design of these studies. They might well ask that the data in the studies be so gathered as to help provide the answers to straightforward questions. Here are a few questions on the capital expenditure side of the budget:

What industries are developing? What support will these industries need in terms of streets, docks, fire control equipment, or other government facilities? If the migration and land use studies indicate new areas to which the population is moving, what new facilities will be desired in the way of schools, transport, parks, and recreation? If this migration is not wholly desirable, what are the improvements that might slow movement from the older areas?

The studies may also help show the trends of operating expenditures for social services, welfare, protection, and general government programs as the population structure and land use patterns change.

On the forecasted revenue side of the budget, a similar set of questions may be asked:

What is the likely growth of various parts of the municipality's economy? Does an analysis of this growth provide enough information to estimate future tax sources? For example, will the value of downtown property decline? Will a decline in the property tax base be offset by growth in the earned income tax? Do the land use and migration studies indicate whether the movement path of the population is toward vacant land that is likely to be developed and added to the municipality's tax base? Can it be assumed that future growth of the property tax-base area will be slower or faster than past trends?

Estimating fiscal resources

The following sections deal in general with the projection of needs and financial and economic resources and conditions into the future. More detailed explanation of this forecasting process will be found in Chapter 4. A summary of useful indicators will be found in Handbook 1, *Evaluating Financial Condition*, published by the International City Management Association.[3]

Because the capital budget is by its very nature a forward-looking study, one of the most important sections of a local government capital budget is the forecast of the municipality's resources and responsibilities over a period of years. This provides the essential fiscal framework for the capital program. Fiscal resources are projected in terms of normally anticipated sources of revenues, less normal expenditures, and existing debt service costs. The financial impact of the desired capital improvements—given their estimated costs, the timing of construction starts and outlays, and the amount of construction funds that may be available as grants from other governmental units—is measured against the forecast of resources. The budget maker's forecast of fiscal resources compared to the projected outlays for the capital improvement program serves the useful function of preparing the community for required fiscal changes and adjustments.

Forecasting operating revenues and expenditures

The projection of fiscal resources includes (1) a projection of recurrent revenues and (2) a projection of normal operating expenditures, existing debt service charges, and recurring capital expenditures. A comparison of these two series provides the forecast of the resources available under the existing tax structure. (Of course, if regular expenditures are growing faster than existing revenue sources, the forecast of net resources can be negative.) The magnitude and timing of outlays on planned capital improvements are measured against the forecast of financial resources. This provides a picture of how much of the capital budget can be supported directly out of current revenues, how any necessary bond financing can be serviced, and what tax increase (if any) will be required. Generally, the fiscal forecast should extend for five or six years if it is to be a useful planning tool.

In order to forecast normal recurring revenues and operating expenditures, the revenue and expense items must be separated into readily definable major categories. The behavior of these categories is subject to historical analysis to ascertain past trends. Historical analysis is one way to project major revenue sources and major expenditures. In many cases, more sophisticated methods may be desirable (see Chapter 4). In any case, the forecasts should not be made on a purely mechanical basis; the budget maker should interview local government officials to see if there are any special factors in the community's fiscal history or in its prognosis that may suggest deviations from past relationships. Some parts of the capital budget itself may influence the trend of revenues. Nevertheless, unless there are strong local characteristics that differ from the overall pattern, the projections should be consistent with the overall trends of local government finance and with the developments of the national economy.

Price inflation

Another likely problem is allowing for the rate of price increases. In a certain sense, the rate may already be accounted for insofar as the historic trends must reflect the rate of past inflation. Moreover, if inflation increases nominal costs and expenditures, it also increases the dollar amount of potential revenues. The effects of inflation generally do make for difficulties in financing local government activities, because not all costs and revenues run parallel. Thus, to the extent possible, the forecaster should adjust the projections for the forecasted increase in price levels.

The projections of the sum of the major revenue sources are presented in a master table; the projected major expenditure items are also presented in this table. A hypothetical illustration of such a forecast is shown in Table 19–5. (The details of how this table is constructed follow later.) Its major function is to project the differences between the totals of future operating revenues and expenditures. This gives an estimate of *future net available fiscal capacity*. Future net available fiscal capacity represents potential funds that may be used either for direct expenditures on capital items or for service charges on additional bonded debt incurred to finance capital improvements. The trend of fiscal capacity over time indicates how much financial resources the government will have available to support desired future capital improvements under the *existing fiscal structure*.

Two main, limiting procedures guide the fiscal forecast section of the capital budget study. First, it is assumed that no new major operating functions will be undertaken by the local government in the period under review. (If this assumption should be relaxed, the budget can still be useful, because it gives an estimate of future fiscal resources that might be available for any new functions.) Second, the revenue forecasts are based on an analysis of existing taxes and tax rates. This is necessary because the revenue projected by the existing tax structure serves as a base for estimating both the additional revenue that might be obtained by an increase in the existing taxes and the level of activity the local economy can carry.

The actual construction of the fiscal plan of the capital budget can be facilitated by dividing the operation into three steps.

1. Analyzing past revenue data and developing a forecast of normal recurring future revenues
2. Analyzing past expenditure data and developing a forecast of normal recurring future expenditures
3. Comparing projected revenues and operating expenses. The difference between these two series provides an estimate of the projected fiscal resources of the local government on the basis of its current revenue

structure. The formal capital improvement program is then related to the local government's fiscal resources. Usually, it is found that additional funds will be necessary to finance the capital program. If so, the budget maker should present alternative financial plans that indicate the timing and fiscal impact of raising these funds through different possible combinations of debt and tax increases.

Forecasting revenues

In the following section, much of the discussion is based on the trend analysis method of forecasting. Trend analysis is, of course, not the only method of forecasting these items. Chapter 4 outlines many sorts of relationships and econometric regression models that can be used to help make forecasts. The planner should use those statistical tools and methods that are best adapted to the problems at hand.

Future revenues may be projected by studying the past data on existing revenue sources. Projections should be based on existing tax rates; this involves forecasting the growth of the existing tax base. Possible local legislated changes in the tax rates are not predicted, because the basic purpose of the fiscal plan of the capital budget is to generate reasonable estimates of what changes in the rates, if any, will be necessary to support the financing of the planned and desired level of future capital projects.

Cleaning the data

In analyzing past trends, it is important to distinguish between the effects of natural economic growth in the tax base and the effects of past legislated changes in the tax system. This is why it is improper simply to chart trends in total revenues. Part of the past increase in revenues could have been caused by a rise in the rates of existing taxes, a change in assessment levels, or the institution of a new tax. The projection of the overall trend of combined revenues can also be misleading if the returns from individual taxes are growing at different rates. Thus, a relatively stable total revenue trend might be the result of a slow decline in the returns from major tax Source A, whereas the revenue from new tax Source B is rapidly increasing. Breaking out the two taxes historically, analyzing them separately for trends, and then combining the results may indicate that after a brief period of stability, forecasted total revenues should start climbing significantly.

Pitfalls in making revenue forecasts

In order to make a useful and consistent analysis of past trends of the various revenue sources, the following factors should be considered:

1. The major revenue sources should be classified in past operating budgets under consistent headings. Sometimes budget classifications change. When this occurs, current classifications should be followed and past revenue classifications should be made consistent with current classifications.
2. The property tax, as a major source of local government revenue, and its projection are worth some study. In analyzing the revenue derived from the property tax, the trend in the total levy should not be overemphasized. The growth in the assessment base is the most significant aspect underlying any forecast. Thus, a sudden jump in the assessment base should lead to some further questioning. The rise may have resulted from an increase in the assessment ratio (e.g., from 40

percent to 60 percent) rather than from true economic growth. In projecting property tax revenues, detailed analysis and knowledge of the local area can prove very useful. The land base study is very valuable. Whether any major developments are pending, how much land is still open for development and improvement, and whether any significant amount of property might be taken off the rolls in the future also should be considered.

3. A newly instituted tax requires careful analysis. Its growth rate can be exaggerated if the base year revenues do not represent a full fiscal year. Moreover, the first years of the imposition of the tax may show a rapid rate of growth in revenues; some of this may be caused by improvement in administration as the local government becomes accustomed to the tax. Such growth is not likely to continue indefinitely at the same rate.

4. Last, in making projections, past trends should be modified by any recently observed changes in the patterns. Thus, for example, the observed compound rate of growth for a local earned income tax over the last ten years was 8 percent. However, in earlier years the growth rate was about 7 percent, and this has gradually increased to almost 9 percent per year. The projection rate might be best set at 9 percent per year or even slightly higher.

Forecasting operating expenditures

Again, as in forecasting revenues, the major emphasis in this section rests on the use of trend analysis. However, the points noted are useful in any case where careful classification and handling of the data may be necessary. Often, the methods cited in Chapter 4 will be superior to the extrapolation of trends in projecting the future. Study of expenditures requires that the numerous individual outlays be grouped into workable categories, that operating expenditures be separated from recurring capital expenditures (which may be made from the general fund), and that service charges on existing debt be isolated to note any special or nonrecurring capital expenditures financed out of current revenues.

Past expenditures are analyzed to determine the trends and relationships of each major component. Where these trends appear consistent with general economic developments, they are used in making forecasts. As in the case of revenue analysis, local government officials should be questioned about significant deviations from past trends to learn whether there are any special factors likely to affect expenditure patterns in the future.

In making expenditure projections, there are certain pitfalls and problems to which the analyst must apply informed judgment. Some of those problems are:

1. In terms of revenue accounts, budget classifications may have changed in the time period under review. If this is the case, the existing budgetary classification should be used, and past data arranged to conform to current usage.

2. When new government functions are introduced, the rate of expenditure growth may be quite high in the early years. It generally can be assumed that the rate of increase will decline after the function gets "on stream." The projections should take this into consideration, and the average historic rate of growth of a particular item should be adjusted if it is a relatively new function.

3. Totally new functions may have no historic record of past expenditures. Such functions should be given a separate line in the forecast. The estimate of expenditures on such functions will have to be developed from interviews with relevant officials and must incorporate the reasonable judgment of the analyst. Methods using regression models are often useful in this case. The amounts forecasted and the rate of growth

can be compared also with the experience of other similar local governments that have already instituted the function.

The framework of the fiscal resource study

How might the fiscal planning budget be worked out? The following section illustrates some of the specific factors that would enter into the construction of the fiscal resource study.

Table 19–5 is the key table for projecting the fiscal resources of a hypothetical city for six years. The base year 1981 is the current operating year. Row 1 shows the estimated current operating revenues for the next six years. (It does not include any grants from higher governments that are to be used for capital improvements.) Row 2 is the projected level of current expenditures. Row 3 is the difference between current revenues and expenditures; this item does not represent a surplus even when it is positive, because the service charges on already existing debt must be subtracted both from this figure and from amounts that are to be expended on such recurring capital items as police cars, typewriters, and sanitation equipment. When these items are subtracted, Row 7, the projected annual net cash flow of the municipality, is obtained. This amount may be used to help finance *new* capital projects and to help cover the service charges on additional debt obligations, which may be floated to finance the capital budget. Row 8 contains the proposed capital expenditures taken from the capital budget itself. Row 9 shows the net new capital funds that will be required to finance the capital budget. It does *not* show the full fiscal impact of the budget over time because this involves an extrapolation of the impact of the bond financing plan chosen on the tax structure of the city. This will be discussed in more detail later in this chapter.

Table 19–5   General fund fiscal projections and the capital budget (000 omitted)

Category	1981	1982	1983	1984	1985	1986	1987
1 Projected operating revenue	6,000	6,500	7,000	7,300	7,700	8,000	8,400
2 Less projected operating expenditures	5,000	5,800	6,300	6,600	7,000	7,300	7,700
3 Gross cash flow from operations	1,000	700	700	700	700	700	700
4 Debt service on existing obligations (interest plus amortization)	500	500	350	300	250	200	150
5 Gross funds flow after debt service charges	500	200	350	400	450	500	550
6 Less projected recurrent capital expenditures	200	300	350	400	450	500	500
7 Net funds[1]	300	(100)	–0–	–0–	–0–	–0–	50
8 Less proposed major capital expenditures	1,000	1,000	1,000	500	500	–0–	–0–
9 Net new financing required[2]	700	1,100	1,000	500	500	–0–	(50)

1 Parentheses indicate deficit.
2 Parentheses indicate surplus.

Supporting schedules for the fiscal forecast

The summary items in the projections for the general fund and the capital budget are derived from more detailed analyses and forecasts. Table 19–5 and Figures 19–1 through 19–8 provide the diagrammatic framework for the following discussion of compiling and organizing the requisite financial data for the decisions to be made on capital financing. Figure 19–1 is a schematic presentation that shows the interrelated steps in compiling these general and detailed data.

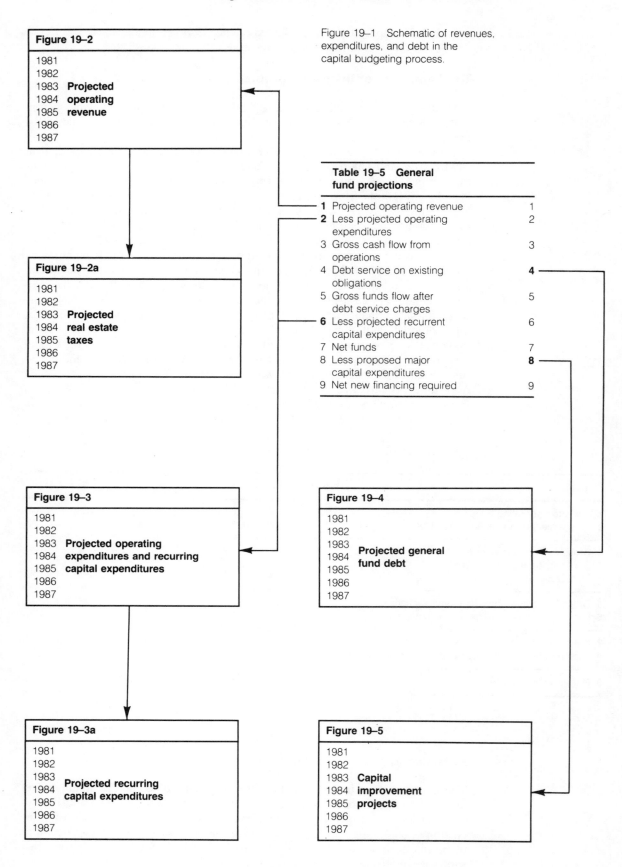

Figure 19–2

1981
1982
1983 **Projected**
1984 **operating**
1985 **revenue**
1986
1987

Figure 19–2a

1981
1982
1983 **Projected**
1984 **real estate**
1985 **taxes**
1986
1987

Figure 19–3

1981
1982
1983 **Projected operating**
1984 **expenditures and recurring**
1985 **capital expenditures**
1986
1987

Figure 19–3a

1981
1982
1983 **Projected recurring**
1984 **capital expenditures**
1985
1986
1987

Figure 19–1   Schematic of revenues, expenditures, and debt in the capital budgeting process.

Table 19–5   General fund projections

1	Projected operating revenue	1
2	Less projected operating expenditures	2
3	Gross cash flow from operations	3
4	Debt service on existing obligations	**4**
5	Gross funds flow after debt service charges	5
6	Less projected recurrent capital expenditures	6
7	Net funds	7
8	Less proposed major capital expenditures	**8**
9	Net new financing required	9

Figure 19–4

1981
1982
1983 **Projected general**
1984 **fund debt**
1985
1986
1987

Figure 19–5

1981
1982
1983 **Capital**
1984 **improvement**
1985 **projects**
1986
1987

Year	Real estate taxes	Personal property taxes	Fines	Depart-mental earnings	Prisons	Welfare earnings	Federal and state grants	Miscel-laneous	Total
1981									
1982									
1983									
1984									
1985									
1986									
1987									

Figure 19–2   Schedule for derivation of projected operating revenues.

Year	Assessed value (A)	Existing millage (B)	Levy (C = A × B)	Collections (D)	Collection as % of levy (E = D ÷ C)
1981					
1982					
1983					
1984					
1985					
1986					
1987					

Figure 19–2a   Schedule of projected real estate taxes.

Figure 19–2 shows the main forecast items that underlie the overall projection of revenues on Row 1 of Table 19–5. Each item that makes up the row for each year is projected separately. Figure 19–2a shows the items that are likely to enter into the forecast of property tax revenues—still a major item in most local budgets.

An analytical breakdown similar to that on the revenue side underlies the global items of expenditure. Thus Figure 19–3 shows the classifications of the major items constituting the operating or recurrent expenditures. Each of these items should be forecast separately to obtain the projection of overall expenditures shown in Row 2 of Table 19–5. The recurrent capital expenditures may be broken down further by the categories shown in Figure 19–3a. The projection

Year	Operating expenditures							Total recurring capital ex-penditures	Total
	Adminis-trative	Judicial	Correc-tions	Welfare	Health and hospital	Miscel-laneous	Total		
1981									
1982									
1983									
1984									
1985									
1986									
1987									

Figure 19–3   Schedule of projected operating expenditures and recurring capital expenditures.

Year	Adminis- trative	Judicial	Correc- tions	Welfare	Miscel- laneous	Total
1981						
1982						
1983						
1984						
1985						
1986						
1987						

Figure 19–3a   Schedule of projected recurring capital expenditures from the general fund.

Year	Balance outstanding as of December 31	Debt retirement	Interest	Debt service
1981				
1982				
1983				
1984				
1985				
1986				
1987				

Figure 19–4   Schedule of projected existing general fund debt.

of existing debt service (see Figure 19–4) is relatively easy to obtain. This is not a forecast but a firm projection because the annual interest charges and amortization on the existing debt are already contractually obligated.

Schedule of capital improvements

After the fiscal resource statement has been developed, the next phase in the construction of the capital budget is the detail of the items and costs of the capital projects for the next six years. (The economic criteria for the selection of projects have been discussed in the opening portion of this chapter.)

The items making up the projected capital improvement program should be presented in a table. Although the format of this table can vary, it should include the following items:

1. A complete list of major capital improvements
2. Estimates of the total cost of each improvement
3. Outside sources of financing such as state or federal grants and private gifts. (The difference between the total cost of any item and the available grants is the net burden that must be borne by the fiscal capacity of the local authority.)
4. The scheduling of construction starts and annual expenditures. (In most cases, the expenditures on a project will be spread over a number of years.)

The optimal timing of municipal debt issues is a special problem in finance and depends on the level and trend in interest rates and the spread between municipals and short-term U.S. Government bonds. Often there may be some savings if the local unit floats all the bonds immediately and invests the proceeds in short-term Treasury issues until they are needed.

Project	1981	1982	1983	1984	1985	1986	1987
Home for elderly							
Addition and reconstruction							
Less: grants							
Net to city							
Prison improvements							
Recreation							
Land acquisition and improvement							
Less: grants							
Net to city							
Street improvements							
Less: total grants							
Net burden on general fund							

Figure 19–5   Schedule of capital improvement projects planned from general fund.

Figure 19–5 indicates the major variables entering into the capital program: the capital projects, costs, outside financing sources, and the timing of the net expenditures. The schedule should show how the total expenditures will be spread over the six-year planning period and how much will be covered by grants.

The financial impact of the capital program

On completion of the list of capital projects, the analyst can construct the master table of the fiscal plan. This represents the integration and the consolidation of the financing plan adopted for the capital program and the projection of fiscal resources as shown previously in Table 19–5, which contained the following information:

1. The six-year forecasts of operating revenues and expenditures (Rows 1 and 2). The difference between these two series is the projected gross cash flow from operations (Row 3).
2. The annual service charge on existing debt (Row 4) and the annual amount of recurring capital expenditures (Row 6). These outlays are subtracted from the gross cash flow from operations.
3. The net funds, if any, that remain (Row 7). This is the amount available for direct expenditures on planned capital projects or for the support of service charges on additional bond financing.
4. Finally, the net cost of the planned capital improvement program (Row 8). This was entered into the table and subtracted from the net cash flow. The final figure (Row 9), when negative (which is generally the case), represents the amount of net new financing that will be required to implement the capital program.

According to the projections, the net funds available to support new projects is $300,000 in 1981. Unfortunately, it is expected that this will turn into a deficit of $100,000 by 1982. For 1983 through 1986, the plan is for the budget to be in balance. In 1987, a modest surplus of $50,000 is projected.

Assuming the city follows through with its capital program, Row 9 of Table 19–5 shows the required new financing. For 1981, $700,000 is committed, and $1,100,000 will be required in 1982. The requirements of the program taper off to $500,000 in 1984 and 1985. There are no new large projects for 1986, nor any requirements for funds; and 1987 actually projects a surplus of $50,000. The total capital financing required from 1981 to 1986 (including funds already committed for 1981) equals $3,800,000.

The next step in capital budget preparation is to devise a financial plan and show its effects on the tax structure of the city. The two basic concepts for financing capital programs are *pay-as-you-go* (*pay-as-you-acquire*) and *pay-as-you-use*. In practice, many plans have a mix of these two basic models.

Financing concepts: pay-as-you-go versus pay-as-you-use

Some years ago, many writers on local finance were advocating pay-as-you-go capital budgeting as a way of saving on interest charges. Pay-as-you-go meant that the local government was to allocate a significant portion of operating revenues each year to a capital reserve fund. The monies in this fund were to be used for annual capital improvements or saved until they were sufficient for large projects. In any case, a regular capital allocation would be made from the operating budget to smooth budget allocations for capital expenditures and eliminate the need for bond financing. Because the municipality would save the interest charges that would have been incurred on the debt, the absolute amount of payments for any given capital program would be less over time than if financing were carried out through the flotation of bonds.

However, pay-as-you-go financing has certain difficulties both in practice and in theory. For pay-as-you-go financing to function well, capital projects must be evenly spaced over time (i.e., large projects must be relatively rare). Yet this characteristic of an even flow of capital expenditures (a lack of "lumpiness") is only likely in large jurisdictions where projects average out over time, and even here, there is a high possibility that projects that demand more than normal expenditure may be implemented. Under strict pay-as-you-go financing, if this should occur, some projects would be delayed until the funds could be accumulated. In the meantime, the community could be denied a very desirable facility, or a vital part of a total system (e.g., a road link or docking facility) would have to be postponed with a resultant loss to the community's economy. Moreover, if public funds are accumulated for future expenditure, the municipality has taken over a savings function for its citizens. The citizens might have more urgent uses for these funds, which might generate higher returns than the interest the government could earn while waiting to build a project.

If the population is relatively mobile, pay-as-you-go financing may not be equitable. Some citizens of a given town may have contributed heavily to its capital improvements; however, before they have a chance to enjoy them, they may move to a different area and have to start paying for capital improvements all over again. Conversely, a new resident moving into a community that has completed the bulk of its capital program will enjoy the use of these facilities without having contributed to their financing. Pay-as-you-go financing may also cause problems with intergenerational equity. Older families will be taxed immediately to pay for capital facilities that may last long past their lifetimes; the use and enjoyment of these facilities will accrue to younger people who may have made very little payment on them.

Most of the problems entailed by pay-as-you-go plans can be avoided by a pay-as-you-use method of financing. In its pristine theoretical form, pay-as-you-use financing means that every long-run improvement is financed by serial debt issues with maturities arranged so that the retirement of debt coincides with the depreciation of the project. When the project finally ends, the last dollar of debt is paid off. If a replacement facility is desired, it should be financed by a new bond issue tailored in the same manner. The interest and debt retirement charges paid by each generation of taxpayers would coincide with their use of the physical assets. These payments parallel the productivity of the social investment. Under pay-as-you-use, each user group pays for its own capital improvements. No one is forced to provide free goods for a future generation or to contribute toward facilities for a town in which he or she will not live, nor will new members of the community reap where they have not sown.

It would appear that the weight of theoretical analysis is in favor of pay-as-you-use financing. The only argument for pay-as-you-go financing rests on the notion of saving on total interest costs over time. This notion generally is erroneous because it ignores the private time value of money; it ignores the fact that the interest borrowing costs of the local government generally are lower than those of the rest of the financial market. Nevertheless, since pay-as-you-go financing carried the cachet of "good planning," it was highly recommended during the 1950s and was adopted by many communities. In actual practice, however, the developing tightness in the fiscal resources of local communities generally forced the subsequent abandonment of most pay-as-you-go budgets.

Illustrating the effects of possible financing plans

Notwithstanding the arguments in favor of pay-as-you-use financing, it is generally worthwhile to show the effects of various financial plans on the projected changes in the required local millage rate and on the projected financial position and credit rating of the community. Figure 19–6 shows the fiscal considerations

---

Plan A—Effect on millage under current revenue financing

	1981	1982	1983	1984	1985	1986	1987
1. Net new financing required for operations and capital budget ($000)							
2. Additional mills required (to the nearest tenth)							
3. Approximate revenue increase ($000)							
4. Total millage							

Plan B—Effect on millage using 100% debt financing (bond financing for capital requirements only)

	1981	1982	1983	1984	1985	1986	1987
1. New debt required to finance capital budget (nearest $100,000)							
2. Amortization of debt (15 year issues)							
3. Add: interest (6% on outstanding balance)							
4. Funds needed for service charges on new debt							
5. Funds needed for increase in current operations							
6. Total revenue requirements							
7. Additional mills required							
8. Approximate revenue increase							
9. Total millage							

Plan C—30% current financing and 70% debt financing

	1981	1982	1983	1984	1985	1986	1987
1. New debt required (nearest $100,000)							
2. Amortization of debt (15 year issues)							
3. Add: interest (6% on outstanding balance)							
4. Funds needed for service charge on new debt							
5. Other funds required (nondebt)							
6. Total revenue requirement							
7. Additional mills required							
8. Approximate revenue increase							
9. Total millage							

Figure 19–6 Schedule of alternative financing plans for capital budget.

of three possible plans for financing. Plan A, pay-as-you-go, involves complete financing out of current sources; Plan B rests completely on bond financing; and Plan C is a mixed plan that finances 30 percent of the net new financial requirement with taxation and the remaining 70 percent with debt. The various plans provide a guideline; the program eventually adopted is, of course, the responsibility of the political decision makers.

Plan A: 100 percent tax finance (pay-as-you-go)

Under this plan, the local government's net new financing requirements are covered entirely by taxation. Row 1 of Figure 19–6, Plan A, would show the annual amount to be financed. Row 2 would show the amount by which the real estate tax rate (in terms of mills) would have to rise to provide the needed funds. (Taxes other than real estate might be used in the actual financing, but the financial impact is usually quite clear if it is presented in terms of the required rise in the millage.) Row 4 would give the total millage required to carry out the ordinary operation and the capital program.

When the capital program is lumpy, pay-as-you-go produces a fluctuating tax rate because the municipality's financial needs fluctuate, whereas the tax base is relatively stable. These variations in tax rates make the costs of improvements very clear to the citizens of the community and probably induce conservative decisions regarding the desirability of improvements. One disadvantage is that fluctuating tax rates add to uncertainty and may therefore hinder good decision making.

Plan B: Debt finance (pay-as-you-use)

In Plan B, the community's net new financial requirements are covered by issuing new debt. Row 1 of Figure 19–6, Plan B, would show the timing of debt issues that coincides with the municipality's capital expenditures. Row 2, the debt amortization requirement, must be based on the normal issue length of serial bonds. (These are normally fifteen to twenty-five years.) Interest payments, calculated at an *average* rate would be shown in Row 3. Row 4 (the sum of Rows 2 and 3) would present total debt service on the new bonds. These charges plus the increased outlays for current operation (Row 5) will be covered by taxation. Generally under pay-as-you-use programs, the millage rate (or equivalent taxes) would remain relatively constant for the first year or so. However, the increased service charges on the net debt generally necessitate raising the millage rate thereafter. Nevertheless, the variations in tax rates induced by this plan are considerably milder than those associated with pay-as-you-go. The use of bond financing allows a much smoother budgetary transition—one of the main advantages of debt financing.

One rating criterion, which has often been suggested in the past, is the benefit/cost ratio, *PV/I*, where the present value of the benefits is divided by the cost of the project. This criterion, too, will work for passing single projects. However, as shown in Table 19–3, where the benefit/cost ratio favors Project A, this ratio can be misleading when the projects differ in size.

Plan C: Tax-debt combination

Any number of mixed plans of debt and immediate raises in taxes is possible. For purposes of viewing the alternatives, the finance officer should present at least one sample plan. Figure 19–6, Plan C, for example, combines 70 percent debt and 30 percent current financing through increased taxes. Generally, the tax rate fluctuations in a combined plan are milder than those in a pay-as-you-go plan but are more pronounced than those in a pay-as-you-use plan.

Feasibility of debt financing

If bond financing is to be used, the debt-carrying capacity of the community must be analyzed. Figures 19–6 and 19–7 show the basic factors used to measure the projected debt of the capital program against the carrying capacity of the municipality. Column C of Figure 19–7 would show the ratio of percentage outstanding general fund debt to the true (or estimated market) value of taxable property. Column E would show the total of the old and projected new debt. Column F then would give the ratio of total projected debt to the value of the local property tax base. The general rule of thumb for the credit worthiness of local government debt is that it should not exceed a 10 percent ratio of funded debt to true property value.

Year	Existing debt outstanding as of Dec. 31 ($000) (A)	True value of assessable property ($ millions) (B)	% of outstanding debt to true valuation (C = A ÷ B)	Projected new debt as of Dec. 31 ($000) (D)	Projected total debt outstanding ($000) (E = A + D)	% of projected debt outstanding to true valuation (F = E ÷ B)
1981						
1982						
1983						
1984						
1985						
1986						
1987						

Figure 19–7 Schedule of projected debt and true value of assessments.

Column A: from Figure 19–3.
Column B: from Figure 19–1a.
Column D: from Figure 19–5.

Another measure of debt capacity is the percentage of debt service charges to current revenues. The framework for forecasting this ratio is shown in Figure 19–8. Column C would give the ratio of the service charges on the existing general fund debt to projected revenues. Column E would give the total service charges on the total of the old and projected new debt. Municipal bond analysts assume that a 20 percent ratio of debt service charged to revenues is within a reasonable range. If a debt plan were adopted, it would be important to note whether the peak debt service charges would go past this point.

User charges and revenue bonds

In constructing the hypothetical capital budget, the funds to be raised for debt service were to come from general taxation. This is the appropriate source of funds when the benefits of the projects accrue to the community as a whole, when it is impossible to measure the precise amount of benefits accruing to particular individuals, or when it is not possible to exclude people from the overall services provided. A new city hall would provide an example of such a generalized project.

Year	Debt service on existing debt (A)	Projected revenue (B)	% of debt service to projected revenue (C = A ÷ B)	Debt service, Plan B (D)	Total projected debt service (E = A + D)	% of total projected debt service to projected revenue (F = E ÷ B)
1981						
1982						
1983						
1984						
1985						
1986						
1987						

Figure 19–8   Schedule of debt service and projected revenue under capital budget financing Plan B.

Column A: from Figure 19–3.
Column B: from Figure 19–1.
Column D: from Figure 19–5.

The benefits generated by some kinds of capital investments, however, accrue more directly to individual users; in such cases the government can charge for these services. Admission fees can be charged for the use of a swimming pool; motorists can be charged tolls for crossing a bridge. Revenue bonds with interest and amortization covered by these user charges may be the appropriate method of financing such facilities. Moreover, given the necessity to constrain government expenditures and the current resistance to increases in the broad-based taxes, it is likely that revenue bonds will be used even more frequently in the future.

If a capital improvement is to be financed partially or fully by revenue bonds, the projected revenues should be sufficient, at a minimum, to cover the maintenance and operating costs of the facility and the interest and service charges on the bonds. The revenue projections should show the ability to cover these costs with some margin of safety.

However, a sufficiency of projected revenues is not always necessary. Sometimes a project shows benefits beyond those the users can be expected to support. For example, a recreational facility in a poor neighborhood may be considered an investment in human capital; it may provide benefits to the whole city in excess of the revenues it generates. The necessary condition for a project to be worthwhile is that the total flow of benefits (including those for which there is no charge), discounted at the social cost of capital, should equal or exceed the total outlay on the project. To the extent that benefits may accrue to nonusers, the project may be partly financed with general debt, subsidized and serviced with general revenues.

Although a user charge system can provide the basis for efficient economic decision making, it often runs into criticism on grounds of equity. User charges generally will weigh more heavily in the budget of a poor person than that of a rich person. Complete reliance on user charges would prevent the poor from taking full advantage of available municipal services. Moreover, the services that should be provided by governments are those that are not fully supplied by the private sector; the community may have social reasons to encourage their consumption among people who cannot afford them. It is clear that, by their nature, a significant part of government services must be subsidized by the community as a whole. The challenge of the public official is to find the optimal balance between efficiency in the supply of public services and equity among the citizens.

Tailoring debt to the cost curve

If a project is financed with a serial bond issue, the maturities can be designed so that the total of the service charges on the debt and the facility maintenance costs (excluding the variable operating costs) are at a reasonably flat level over the life of the project. This is another application of the general rule that each group of users should pay the same level of capital costs over time.

The following brief example illustrates the problem. Suppose the project under consideration costs $15,000,000 and is estimated to last fifteen years with an average interest rate of 5 percent. An approximately flat debt service charge schedule would appear as shown in Table 19–6.

Under this scheme, the principle repayments are higher in later years, but of course interest charges are lower. Thus the total debt service payments are relatively constant for taxpayers each year. The service charges on the debt, however, are not the only capital cost borne by the taxpayers.

Table 19–6 Debt service schedule

Year	Amortization of principal	Interest	Total debt service charges
1	$ 700,000	$750,000	$1,450,000
2	700,000	715,000	1,435,000
3	800,000	680,000	1,480,000
4	800,000	640,000	1,440,000
5	900,000	600,000	1,500,000
6	900,000	555,000	1,455,000
7	900,000	510,000	1,410,000
8	1,000,000	465,000	1,465,000
9	1,100,000	415,000	1,415,000
10	1,100,000	365,000	1,465,000
11	1,100,000	310,000	1,410,000
12	1,200,000	255,000	1,455,000
13	1,300,000	195,000	1,495,000
14	1,300,000	130,000	1,430,000
15	1,300,000	65,000	1,365,000

Suppose repairs, modifications, and maintenance costs (exclusive of operations) are estimated to be $250,000 in the first year, but will rise at about the rate of $50,000 a year to a total of $950,000 in the fifteenth year. In this case, a flat repayment of the principle in the amount of $1,000,000 per year best serves to equalize annual capital costs. The capital cost schedule would appear as shown in Table 19–7.

Table 19–7 Capital cost schedule

Year	Amortization of principal	Interest	Total debt service	Maintenance and repair	Total capital cost
1	$1,000,000	$750,000	$1,750,000	$250,000	$2,000,000
2	1,000,000	700,000	1,700,000	300,000	2,000,000
3	1,000,000	650,000	1,650,000	350,000	2,000,000
⋮					
14	1,000,000	100,000	1,100,000	900,000	2,000,000
15	1,000,000	50,000	1,050,000	950,000	2,000,000

Although the debt service charges decline over the life of the facility, this is a more equitable method of spreading the costs. The early users have the advantage of using new capital and pay somewhat heavier debt service charges. The later users are compensated for the declining efficiency of the installation with lower financing costs.

Miscellaneous capital projects

In recent years, there has been a spate of what may be called "pass-through" financing of bond issues. This has involved local finance officers and planning personnel in some very sophisticated financial dealings.

A pass-through finance project may be defined as one where the state or local government lends its credit and tax-free status to some other institution or private enterprise without taking responsibility for the final outcome. Thus, for example, a nonprofit hospital may wish to finance an expansion of its facilities. The city may float bonds for the necessary amount and turn the funds over to the hospital. The obligation to repay interest and principle rests with the hospital. There may be an insurance fund to help repay the debt; nevertheless the indenture may clearly state that neither the city nor the state nor any political subdivision is in any way pledged to repay the bonds.

Another type of pass-through bond may involve a leveraged lease for a new building to be constructed in a development area. A private individual or consortium may furnish the initial equity capital; the local government will sell bonds to the bank to cover the mortgage; and the leasor undertakes to pay a rental fee sufficient both to cover the mortgage (and thus retire the bonds) and to pay a return to the equity investors. The leasor receives the low, tax-free rate on the mortgage; the bank receives tax-free interest; and the equity holders have the tax advantages provided by the investment tax credit and accelerated depreciation. The gain to the local government is that by putting this package together, an employer has been induced to relocate to a redevelopment area.

Housing authority bonds involve lending funds raised by the sale of tax-free bonds to private housing lenders (e.g., banks and savings and loans associations). These financial institutions will then re-lend the money to private home buyers at a relatively low rate. There was a considerable volume of these bonds issued in the late seventies, but Congress has severely reduced the amount of eligible bonding in this category.

Although these classes of bonds legally are not obligations of the sponsoring governments, local governments should be extremely cautious about entering into such financing schemes. The security and the probability of the repayment plan should be checked meticulously. Having lent the local government's name to the transaction, municipal officials cannot be sure that the municipality will not end up with a "moral obligation" to repay in the event that the primary borrowers default on their payments.

From an overall view, the housing finance bonds appear particularly pernicious. Essentially, they favor one class of borrower over another; they merely shift funds around. If they help one part of the housing market, they hurt another part of the market, or they harm some other "worthy" class of borrowers (e.g., the public utilities) by reducing the available credit and raising the interest rates on the issue of regular bonds. Nevertheless, once Congress authorizes the use of tax-free bonds for such purposes as subsidized private mortgages, it is probably competitively advantageous for any single locality to make use of the device. Indeed, this is probably the worse part of the whole scheme.

The capital budget and the fiscal plan

Several interrelated factors, some of which are economic, and others of which are fiscal, determine the local government's capital budget and fiscal plan.

The initial step is to implement rules for selecting capital projects. This involves some quantification of benefit flows, the proper use of the concept of present value, and the correct estimate of the social discount rate. Only projects with a positive net present value of benefits should be put into the capital improvement program.

Second, the fiscal counterpart of the capital project selection process is the forecast of the fiscal capacity of the responsible local government. Will the predicted growth of local revenues and wealth carry the service charges on the debt incurred to finance the capital improvements? Although the measurement of fiscal capacity is considered an independent test and, indeed, allows for the use of more objective data than the estimated benefits involved in the net present value analysis of project selection, the two tests are probably organically related. For if the project is economically desirable, then in one way or another it should generate sufficient social wealth to finance its carrying costs.

In the case of revenue bonds—which are becoming more prevalent today—the projected level of user charges or rents is substituted for the estimate of community benefits. The level of revenue inflows must cover repair and operating costs and return a sufficient amount to cover the interest charges and the amortization of debt equal to the investment in the project.

Third, on the grounds of intergenerational equity and equity between in- and out-migrants, long-term debt is the indicated method for financing local long-lived capital projects. The operational counterpart of this concept requires that the debt issue be tailored to the useful life of the project so that bonds are retired at the same rate as the capital is worn out. In short, this means that serial bonds should be used and that the periodic amount of bonds retired should be correlated to the time reduction in the economic value of the project. (When this is done properly, there is no need for the use of depreciation in a purely governmental accounting system.)

Serial bond financing leads to intergenerational equity because, in each time period, the receivers of the benefits pay the equivalent of the user costs. The current generation is not constrained to reduce its income to transfer wealth to the future. This would occur if current taxes were used to pay for the capital improvement. Nor is the reverse true; when serial bond financing is used, the current generation cannot enjoy the present services of capital improvements and leave to future generations the burden of retiring a balloon payment at the end of the asset's life.

The problem of equity between new residents and out-migrants is analogous to that of intergenerational equity. When local debt is properly used, the new resident takes up the financing burden in his or her taxes. The resident also has the benefits of the remaining life of the community assets. The out-migrant paid for his or her share of capital use during his or her residency.

Finally, the capital improvement program cannot be thought of only in financial terms. The objective of the program is to plan for a level of social capital such that the municipality maintains a viable economic base and provides those amenities necessary for the well-being of its citizens. The final audit test of a successful program is that, at the end of the planning horizon, the local government shows a relative improvement in indicators of private wealth, economic activity, health, education, and social contentment.

1   For a more detailed discussion, see: Eli Schwartz, "The Cost of Capital and Investment Criteria in the Public Sector," *Journal of Finance* 25 (March 1970):135–42.

2   Sanford M. Groves, *Evaluating Financial Condition: An Executive Overview for Local Government*, handbook no. 1 in *Evaluating Local Government Financial Condition*, by Sanford M. Groves and W. Maureen Godsey, 5 handbooks (Washington, D.C.: International City Management Association, 1980), p. 15.

3   Ibid., pp. 11–19.

4   For further analysis of pay-as-you-go versus pay-as-you-use financing, see: James A. Maxwell and J. Richard Aronson, "The State and Local Capital Budget in Theory and Practice," *National Tax Journal* 20 (June 1967):165–70; and J. Richard Aronson, "A Comment on Optimality in Local Debt Limitation," *National Tax Journal* 24 (March 1971):107–108.

Appendix

Risk management
in a small city

Much of the emphasis to date in public sector risk management has been on the needs and problems of large communities, where resources are sufficient to justify and support a full-time risk manager. Small communities, however, face unique problems in implementing a risk management program because of their limited financial and staff resources. How one small community assessed its risk management needs and implemented a program appropriate to its needs and resources is discussed in the following case study.

Kirksville, Missouri (population: 15,443), is one of many communities where the amount of city funds expended for insurance premiums, deductibles, and employee benefits is second only to salaries as the largest fixed cost; but, like most small communities, it cannot justify a full-time risk manager. Generally, the person most likely to perform some or all of the risk management functions has other duties and responsibilities that overshadow risk management. It is all too easy to assume that insurance will take care of itself while dealing with the more pressing issues of personnel, finance, budgeting, recordkeeping, and other day-to-day administrative activities.

Because of the increased exposure due to the loss of sovereign immunity and the additional role cities play in providing leisure-time activities, code enforcement, workers compensation claims, and other potential loss areas, the old method of letting insurance take care of itself simply will not work. The simultaneous challenges of increased expectations for expanded services, spiraling inflation, and community pressure to reduce expenditures have forced cities to evaluate seriously a more effective use of insurance dollars. Kirksville is currently in the process of correcting the heretofore self-perpetuating deficiencies through the establishment of risk management policies and methods to assure that its insurance program will be appropriately monitored and implemented.

Determining Problem Areas

After extensive research and evaluation of our program, four areas surfaced as the most serious obstacles to the successful implementation of a risk management program using existing staff and resources.

The first problem that had to be addressed was to develop a clear-cut policy on what to insure and for how much. It was fruitless to attack the problem of risk exposure until it was determined to what extent risk could be assumed and where the various exposures existed. A thorough inventory of existing property, buildings and vehicles, and detailed loss records was mandatory to make the best decisions regarding needed changes in risk coverage. This was a time-consuming task and one that proved frustrating because of the unavailability of information.

Once the information had been gathered, the person most responsible for risk management needed to review the data and formulate some recommendations for the city council. Some of the policy considerations included: (1) whether to insure vehicles over a certain age for damages; (2) what level of deductible should the city assume for property and liability insurance; and (3) what type of blanket coverages could be utilized.

After these decisions were made, the individual policies were recorded. This served as the foundation for a risk management manual. The manual outlined all of the major provisions of the policy and was reviewed with the entire management staff.

The second problem dovetailed with the first. After researching and documenting the current inventory of property and vehicles, the inventory data were compared with current insurance policies. We found we had too many agents, policies, and decentralization of knowledge. As of the first part of 1979, the city had twenty-five separate policies with eighteen companies and thirteen different agents. Additionally, it was found that many facilities were not insured: a fire station, the waste-water treatment plant, and the airport T-hangars.

A simple grouping by policy type (i.e., fire, boiler and machinery, inland marine, general liability, and public officials liability) exposed much in the way of duplicate coverage or no coverage at all. Reading policies to determine the exceptions and levels of coverage led to items that needed clarification by city policy; for example: does the general liability policy exclude product liability? This could be a problem if the city operates a utility.

Competitive bidding has been the prescription for many insurance ills in recent years. It is true that competitive rates are desirable, but there are hidden dangers to placing insurance out for bid. The first is the design of the bid specifications. There are boilerplate specifications for certain coverages available. These may or may not reflect the desires of the city. Many communities use a selection board for development of specifications and placement, which is an excellent idea if qualified persons, other than current or future agents, sit on the board.

The recent trend has been not to select agents or individual policies but, through prequalification review, to use agents, brokers, or large brokerage firms. This solution could cause considerable problems in a small community when the prevalent feeling is to "keep the business in town." The key area to review is that of service. If a local agent has provided excellent service in the past and can present a competitive bid proposal, that should be of prime consideration.

One final pitfall of bidding coverage is that of duplicate bids from different agents using the same insurance company. The best way to combat this is to ask for an "agent of record" for any companies that may bid on the package. Kirksville, for instance, experienced this problem with three agents using the same low bid company.

The third area most likely to become a problem in a small community is that of failing to update policy coverage amounts at the time of renewal. This can happen whether a risk management manual is in effect or not; it is simply a part of good risk management. Most property insurance policies contain two important pieces of information on the face of the document. The first is the property covered, for what amount, and on what basis (either replacement cost or actual cash value). The second item is the coinsurance clause. Both of these items can cause an unpleasant surprise at the time of a loss.

The past practice has been to have an independent appraiser establish the actual cash value of an existing structure prior to the award or renewal of the policy. Although a good idea, the cost for this appraisal can be prohibitive for a small community. One less expensive method is for city staff to use a "costimator"—an annual booklet published by some insurance companies that provides a per square foot cost estimate based on utilization and construction material. When awarding or renewing a policy, requesting the "Agreed Amount Endorsement" (that figure derived from the "costimator") can help solve this ongoing problem because the insurer is, in effect, agreeing that the value stated in the policy is an acceptable one.

The mistake of not updating a policy's face value and not having an Agreed Amount Endorsement can cause serious problems when a loss occurs. The coinsurance penalty, very simply stated, is the insured agreeing to absorb a portion of a loss (generally 10 percent to 20 percent) based on the current value of the structure at the time of loss. For example, Kirksville had for many years insured its city hall for $110,000. Based on costimator calculations, the building and contents were worth $775,000. Such underinsurance could have caused a serious financial loss. If a $50,000 loss had occurred, the city could only have recovered $8,871. Under the recently awarded insurance, using Agreed Amount Endorsements, the entire loss can be recovered.

The final challenge for the small community is one of ongoing review and loss control efforts.

A good reporting system, coupled with safety efforts and accident review, can make a community a more attractive client to an insurance company. In fact, even though most premiums are calculated by standard rates, the companies can use such fudge factors as experience, longevity, safety programs, and other catch phrases that allow them to adjust rates.

Kirksville has recently established two committees, the Accident Review Committee composed of five department heads, and the Safety Committee, a spinoff responsibility of the Employees Council. The Accident Review Committee reviews each property or personal injury, makes recommendations to reduce the likelihood of reccurrence, determines if the accident was preventable, and through the appropriate department head, recommends discipline based on approved guidelines.

The Safety Committee brings potentially dangerous situations to the attention of management. Most insurance companies will provide a safety engineer to help educate employees and establish a safety program.

All recommendations from both committees

are brought before the city manager periodically for review in light of fiscal constraints for improvements and severe employee disciplinary actions. To date, a 30 percent reduction in the number of accidents as compared with last year has been experienced.

Results

Risk management for small communities is unique in some ways but many of the methods for larger communities can be applied. The four most important considerations to address are: (1) the establishment of a clear-cut policy from management concerning insurance and safety management; (2) the reduction of excessive numbers of policies and agents to take advantage of blanket rates and policies; (3) the need to review annually policy amounts and coinsurance clauses to keep penalties to a minimum; and (4) the establishment of a good reporting system and loss control efforts.

This appendix is based on coverage in Chapter 17, "Inventory, Purchasing, and Risk Management."

Source: Michael J. Smith, "Risk Management Program," *Current Approaches to Risk Management: A Directory of Practices*, ed. Paula R. Valente, Management Information Service Special Report no. 7 (Washington, D.C.: International City Management Association, 1980), pp. 11–13. This article originally appeared in the *Missouri Municipal Review*, April 1980.

Bibliography

The following bibliography is selective, including basic and introductory references. Many additional books, periodical articles, and other references are cited in the endnotes to the individual chapters.

1 The Finance Function in Local Government

Adrian, Charles R., and Press, Charles. *Governing Urban America*. 5th ed. New York: McGraw-Hill Book Co., 1977.

Banovetz, James M., ed. *Managing the Modern City*. Washington, D.C.: International City Management Association, 1971.

Buchanan, James M. *Public Finance in Democratic Process*. Chapel Hill: University of North Carolina Press, 1967.

Crecine, John. *Financing the Metropolis: Public Policy in Urban Economics*. Beverly Hills, Calif.: Sage Publications, 1970.

Due, John F., and Friedlaender, Ann F. *Government Finance: Economics of the Public Sector*. 6th ed. Homewood, Ill.: Richard D. Irwin, 1977.

Ecker-Racz, L. I. *The Politics and Economics of State-Local Finance*. Englewood Cliffs, N.J.: Prentice-Hall, 1970.

Greene, Kenneth V.; Neenan, William B.; and Scott, Claudia. *Fiscal Interaction in a Metropolitan Area*. Lexington, Mass.: Lexington Books, 1974.

Maxwell, James A., and Aronson, J. Richard. *Financing State and Local Governments*. 3d ed. Washington, D.C.: Brookings Institution, 1977.

Mendosa, Arthur A. *Simplified Financial Management in Local Government*. Athens: Institute of Government, University of Georgia, 1969.

Moak, Lennox L., and Hillhouse, Albert M. *Concepts and Practices in Local Government Finance*. Chicago: Municipal Finance Officers Association, 1975.

Musgrave, Richard A., and Musgrave, Peggy. *Public Finance in Theory and Practice*. 3d ed. New York: McGraw-Hill Book Co., 1980.

Sharkansky, Ira. *Spending in the American States*. Chicago: Rand McNally & Co., 1970.

U.S. Advisory Commission on Intergovernmental Relations. *Federal-State-Local Finances: Significant Features of Fiscal Federalism*. Washington, D.C.: Government Printing Office, 1980.

2 Local Government Expenditures

Aronson, J. Richard, and Schwartz, Eli. *Forecasting Future Expenditures*. Management Information Service Reports, vol. 2, no. S–11. Washington, D.C.: International City Management Association, 1970.

Baumol, William J. "Macroeconomics of Unbalanced Growth." *American Economic Review*, June 1967.

Bradford, D.; Malt, R.; and Oates, W. "The Rising Cost of Local Public Services: Some Evidence and Reflections." *National Tax Journal* 22, no. 2 (June 1969): 185–202.

Buchanan, James M.; and Flowers, Marilyn R. *The Public Finances: An Introductory Textbook*. 4th ed. Homewood, Ill.: Richard D. Irwin, 1975.

Burkhead, Jesse, and Minor, Jerry. *Public Expenditure*. Chicago: Aldine-Atherton, 1971.

Maxwell, James A., and Aronson, J. Richard. *Financing State and Local Governments*. 3d ed. Washington, D.C.: Brookings Institution, 1977.

McKean, Roland N. *Public Spending*. New York: McGraw-Hill Book Co., 1968.

Oates, Wallace E. *Fiscal Federalism*. New York: Harcourt Brace Jovanovich, 1972.

Scott, Claudia DeVita. *Forecasting Local Government Spending*. Chicago: Municipal Finance Officers Association, 1972.

U.S. Advisory Commission on Intergovernmental Relations. *State Mandating of Local Expenditures*. A–67. Washington, D.C.: Government Printing Office, 1978.

3 Local Government Revenues

Aronson, J. Richard, and Schwartz, Eli. *Forecasting Future Revenues.* Management Information Service Reports, vol. 2, no. S–7. Washington, D.C.: International City Management Association, 1970.

Break, George F. *Agenda for Local Tax Reform.* Berkeley: Institute of Governmental Studies, University of California, 1970.

Goetz, Charles J. *What Is Revenue Sharing?* Washington, D.C.: The Urban Institute, 1972.

Juster, F. Thomas, ed. *The Economic and Political Impact of General Revenue Sharing.* Ann Arbor: Survey Research Center, Institute for Social Research, University of Michigan, 1977.

MacManus, Susan A. *Revenue Patterns in U.S. Cities and Suburbs: A Comparative Analysis.* New York: Praeger Publishers, 1978.

Maxwell, James A., and Aronson, J. Richard. *Financing State and Local Governments.* 3d ed. Washington, D.C.: Brookings Institution, 1977.

Meltsner, Arnold. *The Politics of City Revenue.* Berkeley: University of California Press, 1971.

Municipal Finance Officers Association. *Accounting Manual for Federal General Revenue Sharing.* Chicago: Municipal Finance Officers Association, 1974.

Musgrave, Richard A., ed. *Broad-Based Taxes: New Options and Sources.* Baltimore: Johns Hopkins University Press, 1973.

Nathan, Richard P., and Adams, Charles F., Jr. *Revenue Sharing: The Second Round.* Washington, D.C.: Brookings Institution, 1977.

Pechman, Joseph A., and Okner, Benjamin A. *Who Bears the Tax Burden?* Washington, D.C.: Brookings Institution, 1974.

Scott, Claudia DeVita. *Forecasting Local Government Spending.* Chicago: Municipal Finance Officers Association, 1972.

Tax Foundation. *Big City Revenue Structures in Transition.* New York: Tax Foundation, 1972.

U.S. Advisory Commission on Intergovernmental Relations. *General Revenue Sharing: An ACIR Reevaluation.* A–48. Washington, D.C.: Government Printing Office, 1974.

———. *Measuring the Fiscal Capacity and Effort of State and Local Areas.* M–58. Washington, D.C.: Government Printing Office, 1971.

———. *Significant Features of Fiscal Federalism: 1976–1977 Edition. Vol. II—Revenue and Debt.* M–110. Washington, D.C.: Government Printing Office, 1977.

———. *Significant Features of Fiscal Federalism: 1976–1977 Edition. Vol. III—Expenditures.* M–113. Washington, D.C.: Government Printing Office, 1977.

———. *Significant Features of Fiscal Federalism: 1978–79 Edition.* M–115. Washington, D.C.: Government Printing Office, 1979.

———. *State Limitations on Local Taxes and Expenditures.* A–64. Washington, D.C.: Government Printing Office, 1977.

4 Forecasting Local Revenues and Expenditures

Helmer, Olaf. *The Use of the Delphi Technique—Problems of Educational Innovations.* Santa Monica, Calif.: Rand Corp., 1966.

Kmenta, Jan. *Elements of Econometrics.* New York: Macmillan Co., 1971.

Kraemer, Kenneth L. *Policy Analysis in Local Government.* Washington, D.C.: International City Management Association, 1973.

Madere, L. E. *Municipal Budget Projections, Econometric Revenue Forecasting.* City of New Orleans: Office of Economic Analysis, 1977.

Makridakis, Spyros, and Wheelwright, Steven C. *Forecasting: Methods and Applications.* New York: John Wiley & Sons, 1978.

Murphy, James L. *Introductory Econometrics.* Homewood, Ill.: Richard D. Irwin, 1973.

Pindyck, Robert S., and Rubinfeld, Daniel L. *Econometric Models and Economic Forecasts.* New York: McGraw-Hill Book Co., 1976.

Ross, John, and Burkhead, Jesse. *Productivity in the Local Government Sector.* Lexington, Mass.: Lexington Books, 1974.

Sjoquist, David L.; Schroeder, Larry D.; and Stephan, Paula E. *Interpreting Linear Regression Analysis: An Heuristic Approach.* Morristown, N.J.: General Learning Corp., 1974.

Wheelwright, Steven C., and Makridakis, Spyros. *Forecasting Methods for Management.* 2d ed. New York: John Wiley & Sons, 1977.

Wonnocott, Thomas H., and Wonnocott, Ronald J. *Introductory Statistics for Business and Economics.* New York: John Wiley & Sons, 1977.

5 Budgeting

Burkhead, Jesse, and Bringewatt, Paul. *Municipal Budgeting: A Primer for the Local Official.* Washington, D.C.: Joint Center for Political Studies, 1977.

Crecine, John P. *Government Problem Solving: A Computer Simulation of Municipal Budgeting.* Chicago: Rand McNally & Co., 1969.

Friedman, Lewis. *Budgeting Municipal Expenditures: A Study in Comparative Policy Making.* New York: Praeger Publishers, 1975.

Kraemer, Kenneth L., et al. *Integrated Municipal Information Systems: The Use of the Computer in Local Governments.* New York: Praeger Publishers, 1974.

Lee, James. *A Planning, Programming, and Budgeting Manual: Resource Allocation in Public Sector Economics.* New York: Praeger Publishers, 1974.

Lee, Robert D., Jr., and Johnson, Ronald W. *Public Budgeting Systems.* Baltimore: University Park Press, 1973.

Lindholm, Richard W., and Wignjowijoto, Hartojo. *Financing and Managing State and Local Government.* Chapters 5–9. Lexington, Mass.: Lexington Books, 1979.

Lynch, Thomas D. *Public Budgeting in America.* Englewood Cliffs, N.J.: Prentice-Hall, 1979.

Lynden, Fremont J., and Mills, Ernest G., eds. *Public Budgeting: Program Planning and Evaluation.* Chicago: Rand McNally College Publishing Co., 1978.

Moak, Lennox L., and Hillhouse, Albert M. *Concepts and Practices in Local Government Finance.* Chicago: Municipal Finance Officers Association, 1975.

Moak, Lennox L., and Killian, Kathryn W. *Operating Budget Manual.* Chicago: Municipal Finance Officers Association, 1963.

————. *Manual of Techniques for the Preparation, Adoption and Administration of Operating Budgeting.* Chicago: Municipal Finance Officers Association, 1973.

Municipal Finance Officers Association. *An Operating Budget Handbook for Small Cities and Other Governmental Units.* Chicago: Municipal Finance Officers Association, 1978.

————. *Total Municipal Information Systems.* Chicago: Municipal Finance Officers Association, 1970.

Sharkansky, Ira. *The Politics of Taxing and Spending.* Indianapolis: Bobbs-Merrill Co., 1969.

Urban Institute and International City Management Association. *Measuring the Effectiveness of Basic Municipal Services: Initial Report.* Washington, D.C.: The Urban Institute and International City Management Association, 1974.

Wanat, John. *Introduction to Budgeting.* North Scituate, Mass.: Duxbury Press, 1978.

Wildavsky, Aaron. *The Politics of the Budgetary Process.* Boston: Little, Brown & Co., 1964.

6 The Property Tax

Aaron, Henry J. *Who Pays the Property Tax?* Washington, D.C.: Brookings Institution, 1975.

Break, George F., ed. *Metropolitan Financing and Growth Management Policies.* Madison: University of Wisconsin Press, 1978.

Case, Karl E. *Property Taxation: The Need for Reform.* Cambridge, Mass.: Ballinger Publishing Co., 1978.

Church, Albert M., and Gustafson, Robert H. *Statistics and Computers in the Appraisal Process.* Chicago: International Association of Assessing Officers, 1976.

Gold, Steven D. *Property Tax Relief.* Lexington, Mass.: D.C. Heath, 1979.

Holland, Daniel M., ed. *The Assessment of Land Value.* Madison: University of Wisconsin Press, 1970.

International Association of Assessing Officers. *Analyzing Assessment Equity: Techniques for Measuring and Improving the Quality of Property Tax Administration.* Chicago: International Association of Assessing Officers, 1977.

————. *Automated Mass Appraisal of Real Property.* Chicago: International Association of Assessing Officers, 1974.

————. *Improving Real Property Assessment.* Chicago: International Association of Assessing Officers, 1978.

————. *Property Tax Reform: The Role of the Property Tax in the Nation's Revenue System.* Chicago: International Association of Assessing Officers, 1974.

Lindholm, R., ed. *Property Taxation and the Finance of Education.* Madison: University of Wisconsin Press, 1974.

Lindholm, Richard W. *Property Taxation USA.* Madison: University of Wisconsin Press, 1967.

Lynn, Arthur D. *The Property Tax and Its Administration.* Madison: University of Wisconsin Press, 1969.

Netzer, Dick. *Economics of the Property Tax*. Washington, D.C.: Brookings Institution, 1966.

Paul, Diane B. *The Politics of the Property Tax*. Lexington, Mass.: Lexington Books, 1975.

Peterson, George E., et al. *Property Taxes, Housing and the Cities*. Lexington, Mass.: Lexington Books, 1973.

Research and Technical Services Department. International Association of Assessing Officers. *Understanding Real Property Assessment: An Executive Summary for Local Government Officials*. Chicago: International Association of Assessing Officers, 1979.

Schroeder, Larry D., and Sjoquist, David L. *The Property Tax and Alternative Local Taxes: An Economic Analysis*. New York: Praeger Publishers, 1975.

U.S. Advisory Commission on Intergovernmental Relations. *Financing Schools and Property Tax Relief—A State Responsibility*. A–40. Washington, D.C.: Government Printing Office, 1973.

———. *Property Tax Circuit-Breakers: Current Status and Policy Issues*. M–87. Washington, D.C.: Government Printing Office, 1975.

7 Sales Taxes, Income Taxes, and Other Revenues

Commonwealth of Pennsylvania. Department of Community Affairs. *The Administration of Local Earned Income Tax*. Harrisburg: Commonwealth of Pennsylvania, 1971.

Due, John F. *Sales Taxation*. Urbana: University of Illinois Press, 1957.

———. *State and Local Sales Taxation: Structure and Administration*. Chicago: Public Administration Service, 1971.

Lindholm, Richard W., and Wignjowijoto, Hartojo. *Financing and Managing State and Local Government*. Chapters 24–28. Lexington, Mass.: Lexington Books, 1979.

Moak, Lennox L., and Cowan, Frank, Jr. *Manual of Suggested Practice for Administration of Local Sales and Use Taxes*. Chicago: Municipal Finance Officers Association, 1961.

Sigafoos, Robert A. *The Municipal Income Tax: Its History and Problems*. Chicago: Public Administration Service, 1955.

Smith, R. Stafford. *Local Income Taxes: Economic Effects and Equity*. Berkeley: Institute of Governmental Studies, University of California, 1972.

Tax Institute of America. *Business Taxes in State and Local Governments*. Lexington, Mass.: Lexington Books, 1972.

U.S. Advisory Commission on Intergovernmental Relations. *Local Nonproperty Taxes and the Coordinating Role of the State, A Commission Report*. A–9. Washington, D.C.: Government Printing Office, 1961.

———. *Local Revenue Diversification: Income, Sales Taxes and User Charges*. A–47. Washington, D.C.: Government Printing Office, 1974.

8 User Charges and Special Districts

Bird, Richard M. *Charging for Public Services: A New Look at an Old Idea*. Toronto: Canadian Tax Foundation, 1976.

Bollens, J. C. *Special District Governments in the United States*. Berkeley: University of California Press, 1957.

Downing, Paul B., ed. *Local Service Prices and Their Effect on Urban Spacial Structure*. Vancouver: University of British Columbia Press, 1977.

Fisher, Glenn W. *Financing Local Improvements by Special Assessment*. Chicago: Municipal Finance Officers Association, 1974.

Goetz, Charles J. "The Revenue Potential of User-Related Charges in State and Local Governments." In *Broad-Based Taxes: New Options and Sources,* edited by Richard A. Musgrave. Baltimore: Johns Hopkins University Press, 1973.

Mushkin, Selma, ed. *Public Prices for Public Products*. Washington, D.C.: The Urban Institute, 1972.

Pock, Max A. *Independent Special Districts: A Solution to Metropolitan Area Problems*. Ann Arbor: University of Michigan Law School, 1962.

Tax Foundation. *Special Assessment and Service Charges in Municipal Finance*. Government Finance Brief 20. New York: Tax Foundation, 1970.

Turvey, Ralph, ed. *Public Enterprise*. Harmondsworth, Middlesex, England: Penguin Books, 1968.

U.S. Advisory Commission on Intergovernmental Relations. *Local Revenue Diversification: Income, Sales Taxes and User Charges*. A–47. Washington, D.C.: Government Printing Office, 1974.

———. *Regional Decision Making: New Strategies for Substate Districts.* A–43. Washington, D.C.: Government Printing Office, 1973.

———. *Improving Urban America: A Challenge to Federalism.* M–107. Washington, D.C.: Government Printing Office, 1976.

9 Fiscal Problems of Political Boundaries

Aronson, J. Richard, and Schwartz, Eli. "Financing Public Goods and the Distribution of Population in a System of Local Governments." *National Tax Journal* 26 (June 1973):137–60.

Bahl, Roy, ed. *The Fiscal Outlook for Cities.* Syracuse, N.Y.: Syracuse University Press, 1978.

Banfield, Edward. *The Unheavenly City Revisited.* Boston: Little, Brown & Co., 1974.

Downs, Anthony. *Urban Problems and Prospects.* Chicago: Markham Publishing Co., 1970.

Glazer, Nathan, ed. *Cities in Trouble.* Chicago: Quadrangle Books, 1970.

Goodall, Leonard E., and Sprengel, Donald P. *The American Metropolis.* 2d ed. Columbus, Ohio: Charles E. Merrill Publishing Co., 1976.

Hawley, Amos, and Rock, Vincent, eds. *Metropolitan America.* New York: Halsted Press, 1975.

Hirsch, Werner Z. *The Economics of State and Local Governments.* New York: McGraw-Hill Book Co., 1970.

Hirsch, Werner Z., et al. *Fiscal Pressures on the Central City: The Impact of Commuters, Nonwhites, and Overlapping Governments.* New York: Praeger Publishers, 1971.

Meyer, John; Kain, John; and Wohl, Martin. *The Urban Transportation Problem.* Cambridge, Mass.: Harvard University Press, 1965.

Murphy, Thomas P., and Warren, Charles R. *Organizing Public Services in Metropolitan America.* Lexington, Mass.: Lexington Books, 1974.

Netzer, Dick. *Economics and Urban Problems: Diagnoses and Prescriptions.* New York: Basic Books, 1970.

Thomlinson, Ralph. *Urban Structure: The Social and Spatial Structure of Cities.* New York: Random House, 1969.

U.S. Advisory Commission on Intergovernmental Relations. *City Financial Emergencies: The Intergovernmental Dimension.* Washington, D.C.: Government Printing Office, 1973.

10 Fiscal Structure in the Federal System

Break, George F. *Financing Government in a Federal System.* Washington, D.C.: Brookings Institution, 1980.

Cole, Richard L., and Caputo, David A. *Urban Politics and Decentralization: The Case of General Revenue-Sharing.* Lexington, Mass.: Lexington Books, 1974.

Glendening, Parris N., and Reeves, Mavis Mann. *Pragmatic Federalism: An Intergovernmental View of American Government.* Pacific Palisades, Calif.: Palisades Publishers, 1977.

Heller, Walter W. *New Dimensions of Political Economy.* New York: W. W. Norton & Co., 1966.

Maxwell, James A., and Aronson, J. Richard. *Financing State and Local Governments.* 3d ed. Washington, D.C.: Brookings Institution, 1977.

Oates, Wallace E. *Fiscal Federalism.* New York: Harcourt Brace Jovanovich, 1972.

Oates, Wallace, ed. *Financing the New Federalism: Revenue Sharing, Conditional Grants and Taxation.* Baltimore: Johns Hopkins University Press, 1975.

Oates, Wallace E., ed. *The Political Economy of Fiscal Federalism.* Lexington, Mass.: Lexington Books, 1977.

U.S. Advisory Commission on Intergovernmental Relations. *Block Grants: A Comparative Analysis.* A–60. Washington, D.C.: Government Printing Office, 1977.

———. *Block Grants: A Roundtable Discussion.* A–51. Washington, D.C.: Government Printing Office, 1976.

———. *Categorical Grants: Their Role and Design.* A–52. Washington, D.C.: Government Printing Office, 1978.

———. *Community Development: The Workings of a Federal-Local Block Grant.* A–57. Washington, D.C.: Government Printing Office, 1977.

———. *Fiscal Balance in the American Federal System.* 2 vols. Washington, D.C.: Government Printing Office, 1967.

———. *Improving Federal Grants Management.* A–53. Washington, D.C.: Government Printing Office, 1977.

————. *Safe Streets Reconsidered: The Block Grant Experience—1968–1975.* A–55. Washington, D.C.: Government Printing Office, 1977.

————. *Safe Streets Reconsidered: The Block Grant Experience—1968–1975: Part B, Case Studies.* A–55a. Washington, D.C.: Government Printing Office, 1977.

————. *The State and Intergovernmental Aids.* A–59. Washington, D.C.: Government Printing Office, 1977.

————. *Summary and Concluding Observations.* A–62. Washington, D.C.: Government Printing Office, 1978.

11 Fiscal Structure of Local Authorities in Britain

Brittain, Herbert. *The British Budgeting System.* New York: Macmillan Co., 1959.

Clarke, Sir Richard. *New Trends in Government.* Lectures delivered by Sir Richard Clarke at the Civil Service College between 1 March and 5 April 1971. London: Her Majesty's Stationery Office, 1971.

The Finance of Education. Walton Hall, Milton Keynes, Great Britain: Open University Press, 1977.

Hicks, Ursula Kathleen (Webb). *British Public Finances, Their Structure and Development, 1880–1952.* London: Oxford University Press, 1954.

Richards, Peter G. *The Reformed Local Government System.* Reading, Mass.: Allen & Unwin, 1975.

12 Managing Financial Condition

Aronson, J. Richard. *Municipal Fiscal Indicators.* Information Bulletin of the Management, Finance and Personnel Task Force of the Urban Consortium. Washington, D.C.: U.S. Department of Housing and Urban Development, 1979.

Aronson, J. Richard, and King, A. E. "Is There a Fiscal Crisis Outside of New York?" *National Tax Journal* 31, no. 2 (June 1978):153–64.

Aronson, J. Richard, and Schwartz, Eli. *Determining Debt's Danger Signals.* Management Information Service Reports, vol. 8, no. 12. Washington, D.C.: International City Management Association, 1976.

Bahl, Roy, ed. *The Fiscal Outlook for Cities.* Syracuse, N.Y.: Syracuse University Press, 1978.

Clark, Terry N., et al. *How Many New Yorks?* Comparative Study of Community Decision-Making, report no. 72. Chicago: University of Chicago, 22 April 1976.

Coopers & Lybrand. *Financial Disclosure Practices of the American Cities: Closing the Communications Gap.* Boston and New York: Coopers & Lybrand, 1978.

Dearborn, Philip M. *Elements of Municipal Financial Analysis.* Special report, parts 1–4. Boston: First Boston Corp., 1977.

Galambos, Eva C., and Schreiber, Arthur L. *Making Sense Out of Dollars: Economic Analysis for Local Government.* Washington, D.C.: National League of Cities, 1978.

Mansfield, Roger. "The Financial Reporting Practices of Government: A Time for Reflection." *Public Administration Review* 39, no. 2 (March–April 1979):157–62.

Moody's Investors Service, Inc. *Pitfalls in Issuing Municipal Bonds.* New York: Moody's Investors Service, 1977.

Municipal Finance Officers Association. *Is Your City Heading for Financial Difficulty?: A Guidebook for Small Cities and Other Governmental Units.* Chicago: Municipal Finance Officers Association, 1979.

Peterson, George. *The Economic and Fiscal Accompaniments of Population Change.* Syracuse, N.Y.: Metropolitan Studies Program, Syracuse University, 1979.

Peterson, George, et al. *Urban Fiscal Monitoring.* Washington, D.C.: The Urban Institute, 1978.

Sherwood, Hugh. *How Corporate and Municipal Debt is Rated: An Inside Look at Standard and Poor's Rating System.* New York: John Wiley & Sons, 1976.

Smith, Wade S. *The Appraisal of Municipal Credit Risks.* New York: Moody's Investors Service, 1979.

Twentieth Century Fund. *The Rating Game: Report of the Twentieth Century Fund Task Force on Municipal Bond Credit Ratings.* New York: Twentieth Century Fund, 1974.

U.S. Advisory Commission on Intergovernmental Relations. *City Financial Emergencies: The Intergovernmental Dimension.* Washington, D.C.: Government Printing Office, 1973.

13 Debt Management

Calvert, Gordon L., ed. *Fundamentals of Municipal Bonds.* 9th ed. Washington, D.C.: Securities Industry Association, 1972.

Center for Capital Market Research. *Improving Bidding Rules to Reduce Interest Costs in the Competitive Sale of Municipal Bonds.* Eugene: College of Business Administration, University of Oregon, 1977.

———. *Planning, Designing and Selling General Obligation Bonds in Oregon: A Guide to Local Issuers.* Eugene: University of Oregon, 1978.

Davidson, Sidney, et al. *Financial Reporting by State and Local Units.* Chicago: University of Chicago Press, 1977.

Doty, Robert W., and Petersen, John E. "The Federal Securities Laws and Transactions in Municipal Securities," *Northwestern Law Review,* July–August 1976, pp. 283–412.

Hopewell, Michael H., and Benson, Earl D. *Alternate Methods of Estimating the Cost of Inefficient Bids on Serial Municipal Bond Issues.* Eugene: College of Business Administration, University of Oregon, 1975.

Moak, Lennox L. *Administration of Local Government Debt.* Chicago: Municipal Finance Officers Association, 1970.

Municipal Finance Officers Association. *Disclosure Guidelines for Offerings of Securities by State and Local Governments.* Chicago: Municipal Finance Officers Association, 1976.

———. *Guidelines for Use by State and Local Governments in the Preparation of Yearly Information Statements and Other Current Information.* Chicago: Municipal Finance Officers Association, 1978.

———. *Observations Concerning the Rating of Municipal Bonds and Credits.* Chicago: Municipal Finance Officers Association, 1971.

———. *Procedural Statements in Connection with the Disclosure Guidelines for Offerings of Securities by State and Local Governments and the Guidelines for Use by State and Local Governments in the Preparation of Yearly Information Statements and Other Current Information.* Chicago: Municipal Finance Officers Association, 1978.

———. *State and Local Government Finance and Financial Management: A Compendium of Current Research.* Chicago: Municipal Finance Officers Association, 1978.

Mussa, Michael L., and Kormendi, Roger C. *The Taxation of Municipal Bonds.* Washington, D.C.: American Enterprise Institute, 1979.

Rabinowitz, Alan. *Municipal Bond Finance and Administration.* New York: Wiley-Interscience, 1969.

Twentieth Century Fund. *The Rating Game: Report of the Twentieth Century Fund Task Force on Municipal Bond Credit Ratings.* New York: Twentieth Century Fund, 1974.

U.S. Advisory Commission on Intergovernmental Relations. *Understanding the Market for State and Local Debt.* M–104. Washington, D.C.: Government Printing Office, 1976.

14 Cash Management

Aronson, J. Richard. "The Idle Cash Balances of State and Local Governments: An Economic Problem of National Concern." *Journal of Finance* 23 (June 1968):499–508.

Aronson, J. Richard, and Schwartz, Eli. *Improving Cash Management in Municipal Government.* Management Information Service Reports, vol. 1, no. LS–6. Washington, D.C.: International City Managers' Association, 1969.

Deloitte Haskins & Sells Government Services Group. *Implementing Effective Cash Management in Local Government: A Practical Guide.* Chicago: Municipal Finance Officers Association, 1977.

Jones, John A., and Howard, Kenneth S. *Investment of Idle Funds by Local Governments: A Primer.* Chicago: Municipal Finance Officers Association, 1973.

League of California Cities. *Treasury Cash Investment Management.* Sacramento: League of California Cities, 1972.

Monhollon, Jimmie R., and Picou, Glen. *Instruments of the Money Market.* 3d ed. Richmond, Virginia: Federal Reserve Bank of Richmond, 1975.

Orgler, Yair. *Cash Management.* Belmont, Calif.: Wadsworth Publishing Co., 1970.

Twentieth Century Fund. *The Rating Game: Report of the Twentieth Century Fund Task Force on Municipal Bond Credit Ratings.* New York: Twentieth Century Fund, 1974.

U.S. Advisory Commission on Intergovernmental Relations. *Investment of Idle Cash Balances by State and Local Governments: Report A–3.* Washington, D.C.: Government Printing Office, 1961.

———. *Investment of Idle Cash Balances by State and Local Governments: Supplement to Report A–3.* Washington, D.C.: Government Printing Office, 1965.

———. *Understanding State and Local Cash Management.* M–112. Washington, D.C.: Government Printing Office, 1977.

Van Horne, James C. *Financial Management and Policy.* 2d ed. Englewood Cliffs, N.J.: Prentice-Hall, 1971.

15 Collective Bargaining, Wages, and Local Government Finance

Aaron, Benjamin, et al. *Public Sector Bargaining*. Washington, D.C.: Bureau of National Affairs, 1979.

Bent, Alan E., and Reeves, T. Zane. *Collective Bargaining in the Public Sector*. Menlo Park, Calif.: Benjamin-Cummings Publishing Co., 1978.

Corcoran, Kevin, and Kutell, Diane. "Binding Arbitration Laws for State and Municipal Workers." *Monthly Labor Review* 101, no. 10 (October 1978).

Fogel, Walter, and Lewin, David. "Wage Determination in the Public Sector." *Industrial and Labor Relations Review* 27, no. 3 (April 1974).

Gershenfeld, Walter. "An Introduction to the Scope of Bargaining in the Public Sector." In *Scope of Public Sector Bargaining*, edited by Walter Gershenfeld. Lexington, Mass.: Lexington Books, 1977.

Horton, Raymond D. "Productivity and Productivity Bargaining in Government: A Critical Analysis." *Public Administration Review* 36, no. 4 (July–August, 1976):407–14.

Levine, Marin J., and Hagburg, Eugene C. *Labor Relations in the Public Sector: Readings, Cases, and Experimental Exercises*. Salt Lake City: Brighton Publishing Co., 1979.

Lewin, David, et al. *Public Sector Labor Relations: Analysis and Readings*. Glen Ridge, N.J.: Thomas Horton and Daughters, 1977.

Stanley, David. *Managing Local Government Under Union Pressure*. Washington, D.C.: Brookings Institution, 1972.

Stieber, Jack. *Public Employee Unionism*. Washington, D.C.: Brookings Institution, 1973.

Wellington, Harry H., and Winter, Ralph K., Jr. *The Unions and the Cities*. Washington, D.C.: Brookings Institution, 1972.

Zagoria, Sam, ed. *Public Workers and Public Unions*. Englewood Cliffs, N.J.: Prentice-Hall, 1972.

16 Pension Fund Management

Bleakney, Thomas P. *Retirement Systems for Public Employees*. Philadelphia: University of Pennsylvania Press, 1972.

Municipal Finance Officers Association Committee on Public Employee Retirement Administration. *Public Employee Retirement Administration*. Chicago: Municipal Finance Officers Association, 1977.

Munnell, Alicia Haydock, in collaboration with Connolly, Ann M. *Pensions for Public Employees*. Washington, D.C.: National Planning Association, 1979.

Myers, Robert J. *Indexation of Pension and Other Benefits*. Homewood, Ill.: Richard D. Irwin, 1978.

Ott, David J., et al. *State and Local Finances in the Last Half of the Seventies*. Chapters 3 and 4. Washington, D.C.: American Enterprise Institute for Public Policy Research, 1975.

Petersen, John E. *State and Local Government Pension Fund Investments*. Washington, D.C.: Government Finance Research Center, Municipal Finance Officers Association, 1979.

———. *State and Local Pension Financial Disclosure*. Washington, D.C.: Government Finance Research Center, Municipal Finance Officers Association, 1979.

Tax Foundation. *Employee Pension Systems in State and Local Government*. New York: Tax Foundation, 1976.

Tilove, Robert. *Public Employee Pension Funds*. New York: Columbia University Press, 1976.

U.S. Advisory Commission on Intergovernmental Relations. *State and Local Pension Systems, Federal Regulatory Issues*. A–71. Washington, D.C.: Government Printing Office, 1980.

U.S. Congress. House. Committee on Education and Labor. *Task Force Report on Public Employee Retirement Systems*. Washington, D.C.: Government Printing Office, 1978.

U.S. General Accounting Office. Comptroller General of the United States. *Funding of State and Local Pension Plans: A National Problem*. Washington, D.C.: Government Printing Office, 1979.

Winklevoss, Howard, and McGill, Dan. *Public Pension Plans*. Homewood, Ill.: Dow Jones–Irwin, 1979.

17 Inventory, Purchasing and Risk Management

Aljian, George W. *Purchasing Handbook*. 3d ed. New York: McGraw-Hill Book Co., 1973.

Braun, J. Peter. *Total-Cost Purchasing*. Management Information Service Reports, vol. 3, no. S–4. Washington, D.C.: International City Management Association, 1971.

Buttenheim Publishing Corporation. *Municipal Index: The Purchasing Guide for City, Township, and Urban County Officials and Consulting Engineers*. Pittsfield, Mass.: Buttenheim Publishing Corp. Annual.

Coe, Charles K. *Understanding Risk Management: A Guide for Governments*. Athens: Institute of Government, University of Georgia, 1980.

England, Wilbur B. *Modern Procurement Management*. Homewood, Ill.: Richard D. Irwin, 1970.

Georgia Chapter, Society of Chartered Property and Casualty Underwriters. *Municipal Risk Management*. Cincinnati: National Underwriters Company, 1971.

Lakefish, Richard. *Purchasing Through Intergovernmental Agreements*. Management Information Service Reports, vol. 3, no. S–6. Washington, D.C.: International City Management Association, 1971.

Public Management 60, no. 11 (November 1978). Issue devoted to risk management.

Roos, Nestor R., and Gerber, Joseph S. *Insurance Risk Management*. Management Information Service Reports, vol. 2, no. LS–6. Washington, D.C.: International City Management Association, 1970.

Thierauf, Robert J., and Klekamp, Robert C. *Decision Making Through Operations Research*. 2d ed. New York: John Wiley & Sons, 1975.

Todd, J. D. *Effective Risk and Insurance Management in Municipal Government*. Austin: Institute of Public Affairs, University of Texas, 1970.

Valente, Paula R. *Current Approaches to Risk Management: A Directory of Practices*. Management Information Service Special Reports, no. 7. Washington, D.C.: International City Management Association, 1980.

18 Local Government Accounting

American Accounting Association. Committee to Prepare a Statement of Basic Accounting Theory. *A Statement of Basic Accounting Theory*. Evanston, Ill.: American Accounting Association, 1966.

Anthony, Robert N. *Financial Accounting in Nonbusiness Organizations: An Explanatory Study of Conceptual Issues*. Stamford, Conn.: Financial Accounting Standards Board, 1978.

Committee on Governmental Accounting and Auditing. American Institute of Certified Public Accountants. *Audits of State and Local Governmental Units*. Industry Audit Guide. New York: American Institute of Certified Public Accountants, 1974. Related Statements of Position 75–3, 77–2, 80–2.

Coopers & Lybrand and the University of Michigan. *Financial Disclosure Practices of the American Cities: A Public Report*. New York: Coopers & Lybrand, 1976.

Davidson, Sidney, et al. *Financial Reporting by State and Local Government Units*. Chicago: Center for Management of Public and Nonprofit Enterprise, Graduate School of Business, University of Chicago, 1977.

Freeman, Robert J., and Lynn, Edward S. *Fund Accounting*. Englewood Cliffs, N.J.: Prentice-Hall, 1974.

Hay, Leon E. *Accounting for Governmental and Nonprofit Enterprise*. Homewood, Ill.: Richard D. Irwin, 1980.

Henke, Emerson O. *Introduction to Nonprofit Organization Accounting*. Boston, Mass.: Kent/Wadsworth, 1979.

Holder, William. *A Study of Selected Concepts for Government Financial Accounting and Reporting*. Chicago: National Council on Governmental Accounting, 1980.

Municipal Finance Officers Association and Peat, Marwick, Mitchell & Co. *Study Guide to Governmental Accounting, Auditing and Financial Reporting*. Chicago: Municipal Finance Officers Association, 1974.

National Council on Governmental Accounting. *Governmental Accounting, Auditing, and Financial Reporting*. Chicago: Municipal Finance Officers Association, 1968.

"Objectives of Financial Reporting by Nonbusiness Organizations." In *Statement of Financial Accounting Concepts No. 4*. Stamford, Conn.: Financial Accounting Standards Board, 1980.

Touche Ross & Company. *Public Financial Reporting by Local Government: Issues and a Viewpoint*. New York: Touche Ross & Co., 1977.

19 Capital Budgeting

Aronson, J. Richard, and Schwartz, Eli. *Capital Budget Finance*. Management Information Service Reports, vol. 3, no. S–2. Washington, D.C.: International City Management Association, 1971.

Beenhakker, Henri L. *Capital Investment Planning for Management and Engineering*. Rotterdam, The Netherlands: Rotterdam University Press, 1975.

Boness, A. James. *Capital Budgeting: The Public and Private Sectors*. New York: Praeger Publishers, 1972.

Johnson, Robert W. *Capital Budgeting.* Belmont, Calif.: Wadsworth Publishing Co., 1970.

Moak, Lennox L., and Killian, Kathryn W. *Capital Program and Capital Budget Manual.* Chicago: Municipal Finance Officers Association, 1964.

Steiss, Alan Walter. *Local Government Finance: Capital Facilities Planning and Debt Administration.* Lexington, Mass.: Lexington Books, 1975, 1978.

Wilkes, F. M. *Capital Budgeting Techniques.* New York: Wiley, 1977.

List of
contributors

Persons who have contributed to this book are listed below with the editors first and the authors following in alphabetical order. A brief review of experience and training is presented for each author. Because many of the contributors have published extensively, books, monographs, articles, and other publications are omitted.

J. Richard Aronson (Editor and Chapter 19) is Professor of Economics at Lehigh University. He is also Director of the Fairchild-Martindale Center for the Study of Private Enterprise. His educational background includes a bachelor's degree from Clark University, a master's from Stanford University, and a doctorate from Clark. He has taught at Worcester Polytechnic Institute and Clark University and has been a Fulbright Scholar at the University of York, England. His professional activities include studies of fiscal capacity reports and capital budgets for local government units in Pennsylvania.

Eli Schwartz (Editor and Chapter 17) is Professor of Economics and Finance at Lehigh University. He holds the Charles Macfarlane Chair in Theoretical Economics and is Chairman of the Department of Economics. He has a bachelor's degree from the University of Denver, a master's degree from the University of Connecticut, and a doctorate from Brown University. He has taught at Michigan State University, the London School of Economics, and the Autonomous University of Madrid. He has wide experience as a consultant in the financial and economics fields with a number of private and public bodies.

James M. Buchanan (Chapter 2) is General Director, Center for Study of Public Choice, Virginia Polytechnic Institute, and University Professor of Economics, Virginia Polytechnic Institute. His academic experience includes positions as Professor of Economics, University of California at Los Angeles; Director, Thomas Jefferson Center for Political Economy, University of Virginia; and Fulbright Visiting Professor, Cambridge University. He holds a bachelor's degree from Middle Tennessee State College, a master's from the

University of Tennessee, and a doctorate from the University of Chicago. He has been a member of numerous boards and commissions.

Thomas J. DiLorenzo (Chapter 8) is Assistant Professor of Environmental Analysis and Policy, School of Management, State University of New York at Buffalo. He holds the Ph.D. in economics from Virginia Polytechnic Institute and State University. His major research interests are urban public finance, public choice, and the economic organization of local government.

Paul B. Downing (Chapter 8) is Professor of Economics and Policy Sciences at Florida State University. He received a Ph.D. in economics from the University of Wisconsin. He has been employed by various federal agencies and has taught at the University of California at Riverside and the Virginia Polytechnic Institute.

Marilyn R. Flowers (Chapter 2) is Associate Professor of Economics at the University of Oklahoma. Her educational background includes a bachelor's degree from the University of Iowa, a master's from the University of California at Los Angeles, and a doctorate from Virginia Polytechnic Institute and State University. She has also been a professional staff member, Program Analysis Division, Institute for Defense Analysis, and has taught at the Virginia Polytechnic Institute and State University.

Lewis Friedman (Chapter 5) is Associate Professor and Graduate Supervisor, Department of Public Administration, Baruch College of the City University of New York. He holds a bachelor's degree from Hunter College, City University of New York, and a doctorate from Michigan State University. He has served as a consultant to state and local governments and public interest groups.

W. Maureen Godsey (Chapter 12) is Assistant Director, Management Development Center, International City Management Association. She currently directs ICMA's programs in productivity improvement and financial condition analysis. She holds an A.B. in urban economics from the University of California at Berkeley and an M.P.A. in budget and finance from the George Washington University. Prior to joining ICMA, she was a research economist with the U.S. Department of Agriculture.

Sanford M. Groves (Chapter 12) is Assistant City Manager for the city of Paramount, California. Prior to that, he was Director for Public Finance at the International City Management Association, where he directed the association's research and technical assistance programs in public finance. He holds a bachelor's degree in business administration and a master's in public administration from California State University at Fullerton. He has served in various positions in the city of Garden Grove, California, including Assistant to the City Manager and Fiscal Services Manager.

William W. Holder (Chapter 18) is Associate Professor, School of Accounting, University of Southern California. He received his B.S. degree from Oklahoma State University and his master's of accounting and doctoral degrees from the University of Oklahoma. He served on the faculty of Texas Tech University for five years and has had extensive experience with several public accounting firms. He is a certified public accountant and a member of professional CPA associations.

George G. Kaufman (Chapter 13) is John F. Smith, Jr., Professor of Economics and Finance, School of Business Administration, Loyola University of Chicago. He received a bachelor's degree from Oberlin College, a master's from the University of Michigan, and a Ph.D. in economics from the University of Iowa. He has been a research fellow, economist, and senior economist at the Federal Reserve Bank of Chicago; John B. Rogers Professor of Banking and Finance and Director of the Center for Capital Market Research in the College of Business Administration at the University of Oregon; and visiting professor or visiting scholar at numerous institutions. He also served as Deputy to the Assistant Secretary for Economic Policy of the U.S. Treasury.

Julius Margolis (Chapter 9) is Professor of Economics at the University of California at Irvine. He has been the Director of the Institutes of Public Policy Analysis at Stanford University and the University of Pennsylvania. He has held professorships of economics, planning, business, engineering, and public policy at the University of Chicago, Stanford, the University of California at Berkeley, and the University of Pennsylvania and has consulted

with federal, state, and local governments. He received a Ph.D. in economics from Harvard University and holds other degrees from the City College of New York and the University of Wisconsin.

Alan Maynard (Chapter 11) is a Senior Lecturer in Economics, Department of Economics and Related Studies, University of York, Heslington, York, England. He has also taught at the University of Exeter, Italy; at the University of Otago, New Zealand; and at the University of Götenborg, Sweden.

Wallace E. Oates (Chapter 10) is Professor of Economics at the University of Maryland. After receiving his Ph.D. in economics from Stanford University, he engaged in research on state and local finance at Princeton University, then at Maryland. He has written on the provision of public services, taxation, and intergovernmental grants and served as an advisor to federal, state, and local governments.

John E. Petersen (Chapter 16) is Director of the Government Finance Research Center, Municipal Finance Officers Association. Previously, he was Director, Center of Policy Research, National Governors Conference; Washington Director, MFOA; Director of Finance, Securities Industries Association; and Economist for the Urban Institute and the Board of Governors of the Federal Reserve System. He holds a Ph.D. in economics from the University of Pennsylvania, an M.B.A. from the Wharton School, and a bachelor's degree in economics from Northwestern University.

Arnold H. Raphaelson (Chapter 6) is Professor of Economics at Temple University. His educational background includes a bachelor's degree from Brown University, master's degrees from Columbia and Clark Universities, and a doctorate from Clark University. He has taught at the University of Maine and has served as both a professional staff member and a consultant to the U.S. Senate Subcommittee on Intergovernmental Relations.

James D. Rodgers (Chapter 7) is Professor of Economics at the Pennsylvania State University, where he has been a faculty member since 1969. He holds a bachelor's degree from East Texas State University and a doctorate from the University of Virginia. He has recently served as a research director in the area of local non-real estate taxation to the Pennsylvania Tax Commission.

Leonard I. Ruchelman (Chapter 1) is Director of the Institute of Urban Studies and Public Administration at Old Dominion University. His educational background includes a bachelor's degree from Brooklyn College and a doctorate from Columbia University. He has also taught at Lehigh University, where he was director of the Urban Studies Program; at Alfred University; and at West Virginia University.

Larry D. Schroeder (Chapter 4) is Associate Professor of Public Administration and Senior Research Associate with the Metropolitan Studies Program at the Maxwell School, Syracuse University. He holds a doctorate in economics from the University of Wisconsin as well as degrees from Central College (Iowa) and Northern Illinois University.

Bernard F. Sliger (Chapter 3) is President, Florida State University. He holds a bachelor's degree, a master's degree, and a doctorate from Michigan State University. He has taught at Louisiana State and at Southern University, and is also Professor of Economics at Florida State University. His administrative experience includes service as Executive Director of the Louisiana Coordinating Council for Higher Education. He served as a consultant for many private and public groups.

Robert J. Thornton (Chapter 15) is Associate Professor of Economics at Lehigh University. He has previously been employed as a research assistant by the Brookings Institution and most recently was a visiting research fellow at the University of Sussex, England. He

holds a Ph.D. in economics from the University of Illinois.

Barbara H. Tuckman (Chapter 3) is Assistant Professor of Economics and a Senior Research Associate in the Center for Manpower Studies at Memphis State University. Her previous positions include Assistant to the President and Director of the Center for Economic Education at Florida State University. She has also worked for the Federal Trade Commission and for the Wisconsin Department of Revenue. She holds a master's degree from the University of Wisconsin and a Ph.D. degree from Florida State University.

James C. Van Horne (Chapter 14) is A. P. Giannini Professor of Finance, Graduate School of Business, Stanford University. He holds a bachelor's degree from DePauw University and an M.B.A. and a Ph.D. from Northwestern University. He has served as Associate Dean for Academic Affairs, Graduate School of Business, at Stanford; Deputy Assistant Secretary, U.S. Treasury; Director, Stanford M.B.A. Program; Assistant Professor, Michigan State University; and Commercial Lending Representative, Continental Illinois National Bank and Trust Company, Chicago. He is Associate Editor of the *Journal of Financial and Quantitative Analysis* and serves on the board of directors of a number of institutions.

Acknowledgments

A major step in planning this book was to convene three separate sessions in California of city managers, county managers, finance directors, and university teachers in early 1979. Two of the sessions were held at the city hall at Long Beach, with the cooperation of the city of Long Beach, and the third session was held at the Hotel Claremont in Berkeley, with the help of the League of California Cities. These sessions were influential in expanding the coverage of several chapters and adding new chapters to the book. Many of the persons attending these sessions later reviewed chapter drafts and provided helpful suggestions for improvement.

The persons attending the planning sessions (with their affiliations at that time) in Long Beach and Berkeley were: Joseph Arch, Director of Finance, San Leandro; Philip Brubaker, Manager, Tidelands Administration, Long Beach; Jeffrey I. Chapman, School of Public Administration, University of Southern California; Richard B. DeLong, City Manager, San Mateo; John E. Dever, City Manager, Long Beach; William W. Dundore, Director of Finance, Torrance; William H. Dutton, School of Public Administration and Urban Studies, San Diego State University; Virgil L. Elliott, Adjunct Professor, Golden Gate University; James M. Fales, Jr., City Manager, Redwood City; Jack Ference, Director of Finance, Redwood City; Clark Goercker, Associate Director, League of California Cities; Randy H. Hamilton, Dean, Graduate School of Public Administration, Golden Gate University; Roger Heast, Chief Examiner, Civil Service Commission, Long Beach; William T. Hopkins, Assistant City Manager, Anaheim; Carl Husby, Director of Finance, Long Beach; Kenneth L. Kraemer, Public Policy Research Organization, University of California, Irvine; Dale Kunkel, Annenberg School of Communications, University of Southern California; Wesley McClure, former City Manager, San Leandro; Thomas H. McCorkill, Administrative Analyst, Tulare County; Arnold J. Meltsner, Graduate School of Public Policy, University of California, Berkeley; James S. Mocalis, City Manager, San Juan Capistrano; Donald M. Nuttall, Director of Finance, Santa Fe Springs; Stanley Pinkoski, Director of Finance, Concord; John Rehfuss, Chairman, Department of Public Administration and Recreation and Park Administration, California State University, Sacramento; Allen Saltzstein, Department of Political Science, California State University, Fullerton; John Scott, California State University, Long Beach; Sherry Suttles, Executive Assistant to the City Manager, Long Beach; William O. Talley, City Manager, Anaheim; Donald Winkler, School of Public Administration, University of Southern California; and William Zaner, City Manager, Union City.

Other persons who helped in planning the content of this book and in reviewing chapter drafts in various stages of preparation (with their affiliations at that time) were: Kenneth G. Ainsworth, Department of Economics, Allegheny College; Richard R. Almy, Director, Research and Technical Services Department, International Association of Assessing Officers; Wayne F. Anderson, Executive Director, U.S. Advisory Commission on Intergovernmental Relations; C. Dean Be Ler, County Administrator, County of Charles City, Virginia; Robert Bieber, Director, Risk Management, Westchester County, New York; Jane B. Finley, Comptroller, The Babcock Company, Coral Gables, Florida; Michael J. Gable, Director of Finance, Columbus, Ohio; R. Ray Goode, President, The Babcock Company, Coral Gables, Florida; Richard R. Herbert, Editorial Consultant, Washington, D.C.; Howard D. McMahan, President, The Justin Companies, Fort Worth, Texas; Richard Milbrodt, City Manager, South Lake Tahoe, California; John O'Sullivan, Special Assistant to the City Manager, San Clemente, California; and Clinton H. Strong, City Manager, Hopewell, Virginia.

The Municipal Management Series is the responsibility of David S. Arnold, Senior Editor, Publications and Policy Center, ICMA, who worked with Professors Aronson and Schwartz in book planning, manuscript review, and substantive editing. Chisholm Gentry handled the substantive edit for Chapters 6, 9–11, 13–16, and 18. Cheryl L. Crowell, Administrative Editor, ICMA, assisted by Barbara H. Moore, Editor, ICMA, coordinated editorial schedules and handled final editing of the manuscript. Emily Evershed prepared the index.

Illustration credits

Chapter 5   Figure 5–1: John P. McIver and Elinor Ostrom, "Using Budgets To Reveal Preferences: Validation of a Survey Instrument," in *Citizen Preferences and Urban Policy: Models, Measures, Uses*, ed. Terry N. Clark (Beverly Hills, Calif.: Sage Publishing Co., 1976), p. 90; Figure 5–2: Operating budgets and work programs, City of Philadelphia, City of Rochester (New York), 1979–80; Figure 5–3: Adapted from *Recommended Annual Budget for Year Ending 30 September 1980*, City of Tampa, Florida, pp. 43–44; Figure 5–4: *Annual Budget, Fiscal Year 1979–80*, vol.1, *Operating Detail*, City of San Diego, California; Figure 5–5: City of Pittsburgh, Pennsylvania, *Proposed Operating Budget, 1980*, p. 103; Figure 5–6: Adapted from *The Mayor's Management Report*, New York, New York, 15 January 1980, pp. 3–6; Figure 5–8: Institute of Public Administration, Pennsylvania State University, *Sample Program Structure for Medium Size Cities* (State College, Pa.: Institute of Public Administration, Pennsylvania University, 1977); Figure 5–9: Harry P. Hatry et al., *How Effective Are Your Community Services? Procedures for Monitoring the Effectiveness of Municipal Services* (Washington, D.C.: The Urban Institute and International City Management Association, 1977), pp. 86–87; Figure 5–10: City of Wichita, Kansas, *City Manager's Zero Base Budget Message* (Wichita, Kans.: City of Wichita, Office of the City Manager, 1979), p. 21.

Chapter 12   Figure 12–1: Sanford M. Groves and W. Maureen Godsey, *Evaluating Financial Condition*, 5 handbooks (Washington, D.C.: International City Management Association, 1980): Handbook 1, *Evaluating Financial Condition*, p. 6; Figure 12–2: Groves and Godsey, *Evaluating Financial Condition*, Handbook 1, *Evaluating Financial Condition*, p. 8; Figure 12–3: Groves and Godsey, *Evaluating Financial Condition*, Handbook 2, *Financial Trend Monitoring System: A Practitioner's Workbook*, p. 10.

Chapter 14   Figure 14–4: Merton H. Miller and Daniel Orr, "A Model of the Demand for Money by Firms," *Quarterly Journal of Economics* 80 (August 1966): 420; Figure 14–5: U.S., Department of the Treasury, Office of the Secretary, Office of Government Financing, 1977; Figure 14–6: U.S., Federal Reserve Bank of St. Louis, 1980.

Chapter 16   Figure 16–6: Thomas J. Wander, "How Intergovernmental Pooling Can Help Finance Risk," *Risk Management*, September 1979, p. 35.

Index

1
2

3

5
6
7   02706$$$1X   05-04-81 16-43-12
8
9   **I C M A**
10   TS **02706**
11   Tape **1x**
12   Oper 27
13   PR by
14
15

Municipal Management Series

16

Management Policies in
17   **Local Government Finance**
18

Text type
19   FotoTypesetters Incorporated
20   Baltimore, Maryland
21
Printing and binding
22   Kingsport Press
23   Kingsport, Tennessee
24
Paper
25   Unisource Offset, 60#
26
Design
27   Herbert Slobin
28
29